PRODUCTION AND OPERATIONS MANAGEMENT

Everett E. Adam, Jr. and Ronald J. Ebert

Prentice-Hall, Inc.
Englewood Cliffs, N. J. 07632

PRODUCTION AND OPERATIONS MANAGEMENT

Concepts, Models, and Behavior

Library of Congress Cataloging in Publication Data

ADAM, EVERETT E (date).
  Production and operations management.

  Includes bibliographies and index.
  1. Production management. I. Ebert, Ronald J.,
joint author. II. Title.
TS155.A29514   658.5   77-20841
ISBN 0-13-724955-1

Art by Arthur J. Barbour and Margaret A. Barbour

Printed in the United States of America

10 9 8 7 6 5 4 3 2 1

Prentice-Hall International, Inc., London
Prentice-Hall of Australia Pty. Limited, Sydney
Prentice-Hall of Canada, Ltd., Toronto
Prentice-Hall of India Private Limited, New Delhi
Prentice-Hall of Japan, Inc., Tokyo
Prentice-Hall of Southeast Asia Pte. Ltd., Singapore
Whitehall Books Limited, Wellington, New Zealand

Preface

Production and operations management continues to play a vital role in national and world economies. Although the operations function exists in virtually every organization, it is often misunderstood by practitioners and sometimes elusive to students of business and management. Part of the problem lies in the changing nature of the field of study—the historical evolution from shop management to production management to systems analysis and management science. This shift has been paralleled somewhat by changing terminology, from manufacturing management to production management to production/operations or operations management. Originally, the conceptual orientation and emphasis focused on management; in more recent years, the emphasis has shifted to quantitative analysis. As the emphasis has shifted educationally, two gaps have resulted, one in education, the other in practice.

In the educational setting, contemporary operations management students are often left with the feeling that this topic is distinctly different and separate from management itself. In some instances, analysis and quantitative techniques have been emphasized at the expense of an understanding of a basic unifying framework for envisioning the role of operations management in organizations. We hope to fill this void with the unifying theme of this book: planning, organizing, and controlling—the classical process school of management. As we present and integrate problem areas in this familiar framework, operations management may be more readily understood by those with a basic management background. Within this process framework, we integrate the resource conversion (transformation) into goods and services and the modeling and behavioral techniques necessary to accomplish conversion. A distinguishing feature of this book is this integrating approach, which is repeated in nearly every chapter and referred to throughout.

At the same time, we recognize that this schema has its drawbacks. The problem areas of operations management do not fit exclusively into just one of the process areas; product quality, for example, is not solely a control problem; it involves planning and organizing as well. In light of these difficulties we have had to decide how best to introduce primary production/operations management problem areas within the process subfunctions. In a few instances, our decision had to be somewhat arbitrary to carry through with the basic theme. In other instances, when the problem area is clearly dominant within the planning, organizing, or controlling subfunction, the organization was obvious. Throughout the book, problem areas in each subfunction are explicitly mentioned. On balance, we believe the continuity offered by this approach far outweighs its drawbacks. In fact, the alert student will recognize the difficulties in categorizing and use them to think more carefully about the entire field of production/operations management.

Within the process framework, we have found it useful to approach the planning subfunction somewhat differently than is usually the case. We divide this subfunction into two major parts: planning the conversion system and planning the use of the conversion system. Planning the conversion system revolves around its design; planning the use of the conversion system focuses on utilizing it once it's in existence. Although this distinction may be somewhat artificial, it allows us to integrate problem areas more logically than has been done in the past.

In the eyes of many practitioners there is often a large gap between what they must deal with operationally and what they studied in production/operations books. This is particularly true for those who were introduced to production/operations management as a quantitative/systems analysis discipline. In the first place, practitioners' problems are not all as readily solved by quantitative models as some of the introductory treatments seem to imply. Second, the systems approach to operations, for some reason, has tended to underemphasize the role of human behavior as an integral part of productive systems. For these reasons we have tended both to deemphasize the quantitative aspects of production/operations management and to introduce some important behavioral applications into the discipline. When problems are behavioral (quality motivation, for example), we introduce such contemporary techniques as behavior modification and attitude change procedures to deal with them; when they are quantitative (inventory control, for example) we stress such techniques as economic and optimal analysis.

Throughout the book, we have attempted to preserve the basic production/operations management issues and concepts. We have tried to discuss them in a way that can be understood by readers with minimal mathematical skills. Then, if desired, readers can use the chapter supplements to build upon these fundamentals. Each supplement emphasizes technique and methodology as it relates to a fundamental topic in the chapter, but it does so at a more rigorous quantitative level. Thus, computer simulation, linear programming, the mathematics of forecasting, some optimization techniques, and other related materials included in the supplements can be an integral part of the course at the option of the user. The book can also stand alone, however, without the supplements.

Another source of difficulty in understanding contemporary operations management is caused by the apparent shift from goods-producing to service organizations. As service industries continue to increase in importance, the role of production/operations management in the service sector takes on added significance. Historically, much of our production management technology was developed and refined in manufacturing organizations. To what extent is this technology transferrable to service organizations? When technologies can be transferred, we have demonstrated the possibility. We have also, however, pointed out those deficiencies in existing technology that make a transfer difficult. Our view is that operations in a broad term encompassing manufacturing, agriculture, and services—not a term that simply replaces traditional production or is applicable only to services.

The major purpose of this book is to introduce the basics of production/operations management in an understandable way. With this in mind, we have stressed continuity in our general strategy. After giving the reader an historical perspective of management and operations management, we discuss the role of analysis in production/operations management. In the next fourteen chapters (Parts II through V), the material is organized around the planning, organizing, and controlling theme. In the beginning of each of these chapters, a major production/operations activity is discussed and analyzed in isolation so the reader may have an unclouded perspective of the basic activity under consideration. As the chapter progresses, however, we show how this activity interrelates with the others. In short, Chapters 4 through 17 present the core production/operations management activities. In Part VI, the emphasis shifts to synthesizing—integrating the production/operations management process into a more realistic and meaningful whole. Overall, the reader proceeds from the parts to the whole, first learning the concepts and terminology of each subfunction and then seeing how they relate to one another and work together. We believe these fundamentals can be grasped by students with a minimal knowledge of statistics, quantitative methods, management, and organizational behavior.

In general, our intent is to provide a student-oriented presentation at an introductory level. To this end, we present the material in a simple, straightforward fashion. The emphasis is on terminology and general concepts, rather than the specifics of different solution techniques and methodologies. At the end of each chapter, the reader will find a glossary and a case; these reemphasize the terminology and basic concepts in the chapter. Although some of the review questions and problems at the end of each chapter are intended to challenge understanding slightly beyond the level in the chapter itself, most directly reinforce the basics.

Distinguishing features of this book are *an integrating framework,* featuring the management process, resource conversion, and concepts, models, and behavior; *behavioral applications* within production/operations; inclusion of the service sector via an *operations orientation;* and *a student emphasis* featuring an introductory treatment, continuity among chapters, and learning enhancement within chapters with numerous examples, chapter summaries, cases, glossaries, review and discussion questions, and problems.

We are especially indebted to the following people, whose comments helped us throughout the development of this book: Professors Douglas A. Elvers, University of North Carolina; Albert R. Wood, University of Western Ontario; and Larry Ritzman, The Ohio State University. We also wish to acknowledge the resource support of the University of Missouri—Columbia.

March 1978
Columbia, Missouri

EVERETT E. ADAM, JR.
RONALD J. EBERT

Contents

ORGANIZING FOR CONVERSION III

PLANNING THE USE OF THE CONVERSION SYSTEM IV

DYNAMICS OF OPERATIONS MANAGEMENT

To   Joy, Scott, and Kevin
      Mary, Kristen, and Matt

Part 1

MANAGEMENT AND OPERATIONS

1

Management

Managing nuclear power stations, automobile manufacturing facilities, multibranch banks, and long-term health care facilities are among the diverse tasks facing today's operating management. A society concerned with energy sources, consumer goods and services, and care for the elderly wants these goods and services delivered effectively and efficiently. Management faces challenges from a more educated, affluent, and concerned society today than ever before. No longer can we produce anodized aluminum for decorative automotive dashes without considering passenger safety and questioning where and how to dispose of resulting acid baths and fumes. Never before have the challenge and the costs of failure been greater; and never have the techniques and knowledge to meet these challenges been more available to operating managers.

The complexities of contemporary society make all of us dependent on organizations and the people who manage them; yet we often fail to understand and appreciate the process of management. Manufacturing consumer goods involves considerable direction of human and material resources. Likewise, the services that we expect from both the private and public sectors require managers and administrators to assure that these services are of specified quality and quantity. Everywhere we turn we see the results of organized group effort in complex organizations. But the people who lead these organizations, whether we call them managers, administrators, or supervisors, are commonly taken for granted.

MANAGEMENT AS A DISCIPLINE

As the name implies, operations management involves management. Before we focus on the development of operations management, however, let us examine the more general concept of management by briefly tracing its history, explaining current schools of management thought, and establishing the framework for analysis that we will use throughout the book.

For those of you who have worked as managers or have previously been introduced to the discipline of management, this chapter will be a review. As you read the material, think in terms of real management situations you have experienced and recall concepts you have learned. These concepts can readily be related to your own real-life and classroom experiences.

Ask yourself some probing questions about what constitutes this thing called management, administration, or supervision. What is management? Who is a manager? Who are some managers I know? What have they told me about their jobs? In my own work experience, what have I observed managers do? Perhaps you will want to jot down some answers to these questions. If you are aware of your own opinions, you'll be able to compare them with others later on.

HISTORY OF MANAGEMENT

Historically, management has not always been as visible as it is today, although it has been practiced for centuries. Records and artifacts from ancient Egyptian and Greek cultures indicate that management concepts and techniques played an important role in civilized societies thousands of years before the birth of Christ. The Egyptian pyramids, for example, vividly illustrate that tens of thousands of people worked for many years on large-scale construction projects. These certainly required substantial organizational and planning abilities, as well as skills in directing and controlling the actual construction. Surely management skills must have been necessary for ancient Egyptians to communicate with thousands of people every day without modern telephone, telegraph, or transportation technology.

The Bible provides even further examples of management practices. When Moses organized the scattered tribes of his people and led them out of Egypt, he showed considerable leadership and management abilities. During years of plenty, Joseph marked and stored extra grain so that it could be distributed on a first-in, first-out basis in the lean years that followed. Today we call this "inventory control." In the New Testament, writings about Christ provide a human relations model that is emulated by many managers today.

In more recent history, too, leaders have used techniques and skills that would be valued by modern management. The eleventh-century invasion and conquest of England by William the Conqueror required tremendous organizing and planning efforts. Marco Polo's thirteenth-century travels to establish trade between the Orient and the Western world posed significant logistics management problems in the acquisition, movement, and maintenance of supplies and equipment. In the fifteenth century, Joan of Arc displayed considerable talent for organizing as she led the movement to purge her French homeland of foreign rulers. Written accounts of the late 1700s and 1800s reveal the emergence of several managerial developments, especially with regard to the scientific study of work. Adam Smith introduced the concept of specialization of labor; he recommended breaking jobs down into subtasks and reassigning workers to specialized tasks.

In the early twentieth century, Frederick Taylor implemented Smith's theories by dividing jobs into two categories: those performed by operative workers and those performed by managers or supervisors. Thus was born the scientific management movement. Taylor's work and that of others associated with scientific management emphasized a micro, a very narrow, approach toward studying jobs and people in jobs. Scientific management, however, perceived workers primarily as mechanistic, economically motivated beings. The more money workers received, management reasoned, the more output they would produce. The more output they produced, the more money they would receive. Thus emerged a very simple view of people at work.

During the Depression, management modified its views, having discovered that workers have multiple, not just economic, needs. Thus managers began taking a more enlightened approach toward the subordinate-supervisor relationship, an approach known as human relations.

Thus began a rapid forty years in the development of management thought. Psychologists, sociologists, and other social scientists began in earnest to study people in their working environments. Knowledge concerning human behavior in organizations has grown rapidly since the 1930s. Additionally, the scientific management approach has benefited from the work of economists, mathematicians, and computer scientists. Many of these later, more analytical, approaches were the result of Allied operations research applications in World War II.

Although management techniques have been practiced for centuries, management did not emerge as a discipline until relatively recently. Over the years, however, distinct theories of management have evolved, and today the discipline consists of three primary schools of thought. We turn to these now.

SCHOOLS OF MANAGEMENT THOUGHT

The various schools of management thought can be classified in numerous ways; we have chosen a classification scheme that we believe is general and largely self-explanatory. In this scheme, we fit the various theories of management into three broad categories: the *classical*, the *behavioral*, and the *modeling* schools. Our choice of this classification scheme, rather than another, is somewhat arbitrary, but we hope it will help you understand the major contributions to management thought without getting bogged down in semantics or too-technical details. With this in mind, let's find out what these schools of management thought are all about.

Classical

Classical management thought encompasses the scientific management and process theories.

Scientific management   The basis of scientific management is a focus on economic efficiency at the production core of the organization. Of central importance is the belief that rationality on the part of management will obtain economic efficiency. This school emphasizes the closed-system logic of engineering, technology, and economics. (A closed system is one that is self-contained, relies little on support from its environment, and operates essentially in a world of certainty.) People at work were considered to be motivated by money alone. Economic efficiency was the single measure of organization performance. Further, it was assumed that by buying the talents of an expert who specialized in engineering technology, management could purchase the rationality it needed. In short, the scientific management school of thought considers the organization to be a closed system unaffected by outside disturbances or influences.

Economic efficiency, a vital measure of performance according to the classical school, is a term that has been retained even by organizations that do not agree with the scientific management approach. Consequently, it is an important concept to understand. Efficiency refers to the ratio of outputs to inputs. Organization efficiency typically is a ratio of product or service outputs to land, capital, or labor inputs.

$$\frac{\text{Efficiency}}{(\%)} = \frac{\text{Output}}{\text{Input}} \times 100\% \qquad (1\text{-}1)$$

EXAMPLE

Management is concerned with labor efficiency, especially when labor is costly. To determine how efficient labor is in a given situation, management sets an *individual standard,* a goal reflecting an average worker's normal amount of output per unit of time under normal working conditions. Say that the standard in a cafeteria is the preparation of 200 salads in one hour. If labor input produces 150 salads per hour, how efficient is the salad operation?

$$\text{Labor efficiency} = \frac{\text{Labor output}}{\text{Labor input}} \times 100\% = \frac{150 \text{ salads}}{200 \text{ salads}} \times 100\%$$

$$= 75\%$$

Compared to standard, this operation is 75 percent efficient in the preparation of salads.

Although we cannot accept scientific management as an all-inclusive definition, we certainly recognize its influence in many operations today. Labor standards, wage incentives, time and motion studies, and layout analysis are all management techniques used in automobile and other goods-producing firms. Economic efficiency through labor cost analysis and control are employed in city government, hospitals, and other service organizations.

EXAMPLE

Recently a small city established a standard number of waste collections for a truck and three workers in any one day. Upon completion of this standard, the workers return to the office. They must remain there until the work day is over, but they may use the time until the end of their shift as they wish (they are responsible for collections missed). It is our understanding that this system works very well. Collection is more efficient, quality is maintained, and job turnover is reasonably low.

As our economy becomes more service-oriented, we can expect managers to be held accountable for resource utilization. Like the city manager in our example, they will increasingly rely on proven scientific management techniques to assist them in reaching their goals, including economic efficiency.

Perhaps the most significant contribution to scientific management was Frederick Taylor's concept that *planning* and *doing* in production should be separated. He believed that some workers (managers, in modern terminology) should schedule work, purchase materials, analyze jobs, and perform other nonproduction tasks. Others (operative or production workers) should perform the manual tasks necessary to transform materials into finished goods. Taylor believed that the two sets of tasks should be separated and performed by people with distinctly different skills. Before Taylor, all an industrial society's tasks were performed by the same person—much like a small family farm is operated by a farmer today.

Process

The *process* school of management thought is also referred to as the administrative or functional approach to management. Management is viewed as a continuous process involving the functions of planning, organizing, and controlling by a manager, who influences others through the functions he or she performs. In performing these functions the manager adheres to certain basic principles. This definition of management, with the process emphasis, will be the one most frequently referred to in this book.

The process school was actually developed independently in the early 1900s in at least three different societies. In the United States, Ralph C. Davis, a professor and management consultant, documented the essence of this approach. In the United Kingdom, Luther Gulick and Lyndall Urwick wrote and collected papers concerning the sciences of administration, and Oliver Sheldon first recorded the process approach. Meanwhile, Henri Fayol, a French metallurgist, also described how the management process worked. Although his work was done in the early nineteenth century, it was not widely translated into English until 1949, so that only recently have we been able to give it careful attention. Since Fayol's ideas are representative of this school, let's look at some of them.

Fayol suggested fourteen principles that should guide managers in their actions. Rather than list all fourteen, we will show two that may serve to illustrate his concept of management principles.

1. *Authority and Responsibility.* Authority is the "right to give orders and the power to exact obedience," and responsibility is the duty to command. Fayol recognized the difference between official authority, associated with position; and personal authority, associated with the office holder's own personality, experience, moral worth, and other personal characteristics. The principle he seemed primarily to emphasize, however, was that authority should equal responsibility; that is, managers should not assign responsibilities without delegating commensurate authority.

2. *Unity of Command.* Fayol felt that if one subordinate must report to two supervisors, severe breakdowns in authority and discipline result. Each employee therefore should have only one supervisor. Unity of command does not imply the optimum number of subordinates who should report directly to each supervisor; that concept ("span-of-control") is discussed separately.

Fayol further elaborated on the management process by identifying five functions in which managers engage:

1. *Planning* includes all those activities that result in developing a course of action. These activities guide future decision making.
2. *Organizing* involves all activities that result in some structure of tasks and authority.
3. *Commanding* is concerned with directing the activities of subordinates.
4. *Coordinating* includes those activities that bind together all individual efforts and direct them toward a common objective.
5. *Controlling* activities are those that assure that the performance in the organization takes place in accordance with planned performance.

Other managerial functions identified by process writers are staffing, directing, and communicating. These functions overlap and are not necessarily performed in any fixed order.

It is clear that managers do perform these as well as other functions in organizations today. Similarly, there are principles that managers accept as guides to action in modern complex organizations. Although these principles are not necessarily self-evident or universal truths, as has been implied by some classical contributors, the process school has nevertheless contributed to our understanding of management by identifying many management functions and principles.

The process orientation is similar in some ways to the scientific management orientation. Both are concerned with efficiency; both adopt a limited concept of human behavior; and both operate within a closed system. Modern management has outgrown many of the concepts advocated by these schools; but even with their limitations, much of their thought is relevant to management today.

Behavioral

Human relations   The behavioral school began with a human relations movement that started in the 1930s. The human relations movement emerged quite unexpectedly from some research studies in a manufacturing plant. The research was originally intended to examine the effects of changes in the physical work environment on production output—a typical scientific management study. Some social scientists on the research team, however, observed that changes in output were often due to factors other than just physical changes in the work area. Specifically, workers seemed to respond favorably to the individual care, attention, and interest that the experimenters had shown toward their work. Productivity increased. The main outgrowth of this research was a new attitude that seriously questioned scientific management's man-as-machine concept.

Human relations proponents recognize that people are complex and have multiple needs, and that the subordinate-supervisor relationship directly affects productivity. Perhaps the major contribution of the human relations school was in raising just that question—should an employee be viewed as a machine or as a person with multiple needs and complex behavioral responses?

Behavioral science   The answer to the human relations question has been
and social systems   provided by *behavioral science* and *social systems* theories: people in their work environment, as elsewhere, are extremely complex. Behavioral scientists—psychologists, sociologists, and cultural anthropologists—have added substantially to our understanding of people at work. Theories concerning such behavioral processes as leadership, motivation, communication, and attitude change have been supported with a great deal of experimental evidence from both laboratories and actual organizations. Applied psychologists have developed *behavioral science* theories of the individual; social psychologists, sociologists, and cultural anthropologists have developed *social systems* theories of people in groups at work. Role relationships, group structure, formal and informal power, and cultural differences have all been found to affect performance. In light of these developments, modern managers have modified their views.

Our study of operations management would certainly be superficial if we chose to ignore the contributions from the behavioral sciences. Although we cannot accept the view that management is solely concerned with human relations (just as we cannot accept everything about the classicists' closed-systems approach to management), we can and must accept many of the behavioral scientists' findings. Each theory of management, although incomplete in itself, contributes substantially to our understanding and practice of the discipline.

Modeling

The modeling school is concerned with decision making, systems theory, and mathematical modeling of systems and decision-making processes.

Decision making The decision-making orientation considers making decisions to be the central purpose of management. Simply stated, the view of this approach is that management *is* decision making. Managers subscribing to this approach make use of studies dealing with human information needs, information processing, assessing risk, and generating decision alternatives to help them make final choices. The decision theory approach can be expanded to include all decision processes throughout the organization.

Systems theory Advocates of systems theory stress the importance of studying organizations from a "total systems" point of view. They consider the organization to be a system of highly interrelated and interdependent parts. When management makes a change in one subsystem, far-reaching effects can be felt in other parts of the total system. A policy change in marketing, for example, can affect finance, production, and personnel subsystems. According to this school, identifying subsystem relationships, predicting effects of changes in the system, and properly implementing system change are all part of managing the total organization.

Mathematical modeling With its foundations in operations research and management science, mathematical modeling focuses on creating mathematical representations of management problems and organizations. For a particular problem, the variables are expressed mathematically, and the model is then used to demonstrate different outcomes that would result from various possible managerial choices. The modeling approach can also be used to examine organization decisions from a systems viewpoint. After relationships among subsystems have been represented mathematically, management can use a model to determine the consequences possible management decisions would have on various subsystems throughout the organization. Often mathematical modeling is used simply to clarify relationships and provide information that might be useful for management decisions.

EXAMPLE

The breakeven volume of output is that volume at which the total revenue received equals the total cost of production. Let fixed cost be *a*, unit variable cost *b*, and unit revenue *c*. At what volume of output *x* (expressed in units of product) will the organization break even? Using the linear mathematical breakeven model, equation 1-2, we can find the output level *x* at which total revenue equals total cost.

$$\text{Total revenue} = \text{Total cost}$$
$$cx = a + bx \qquad \text{(1-2)}$$

If a city license bureau has fixed operating costs of \$500,000 per year, incurs variable costs of \$1 for each customer it services, and receives \$2 in revenue from each customer, how many customers must it service to cover all its costs of operation? The breakeven volume is determined as follows:

$$cx = a + bx$$
$$\$2x = \$500,000 + \$1x$$
$$x = \$500,000$$

Breakeven volume is 500,000 customers.

This is one simple example of a general approach to management that works very effectively in management situations lending themselves to logical analysis. Breakeven analysis, inventory control, physical distribution, and resource allocation are easily converted into mathematical terms. No one has ever had much success, however, in fitting people into mathematical models. We're too varied and unpredictable.

The modeling school extends the rational, logical, technical orientation of that part of classical theory known as scientific management. Relationships among variables do exist in organizations, and mathematical modeling can be used to describe them. Thus the modeling school has been and continues to be a major contributor to management thought. As we have noticed with all the other schools of thought, however, modeling theories alone cannot supply a total approach to management. Modeling theories have a limited concept of human beings; when mathematical relationships are stressed, managerial activities may be neglected, and these activities cannot always be modeled.

Our perceptions of management responsibilities and concepts have evolved through the years, and we have gained insights from a variety of sources with different orientations. Table 1-1 gives a summary sketch of the schools of management thought.

TABLE 1-1

OVERVIEW OF SCHOOLS OF MANAGEMENT THOUGHT

School	Some important assumptions	Primary focus	General contributions to management
Classical Scientific management Process orientation	People motivated by economics alone Managerial rationality Organization a closed system (certainty)	Economic efficiency Physical aspects of work environment Scientific analysis of work tasks Applications of techniques to work tasks Management processes	Demonstration of benefits from specialization of labor, division of labor, job analysis, separation of planning and doing Identification of principles and functions of management
Behavioral Human relations Behavioral science Social systems	People complex; possess multiple needs Human beings social creatures Organization an open system	Behavior of individual in work environment Interpersonal and social aspects of work environment Interactive relationships of organization with its environment	Identification of behavioral variables that relate to organizational behavior Development of theories relating organizational behavior to human characteristics and organizational variables
Modeling Decision making Systems theory Mathematical modeling	Decision making processes the primary managerial behaviors Organization an open system Organization a complex of interrelated subcomponents Main elements of organizations can be abstracted, interrelated, and expressed mathematically	Information acquisition, utilization, and choice processes Identification of organization boundaries, interrelationships among subsystems, and relationships between organization and larger environment Quantification of decision problems and systems Optimization of small set of situations	Development of guides for improving decision making Development of approaches for predicting and explaining system behavior Development of explicit rules for management decisions Development of methods for analyzing organizational systems or subsystems

The Contingency Approach: An Integrative Thrust

The schools of management thought we have discussed are widely documented, and each has established its niche in the history of management. Where do we go from here? Some developments during the past decade suggest the beginnings of a new thrust in management, the *contingency* approach.[1]

Although the contingency approach to management is still in its infancy, its underlying philosophy has some appeal both conceptually and pragmatically. The contingency approach is integrative, focusing on fitting together the ideas and concepts of the different schools of thought rather than dwelling on their differences; it "integrates the ideas from a wide range of disciplines to make it possible to be more prescriptive about how to manage under different sets of circumstances."[2]

The need for an integrative thrust arises from the often contradictory, incomplete, or incompatible managerial actions suggested by existing schools of thought. Consider the following specific examples.

- Employee participation in decision making facilitates organizational effectiveness in some situations but is dysfunctional in others.
- Autocratic leadership is most effective under some conditions, but an employee-centered leadership style results in higher group performance under other conditions.
- For some organizations a hierarchical structure is most appropriate; but others find it to be unsuitable for adapting to the demands of a dynamic external environment.

Satisfactory resolutions of these and many more issues have not emerged from existing schools of management thought. When should the prescriptions offered by the different orientations be applied? Under what circumstances? In answering these questions, the contingency approach assumes that no single existing approach is "best." Instead, existing ideas must be applied selectively, depending upon the circumstances confronting the manager. In fact, the contingency approach goes even further:

> . . . to say that "the correct way to apply an idea depends upon the circumstances" says nothing to anyone—it is indeed vacuous. . . . It is necessary to specify the individual and organizational conditions which modify managerial activity; that is, to specify the circumstances on which correct applications of a concept depends.[3]

Specifying the circumstances in which specific actions are appropriate and those in which they are inappropriate is the challenge we face. This challenge is immense; ideas from many disciplines—organizational behavior, organization theory, economics, sociology, and psychology—must be

---

[1] For an introduction to the contingency approach to management, see Don Hellriegel and John W. Slocum, Jr., *Management: A Contingency Approach* (Reading, Mass.: Addison-Wesley Pub. Co., Inc., 1974).

[2] Henry L. Tosi and Stephen J. Carroll, *Management: Contingencies, Structure, and Process* (Chicago: St. Clair Press, 1976), p. 17.

[3] Tosi and Carroll, *Management: Contingencies, Structure, and Process*, p. 17.

integrated. Efforts to meet the challenge posed by the contingency approach have just begun; but the potential rewards seem great, and we expect continued interest in this new approach.

A FRAMEWORK FOR ANALYSIS

Classical, behavioral, and modeling schools all have contributed substantially to our understanding of management as taught and practiced today. In this book, we hope to draw from these schools a framework for analysis for our study of operations management.

As part of the ongoing process of management, managers perform functions that involve planning, organizing, and controlling. The process approach is very helpful in structuring our thinking about management since it both examines separate activities in detail and allows for interdependence of systems (see Figure 1-1).

People in their working environments exhibit behavioral dimensions that are not readily explained either in the closed system of the classical approach or by the logical analysis of the modeling approach to management. Certainly managers must take into account individual and group behavior of subordinates, peers, superiors, and other groups in their managerial activities. (Behavior in this sense refers to the actions of all participants in the organization, both subordinates and managers.) As managers plan, organize, and control their operations, they must take into account the behavioral implications of their activities. Thus, the process and behavioral approaches necessarily interact.

Many of the planning, organizing, and controlling activities of the managerial process can be modeled. But although these models of decision making, functional problems, and systems are related to the behavioral dimensions of subordinates and supervisors, integration of the modeling

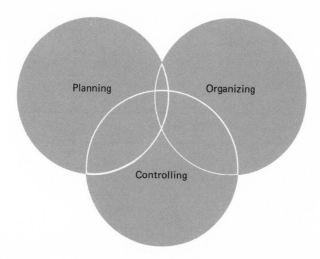

Figure 1-1 **The management process**

and behavioral approaches to management is difficult. Both schools developed at about the same time, but they have adopted very different scientific methodologies. The kinds of measurements used in the empirical, experimental approach of the behavioral school differ somewhat from those used in the mathematical, computerized approach of the modeling school. It is our observation that the modeling and behavioral approaches have found more in common with the process school than they have with each other. Nevertheless, in private and public organizations managers need to draw from the modeling school for those activities that can be modeled, taking into account any behavioral consequences. We suggest an integration of the three schools as a framework for analysis in operations management (see Figure 1-2). Throughout the balance of this book, this framework will provide the structure for examining operations management problems, concepts, and techniques.

SUMMARY

Management activities are centuries old; they can be traced in records of ancient civilizations. Never, however, have managerial functions been as necessary or as complex as they are today. Whatever their titles, managers, administrators, and supervisors of both public and private organizations make it possible for modern industrialized societies to function.

Management thought can be classified into *classical, behavioral,* and *modeling* schools. The classical school emphasizes the scientific management and process approaches to management; it defines management as the process that results as one person influences others through the functions of planning, organizing, and controlling.

The behavioral school focuses on a realistic concept of people in their working environments, realizing that workers have multiple needs and feelings. This concept centers managers' attention on individual and group behavior in organizations. Contributions from human relations studies, behavioral science, and social systems theories contribute to management's awareness of people at work.

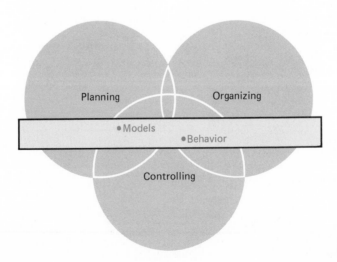

Figure 1-2 **A framework for analysis**

The modeling school emphasizes relationships among variables in organizations. This rational, quantitative approach reflects contributions from decision-making, mathematical, and systems theories. The modeling approach is best applied to routinized aspects of an organization; one must be able to identify and model distinct relationships among organization variables.

We suggest an integration of the three schools as a framework for analysis in operations management. Any one of them taken alone would ignore significant contributions of the other two schools of management thought. Throughout the balance of the book, this framework for analysis will be our guide as we examine operations management problems, concepts, and techniques.

REVIEW AND
DISCUSSION
QUESTIONS

1. Compare and contrast the three broad categories of management thought: classical, behavioral, and modeling schools.

2. The Egyptian pyramids and Moses's organizational ability are two historical examples of the early existence of management. Give two other historical examples of nonbusiness management.

3. Describe classical management's scientific management theory.

4. A problem with modern assembly line techniques seems to be that workers are apathetic. How could scientific management be used as a basis for solving this problem? How could a human relations philosophy help solve it?

5. Together, Frederick Taylor's scientific management theory and Henri Fayol's process theory comprise classical management thought.
   (a) What are some differences between Taylor's and Fayol's theories?
   (b) What are two limitations of classical management?

6. Why is there a need for a behav-ioral school of management thought? Preferably from your own experience or observation, provide a supervisor-subordinate situation that supports your answer.

7. Explain the decision-making theory of management.

8. Sometimes management has been defined as "getting things done through others."
   (a) Which management theories most closely support this definition?
   (b) Why do proponents of mathematical modeling feel that this definition is oversimplified?

9. Which school of management thought do you think is best? Why?

10. What might the contingency approach to management add to existing thought? Provide an example that you think would fit the contingency approach.

11. Relate the framework for analysis (Figure 1-2) to each school of management.

PROBLEMS

1. A machine shop has an opportunity to build metal "tees" for a company that is marketing Tee-Ball, a new development in Little League baseball. Fixed costs are estimated to be $1,500, variable costs $2.50 per tee, and the projected bid price $4.50 per tee. How many tees must the machine shop build to break even?

2. A state university has fixed operating costs of $4,500,000 per year and variable costs of $1,200 per student. Tuition is currently $460 per year; the balance of the funds come from the state and federal governments. Projected enrollment for next year is 3,500 students. Use breakeven analysis to determine

the amount of money that the university must receive from government to break even.

3. **An insurance claims office's group labor standard is 150 claims processed per day. So far this week, 160, 125, 140, and 100 claims have been processed daily. The claims backlog is building. Prepare a graph of daily efficiency. What does the graph indicate?**

GLOSSARY

Authority: the right to give orders and the power to exact obedience; may be obtained by position or such personal characteristics as personality, experience, and moral character

Behavior science: theory that people in their work environments are complex and that such processes as leadership, motivation, communication, contingency relationships, and attitude change have a direct impact upon the individual's productivity

Breakeven: that volume of output at which the total revenue received equals the total cost of production

Classical school of management: focuses on efficiency at the production core and on the separation of planning and doing work; emphasizes management principles and functions

Closed system: one that is self-contained, relies little on its environment, and operates in a world of certainty

Commanding: directing the activities of subordinates

Controlling: all those activities assuring that performance in the organization takes place in accordance with planned performance

Coordinating: all activities that bind together individual efforts and direct them toward a common objective

Decision-making approach: stresses decisions as the central purpose of managers

Efficiency: some measure of outputs over inputs

Human relations: concept that people are complex and have multiple needs and that the subordinate-supervisor relationship directly affects productivity

Individual standard: a goal reflecting an average worker's normal amount of output per unit of time under normal working conditions

Logistics management: all aspects of procurement, movement, maintenance, provision of services, and disposition of supplies, equipment, facilities, and personnel

Mathematical modeling: the creation of mathematical representations of management problems and organizations in order to determine outcomes of proposed courses of action

Organizing: all activities that result in some structure of tasks and authority

Planning: all those activities that result in developing a course of action and guide future decision making

Process management: one theory of the classical school; it views management as a continuous process involving the functions of planning, organizing, and controlling so as to influence the actions of others

Responsibility: the duty to be accountable for a specific set of events

Scientific management: one of several classical theories of management; it emphasizes economic efficiency at the production core through management rationality; assumes the economic motivation of workers and urges the separation of planning and doing work

Social system: one set of behavioral theories examining group relationships and their effect upon productivity

Span-of-control: number of subordinates who report directly to the supervisor

Specialization of labor: concept of breaking jobs down into specialized subtasks and reassigning work according to the task involved

System theory: identifies organization boundaries, interrelationships among subsystems, and relationships between the organization and the larger environment

Unity of command: concept of having only one supervisor for each employee

Academy of Management Journal 15, no. 4 (December 1972).

Barnard, Chester I. *The Functions of the Executive.* Cambridge: Harvard University Press, 1938.

Donnelly, James H., Jr., James C. Gibson, and John M. Ivancevich. *Fundamentals of Management: Functions, Behavior, Models.* Dallas: Business Publications, Inc., 1971.

Fayol, Henri. *General and Industrial Management.* Translated by Constance Storrs. London: Pitman Pub. Corp., 1949.

George, Claude S., Jr. *The History of Management Thought.* 2nd ed. Englewood Cliffs, N.J.: Prentice-Hall, Inc., 1972.

Hellriegel, Don and John W. Slocum, Jr. *Management: A Contingency Approach.* Reading, Mass.: Addison-Wesley Pub. Co., 1974.

Mee, John F. *Management Thought in a Dynamic Economy.* New York: New York University Press, 1973.

Minor, John B. *Management Theory.* New York: Macmillan Pub. Co., Inc., 1971.

Simon, Herbert A. *The New Science of Management Decision.* New York: Harper & Row, 1960.

Smith, Adam. *The Wealth of Nations.* New York: Random House, Inc., 1937.

Thompson, James D. *Organizations in Action.* New York: McGraw-Hill Book Co., 1967.

Tosi, Henry L. and Stephen J. Carroll. *Management: Contingencies, Structure, and Process.* Chicago: St. Clair Press, 1976.

2 Operations Management

Manufacturing management, production management, and *operations management* all describe the same general discipline, and the order of the terms reflects the evolution of modern operations management. The traditional view of manufacturing management began in the eighteenth century with Adam Smith's recognition that the subdivision and specialization of labor can result in economic benefits. From then until about 1930, the traditional view prevailed, and many techniques we still use today were developed. Among these were the recognition of differential skills, the development of the scientific approach to studying work, motion and time studies, and scheduling techniques. A brief sketch of these and other contributions to manufacturing management is highlighted in Table 2-1.

Production management became the more widely accepted term from the 1930s through the 1950s. As Frederick Taylor's work became more widely known and other contributors to management adopted the scientific approach, techniques were developed that focused on economic efficiency at the core of manufacturing organizations. Work measurement, incentives, and other techniques traditionally associated with industrial engineering were applied to management situations. People in their physical environments were "put under a microscope" and studied in great detail. Jobs were carefully analyzed and reorganized to achieve greater efficiency.

The Hawthorne studies in the late 1930s encouraged psychologists and sociologists to join in the study of people at work. An expanded view of human beings differing considerably from Taylor's "machine-man" concept was developed. This human relations approach toward employees in the 1940s and 1950s, and its concern with the individual's feelings and needs, changed our concepts of both employees and management. Production managers were forced to become aware of both subordinate-

TABLE 2-1

HISTORICAL SUMMARY OF OPERATIONS MANAGEMENT

Date (approximate)	Contribution	Contributor
1776	Specialization of labor in manufacturing	Adam Smith
1832	Division of labor by skill; assignment of jobs by skill; basics of time study	Charles Babbage
1900	Scientific management; time study and work study developed; dividing planning and doing of work; emphasis on research, logic in production process	Frederick W. Taylor
1900	Motion study of jobs	Frank B. Gilbreth
1901	Scheduling technique for employees, machines, jobs in manufacturing	Henry L. Gantt
1915	Economic lot sizes for inventory control	F.W. Harris
1931	Statistical inference applied to product quality; quality control charts	Walter A. Shewhart
1935	Statistical sampling applied to quality control; inspection sampling plans; single, double sampling	H.F. Dodge and H.G. Romig
1940	Operations research applications in World War II	P.M.S. Blacket and others
1947	Linear programming	George B. Dantzig, William Orchard-Hays, and others
1950	Mathematical programming, nonlinear and stochastic processes	A. Charnes, W.W. Cooper, H. Raiffa, and others
1955	Digital computer; large scale computations available	IBM
1960	Organizational behavior; continued study of people at work; integration into production/operations management	L. Cummings, L. Porter, and others

supervisor relationships and techniques for increasing efficiency in production. The production manager's dual role as a manager of people and a manager of methods and techniques is still apparent in operations management today.

Organizations Viewed as Systems

What is a system? Often used loosely, the term can mean different things to different people. In a very general sense, a *system* is a collection of objects united by some form of regular interaction and interdependence. Systems can vary from very large physical collections of subcomponents, such as nationwide communications networks, to more minute abstract examples—someone's "system" for processing paperwork in an office, for example. In some professional fields, such as process engineering and biology, *system* has a much more precise definition. Regardless of the precision of the term, however, models are often developed to represent a system or some aspect of it. These models, which show functional relationships, are used to facilitate communication among people who are mutually interested in whatever system is under consideration.

Figure 2-1 illustrates an operations planning system for a construction company. Notice that in this system, major planning activities precede actual construction activities. The solid lines represent the primary direction of the planning process; the dotted lines represent feedback among planning activities. The system concept in construction planning requires that subfunctions be planned so that they relate to each other in a specific order. This example illustrates only one of the many meanings that can be intended when the word *system* is used.

The systems concept can help develop our understanding of the operations of an organization. Consider this simple systems model.

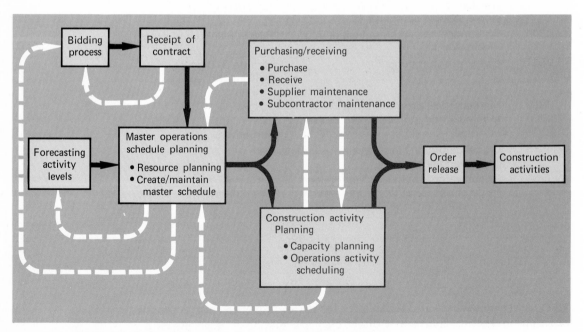

Figure 2-1 **Operational planning system for a construction company**

EXAMPLE

21

Chapter 2
Operations
Management

A business organization can be defined as an identifiable entity created to accomplish specific purposes. It exists within, and is part of, a larger environment. The organization itself consists of numerous subcomponents (subsystems), all of which interact in pursuing the organizational goals.

Several important systems concepts underlie this definition. The organization:

- has identifiable goals that may be expressed in terms of profit, service, or other accomplishments,
- has boundaries that limit the nature and types of activities it performs,
- is part of a larger environment (another system),
- is made up of subcomponents that are interrelated in many complex ways,
- engages in efforts and actions to ensure that its goals are being satisfactorily attained.

Its goals identify an organization's fundamental reasons for existence; they tell what it is trying to accomplish. A business firm's goals often describe both the general nature of its products (goods and/or services) and what it wishes to accomplish for its customers, employees, and owners. A firm's statement of goals is important because it directs and guides day-to-day activities and alerts management when the firm is headed off course. By comparing actual accomplishments with stated goals, management can decide when changes are needed to redirect the organization's efforts.

The boundaries of an organization are largely determined by society's acceptance of its goals. The business firm cannot exist without the consent and support of the larger environment. Figure 2-2 shows several environmental elements affecting the firm's success. If consumers don't buy the product, if other businesses won't supply needed materials, if governmental regulations are too rigid, the business firm will cease to exist.

A systems model of the organization itself identifies the subsystems, or subcomponents, that make up the firm. Some of these are illustrated in Figure 2-3. The production/operations subsystem is one of many interdependent subsystems in most organizations. As Figure 2-3 shows, a business firm might well have accounting, personnel, engineering, finance, marketing, purchasing, and physical distribution functions in addition to production/operations. These functions are not independent but are interrelated to one another in many complex ways. (The arrows indicate interdependence.) You can see that marketing interacts with purchasing and finance; what you cannot see so clearly is that marketing interacts with all other subsystems as well. Decisions made in the production/operations subsystem often affect the behavior and performance of other subsys-

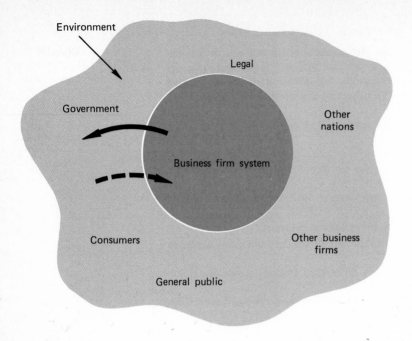

Figure 2-2 **The business firm and the environment**

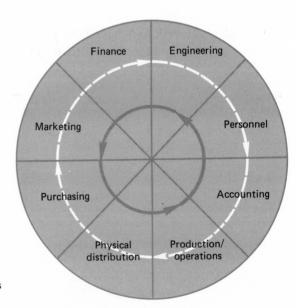

Figure 2-3 **The business firm: a systems view**

tems. Likewise, decisions in the other subsystems affect production/operations as well as one another. Finally, you should understand that the boundaries separating the various subsystems are not clear and distinct. Where do the responsibilities of production/operations end and those of physical distribution begin? The answers to such questions are often unclear and sometimes never resolved.

The final major concept in the systems model of organizations is control. Control in the business firm involves measurement of outputs, evaluation or comparison of actual accomplishments with desired accomplishments, and adjustments of inputs. The results of this comparison are fed back to management, as shown in Figure 2-4. The "feedback loop" enables management to decide whether or not adjustments in organizational activities are needed; it is an essential element in exercising timely control over the firm's behavior.

EXAMPLE

There are many different kinds of control in technologically advanced societies. Consider the technological control feature in a high quality automobile that features year-round constant interior temperature. Say that desired temperature is 72°F. If the temperature in the early morning is actually 58°F, when the car is started actual temperature is monitored, a comparison to desired temperature made, and the adjustment made by the heater. In the evening, the temperature in the car might be 84°F. The monitoring, comparison, and adjustment takes place again, this time by air conditioning.

A similar kind of control exists in organizations. Some executives use a simple system to make sure future organization activities take place in accordance with the organization's plans. Required activities are noted on a calendar date when they are supposed to be performed. At the beginning of each day, the executive checks the calendar to see what activities are planned for the day. He or she seeks information to compare actual progress to date with planned progress. If adjustments are needed, they can be made immediately. Even if no adjustments are necessary, the control process is functioning, since the executive knows that performance is taking place according to the organization's plans.

Figure 2-4 The business firm: feedback for control

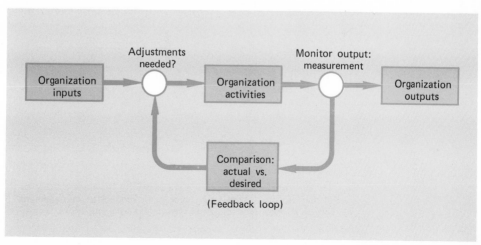

(Feedback loop)

The Operations Subsystem

Generally speaking, the operations subsystem is that part of the organization that exists primarily for generating or producing the organization's products. In some business firms the product is a physical good (refrigerators, breakfast cereal), while in others it is a service (insurance, health care for the elderly). Why do such diverse companies as manufacturing organizations, financial institutions, and health care facilities have an operations subsystem? All of them have a *conversion process* (see Figure 2-5). Necessary for this process are the inputs needed to make the product, the process by which these inputs are converted, the product resulting from the conversion of the inputs, and feedback loops in the operations subsystem. The product or service is converted into cash to acquire more resources. Thus the conversion process remains alive.

Try to recall examples of real organizations as you think about the conversion process shown in Figure 2-5. Perhaps you have worked in a department store, on a farm, for a construction company, or in an automobile assembly plant. What were the inputs? A department store's inputs include the land upon which the building is located; your labor as a stock clerk; capital in the form of the building, equipment, and merchandise; and the management skills of the store managers (see Figure 2-6).

On a farm the conversion process is the technical transformation[1] that occurs when the farmer's inputs (land, equipment, labor, and so on)

Figure 2-5 **The conversion process**

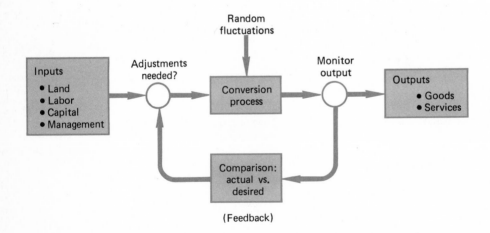

(Feedback)

[1]The transformation process is essentially the same concept as the conversion process. See Martin K. Starr, "Evolving Concepts in Production Management" (Chicago: *Proceedings of the 24th Annual Meeting, Academy of Management,* 1964).

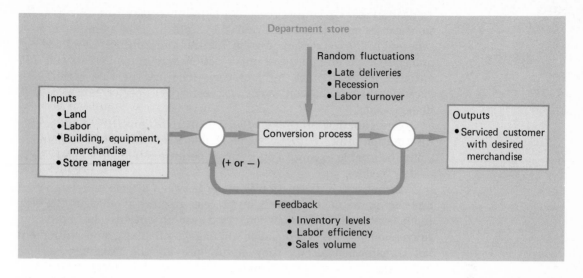

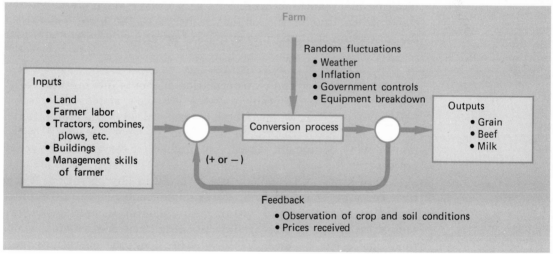

Figure 2-6 **The conversion process for a department store and a farm**

are converted into such outputs as corn, wheat, or milk. The exact form of this conversion process varies from industry to industry, but it is an economic phenomenon that exists in every industry. Economists refer to this transformation of resources into goods and services as the "production function"; if you are familiar with microeconomics, you may recall the total product, cost, and supply curves that represent the production side of market equilibrium.

The random fluctuations indicated in Figure 2-5 consist of unplanned and/or uncontrollable environmental influences that might cause actual output to differ from planned output. A Chrysler assembly plant might be plagued with production equipment failures, material shortages, or wildcat strikes by United Auto Workers union members. Random fluctuations can be acts of God (fire caused by lightning, for example) or problems inherent in the conversion process. Inherent variabilities of material, labor, and equipment and material imperfections and human errors can all affect output quality. In fact, random variations are the rule rather than the exception in production processes; error-free performance is virtually nonexistent.

The function of the feedback loop in Figure 2-5 is to provide an information link. Without some feedback of information, management would be unable to control operations, because it wouldn't know the results of its decisions.

Sometimes a distinction is made between direct conversion of inputs and the inputs in the conversion process. In stock production the economic input (material) is directly converted into an output. The inputs into the conversion process (land, labor, management, plant, and equipment) are not transformed at all; they simply provide the necessary services for production. This is a fine point in economics, but it can be useful when thinking of production/operations as a conversion process. We will not elaborate on this distinction but rather take the more general view of the conversion of inputs into outputs of goods and services.

Technological
impact in
conversion

The transformation of inputs into outputs varies considerably with the technology employed. By *technology*, we mean both the general set of transformation activities taking place and the level of scientific sophistication in plant, equipment, skills, and product (or service) in the conversion process.

Both kinds of technology are involved in any operation. A trucking firm and an accounting firm, for example, require quite different transformation activities, and within both kinds of firms various levels of sophistication can be employed. In trucking firms, for example, a conscientious choice can be made as to whether long-line operations will have permanent or portable refrigeration and heating in all, none, or some trailers. The level of technological sophistication in any firm affects both the services that can be offered to customers and operating efficiency. Generally, the more scientifically advanced the technology, the more capital required.

MANAGING THE
OPERATIONS
SUBSYSTEM

We have described the operations subsystem; the real problem, however, is not to identify it but to operate it effectively. The conversion process must be managed by someone, and that someone is the operations manager.

The operations manager's job is to manage the process of converting inputs into desired outputs. Look again at Figure 1-2 in Chapter 1. All the elements in our framework for analysis are the operations manager's responsibility.

Planning
The operations manager selects the objectives for the operations subsystem of the organization and the policies, programs, and procedures for achieving the objectives. This stage includes efforts directed toward product planning, facilities design, and the use of the conversion process.

Organizing
The operations manager establishes an intentional structure of roles within the operations subsystem. He or she determines and enumerates the activities required to achieve the operations subsystem's goals and assigns authority and responsibility for carrying them out.

Controlling
The operations manager assures that the plans for the operations subsystem are accomplished. Performance of the subsystem is monitored, and steps are taken to improve performance when there are deviations from planned actions. Thus, to achieve the desired output goals, the operations manager must manage the resource inputs and the conversion processes pictured in Figure 2-7. What inputs are needed? How and where will they be obtained? The answers to these and many other input questions require considerable planning and organizing efforts by the operations manager. What type of conversion process should be selected? What should be its capacity? Where will it be located? What investment will be required? These and many other kinds of issues must be resolved in planning for and organizing the conversion process.

The operations manager must also exercise control. Outputs must be measured to see if they conform to what has been planned. If they do, adjustments aren't needed. If the information feedback indicates substantial differences between planned and actual outputs, then inputs or parts of the conversion process must be adjusted. Suppose automobile production one week averaged 51 cars per working hour, but planned output was 59 cars. Investigation reveals that on four occasions some gear box subassemblies were not sent to the main assembly line. These shortages resulted in reduced output levels for the week. Adjustments must be made through the feedback loop to alleviate the shortage. Perhaps inputs have

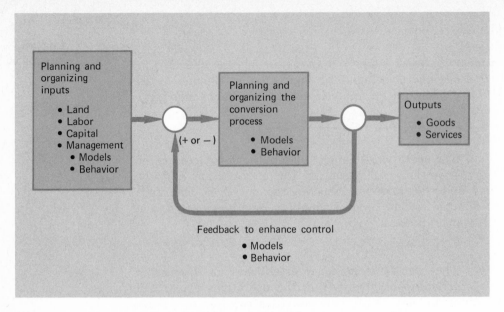

Figure 2-7   Planning, organizing, and controlling the conversion process

to be readjusted and more direct labor and materials devoted to gear box subassemblies. Actual solutions to such problems might not be so simple, but feedback and control measures can often help identify the sources of problems and suggest ways to solve them.

Behavior   In executing planning, organizing, and controlling functions, operations managers are clearly concerned with how their actions affect subordinate behavior. They also want to know how the behavior of subordinates can affect management's planning, organizing, and control actions. Usually, *behavior* refers to subordinate behavior in the supervisor/subordinate relationship. In operations we are also interested in the behavior of the supervisor, typically the operations manager. Of particular interest is the manager's decision making behavior.

Models   As operations managers plan, organize, and control the transformation process, they encounter many problems and must make many decisions. These difficulties are frequently simplified by using models. Types of models and examples of their uses will be illustrated in some detail as we cover the functional problems of operations management.

Problems of the Operations Manager

Operating managers are concerned with many different problem areas: cost control in brokerage houses, quality of services in hospitals, rates of production output in furniture factories. Although operations managers occupy positions at several levels of their organizations, and although they work in different kinds of organizations, they all share some kinds of problems. A recent Canadian study of plant superintendents, work managers, production managers, and others with related duties showed that most of their problems had to do with planning, organizing, and controlling (Figure 1-2) and the conversion process (Figure 2-7). Figure 2-8 gives a distribution of the participants' executive positions and roles. About 25 percent of the participants were plant superintendents or works managers, about 25 percent production managers, and the other 50 percent from a range of other production-related roles in their companies. Figure 2-9 shows results of interviews with many of these managers. You can see that hardly any of their problems are uniquely identified with only one of the three functions of management. Four of the fifteen major problem areas are most frequently encountered in *planning* (production planning, production scheduling, forecasting, and budgeting); three are very often dealt with in *organizing* (labor/industrial relations, process design, and job design); and four are principally *control* problems (cost, production, quality, and inventory). Since we are dealing with a system that has highly interrelated components, however, these problem areas are interrelated, and none is related strictly to planning *or* organizing *or* controlling. It will become clear as we progress in our study of operations management that all these problem areas are encountered to some extent as the operations manager plans, organizes, and controls the operations subsystem and manages the conversion process.

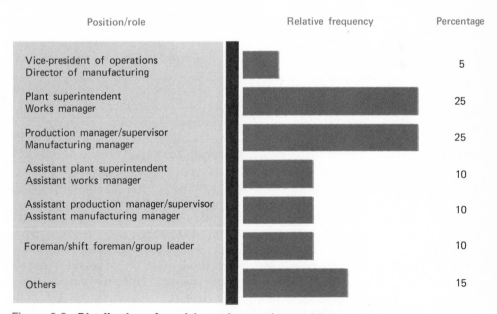

Figure 2-8 Distribution of participants' executive positions and roles
Adapted from Robert R. Britney and E. F. Peter Newson, *The Canadian Production/Operations Management Environment: An Audit* (School of Business Administration Research Monograph, London, Ontario: University of Western Ontario, April 1975).

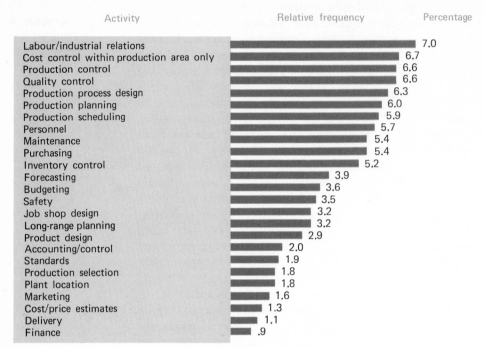

Activity	Relative frequency	Percentage

Activity	Percentage
Labour/industrial relations	7.0
Cost control within production area only	6.7
Production control	6.6
Quality control	6.6
Production process design	6.3
Production planning	6.0
Production scheduling	5.9
Personnel	5.7
Maintenance	5.4
Purchasing	5.4
Inventory control	5.2
Forecasting	3.9
Budgeting	3.6
Safety	3.5
Job shop design	3.2
Long-range planning	3.2
Product design	2.9
Accounting/control	2.0
Standards	1.9
Production selection	1.8
Plant location	1.8
Marketing	1.6
Cost/price estimates	1.3
Delivery	1.1
Finance	.9

Figure 2-9 **Major problem areas of operations management**

Source: Robert R. Britney, "Continuing Education in Production/Operations Management,"
Paper presented at the 34th Annual Meeting, Academy of Management, Seattle, 1974.

THE STRATEGIC ROLE OF OPERATIONS

As one studies and practices operations management, it is easy to become preoccupied with the detailed economic and engineering aspects of the conversion process and lose sight of its fundamental purpose for existence. When this occurs, and it often does, the results can be disastrous from an overall organizational viewpoint. Economy and efficiency of conversion operations are secondary goals, not primary goals, of the overall organization. Primary overall goals are related to market opportunities. Indeed, an overemphasis on operations efficiency and economy can detract from primary goal accomplishment. We must therefore consider the broader strategic role of operations in the organization.

Consider the firm with a product quality control system geared to one orientation at the time that emerging market opportunities require another. Say that current products for existing markets warrant low to medium reliability. They need little or no product-life testing and only periodic performance checks of large volumes of output. When a new market opportunity emerges, the firm might attempt to use its existing quality control system for the sake of efficiency and economy. If the market success of the new product depends on greater product precision, reliability, and a more intensive quality control effort than currently exists, however, an entirely different quality control technology may be necessary. Left as is, the quality control system overlaid on a new product can lead to a marketing disaster. If the company wishes to capitalize on the new market opportunity, it must be willing and able to implement the necessary quality control technology, even if it involves extensive, costly changes.

In other instances, firms get themselves locked into situations that are detrimental to pursuing new market opportunities, and they are placed at a competitive disadvantage for long periods of time. This often happens with such basic operations design decisions as how many facilities to build and where to locate them. Should we build one large facility to benefit from economies of scale in operations? Or should we build several smaller specialized facilities to provide better delivery service to various market segments? Each decision has advantages, but each also has long-run implications for the types of future market opportunities it can accommodate. If, for example, a firm decides on four small facilities, each specializing in a particular family of products, the capital requirements of this decision may strain the company financially. Should market demand increase for one of the products, the firm may be unable both to compete with larger firms in the industry and to acquire funds for expansion.

There is no all-inclusive rule for resolving all these operations design decisions. What can be done, however, is to point out the tradeoffs that exist for the decision alternatives and to assess them within a broader strategic perspective.

Alternatives and Tradeoffs

Several critical operations decisions and their associated tradeoffs are shown in Table 2-2. As you can see, the decisions involve not only physical facilities and equipment but the mix of human skills and types of organizational arrangements as well. All these decision areas in combination determine the organization's basic overall orientation, its ability to perform effectively and to respond to opportunity, and the extent to which it is constrained from undertaking new endeavors. After outlining the decisions and alternatives, how does one proceed to make choices among them? This task can be guided by a broader strategic perspective.

A Strategic Perspective

In Figure 2-10 we see the basic downward flow leading to conversion operations and results. The general thrust of the process is guided by competitive and market conditions in the industry, which provide the basis for determining the organization's strategy. Where is the industry now, and where will it be in the future? What are the existing and potential markets? What market gaps exist, and what are the prospects for filling them? A careful analysis of market segments and the ability of our

TABLE 2-2

**SOME IMPORTANT TRADE-OFF DECISIONS IN MANUFACTURING—
OR "YOU CAN'T HAVE IT BOTH WAYS"***

Decision area	Decision	Alternatives
Plant and equipment	Span of process	Make or buy
	Plant size	One big plant or several smaller ones
	Plant location	Locate near markets or locate near materials
	Investment decisions	Invest mainly in buildings or equipment or inventories or research
	Choice of equipment	General purpose or special purpose equipment
	Kind of tooling	Temporary minimum tooling or "production tooling"
Production planning and control	Frequency of inventory-taking	Few or many breaks in production for buffer stocks
	Inventory size	High inventory or a lower inventory
	Degree of inventory control	Control in great detail or in lesser detail
	What to control	Controls designed to minimize machine downtime or labor cost or time in process, or to maximize output of particular products or material usage
	Quality control	High reliability and quality or low cost
	Use of standard	Formal or informal or none at all
Labor and staffing	Job specialization	Highly specialized or not highly specialized
	Supervision	Technically trained first-line supervisors or nontechnically trained supervisors
	Wage system	Many job grades or few job grades; incentive wages or hourly wages
	Supervision	Close supervision or loose supervision
	Industrial engineers	Many or few such men
Product design/engineering	Size of product line	Many customer specials or few specials or none at all

*Wickham Skinner, "Manufacturing—Missing Link in Corporate Strategy," *Harvard Business Review* 47, 3 (May–June 1969), p. 141. Copyright 1969 by the President and Fellows of Harvard College.

Decision area	Decision	Alternatives
	Design stability	Frozen design or many engineering change orders
	Technological risk	Use of new processes unproved by competitors or follow-the-leader policy
	Engineering	Complete packaged design or design-as-you-go approach
	Use of manufacturing engineering	Few or many manufacturing engineers
Organization and management	Kind of organization	Functional or product focus or geographical or other
	Executive use of time	High involvement in investment or production planning or cost control or quality control or other activities
	Degree of risk assumed	Decisions based on much or little information
	Use of staff	Large or small staff group
	Executive style	Much or little involvement in detail; authoritarian or nondirective style; much or little contact with organization

competitors and ourselves to meet the needs of these segments are the bases for determining the most effective direction for an organization's future efforts.

After assessing the potential within the industry, management must develop an overall organizational strategy. Profit or return on investment and product and service offerings (product types, volumes, and quality anticipated within market segments) must be considered. Do we intend to concentrate organizational efforts on one standardized product that will be produced in large volume and sold at low price to a mass audience? Or do we foresee a large group of high-priced specialized products, each with a low market potential but reasonable overall revenue prospects? What will be the source of funds to finance delivery? How can we obtain funds from financial markets? These basic strategic decisions, based on market and competitive opportunities, should be our guide in establishing operations policy.

Once the competitive and market conditions are assessed, financial policy needs to be established. Management must determine the source of funds for initially financing operations, a policy for future funding, an integrated profit and dividend plan, and essential budgeting procedures for control. Financial policy can be established at the same time operations strategies are being set. Both react to and are integrated with the competitive

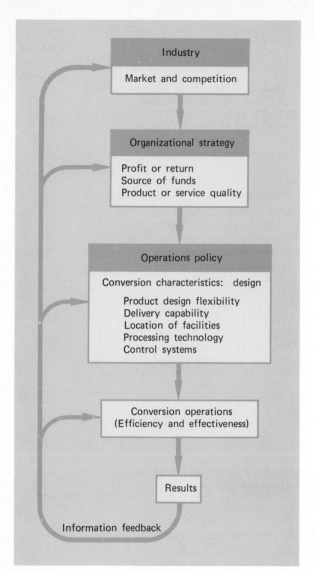

Figure 2-10 **Operations as a strategic element in accomplishing organizational goals**

and market conditions. Marketing, finance, and operation strategies and policies can be set only if they interact and consider each other.

In determining the design characteristics of the conversion process, management must implement an operations policy that reflects the organization's overall strategy. Suppose we elect to pursue several specialized segments of the electronics instrumentation market by featuring a small volume of high-priced, custom-engineered products of high reliability. This choice has important implications for each of the conversion characteristics and decision areas we have discussed. We might choose to buy basic product subcomponents rather than make them in several small plants located near specific market segments. This decision could involve relatively low investment in buildings but high investment in general-purpose equipment and research. Production planning and control could be oriented toward low inventory levels, with emphasis on high product reliability and on-time deliveries. A specialized professional work force under relatively loose supervision could be appropriate. Within each facility, the "design-as-you-go approach" to product engineering could be employed for meeting customers' specialized product needs. The highly technical nature of the product could dictate the need for a relatively large engineering and product development staff.

Once the basic characteristics of the conversion process are determined, facilities must be established and operated in a manner consistent with the strategic mission of the organization. It is at this level of activity that the operations manager becomes concerned with questions of efficiency and effectiveness. Both are critical for organizational success.

For consistency in our discussion of operations strategy, we have drawn all our examples from manufacturing. Strategy in service operations, however, is just as important as it is in manufacturing operations. Managers of hospitals, hotels, long-term health care facilities, and entertainment operations must ask similar questions and raise similar issues if they want to have successful organizations.

Operations Objectives

The overall objective of the operations subsystem is to provide conversion capabilities for meeting the organization's basic goals. Most organizations' primary goal is the attainment of a desired profit or return. This goal is then translated into operations subgoals, which specify:

1. product (service) characteristics
2. process characteristics
3. customer service
   a. producing quantities to meet expected demand
   b. meeting the required delivery date for goods or services
4. product (service) quality
5. efficiency
   a. effective employee relations and labor cost control
   b. material cost control
   c. cost control in facility utilization
6. adaptability for future survival

When the organization's primary goal is not-for-profit, the operations subgoals are essentially the same, but they differ in emphasis.

These operations objectives are directed toward satisfying existing market opportunities and employees' needs and maintaining a healthy posture for the future. In trying to accomplish these objectives, we must be concerned about efficiency, because the organization's resources are limited. The conversion system therefore seeks to be both effective (in meeting its objectives) and efficient (in not expending resources unnecessarily).

What new demands are being made of operations managers today? How will their jobs change in the future? Answers to such questions are speculative, but we can find some clues by observing recent trends in overall economic activities.

Shifts in Economic Activity

Are people doing the same kinds of work today that they have done in the past?

The question is important because operations management will usually be found where economic activity is occurring. Table 2-3 provides us with some answers. We can see that there has been an employment shift from agriculture and other extractive (mining and contract construction) industries to the service sector, agriculture decreasing from 38 percent of the employed workers in 1900 to 5 percent in 1974, and service workers increasing from 28 percent in 1900 to 61 percent in 1974. The percentage of workers employed in industry has remained essentially the same. Will this trend continue? We suspect not. It is quite possible that the percentage of workers in the service sector will gradually continue to grow, but we believe this growth will be relatively slow. Probably it will come from workers shifting from industry to the service sector, while the percentage of agricultural workers will remain around 5 percent.

TABLE 2-3

DISTRIBUTION OF EMPLOYED WORKERS BY MAJOR SECTORS OF THE ECONOMY, 1900–1974 *

Year	Agriculture and other extractive industries	Industry	Services	Total
1900	38%	34%	28%	100%
1910	34	37	29	100
1920	30	39	31	100
1930	27	35	38	100
1940	25	34	41	100
1950	15	40	45	100
1960	11	39	50	100
1970	5	36	59	100
1974	5	34	61	100

*U.S., Bureau of the Census; Victor Fuchs, *The Service Economy* (New York: Columbia University Press, 1968), p. 207, with permission of the NBER; *Statistical Abstract of the United States 1972*, pp. 227–30; U.S., Department of Labor, Bureau of Labor Statistics, 1975.

TABLE 2-4

EMPLOYMENT IN THE SERVICE SECTOR, 1929 AND 1974 (in thousands)*

Service	1929	1974	1974 divided by 1929
Wholesale and retail trade	6,123	16,674	2.7
Finance, insurance, real estate	1,509	4,091	2.7
Repair services	3,440	13,021	3.7
Government	3,065	13,739	4.4
Transportation, communication, utilities	3,916	4,644	1.1
Total, all services	18,053	52,169	2.8
Total employed (labor force)	47,630	85,936	1.8

*U.S., Department of Labor, Bureau of Labor Statistics, 1972 and 1975.

One point is clear. The largest sector of the United States economy today is in services. Let's examine the service sector a little closer, since its growth has significant implications for operations management. Look at Table 2–4. Over the years 1929 to 1974, the most significant growth in actual employment has come in government, where there has been an increase of over 10.6 million workers. For the same period, wholesale and retail trade services have increased by over 10.5 million workers and repair services by over 9.5 million workers. In number of actual workers, the total labor force has increased some 38 million workers, with 34 million of this increase occurring in the service sector.

The United California Bank annually forecasts the growth of the major sectors of the U.S. economy in current dollars. Table 2-5 shows what changes took place in the decade of the 1960s and what is expected in the 1970s. A 25 percent increase in current dollar growth is forecast for the years from 1972 to 1982, with growth percentages in agriculture and extractive (mining and contract construction) industries and in manufacturing. Their growth is expected to be higher than overall growth or growth in the services group (transportation, trade, insurance, services, and government). This leads one to believe that major shifts of activity to the service sector (based on employment shifts) have already occurred.

More economic activity in the service sector suggests that many of you may find yourselves employed in service industries in the future. In this book we will take the position that operations management concepts, skills, and techniques are transferable *across* the industry/service sectors and *within* industries and services. Our examples and explanations will therefore apply to both kinds of operations, even if only one is mentioned. Unfortunately, our view is not widely shared:

People think of service as quite different from manufacturing. Service is presumed to be performed by individuals for other individuals, generally

TABLE 2-5

CHANGES IN U.S. MAJOR INDUSTRIES (billions of current dollars)†

Industry	1962	1972	1982	Percent of change 1972–1982
Agriculture, forestry, fishing	$ 23	$ 38	$ 100	163%
Mining	13	18	35	94
Contract construction	25	56	140	150
Manufacturing, nondurables	67	120	280	133
Manufacturing, durables	92	171	415	143
Transportation, communications, and utilities*	49	102	250	145
Wholesale trade*	37	78	155	99
Retail trade*	56	117	225	92
Finance, insurance, real estate*	76	164	375	129
Services*	58	133	350	163
Government and other	64	158	275	74
Total gross national product	$560	$1,155	$2,600	125%

†1975 Annual Forecast, Research and Planning Division, United California Bank, Los Angeles, California.
*A member of the "service producing industries," as defined by the Department of Commerce.

on a one-to-one basis. Manufacturing is presumed to be performed by machines, generally tended by large clusters of individuals whose sizes and configurations are themselves dictated by the machines' requirements. Service (whether customer service or the services of service industries) is performed "out there in the field" by distant and loosely supervised people working under highly variable, and often volatile, conditions. Manufacturing occurs "here in the factory" under highly centralized, carefully organized, tightly controlled, and elaborately engineered conditions.[2]

Modern management needs to transfer manufacturing concepts, techniques, and skills to the service sector. With an understanding of operations management, managers of service operations might well be able to bring about needed improvements in quality, effectiveness, and efficiency in their organizations.

New Challenges for Operations Management

What new problems and challenges will face production/operations managers? Changes in economic activity suggest that operations are becoming more labor intense. Does this mean we should throw out estab-

[2]Theodore Levitt, "Production-Line Approach to Service," *Harvard Business Review* 50, no. 5 (September–October 1972), p. 42.

lished, proven management techniques that have helped solve problems in manufacturing over the years? We think not. Rather, the challenge operations managers face lies in identifying problems, selecting appropriate models or techniques for solving them, and implementing the models or techniques successfully in unaccustomed settings.

Changes in the business world highlight the need for skilled operations managers to apply their tools to new problems. Three important trends in business that present challenges to production/operations managers have been identified:

> For one thing, shorter product life, more new technological choices concerning equipment processes, increased foreign competition, reduced margins, more customer specials, labor unrest, more knowledgeable workers, bigger and riskier capital investment decisions—all add up to needs for better production management and an enlarged role for production and operations executives in the success of the firm. For another thing, there is a growing concern with the apparent unwillingness of many MBAs (from almost any school) to "roll up their sleeves," to "get into important gritty details," and to "learn the business from ground-level experiences in manufacturing and selling in their early years before it is too late." And, finally, note a revived concern with the production and operating side of the business. "That's where we make or lose our money" would be a typical statement.[3]

Traditionally, manufacturing has been the focus of problems in this discipline, and it is there that most of our techniques have been developed. Now it is time for production/operations managers, as they assume enlarged roles in their organizations, to apply these techniques to problems they haven't met before. New managers must gain product and process knowledge at the ground level of their businesses, and they must be aware of a revived concern about cost control and productivity gains in operations.

CONTEMPORARY OPERATIONS MANAGEMENT TOPICS

Modern operations management is a complex proposition. To deal with it, we have divided this book into five major parts (see Figure 2-11). In each part, we relate specific operations management considerations to the contemporary issue under discussion. Our approach to production/operations management (P/OM) focuses on the functions of management, along with models and behavior, as they relate to the conversion side of the operation.

By organizing our coverage around the management subfunctions of planning, organizing, and controlling, we strive for an integrative perspective. By relating each problem area to a common theme, we hope to suggest a continuity of thought that will help you grasp the fundamentals of operations management. Within this framework, we have found it useful to approach the planning subfunction somewhat differently than is usually the case. We divide this subfunction into two major parts: planning the

[3]Wickham Skinner, "New Directions for Production and Operations Management" (*P/OM Division Communication 2, Academy of Management,* July 1972).

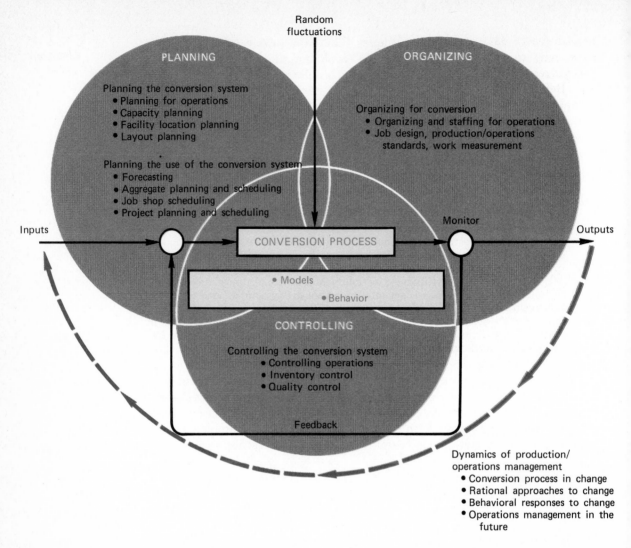

Figure 2-11   **General model for production/operations management (P/OM)**

conversion system and planning the *use of* the conversion system. Planning the conversion system revolves around its design; planning the use of the conversion system focuses on utilizing it once it's in existence. Although this distinction may be somewhat artificial, it allows us to integrate problem areas more logically than has been done in the past.

One major topic, for example, is controlling the conversion system (Part V). In this section we deal with cost control, inventory control, and quality control—all necessary activities of operating managers. As we discuss each of these separately, we develop relevant concepts and terminology, identify problems, and present problem-solving techniques. When problems are behavioral (quality motivation, for example), we introduce contemporary techniques like behavior modification and attitude change procedures to deal with them. When problems are process-oriented, we show why models and such methods as sampling theory and control procedures are appropriate.

Before considering specific operations problems, however, we must introduce a general orientation for analysis. This includes an acquaintance with some basic methods of analysis that can later be applied to resolve specific operation problems. It is this analytic orientation that we consider next.

SUMMARY

Systems concepts can be useful for understanding organizations and the role of the operations function within them, and pictorial models of these systems show the basic nature of the operations subsystem and its interaction with the environment. Operations management makes use of these systems and models in directing the conversion process, which converts inputs into desired outputs. Operations managers must become involved in planning, organizing, and controlling operations. As they make decisions and decide among alternatives, they must consider the organization's goals and overall strategy.

Historical shifts in economic activity and predicted changes in the growth of major industries indicate the increasing importance of the service sector. These changes present some new challenges to operations management, and transferring our knowledge of production management into the service sector setting is chief among them.

CASE

Operations Management in a Veterinary Clinic

See if you can identify the inputs, outputs, and conversion processes that exist in a veterinary clinic consisting of three veterinarians, a clerical staff, and two animal control assistants. Identify the primary operations management activities (use Figure 2-9 as a guide) that exist in this setting. Lay them out in a framework similar to the one in Figure 2-5. You should consider how the addition of an operations manager to the clinic staff would affect the cost and effectiveness of medical services. Normally, in a situation like this the operations manager would be one of the veterinarians. Could you explain to them why they should hire *you* to manage operations of the clinic?

REVIEW AND DISCUSSION QUESTIONS

1. Figure 2-6 shows the conversion processes for a department store and a farm. Can you list different levels of technology within both kinds of organizations?

2. Describe the three basic functions of an operations manager.

3. Organization goal accomplishment requires that a strategic element of operations is the consideration of the firm's industry, strategy, operations policy, and con-

version. How do these elements relate to one another? How do they relate to organization goal accomplishment?

4. How does production/operations policy interrelate with accounting and financial policy and marketing policy? What does this interrelationship accomplish?

5. Explain how control works in the operations subsystem. A schematic model (a diagram) might be

helpful in organizing your discussion.

6. Using Figure 2-5, explain the conversion process in a fast food outlet (McDonald's, for example) and a public swimming pool.

7. (a) What are operations subgoals?
   (b) What is the overall objective of the operations subsystem?
   (c) How do they relate to each other?

8. What are some employment shifts and economic growth trends that might help production/operations managers deal with the future?

9. Relate the conversion diagram in Figure 2-5 to the first 15 problem areas listed by operations managers in Figure 2-9.

10. What are some changes in the business world that present new challenges to production/operations managers?

11. Provide an example from any organization you choose for each of the first 5 problem areas in Figure 2-9.

12. As an industrialized nation becomes more affluent, people have more leisure time and demand more services than they used to. Many workers enter the labor force later and leave it earlier. How do these changes affect the role of the traditional production/operations manager?

GLOSSARY

Control: measurement of outputs, comparison of actual with desired accomplishments, and adjustment of inputs

Conversion process: changing labor, capital, land, and management inputs into outputs of goods and services

Feedback: that part of the control process that allows management to decide whether or not adjustments in organizational activities are needed

Operations management: management of the conversion process, which converts land, labor, capital, and management inputs into desired outputs of goods and services

Operations subsystem: that part of the organization that exists primarily for generating or producing the organization's physical goods or services

Random fluctuations: unplanned and/or uncontrollable environmental influences (strikes, floods, etc.) that cause planned and actual output to differ

System: a collection of objects united by some form of regular interaction and interdependence

SELECTED READINGS

Britney, Robert R. and E. F. Peter Newson. *The Canadian Production/Operations Management Environment: An Audit.* School of Business Administration Research Monograph. London, Ontario: University of Western Ontario, April 1975.

Koontz, Harold and Cyril O'Donnell. *Principles of Management: An Analysis of Managerial Functions.* 4th ed. New York: McGraw-Hill Book Co., 1968.

Levitt, Theodore. "Production-Line Approach to Service." *Harvard Business Review* 50, no. 5 (September–October 1972).

Roethlisberger, Fritz and William J. Dickson. *Management and the Worker.* Cambridge, Mass.: Harvard University Press, 1939.

Skinner, Wickham. "Manufacturing—Missing Link in Corporate Strategy." *Harvard Business Review* 47, no. 3 (May–June 1969).

Starr, Martin K. "Evolving Concepts in Production Management." Chicago: *Proceedings of the 24th Annual Meeting, Academy of Management,* 1964.

Operations Analysis

3

One of the distinguishing features of contemporary operations management is its use of systematic formal analysis. Formally analyzing problems allows managers to plan, organize, and control the conversion process in a systematic way; it gives them information and guidance for the decisions they have to make. As they analyze problems or alternatives, managers often make use of modeling techniques. In this chapter, we introduce the analytic orientation that typifies much of production/operations management (P/OM). As you read it, you will see that analysis and modeling are closely related (see Figure 3-1).

DECISION MAKING

In Chapter 1 we examined the decision-making school of management thought and concluded that although management is not synonymous with decision making, managers do become involved in the decision-making process. Faced with difficult and complex problems, managers must often take decisive action under severe time constraints. To help them, a variety of decision-making and analysis aids have been developed over the past sixty years. This abundance of decision-making aids distinguishes P/OM from many of the other subsystems of the organization. It is difficult to find another area of management in which more effort has been devoted to finding formal methods of analysis, and it is equally difficult to find areas where these developments are more widely employed. How does analysis help a manager make decisions? The answer becomes clearer when we examine the process of decision making.

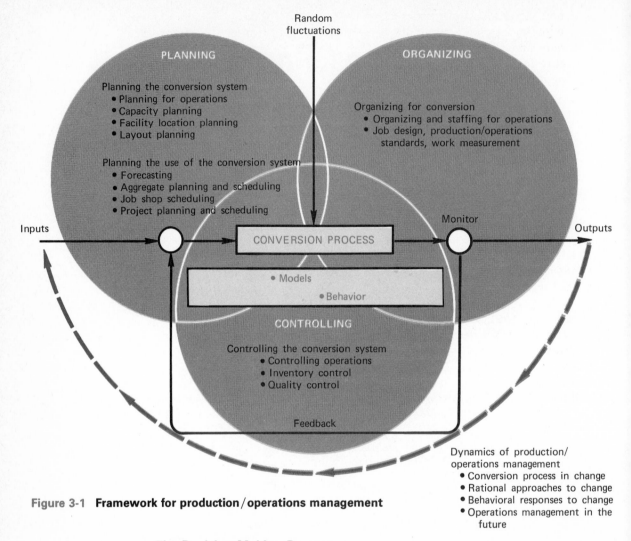

Figure 3-1 **Framework for production/operations management**

The following labels appear within the figure:

Random fluctuations

PLANNING

ORGANIZING

Planning the conversion system
• Planning for operations
• Capacity planning
• Facility location planning
• Layout planning

Planning the use of the conversion system
• Forecasting
• Aggregate planning and scheduling
• Job shop scheduling
• Project planning and scheduling

Organizing for conversion
• Organizing and staffing for operations
• Job design, production/operations standards, work measurement

Inputs

CONVERSION PROCESS

Monitor

Outputs

• Models
• Behavior

CONTROLLING

Controlling the conversion system
• Controlling operations
• Inventory control
• Quality control

Feedback

Dynamics of production/operations management
• Conversion process in change
• Rational approaches to change
• Behavioral responses to change
• Operations management in the future

The Decision-Making Process

Decisions usually involve several identifiable stages. First is the recognition that a problem, an obstacle to achieving a goal, exists. Second, attempts are made to identify alternatives, evaluate them, select one alternative, and implement the decision. Although it has a role to play throughout the process, formal analysis is used most extensively in the evaluation and choice stages. Some additional, "in between" steps are also involved in the decision-making process: identifying criteria, identifying relevant variables, and experimenting. To evaluate alternatives, managers must choose a criterion to distinguish between "good" and "bad" choices, and they must know how all the alternatives would affect the organization. The parts of the organization that would be affected are called the *relevant variables.* After identifying criteria and relevant variables, managers use some experimentation to estimate the impact each alternative would have if it were adopted. This experimentation may range from very informal to highly formal. Figure 3-2 shows the stages managers go through in making a decision.

Management Science Approach to Decision Making

Management science is a contemporary term encompassing both a philosophy and an approach to analyzing and solving organizational problems. Philosophically it assumes that explainable causes underlie organization problems and that systematic study of these problems can suggest how they may be resolved. The management science approach relies heavily on the scientific method of problem solving and on the use of quantitative models. *A model is a representation of something real; it shows relationships among variables and can be used to predict or explain.* Coupling the scientific method with quantitative models provides a powerful basis for analysis. Analysts can build a model of the operating system or of one or more system subcomponents. Then they can experiment with the model to see how it performs under various conditions. The idea behind all this is to find ways of improving the real operating system without tampering with it directly. Actually changing the real system to observe whether or not improved performance occurs is potentially dangerous. Real changes in productive systems can be costly to make, and once made they can have

Figure 3-2 **The decision-making process**

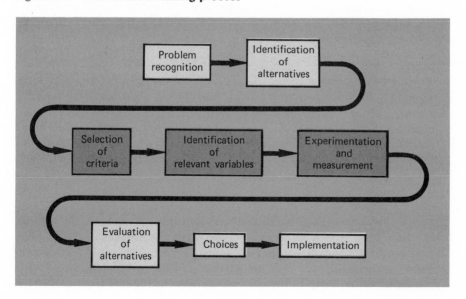

unexpected costly consequences, which may be irreversible. Predicting system responses to various changes before those changes are actually made is the purpose and goal of the management scientist.

With a model, the effects of experimental changes can be measured and observed more rapidly, more conclusively, and in some respects at less risk than would be possible by manipulating the real system. The difficulty is that sometimes the model may not accurately reflect the real system. If it doesn't, changes that looked good in the model may turn out to be disappointing when they're actually implemented. Did the analyst build into the model all the relevant aspects of the real system? It's a good idea to find out with a validity check. Either or both of these steps can help make sure the model is accurate:

1. People responsible for the function being modeled should approve the model's operation.
2. The model and the function being modeled should be operated together in real time to make sure they're equivalent.

For our purposes, operations research and management science are synonymous. Both can help operations managers solve many of the problems they confront. But which problems should be tackled by management science and which by another approach is a decision that has to be based on experience and judgment—two qualities that can hardly be modeled.

THE ROLE OF MODELS IN ANALYSIS

Models are used extensively by practitioners in operations analysis because they can aid in decision making. In spite of their utility, however, we must recognize them for what they are—artificial representations of things that are real. As such, they have shortcomings. They fall short of fully duplicating their real world counterpart.

> ### EXAMPLE
> Descriptions of the conversion process in this book are one kind of model, a *written* model. These descriptions are not, of course, the conversion process itself. The conversion process is an ongoing, real-life action that is occurring right now in most organizations; our descriptions merely explain that process.

This incompleteness of models should not be interpreted as a strictly negative feature. In fact, it can be desirable, because it clears away extraneous elements and concentrates on the heart of the problem. Real decision problems are complicated enough without trying to reconstruct all their complexities into a model. Instead, what we want, and what the modeling process gives us, is a simplified version of the situation, a representation in which all the minor considerations have been stripped away so the major factors are clearly visible.

Types of Models in Production and Operations Management

Models of relationships, like the relationships themselves, can be sophisticated or simple, rigorous or inexact. In production and operations management, we use several types of models of varying levels of sophistication.

Verbal models   Verbal or written models are descriptive. *They express in words the relationships among variables.* Suppose a passing motorist asks you to give him directions to the nearest gas station. Rather than actually driving along the roads to show him the way, you *abstract* the situation by methodically describing road signs, traffic lights, perhaps landmarks. If you tell him the way, you are giving him a verbal model. If you write the directions in words (not pictures), you are giving him a descriptive model.

Schematic models   *Schematic models show a pictorial relationship among variables.* If you gave the passing motorist a map showing the way to the nearest gas station, you would be giving him a schematic model. Charts and diagrams are also schematic; they are very useful for showing relationships among variables, as long as all the legends, symbols, and scales are explained.

Iconic models   *Iconic models are scaled physical replicas of objects or processes.* Architectural models of new buildings, highway engineering replicas of a proposed overpass system, and prototypes of chemical facilities are iconic models. In chemical engineering, scaled operating physical replicas of new chemical processing facilities are often constructed. These are operated before actual construction to assess whether the hypothesized relationships among chemicals, temperature, and other variables really hold.

Mathematical models   *Mathematical models show functional relationships among variables.* You are probably familiar with word problems from high school and college algebra in which variables were called x, y, and z to determine such relationships as age, weights, and distances. In any equation, x, y, and similar symbols are abstractions (they represent real variables), and they are used to illustrate a precise functional relationship among the variables.

$$x + y = 10$$

indicates a precise relationship between x and y;

$$x - y = 10$$

indicates quite a different precise relationship.

Choosing the Right Model

What is the most appropriate form of model? The answer depends on the purpose of the analysis and the nature of the problem under consideration. The selection of a model and the level of detail to be included are guided by one overriding consideration: what kind of information do I need to make a decision?

Consider an office layout problem. Two different models may be appropriate. First, we may use a mathematical model to show how work volume flows among the different work centers in the office. This would give us a general idea of where the work is concentrated and where congestion might be a problem. Then we might use a schematic model to specify exact positioning of equipment and determine space relationships. The level of the schematic model could vary anywhere from a rough sketch to scaled replicas of equipment, walls, and even wiring. As a result of the entire modeling effort, we could recommend an efficient layout design.

Mathematical Models in P/OM

Optimization

To solve an operating problem, you must analyze it. Operations managers often use formal models to help them analyze problems and suggest solutions. If a solution procedure *ensures* finding the *best* solution, it is called an optimization technique. There are many kinds of solutions procedures, but the one analysts use is called an *algorithm*. Although it does not always lead to an optimal solution, an algorithm consists of a series of steps to follow in solving a problem. In operations management we strive for optimization algorithms, series of steps ensuring the best solution, as aids in problem solving.

Heuristics

In other cases, a systematic procedure known as a heuristic is used. Heuristics are procedures for reducing the amount of search needed to find a *satisfactory*, but not necessarily the *best*, solution to a problem. *Heuristics involve the systematic application of "rules of thumb" that will result in a solution that is nearly best.* Heuristics are useful for problems for which optimal algorithms have not yet been developed. Among their uses are the assembly line balancing problem (discussed Chapter 7).

Modeling Benefits

The extensive use of models, especially schematic and mathematical models, is sometimes questioned by students and practitioners of P/OM. The application of well-defined models often requires data that are difficult to obtain and some rather stringent assumptions. It is true that assumptions are sometimes questionable, costs and other data are difficult to define explicitly, and forecasts of future events are not easily obtained. Even so, using a particular model to help make a difficult decision is frequently justified. Even if the results seem unrealistic, the knowledge gained from working with models and attempting to apply them can yield valuable insights into the problem in question. In fact, several specific benefits can result from studying explicitly defined models. They:

1. force managers to recognize a problem area and decide what types of decisions are required. Simply recognizing the decision points can be a major step forward in many situations;
2. make managers recognize the factors involved in the problem and determine what variables can be controlled to affect performance of the system;
3. force us to recognize *relevant* costs and gain some knowledge of their magnitudes;
4. enable us to identify the relationships of costs to the decision variables, recognize important tradeoffs among costs, and gain knowledge of the overall interaction of variables and costs.

Studying formal models also makes managers think about their assumptions and the possible effects of them on the application of a solution. Managers have to recognize the rigidity of the assumptions in various models and evaluate the extent to which this rigidity deters practical applications of the models.

Breakeven Analysis

Sometimes a simple formal analysis can be used to clarify one of the most fundamental sets of relationships encountered in operations management. *Breakeven analysis is a graphical or algebraic representation of the relationships among volume, cost, and revenues in an organization.* It has great usefulness in operations management.

As the volume of output from a productive facility increases, costs and revenues also increase. Costs can generally be divided into two categories, fixed and variable. Fixed costs are those incurred regardless of output volume. They include heating, lighting, and administrative expenses that are the same whether one or one thousand units of output are produced. Variable costs are those that fluctuate directly with volume of output; higher output results in higher variable costs. Typically, they are the costs of direct labor and material. In Figure 3-3, total revenues and total costs are shown as linear functions of output volume. The chart shows that both total costs and total revenues increase with higher levels of output. Costs exceed revenues over the initial range of volume up to point V_{BE}. Point V_{BE} is *the breakeven point—that level of operating volume at which total cost is equal to total revenues from operations.* Thereafter, revenues exceed costs of operation.

Breakeven analysis is useful for identifying the level of operations (output) that must be reached in order to recover all the costs of operation from revenues. The breakeven point depends on the selling price of the product and the operating cost structure. Operating costs vary from company to company depending on the type of conversion technology, administrative structure, and operating policies they employ. Some conversion processes require large capital outlays and high overhead expenses but low unit variable costs. They require a large volume of output to reach breakeven, but once they have attained it profitability increases rapidly. Other conversion processes have low fixed costs and high unit variable costs. Figure 3-4 shows both kinds of cost structures.

Breakeven with discontinuous revenues and costs

Revenues and/or costs may be curvilinear rather than linear functions (with constant slope) over some ranges of output volume, and the functions may not be continuous with increasing volume. Indeed, a major purpose

Figure 3-3
Breakeven chart

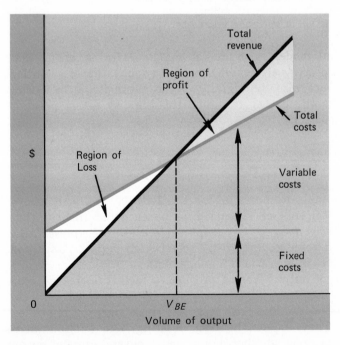

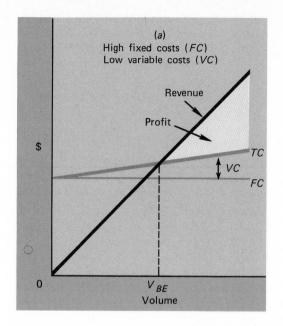
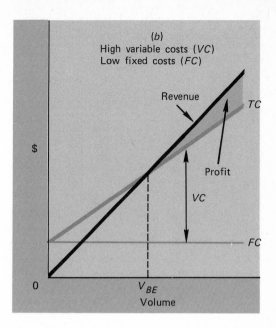

Figure 3-4 **Cost structures and breakeven charts for two contrasting conversion processes**

of breakeven analysis is to reveal how the organization's costs and revenues change with volume of output. The analysis can then be used to help make decisions about the organization's output goals.

Consider the situation in Figure 3-5. The organization has two facilities, A and B, which may be operated during the coming year. Facility A, working a single shift, has a breakeven volume of BE_1 units. Thereafter, profitability increases up to the output V_A. If greater profit is desired, facility B must be opened and additional fixed costs incurred. The overall operation (facilities A and B) will not be profitable until a volume of BE_2 units is achieved. Output volumes above BE_2 result in higher profit rates until volume V_B is reached. To achieve outputs above V_B, second shift operations are necessary, and variable costs increase accordingly. Beyond V_B, profits continue to increase, but at a slower rate.

Information from the breakeven chart can now be used for aiding managerial decisions. Once the desired level of profitability for the year has been stated, we can show the volume of output necessary for achieving it. We can also identify how many facilities and shifts will be needed, and we can estimate operating costs and working capital requirements. This discussion shows that breakeven analysis can be aided by using a schematic model. It is also possible to present the analysis in a mathematical model using equations to represent the relationships among output volume, cost, and sales revenues.

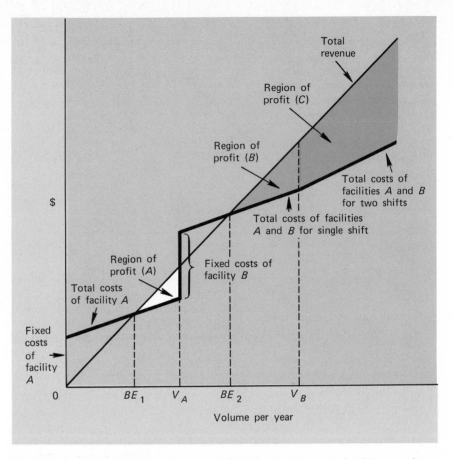

Figure 3-5 **Breakeven chart for operating one facility, two facilities, and two facilities on double shifts**

SELECTING DECISION CRITERIA   The decision-making process ultimately involves choosing one of several alternatives. Rational decision making includes a careful evaluation of all the possibilities. What constitutes a "good" alternative or a "bad" one? The answer to this question is often not clear. Alternative A may be good in one sense but not so good in another. The same may be true for alternative B. An alternative may be good or bad depending upon the dimension being considered, and it might have both desirable and undesirable features. Somehow we must decide; we must have *criteria* that will help us compare alternatives.

The criteria managers use are those system characteristics deemed most crucial for meeting system objectives. A formal analysis not only identifies these characteristics but attempts to measure the performances of each alternative for each objective. The criteria measurements then become formal indicators by which alternatives are evaluated. One of the primary reasons for formal analysis in decision making is to determine the criteria values of each decision alternative. Were the criteria values of alternatives already known, formal analysis would be unnecessary.

====== EXAMPLE ======

The manager of banking operations at Downtown National Bank has been allocated a budgetary increase of $10,000 for the purpose of streamlining bank operations. Her job is to improve service to customers with minimum additional resource expenditures during the coming year. As part of this program the manager has identified, and is considering, two decision alternatives: *A*, employ an additional teller during peak business hours, or *B*, change existing business hours from 9 to 4 o'clock to 9 to 5 o'clock daily. A formal analysis of both alternatives was made using two criteria, average customer waiting time, and annual added cost of operations. The analysis revealed the following:

Alternative	Reduction in average customer waiting time (minutes)	Additional operating cost per year
A	2.73	$10,000
B	.68	10,000

Since the alternatives are equally attractive in terms of the cost criterion, the manager chooses alternative *A* because it reduces customer waiting time more than alternative *B* does.

Notice that many additional factors could also have been considered. These two alternatives, for example, may differ in terms of the number of new customers they would attract. The operations manager has necessarily discarded some criteria and selected only those she believes to be realistic and reasonable. On the basis of the alternatives' effectiveness according to established criteria, the manager was able to make a decision.

Conflicting Criteria

Identifying the criteria and measuring the criteria values for each alternative do not always resolve the decision problem. Often a very difficult phase of decision making remains. This occurs when the chosen criteria values conflict, usually when there are multiple criteria. Suppose the analysis in our banking example had shown the following:

Alternative	Reduction in average customer waiting time (minutes)	Additional operating cost per year
A	2.73	$10,000
B	.68	2,000

Alternative *A* is most attractive in terms of reducing average customer waiting time. *B*, however, is far less costly. The operations manager is concerned with both cost and service. Now which alternative is better? There is no simple answer; the manager will have to use her experience and judgment. She may attempt to combine the two criteria into a single measure of desirability, the cost per minute of reduced waiting time.

Alternative	Cost per minute of reduced waiting time
A	$\dfrac{\$10,000}{2.73 \text{ minutes}} = \$3,663$
B	$\dfrac{\$\ 2,000}{.68 \text{ minutes}} = \$2,941$

Alternative *B* is more efficient in terms of offering greater reductions in waiting time for each dollar expended. In addition, $8,000 is still available to spend on other service improvement opportunities that may exist. If additional opportunities are not available, alternative *A* may become more attractive than *B*.

The perplexing problem of conflicting criteria is commonly encountered by operations managers. It becomes even more challenging as our economy continues to shift from manufacturing toward service industries. Many of the criteria that were appropriate for manufacturing analysis are not suited to analysis of labor-intense service industries.[1] Still, service industries managers can use formal analysis to identify relevant criteria and measure the criteria values of each alternative before they make decisions.

CLASSIFYING DECISION PROBLEMS

Since many different kinds of decision problems are encountered by the operations analyst, it's a good idea to have a convenient starting point, or frame of reference, for initiating the analysis effort. Classifying problems into different types makes it easier to select models and criteria to use in the analysis. We'll consider two ways of classifying problems: by the degree of uncertainty of outcomes and by the degree of interdependence among decisions.

[1] Recognizing the measurement problem that exists in the service sector, the National Science Foundation has developed a program for research into productivity measurement in service industries. See, for example, *Proceedings of the Grantees Conference on Research on Productivity Measurement Systems for Administrative Services*, ed. William A. Ruch, National Science Foundation Program 75-14 (Washington, D.C., November 1977).

When we know for sure what the outcome for each decision alternative will be, we are dealing with a problem under conditions of *certainty*. When a decision alternative can result in more than one possible outcome and we know the relative chances (probabilities) of each outcome's occurrence, we are facing a decision problem under conditions of *risk*. Finally, when an alternative has more than one possible outcome and we do not know their relative chances of occurrence, we face a decision problem under *uncertainty*.

These three categories possess both common features and some important differences. These characteristics are shared by all three:

1. there are two or more alternatives,
2. possible outcomes for each alternative are identified, and
3. a decision criterion is identified as a basis for evaluating the alternatives.

The three differ in:

1. the extent to which the ultimate outcome of the decision is known,
2. the extent to which the chances of each outcome's occurrence (state of nature) is known, and
3. the computational procedure used for evaluation.

Some examples may clarify the problems of certainty, risk, and uncertainty.

=========== EXAMPLE: CERTAINTY ===========

A chain of supermarkets is going to open a new store at one of four possible locations. Management wishes to select the location that will maximize profitability over the next ten years. An extensive analysis was performed to determine the costs, revenues, and profits for each alternative. The results are shown below.

Location	Ten-year profit ($ millions)
1	.70
2	.95
3	.60
4	.84

Management has a high degree of confidence in these figures. The decision criterion (profit) has been explicitly identified and accurately calculated for each alternative. Management's strategy is to select the alternative with the highest criterion value, in this case location 2.

=== **EXAMPLE: RISK** ===

An extensive analysis of the supermarket chain's problem reveals that the profit associated with each alternative is not known for sure. Management is convinced that the ten-year profitability of each location alternative will depend upon future regional population growth. Therefore, the ultimate outcome is not totally within the control of management; it also depends on external considerations. Three possible levels of population growth have been identified: low, medium, and high. The profitability associated with each alternative under each possible level of population growth has been estimated below.

| | Ten-Year Profit ($ million) Rate of population growth | | |
| | | | |
Location	Low (5% or less)	Medium (above 5% but below 10%)	High (10% or more)
1	$.3	$.8	$ .9
2	.2	.6	1.1
3	.4	.5	.6
4	.6	.7	.8
Probability (*p*)	.2	.3	.5

At the bottom of the table, the analyst has recorded the probability of occurrence for each possible level of population growth. Decision strategy in this situation is more difficult than it is under conditions of certainty.

=== **EXAMPLE: UNCERTAINTY** ===

If the supermarket chain's management knows that profitability depends on future population growth, but it doesn't know the probabilities of low, medium, or high growth, it is faced with a decision problem under uncertainty. Obviously, strategy is much harder to come by in this case.

Under conditions of certainty, the best location alternative is easily identified. Location 2 clearly yields the highest profit. Under conditions of risk, however, the choice is not so easy. We do not know which location will be best because the rate of future population growth is unknown. In analyzing this situation, we have to arrange the data differently than we did under certain conditions. Look at the table in the example. (A table arranged like this is called a *matrix*.) The levels of profit for low, medium, and high population growth are listed separately for each location. Which alternative is best? If population growth turns out to be low, location 4 is best ($.6 million). If growth is medium, location 1 is best ($.8 million), and if it is high, location 2 is best ($1.1 million). In the analyst's language, the three rates of population growth are called *states of nature*.

You may have noticed something important about location 3. For every population rate (state of nature), location 4 has a better outcome than location 3. When one alternative is equal to or better than another for every possible state of nature, analysts say that it *dominates* that alternative; in this case, 4 dominates 3. Therefore 3 can be eliminated immediately.

To help guide our decision, we use a procedure that calculates both the profits for each alternative and the chances of obtaining those profits. This procedure uses a modified criterion called *expected value*, an averaging technique in which each possible outcome is weighted by its chances of occurring. The expected value procedure follows these steps:

1. Select one alternative.
2. List all possible outcomes for this alternative.
3. Multiply each of these outcomes by its chance of occurrence.
4. Add the products obtained in step 3 (this is the expected value for that alternative).
5. Repeat steps 1 to 4 for each of the remaining alternatives.
6. Select the alternative with the highest expected value (for profits) or lowest expected value (for costs).

This procedure has been applied to our example in Table 3-1. The expected value criterion is highest for alternative 2. Although profits for location 2 vary from lower than the others ($.2 million) to higher ($1.1 million), it is the best choice because it yields the highest long-run profit of all ($.77 million). If management faced this situation many times and always chose alternative 2, its average profit would be higher than for any other alternative. The expected value criterion is helpful in many decisions faced by the operations manager, and we will use it frequently.

Decision problems under uncertainty can also be structured in matrix form. Since the probabilities are not known, however, rational strategies for decision making are not well-defined or straightforward. Analysts use three approaches in these circumstances. The first, *maximax*, is an optimistic

TABLE 3-1

CALCULATION OF EXPECTED VALUE ($ MILLION)

Alternative	Outcomes × Chances			Summation	Expected value (profit)
1	$.3 × .2 = .06	$.8 × .3 = .24	$ .9 × .5 = .45	.06 + .24 + .45	= $.75
2	.2 × .2 = .04	.6 × .3 = .18	1.1 × .5 = .55	.04 + .18 + .55	= .77
3	.4 × .2 = .08	.5 × .3 = .15	.6 × .5 = .30	.08 + .15 + .30	= .53
4	.6 × .2 = .12	.7 × .3 = .21	.8 × .5 = .40	.12 + .21 + .40	= .73

approach; the analyst considers only the best outcome for each alternative. In Table 3-1, the outcomes considered would be $.9 million for alternative 1, $1.1 million for alternative 2, $.6 million for alternative 3, and $.8 million for alternative 4. Among these, alternative 2 yields the highest profit, and that is the one that would be chosen.

The second approach under uncertainty is *maximin*, a pessimistic approach. With this approach, the analyst considers only the worst possible outcome for each alternative and chooses the "best of the worst." In Table 3-1, the figures would be $.3 million for alternative 1, $.2 million for alternative 2, $.4 million for alternative 3, and $.6 million for alternative 4. The best of these is 4.

The third approach is called the *principle of insufficient reason*. This assumes that since we know absolutely nothing about the probabilities of any state of nature, we should treat each with equal probability and choose on the expected value basis. Using this approach, we would choose alternative 4.

Interdependence Among Decisions

Another way of classifying decision problems is in relation to their duration, the number of decision stages that must be considered. At one extreme are single-stage, or static, problems; at the other are multistage, or sequential, problems. Although real problems don't always fall into either of these two pure types, we usually treat them as such for purposes of analysis. Both types are encountered in operations management.

Static problems are essentially "one-time-only" decisions. Inventory, "make vs. buy," product mix, and location of new facility decisions are often treated as static problems. Our supermarket chain example was treated this way.

With static problems, the analyst focuses on the immediate consequences of the decision without much formal concern about how these consequences affect other future decisions. To simplify the situation, the decision is treated as if it were independent of other decisions.

Multistage treatments, on the other hand, explicitly consider how several sequential decisions are related to one another. The outcome of the first decision affects the attractiveness of the choices at the next decision stage, and so on down the line at each decision point. With multistage problems, the concern is not how to get the best outcome at any single stage but how to make a *series* of choices that will finally result in the best overall set of outcomes from beginning to end. Sequential decision problems are commonly encountered by the operations manager in project management, capacity planning, and aggregate scheduling.

One method for dealing with sequential problems is decision tree analysis. Decision trees are used to structure and analyze decision problems in a systematic way. Not only the results of a decision tree analysis are useful. The process of structuring a decision problem into a decision tree framework is itself very helpful in clarifying the problem. The manager must clearly identify decision alternatives, identify chance events that can influence the outcomes, and explicitly assess the chances that various outcomes will occur. The very process of clarifying these aspects of the problem can lead to more enlightened decisions, even if the analysis is not carried to completion. Typically, the analysis uses an expected value criterion to identify the best course of action.

Decision trees are most beneficial when applied to sequential, multi-stage problems involving a sequence of time-phased decisions. Decision tree analysis consists of these steps:

1. Tree diagramming
   (a) Identify all decisions (and their alternatives) to be made and the order (sequence) in which they must be made.
   (b) Identify the chance events that can occur after each decision.
   (c) Develop a tree diagram showing the sequence of decisions and chance events.
2. Estimation
   (a) Obtain a probability estimate of the chances of each outcome's occurrence.
   (b) Obtain estimates of the consequences of all possible outcomes and actions.
3. Evaluation and selection
   (a) Calculate the expected value of all possible actions.
   (b) Select the action offering the most attractive expected value.

The decision tree in Figure 3-6 shows the sequence of decisions and chance events flowing from left to right. Squares are used to denote decision points. Each branch emanating from a decision node (the square) represents a decision alternative. Chance event nodes (the circles) represent the occurrence of a chance event, which can lead to any of several outcomes. Each possible outcome of the chance event is represented by a branch flowing out from the circle.

The first decision in Figure 3-6 involves two alternatives, *A* and *B*. If alternative *B* is chosen, it will be followed by a chance event, which will determine which of three ultimate outcomes will occur. If alternative *A* is chosen, it will be followed by a chance event with two possible outcomes. Regardless of what outcome occurs after decision *A*, a second decision must then be made. After the second decision is made, other chance events will occur for each alternative, each chance event leading to a different ultimate outcome.

━━━━━━━━━━━━━━ **EXAMPLE** ━━━━━━━━━━━━━━

The city transit system in Smalltown has been operating its bus system at a $400,000 deficit annually. The city council has decided to raise bus fares to help offset the operating deficit. The director of City Transit believes the fare increase will decrease ridership unless transit system services are expanded. The director suggests that expanded services be offered simulta- neously with the fare increase to offset negative community reaction. He believes this action will result in one of three levels of ridership: increased, sustained, or reduced.

An influential council member suggests an alternative plan. He would increase the fare now but delay the expanded service decision for two years. If this is done, the director is sure, ridership will not increase during the next two years; it will either decrease or be sustained at current levels. If service is expanded two years after the fare increase, ridership may be increased, sustained, or reduced. If service is not expanded in two years, however, the most optimistic estimates are that ridership will either be sustained or reduced, not increased. The director has decided to use a decision tree analysis to evaluate this problem for an eight-year time horizon (the desired length of the planning period).

Tree diagramming Figure 3-6 shows the initial tree diagram developed by the director. In Figure 3-7, labels have been added to each branch of the tree. At the left side of the diagram, we see the first decision and its two alternatives. If service is expanded now (alternative *B*), annual ridership during each of the next eight years will either increase, remain unchanged, or decrease. The annual operating deficit (ultimate outcome) depends on the outcome of the chance event. If service is not expanded now (alternative *A*), annual ridership during the next two years is expected to be either reduced or sustained at the current level. After two years, a second decision must be made. Service will either be expanded or not be expanded (alternatives *C* and *D*). If service is not expanded (*D*), ridership during the next six years will either be sustained or reduced. If service is expanded (*C*), it is also possible that ridership might increase above the current level.

Estimation The next stage of the decision tree analysis involves estimating the outcomes and probabilities of chance events. Probability estimates are needed *wherever a chance event appears* in the diagram. Notice that probabilites for the chance event *f* sum to 1.0. This is because one and only one of these three outcomes must occur. The cost of expanding service is $300,000 if done now and $450,000 if done two years from now.

Figure 3-6   Decision tree diagram

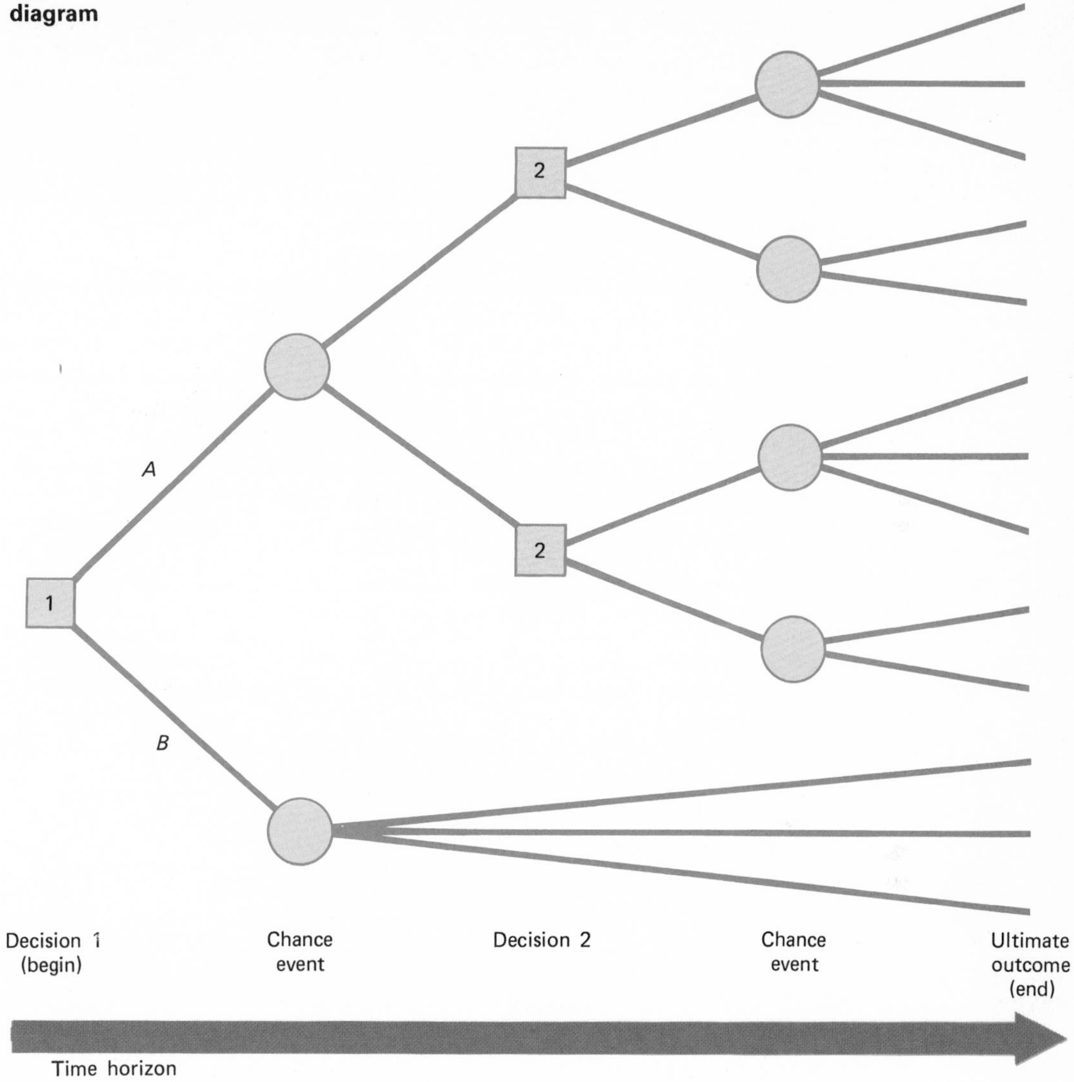

Decision 1
(begin)

Chance
event

Decision 2

Chance
event

Ultimate
outcome
(end)

Time horizon

EXAMPLE

Consider the chance node following decision alternative *B*. The director believes that by expanding services now, the chances for increased ridership are .2, for sustained ridership .5, and for reduced ridership .3 for each of the next eight years. With alternative *A*, the chances for sustained ridership are .3 and for reduced ridership .7 in years one and two. Similarly, probabilities have been estimated for each possible outcome for the chance events that follow alternatives *C* and *D*. The various probability estimates for all chance events are shown in Figure 3-8, as are the cost consequences of all outcomes and actions.

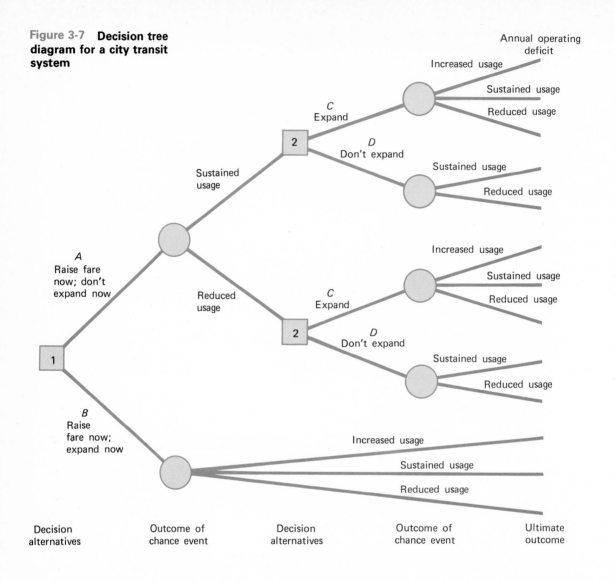

Figure 3-7 **Decision tree diagram for a city transit system**

Annual operating deficit

Increased usage

Sustained usage

Reduced usage

C
Expand

Sustained usage

Reduced usage

Sustained usage

D
Don't expand

2

Increased usage

Sustained usage

A
Raise fare now; don't expand now

Reduced usage

C
Expand

Reduced usage

2

Sustained usage

D
Don't expand

Reduced usage

1

B
Raise fare now; expand now

Increased usage

Sustained usage

Reduced usage

| Decision alternatives | Outcome of chance event | Decision alternatives | Outcome of chance event | Ultimate outcome |

Evaluation and selection

The final phase of the decision tree analysis is to calculate the expected values of all possible actions. For the transit system's problem, we will calculate the expected cost of each chance event node and decision square in the diagram. That will allow us to identify the set of actions that will lead to minimum expected cost for the eight-year decision horizon. We begin by calculating expected costs of nodes at the right side of the diagram, at the last stage of the problem, and then work backwards.

Look at Figure 3-8 again. Suppose the city had taken a course of action that resulted in its being located at node *a*. This would be the case if service was not expanded initially, ridership was sustained in years one and two, and service was expanded after two years. What will happen to ridership in years three through eight? We don't know for sure; this is a chance event. We can, however, calculate the *expected cost* of the outcomes that follow node a:

$$EC_a = (.4)(\$600) + (.5)(\$1,800) + (.1)(\$3,000)$$
$$= 240 + 900 + 300$$
$$= \$1,440$$

This tells us that if we ever do reach node a, the expected cost of all possible outcomes thereafter is $1,440,000. We can similarly calculate the expected costs associated with nodes b, c, and d.

$$EC_b = (.5)(\$1,500) + (.5)(\$2,400) = \$1,950$$
$$EC_c = (.2)(\$600) + (.4)(\$1,800) + (.4)(\$3,000) = 2,040$$
$$EC_d = (.2)(\$1,500) + (.8)(\$2,400) = 2,200$$

Figure 3-8 **Tree diagram with probabilities, outcomes, and costs (cost figures in $ thousands)**

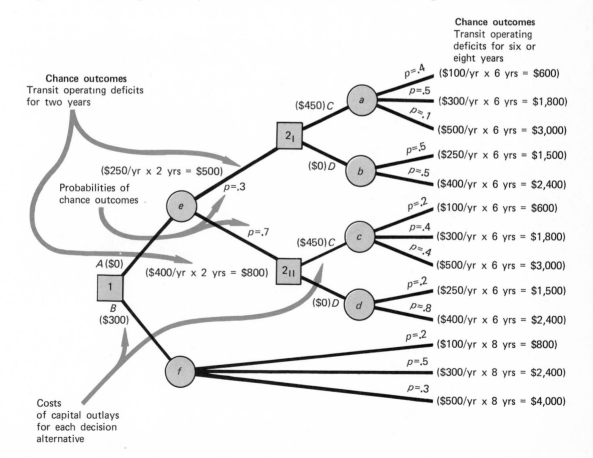

Now compare the expected costs of nodes a and b. Node a has a more desirable expected cost because it is lower than the expected cost of b. We now move to the left in the diagram to determine what decisions (and costs) have to be made to reach nodes a and b. First consider node a. At decision square 2_I, decision C (costing $450,000) leads to node a with expected cost of $1,440,000 thereafter. The overall expected cost, then, of C and a is $1,890,000. Now consider node b, which can be reached in only one way, by choosing alternative D at decision square 2_I. Since D requires no cost, the overall expected cost of D and b is $1,950,000. If you are located at decision square 2_I, which route is more attractive thereafter, C and a or D and b? Given this choice you should pick alternative C (expand service), which offers a lower expected cost than D at square 2_I. The expected cost of this course of action is recorded under decision square 2_I in Figure 3-9. Also, alternative D has been crossed out, indicating it is less desirable than alternative C. The significance of these calculations is as follows: if the city takes a course of action that results in having

Figure 3-9 **Decision tree showing expected costs and best decision strategy**

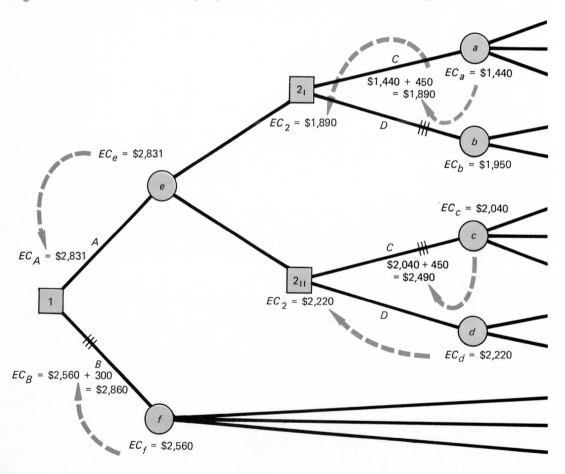

to make the decision offered at square 2_I, the best choice is alternative C, which has the minimum expected future cost of $1,890,000.

Let us now repeat this analysis for decision square 2_{II}, which involves nodes c and d. Given the choice of reaching nodes c and d, we would prefer d. If we had not expanded service initially and if ridership for years one and two were reduced, we would find ourselves located at decision node 2_{II}. The desired course of action thereafter would be alternative D, which has an expected cost of $2,220,000.

Now consider the consequences of being located at node e. There is a .3 chance of sustained ridership for two years with an operating deficit (cost) of $500,000, followed by the decision to expand service at an expected cost of $1,890,000. There is also a .7 chance of reduced usage costing $800,000, after which a "no expansion" decision would be made with an expected cost of $2,220,000. The expected cost of node e is calculated as follows:

$$EC_e = (.3)(\$500 + \$1,890) + (.7)(\$800 + \$2,220)$$
$$= 717 + 2,114$$
$$= \$2,831$$

The expected cost for node f is:

$$EC_f = (.2)(\$800) + (.5)(\$2,400) + (.3)(\$4,000)$$
$$= 160 + 1,200 + 1,200$$
$$= \$2,560$$

This tells us that if we reach node f, the expected consequences are costs of $2,560,000; if we reach node e and select the optimal set of decisions thereafter, the expected consequences are costs of $2,831,000. In order to reach node f, decision B must be made initially at an additional cost of $300,000. The expected cost of reaching node f is therefore $300,000 plus $2,560,000 or $2,860,000. We have now determined the best course of action for the entire problem. First, the decision should be made to not expand the transit services initially. If the ridership is sustained during the ensuing two years, the system should be expanded. If ridership is reduced during years one and two, service should not be expanded for years three through eight. The expected cost of this course of action is $2,831,000. The expected costs are shown in Figure 3-9.

BEHAVIOR

Almost by definition, operations analysis requires that paramount consideration be given to models used by the operations analyst. But behavioral considerations play a vital role in operations analysis too, and they raise some important questions. Can formal analysis be beneficial from a behavioral standpoint? What are the advantages and disadvantages of formal analysis when compared to intuitive human judgment? What can the operations manager expect from the analyst?

Characteristics of Intuitive Analysis

In recent years a considerable amount of research has been devoted to finding out how well people can perform certain types of analysis. Without reviewing this research in great detail, we can summarize some important findings.

Estimating
probabilities

People are not always objective when they estimate probabilities; they tend to overestimate the chances of obtaining a desirable outcome and underestimate the chances of undesired outcomes. A correct analysis, of course, is one in which estimates are made without regard to the desirability of the outcome. Probabilities are needed, you may remember, to perform an expected value analysis. Obviously, if the probabilities are wrong, the expected value will be wrong too. In cases like these, the human behavioral tendency to over- or underestimate probabilities could greatly affect the results of a formal analysis.

Processing
information

Another area of study shows that humans tend to be conservative information processors. Given several pieces of information that must be combined into a summary conclusion, people tend to underestimate the amount of information that is present. Suppose you are trying to determine the chances that a decision will lead to a particular outcome. Various pieces of information are given to you. If properly combined, the information should lead to the conclusion that this outcome has a probability of .90 of occurring. People seem reluctant to arrive at such a conclusion. They generally estimate the chances to be much less than .90. A formal analysis using probability and statistical techniques can be helpful in avoiding this sort of inaccuracy.

Sequential
decisions

Potential human inaccuracies may occur in sequential decision problems too. Problems of this type require consideration of several future time periods when a current decision is being made. Research indicates that people do not look far enough into the future when making these decisions; they use an inadequate time horizon. Formal analyses help overcome this inadequacy by identifying the number of future time periods that should be considered.

Interpersonal
relationships

Another behavioral aspect of concern is the interpersonal relationships between the analyst and the operations manager. The analyst often spends more time and effort examining a specific problem than does the manager. Consequently, the analyst may observe subtleties or recognize irrelevancies that the manager might not be aware of. The analyst can therefore provide an important service by acting as an information filter, clarifying relevant and irrelevant aspects of the problem for the manager. The relationship between the analyst and the manager depends, of course, on several factors: the personalities of the people involved, the jobs being performed, and the overall organizational climate that exists.

Communication   Communication between the analyst and the manager may be the single most important determiner of success or failure of formal analysis efforts in organizations. Most analysts tend to think in terms of models and techniques. In addition, *good* analysts try to blend their thinking into the broader perspective of the organization. Effective analysts have the ability to strip away the elegant technical details of their efforts and present their recommendations to management in understandable ways. The potential communications gap between managers and analysts is an obstacle that should be recognized and dealt with in the organization. Analysis, even if it is accurate, cannot be effective unless it is used to help make decisions—and it won't be used unless mutual respect and understanding exist.

Since models and analysis are critical tools in manufacturing and service industries, can we assume they are widely used? How large are the organizations that use models, analysis, management science, and operations research (OR) techniques?

APPLICATION OF MANAGEMENT SCIENCE

Overall Usage of Management Science Techniques

Table 3-2 summarizes the results of several studies on the use of operations research in manufacturing. In each of the first three studies OR was used in only a fraction of the production processes in the organizations surveyed, as indicated in the last column of the table. The Gaither study (1975) surveyed *only* manufacturing firms; 48 percent indicated they used OR techniques. Gaither did not ask about use in production, but we would guess that those firms using the techniques used them heavily in production applications, since they are manufacturing firms. Overall, these studies indicate that somewhere around one-half to two-thirds of firms responding to the surveys use management science techniques. The Gaither study also suggests (Table 3-3) that the larger the firm, the greater the use of OR techniques.

Why do so many firms not use operations research? Perhaps there is a lack of understanding about analysis techniques that inhibits higher usage. Perhaps experiences with analysis have been unsatisfactory, or the costs of analysis may have been prohibitive.

TABLE 3-2

THE USE OF OPERATIONS RESEARCH (OR) AS A PERCENTAGE OF SAMPLE SIZE*

Study	Year	Sample size	Use of OR in total organization	Use of OR in production
AMA	1957	631	51%	24%
Hovey and Wagner	1958	90	68	32
Schumacher and Smith	1964	65	75	68
Gaither	1975	275	48	—

*Modified from Norman Gaither, "The Adoption of Operations Research Techniques by Manufacturing Organizations," *Decision Sciences* 6, no. 4 (October 1975), pp. 799 and 803.

TABLE 3-3

USE OF OPERATIONS RESEARCH BY MANUFACTURING FIRM SIZE*

Firm size (number of employees)	Number of nonusing firms	Number of using firms	Percentage using firms
250–499	98	69	41
500–999	28	35	56
1,000–4,999	16	24	60
5,000 and above	0	5	100
All firms	142	133	48

*Modified from Gaither, p. 806.

Use of Specific Operations Research Techniques

In Chapter 2, we presented a study of the most significant problems of production managers. A similar study of manufacturing managers addressed their use of specific operations research techniques for manufacturing problems. The results, shown in Table 3-4, indicate that OR techniques are used most frequently for problems of planning and control. The table also shows (across the bottom) the ranking of the five most-used techniques. The first four are presented in this book; the second (computer simulation) is discussed in the supplement to this chapter.

Perhaps the question of whether or not to use operations research can best be answered by firms that use it. Table 3-5 shows the results of a study of such firms; you can see that the majority felt that the results were either good or very good. The problems encountered by firms using

TABLE 3-4

THE NUMBER OF FIRMS APPLYING OPERATIONS RESEARCH TECHNIQUES TO MANUFACTURING PROBLEMS*

Manufacturing problems	Linear or nonlinear programming	Computer simulation	PERT, CPM	Exponential smoothing, regression analysis	Queueing theory	Total number of firms	Rank
Production planning and control	41	25	40	23	7	136	1
Project planning and control	1	4	85	1	0	91	2
Inventory analysis and control	20	29	5	22	8	84	3
Analyzing capital investment projects	21	25	5	5	0	56	4
Quality control	15	12	2	27	0	56	4
Maintenance planning	8	5	33	3	2	51	6
Capacity allocation	29	13	0	2	2	46	7
Product mix	31	11	0	2	0	44	8
Material allocation	19	14	1	4	0	38	9
Equipment design analysis	4	21	2	4	1	32	10
Facility location	13	9	6	2	1	31	11
Line balancing	14	6	1	4	6	31	11
Chemical or ingredient blending	19	3	0	4	0	26	13
Logistics studies	13	5	2	1	2	23	14
Machines per operator	11	5	0	0	7	23	14
Service crew size	2	8	0	0	10	20	16
System reliability	0	11	0	5	1	17	17
Holding area size	4	6	0	0	4	14	18
Waiting lines	0	3	0	0	11	14	18
Facilities layout	3	3	2	0	2	10	20
Reducing trim waste	6	2	0	0	0	8	21
Total	274	220	184	109	64		
Rank	1	2	3	4	5		

* Gaither, p. 809.

OR techniques are listed in Table 3-6. Most had to do with a combination of modeling (technical) and behavioral issues, many of which we have discussed in this chapter.

TABLE 3-5

OVERALL RESULTS ACHIEVED BY OPERATIONS RESEARCH PERSONNEL*

Firm size (employees)	Poor	Fair	Good	Very good	Excellent
250–499	0.0%	4.3%	51.1%	34.1%	10.5%
500–999	0.0	6.9	48.3	31.1	6.9
1,000–4,999	0.0	16.7	44.4	22.2	16.7
5,000 and above	0.0	0.0	40.0	40.0	20.0

* Modified from Gaither, p. 810.

TABLE 3-6

PROBLEMS ENCOUNTERED WHILE USING OPERATIONS RESEARCH TECHNIQUES*

Problems	Firms	Rank
Production personnel are inadequately trained.	54	1
Competent personnel with quantitative training are scarce.	44	2
Staff personnel do not sell these approaches and solutions.	33	3
Returns from expenditures on these techniques are inadequate.	26	4
Data for these models are inadequate.	22	5
Staff personnel are reluctant to assist in the implementation of quantitative solutions.	20	6
Top management does not understand.	20	7
It takes too long to get answers.	18	8
The computer is inadequate.	13	9
Quantitative personnel are too impractical.	11	10
These models make too many unrealistic assumptions.	10	11
The turnover of quantitative personnel is high.	6	12

* Gaither, p. 811.

SUMMARY   This chapter has highlighted the role of analysis in P/OM. Analysis is often needed to solve complex decision problems that arise in managing the conversion process. Relying heavily on the development and use of models, formal analysis requires careful selection of decision criteria. The choice of criteria depends on the type of problem under consideration. Breakeven analysis is helpful in structuring the relationships among volume, costs, and revenues of an organization; decision tree analysis can be used in many multistage problems.

In conclusion, we wish to emphasize that analysis usually does not dictate the final decision. Real problems are so complex that a combination of judgment, experience, and analysis is often necessary to solve them adequately. Practitioners of analysis recommend a formal analysis of subcomponents tempered by real world considerations; such a combination encourages a practical conclusion. Once the conclusion has been reached, managers can decide what criteria to use, what goals to reach for, what plan to follow in future decisions. A plan of action evolves.

Sometimes formal analysis is done by the P/OM manager. In other cases, the analysis effort is so complex that a specialized staff is created to perform it. In these cases, the manager must understand what can be expected from the staff; he or she must guide its overall efforts and evaluate its recommendations from the broader perspective of the total P/OM efforts of the organization.

Safety Sight Company

CASE

Safety Sight Company owns two plants that manufacture bicycle headlights. The Edgewater plant has been fully operational in recent years; the Garland facility has been shut down for the past two years. Management anticipates a large increase in demand for bicycle lights, and future production plans are now being developed. Revenue from the sale of headlights is expected to average $8 per unit over the foreseeable future.

The Edgewater plant has been operating a single shift with fixed costs of $2.5 million and a production capacity of 500,000 units annually. Unit variable costs have been $1.60 for this range of output. Greater output volume could be achieved by starting up a second shift. If that were done, it is estimated that unit variable costs on the new shift would be either $6.3, $5.7, or $5.1 with probabilities of .09, .33, and .58, respectively. Production capacity on the second shift would be 500,000 units annually.

To achieve larger volumes of output, the Garland facility could be reopened. The exact annual fixed cost of operating this facility is unknown. Three recent estimates were: $1.8, $1.65, and $1.55 million with probabilities of .4, .5, and .1, respectively. Unit variable cost for first shift operations is expected to be $1.60, the same as for the Edgewater plant. The first shift capacity of the Garland plant is expected to be 500,000 headlights per year.

Management is considering two alternatives: operate the Edgewater plant on two shifts, keeping the Garland plant shut down; and operate both plants on a single shift. Management is sure either alternative will provide capacity to meet the new expected demand. What should they do?

1. Discuss the advantages and disadvantages of these models in operations management:
   (a) verbal
   (b) schematic
   (c) iconic
   (d) mathematical

2. The stages of the decision-making process are presented in Figure

3-2. For each stage, identify the roles of the operations analyst and the operations manager.

3. By definition, models are incomplete representations of the things being modeled. Discuss the reasons for this fact and its implications from a managerial point of view.

4. Develop a model of the operations function of a large apartment complex or a dormitory. Discuss the ways in which your model is useful and the ways it is limited.

5. What criteria do you think should be used to evaluate the operations of a university's school of business?

6. Show the similarities and differences among the criteria you would recommend for evaluating the operations functions in a neighborhood dry cleaning establishment and a toy manufacturing company.

7. Explain in detail the meaning and limitations of the expected value decision criterion.

8. Give examples illustrating personal everyday decision problems under conditions of certainty, risk, and uncertainty.

9. What are the problems of data and information availability you might have in conducting a decision tree analysis?

10. Describe and show differences among: decision, decision alternative, chance event, state of nature, and outcome.

11. How would the results of a decision tree analysis be affected if people made erroneous probability estimates? Demonstrate with an example.

12. In many organizations, operations managers employ an analysis staff that includes operations research specialists.

    (a) What are some potential sources of conflict between manager and analyst?

    (b) What actions could be taken to reduce this conflict?

13. Discuss the role relationships between the operations analyst and various managers throughout the organization.

14. To what extent are management science and operations research used in organizations? What factors tend to encourage or discourage their use?

15. Some managers have expressed disappointment with the results of management science/operations research efforts in their organizations. What might be the causes of these disappointing results?

PROBLEMS

1. A manufacturer of plastic moldings incurs a material and labor cost of $1.40 to produce each molding. Fixed costs of operation are $430,000 per year, and moldings are sold for $2.90 each.
   (a) Develop both a schematic and a mathematical model of the volume-cost-revenue relationships.
   (b) Using both models, determine the breakeven volume of operations.

2. Suresnap fishing reels require variable production costs of $12 per unit. Fixed costs are $200,000 for first shift operations, which have a capacity of 30,000 reels. Distributors purchase reels for $20 each. Suresnap can double capacity by operating a second shift at an additional cost of $80,000. Using a schematic model, evaluate the alternative levels of plant operation.

3. A delivery company is considering the purchase of a used truck. Its useful service life is estimated to be 3 years with a probability of 0.4, 4 years with a probability of 0.5, and 5 years with a probability of 0.1. What is the expected useful life of the used truck?

4. A local entertainment company is contemplating construction of a new

theater. **Three location sites are under consideration, and their relative attractiveness depends on the number of competing theaters that will be built in the next 5 years. Four possible industry growth rates, their chances of occurrence, and anticipated 5-year profitability (in thousands of dollars) are shown in this table. Which site is best on an expected value basis?**

Five-Year Profitability
Industry growth rate

Site	Low	Medium	High	Very high
A	$200	$120	$ 40	$ 8
B	160	240	120	40
C	40	80	200	280
Probability	0.4	0.3	0.2	0.1

5. **Four alternative manufacturing methods are being considered for a new product. Profitability, which depends on method of manufacture and level of consumer acceptance, is anticipated as shown here.**

Profits (thousands of dollars) From New Product
Projected consumer acceptance

Manufacturing method	Low	Moderate	High	Very high
I	$100	$300	$400	$450
II	200	300	400	500
III	250	300	350	400
IV	100	200	300	600
Probability	0.3	0.3	0.2	0.2

(a) **What is the best manufacturing method according to each of these criteria:**
   1. expected value
   2. maximin
   3. maximax
   4. insufficient reason
(b) **Which manufacturing method should be selected? Why?**

6. **Which of the decision alternatives in the following table is the most attractive? Why? (Outcomes are expressed in terms of operating costs in thousands of dollars.)**

Decision alternatives	Chance event E_a	E_b	E_c
I	$700	$200	$200
II	300	300	300
III	200	100	700
Probability	0.2	0.5	0.3

7. **Management, facing a two-stage decision problem, wants to pick a sequence of actions to maximize revenues. The first decision (I) has three alternatives: A, with revenues of $20; B, with revenues of $30; and C, with revenues of $40. The chance event following the initial decision has either two or three states of nature, depending on the initial decision. The probability of each state of nature is shown in Figure 3-10. Thereafter, a second decision, resulting in further revenues, must be made. What is the best decision sequence?**

8. **A trucking company has decided to replace its existing truck fleet. Supplier A will provide the needed trucks at a cost of $600,000. Supplier B will charge $450,000, but its vehicles may require more maintenance and repair than those from supplier A. The trucking company is also considering modernizing its maintenance and repair facility either by renovation or renovation and expansion. Although expansion is generally more expensive than renovation alone, it enables greater efficiency of repair and therefore reduced annual**

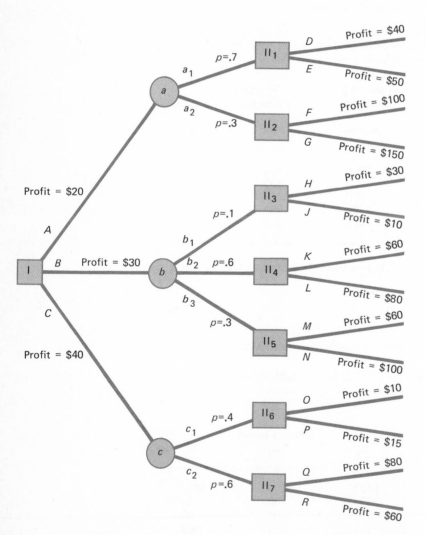

Figure 3-10 **Two-stage decision problem**

operating costs of the facility. The estimated costs of renovation alone and renovation and expansion, as well as the ensuing operating costs, depend on the quality of the trucks that are purchased and the extent of the maintenance they require. The trucking company has therefore decided on the following strategy: purchase the trucks now; observe their maintenance requirements for one year; then make the decision as to whether to renovate or to renovate and expand. During the one-year observation period, the company will get additional information about expected maintenance requirements during years 2 through 5.

If the trucks are purchased from supplier A, first year maintenance costs are expected to be low ($20,000) with a probability of 0.6 or moderate ($30,000) with a probability of 0.4. If they are purchased from supplier B, maintenance costs will be low ($20,000) with a probability of 0.3, moderate ($30,000) with a probability of 0.6, or high ($35,000) with a probability of 0.1. The costs of renovation, shown here, depend on the first year's maintenance experience.

One-year maintenance requirements	Renovation costs	Renovation and expansion costs
Low	$100,000	$200,000
Moderate	150,000	300,000
High	200,000	400,000

Expected maintenance costs for years 2 through 5 can best be estimated after observing the maintenance requirements for the first year.

Maintenance Costs for Years 2 through 5

Supplier	First year maintenance	Renovate Maintenance years 2 through 5		Renovate and expand Maintenance years 2 through 5	
		Low	Moderate	Low	Moderate
A	Low	$100,000	$150,000	$40,000	$ 60,000
	Moderate	100,000	150,000	40,000	60,000
		Moderate	High	Moderate	High
B	Low	150,000	200,000	50,000	90,000
	Moderate	150,000	200,000	50,000	90,000
	High	250,000	300,000	70,000	100,000

Probabilities of various maintenance levels in years 2 through 5 depend on the types of trucks selected and the maintenance experience during year 1:

| Supplier | First year maintenance | \| Maintenance level, years 2–5 | | |

Probabilities of Maintenance Effort, Years 2 through 5

Supplier	First year maintenance	Low	Moderate	High
A	Low	0.7	0.3	—
	Moderate	0.4	0.6	—
B	Low	—	0.5	0.5
	Moderate	—	0.4	0.6
	High	—	0.3	0.7

Use decision tree analysis to determine the decision strategy that minimizes expected costs.

Algorithm: solution procedure consisting of a series of steps that may or may not provide an optimal problem solution

Breakeven analysis: graphical or algebraic representation of the relationships among volume, cost, and revenues in an organization

Certainty: in decision problems, a condition in which the state of nature is known for sure for each alternative

Chance event: a happening with several possible outcomes, one of which will occur; the decision maker has no knowledge of or control over which outcome will occur

Criterion: measure of desirability used to distinguish between good and bad alternatives

Decision tree: device used to structure and analyze a decision problem; used to lay out systematically the sequence of decision points, alternatives, and chance outcomes in diagram form

Expected value: averaging technique in which each possible outcome is weighted by its chances of occurring

Experimentation: systematic manipulation of variables used to establish cause-effect relationships

Heuristic: simplification procedure in which a set of rules is systematically applied in order to find a satisfactory problem solution

Iconic model: a scaled physical replica of an object or process

Management science: scientific approach to the study of management, often using a mathematical modeling orientation; frequently used interchangeably with "operations research"

Model: a representation of something real; it shows relationships among variables and can be used to predict or explain

Operations research: an interdisciplinary approach to the systematic research of operations

Optimization: solution procedure that ensures finding the best solution to a problem

Relevant variables: system components, the values of which will be changed depending on the decision that is made

Risk: in decision problems, a condition in which the ultimate state of nature is not known for sure, but probabilities are known for each state of nature

Schematic model: pictorial or graphical representation of an object or system

Sequential decision problem: decision problem consisting of a series of interrelated decisions

States of nature: in decision problems, different conditions that can occur as a result of an uncontrollable chance event

Uncertainty: in decision problems, a condition in which the probabilities of the states of nature are not known

Validity: in modeling, the process of assuring that the model adequately reflects the system being studied

SELECTED
READINGS

American Management Association, Inc. *Operations Research Reconsidered.* Report no. 10 (New York: AMA, Inc., 1957).

Bross, I. D. *Design for Decision* (New York: Macmillan Pub. Co., 1953).

Ebert, R. J. and T. R. Mitchell. *Organizational Decision Processes: Concepts and Analysis* (New York: Crane, Russak and Co., Inc., 1975).

Fishburn, P. C. "Decision Under Uncertainty: An Introductory Exposition." *The Journal of Industrial Engineering* 17, no. 7 (July–August 1966), pp. 341–53.

Gaither, Norman. "The Adoption of Operations Research Techniques by Manufacturing Organizations." *Decision Sciences* 6, no. 4 (October 1975), pp. 797–813.

Hovey, R. W. and H. M. Wagner. "A Sample Survey of Industrial Operations Research Activities." *Operations Research* 6 (November-December 1958), pp. 876–79.

Magee, J. F. "Decision Trees for Decision Making." *Harvard Business Review* 42, no. 4 (July–August 1964), pp. 126–38.

Meier, R. C., W. T. Newell, and H. L. Pazer. *Simulation in Business and Economics* (Englewood Cliffs, N.J.: Prentice-Hall, Inc., 1969).

Michael, G. C. "A Review of Heuristic Programming." *Decision Sciences* 3, no.3 (July 1972), pp. 74–100.

Morris, W. T. "On the Art of Modeling." *Management Science* 13, no. 2 (August 1967), pp. 707–17.

Rosenzweig, J. E. "Managers and Management Scientists (Two Cultures)." *Business Horizons* 10, no. 3 (Fall 1967), pp. 79–86.

Schumacher, C. C. and Barnard E. Smith. "A Sample Survey of Industrial Operations Research Activities II." *Operations Research* 13 (December 1965), pp. 1023–27.

Simon, H. A. *The New Science of Management Decision* (New York: Harper & Row, Pub., 1960).

Supplement to Chapter 3

COMPUTER SIMULATION

Simulation is a commonly used technique in operations analysis. Our purposes in this section are to present some fundamental simulation terminology and to introduce the "Monte Carlo" technique, which is used extensively in computer simulations.

EXAMPLE

The manager of a drive-in banking facility is concerned about complaints from customers regarding the length of time they must wait to complete their transactions. A management consultant has offered a proposal that promises to speed up services. For a fee of $5,000, the consultant will analyze the job content of the bank teller and retrain the teller. He promises this will reduce average time to service a customer by at least 10 percent. The manager of the bank feels that this expenditure is not warranted unless it results in reducing average customer waiting time by at least fifteen percent, and she assigns an analyst the task of determining whether or not the consultant should be hired.

The first step taken by the analyst is to decide what *components* of the system to include in a model. In this case, the analyst selects three basic components, one representing customer arrivals, one representing teller services to customers, and one representing customer departures. These are shown in Figure S3-1.

Using this simplified representation of the bank, the analyst:

1. builds a model that includes the components of Figure S3-1,
2. gathers appropriate data to represent the behavior of arrivals and services as they now exist,
3. runs the model to insure that the average simulated waiting time closely approximates the current real average waiting time,
4. modifies the "teller services" component of the model to reflect the improvement in teller service time that is expected from the consultant's proposal,

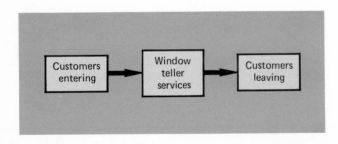

Figure S3-1 Components of a drive-in subsystem

5. reruns the simulation under these new conditions to measure average waiting time, and
6. compares the average customer waiting times under the existing and new service time conditions.

Model Building

The model begins to operate at a reference point called *time zero,* the arrival time of the first imaginary customer. The simulator records the time of this arrival. Since no other customers are being serviced, the new arrival does not have to wait, and service begins immediately. How long will it take? The simulator generates a representative service time (we will discuss this shortly). When the service time has elapsed, the customer leaves the system. While the first customer was being serviced, however, a second or even a third customer may have arrived. If so, they would have had to wait in line while the first customer was being serviced. The simulator keeps track of waiting times for each customer. Figure S3-2 illustrates a flow of arrivals and services on a time scale similar to that used in the simulator.

This figure shows that the first customer arrived at time zero, did not have to wait for service to begin, and ended the transaction at time 2.5. The second customer did not arrive until time 5.5. Service was begun immediately and was completed at time 9. At time 10.5, the third customer arrived and began a transaction at the teller's window. Meanwhile, at time 14 customer four arrived and had to wait in line. At time 16, customer three left, and customer four began a transaction. Customer four had to wait two minutes before beginning the transaction with

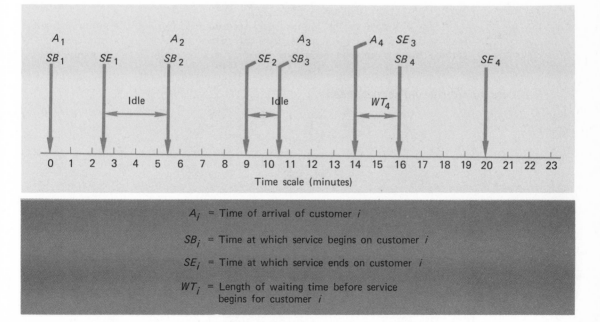

A_i = Time of arrival of customer i

SB_i = Time at which service begins on customer i

SE_i = Time at which service ends on customer i

WT_i = Length of waiting time before service begins for customer i

Figure S3-2 Flow of simulation events: time-phased

the teller. At time 20, customer four was served and the queue (waiting line) was empty again. Using this general approach, the analyst intends to simulate many (about 2,000) customer arrivals and services, always recording and accumulating waiting times. At the conclusion of the simulation, the analyst can calculate the average waiting time per customer.

Data Gathering

How does the simulator generate arrival times and service times for each simulated customer? The analyst must build into the model a procedure based on real world arrival and service data. Since we want a simulated pattern of the real drive-in window, the analyst sets up a procedure for observing a large sample of customers (say 1,000) at the actual drive-in facility. He records the elapsed time between arrivals of successive customers, the length of time required to service each customer, and customer waiting times. The results of part of this data-gathering effort are shown in Figure S3-3.

Although time between arrivals varied widely, the analyst groups the data into only seven classification intervals and uses the midpoint of the interval to represent the entire class. The same is true for the observed service times. The two resulting relative frequency distributions (frequency is symbolized $f(x)$ on the figures) are expected to provide adequate approximations of arrival and service patterns. These distributions are built into the simulation model. They are used in the model to generate the arrival time and the time required to service each customer by a procedure known as the Monte Carlo technique.

Monte Carlo Technique

The objective of the Monte Carlo technique is to have the simulator select service times (and arrival times) that fall into a specified pattern. We want the service time for our next simulated customer, for example, to be randomly selected

Figure S3-3 **Data for arrivals and service times**

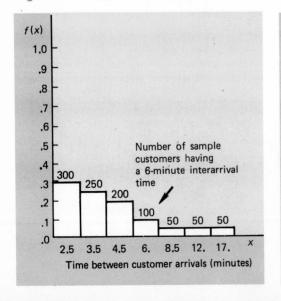

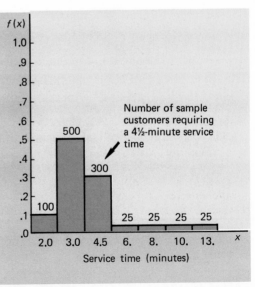

from the service time distribution in Figure S3-3. If we randomly select service times for each of many simulated customers, the simulator will replicate the pattern of service times that occurs in the real system. Notice that we want the service time to be randomly selected by the simulator. We do not know in advance whether the next service time will be 2, 3, 4.5, 6, 8, 10, or 13 minutes. Any of these is possible, but we want some to be selected more often than others because some occur in real life more often than others. In fact, we want our simulator to have a .1 chance of selecting a 2 minute service time, a .5 chance of a 3 minute service time, and so on. The Monte Carlo technique accomplishes this goal in two steps:

1. the frequency distribution is converted into a *cumulative* frequency (shown as $F(x)$ in Figure S3-4), and
2. uniformly distributed random numbers are used to enter the cumulative distribution.

A cumulative distribution for service time and one for time between arrivals are shown on the right side of Figure S3-4. Notice that the vertical axis of each cumulative distribution has a maximum value of 1.0 and a minimum value of 0.0. This range of values is subdivided among the various classification intervals in proportion to their chances of occurrence. Look at the cumulative frequency distribution for service time, for example. All the values on the vertical axis between 0.0 and 0.1 are associated with a service time of two minutes. This range of values (0.0 to 0.1) represents 1/10 (or 10 percent) of all possible values on the vertical axis. Similarly, all the values greater than 0.1 up to 0.6 on the vertical axis are associated with a service time of three minutes. This range of values (greater than 0.1 to 0.6) represents 5/10 (50 percent) of all possible values on the vertical axis. Continuing in this manner, we can see that each possible service time has been allocated a range of vertical axis values in proportion to its chances of being selected as the next service time. These allocations are listed in Table S3-1.

The next step in the Monte Carlo technique involves the use of random numbers. In most computers, there are standard procedures for obtaining random numbers, and they are also readily available in tables (see Appendix A). Random numbers are uniformly distributed, each with an equal chance of occurring. For our example, we want to use random numbers between 0.001 and 1.000. Since 10 percent of the random numbers have values between .001 and .100, there is a 10 percent chance of drawing a random number between .001 and .100. Likewise, the chances of getting a random number whose value lies between .101 and .600 are 50 percent. This is fortunate because the total range of uniform number values coincides with the values on the vertical axis of the cumulative distribution. By randomly selecting one number from the uniform distribution, we can find the corresponding value on the vertical axis of the service time cumulative distribution. Then we can identify the service time associated with this value. Thus we have randomly selected the length of service time for the next customer. This procedure can be repeated with the cumulative distribution of time between arrivals to generate the time that will elapse between the arrivals of the last customer and the next customer. *This is the Monte Carlo method for generating random occurrences from a probability distribution.*

Let's examine the use of this technique by simulating the arrival and servicing of six drive-in customers. From a table of uniformly distributed random numbers, we have found the numbers on the next page. In Table S3-2 are the calculations for each customer.

Relative frequency

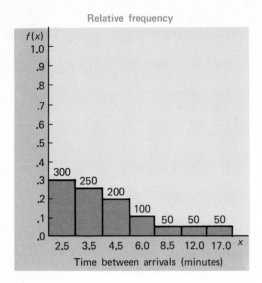

Cumulative frequency

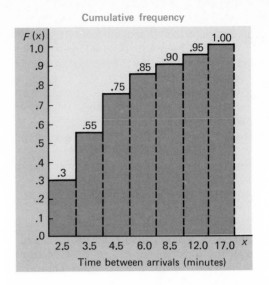

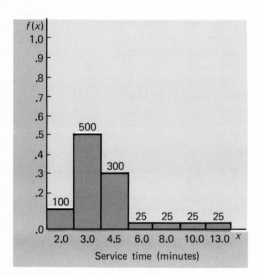

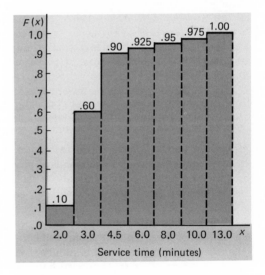

Figure S3-4 **Relative and cumulative frequency distributions**

Uniform Random Numbers

.964	.952	.342
.843	.476	.682
.876	.841	.852
.847	.943	

TABLE S3-1

PROPORTIONS OF PROBABILITIES ALLOCATED TO SERVICE TIMES

Service time (minutes)	Range of vertical axis values	Percent of total vertical axis values
2.0	0.000–0.100	10.0
3.0	0.101–0.600	50.0
4.5	0.601–0.900	30.0
6.0	0.901–0.925	2.5
8.0	0.926–0.950	2.5
10.0	0.951–0.975	2.5
13.0	0.976–1.000	2.5
Total		100.0

TABLE S3-2

SIMULATION DATA FOR SIX SIMULATED CUSTOMERS

Simulation characteristic	Minutes for customer					
	1	2	3	4	5	6
Time between arrivals of customers i and $i-1$	—	6.0	8.5	3.5	12.0	4.5
Time of arrival (on simulator clock)	0.0	6.0	14.5	18.0	30.0	34.5
Length of service	10.0	4.5	10.0	4.5	3.0	4.5
Time when service begins (on simulator clock)	0.0	10.0	14.5	24.5	30.0	34.5
Customer waiting time	0.0	4.0	0.0	6.5	0.0	0.0
Time when service ends (on simulator clock)	10.0	14.5	24.5	29.0	33.0	39.0

Total waiting time = 0.0 + 4.0 + 0.0 + 6.5 + 0.0 + 0.0
= 10.5 minutes
Average customer waiting time = 10.5/5 = 2.1 minutes

Begin by assuming that customer number 1 ($i = 1$) arrives at time zero on the simulator clock. We determine the length of time required to service this customer by using the first random number, .964. This number, when used in the cumulative service distribution (Figure S3-4), is associated with a service time of 10 minutes, which has been recorded in Table S3-2 as the length of service for the first customer. Service begins on this customer at time zero (no waiting), assuming no other customers were in the system when the first customer arrived. Service on this customer therefore ends at time 10.0 on the simulator clock. All the entries for customer 1 have now been filled in.

To determine the arrival time of the second customer ($i = 2$), we proceed down the random number list to .843. From the cumulative distribution of time between arrivals we find that .843 is associated with 6.0 minutes. This means that the second customer arrives 6.0 minutes after the arrival of the first customer. Thus, the second customer arrives at time 6.0 on the simulator clock. We can also determine the length of time that will be required to service the second customer by using the next random number, .876, in the cumulative service time distribution. If .876 represents a service time of 4.5 minutes for the second customer, at what time on the simulator clock does service begin? Not until time 10.0, when the teller finishes servicing the first customer. This means that the second customer must wait in line from time 6.0 until time 10.0, an elapsed waiting time of 4.0 minutes. Service to customer 2 is completed at time 14.5 on the simulated clock.

The same procedure may now be repeated for each customer in the simulation. Whenever a new arrival time is needed, the analyst merely selects the next random number on the list and uses it to enter the cumulative "time between arrivals" distribution. Then the next random number is used to generate a service time. The simulator clock is a convenient device for keeping track of the time-phased sequence of events. After simulating any desired number of customer transactions, the analyst can calculate the average waiting time for this system.

Using the Monte Carlo technique and a computer, the analyst in our example simulates 2,000 customers. The logic of the simulation model is shown in the flow diagram in Figure S3-5. The pattern of simulated waiting times closely parallels those that had been observed during the data gathering phase of analysis. The results of the analyst's simulation run (shown later) indicated an average customer waiting time of 4.22 minutes. The analyst concluded, therefore, that the model was a reasonable representation of the real system of drive-in operations. Notice that 4.22 minutes for 2,000 customers is considerably different from our hand calculated figure of 2.1 minutes for 6 customers in Table S3-2. Computers allow us to use large samples and reduce errors resulting from small sample sizes.

Modifying Teller Services and Waiting Times

The consultant's proposal guarantees a 10 percent or more reduction in service time. How would such a reduction affect average waiting time? To estimate the answer, the analyst uses the simulation model. He modifies the old service time distribution to reflect a 10 percent reduction in each service time interval. The modified distribution is shown in Figure S3-6.

The modified service time distribution is then used in a new simulation run. Based on a run length of 2,000 customers, average waiting time was found to be 2.43 minutes.

The results of the two simulation runs are summarized in Table S3-3. The analyst compared average customer waiting times under the existing and the proposed systems, and he found that if average service time is decreased by 10 percent, waiting time would be reduced by 42 percent. The analyst therefore recommended that the consultant be hired.

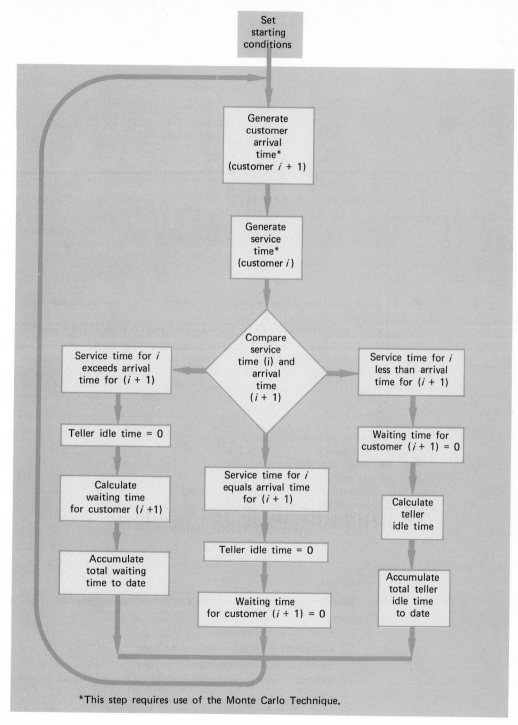

*This step requires use of the Monte Carlo Technique.

Figure S3-5 **Flow diagram of simulation model logic**

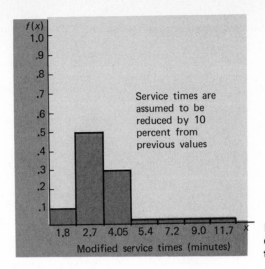

Figure S3-6 **Modified distribution of service times**

TABLE S3-3

SUMMARY DATA FOR 2,000 SIMULATED BANK CUSTOMERS

	Run 1 Original service time distribution	Run 2 Reduced service time distribution	Change
Number of simulated customers	2,000	2,000	—
Average waiting time per customer (minutes)	4.22	2.43	−42%
Average idle time of teller per customer served (minutes)	1.04	1.42	+36%

SUMMARY

Monte Carlo simulation involves the following steps:

1. Formulate the problem.
2. Collect and process real world data.
3. Formulate the mathematical model.
4. Estimate the model parameters and conditions from the real world data.
5. Test the model. Make an initial evaluation of model adequacy.
6. Formulate a computer program.
7. Validate the model. Compare model results with historical data. Are predictions from the model reasonable?

8. Design and run the experiment to solve the problem formulated in step 1.
9. Interpret, analyze, and utilize the simulation results.

Each of these nine steps was used in the bank teller example. Although most real problems are more complex than the bank manager's, the solution steps are the same, and the Monte Carlo simulation technique can be expanded to handle even very complicated decision problems.

1. What are "model components" in a simulation model? How does the modeler decide which components to include in a model?

2. Give a detailed description of how the Monte Carlo technique works in a simulation model.

3. Simulation models vary in degree of sophistication, completeness, and detail. Using your own example, show how the sophistication decision affects the amount of real world data gathering effort necessary for using the model.

4. What factors should be considered in deciding on simulation run length?

5. Give an example showing how a simulation model can be developed for experimenting on different operating policies. In your example, describe the situation and identify the data requirements, your procedure for validating the model, and the output measures you have selected.

6. Develop a flow chart showing the logic of the model in question 5.

Bierman, H., Jr., C. P. Bonini, and W. H. Hausman. *Quantitative Analysis for Business Decisions*. 5th ed. Homewood, Ill.: Richard D. Irwin, Inc., 1977.

Meier, R. C., W. T. Newell, and H. L. Pazer. *Simulation in Business and Economics*.

Englewood Cliffs, N.J.: Prentice-Hall, Inc., 1969.

Naylor, T. H., J. L. Balintfy, D. S. Burdick, and K. Chu. *Computer Simulation Techniques*. New York: John Wiley & Sons, Inc., 1966.

II

PLANNING THE CONVERSION SYSTEM

Planning for Operations

4

Planning for operations is the *establishment of a program of action for resource conversion into goods and services.* Before any actual resource conversion takes place, the operations manager identifies what resources will be necessary, determines how the conversion process will have to be designed, and anticipates any problems that may come up in operating the facility and delivering the product or service.

Once the conversion process has begun, planning must be integrated with the organizing and controlling functions. All are basic to the management process in operations. In their planning efforts, operations managers use modeling approaches and apply behavioral science techniques. The operations manager doesn't devote the first three hours of the day to planning, then two hours to organizing, then five to controlling. Rather, these functions are intertwined throughout the day and week. At one instant the manager might be on the shop or office floor taking corrective action to overcome some operating error (controlling). Suddenly he or she may realize the need to develop a better program of action for scheduling jobs (planning). Similarly, when the operations manager is determining the content of jobs (organizing), the need for replanning may be evident. These interfaces of planning, organizing, and controlling are depicted by their overlapping areas in Figure 4-1. Although this chapter concentrates on major planning concepts, you should remember that without careful controlling and organizing, even the best planning would do little good.

Like most other processes, planning involves a series of steps, distinct phases that follow one another in an ordered pattern. These steps have **PLANNING CONCEPTS**

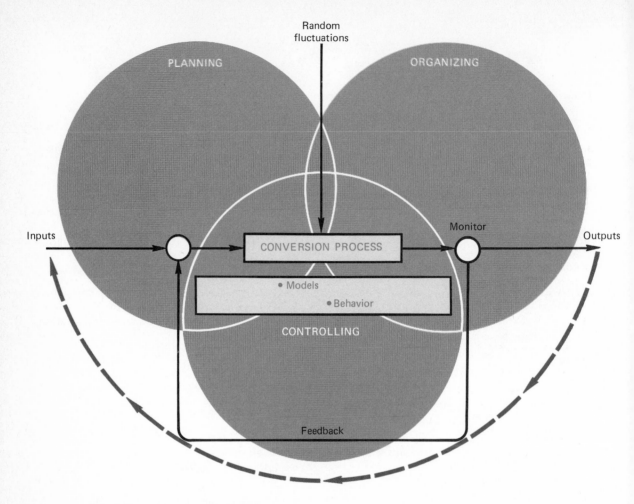

Figure 4-1 **Operations management functions**

been discovered and refined over the years by all the major management schools of thought that we discussed in Chapter 1. We have summarized them in Table 4-1, and you may find it helpful to refer to this table as you read the rest of the chapter.

Analysis of the Work Process

There is no substitute for knowledge about the work process when one is setting out to plan or develop a program for action. Frederick Taylor emphasized the scientific study of people and machines at work, closely examining the activities being performed on the production (shop) floor. As a result of his observations, he isolated three leading functions of the planning department of an organization:

TABLE 4-1

SELECTED PLANNING CONCEPTS

Planning concept	Management school	Contributor	Brief concept definition
Manager's planning responsibility	Classical	Frederick Taylor	Concern with analysis of the work process and standardization of the work process
Standardization of the work process	Classical	Frederick Taylor, R. C. Davis	Standardization can be accomplished through policies, procedures, and work routinization
Policies	Classical	Henri Fayol, others	A statement serving as a guide to action
Procedures	Classical	Henri Fayol, others	A rule for a specific condition that leads to action
Work routinization	Classical	Frederick Taylor	Regulating; making work processes habitual and uniform
Goals	Social system	Chester Barnard	The objectives that the organization seeks to accomplish
Planning time horizon	Decision-making	Herbert Simon	That distance into the future to which a decision maker looks when evaluating the consequences of a proposed action
Forecasting	Decision-making	Many	Determining an estimate of future events
Generating alternative programs of action	Social system and decision-making	Richard Cyert, James March, Herbert Simon	Searching for alternatives until a satisfactory set is obtained

1. complete analysis of all orders taken by the company for machines or work,
2. analysis of all inquiries for new work received in the sales department and promises for time of delivery, and
3. cost of all items manufactured with complete expense analysis and complete monthly comparative cost and expense exhibits.

These activities are performed in many production/operation processes, and, depending upon the volume and complexity of activities, several managers often perform them. The marketing manager should know about the salesperson's job, product markets, and distribution systems if the overall marketing effort is to be effectively planned. The financial manager must have an understanding of money markets, alternative funding approaches, and the effects of operating decisions on the financial structure, profitability, and cash flows of the organization. To understand production/operations, marketing, and finance, the managers of these subsystems must be involved in the analysis and documentation of their activities. Taylor suggests that providing this analysis and documentation is the function of the planning department. Although we agree that there is a need for analysis and documentation, we question whether establishing a separate planning department is always sound, however.

Standardization of the Work Process

Organizations are usually dynamic, changing to such pressures as new market demands, new owner demands, new employees, and government restrictions. Often reactions to changes in the environment can result in oscillations that leave the organization unstable—out of control. If decision makers overreact to changes and pressures with erratic or unpredictable decisions, severe mismanagement can result. To minimize this possibility, management attempts to standardize the work process by establishing *policies, procedures,* and *work routinization.*

Policies

A policy is a statement serving as a guide to action. Policies are somewhat general in nature; they are simply guides for administrators to follow. Since they affect everyone in the organization, policies should be:

1. written down, particularly if they deal with personnel,
2. readily available,
3. understood by managers and subordinates, and
4. general enough to be stable over time.

Suppose that one policy in your organization is: "Schedule jobs in the plant to meet delivery dates." This manufacturing policy reflects the organization's goal of providing good service to customers. Notice that the policy does not state how to accomplish the goal; it provides a guide for selecting scheduling rules, which are much more specific. A scheduling rule reflecting policy goals might be: "Schedule jobs in the stamping department on a due-date basis, with the exception of Jones Printing Company jobs, which should always be scheduled first."

There are as many types of policies as there are functional areas in an organization—policies, for example, in marketing, finance, personnel, production or operations, and engineering. Within any one functional area, there are numerous policies, many of which are documented in a manual for that function. No matter what area a policy is created for, it should have these characteristics:

1. *Flexibility.* A policy must strike a reasonable balance between stability and flexibility. Policies must change with conditions.

2. *Comprehensiveness.* A policy must be a general guide, comprehensive enough to cover most situations that might arise.
3. *Coordination.* A policy must provide for coordination of interrelated subunits.
4. *Ethics.* A policy must conform to the society's canons of ethical behavior.
5. *Clarity.* A policy must be written clearly and logically.

Procedures

Work processes are standardized through procedures. *A procedure is a specific rule that must be followed.* One scheduling rule for a stamping department was illustrated in our discussion of policy. The difference between a policy and a procedure can be seen in two statements about hiring. "If one of two or more equally qualified applicants is Mexican-American, and we currently have inadequate minority representation, give preference to the Mexican-American" is a procedure, a specific rule requiring management to achieve an overall ethnic balance. "All personnel selection should be nondiscriminatory" is a statement of policy, a much more general guide from which the procedure was derived.

Work routinization

Work processes are standardized through regulation of activities. *Work routinization is the regulation of habitual uniform work processes.* Variability of work content and behavior is reduced through techniques designed to stabilize the work process. Typical, but certainly not all-inclusive, are these standardizing methods and techniques:

1. *Personnel.* Job descriptions, application forms, testing procedures for selection, personnel evaluation procedures and forms, wage and salary schedules.
2. *Marketing.* Travel expense reports, product pricing schedules, establishment of sales quotas, appropriate channels of distribution for given conditions.
3. *Operations.* Automation, job design, work measurement, material handling specifications, quality standards, quantity standards, product design.
4. *Finance.* Loan application forms, daily cash balance reports, weekly cost reports, profit center analyses, discounted cash flow for investment analyses.

As with other concepts we've discussed, Frederick Taylor was among the first to discuss the value of standardized work processes.[1] Many organizations have built on his theories and have found that regulated planning makes for a more efficient operation.

[1] See Frederick W. Taylor, *Shop Management,* p. 111, where he states that the primary functions of the planning department should include time study, line balancing, pay schedules, standards, and systematic part identification.

Establishing Goals

The planning function begins with the establishment of goals, objectives the organization seeks to accomplish. Goals give direction to the organization's efforts. But an organization may have many goals, and at times they may conflict. Furthermore, some goals may apply to certain situations and not to others. When goals are established, therefore, careful thought should be given to their *priority, time,* and *structure.*

Priority of goals

An organization must decide which of its goals are primary and which are secondary; secondary goals are derived from and support primary goals. One primary goal of any organization is survival. A secondary goal, such as providing a 6 percent dividend yield to stockholders, is dependent on the primary goal, since an organization obviously cannot provide a dividend if it doesn't survive. At the same time, the secondary goal supports the primary goal; a good dividend helps ensure the organization's survival. Thus the organization's goals, while ordered in terms of priority, are complementary. Other secondary goals might include profitability, growth, and quality service.

Timing of goals

Goals can be short-term, intermediate, or long-term. A short-term goal is normally for a year or less, for example to achieve designated sales volumes monthly or annually. Intermediate goals are usually of one to five years' duration, for example to add plant capacity by selecting a new site, purchasing land, and building and staffing the new facility. Long-term goals have longer than a five-year time horizon, for example to establish vertical manufacturing integration.

=== **EXAMPLE** ===

Vertical manufacturing integration was established within AMAX Aluminum Company, where aluminum fabrication operations were purchased and grouped. By becoming a primary aluminum producer in the 1960s and 1970s, AMAX was able vertically to integrate backwards. One interesting side benefit was the possibility of avoiding antitrust action that might have resulted had the integration gone from metal source to purchasing firms for a captive market. AMAX's integration illustrates the pursuit of a long-term goal requiring more than five years. It was supported by intermediate goals and was implemented through a series of short-term goals.

Structure of goals

Structuring goals is the process of breaking them down into units, such as finance, marketing, and production, and assigning goals to each unit. Overall corporate profitability goals, for example, might be translated into cash management goals for the finance department, sales volume goals for the marketing area, and cost control goals for production employees. Structuring according to primary and secondary goals is also effective.

In structuring goals, management must also distinguish between employees' personal goals and the organization's goals. This distinction is important because it is another important source of potential goal conflict. A personal goal of leisure time might not be compatible with an organization goal of achieving higher output volume through overtime operations. Furthermore, the organization can and very well may have conflicting goals with government, competitors, stockholders, suppliers, and creditors.

Besides all this, goals must be measurable and have a semblance of unity. Establishing measurable goals that are supportive but not conflicting is both necessary and difficult. In fact, goal formation is one of the most difficult parts of planning.

Setting goals The process of setting goals varies with management style and organization constraints. Typically, goal setting procedure initiates at the top of the organization, the Board of Directors and top executives determining broad guidelines. Normally, the goal setting process, as opposed to goals themselves, is established at this level.

As the broad goals of survival and performance filter down through the organization, they become more specific. If, for example, top management has determined certain growth objectives, the general goal for operations might be to increase capacity 10 percent and output 15 percent in the next two years. Finance and marketing would also have general goals in line with the overall objective. At a level much lower in the organization, the operations goal might be to build and staff, within eighteen months, a 100,000 square foot manufacturing plant in Maryland to support expansion.

Generally, an organization's final goals represent a consensus of executives and managers, who provide general guidelines, and subordinates, who offer their suggestions in turn. The process, starting from the top, flows downward in the organization and then flows back upward; the final goals are somewhat different in form than they were when first conceived. If you are familiar with the annual budget-setting process, you know that a budget, which represents financial operating goals, is established in this manner.

The Planning Time Horizon

The planning time horizon is that time in the future a decision maker looks toward in evaluating the consequences of a proposed action. Many decisions require managers to look into the future; planning decisions are among them.

Goal setting, budgeting, forecasting, and policy making are all aspects of planning that use a time horizon. Imagine the time horizon as a continuum. At one end is top management, whose involvement in long-term planning often involves a time horizon of five years or more. At the other end of the time horizon continuum are first line supervisors, who are involved in short-term planning, often on a day-to-day basis. In the middle of the time horizon continuum we find people in middle management, who are involved in one- to five-year intermediate planning; they receive inputs from lower managers and review from top management.

What happens if inappropriate planning horizons are used? Basically, an organization can either miss sound business opportunities or incur excessive operating costs. Failure to plan for a changing market or failure to develop contingency plans for directing the efforts of manufacturing and engineering can result in missing significant business opportunities.

EXAMPLE

In the early 1970s, American and Canadian automobile manufacturers were unable to react to consumer demand for small cars and thus lost markets to foreign competition. Perhaps a contributing factor toward the delay was the American/Canadian time horizon for retooling. Although the annual model year time horizon would seem to allow adequate time for market adjustments, major retooling is actually done only every three or four years. Since the automobile companies have such substantial sunk costs in retooling and design, they were unable to respond quickly. Clearly, a shorter planning time horizon and lesser tooling commitment would have been beneficial for the industry.

We can see that using inappropriate time horizons can easily result in excessive costs and lost opportunities for profit. How does a manager avoid this? One way is to use managerial experience to learn the appropriate time horizon for various situations. Managers may also profit by learning traditional practices of the industry, by sharing the experiences of others, and in some cases by participating in business simulation games that emphasize the importance of time horizons in decision making. Perhaps the most important thing that the manager can do is to become aware of the concept itself, to recognize that the planning time horizon affects outcomes.

Forecasting Future Events

Planning means considering the future. In order to plan for future events, we must have some idea about what they will be. Just as many of us plan our weekends according to the weather forecast, businesspeople plan future actions according to forecasts of future market conditions. In business, *forecasting is predicting, determining an estimate of future events.* Business forecasts can be derived from intuitive estimation, simple

TABLE 4-2

97
Chapter 4
Planning for
Operations

A DECISION THEORY FRAMEWORK FOR PLANNING

Alternative actions	Event 1	Event 2
Plan *A*	Outcome *A1*	Outcome *A2*
Plan *B*	Outcome *B1*	Outcome *B2*
Plan *C*	Outcome *C1*	Outcome *C2*

modeling, or sophisticated modeling. As model complexity increases, so do forecasting costs and, usually, forecasting accuracy.

Since planning involves developing alternative programs of action for different possible future events, planners depend on reasonable forecasts. Table 4-2 represents a simplified decision theory framework. It shows, for example, that if plan *B* is developed as an alternative and eventually chosen as a course of action, and if event *2* is the state of nature that occurs, the result will be outcome *B2*. Various combinations of events and actions yield predictable outcomes. Once future events or states of nature have been estimated, plans can be developed to include consideration of forecasted events. To select a course of action, managers must:

1. identify possible events,
2. estimate outcomes for these events, and
3. establish probabilities of occurrence.

Thereafter, other methods can evaluate which alternative actions are most acceptable.

Forecasting problems concern overall markets, competitor actions, financial markets, and general business conditions. In production/operations, forecasters deal with specification of final product demand, individual component part demand, and technology requirements. Solutions to all these problems are not easily come by, and no one has yet devised a perfect forecaster. Usually we have to rely on a combination of judgement, wisdom, economic indications, and econometric and statistical models. But forecasting is nevertheless a critical phase of planning; good forecasting results in low forecast error, fewer alternatives that must be generated for possible states of nature, and simplified evaluation of alternative programs of action.

Generating Alternative Programs of Action

After possible states of nature have been forecasted, alternative programs of action can be developed. A fundamental question (seldom answered satisfactorily) is: how many alternatives should one generate? How much time, effort, and money should one spend to generate alternatives? The answer is that there is no optimal number of alternatives. Much depends on how valuable the outcomes may be; obviously, more time and money should be spent on potentially very profitable outcomes than on less profitable ones. Certainly, it would be unwise to spend so much money on planning that profits are eaten up. On the other hand, there have to be enough alternatives for decision makers to be flexible.

Since it's impossible to find the *optimal* number of alternatives, managers look for a *satisfactory* set. This is especially true for highly complex business problems. *Satisficing,*[2] a term sometimes used to describe behavior that limits the search for alternative solutions, allows managers or administrators to search until a satisfactory alternative is found and then stop. Having found a satisfactory alternative to one problem, they continue on to another.

There are similarities between limiting the search for alternatives in decision making and searching for alternative courses of action in planning. Satisficing is most readily observable in short-term planning, because time pressures severely limit search activity. Often, planners don't have the choice of buying additional information or taking the time to develop a good set of alternatives. They must find one good alternative quickly and be satisfied with that.

PLANNING FOR OPERATIONS

The fundamentals of planning apply to operations management too. Operating managers in manufacturing, the extractive industries, and the service sector make two sets of planning decisions. If you look at Figure 4-2, you'll see that operating managers must make decisions about planning both the conversion system and the use of the conversion system. *Planning the conversion system involves establishing a program of action for acquiring the necessary physical facilities to be used in the conversion process. Planning the use of the conversion process involves establishing programs of action for the actual transformation of the resource inputs into outputs of goods and services, given an existing physical facility.* As Figure 4-2 shows, models and behavioral techniques are applicable to both of these planning areas.

Table 4-3 lists the types of planning decisions that must be made in operations. Our discussion of them in this chapter will be brief and introductory; later, we'll discuss both the planning situations and modeling and behavioral techniques to confront them.

Planning Conversion Facilities

Capacity planning   The idea behind capacity planning is to be able to make as many units as the organization will be able

[2]James C. March and Herbert A. Simon, *Organization* (New York: John Wiley & Sons, Inc., 1950) and Richard M. Cyert and James C. March, *A Behavioral Theory of the Firm* (Englewood Cliffs, N.J.: Prentice-Hall, Inc., 1963).

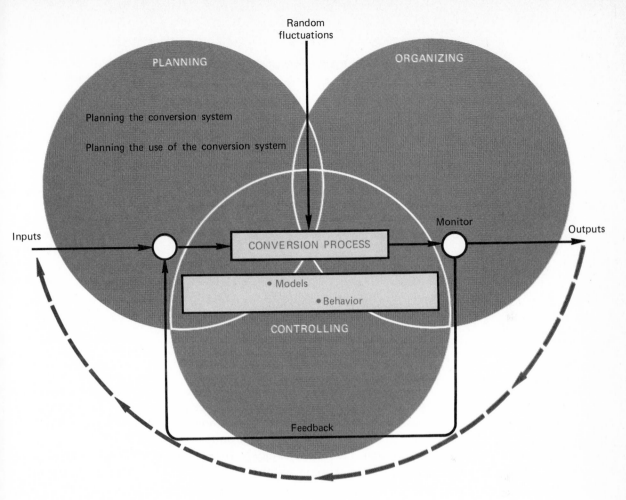

Figure 4-2 **Major operations planning decisions**

to sell. The first thing to be done, then, is to convert forecasts of sales demand from dollar amounts into the units the organization provides, whether they are manufactured items, beds occupied in a hospital, or meals served in a cafeteria. Then the forecasted number of units is compared to existing capability of meeting these demands over time. Management may decide that future demands require adding capacity, deleting some capacity, or making no changes in the existing facility. Capacity planning requires a time horizon that is dependent upon the technology. A barbershop can normally add another chair and barber quicker than a steel producer can add another oxygen-fired blast furnace. Generally, capacity planning is one of the first operations planning questions to be addressed, since it has implications for future facilities and their use.

Location of facilities   Once a need is established for additional capacity, a facility must be designed and a location chosen. The location depends upon a multitude of factors—trans-

================= TABLE 4-3 =================

OPERATIONS PLANNING DECISION SITUATIONS

Major planning decision	Specific planning situations
Planning conversion facilities (planning the conversion system)	Capacity planning Location of facilities Process planning Facility layout planning Product planning: research and development
Planning the use of the conversion system	Forecasting Production planning for aggregate output job shop scheduling production control Project planning and scheduling Personnel planning Manufacturing policy

portation requirements, necessary delivery times from suppliers and to customers, the labor market, natural resources required for production, utility costs, land availability, and socioeconomic factors in retaining a work force. All these factors help determine the kinds of technological processes that can be handled. Obviously, the location of a TWA overhauling and repair facility would depend on a different set of considerations than would the location of a paper mill for International Paper Company.

Process planning   For any given production/operations process, there are alternative methods of conversion. Management has to decide which plans offer the best hopes of meeting their goals. What degree of automation shall we use? How much capital investment? How shall we use labor?

================= EXAMPLE =================

Kawneer Co., Inc., was planning a new aluminum fabrication plant to produce decorative trim parts for the automotive and appliance industry. Process planning resulted in the design and selection of alternative methods of material handling. Suggestions included an overhead crane to move raw materials, an automated run-out for handling hot extrusions, fixed conveyors, mobile conveyors, gravity conveyors, a roof-mounted oven with overhead conveyors, forklift trucks, and a manual transfer system. Kawneer's process planning for material handling required about three months of effort for a 200,000-square-foot plant.

From the various process plans presented to them, management makes process selection decisions, which are usually interactive. Since Kawneer's management, for example, chose the process plan to roof-mount a paintbaking oven, they also had to plan for a fixed overhead conveyor to transport parts through the roof and into and out of the oven. They had to eliminate plans that involved manual loading and unloading of the oven. The technical and economic aspects of process planning are often analyzed by an industrial engineering staff or, in their absence, by operations managers.

Facility layout planning
In layout planning, alternative layouts of equipment and work stations are analyzed and evaluated. How efficiently will work orders flow through different layout configurations? Which one should we select? In facility layout planning, we are concerned with fixing the locations of elements *within* the plant or building walls, unlike capacity planning and plant location, which are concerned with matters external to the actual facility's walls. Should the boiler room be closer to the chemical baths or to the restrooms? Where should equipment be placed within the boiler room? Techniques for planning layouts vary from scaled-down templates, which are moved about on a piece of paper, to elaborate computerized models, which evaluate layouts against one another and print out the best one.

Product planning: research and development
Product ideas do not just happen; they are planned and developed. For existing products as well as new ones, applied research and development are necessary. Management must plan programs to select, develop, produce, and market their products or services, and they must continually assess the economic and technical risks involved. Many organizations fail long before their time because they do not plan for new products and services before current products or services become obsolete. This is just as true for an outmoded urban transit system as it is for second-generation computers.

Planning the Use of the Conversion Facility

Forecasting
In most operations, future demand for output is not known with certainty. Demand forecasts are therefore necessary, not only for short-term inputs but for phasing in production of future demand quantities. With the help of good forecasts, management can plan for smooth transitions from current output to future output. Forecasting, like other aspects of planning, varies in sophistication from intuitive estimates to complex econometric and statistical models. Accurate forecasting can significantly reduce production variation and thus reduce production costs.

Production
planning for
aggregate output

Once a forecast of aggregate demand in units has been achieved, aggregate (overall) production must be planned. Figure 4-3 illustrates a constant-level production plan for meeting a seasonal demand. This aggregate plan calls for producing 100 units per month with a constant work force. Typically, an aggregate plan consists of two basic decisions: establishing the overall production rate and determining the overall number of workers to be employed during each month or period in the chosen planning horizon. To plan for these two decisions, the manager must consider hiring and layoff costs, overtime costs, inventory levels, and similar production-level related costs. The operations manager plays an important role in determining final programs for action at the aggregate planning level.

Production
planning for job
shop scheduling

Besides the broad overall focus of the aggregate planning problem, managers must also plan the more micro problem of job shop scheduling. In a job shop, jobs are basically made to order, and production/operations are intermittent. Because of the diversity of the products they produce, job shops characteristically operate with much shorter planning horizons and face greater uncertainties about demand than do standard product shops. Two short-range tasks must be performed for job shop scheduling: determining which jobs to run first, second, and so on (job scheduling)

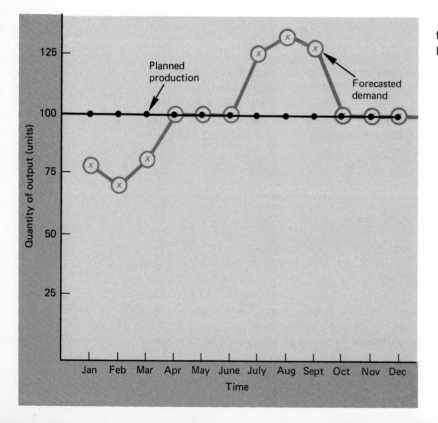

Figure 4-3 **An aggregate forecast and production plan**

and determining which machines or work centers should handle which jobs (job assignment). Often, job shop planning includes development of specific rules for scheduling jobs through the facility, for example scheduling the *shortest* jobs first. (Surprisingly, scheduling the shortest jobs first often increases the number of jobs the shop can do.)

Production planning for production control

Production planning is a prerequisite to effective production control. There are two stages of production planning and control, the preliminary stage and the action stage. In the preliminary, or planning stage, forecasts are converted into a master schedule, supplementary planning is carried out, jobs are assigned to work centers, and jobs are sequenced and scheduled. Work levels are checked to assure that capacity is not being exceeded. In the action stage, job assignments are released for the first time to shop foremen or operations managers through an activity called *dispatching*. Before dispatching, planning for production is a staff function. After dispatching, the planning staff continues with instruction, surveillance, and correction; the foremen and operations managers are responsible for conversion in their roles as line supervisors. During conversion, some supplementary planning is carried out by both line and staff personnel; feedback about shop performance comes back to the production planning staff. Since this feedback allows for new programs of action if necessary, it is the essence of the production control activity. It is helpful to remember that line personnel directly carry out the organization goals, while staff are supportive of and advisory to line personnel. The production planning for production control process thus repeats itself.

Project planning and scheduling

Aggregate, job shop, and production planning are repetitious, ongoing processes. But planning is also required for unique, one-time projects. If an important major project needs close coordination to be successfully completed, project planning techniques may be useful. They require:

1. identifying and specifying all activities to be performed,
2. establishing the order in which the activities must be performed (precedence relationships),
3. establishing time estimates for the activities, and
4. calculating expected completion times and dates.

Project planning techniques vary from simple bar graphs to sophisticated computerized algorithms; all, however, are planning tools for future coordination and control.

Personnel planning

Since most of the jobs in any organization are done by people, personnel planning is vital. It begins early, when facility location and layout are being considered.

Once the facility is ready, workers must be hired who can do the specific jobs required by the technology of the conversion process. Personnel management, which can be handled by the staff or by the operations manager, prepares job descriptions, recruits and selects employees, provides initial orientation, and often assists in employee evaluation. As part of the aggregate planning function, operations managers convert production level specifications into employee requirements; they determine what labor skills are needed and see to it that employees have those skills. Obviously, staffing for operations is critical. If laborers, maintenance people, engineers, and managers don't have the skills they need, the facility will not operate effectively, if it operates at all. Furthermore, personnel planners must gather wage and salary surveys and establish wage schedules, and often they must negotiate with unions. Personnel planning is a big job. It must begin early in the planning process, especially for critical technical and professional personnel, and must continue throughout the entire planning process.

Manufacturing
policy

Manufacturing or operations policies are overall guides established for converting resources into goods and services; they concern operating technology, quantity and quality standards, service levels, and cost control. A typical operations policy for a dry cleaning facility, for example, might be, "minimize the idle time of employees who service customers." Perhaps this policy could be followed by asking employees to perform certain production tasks, such as packaging clean garments, when the store is empty. A manufacturing policy might be, "ship as much finished goods inventory as possible by the last week of the month." Possibly the manager might set up procedures that would vary from customer to customer; some orders, then, could be shipped ahead of schedule and some later. Manufacturing and operations policies are a necessary phase in planning the use of the conversion facility.

Production/Operations Objectives

What are the specific goals in production/operations? Some insight into this question can be found in Britney and Newson's audit of the tasks of Canadian operations managers.[3] Most frequently, managers who were sampled spent time on labor/industrial relations, cost control, production control (assuring that adequate quantities are available for delivery on schedule), and quality control. Judging from the audit and from experience, we can say that primary short-term production/operations objectives are:

[3]Robert R. Britney and E.F. Peter Newson, *The Canadian Production/Operations Management Environment: An Audit,* School of Business Administration Research Monograph (London, Ontario: University of Western Ontario, 1975), pp. 15–19.

1. Establish product (service) characteristics.
2. Establish process characteristics.
3. Deliver the required service to the customer by
   (a) producing quantities to meet expected demand and
   (b) meeting the customer specified delivery date for the goods or services.
4. Produce the goods or services at the desired quality level.
5. Meet the above goals efficiently by
   (a) effective employee relations and labor cost control,
   (b) material cost control, and
   (c) cost control in facility utilization.
6. Maintain adaptability for future survival.

These short-term objectives support survival of the production process. The long-run production/operations goal is to utilize resources in a manner that meets long-run market demand for the firm. If successful, this process will generate the necessary funds to acquire additional resources, and the cycle of producing to meet market demand can begin again. The production/operations function survives, then, on effectiveness and efficiency criteria, and these criteria are what our objectives are all about.

Models for Planning

It is not surprising to find that planning models are most often presented in verbal or diagrammatic form. Planning requires consideration of so many variables, and interrelationships among them, that precise quantification is almost impossible. Recently, however, researchers have made inroads toward quantifying selected aspects of planning. Two of these quantified approaches are goal programming and the use of a goal consistency model. We won't discuss the technical aspects of these models; our purposes are to point out their existence and to show how they apply to the planning process.

Goal programming Sometimes multiple goals can lead to goal conflict. After an extensive planning effort you may find, for example, that a marketing subgoal conflicts with one in operations or finance. Similarly, within a single functional area, such as operations, two subgoals may conflict. A goal of reducing annual operation costs by 10 percent may be incompatible with a goal of increasing output by 15 percent. When resources are limited and all the subgoals cannot be simultaneously accomplished, a method of analysis called *goal programming* can help determine the best course of action. This technique is a special version of linear programming, an optimization method we discuss in the supplement to Chapter 5.

To use goal programming, managers must clearly identify each goal and subgoal. Then each must be given a priority ranking reflecting its relative importance and specifying whether overaccomplishment or underaccomplishment is to be allowed. Finally, limitations of resources necessary for accomplishing the goals must be identified. Having done all this, managers can use the goal programming technique to allocate their resources and meet the priorities they've established. Usually, they will find that some subgoals can be fully accomplished and others can be only partially realized. But managers have the comfort of knowing that although they have been unable to accomplish all goals, they have been able to identify the best uses of limited resources and minimize goal conflict.

Goal programming has been suggested for use in several types of organizations: in an academic setting to meet teaching, research, and service goals, and in determining a distribution network to achieve a balance among goals relating to customer service, operating costs, and adherence to union agreements, to name just two.

Goal consistency   Goal programming prescribes an *optimal* course of action; the goal consistency model does not. Its purpose is to help the planner to be consistent in estimating relationships among elements of a plan.

Most plans begin with rather general goal statements. As the plan is refined and elaborated, its elements become more specific. Ideally, successively detailed elements of the plan are hierarchically linked, ultimately in support of the broadly stated goals that initiated the planning effort in the first place. Figure 4-4 shows an example of a hierarchy of elements. First the overall goal, increasing productive output, is established. Then subgoals that will lead to accomplishment of the overall goal are identified. Next, the planner identifies those policy areas (two in this example) in which decisions can be made to accomplish subgoals. Finally, the plan becomes even more detailed by showing specific action alternatives for each policy area.

A complete plan identifies many specific action alternatives (five in Figure 4-4) that could ultimately lead to accomplishment of the overall goal. If resources are limited, however, only some of the action alternatives can be selected. Which ones? Normally the operations manager carefully examines the alternative actions and, using experience as a guide, ranks them according to how well they would help accomplish the overall goal.

As you can see in Figure 4-4, however, there's another step. After all the subelements of the plan have been listed, the manager assigns numeric importance ratings to them. In Figure 4-4, these ratings are represented by the numbers $1a$ through 5; here, a total of 11 ratings is used. Estimates $1a$ and $1b$, when assigned specific numerical ratings, will indicate how strongly redesigning the assembly line and changing the packing operation would influence the job design. Estimate $2a$ will reflect the importance of job design to achieving reduced labor turnover and estimate $2b$ the importance of job design to reducing scrap. Estimates 4 and 5 will show the relative importance of the two subgoals to increasing productive output, the overall goal. When all the subelements have been

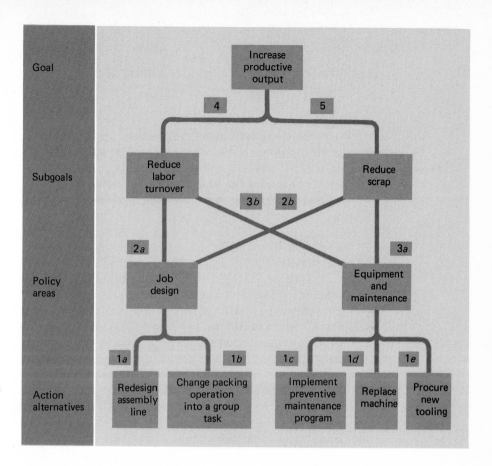

Figure 4-4
Hierarchy of elements in a plan (numeric weightings to be assigned to each square)

numerically ranked, according to the manager's intuition and judgment, the manager can calculate a goal accomplishment rating for each action alternative and determine which is best.

Sometimes the final rankings differ from the manager's original rankings. If they do, something's wrong, and the plan needs closer evaluation. Maybe too little care was taken in identifying goals, subgoals, policy areas, and/or alternatives; some may have been omitted. Perhaps an action area is less important for attaining a subgoal than was originally believed. It may be that some of the relationships among elements were originally misunderstood or incorrectly represented in the diagram. In any event, the elements and their relationships must be further clarified, importance weightings re-estimated, and the entire process repeated until the inconsistencies are resolved.

The goal consistency procedure offers several benefits. It:

1. provides a guide for clarifying what elements should be considered in planning,
2. tests the planner's understanding of how the elements are interrelated, and
3. provides a basis for uncovering sources of inconsistency in intuitive judgment.

Although this method has not yet received wide application, it seems to offer promise as a useful planning tool.

PRACTICAL
GUIDES IN
PLANNING FOR
OPERATIONS
Previous sections of this chapter have focused on conceptualizing the planning process. Before we examine the details of operations planning, the subject of the next several chapters, we want to leave you with some practical guides for planning in operations: planning in industrial firms, phases of planning, practical tips, and possible pitfalls.

Planning Field Studies

Just because planning seems practical, we cannot assume that all companies readily plan and plan well. Table 4-4 shows the results of a planning study of 35 firms in the paint and varnish industry. Each of the 35 is classified in two ways: by the strategy that is emphasized in planning (marketing or research) and by the number of employees (small, medium, or large). The level of planning sophistication covers a broad range across which the firms are rather evenly distributed. Notice that a strong majority do *not* have highly sophisticated operational plans. Comparing the highly sophisticated with the highly unsophisticated firms, we notice some correlation in firm size; six of the eight highly sophisticated firms employed more than 250 people, while four of the five highly unsophisticated firms employed fewer than 50 people. To the extent that this study in the paint and varnish industry represents other industries, a wide disparity in planning emphasis can be observed across firms and organizations.

In another study, a questionnaire was administered to some 280 chief executives throughout the world.[4] The executives were asked to rate the relative perceived importance of external relations, meetings, planning, inspection and control, people, personal development, and other activities. Over 65 percent ranked planning first in importance, although they indicated they were not able to spend as much time in planning as they felt its importance warranted. In general, United States executives seemed to stress planning more than executives from other countries.

Phases of Planning

In view of its importance, and with an understanding of planning fundamentals, what can one use as a guide to effective planning? Although there is no one method that is best for every circumstance, these steps are usually helpful:

[4]H. Stieglitz, *The Chief Executive and His Job,* Personnel Policy Study No. 214 (New York: National Industrial Conference Board, 1969).

TABLE 4-4

PLANNING IN THE PAINT AND VARNISH INDUSTRY*

Level of sophistication of operational plans	Strategy emphasis		Number of employees		
	Marketing	Research	1–49	50–249	250+
Highly sophisticated	1	7	1	1	6
Sophisticated	1	6	4	2	1
Minimal sophistication	7	0	2	1	4
Unsophisticated	8	0	2	5	1
Highly unsophisticated	4	1	4	1	0
Subtotals	21	14	13	10	12
Total		35		35	

*Adapted from R. J. Litschert, "Some Characteristics of Long-Range Planning: An Industry Study," *The Academy of Management Journal* 11 (1968), pp. 321, 322, 327.

1. *Establish goals.* Goals must be set so that direction can be given to the organization. Management must establish primary and secondary goals and resolve goal conflicts as much as possible. In establishing goals, attention should be given to measuring performance so that subsequent goal accomplishment can be evaluated.

2. *Forecast events.* Premises for future action must be specified, and the assumptions upon which the plans are developed must be clearly stated. These steps require forecasts of the external and internal environment. The forecasting procedure depends upon the type of planning being undertaken; it varies from general business forecasting for strategic planning to more routinized statistical forecasting for operational planning.

3. *Generate alternatives.* After future events have been forecasted, the manager must generate alternatives with the established goals. From these alternatives a course of action will be selected, depending on which future events occur. This is contingency planning or contingency decision making. "If _____ happens, then I want to proceed according to alternative _____" is the basic approach.

4. *Establish policies.* Managers need to establish general guides for manufacturing and operations so resources can be converted into goods and services. The conversion process operates more effectively and efficiently with policies than it does without them. Policies facilitate coordinated effort and help reduce unwarranted variability in decision making.

5. *Operationalize the plan.* Operationalization is preparing for action. In the operationalizing phase of planning, policies are used as guides for establishing procedures and rules; budgets are established; standards are set for operations; measurement techniques are determined; and the operational basis for control is established. This phase involves getting out of the ideal realm of planning and into the real world of day-to-day

activities by communicating plans to the work group. Once plans have been communicated and the bases for control and future direction have been established, action can begin.

Suggestions for Effective Planning

Once you understand the general concepts of planning, how do you put them into effect? Here are some practical suggestions:

1. Use planning to increase employees' understanding of their jobs and job responsibilities. Effectively communicated policies will avoid considerable confusion and duplication of individual and group efforts.
2. Encourage participation in establishing goals, especially from subordinates. Although all goals cannot be set with subordinate participation, many can be. Including subordinates in planning will certainly reduce resistance to change and assist in motivation.
3. Limit arbitrary action of supervisors by effective planning. Effective planning establishes guides and encourages rational decisions.
4. Encourage through planning the consideration of many variables and alternatives before action begins. The planning process can lead to better decision making. Good planning should foster contingency decision making.
5. Operationalize plans. Budgets are expectations expressed in quantitative terms; use them. Translate policies into rules and procedures. Establish timetables; completion dates are an important part of operations planning. Establish standards that future performance can be measured against. In general, the planning process should be transferred from the ideal into practical guides.
6. Allow planning to interact with organizing and controlling activities. These functions are not performed in a vacuum; they interact. Feedback from control assists in planning, just as the relationships between jobs and groups of people do in organizations. Effective planning leads to effective organizing and controlling.

Reasons for Planning Failure

Prevoyance, a term introduced by Henri Fayol, demands two considerations in planning: assessing the future and making provisions for it. Many failures in planning evolve because basic planning concepts have been misapplied or not used at all.

A survey of decision making and planning practices in over 350 European and American corporations indicates that most planning failures can be traced to one or more of the following factors:

1. Corporate planning is not integrated into the total management system.
2. Planning is not systematic; there is a lack of understanding of the different dimensions of planning.
3. Various levels of management are not engaged or involved in planning.
4. Responsibility for planning is vested solely in planning departments.
5. Management assumes that because a plan exists it will be put into practice.

6. Too much is attempted at one time.
7. Management "plans its work but fails to work its plan."
8. Extrapolation and financial planning are confused with general planning procedures.
9. Information inputs are inadequate.
10. Too much emphasis is placed on a single aspect of planning.[5]

SUMMARY

The production/operations manager must plan a program of action in advance of actual resource conversion. To do this, the manager must understand such classical planning concepts as goal setting, policy making, forecasting, timing, and analysis and standardization of work.

In practice, the operations manager must plan both the conversion process (the facility) and the use of the conversion process. This is done through the wide variety of planning situations illustrated in Table 4-3. With effective planning, the chances of personal and organizational success increase substantially.

To plan effectively, managers must remember that employees are human beings. Both in the planning process itself and in implementing the plans once they're made, behavioral phenomena must be taken into account. The planning process involves human initiative to start the process and human judgment and intuition to deal with and consider future events.

Distinctly different from the planning process itself is the effect of planning on the organization. Managers should plan the work, then work the plan. Although a good plan specifies managerial and subordinate roles, you must remember that people are different from one another and cannot always be expected to conform just because the plan says they should. Planning a 5 percent allowable defective product level in production does not assure that that level will always be achieved. A good plan allows for variability by specifying both managerial and subordinate behavior in unexpected situations. By allowing 5 percent defective levels, a plan shows the direction employees should be heading, indicates the product quality management expects, and at the same time allows for variability in human behavior.

Employees' limitations can be overcome to some degree by modeling selected aspects of production planning. Models can assist managers by evaluating data rapidly and accurately. They can provide design standards against which planning alternatives can be compared. The modeling approach is feasible in situations in which major relationships are known and can be specified in model form. Recently, the digital computer has been a very important factor in the development of a modeling framework.

Table 4-5 lists behavioral and modeling approaches to typical production/operations planning situations. Although you are not yet familiar with some of the techniques, you may want to refer to this table as we proceed with our analysis of planning in production/operations management (P/OM).

We hope you are now aware of the importance of planning in operations management. Much of your success or failure as an operations manager, and of operations managers who might eventually report to you if you're a general manager, will depend upon your ability to plan effectively.

[5]Kjell A. Ringbakk, "Why Planning Fails," *European Business*, no. 29 (Spring 1971), pp. 15–26.

TABLE 4-5

AN OVERVIEW OF PRODUCTION/OPERATIONS MANAGEMENT SOLUTION PROCEDURES*

Planning situations	Solution approaches	
	Behavior	Models
Planning conversion facilities		
Capacity planning	Intuitive evaluation of past, current, and future capacity requirements	Long-run economic capacity planning analysis
Location of facilities	Evaluation of labor markets, unionization, natural resources, tax considerations, environment for quality of living	Economic location models, transportation model of linear programming, computer simulation
Process planning	Participative approach to planning, evaluation of alternative technologies, management/engineering interaction	Assembly charts, route sheets, flow process charts, form charts
Facility layout planning	Mixed layout strategies, layout flexibility desirable, management/engineering interaction, trial and error approaches	Templates, CRAFT, ALDEP, CORELAP for layout; heuristics for assembly line balancing
Product planning: research and development	Assessment of technological success, assessment of economic success, assessment of product and project overall success, R&D management, creativity, brainstorming	Net present value, expected value in project selection, project screening models, R&D management models
Planning the use of the conversion facility		
Forecasting	Human intuitive forecasting, predictions, forecast error evaluation	Regression, exponential smoothing, moving averages, adaptive models, Box-Jenkins
Production planning for aggregate scheduling	Information processing, multistage decision making	Linear programming, HMMS model, computer direct search techniques
job shop scheduling	Management decision rules, establishing customer priorities, dispatching, corrective action on shop floor, job shop configurations	Shortest processing time rule, assignment method, GANTT chart, minimum flow time, minimum lateness

*Most of these solution procedures were not explained in this chapter; they are used to clarify the behavioral and modeling approaches to planning in P/OM. The solution procedures will be developed in chapters that follow.

| | Solution approaches | |
Planning situations	Behavior	Models
production control	Scheduling, supplementary planning, dispatching, corrective action in shop, materials releases, shipping schedules	GANTT charts, MRP, COPICS
Project planning and scheduling	Activity identification, estimation of activity times, establishing precedence, relations among activities, project budgeting and control decisions	PERT, PERT/COST, stochastic PERT, CPM, GANTT charts
Personnel planning	Selection, recruiting, training, establishing personnel requirements, layoff planning, evaluation procedures, discipline, rewards	Human resources accounting, job analysis, job descriptions, wage and salary models, personnel requirements analysis
Manufacturing policy	Establishing manufacturing goals, presenting manufacturing position to general management thus influencing overall organization goals, establishing procedures, interpreting policy	Economic, cost, and technological analysis of policy alternatives

Glaskowe Manufacturing, Inc.

CASE

Glaskowe Manufacturing, a twenty-year-old firm producing parts for the automotive industry, is headquartered in a midwestern city. About 70 percent of production is sold to Chrysler, Ford, and General Motors. The remaining 30 percent is sold to other automotive, truck, and heavy equipment producers.

Glaskowe has six plants operating in the midwestern and southern United States. The owner and principal stockholder, Thomas Gillet, has approved $2.5 million for a new manufacturing facility to be located near Macon, Georgia. It is currently the fall of 1977, and Mr. Gillet would like the plant to be in operation by September 1, 1978, for the 1979 automotive model year. An experienced process engineer, Tim Anderson, has been working on this project for six months as project director.

A June business school graduate from an eastern university, Cy Wilson, has just been hired by Glaskowe and assigned to Tim Anderson to help see the project through. Tim explains to Cy, "Our responsibility is to have a manufacturing plant and equipment ready for operations September 1,

1978. You and I will not operate it; our Atlanta plant will staff and start up the plant. Since Atlanta is busy with current production, you and I will select, purchase, and coordinate all the plant and equipment necessary for production."

After a couple of days of becoming familiar with Glaskowe operations, Cy gets his first assignment. Tim informs him, "Cy, Monday I want you to go to our Atlanta plant for a week. Meet the people and spend some time learning our manufacturing technology. Here is a list of things we'll be working on when you return. I want you to size our air compressors and get them on order when you come back. Report to Fred Smith, the plant manager, who is expecting you."

On the airplane to Atlanta, Cy decided he would return with a plan of attack for this project. He didn't believe that buying air compressors was critical right now, nor was he sure at all that the process engineer had all the key activities identified. While in Atlanta, Cy was going to do some real planning for this project.

MACON PHYSICAL PLANT

Activity	Project engineer's estimated duration (weeks)
Order equipment	
Conveyors—fixed and variable path	12
Overhead crane	16
Chemical baths	8
250-ton press	32
Stamping presses	16
Chemical storage tanks	8
Air compressors	10
Boilers	12
Schedule construction	3
Oversee construction	26
Finalize facility layout	6
Purchase sprinkler system	8
Hire architect	2
Advertise for personnel	
Maintenance, tool room	8
Manufacturing labor	4
Clerical	4
Foremen and supervisors	8
Select personnel	4
Size boilerroom	3
Select contractor through competitive bids	6
Select products for transfer from Atlanta plant	4

Case questions:
1. What type of planning problem is this?
2. What general approach might Cy take in formulating a plan?
3. What activities might Cy add or delete?
4. Do you expect a new employee, fresh from college, to have his ideas readily accepted? How should Cy approach Tim?

1. Explain the differences among the priority, timing, and structuring dimensions in establishing goals.

2. Using the phases of planning as your guide, develop a study plan for a course in production/operations management from a student's perspective.

3. Think of a situation you have observed in which poor planning was evident. Which of the reasons for planning failure were the causes of the situation?

4. (a) How does the goal consistency model (or procedure) work?
   (b) What benefits could the model provide?

5. Management attempts to standardize the work process by establishing policies, procedures, and work routinization. Explain how management goes about doing this.

6. You are a student confronted with the possibility that on the same day two weeks from now you will have to take one exam in statistics and another in finance. One week from now, the exam schedule will be finalized. What are several alternative actions for and estimated outcomes of this situation? View the situation as a decision theory problem and construct a matrix (table) showing your framework. Which plan would you recommend now? Would you change your plan if you discover next week that your exams are scheduled for different days?

7. (a) Explain the differences between planning the conversion facility and planning the use of the conversion facility.
   (b) Which planning decision situation seems to you to be the most critical? Why?

8. If you were beginning a new venture, opening a wine and cheese shop in a shopping mall, what would your short-term production/operations objectives be?

9. A hospital administrator must plan the use of the conversion process. How would aggregate output planning and personnel planning interrelate in the hospital administrator's specific situation?

10. Look again at the planning field study of the paint and varnish industry that we discussed in this chapter. What insights did you gain from this study? (Support your statements with specific data.)

Dispatching: releasing job assignments to shop foremen or operations managers

Forecasting: predicting; determining an estimate of future events

Goals: objectives the organization seeks to accomplish

Goal priority: the ranking of primary and secondary goals

Goal structuring: process of breaking goals down into units, such as finance, marketing, and production, and assigning goals to each unit; also distinguishing between personal and organizational goals

Goal timing: short-term (one year or less), intermediate (one to five years), or long-term (more than five years) dimension of goals

Manufacturing policy: overall guides established for converting resources into goods and services

Operationalization: preparing to put plans into action by establishing procedures, setting standards, determining measurement techniques, and establishing budgets and operational control

Planning conversion facilities: see "Planning the conversion system"

Planning for operations: establishing a program of action for converting resources into goods or services

Planning the conversion system: establishing a program of action for acquiring the necessary physical facilities to be used in the conversion process

Planning the use of the conversion process: establishing programs of action for the actual transformation of the resource inputs into outputs of goods and services, given an existing physical plant

Planning time horizon: that time in the future a decision maker looks toward in evaluating the consequences of a proposed action

Policy: a statement serving as a guide to action

Procedure: a specific rule that must be followed

Project: a one-shot set of activities with a distinct beginning and ending

Scheduling: time sequencing of events

Work routinization: the regulation of habitual uniform work processes

SELECTED READINGS

Britney, Robert R. and E.F. Peter Newson. *The Canadian Production/Operations Management Environment: An Audit.* School of Business Administration Research Monograph. London, Ontario: University of Western Ontario, April 1975.

Cyert, Richard M. and James C. March. *A Behavioral Theory of the Firm.* Englewood Cliffs, N.J.: Prentice-Hall, Inc., 1963.

Donnelly, James H., James L. Gibson, and John M. Ivancevich. *Fundamentals of Management: Functions, Behavior, Models.* Dallas, Texas: Business Publications, Inc., 1971.

Drucker, Peter F. *Management: Tasks, Responsibilities, Practice.* New York: Harper & Row, 1974.

Fayol, Henri. *General and Industrial Management.* London: Pitman Pub. Corp., 1949.

Gulick, L. and L. Urwick, eds. *Papers on the Science of Administration.* New York: Institute of Public Administration, 1937.

Kast, Fremont E. and James E. Rosenzweig. *Organization and Management: A Systems Approach.* New York: McGraw-Hill Book Co., 1970.

Lee, S.M. "Decision Analysis Through Goal Programming." *Decision Sciences* 2, no. 2 (April 1971): 172–80.

———— and E.R. Clayton. "A Goal Programming Model of Academic Resource Allocation." *Management Science* 18, no. 8 (April 1972): B-395–B-408.

Litschert, R.J. "Some Characteristics of Long-Range Planning: An Industry Study." *The Academy of Management Journal* 11, no. 3 (September 1968): 315–28.

Ringbakk, Kjell A. "Why Planning Fails." *European Business,* No. 29 (Spring 1971): 15–26.

Stieglitz, H. *The Chief Executive and His Job.* Personnel Policy Study No. 214. New York: National Industrial Conference Board, 1969.

Taylor, Frederick W. *The Principles of Scientific Management.* New York: Harper & Row, 1911.

————. *Scientific Management.* New York: Harper & Row, 1919.

————. *Shop Management.* New York: Harper & Row, 1911.

Capacity Planning

5

Chapter 4 discussed the basic concepts of planning. In this and the next two chapters, we will apply these ideas to specific problem areas that are the particular concern of the production/operations manager. Our main emphasis will be on short- and long-range aspects of three planning problems, operations capacity, location of facilities, and layout. Their places in our familiar P/OM model are indicated in Figure 5–1.

The *capacity* of operations refers to the productive capability of a facility; it is usually expressed as volume of output per time period. Operations managers are concerned with capacity for several reasons. First, they want sufficient capacity to provide the output needed for meeting current and future customer demand. Second, the available capacity affects the efficiency of operations, including the ease or difficulty of scheduling output and the costs of maintaining the facility. Finally, the acquisition of capacity is an investment by the organization. Since we seek a good return on investment, both the costs and the revenues of a capacity decision must be carefully evaluated.

At first glance, the concept of capacity seems straightforward. But as plans for capacity are developed, one begins to uncover some hidden complexities. Output capability is highly dependent, for example, on both the type of conversion technology (processes) that exists and on the type of product (product mix) being produced. Later, you will see that these two factors, technology and product mix, make it difficult to measure capacity in meaningful terms.

THE CAPACITY PLANNING ENVIRONMENT

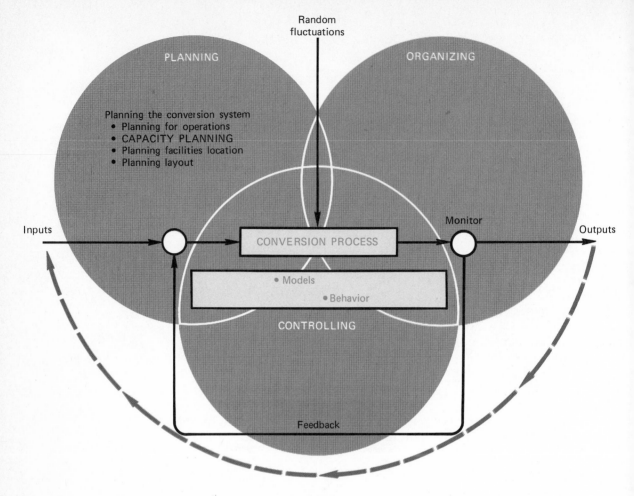

Random fluctuations

PLANNING

ORGANIZING

Planning the conversion system
• Planning for operations
• CAPACITY PLANNING
• Planning facilities location
• Planning layout

Inputs

Monitor

Outputs

CONVERSION PROCESS

• Models
• Behavior

CONTROLLING

Feedback

Figure 5-1 **Production / operations management activities**

Capacity planning decisions normally involve these activities:

1. an assessment of existing capacity,
2. estimates of future capacity needs (product, human, and technological) over a selected planning horizon,
3. identification of alternative ways to modify capacity,
4. financial, economical, and technological evaluation of capacity alternatives, and
5. selection or choice of a capacity alternative.

Measuring Capacity

For some organizations capacity seems simple to measure. United States Steel can refer to tons of output per year. General Motors Corporation can speak of number of automobiles per year. But what about organizations with more diverse product lines? How do you measure the capacity of a law firm or a veterinary clinic? In part, the answers depend on the diversity of the product mix. Even within General Motors, output consists of automobiles, trucks, and refrigerators. When the units of output are identical, or nearly so, a common unit of measure may be selected: megawatts of electricity, tons of gravel, number of autos, or barrels of beer. In these cases, capacity is measured in units of *output.*

On the other hand, when product mix is diverse it is hard to find a common unit of output measure that makes sense. As a substitute, capacity can be expressed in terms of *input* measures. A legal office may express capacity in terms of the number of attorneys employed. A custom job shop or an auto repair shop may indicate capacity by available labor hours and/or machine hours per week, month, or year.

An estimate of capacity, then, may be measured in terms of the inputs or the outputs of the conversion process. Some common examples of capacity measures used by different organizations are shown in Table 5-1. The most common measure of capacity is a *throughput* measure of the organization, a measure closer to output than to inputs. Throughput measures capacity in terms of time—as a *rate* of output or input per *time unit.* The custom in many industries is to operate on a standard forty-hour work week, and measures of processing capacity are normally interpreted within this context. During peak demand periods, however, extra hours are worked, and capacity is therefore greater. The weekly

=== TABLE 5-1 ===

MEASURES OF OPERATING CAPACITY

Organization	Measure
Output	
Automobile manufacturer	Number of autos
Brewery	Barrels of beer
Cannery	Tons of food
Steel producer	Tons of steel
Power company	Megawatts of electricity
Input	
Airline	Number of seats
Hospital	Number of beds
Job shop	Labor and/or machine hours
Merchandising	Square feet of display or sales area
Movie theater	Number of seats
Restaurant	Number of seats or tables
Tax office	Number of accountants
University	Number of students and/or faculty
Warehouse	Square feet or cubic feet of storage space

processing capacity of a tax firm, for example, increases during the months from January through April. What is its "real" capacity? A manufacturing facility may prefer to operate an eight-hour shift daily, but it may sometimes operate as many as three shifts around the clock. What is the capacity of the firm? Some organizations solve the problem by using multiple measures like "preferred or normal capacity" as contrasted with "maximum capacity." "Maximum capacity" is of questionable meaning, though, because firms can seldom operate at true maximum, particularly for sustained periods of time.

Capacity defined   *Capacity is the maximum rate of productive or conver-sion capability of an organization's operations.* Capacity incorporates the concept of rate of conversion within an operations setting.

It's often difficult to get a realistic measure of capacity because of the day-to-day variations that are encountered. Employees are sometimes absent or late, equipment breakdowns occur, facility downtime is needed for maintenance and repair, machine setups are required for product changeovers, and vacations must be scheduled. Since all these uncertainties and variations cause "true" capacity to vary from time to time, they must all be considered in any estimate of capacity. You can see, then, that the capacity of a facility can rarely be measured in precise terms. Such measures as are used must be interpreted cautiously.

Estimating Future Capacity Needs

Capacity requirements can be evaluated from two extreme perspectives, short-term and long-term.

Short-term   Managers often use forecasts of product demand to
requirements   estimate the near-term work load the facility must
                 handle. (Techniques for forecasting will be presented in Chapter 10.) By looking ahead up to twelve months, we can anticipate output requirements for our different products or services. Then we can compare requirements to existing capacity and detect when capacity adjustments will be needed. A company making two products may observe forecasted demands by constructing a chart like the one in Figure 5-2. Some products may have a seasonal pattern with low demand in winter and higher demand in early spring and summer (product *A*). Others, like product *B,* may show a general upward (or downward) trend. Is existing capacity adequate for meeting *overall* demand? If not, what adjustments in capacity can be made? We will answer these questions shortly.

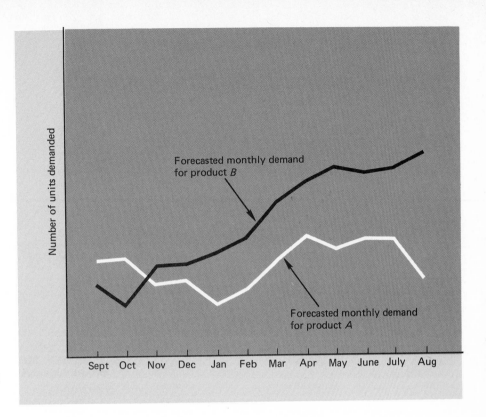

Figure 5-2
Examples of short-run demand patterns

Long-term requirements

Longer-term capacity requirements are more difficult to determine because of uncertainties in future market demand and technologies. Forecasting five or ten years into the future is a risky and difficult task. What products or services will we be producing then? Some new products will have been added; others will have become obsolete and died. Today's product may not even exist in the future. Demand for products changes with time; to describe the chronological stages of demand for a product, we use the term *product life cycle* (see Figure 5-3). Planners attempt to answer questions about future demand for their product by identifying future stages of its life cycle.

At what stage of the life cycle will current products be during the planning horizon? The answer to this question has an important impact on capacity requirements. What new products do we think will be adopted in the future, and what are their expected or planned growth rates? It is obvious from these questions that capacity requirements are dependent on marketing plans and forecasts.

Changes in *processing* technology must also be anticipated. Even if our products remained unchanged, the methods for generating them may change dramatically. Electro-visual advances, for example, may permit university courses to be conducted without the need for faculty. Such a

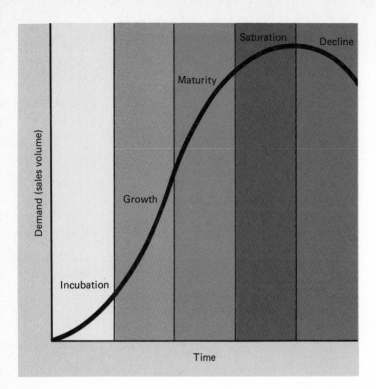

Figure 5-3 **Stages of a product life cycle**

change in processing technology may enable capacity increases to occur without changing the basic product. The development of the digital computer exemplifies a technology change that dramatically increased information processing capacity. Although changes in technology are difficult to antici-pate, their consequences can be so dramatic that planners make great efforts to forecast them. Forecasting technological changes rests on under-standing the current scientific state of the art and then assessing probabil-ities for future developments. At best, technological forecasting is structured guessing by the best scientific and engineering personnel available to the organization. Just as capacity requirements depend upon market plans and forecasts, capacity depends upon technology plans and forecasts.

Strategies for Modifying Capacity

After existing capacity has been measured and future capacity re-quirements assessed, alternative ways of modifying capacity must be identified. Planners must devise both short-run and long-term modification strategies.

Short-run responses   For short-run periods of up to one year, the fundamen-tal capacity of the conversion process is of fixed size. Major facilities are seldom opened or closed as a regular monthly or yearly practice. Many short-run adjustments for increasing or decreasing capacity are possible, however. Which adjustments to make depend on whether the conversion process is primarily labor or capital intensive and whether the product is one that can be stored in inventory.

Capital-intensive processes rely heavily on physical facilities, plant, and equipment for performing the conversion operations. Short-run capacity can be modified by operating these facilities more or less intensively than normal. Rather than operate a single shift each day, management may decide to shut down the facility temporarily during slack demand periods. The potential productive capacity (the *useful economic life*) is thereby deferred until demand picks up. During periods of peak demand, the same facility may be geared up for around-the-clock operations. The problem with modifying short-run capacity is that temporary changes of this type can be very expensive. The costs of facility setup, changeover, maintenance, procurement of raw materials, manpower procurement, scheduling, and inventory management can all be increased by such capacity changes.

Labor-intensive conversion processes are dominated by human skills rather than by such physical resources as plant and equipment. In labor-intensive processes, short-run capacity can be changed by laying off or hiring people or by having employees work overtime or be idle. These alternatives are also expensive, though, since hiring costs and severance pay may be necessary, premium wages may have to be paid, and the risk of losing scarce human skills may increase.

Present strategies for changing capacity also depend upon the extent to which the product can be stored in inventory. Such physical products as appliances, clothing, and canned foods can often be produced ahead of demand and stored in anticipation of later need. For products that are perishable (raw foods) or subject to radical style changes, finished goods inventories may not be feasible. Also in this category are nonstandard or custom-made products whose specifications are not known in advance. This is particularly true for many service organizations offering such products as insurance protection, emergency operations (fire, police, etc.), and taxi and barber services. In these cases, finished goods cannot be produced and stored in inventory prior to demand; the service is consumed at the same time it is generated. Instead, *input* resources can be expanded or shrunk temporarily in anticipation of demand. Tax accounting firms increase working hours and the number of employees during peak demand periods. The U.S. Postal Service does the same thing during peak letter delivery periods such as the Christmas season. Construction contractors adopt a similar strategy during the fair weather months. These are just a few of many ways the operations manager can temporarily change capacity. Several of the most common strategies are summarized in Table 5-2.

Sometimes capacity cannot be suitably changed. There are limits in expanding or shrinking input resources, because some key personnel, equipment, administrators, and the basic physical facility are fixed overhead costs. When capacity cannot be changed, perhaps existing capacity can be used more efficiently. For ideas, the operations manager may seek

━━━━━━━━━━━━━━━ TABLE 5-2 ━━━━━━━━━━━━━━━

TEMPORARY CAPACITY CHANGES

Capacity change	Operations manager's activity
Inventories	Finished goods may be stockpiled during slack periods to meet later demand.
Backlogs	During peak demand periods, customers may be willing to wait some time before receiving their product. Their order request is filed, and they receive their product after the peak demand period.
Employment levels	Additional employees are hired and employees are laid off as demand for output increases and decreases.
Work force utilization	Employees work overtime during peaks and are idle or work fewer hours during slack demand periods.
Employee training	Instead of each employee specializing in one task, each is trained in several tasks. Then, as skill requirements change, employees can be rotated among different tasks. This is an alternative to hiring and layoffs for getting needed skills of specific types.
Process design	Sometimes job content at each work station can be changed to allow productivity increases. Work methods analysis can be used to examine and redesign jobs.
Subcontracting	During peak periods, other firms may be hired temporarily to make the product or some of its subcomponents.
Maintenance deferral	Under normal conditions the facility may be shut down at regular intervals to perform preventive maintenance on facilities and equipment. During peak periods, such maintenance programs are temporarily discontinued. Thus the facility can be operated when it would, without preventive maintenance, have had to be idle.

help elsewhere in the organization. Marketing personnel may be able to increase their efforts, and advertising and promotional campaigns may be used to stimulate demand for certain products during slack demand periods.

Long-run responses: expansion

From World War II through the 1960s, the U.S. economy was one of abundance and growth. In the decade of the 1970s, we have encountered problems of resource scarcity and economic shrinkage. While some sectors of the economy grow, others diminish. Organizations today cannot be locked into thinking only about *expanding* capacity; they must also consider optimal approaches to *contracting* capacity. Let's consider the first of these long-run responses, expansion.

================================== EXAMPLE ==================================

A warehousing operation foresees the need for an additional 100,000 square feet of space by the end of the next five years. One option is to add an additional 40,000 square feet now and another 60,000 square feet three years from now. Another option is to add the entire 100,000 square feet now.

Estimated costs for building the entire addition now are $16 per square foot. If expanded incrementally, the initial 40,000 square feet will cost $18 each. The 60,000 square feet to be added later are estimated at $24 each. Which alternative is better? At a minimum, the lower construction costs plus excess capacity costs of total construction now must be compared to higher costs of deferred construction. The operations manager must consider the costs, benefits, and risks of each option.

Just now we are not concerned with solving the manager's specific problem. Instead, we wish to point out the kinds of issues that must be considered. First, why are costs lower on a square-foot basis if we expand now than they will be later? The answer is that there are economies of scale in initial construction. The builder must bring in people, equipment, materials, and supplies to the construction site. Once these major fixed expenses have been paid, it is relatively inexpensive to go ahead and add on some additional square footage. Thus, the cost of a large expansion now is less than the cost of a small expansion now (on a cost per square-foot basis). The cost of future expansion is even higher because of anticipated inflation. To help analyze an investment decision like this, we would use a *present value analysis*. This technique considers the time value of investment funds and provides a rational approach for evaluating investment alternatives. Although present value analysis plays an important role in expansion decisions, it is used even more frequently in decisions related to equipment and facility renewal or replacement. Present value analysis is discussed more fully in Chapter 19.

The benefits and risks of the expansion alternatives pose an interesting decision problem. By building the entire addition now, we avoid higher building costs; we avoid the risk of accelerated inflation (and even higher future construction costs); and we avoid the risk of having to turn down additional future business because of inadequate capacity. But there may also be disadvantages to this alternative. First, our organization may not be able to muster the large financial investment initially needed. Second, if we expand now we may find later that our demand forecasts were bad; we may find that ultimate demand is lower than expected and we have overbuilt. Finally, even if forecasted demand is ultimately realized, it may not fully materialize until the end of the five-year planning horizon. If so, we will have invested in an excess capacity facility on which no return is realized for several years. Since our funds could have been invested in some other ways during this time, we have foregone the opportunity of earning returns elsewhere on our investment.

The general patterns of capacity utilization costs and incremental expansion can be seen in Figure 5-4. Part (a) shows the minimum cost output rate, p_1^*, for the existing productive facility at time one. Production can fall temporarily to a lower level, p_1^-, but if it does, machine and labor resources will be underutilized and costs will therefore increase. Output could be increased to higher levels, such as p_1^+, but then costs would increase because of excessive overtime, inadequate preventive maintenance, and higher congestion in existing facilities.

If we anticipate that demand will be permanently higher, then the facility should be expanded to reap the benefits of economies of scale offered by a larger facility. Typically, expansion occurs in increments over

(a) Existing facility at time 1

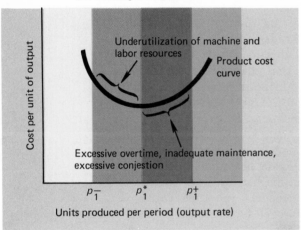

Figure 5-4 Product costs related to facility capacity

(b) Incremental increases in future capacity

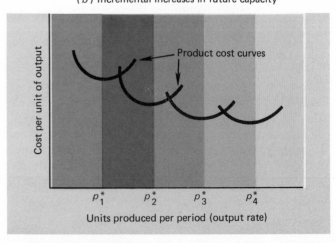

time rather than in a single lump. Part (b) shows optimum output rates for each stage of expansion as permanent demand increases. Capacity could be expanded in one step, from p_1^* to p_4^*, but in that case the risks of overexpanding would be increased.

Long-run responses: contraction and constant capacity

Sometimes long-range planning indicates that future capacity requirements are lower than existing capacity can already produce. When this happens, we can either reduce capacity or find new ways of using what exists.

Capacity contraction most often involves selling off existing facilities, equipment, and inventories and firing employees. As serious declines in demand occur, we may terminate operations gradually. Again, as we must when we consider expansion, we must determine the costs, benefits, and risks of these alternatives. Since large sums of money are often involved, present value and capital investment analyses can be useful in guiding our contraction decisions. When contraction involves shutting down some but not all of our facilities, location analysis may be helpful. This topic will be examined in the next chapter.

Organizations permanently reduce capacity or shut down facilities only as a last resort. Instead, they seek new ways to maintain and use existing capacity. Why? Because a great deal of effort, capital, and human skills have gone into building up a technology. Often this technology and skill base is transferable to other products or services. The technology for making Wheaties, for example, is applicable to other products; General Mills also makes Lucky Charms and a large variety of other breakfast foods. Furthermore, breakfast food technology can be applied to making many other products such as pet food and pretzels.

─────── **EXAMPLE** ───────

In a visit to the Davenport, Iowa, manufacturing facility of Ralston Purina we found brand-labeled cereals for grocery chains being made in one area, Purina Dog Chow being made in another area, and a large distribution warehouse in yet another area. All manufacturing involved conversion of grains into foods, and the entire facility was under one operations manager.

As one product reaches the decline phase of its life cycle, it can be replaced with others without increasing capacity (Figure 5-5). This phasing in and out of new and old products does not occur accidentally; it requires planning. Research and development departments are continually searching for prospective new products. Market research tests the market potential of new product proposals. All these efforts are intermeshed in long-range planning to determine how existing capacity can be used and adapted to meet future product demand. After identifying future capacity

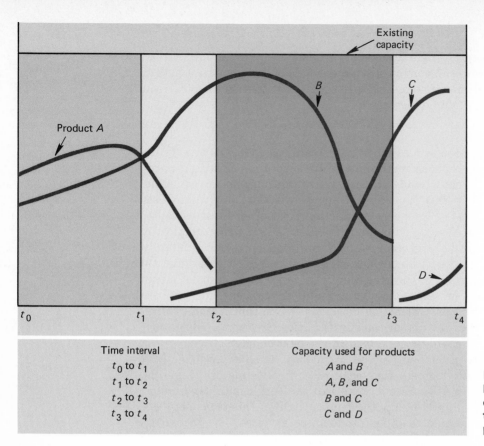

Time interval	Capacity used for products
t_0 to t_1	A and B
t_1 to t_2	$A, B,$ and C
t_2 to t_3	B and C
t_3 to t_4	C and D

Figure 5-5
Ideal use of capacity by time-phasing products

requirements, managers should evaluate various ways of modifying capacity. For analyzing alternatives, production/operations managers have found models to be useful.

CAPACITY
PLANNING
MODELING

Modeling Alternatives

What models are available to assist in capacity planning? We have already mentioned that *present value analysis* is helpful whenever capital investments must be considered. (This will be covered in Chapter 19.) *Aggregate planning models* are useful for specifying how best to use existing capacity in the short run. (These models are presented in Chapter 11.) *Breakeven analysis*, discussed in Chapter 3, can provide the breakeven volumes required as a minimum when various expansion alternatives are being costed against projected revenues. In the following pages we present two useful models for evaluating short-run capacity utilization: *linear programming* and *computer simulation*. Then we'll apply a *decision tree analysis* to the long-run capacity problem of facility expansion. Although we could discuss even more models, these last three serve to illustrate the diversity of capacity-related problems confronting the operations manager.

Our first example of model applications will illustrate the difficulties of measuring capacity in a multiproduct firm. As we discuss MultiBand's situation, we'll show you a way of finding the best use of capacity during a short-run planning horizon.

===== EXAMPLE =====

MultiBand Enterprises manufactures two products, a portable radio (PR) and a citizens' band (CB) radio. The marketing manager states, "We can sell all that can be produced in the near future." She then asks the operations manager, "What is your production capacity per month?" The operations manager replies that his output capacity depends on which product is produced. "Three kinds of labor are required for making our products: subassembly, assembly, and inspection labor. The two products require different amounts of each kind of labor, so our capacity for next month depends on which products we produce. Next month we will have 316 hours of subassembly labor available, 354 hours of assembly labor, and 62 hours of inspection labor." The operations manager knows that each CB radio requires .4 hours of subassembly labor time, .5 hours of assembly labor, and .05 hours of inspection. A portable radio can be produced using .5 hours of subassembly labor, .3 hours of assembly labor, and .10 hours of inspection labor.

The vice-president says, "We know that each CB that we produce and sell contributes $50 towards profit and overhead. Each PR has a $40 contribution margin." What is MultiBand's output capacity, and what mix of CBs and PRs should be manufactured next month?

The *product mix problem,* as it's called, is faced whenever a firm has limited resources that can be used to produce any of several combinations of products. MultiBand's product mix problem is summarized in Table 5-3.

What is MultiBand's output capacity? It depends on the product mix. If all resources next month are devoted to producing CBs, there will be enough subassembly time to produce (316 hours) ÷ (.40 hours/unit) = 790 units; enough assembly time to produce 354 ÷ .50 = 708 units; and inspection time for 62 ÷ .05 = 1,240 CBs. Since a salable CB requires all three kinds of labor, the maximum number of CBs possible is the smallest of these quantities, 708 units. On the other hand, we could produce only PRs. If each resource is devoted totally to PRs, there will be enough subassembly, assembly, and inspection time for producing 632, 1,180, and 620 PRs; the maximum number of completed PRs is 620.

We can summarize MultiBand's capacity utilization alternatives like this:

1. 708 CBs can be produced; this would use all available assembly time; *or*

====== TABLE 5-3 ======

AVAILABLE RESOURCES AND POSSIBLE USES BY MULTIBAND

Resource	Amount of resource needed to produce one unit of product (hours)		Total amount of resource available (hours)
	CB	PR	
Subassembly labor	.40	.50	316
Assembly labor	.50	.30	354
Inspection labor	.05	.10	62

2. 620 PRs can be produced; this would consume all available inspection time; *or*

3. some combination of PRs and CBs can be produced during the month.

What is the *best* mix of CBs and PRs to produce? In other words, what is the best way to use existing capacity in the short run? This question can be answered by using a linear programming model, which is described and applied to the MultiBand problem in the supplement to this chapter. Several steps must be taken before this method can be applied.

First, the decision variables must be identified. For MultiBand there are two decision variables, the number of CBs and the number of PRs to be produced next month. Usually in production/operations management applications of linear programming, the decision variables are the products.

Second, some criterion for choice must be specified to indicate (and measure) the "goodness" or "badness" of each decision alternative. Multi-Band's criterion is total contribution margin, as shown in equation 5-1.

$$
\begin{array}{lll}
\text{Total} & \text{Contribution} & \text{Contribution} \\
\text{contribution} = & \text{margin from} + & \text{margin from} \qquad \text{(5-1)} \\
\text{margin} & \text{all CBs} & \text{all PRs} \\
& \text{produced} & \text{produced} \\
& TCM = \$50\ CB & + \$40\ PR
\end{array}
$$

The value of the criterion, *TCM*, depends on how many CBs and PRs we decide to produce. We wish to select values for CB and PR so that *TCM* is as large as possible; that is, we wish to maximize *TCM*.

Third, the restrictions limiting the number of products that can be produced must be identified. These are shown below for CBs and PRs.

Resource (labor)	Amount of resource used (hours)	Amount of resource available (hours) (resource restriction)	
Subassembly	.40 CB + .50 PR	≤ 316	(5-2)
Assembly	.50 CB + .30 PR	≤ 354	(5-3)
Inspection	.05 CB + .10 PR	≤ 62	(5-4)

The subassembly resource consists of 316 total hours that can be used to make either CBs or PRs. Each CB consumes .40 hours, and each PR consumes .50 hours. The subassembly resource restriction reflects the fact that no more than 316 hours are available for whatever mix of CBs and PRs the manager selects. The other two restrictions are interpreted the same way.

Fourth, a systematic procedure to evaluate possible combinations of products must be applied. The combination that results in the highest value of TCM is the one that's selected. By applying a linear programming procedure, we find that the optimal solution for MultiBand is to produce 632 CBs and 126 PRs (approximately) next month. This will result in a contribution margin of:

$$TCM = \$50(632) + \$40(126)$$
$$= \ 31,600 \ + \ 5,040$$
$$= \ 36,640$$

This product mix will consume all available subassembly and assembly hours, will result in about 18 hours of unused or idle inspection time, and will provide a higher total contribution margin than any other combination of CBs and PRs. Since it represents optimal use of existing capacity, this product mix illustrates the most powerful feature of linear programming: *an optimal allocation of resources to maximize profits or minimize costs is always guaranteed.*

Computer Simulation Used to Evaluate Capacity

In many systems, proper scheduling of the conversion facilities can lead to better utilization of existing capacity. Sometimes a careful analysis reveals that a greater output rate exists than was thought possible. Such an analysis was performed at the University of Massachusetts Health-Service Outpatient Clinic.[1] During the first year of this study, the average number of patients seeing a physician each day was about 180. The clinic

---

[1]This case history is based on the study by E.J. Rising, R. Baron, and B. Averill, "A Systems Analysis of a University-Health-Service Outpatient Clinic," *Operations Research* 21, no. 5 (September–October 1973), pp. 1030–47.

rotated twelve physicians throughout an eight-hour day, but no more than seven doctors could be made available at any given time. A total of 52 physician-hours was available daily. The facility experienced overcrowding and confusion in waiting rooms, and the professional staff felt overworked and harassed. During the day, when few walk-in patients came and when appointment patients failed to appear, physicians were sometimes idle. Often, physicians were still seeing patients up to an hour past closing time.

A team of analysts set out to find better ways to use the existing capacity and resources of the clinic. Their strategy was to build a Monte Carlo simulation model (Chapter 3) of the clinic and to use the model experimentally to improve the clinic operations. First they examined clinic records to estimate the demand on the system—the number of patient visits per week during regular clinic hours. Patients were one of two types, walk-in or appointment. The historical pattern of patient arrivals was examined by day of week and by time of day.

The daily patterns are shown in Figure 5-6. Existing demand patterns seemed to be both stable and predictable, and they revealed that every day uneven demand resulted in both occasional slack periods and periods of very high patient loads. The analysts used the simulation model to test experimentally the effects of various patient scheduling policies. The simulation showed the extent to which the outpatient system could be improved if appointment patients were scheduled during days and hours in which low numbers of walk-in patients were expected.

The recommendations of the simulation experiment were actually implemented at the clinic during the following year, and several improvements in its operation resulted. Customer (patient) service was improved—patient waiting time was reduced; the number of patients seen by physicians

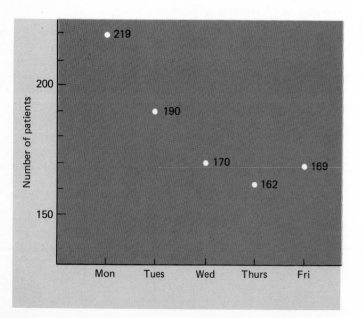

Figure 5-6 Numbers of patients seeing physicians daily

was increased more than 13 percent; and the average time that a patient spent with a physician went up by 5 percent. The total number of physician hours allocated to patients decreased by 5 percent; less overtime was required; and the doctors' morale improved. Clearly, the clinic's existing capacity was increased because resources were scheduled and used more wisely. Just as clearly, a simulation model of other kinds of organizations could result in better uses of resources and increased output for them too.

Computer simulation has also been used to explore the capacity decision of an airline system.[2] The purpose was to identify and evaluate alternative ways of modifying capacity, rather than to find the best way of using existing capacity. Thus, the simulation addresses a comprehensive problem and illustrates the variety of capacity factors that should be considered. Scale of operations, for example, should be selected so as to accomplish some higher level system goal, such as maximizing net earnings or return on investment. Earnings, in turn, depend on revenues and costs. Thus, we need estimates of passenger demand for different possible levels of airline service and estimates of revenues and costs associated with alternative ways of providing different levels of service. In an airline system there are at least two ways of modifying capacity on a route, by increasing flight frequency or by increasing the seating capacities on existing flights. The capacity decision, then, involves consideration of fleet size and the mix or types of vehicles in the fleet. These options have implications for operating costs, passenger demand, and revenues, all of which must be related in the model to net earnings. The various options can then be used to aid in the airline's capacity decision.

Decision Tree Analysis and Facility Expansion

The linear programming and computer simulation models focused on the short-run question of how to use existing capacity; but the planner also faces long-run decisions. One such decision has to do with facility expansion; for analyzing expansion decisions, we often use decision tree analysis, as described in Chapter 3. As you may recall, the procedure involves:

1. laying out decision alternatives,
2. identifying chance events and their probabilities of occurring,
3. identifying monetary consequences of decisions and chance events,
4. calculating the expected value of each decision alternative, and
5. selecting the alternative that has the most attractive expected value.

Let's use an example to help make a long-run decision about how to expand the capacity of an existing facility.

[2]See the simulation study reported by W. Gunn, "Airline System Simulation," *Operations Research* 12, no. 2 (March–April 1964), pp. 206–29.

━━━━━━━━━ **EXAMPLE** ━━━━━━━━━

The Reliable Storage Company has a large warehousing operation. In developing long-range plans, they are considering expansion of storage capacity. Estimates of future storage demand, increased revenues, and costs of expansion have been obtained for the ten-year planning horizon. Management has narrowed the expansion alternatives to three choices: (1) expand now by adding 100,000 square feet of storage space, (2) add 40,000 square feet now and 60,000 square feet three years later, (3) add 40,000 square feet now and nothing later.

If the entire expansion is done now, construction costs will be lower than they will be later. Further, there will be a greater chance for higher business revenues since enough space will be added to take in new business. There is a chance, however, of overexpanding; if the entire expanded facility is not needed, idle capacity will result. The more conservative alternatives are to expand modestly now, wait and see if demand continues to increase as expected, and expand or do not expand accordingly. This approach reduces the risk of investing funds in an idle, overexpanded facility. However, the "wait and see" alternatives have two disadvantages. First, limited storage capacity in the first three years may result in lost opportunities for more business. Second, future construction costs are expected to be considerably higher than those at present levels. Estimates of relevant factors for this decision are shown in Table 5-4 on page 136.

For years one through three, it is estimated that the probability of high annual demand is 0.7; the probability of low demand is 0.3. For years four through ten, the probability of high demand is 0.6, and the probability of low demand is 0.4.

Figure 5-7 shows Reliable's initial decision tree. The time sequence flows from left to right; two initial decision alternatives appear at the far left at stage t_0. This decision is followed by a chance event, high or low demand in years one through three, at stage t_1. The next stage, at time t_2, is the choice of expanding or not expanding after three years. This choice will be available only if our initial decision (at time t_0) was partially to expand the warehouse. The next stage, t_3, represents the chance event of demand level in years four through ten. Demand in these years will be either high or low. Stage t_4 represents all the twelve possible eventual outcomes of the decision problem.

First we calculate the cash flows for *each of the end branches only*, (1) through (12). Branch (1) represents seven years of high demand with cash inflows of $210,000 per year (see Table 5-4). The total cash flow is $7 \times \$210,000 = \$1,470,000$. By similar calculations, we have arrived at the cash flow values for all twelve end branches shown in Table 5-5.

Moving leftward in Figure 5-7 to stage t_3, we now calculate the expected value of each chance node a through f. First consider node a. If our decision process ever leads us to node a, what expected cash inflow would result thereafter? We will attain either outcome (1), with probability

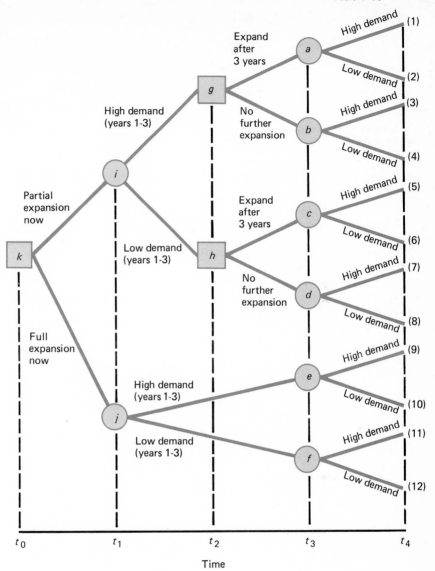

Years 4 - 10

Expand
after
3 years — *a* — High demand (1)
— Low demand (2)

g

High demand
(years 1-3)

No
further
expansion — *b* — High demand (3)
— Low demand (4)

i

Partial
expansion
now

Low demand
(years 1-3)

h

Expand
after
3 years — *c* — High demand (5)
— Low demand (6)

No
further
expansion — *d* — High demand (7)
— Low demand (8)

k

Full
expansion
now

j

High demand
(years 1-3) — *e* — High demand (9)
— Low demand (10)

Low demand
(years 1-3) — *f* — High demand (11)
— Low demand (12)

t_0 t_1 t_2 t_3 t_4

Time

Figure 5-7 Decision tree for Reliable Storage Company expansion

0.6, or outcome (2), with probability 0.4. The *expected* cash inflow is the sum of the possible inflows, each weighted by its chances of occurrence.

Expected cash inflow =	Cash inflow from	Probability of branch
for node *a*	branch *a* − (1) ×	*a* − (1)
	+ Cash inflow from	Probability of branch
	branch *a* − (2) ×	*a* − (2)
	= $1,470,000 × 0.6	+ $840,000 × 0.4
	= $1,218,000	

The expected value for each node at stage t_3 is calculated in Table 5-6.

135

TABLE 5-4

DATA FOR EXPANSION DECISION OF RELIABLE STORAGE COMPANY

Decision alternative	Cash outlays for expansion		Expected increase in after-tax cash flow per year			
			Years 1–3		Years 4–10	
	Expansion cost now	Expansion cost three years from now	If demand is high	If demand is low	If demand is high	If demand is low
Full expansion now	100,000 sq ft @ $16/sq ft = $1,600,000	0	$180,000	$90,000	$240,000	$120,000
Expand 40,000 feet now and 60,000 feet in three years	40,000 sq ft @ $18/sq ft = $720,000	60,000 sq ft @ $24/sq ft = $1,440,000	75,000	36,000	210,000	120,000
Expand 40,000 feet now; no further expansion	40,000 sq ft @ $18/sq ft = $720,000	0	75,000	36,000	75,000	36,000

TABLE 5-5

CALCULATION OF CASH FLOW VALUES FOR END BRANCHES

Branch	Annual cash flow		Number of years		Total cash flow value for branch
(1)	$210,000	×	7	=	$1,470,000
(2)	120,000	×	7	=	840,000
(3)	75,000	×	7	=	525,000
(4)	36,000	×	7	=	252,000
(5)	210,000	×	7	=	1,470,000
(6)	120,000	×	7	=	840,000
(7)	75,000	×	7	=	525,000
(8)	36,000	×	7	=	252,000
(9)	240,000	×	7	=	1,680,000
(10)	120,000	×	7	=	840,000
(11)	240,000	×	7	=	1,680,000
(12)	120,000	×	7	=	840,000

Continuing backwards to stage t_2 in Figure 5-7, we consider the decision points g and h. If the decision maker is positioned at decision node g in the tree diagram, two choices are available. The warehouse can be expanded after three years, or no further expansion can take place. The

TABLE 5-6

CALCULATION OF EXPECTED VALUES FOR NODES *a* THROUGH *f*

Node	Possible outcome branches	Total cash inflow for branch	Probability of this branch	Cash inflow × probability	Expected cash inflow for node
a	a − (1) a − (2)	$1,470,000 840,000	0.6 0.4	$882,000 336,000	+ $1,218,000
b	b − (3) b − (4)	525,000 252,000	0.6 0.4	315,000 100,800	415,800
c	c − (5) c − (6)	1,470,000 840,000	0.6 0.4	882,000 336,000	1,218,000
d	d − (7) d − (8)	525,000 252,000	0.6 0.4	315,000 100,800	415,800
e	e − (9) e − (10)	1,680,000 840,000	0.6 0.4	1,008,000 336,000	1,344,000
f	f − (11) f − (12)	1,680,000 840,000	0.6 0.4	1,008,000 336,000	1,344,000

first choice, further expansion, requires an outlay of $1,440,000 and will lead to node *a*, which provides an expected cash inflow of $1,218,000. There is therefore a net cash *outflow* for this choice ($1,218,000 inflow − $1,440,000 outflow = $222,000). Using this procedure, we can identify the best alternatives available at decision points *g* and *h*, as we have done in Table 5-7. The results in Table 5-7 tell us that if we reach decision point *g* or *h*, our best decision thereafter is to choose no further expansion.

Next we have calculated the expected value of chance nodes *i* and *j*, as shown in Table 5-8. Node *i* offers an expected cash inflow of $415,800; *j* offers $1,803,000. Finally, we can evaluate the expected cash flows for the two decision choices at *k*, stage t_0. The calculations shown in Table 5-9 indicate that full expansion now is the preferred alternative.

Let us now summarize the optimal decision strategy based on decision tree analysis. At t_0, full expansion of the facility should be selected. During years one through three, demand will be either high or low. Thereafter, demand will be either high or low for seven more years. The expected net cash flow is $203,000, which is the most attractive alternative.

Many decision problems are much more complicated than our example might indicate. We could, for example, have included more decision alternatives, a larger number of possible demand levels, or more complex probability estimates.[3] In spite of its simplicity, though, our example

[3] A Bayesian analysis could be used to introduce revised probabilities based on additional information. For examples see H. Bierman, Jr., C.P. Bonini, and W.H. Hausman, *Quantitative Analysis for Business Decisions*, 5th ed. (Homewood, Ill.: Richard D. Irwin, Inc., 1977).

TABLE 5-7

DETERMINATION OF BEST ALTERNATIVES FOR NODES *g* AND *h*

Decision node	Decision alternatives	Expected† cash inflow		Expected‡ cash outflow		Expected net cash flow	Best decision choice (*)
g	Expand after three years	(Node *a*) $1,218,000	−	$1,440,000	=	−$222,000	
	No further expansion	(Node *b*) 415,800	−	0	=	415,800	*
h	Expand after three years	(Node *c*) 1,218,000	−	1,440,000	=	− 222,000	
	No further expansion	(Node *d*) 415,800	−	0	=	415,800	*

†From Table 5-6
‡From Table 5-4

TABLE 5-8

CALCULATION OF EXPECTED VALUES FOR NODES *i* AND *j*

Node	Possible outcome branches	Expected cash inflow from branch	Probability of this branch	Cash inflow × probability	Expected cash inflow for node
i	i − g	$415,800*	0.7	291,060	$ 415,800
	i − h	415,800*	0.3	124,740	
j	j − e	180,000 × 3 = 540,000 +1,344,000 (node *e*) 1,884,000	0.7	1,318,800	$1,803,000
	j − f	90,000 × 3 = 270,000 +1,344,000 (node *f*) 1,614,000	0.3	484,200	

*From Table 5-7

TABLE 5-9

DETERMINATION OF BEST ALTERNATIVE AT NODE k

Decision node	Decision alternatives	Expected‡ cash inflow		Expected† cash outflow		Expected net cash flow	Best decision choice (*)
k	Partial expansion now	(Node i) $415,800	–	$720,000	=	– $304,200	
	Full expansion now	(Node j) 1,803,000	–	1,600,000	=	203,000	*

‡From Table 5-8
†From Table 5-4

illustrates how decision tree analysis can be applied to the long-run capacity expansion problem.

Relationship of Capacity and Location Decisions

Often, the capacity decision is inseparable from the facility location decision. This condition exists because demand for many services depends on system location and, of course, desired capacity depends upon demand; therefore, we have a circular relationship. Commercial banks, for example, simultaneously expand capacity and future demand for services by using branching strategies. Branch location and size decisions are made after management has considered neighborhood population densities and growth projections, geographic locations of market segments, transportation (traffic) flows, and the locations of competitors. The addition of a new branch offers greater convenience to some existing customers and, management hopes, attracts new ones as well. Obviously this decision affects the revenues, operating costs, and capital costs of the organization.

In the public sector, the capacity decision involves similar considerations. Emergency services provided by a municipality, for example, are periodically expanded by adding new emergency stations. An analysis of the geographic dispersion of demand for services is undertaken as the population grows and shifts. Attempts are made to locate stations in the high need areas where emergency services can provide the greatest benefits. The costs of operation and facilities are also considered in choosing a location. Although the capacity decision may not involve direct revenues from the emergency services, cost savings for citizens can be considered a form of indirect revenues. These cost savings can be realized through reduced tax burdens or lower insurance rates in areas with high levels of emergency service protection.

BEHAVIOR CONSIDERATIONS IN CAPACITY PLANNING

Post-Keynesian economic theory has stressed the relationship between business executives' expectations concerning the future of the economy and their subsequent investment in plant and equipment. Favorable expectations result in increased investment in plant and equipment, and thus capacity is increased. Unfortunately, the psychology associated with the interpretation of economic data by individual business people is difficult to measure, and tracing subsequent behavior to changes in beliefs about the future is similarly difficult to document. Surveys by purchasing agent associations do, however, lend some support to the argument that expectations affect investment. They indicate that as expressed attitudes change over time, so do capital goods purchases, lead times, and subsequent capacity.

In the United States, individuals and groups—both within and without official government channels—are involved in establishing policy. One particularly important policy to businesspeople has to do with the investment tax credit, a tax incentive to induce increased expenditures for plants and equipment. If tax incentives are granted, new and modernized facilities are built, and capacity duly increases. The President, members of the Council of Economic Advisors, members of Congress, and constituents all exert influence on the congressional committee establishing tax policy. The behavioral overtones of all this political-economic activity affect policy outcomes, and policy outcomes directly affect the operations manager's capacity planning decisions.

For any one organization, behavioral considerations receive only minor emphasis in our coverage of operations capacity planning. The main reason for this is that capacity decisions are dominated by considerations of product characteristics, economic factors, and processing technology. At this broad level of planning it is difficult to show how specific aspects of employee behavior relate to the capacity decision in any precise way. This situation changes, however, with two other aspects of operations planning, facility location and layout. We shall discuss them in the chapters that follow.

SUMMARY

Capacity is the maximum rate of productive or conversion capability of an organization's operations. Capacity planning decisions involve assessing existing facilities, estimating future needs, identifying alternatives (strategies), evaluating alternatives, and selecting a capacity alternative.

Capacity is usually measured in terms of an output rate. For some companies with diverse products and for service organizations, however, about the only measure of capacity becomes the maximum inputs rather than outputs. Sometimes throughput, which measures capacity in terms of rate of output or input per time unit, is used instead.

In both estimating future capacity needs and evaluating strategies for modifying capacity, short-term and long-term time horizons must be considered. To assist in reaching an acceptable capacity decision, such modeling approaches as linear programming, computer simulation, and decision tree analysis are helpful. Although modeling should not totally overshadow the behavioral implications of reaching a capacity decision, the fact remains that capacity planning benefits most significantly from the logical analysis implicit in modeling. Product characteristics, economic factors, and processing technology are paramount in the capacity planning process.

CASE

Paradise Land Management Company

Paradise Land Management owns and operates hotels and apartment complexes near a major metropolitan area. They wish to expand operations in the near future, the goal being to increase net earnings before taxes. Two alternative expansion opportunities are under consideration, the Densmore complex and the Highgate project. Both projects involve the purchase of land on which apartment buildings would be constructed and operated.

The site for the Densmore complex is situated in a respected, quiet, sparsely populated residential neighborhood. The building site for the 70-unit complex can be purchased for $60,000. Building costs are estimated at $1,680,000. Annual maintenance costs would amount to $30,000. Apartment units would rent for $410 per month. Nearby, Paradise plans to construct a recreation facility. It would cost $100,000 and would service both Densmore residents and the residents of Paradise West, the only existing apartment complex in the neighborhood. Paradise West, with 120 units renting for $290 per month, has had an average occupancy rate of 84 percent for the past three years. The addition of Densmore and the recreation facility is expected to increase Paradise West's occupancy rate to 90 percent with probability of 0.6, or to 95 percent with a probability of 0.4. Densmore's occupancy rate is expected to be 90 percent (probability of 0.5), 85 percent (probability of 0.3), or 80 percent (probability of 0.2).

The Highgate project calls for 400 units to be constructed on a site costing $220,000 in a high density population neighborhood with many competing apartments. Building costs would be $4,200,000. Rental revenue per unit would be $240 per month; annual operating costs would be $150,000. The probability of a 90 percent occupancy rate is 0.2, of an 80 percent rate 0.5, and of a 70 percant rate 0.3.

What factors should be analyzed in making this capacity decision?

REVIEW AND DISCUSSION QUESTIONS

1. Define and give examples of these measures of capacity:
   (a) normal
   (b) maximum
   (c) throughput

2. Define and describe the operating capacity of a college of business administration. How should its capacity be measured?

3. Discuss the fundamental differences in short-run versus long-run capacity decisions. What are the major considerations in each?

4. Outline the merits and drawbacks of incremental capacity changes and large lump changes.

5. Create an example illustrating how the product life cycle concept can be helpful in planning for capacity utilization of a manufacturing company.

6. How is product mix related to the capacity utilization decision?

7. What costs would be affected if you closed one of several warehouses (capacity contraction) in a distribution system? How might revenues be affected?

8. What analytical approaches and models are useful in aiding capacity decisions? Under what circumstances would each model be most beneficial relative to the others?

9. Capacity will be modified in response to demand. Demand will be modified in response to capacity. Which of those two statements is correct? Why?

10. Suppose you were considering expansion of your local fire fighting system. Show what factors should be considered and how you would relate them to one another in your analysis.

PROBLEMS

1. Annual demand for a manufacturing company is expected to be as follows:

Units demanded:	8,000	10,000	15,000	20,000
Probability:	0.5	0.2	0.2	0.1

Revenues are $35 per unit. The existing manufacturing facility has annual fixed operating costs of $200,000. Variable manufacturing costs are $7.75 per unit at the 8,000 unit output level, $5.00 at the 10,000 unit level, $5.33 at the $15,000 level, and $7.42 at 20,000 units of output.

An expanded facility under consideration would require $250,000 fixed operating costs annually. Variable costs would average $9.40 at the 8,000 unit level, $5.20 at the 10,000 unit level, $3.80 at the 15,000 unit level, and $4.90 for the 20,000 level.

If we wish to maximize net earnings, which size facility should we select?

2. Suppose that for problem 1 annual demand expectations were as follows:

Units demanded:	8,000	10,000	15,000	20,000
Probability:	0.25	0.25	0.25	0.25

Is the best alternative under these conditions the same as the best in problem 1? Explain.

3. A manufacturer of dishware is considering three alternative plant sizes. Demand depends upon the selling price of the product; costs of manufacture also depend on the size of the plant selected. Demand is expected to be:

Demand Probabilities

Annual demand (sets of dishware)	Selling price per set of dishware		
	$40	$37	$35
10,000	0.2	0.1	0.05
20,000	0.4	0.4	0.25
30,000	0.3	0.4	0.40
40,000	0.1	0.1	0.30

Anticipated operating costs for the three plant sizes for different levels of operation are:

Variable Manufacturing Costs per Unit

Level of plant operation (units of output)	Plant size		
	Small	Medium	Large
10,000	$21	$25	$32
20,000	16	14	18
30,000	19	13	12
40,000	26	18	14
Annual fixed cost of operation	$300,000	$420,000	$500,000

Which alternative is most attractive on the basis of annual net earnings?

4. How would your answer to problem 3 change if variable manufacturing costs were changed to those shown next?

Variable Manufacturing Costs per Unit

Level of plant operation (units of output)	Plant size		
	Small	Medium	Large
10,000	$21	$20	$25
20,000	19	16	18
30,000	19	15	10
40,000	23	18	12

5. Nitelite Taxi Company is considering two alternative methods of expanding services. One proposal would add four new taxis and drivers to the fleet during the prime daytime hours. This would increase annual fixed operating costs $40,000. Variable operating cost per passenger would average $.50; revenue would average $4.20 per passenger.

The second proposal would add only two new taxis and drivers to work overtime as demand dictates. Fixed operating costs for this alternative are $30,000. Total variable costs are expected to average $1.00 per passenger up to the point where 10,000 customers have been served. If more than 10,000 passengers are served during the year, total variable costs (TVC) will be

$$TVC = (\$.0002)(x - 10{,}000)^2 + 1.0x$$

where x is the number of passengers served during the year. Evaluate and discuss the merits of both alternatives.

6. Micro Distributors is considering an addition of 500,000 square feet of warehouse space to an existing facility during the next two years. Three expansion proposals are being considered: (1) add 100,000 square feet now and 400,000 square feet two years from now, (2) add 200,000 square feet now plus 300,000 square feet in two years, or (3) do the entire addition now. Construction estimates show considerable cost savings for making the additions as soon as possible.

Construction Estimates

	Now		Two years from now	
Alternative	Amount of expansion (thousands of square feet)	Cost ($million)	Amount of expansion (thousands of square feet)	Cost ($million)
1	100	1.00	400	3.2
2	200	1.75	300	2.6
3	500	3.30	—	—

Micro's marketing personnel suggest a wait and see approach with incremental expansion; they favor alternatives 1 and 2. Although expansion is expected to create additional demand, other forces outside Micro's control may result in lower demand, in which case Micro would be left with excessive, unproductive warehousing capacity. A mild expansion now would permit a two-year observation of demand before deciding on additional expansion.

A ten-year planning horizon was chosen. These estimates of demand and net operating revenues were obtained:

Estimates for First Two Years

	Alternative 1		Alternative 2	
Level of demand	Low	High	Low	High
Total net operating revenue ($million)	1.0	1.3	0.8	1.4
Probability	0.4	0.6	0.3	0.7

Estimates for Years 3–10

	Alternative 1				Alternative 2			
	If expanded after 2 years		If not expanded after 2 years		If expanded after 2 years		If not expanded after 2 years	
Level of demand	Low	High	Low	High	Low	High	Low	High
Total net operating revenue ($million)	2.4	7.2	3.8	5.8	2.4	7.2	3.2	6.4
Probability (if demand was high in years 1 and 2)	0.2	0.8	0.3	0.7	0.2	0.8	0.3	0.7
Probability (if demand was low in years 1 and 2)	0.3	0.7	0.8	0.2	0.4	0.6	0.7	0.3

For alternative 3, ten-year operating revenue is estimated at $9,000,000 with probability of 0.5; $6,000,000 with probability of 0.3, and $2,000,000 with probability of 0.2. Which alternative is best? Justify your recommendation.

Capacity: productive capability of a facility, usually expressed as volume of output per time period; maximum rate of productive or conversion capability of an organization's operations

Linear programming: mathematical technique that guarantees the optimal allocation of resources to maximize profits or minimize costs

Present value analysis: method for measuring the worth of an investment in which future cash inflows (and outlays) are converted into an equivalent present value

Product life cycle: concept used to describe the chronological stages of demand for a product

Product mix problem: decision situation involving limited resources that can be used to produce any of several combinations of products

Technology of operations: physical, human, and/or mental processes that are required by the organization to convert input resources into products or outputs

Throughput: capacity measurement in terms of rate of output or input per time unit

Useful economic life: potential productive capacity of a facility

Bierman, H., Jr., C.P. Bonini, and W.H. Hausman. *Quantitative Analysis for Business Decisions.* 5th ed. Homewood, Ill.: Richard D. Irwin, Inc., 1977.

Dantzig, G. *Linear Programming and Extensions.* Princeton, New Jersey: Princeton University Press, 1963.

Erlenkotter, D. "Capacity Expansion With Imports and Inventories." *Management Science* 23, no. 7 (March 1977): 694–702.

Gavett, J.W. *Production and Operations Management.* New York: Harcourt, Brace, Jovanovich, Inc., 1968.

Gunn, W. "Airline System Simulation." *Operations Research* 12, no. 2 (March–April 1964): 206–29.

Hinomoto, H. "Capacity Expansion with Facilities Under Technological Improvement." *Management Science* 11, no. 5 (March 1965): 581–92.

Magee, J.F. "How to Use Decision Trees in Capital Investment." *Harvard Business Review* 2, no. 5 (September–October 1964): 79–96.

Manne, A.S. "Capacity Expansion and Probabilistic Growth." *Econometrica* 29, no. 4 (October 1961): 632–49.

Manne, A.S., ed. *Investments for Capacity Expansion.* Cambridge, Mass.: The M.I.T. Press, 1967.

Markland, R.E. "Analyzing Geographically Discrete Warehousing Networks by Computer Simulation." *Decision Sciences* 4, no. 2 (April 1973): 216–36.

Nord, O.C. *Growth of a New Product—Effects of Capacity Acquisition Policies.* Cambridge, Mass.: The M.I.T. Press, 1963.

Scherer, F.M. "The Determinants of Industrial Plant Size in Six Nations." *Review of Economics and Statistics* 55, no. 2 (May 1973): 135–45.

Rising, E.J., R. Baron, and B. Averill. "A Systems Analysis of a University-Health-Service Outpatient Clinic." *Operations Research* 21, no. 5 (September–October 1973): 1030–47.

Schultz, R.S. "Profits, Prices, and Excess Capacity." *Harvard Business Review* 41, no. 4 (July–August 1963): 68–81.

Woodward, J.T. "Capital Expenditure Programs and Sales Expectations for 1975." *Survey of Current Business* 55, no. 3 (March 1975): 11–17.

Supplement to Chapter 5

LINEAR PROGRAMMING: THE GRAPHICAL AND SIMPLEX METHODS

The purpose of this section is to present a mathematical optimization technique called linear programming. We'll consider three linear programming (LP) methods: graphical, simplex, and transportation. The graphical method is of limited practical value but is helpful for visualizing the underlying concepts of LP. The simplex method can be used to solve any LP problem. The transportation (or distribution) method can be used only on a special type of problem with particular characteristics; it is presented as a supplement to Chapter 6. When such a problem is identified, the transportation method is computationally more convenient to use than the simplex method.

In general, linear programming can be applied to decision problems with these characteristics:

1. *Decision variables.* The numeric values of two or more decision variables are to be determined. (Decision variables are factors under the decision maker's control that, if modified, result in outcomes different from each other.)
2. *Goal.* The goal is to find the best decision values, those that will maximize (or minimize) the objective function.
3. *Objective function.* The objective (criterion) function is a mathematical equation that measures the outcome of any proposed alternative. In LP, the objective function must be linear, as you will see below.
4. *Restrictions.* The values that can be chosen for decision variables are restricted (constrained); complete freedom of choice does not exist. Allowable (feasible) values of decision variables are defined by linear constraint equations.

The General Linear Programming Problem

The general linear programming problem can be stated in any of several forms. Although you cannot be expected to understand this section until after you have read the graphical method and perhaps even the simplex method, we believe it is helpful to state the problem without explaining it at this point. That way we'll have a clear idea of where we're headed.

The following three forms are equivalent statements of the linear programming problem; your understanding of one or more of the forms will depend upon your background in mathematics.

1. *Maximize*

$$Z = C_1 X_1 + C_2 X_2 + \dots C_n X_n \text{ where the } X_1, X_2 \dots, X_n$$

is a set of variables whose values are to be determined. The C_1, C_2, ..., C_n are value coefficients reflecting the contribution each unit of the corresponding variable makes to the objective function. Notice that Z is a linear function of the variables X_i; when X_i increases by one unit, the value of Z increases by an amount $C_i X_i$.

Subject to

$$A_{11}X_1 + A_{12}X_2 + ... + A_{1n}X_n \leq B_1$$
$$A_{21}X_1 + A_{22}X_2 + ... + A_{2n}X_n \leq B_2$$
$$\vdots \qquad \vdots \qquad \vdots \qquad \vdots$$
$$A_{m1}X_1 + A_{m2}X_2 + ... + A_{mn}X_n \leq B_m$$
$$X_1, X_2, ..., X_n \geq 0$$

Where each equation is a constraint imposed on the value of the variables, the $A_{11}, A_{12}, ..., A_{mn}$ are coefficients, and the $B_1, B_2, ..., B_m$ are initial amounts of resources available. Notice that each constraint is a linear function; when X_j increases by one unit, A_{ij} units of resource B_i are consumed.

2. *Maximize*

$$\sum_{j=1}^{n} C_j X_j$$

Subject to

$$\sum_{j=1}^{n} A_{ij}X_j = B_i \qquad i = 1, 2, ..., m$$
$$X_j \geq 0 \qquad j = 1, 2, ..., n$$

3. *Maximize*

$$\mathbf{CX}$$

Subject to

$$\mathbf{AX} = \mathbf{B}$$
$$\mathbf{X} \geq 0$$

where you find a $(n \times 1)$ matrix $\mathbf{X}$
when $\mathbf{C}$ is a $(1 \times n)$ matrix,
$\quad$ $\mathbf{A}$ is a $(m \times n)$ matrix, and
$\quad$ $\mathbf{B}$ is a $(m \times 1)$ matrix.

Graphical Method

The purpose of the graphical method is to provide an intuitive grasp of the concepts that are used in the simplex technique. The general procedure is to convert a descriptive situation into the form of a linear programming problem by deciding what all variables, constants, objective functions, and constraints are for the situation. Then the problem is graphed and interpreted. To use the graphical method, one must:

1. identify the decision variables,
2. identify the objective (or criterion) function,
3. identify resource restrictions (constraints),
4. draw a graph that includes all restrictions,
5. identify the feasible decision area on the graph,
6. draw a graph of the objective function and select the point on the feasible area that optimizes the objective function, and
7. interpret the solution.

In explaining these steps we refer to the case of MultiBand Enterprises that was used in Chapter 5. For your convenience the situation is repeated here.

EXAMPLE

MultiBand Enterprises manufactures two products, a portable radio (PR) and a citizens band (CB) radio. The marketing manager states, "We can sell all that can be produced in the near future." She then asks the operations manager, "What is your production capacity per month?" The operations manager replies that his output capacity depends on which product is produced. "Three kinds of labor are required for making our products: subassembly, assembly, and inspection labor. The two products require different amounts of each kind of labor, so our capacity for next month depends on which products we produce. Next month we will have 316 hours of subassembly labor available, 354 hours of assembly labor, and 62 hours of inspection labor." The operations manager knows that each CB radio requires .4 hours of subassembly labor time, .5 hours of assembly labor, and .05 hours of inspection labor. A portable radio can be produced using .5 hours of subassembly labor, .3 hours of assembly labor, and .10 hours of inspection labor.

The vice-president, says, "We know that each CB that we produce and sell contributes $50 towards profit and overhead. Each PR has a $40 contribution margin." What is MultiBand's output capacity, and what mix of CBs and PRs should be manufactured next month?

Step 1:
Identify decision variables

Citizens band (CB) radios and/or portable radios (PR) can be manufactured by MultiBand. *These are the two decision variables.* The problem is to decide how many CBs and PRs to produce.

Step 2:
Identify objective function

Each CB will provide $50 contribution to profit and overhead, and each PR will contribute $40. MultiBand's total contribution gain will be

$$TC = (\$50)(CB) + (\$40)(PR) \qquad \text{(S5-1)}$$

This *linear* objective function states that total gain (or total contribution, *TC*) depends on the decision as to how many CBs and PRs to produce. MultiBand would like total contribution to be as large as possible; it wishes to *maximize TC*.

Step 3:
Identify resource
restrictions

To produce radios, MultiBand needs three types of labor: subassembly, assembly, and inspection. The available quantities of these three resources are 316 employee hours of subassembly labor, 354 hours of assembly labor, and 62 hours of inspection labor. A CB radio requires 0.4 hours of subassembly labor, 0.5 hours of assembly time, and 0.05 hours of inspection. The manufacture of a PR requires 0.5 hours of subassembly labor, 0.3 hours of assembly time, and 0.1 hours of inspection. Thus we have three restrictions, one for each labor resource. The total number of CBs and PRs that can possibly be produced is limited by the amounts of resources that are available. The restrictions on the use of these three resources are expressed as linear inequalities.

Resource (labor)	Resource consumption		Resource availability (hours)
Subassembly	0.4 CB + 0.5 PR	≤	316
Assembly	0.5 CB + 0.3 PR	≤	354
Inspection	0.05 CB + 0.1 PR	≤	62

Step 4:
Draw a graph of all
restrictions

Look at Figure S5–1. The horizontal axis of the graph shows various quantities of CBs that could be produced. The vertical axis shows quantities of PRs. The *solution space* (the part of the graph where the answer to the problem can be found) consists of all points on or to the right of the vertical axis; and on or above the horizontal axis, since negative values of CBs or PRs have no meaning. Each point in this space represents some combination of PRs and CBs.

Let's draw the line for the subassembly labor restriction. If the entire 316 subassembly hours were devoted to producing CBs, how many could be produced? Since each CB requires 0.4 hours, then 316 hours ÷ 0.4 subassembly hours per CB = 790 CBs. This combination of producing zero PRs and 790 CBs is plotted as point *a* on the graph. Another alternative is to produce no CBs. In that case, we have enough subassembly labor to produce 316 hours ÷ 0.5 subassembly hours per PR = 632 PRs. This combination of products (zero CBs and 632 PRs) is represented by point *b* on the graph. Now, since all restrictions are linear, the line can be drawn connecting points *a* and *b*. Each point on this restriction line represents some combination of CBs and PRs, and each point totally consumes all existing subassembly labor time. In linear programming, all restrictions must be represented by straight lines, never by curves. This is what we mean by a linear function. Points falling above or to the right of line *ab* are *infeasible* combinations of CBs and PRs, since they require more than 316 hours of subassembly.

In a similar manner, we can draw the line representing full use of assembly labor. Look at Figure S5–2. If no PRs are produced, there is enough assembly labor to produce 708 CBs (354 hours ÷ 0.5 assembly hours per CB). This product mix, zero PRs and 708 CBs, is shown as point *c* in Figure S5–2. If no CBs are

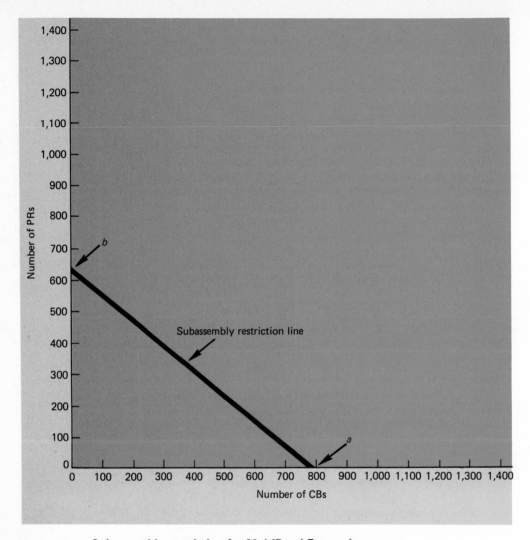

Figure S5-1 Subassembly restriction for MultiBand Enterprises

produced, 1,180 PRs can be made with available assembly labor (point *d*). Line *cd* is the assembly labor restriction line. Similarly, line *ef* is the restriction line for inspection labor.

Step 5:
Identify feasible
decision area

When management decides how many PRs and CBs to produce, they cannot abide by just one or two of the restrictions. They must adhere simultaneously to all three relevant restrictions. The feasible points that satisfy all these restrictions lie within the white area in Figure S5-3. This feasibility area is bounded by the corner points 0, *f*, *g*, *h*, and *c*.

Step 6:
Draw objective
function and select
the optimum point

Although all points in the shaded area are *feasible* decision alternatives, they are not all equally attractive. Some provide a greater total contribution than others. At point *c* (708 CBs, zero PRs), for example, total contribution is ($50)(708) + ($40)(0) = $35,400. But 300 CBs and 300 PRs would only give a total contribution of ($50)(300) + ($40)(300) = $27,000. We must now pick out the *best* point from among the infinite number of points in the feasible area. Our task is simplified, however, because *the best point will lie at one of the corner (extreme) points of the feasibility area.* Therefore, one of points 0, *f*, *g*, *h*, or *c* is optimal. We could calculate the total contribution for each of these five points and select the one that has the highest value.

Restrictions for MultiBand Enterprises

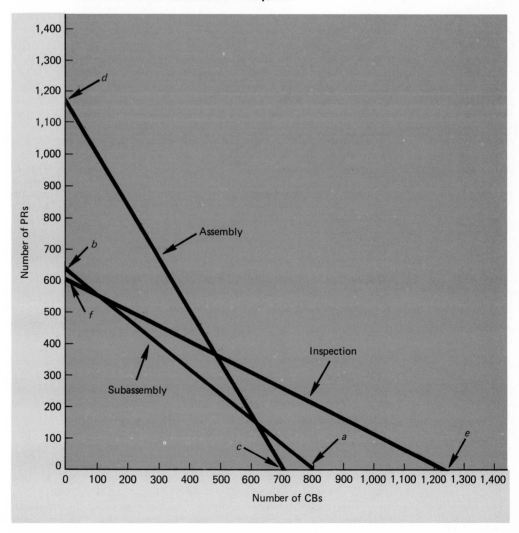

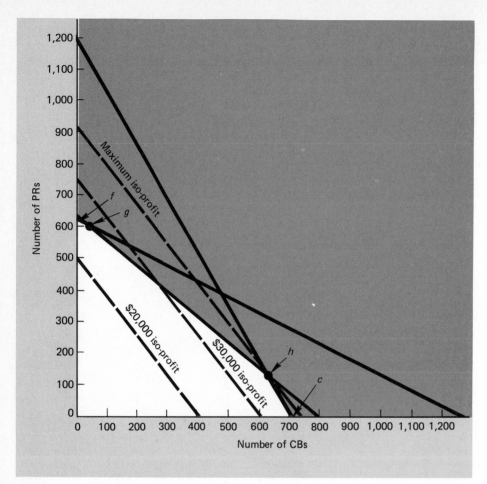

Figure S5-3
Area of feasible solutions for MultiBand Enterprises

A graphical procedure also exists for finding the best point. It requires adding one more line to the graph, an *iso-profit*, or *constant-profit,* line. On an iso-profit line, all the points give the same profit. Suppose we want to find the iso-profit line representing a $20,000 contribution. Using equation S5–1, we find:

$$\$20{,}000 = (\$50)(CB) + (\$40)(PR)$$

Many combinations of CBs and PRs, all lying on the same line, provide this contribution. On Figure S5–3, we have drawn a dotted line connecting all the points at which a $20,000 profit would be contributed. You can see, for example, that a combination of zero CBs and 500 PRs would contribute $20,000. So would a combination of zero PRs and 400 CBs. All the points that fall on this dotted line fall in the feasible area, so it is clearly possible for MultiBand to realize a $20,000 profit. In fact, even greater profits can be achieved. Look at the $30,000 iso-profit line. Some of the points on this line fall outside the feasible area and thus are not legitimate alternatives. Other parts of the line, however, fall in the white area. A $30,000 contribution is therefore attainable.

Two features of these iso-profit lines are particularly noteworthy. First, they are parallel to one another. Second, the farther the lines are removed from the origin of the graph, the greater their contribution. Since all the lines have the same slope, our final step is to continue constructing iso-profit lines that are successively farther away from the origin. This procedure stops when any further movement away from the origin would cause the iso-profit line to lie outside the feasible area. In our example, such a line would pass through point *h*. This point gives the *maximum* contribution; it is the *optimal* decision. When the problem is to maximize the objective function, the iso-profit curve should be the furthest from the origin; when the problem is to minimize, the iso-cost curve should be the closest one to the origin.

The optimal decision at point *h*, interpolated from the graph, calls for the production of about 630 CBs and 125 PRs. The approximate value of this decision is

$$TC = (\$50)(630) + (\$40)(125) = \$36{,}000$$

A more precise evaluation of the solution is obtained by noting the characteristic of the optimal point *h*. This point lies simultaneously on two restriction lines, the subassembly labor line and the assembly labor line. By using simultaneous linear equations, we find the values for PR and CB that satisfy both equations. This occurs when PR = 126.15 and CB = 632.31. The value of this decision is

$$TC = (\$50)(632.31) + (\$40)(126.15) = \$36{,}661.06$$

Step 7: Interpret the solution

The optimal number of PRs and CBs is now known. How much of our three resources will be used for this product mix? Will any of the resources be unused? We can answer these questions both graphically and algebraically. Observation of the graph shows that the optimal point (*h*) lies on the subassembly and assembly labor restriction lines, which represent the *maximum* amounts of these resources that are available for use. Therefore, the maximum amounts of these two resources are being used in the optimal solution. There is no unused subassembly or assembly labor. Now consider the usage of inspection labor. The optimal solution falls below the inspection labor line. This means that all available inspection labor is not used in the optimal solution; some amount of inspection labor will be unused or idle. We can algebraically compute the unused labor:

Unused inspection labor = Available inspection labor − Used inspection labor

= 62.0 hours − [(0.05 hours/CB)(632.31 CBs) + (0.10 hours/PR)(126.15 PRs)]

= 62.0 − [31.62 + 12.62]

= 17.76 hours

Similarly, we confirm that subassembly and assembly labor are fully utilized:

Unused subassembly labor = Available subassembly labor − Used subassembly labor

= 316.0 hours − [(0.4 hours/CB)(632.31 CBs) + (0.5 hours/PR)(126.15 PRs)]

= 316.0 − [252.92 + 63.08]

= 0.0 hours

153
Chapter 5
Capacity Planning

Unused assembly labor	=	Available assembly labor	− Used assembly labor
	=	354.0 hours	− [(0.5 hours/CB)(632.31 CBs) + (0.3 hours/PR)(126.15 PRs)]
	=	354.0	− [316.16 + 37.84]
	=	0.0 hours	

With the graphical method, we can determine what the different coefficients and variables represent and how the constraints and objective function interact. It allows us to see that the optimal solution will always be at an extreme point. The method can be used for problems with two or three decision variables. Since most operations management applications involve larger problems, the graphical method is of limited utility; it is useful, however, for visualizing the basics of linear programming.

Simplex Method

The simplex algorithm is a mathematical procedure for finding the optimal solution to a linear programming problem. It begins with an initial solution, which is progressively improved in a series of stages. To use this procedure, the analyst should:

1. set up the problem in a linear programming framework,
2. create an initial solution,
3. evaluate the existing solution,
4. evaluate variables that could be introduced to improve the solution,
5. select the most advantageous variable to introduce,
6. determine which variable is to leave the solution,
7. revise the solution matrix, and
8. repeat steps 3–7 until no further improvement is possible.

**Step 1:
Setting up the
problem**

A standard format, a statement of the objective function and constraints, is used to set up the problem. In general form, the LP model is a maximization problem of n variables and m restrictions set up as follows:

To Maximize:

$$Z = C_1 X_1 + C_2 X_2 + \ldots + C_n X_n$$

Subject to Constraints:

$$A_{11} X_1 + A_{12} X_2 + \ldots + A_{1n} X_n \leq B_1$$
$$A_{21} X_1 + A_{22} X_2 + \ldots + A_{2n} X_n \leq B_2$$
$$\vdots \qquad \vdots \qquad \qquad \vdots \qquad \vdots$$
$$A_{m1} X_1 + A_{m2} X_2 + \ldots + A_{mn} X_n \leq B_m$$

The above restrictions are stated as *inequalities*. The simplex procedure requires that each restriction be converted into an *equality*. This is accomplished by adding a slack variable to each restriction.

$$A_{11}X_1 + A_{12}X_2 + \ldots + A_{1n}X_n + S_1 = B_1$$
$$A_{21}X_1 + A_{22}X_2 + \ldots + A_{2n}X_n + S_2 = B_2$$
$$\vdots \qquad \vdots \qquad\qquad \vdots \qquad \vdots \qquad \vdots$$
$$A_{m1}X_1 + A_{m2}X_2 + \ldots + A_{mn}X_n + S_m = B_m$$

S_1 is the slack variable representing the unused or idle quantity of the first resource. It is that portion of B_1 which is not devoted to real products $X_1 \ldots X_n$. Similarly, S_2 is the amount of resource two that is not used. One slack variable is uniquely associated with each resource that was converted from an inequality to an equality. In the simplex procedure these slack variables, S_i, are treated in the same manner as the original variables, X_i. However, each slack variable has a zero coefficient in the objective function. In the above formulation, therefore, the problem has a total of $n + m$ variables.

In formulating the problem, the conventional practice is to restate the objective function and restrictions so that each includes all of the slack variables. Let's express the MultiBand Enterprises problem in the format described below.

To Maximize:

$$Z = (\$50)CB + (\$40)PR + \$0S_1 + \$0S_2 + \$0S_3$$

Subject to:

Subassembly labor	$(0.4)CB + (0.5)PR + 1S_1 + 0S_2 + 0S_3 = 316$
Assembly labor	$(0.5)CB + (0.3)PR + 0S_1 + 1S_2 + 0S_3 = 354$
Inspection labor	$(0.05)CB + (0.1)PR + 0S_1 + 0S_2 + 1S_3 = 62$

The restriction inequalities have been converted to equalities by inserting the slack variables S_1, S_2, and S_3. Every variable (real and slack) appears in all the equations. Later, when we get to a final solution, S_1 will represent the number of subassembly labor hours not used for the real products CB and PR, S_2 will represent unused assembly hours, and S_3 will represent unused inspection hours.

Step 2:
Creating an initial solution

An initial solution is created by forming the matrix (table) shown in Table S5-1. We begin at the origin, with no real variables and only the slack variables in solution.

Within the dotted rectangle are the coefficients, A_{ij}, of the variables in the restriction equations, i referring to a row and j to a column. The coefficients are arranged in rows and columns just as they appear in the constraint set for the MultiBand problem. At the top of each column is the decision variable, X_j, to which the coefficients in that column apply. For example, the variable CB has coefficients 0.4, 0.5, and 0.05 in restriction equations one, two, and three, respectively. In the first row of the dotted rectangle are the coefficients of the five variables in the first restriction equation. Notice the zero coefficients

TABLE S5-1

INITIAL SOLUTION MATRIX FOR MULTIBAND ENTERPRISES

C_j	In solution	X_j					Production
		$50	$40	$0	$0	$0	
		CB	PR	S_1	S_2	S_3	
$0	S_1	0.4	0.5	1.0	0.0	0.0	316
0	S_2	0.5	0.3	0.0	1.0	0.0	354
0	S_3	0.05	0.1	0.0	0.0	1.0	62
							B_i
	Z_j	$0	$0	$0	$0	$0	$0
	$C_j - Z_j$	50	40	0	0	0	
			A_{ij}				

for S_2 and S_3 in the first row. These mean that S_2 and S_3 do not consume any subassembly labor, since they are slack variables for assembly and inspection.

Around the outer perimeter of the dotted rectangle we find some additional notation. The in solution column lists *the variables that are in the initial or first-stage solution. The number of variables in solution is equal to the number of restrictions.* This will also be true for each succeeding stage of the problem. The production column shows the quantity of each variable that is in solution. Thus, the initial solution shows 316 units of S_1, 354 units of S_2, and 62 units of S_3 being produced. Since those are fictitious variables, nothing is really being produced. The next step will clarify this point.

| Step 3: Evaluating the existing solution | Refer again to Table S5-1 and find the C_j values representing the objective function coefficients of each variable. These are used to evaluate the existing solution. The value of the objective function for the existing solution is |

$$Z = (\$50)(0) + (\$40)(0) + (\$0)(316) + (\$0)(354) + (\$0)(62)$$
$$= \$0$$

This initial solution leaves all three resources idle, since none of the resources is used for real products. The economic value of this solution is recorded at the bottom of the production column.

| Step 4: Evaluating the effects of introducing other variables into solution | Is it possible to improve upon the initial solution? It might be if a new variable is introduced. Before introducing a new variable, however, we need a procedure for evaluating the economic effects of each variable that could be introduced. This is the purpose of the Z_j and $(C_j - Z_j)$ rows of Table S5-1. C_j represents the amount of *increase* in the objective function if one unit of variable j is added into solution. |

Z_j represents the amount of *decrease* in the objective function if variable j is introduced. $(C_j - Z_j)$ is the net increase. At the bottom of Table S5-1, beneath each variable, the $(C_j - Z_j)$ for each variable is recorded. The C_j values are obtained readily from the objective function, but determination of the Z_j values requires some explanation.

Z_j is obtained by considering the *substitution* rates between variable j and the variables that are currently in solution. These substitution rates are given by the coefficients under variable j in Table S5-1. Consider the CB radio column. If one CB is introduced, then 0.4 subassembly hours, 0.5 assembly hours, and 0.05 inspection hours can no longer be idle. Each unit of CB that is added requires "giving up" 0.4 of an S_1, 0.5 of an S_2, and 0.05 of an S_3 that is currently being produced. If we give up the production of S_1, S_2, or S_3, how would the value of the objective function be changed? Since \$0 is contributed by each unit of S_1, S_2, and S_3, the amount of decrease in the objective function is

$$Z_{CB} = (\$0)(0.4) + (\$0)(0.5) + (\$0)(0.05) = \$0$$

In a similar manner, the Z_j and $(C_j - Z_j)$ values for all variables in the MultiBand problem are calculated in Table S5-2. These same values were recorded at the bottom of Table S5-1.

Step 5:
Selecting a new
variable

By examining the $(C_j - Z_j)$ row of the solution matrix, we see that further improvement is possible. If we add a unit of CB into the solution, the objective function will be increased by \$50. Or, if we add a unit of PR, the solution will improve by \$40. Additional units of S_1, S_2, or S_3 will have no effect on the objective function, since each has a $(C_j - Z_j)$ value of zero. At each stage of the problem, we can introduce only one new variable. Each new variable must be evaluated so that the most attractive one can be chosen. In this case, CB is the most advantageous variable on a per unit basis, so it is the one that should be selected.

Step 6:
Determine which
variable is to leave
solution

In this problem we can have only three variables in solution at one time. If a new variable is introduced, an existing variable must leave solution. Since we wish to introduce CB, either S_1 or S_2 or S_3 must leave. To find the variable that should leave solution, we focus on the substitution rates between CB and S_1, S_2, and S_3 (the variables in solution). The relevant portion of the solution matrix is shown in Table S5-3.

By introducing *one* unit of CB, we increase the objective function by \$50. Since we're trying to maximize, we wish to add as many units of CB as resources will allow. We must therefore determine how many CBs can be introduced. Each CB requires giving up 0.4 S_1. There are 316 S_1s available to give up. If we consider only subassembly labor, then, a maximum of 790 CBs can be introduced. If we consider assembly labor, a maximum of $(354)(0.5) = 708$ CBs can be put into solution. There are enough idle inspection hours (S_3) to allow 1,240 CBs to be introduced. Since *all* restrictions must be met, we can see that available resources are adequate for adding 708 units of CB into solution. If we do this, all assembly labor will be used for producing CBs; none will be idle. Thus, assembly labor is the resource that keeps us from introducing more than 708 CBs; it is the *limiting* resource at this stage.

Let's summarize. We will add 708 units of CB into solution. To do this, we must give up all 354 units of S_2; that is, we give up all the S_2s that were

---

CALCULATION OF Z_j AND $(C_j - Z_j)$ FOR MULTIBAND ENTERPRISES

	If CB is introduced	If PR is introduced	If S_1 is introduced	If S_2 is introduced	If S_3 is introduced
Decreased production of S_1 (a) Decrease in value of objective function	0.4 $0.4 \times \$0 = \$0$	0.5 $0.5 \times \$0 = \$0$	1.0 $1.0 \times \$0 = \$0$	0.0 $0 \times \$0 = \$0$	0.0 $0 \times \$0 = \$0$
Decreased production of S_2 (b) Decrease in value of objective function	0.5 $0.5 \times \$0 = \$0$	0.3 $0.3 \times \$0 = \$0$	0.0 $0 \times \$0 = \$0$	1.0 $1.0 \times \$0 = \$0$	0.0 $0 \times \$0 = \$0$
Decreased production of S_3 (c) Decrease in value of objective function	0.05 $0.05 \times \$0 = \$0$	0.1 $0.1 \times \$0 = \$0$	0.0 $0 \times \$0 = \$0$	0.0 $0 \times \$0 = \$0$	1.0 $0 \times \$1.0 = \$0$
Z_j = Total decrease in value of objective function (a) + (b) + (c)	$Z_{CB} =$ $\$0 + \$0$ $+ \$0 = \$0$	$Z_{PR} =$ $\$0 + \$0$ $+ \$0 = \$0$	$Z_{S_1} =$ $\$0 + \$0$ $+ \$0 = \$0$	$Z_{S_2} =$ $\$0 + \$0$ $+ \$0 = \$0$	$Z_{S_3} =$ $\$0 + \$0$ $+ \$0 = \$0$
C_j	$C_{CB} = \$50$	$C_{PR} = \$40$	$C_{S_1} = \$0$	$C_{S_2} = \$0$	$C_{S_3} = \$0$
$C_j - Z_j$	$C_{CB} - Z_{CB} =$ $\$50 - \$0 = \$50$	$C_{PR} - Z_{PR} =$ $\$40 - \$0 = \$40$	$C_{S_1} - Z_{S_1} =$ $\$0 - \$0 = \$0$	$C_{S_2} - Z_{S_2} =$ $\$0 - \$0 = \$0$	$C_{S_3} - Z_{S_3} =$ $\$0 - \$0 = \$0$

DETERMINING WHICH VARIABLE IS TO LEAVE SOLUTION

In solution	Pivot column CB	Production	Maximum number of CBs that can be added
S_1	0.4	316	$316 \div 0.4 = 790$
S_2	0.5	354	$354 \div 0.5 = 708$
S_3	0.05	62	$62 \div 0.05 = 1{,}240$

formerly in solution, and S_2 is the variable that leaves solution. In the revised solution, we will be producing 708 CBs and no PRs. Graphically, this is shown as point c in Figure S5-3.

Step 7: Revise the solution matrix	After introducing a new variable into solution, we must go back to Table S5-1 and revise each row of the solution matrix to reflect the changes we have made. The column headings will be the same, but the row headings, restriction

coefficients, and production quantities must be changed. In technical terms in the graphical procedure, we are now moving *from the origin to an adjacent extreme point.*

First, we identify the *pivot element,* the coefficient at the intersection of the column entering solution and the row leaving solution. (See Table S5-4, part *a.*) The row and column containing this pivot element are called the *pivot* row and the *pivot* column.

Next we calculate the coefficients for the entering row CB (part *b* of Table S5-4). This is done by dividing each of the old coefficients of the pivot row, S_2, by the pivot element. The old S_2 (pivot) row coefficients (including Production) are 0.5, 0.3, 0.0, 1.0, 0.0, and 354. Dividing each by the pivot element (0.5), we get the resulting row coefficients: $0.5 \div 0.5 = 1$; $0.3 \div 0.5 = 0.6$; $0. \div 0.5 = 0$; $1. \div 0.5 = 2$; $0. \div 0.5 = 0$; and $354. \div 0.5 = 708$. These results are summarized in part *b* of the table.

The new coefficients must now be found for the first and third rows of the matrix. These rows did not include the pivot element, so they are called *nonpivot* rows. The rule for modifying a nonpivot row is: *From each old nonpivot row coefficient, subtract the product of the corresponding pivot row coefficient and the pivot ratio.*

===== TABLE S5-4 =====

PIVOT ELEMENT AND CALCULATION OF NEW COEFFICIENTS FOR ENTERING VARIABLE

	(a) Pivot element in initial matrix		
	CB	Production	
S_1	0.4	316	
S_2	(0.5)	354	← Variable leaving solution
S_3	0.05	62	
	↑ Variable entering solution		

In solution	CB	(b) Coefficients for new row				Production
		PR	S_1	S_2	S_3	
S_1 CB S_3	1.0	0.6	0.0	2.0	0.0	708

The *pivot ratio* is formed by dividing the old nonpivot row coefficient in the pivot column by the pivot element. This rule can be expressed as an equation:

$$\text{New row coefficient} = \text{Old row coefficient}$$
$$- (\text{Corresponding pivot row coefficient} \times \text{Pivot ratio}) \qquad \text{(S5-2)}$$

where

$$\text{Pivot ratio} = \frac{\text{Old nonpivot row coefficient in pivot column}}{\text{Pivot element}}$$

For old row S_1 (Table S5-1), the pivot ratio is calculated as follows:

$$\text{Pivot ratio} = \frac{0.4}{0.5} = 0.8$$

Using equation S5-2, we have calculated the new row coefficients for row S_1 in Table S5-5.

To calculate new row coefficients for row S_3, we use the pivot ratio .05 ÷ 0.5 = 0.1. The new coefficients, calculated by the procedure described above, are recorded in the second simplex tableau (Table S5-6).

This second-stage solution calls for using the three resources as follows: use enough of the three types of labor to produce 708 CB radios; allow 32.8 hours of subassembly labor to be idle; and permit 26.6 hours of inspection labor to be idle. The overall result of doing this is a gain in contribution to profit and overhead of $35,400, a considerable improvement over the initial solution. In Figure S5-3 in the graphical method, we now are at point *c*.

TABLE S5-5

CALCULATION OF NEW ROW COEFFICIENTS FOR ROW S_1

(a) Old row coefficient	0.4	0.5	1.0	0.0	0.0	316
(b) Corresponding pivot row coefficient	0.5	0.3	0.0	1.0	0.0	354
(c) Pivot row	0.8	0.8	0.8	0.8	0.8	0.8
(d) (b) × (c)	0.5 × 0.8 = 0.4	0.3 × 0.8 = 0.24	0 × 0.8 = 0	1.0 × 0.8 = 0.8	0 × 0.8 = 0	354 × 0.8 = 283.2
(e) (a) − (d) = New row coefficient	0.4 − 0.4 = 0	0.5 − 0.24 = 0.26	1.0 − 0 = 1.0	0 − 0.8 = −0.8	0 − 0 = 0	316 − 283.2 = 32.8

SECOND SIMPLEX TABLEAU (SOLUTION MATRIX) FOR MULTIBAND ENTERPRISES

c_j	In solution	$50 CB	$40 PR	$0 S_1	$0 S_2	$0 S_3	Production
$0	S_1	0.0	0.26	1.0	−0.8	0.0	32.8
$50	CB	1.0	0.6	0.0	2.0	0.0	708.0
$0	S_3	0.0	0.07	0.0	−0.1	1.0	26.6
	Z_j	$50	$30	$0	$100	$0	($0) × (32.8) +
	$C_j - Z_j$	0	10	0	−100	0	($50) × (708.) +
			↑				($0) × (26.6) = $35,400

So far we have made one complete cycle through the simplex procedure. Now we can return to step 3 ("evaluate the existing solution") and repeat the entire process. The existing solution in Table S5-6 becomes the starting point. Can this solution be improved? To answer this, we calculate the Z_js as before; they are recorded in Table S5-6.

$$Z_{CB} = (\$0)(0) + (\$50)(1.0) + (\$0)(0) = \$50$$
$$Z_{PR} = (\$0)(0.26) + (\$50)(0.6) + (\$0)(0.07) = \$30$$
$$Z_{S_1} = (\$0)(1.0) + (\$50)(0) + (\$0)(0) = \$0$$
$$Z_{S_2} = (\$0)(-0.8) + (\$50)(2.0) + (\$0)(-0.1) = \$100$$
$$Z_{S_3} = (\$0)(0) + (\$50)(0) + (\$0)(1.0) = \$0$$

Interpreting the $(C_j - Z_j)$ row, we find that no change in the objective function will occur by adding into solution a unit of CB, S_1, or S_3. Adding a unit of S_2 into solution will cause the objective function to *decrease* by $100, an undesirable change. PR, however, can be introduced; the objective function will be increased by $10 for each PR that is added. Therefore, we introduce PR, and the PR column becomes the new pivot column.

How many PRs can be added? This question is answered by repeating step 6, as we did before. Consider the substitution rates between the entering column PR and the variables in solution $(S_1, CB, and S_3)$. Each PR requires giving up 0.26 of an S_1, 0.6 of a CB, and 0.07 of an S_3. The maximum number of these variables available to be replaced is calculated in Table S5-7. The maximum number of PRs that can be added is the smallest of (126.15, 1180.0, 380.0). Thus, 126.15 PRs can be added, and when it is, S_1 will go to zero and leave solution. Therefore, S_1 becomes the pivot row in the second simplex tableau.

Step 7, revising the solution matrix, proceeds as previously described. The pivot element, 0.26, is found at the intersection of the PR column-S_1 row in Table S5-6. Each coefficient in the pivot row is divided by the pivot element, and the row coefficients for the new PR row are: $0 \div 0.26 = 0$; $0.26 \div 0.26 = 1$; $1.0 \div 0.26 = 3.846$; $-0.8 \div 0.26 = -3.077$; $0 \div 0.26 = 0$; and $32.8 \div 0.26 = 126.15$. These

DETERMINING WHICH VARIABLE IS TO LEAVE SOLUTION WHEN PR IS ADDED

In solution	Pivot column PR	Production	Maximum number of PRs that can be added
S_1	0.26	32.8	$32.8 \div 0.26 = 126.15$
CB	0.6	708.0	$708.0 \div 0.6 = 1{,}180.0$
S_2	0.07	26.6	$26.6 \div 0.07 = 380.0$

results are recorded as the PR row coefficients in the third simplex tableau in Table S5-8.

Next, the coefficients are calculated for the first of the *nonpivot* rows, CB. The pivot ratio is $0.6 \div 0.26 = 2.308$. Equation S5-2 is now used to calculate the new CB row coefficients in Table S5-9. Using the same procedure on nonpivot row S_3 results in the coefficients in Table S5-8. The pivot ratio for row S_3 was $0.07 \div 0.26 = 0.2692$. After calculation, the new row coefficients, the C_j and $(C_j - Z_j)$ values were calculated and recorded in the third simplex tableau. The $(C_j - Z_j)$ row reveals that the objective function cannot be increased any further. When all of the $C_j - Z_j$ row cells are zero or negative, the optimum solution has been reached. Adding additional units of CB, PR, or S_3 will result in no change in the objective function. If either S_1 or S_2 is added into solution, the value of the objective function will decrease. We have therefore found the optimal solution that maximizes contribution to profit and overhead: to produce 126.15 PRs, 632.30 CBs, and allow the remaining 17.77 hours of inspection labor to be idle (S_3). This solution corresponds to point h on the graph in Figure S5-3.

THIRD SIMPLEX TABLEAU (SOLUTION MATRIX) FOR MULTIBAND ENTERPRISES

C_j	In solution	$50 CB	$40 PR	$0 S_1	$0 S_2	$0 S_3	Production
$40	PR	0.0	1.0	3.846	−3.077	0.0	126.154
50	CB*	1.0	0.0	−2.308	3.846	0.0	632.298
0	S_3	0.0	0.0	−0.2692	0.1154	1.0	17.77
	Z_j	$50	$40	$38.44	$69.22	$0	($40) × (126.154) + ($50) × (632.298)
	$C_j - Z_j$	0	0	−$38.44	−$69.22	$0	+ ($0) × (17.77) = $36,661.06

*Row coefficients obtained from Table S5-9.

CALCULATION OF NEW ROW COEFFICIENTS FOR ROW CB

(a) Old row coefficient	1.	0.6	0.	2.	0.	708.
(b) Corresponding pivot row coefficient	0.	0.26	1.	−0.8	0.	32.8
(c) Pivot ratio	2.308	2.308	2.308	2.308	2.308	2.308
(d) (b) × (c)	0. × 2.308 = 0	0.26 × 2.308 = 0.6	1. × 2.308 = 2.308	−0.8 × 2.308 = −1.846	0. × 2.308 = 0	32.8 × 2.308 = 75.702
(e) (a) − (d) = New row coefficient	1. − 0. = 1	0.6 − 0.6 = 0	0. − 2.308 = −2.308	2. − (−1.846) = 3.846	0. − 0. = 0	708. − 75.702 = 632.298

Some Additional Considerations

Minimization For purposes of illustration, we have used a maximization problem to present the simplex method. *Minimization* problems are also frequently encountered, and the same basic procedure is applied. The $(C_j - Z_j)$ values in step 4, however, have the reverse meaning in minimization problems; that is, as long as a negative $(C_j - Z_j)$ exists, further improvement is possible. The variable having the largest negative value is selected for introduction into solution. When all $(C_j - Z_j)$ are zero or positive, no further minimization is possible.

An alternative way to solve minimization problems is to multiply all C_j coefficients by −1 and then use the same maximizing procedure that was used for maximization LP problems.

Artificial variables Another circumstance arises when the problem restrictions are not of the "less-than-or-equal-to" variety used in our example. Two other types of restrictions are commonly encountered. First is the equality of the form:

$$A_1 X_1 + A_2 X_2 = B_1$$

In this case, a slack variable need not be added since an equality already exists. However, a different kind of variable, an artificial variable, must be added to the left side:

$$A_1 X_1 + A_2 X_2 + A = B_1$$

The purpose of the artificial variable is to create an identity matrix in the initial tableau. It is undesirable to have the artificial variable appear in the final solution. Therefore, the coefficient of A in the objective function is made to be an arbitrarily large positive value in a minimization problem or an arbitrarily large negative number in a maximization problem. This assures that A will be driven out of solution by the simplex procedure.

Surplus variables   Another type of restriction is the "greater-than-or-equal-to":

$$A_1 X_1 + A_2 X_2 \geq B_1$$

Both a surplus (negative slack) and an artificial variable must be added. The surplus variable converts the expression into an equality:

$$A_1 X_1 + A_2 X_2 - S = B_1$$

Then, since S has a coefficient of -1, an artificial variable must be added to the left side to create an identity matrix:

$$A_1 X_1 + A_2 X_2 - S + A = B_1$$

Once all the restrictions have been converted into appropriate form by adding the necessary artificial and slack variables, the previously described simplex procedure can be applied.

The Power of Linear Programming

The power of linear programming lies in the fact that *an optimal solution is guaranteed—and guaranteed in a finite number of steps.* Since only extreme points are compared, the simplex procedure starts at the origin and checks adjacent extreme points until profits fall or costs rise with a further step (iteration). At that point the optimal has been found. The number of iterations required to solve an LP problem roughly equals the number of constraints. LP is a powerful resource allocation technique, a technique that is often used to approximate nonlinear functions by embedding the simplex technique into nonlinear solution procedures.

There are several basic operations research and management science texts, some devoted entirely to linear programming. They can provide details on problem formulation, solution, and economic interpretation of linear programming problems.

1. **Of what value is the graphic method of LP?**

2. **Define and illustrate:**
   (a) a linear objective function
   (b) a linear constraint
   (c) a nonlinear objective function
   (d) a nonlinear constraint

3. **What is meant by the term "feasibility area" (region of feasibility)** in a linear programming model? What is the significance of the corner points?

4. **In the simplex method, what is the "standard format" of problem formulation? Give an example.**

5. **What is a "slack variable"? Why is it used? How many will there be in an LP problem?**

6. How many variables will be in solution at any stage of an LP problem?

7. What is the significance of the

$$C_j - Z_j$$

row of the LP solution matrix?

8. After determining which variable to introduce next into solution, how do you determine how many units of that variable to introduce?

9. In the simplex method, what indicates that an optimal solution has been reached?

10. Define and illustrate:
   (a) artificial variable
   (b) surplus variable

11. Under what conditions would an LP problem use artificial, surplus, and slack variables? Give examples of each.

1. Solve the following problem using the graphic method of LP.

   Maximize $P = 2A + 2B$

   Subject to: $2A + 4B \leq 16$

   $5A + 3B \leq 15$

   If the objective function is changed to $P = 2A + 5B$, what is the optimal solution?

2. Consider the following LP problem:

   Minimize $C = 7X + 4Y$

   Subject to: $5X + 2Y \geq 20$

   $2X + 4Y \geq 24$

   (a) Using the graphic method, find the optimal solution.
   (b) If the objective function is changed to $C = 8X + 2Y$, what is the optimal solution?

3. Product A offers a profit of $4 per unit; product B yields $2.50 profit per unit. To manufacture the products, leather, wood, and glue are required in the amounts shown below.

   ### Resources Required for One Unit

	Product	
Resource	A	B
Leather (lbs)	1/2	1/4
Wood (board ft)	4	7
Glue (oz)	2	2

   The resources on hand include 2,000 pounds of leather, 28,000 board feet of wood, and 10,000 ounces of glue.
   (a) State the objective function and constraints in mathematical form.
   (b) Find the optimal solution graphically.
   (c) Which resources are fully consumed by the optimal solution?
   (d) How much of each resource remains unused in the optimal solution?

4. Rapid Copy Service has a large backlog of printing jobs to be done. There

are 10,000 standard lots of class A jobs and 18,000 standard lots of class B jobs. The cost of processing a standard class A job is $.72, of a class B job, $.33. The manager wishes to minimize processing costs for the coming month; however, some constraints must be met. First, the marketing department has requested that a minimum of 80 percent of the class A jobs and 60 percent of the class B jobs be completed this month. Second, wage payments are already committed for 4,200 direct labor hours for next month in the processing center. A class A job consumes .16 labor hours, and a class B job requires .23 labor hours. The manager wishes to fully utilize the direct labor during the month. How many jobs of each class should be processed?

5. Fatten Fast Feed Company produces a hog feed made from two basic ingredients, X and Y. A ton of Y can be purchased for $120; a ton of X costs $80. Each ingredient contains three types of nutrients, A, B, and C.

Nutrient Content (units per ton)

Nutrient

Ingredient	A	B	C
X	450	73	69
Y	257	61	208

A ton of hog feed must contain at least 3,600 units of nutrient A, 730 units of nutrient B, and 1,250 units of nutrient C. What proportions of X and Y should be selected to minimize the cost of hog feed?

6. Real Deal Distributors packages and distributes merchandise to retail outlets. A standard shipment can be packaged in small, medium, or large containers. A standard shipment of small containers yields a profit of $4; medium containers yield a profit of $12, and large containers yield a profit of $16. Each shipment is prepared manually, requiring packing materials and time. Each shipment must also be inspected.

Resource Requirements per Standard Shipment

Container size	Packing time (hours)	Packing material (lbs)	Inspection time (minutes)
Small	1.0	2.0	1.5
Medium	2.0	4.0	3.0
Large	4.0	7.0	3.0
Total amount of resource available	1,200	2,400	1,200

(a) Formulate this problem in a simplex format.
(b) What is the optimal number of each container size to produce?

7. Getco Sales Associates sends sales representatives to call on three types of clients: retail, industrial, and professional. Sales revenues of $2,000 result from calling on a retail client, $5,000 from an industrial contact, and $20,000 from each professional client. This month a total of 3,200 hours of sales

representative time is available for calling on customers, and $10,000 is available for travel expenses. Management will not allow more than 20 percent of total sales force time to be devoted to retail clients, and they will not allow more than 30 percent of the travel expense budget to be used for calling on professional clients. Six hours of travel and selling time are required to call on a retail client, 11 hours for an industrial client, and 25 hours for a professional client. Travel expenses are $10 for each retail contract, $14 for each industrial client, and $35 for each professional call. What is the optimal client mix for the coming month?

8. Greenthumb Landscape Company employs senior and junior tree specialists who are assigned to various landscaping jobs. Daily wages are $70 for each senior specialist and $45 for each junior specialist. Working alone, a senior specialist processes an acre of work in four days. A junior specialist requires seven days to process one acre. However, if both types of workers are assigned to a project, two days of senior work and three days of junior work will complete one acre. Greenthumb receives $600 revenue for each acre it processes. Supervisory requirements depend on the type of tree specialist assigned to a project; .8 days of supervisor time is required for each acre processed by a senior specialist; 1.0 days of supervision is needed for an acre processed by a junior specialist; and 2.0 supervisor days per acre are needed for projects using both junior and senior specialists. In total, 450 work-days of supervision, 1,200 work-days of junior specialist labor, and 1,000 work-days of senior specialist skills are available. How should the work force be utilized to maximize the profit?

Anderson, D.R., D.J. Sweeney, and T.A. Williams. *An Introduction to Management Science.* St. Paul, Minn.: West Publishing Co., 1976.

Cabot, A.V. and D.L. Harnett. *An Introduction to Management Science.* Reading, Mass.: Addison-Wesley Pub. Co., Inc., 1977.

Dantzig, G.B. *Linear Programming and Extensions.* Princeton, N.J.: Princeton University Press, 1963.

Wagner, H.M. *Principles of Management Science.* Englewood Cliffs, N.J.: Prentice-Hall, Inc., 1970.

SELECTED
READINGS

6 Facility Location Planning

Adding a new facility is one of the most common ways of expanding productive capacity. The problem is where to locate it. This problem is encountered by service and goods-producing organizations in both the public and private sectors. Banks, restaurants, recreation agencies, and manufacturing companies are all concerned with selecting locational sites that will best enable them to meet their long-term goals. Facility location is clearly an important part of operations planning.

Facility location planning may be viewed as a part of planning the conversion system, as we show in Figure 6-1. The success of this planning activity will both affect and be affected by organizing and control activities. Since the operations manager fixes many costs with the location decision, both the efficiency and the effectiveness of the conversion process are dependent upon location. Leading to this decision are analyses with both modeling and behavioral dimensions. Let's examine the facilities location activity in more detail.

NEED FOR FACILITY LOCATION PLANNING

Location Effects on Costs and Revenues

Public and private organizations are concerned with revenue and cost behavior, both of which can be affected by location. We need to understand how each of these profitability components depends on where the facility is situated.

Revenues

In some industries, revenues depend on having the facility near potential customers. For manufacturing

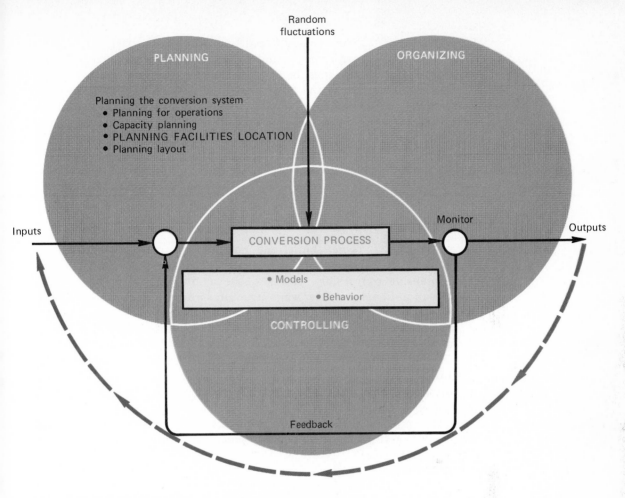

Figure 6-1 **Production/operations management activities**

firms that supply customers (who are often themselves manufacturers and assemblers), delivery time can be crucial. It would be a big advantage, for example, for a tool and die making shop that specializes in extrusions to be in the same city as the primary metal extruder, especially if the extruder happens to be the shop's major customer.

In service industries, the situation is somewhat different. For *stored services*, those not directly consumed, location is not so important. Federal Reserve banks, automotive repair shops, and manufacturers who repair appliances are often quasi manufacturers in the conversion process, and they don't necessarily have to be located near consumers. On the other hand, for firms that offer *directly consumed services*, location can be critical. Movie theaters, restaurants, banks, apartments, dry cleaning stores, and even public recreation areas obviously must be located at sites that are convenient to the public; if they aren't, customers will go somewhere else, and revenues will decline.

Fixed costs　　　New or additional facilities entail fixed initial costs, which are usually incurred only once during the life of the product and which must be recovered out of revenues if the investment is to be profitable. New and additional facilities cost money to acquire, whether they consist of new construction, addition to existing facilities, purchase and renovation of other existing plants, or rental. And once they're acquired, more money must be spent on equipment and fixtures. The magnitude of these costs may well depend on the site that is selected. A choice merchandising corner location in downtown Washington, D.C. requires a totally different capital outlay from one in Greencastle, Indiana. Construction costs also vary greatly from one place to another.

Variable costs　　　Once built, the new facility must be staffed and operated, and these costs depend on location. For labor-intensive conversion processes, the availability of labor and differences in national and local wage structures are major concerns. Management must also consider proximity to raw materials sources (inputs) and to finished goods markets (outputs), either of which can cause transportation and shipping costs to go up or down.

Seldom does an organization find a single site that is best in terms of all revenue and cost variables. The location offering the highest revenue potential may also incur higher variable costs of operation. An optimal location choice requires consideration of all these revenue and cost factors. Tradeoffs must be made among fixed costs, variable costs, and revenue potential; the final locational choice should be the one that offers the best overall balance.

EXAMPLE

Suppose you are selecting a location for a new apartment building. Choosing a site near existing apartments may result in high initial property costs and stiff competition. On the other hand, future costs of advertising vacancies may be substantially lower because apartment seekers are already drawn to the area, and revenues may be high because of existing shopping, barber, and similar services in the area. How do you decide?

Manufacturing industries face many similar decisions. Companies may be attracted to a new geographic location by more favorable labor rates. This happened in textile and other manufacturing industries, and they shifted from the northern U.S. to the South and from the U.S. to foreign locations. It is also true, however, that differences in local culture and work ethics often exist. Sometimes these require great capital investment in equipment and processing technology to overcome the scarcity of specialty skills and to sustain the overall rate of output. Costs of automation, therefore, can counterbalance labor savings.

In evaluating any potential site, then, we must consider all these principal revenue and cost factors. Sometimes we can use a breakeven analysis, a method discussed in Chapter 3. Look at Figure 6-2. For location *a*, fixed costs are low, variable operating costs are high, and expected revenue per unit is low because of locational inconvenience to the customer. The high fixed cost of location *b* is offset by low variable costs and the greater revenue per unit that can be commanded for locational convenience. In spite of high fixed costs, then, the breakeven volume is substantially lower for location *b* than it is for *a*.

Reasons for Locational Changes

In Chapter 5 we discussed how the need for additional capacity can result in our seeking a new location. There are also other reasons for relocating or locating new facilities:

1. Changes in input resources may occur. The cost or location of labor, raw materials, and supporting resources (such as subcontractors) may change.
2. Shifts in geographical demand may occur. As product markets change, it may be desirable to change facility locations.
3. Mergers of companies may result in redundant facilities, some of which must be phased out.
4. The introduction of new products may necessitate locational changes, so that new input resources and product markets can be reached more economically.

Figure 6-2 **Breakeven analysis for overall comparison of two alternative sites**

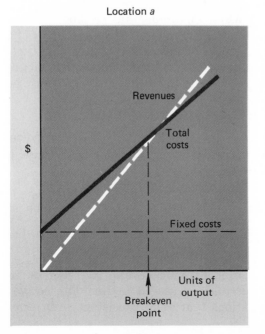

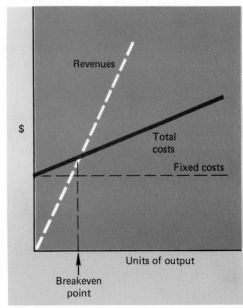

All these reasons for changing facility location—and there are other reasons we haven't listed—show the dynamic environment the operations manager must function in. In our general operations activities model developed in Chapter 2 and reproduced in part as Figure 6-1, we've enclosed the manager's planning, organizing, and control activities in an outer feedback loop that reflects the *dynamics of operations management.*

Characteristics of the Location Decision

In general, organizations tend to grow gradually. New facilities are usually added periodically, one at a time, rather than in one large-scale overall change. By adding facilities as they are needed, the firm can take advantage of new opportunities that arise periodically. Since new facilities usually require large capital expenditures, management must evaluate location alternatives very carefully and in great detail. Unless local conditions have changed substantially, existing sites are favored because they pose fewer uncertainties. The quality of transportation services, local labor availability, local tax conditions, and community receptivity to business are already known. For these reasons, many organizations choose to expand facilities at existing sites or to build nearby. This is especially true for small businesses with capable, but not many, good managers and for businesses that have been successful in one or a few locations.

**GENERAL
PROCEDURES
FOR FACILITY
LOCATION
PLANNING**

The Preliminary Study

A screening study is usually initiated early in the planning process to identify feasible sites. This effort is of a general nature. For some kinds of facilities, particular environmental or labor considerations are crucial. Breweries, for example, require an adequate supply of clean water. Aircraft manufacturers must be located near a variety of types of subcontractors; primary aluminum producers need substantial amounts of electrical power. Some main resources and local factors that must be considered are listed here.

Resources	**Local conditions**
Labor skills and productivity	Community receptivity to business
Land availability and cost	Construction costs
Raw materials	Organized industrial complexes
Subcontractors	Quality of life: climate,
Transportation facilities	housing, recreation, schools
(highways, rail, air, water)	Taxes
Utility availability and rates	

Sources of information

After identifying several key factors, management undertakes a search to find alternative geographic locations that seem consistent with general requirements. Obviously inappropriate alternatives are eliminated from further consideration. Where does all this information come from? Local chambers of commerce provide literature promoting expansion possibilities in various state and local communities. The *Wall Street Journal* and numerous trade publications contain advertisements placed by cities and communities wishing to attract new commerce. The National Industrial Conference Board, federal Departments of Commerce, the Small Business Administration, and the U.S. Census of Manufacturers are among the many sources that provide both general and detailed information for location of facilities. These data include geographic breakdowns of labor availability, population, transportation facilities, profiles of existing types of commerce, and similar information.

Detailed Analysis

Preliminary screening usually narrows serious alternative sites to just a few. At this stage a more detailed analysis ensues. The factors that are examined in detail depend upon the type of business and facility under consideration. At each potential site a labor survey may be conducted to assess the availability of local skills. Where community reaction remains a serious uncertainty, or where the strength of local consumer response is questionable, pilot studies or systematic surveys may be undertaken. Community response would be important, for example, in deciding where to locate a nuclear reactor, a recreation area, a commercial bank, a state prison, or a restaurant. For assessing existing attitudes toward the presence of a facility, and for developing strategies to gain favorable acceptance in the community, survey research techniques can be very helpful.

When the few remaining location alternatives are about equally attractive, for many industries the final decision hinges on transportation costs. These costs are important because a facility located far from its raw materials or product markets will have to invest in truck fleets and/or will incur higher daily operating costs for transportation. Analysis of transportation costs has been the main area in which models have been applied to the location problem.

Many types of quantitative models are used to help determine the best locations of facilities. Sometimes, models are tailor-made to meet the specific circumstances of a unique problem. In New York City, for example, a mathematical model was developed for use as a policy tool for fire department management.[1] In many cities, the problem is to determine the best locations of fire companies. Public officials wish to balance available fire fighting service to reduce risks of property damage

FACILITY LOCATION MODELS

---

[1]This model is reported by K. L. Rider, "A Parametric Model for the Allocation of Fire Companies in New York City," *Management Science* 23, no. 2 (October 1976), pp. 146–58.

and fatalities. Among the regions of the city are different compositions of residential and commercial structures, alarm rates, hazard ratings, and street configurations. Furthermore, since many of these characteristics change with time, the problem is dynamic; a good location pattern now may not be so good in future years. The mathematical model for evaluating fire company locations takes into account many of these factors. The expected travel times (to be minimized) of fire companies are related mathematically to all these characteristics of regions in which they might be located: size of the area to be serviced, number of fire companies in the region, average number of companies busy in the region, street configuration, and travel characteristics of the fire company. Needless to say, although this specialized model may be highly effective for locating emergency services in an urban setting, it is not generally applicable to the locational problems encountered by many other operating systems.

There are some more widely known, general models that can be adapted to the needs of a variety of systems. In the sections below we briefly introduce three types of models that have had application to the location problem: the "simple median model," linear programming, and simulation. All these models focus on transportation costs, although each considers a different version of the basic problem.

Simple Median Model

Suppose we wish to locate a new manufacturing plant that will annually receive shipments of raw materials from each of two existing sources, RM_1 and RM_2. The plant will create finished goods that must be shipped to each of two existing distribution warehouses, DW_1 and DW_2. Given these four existing facilities, shown in Figure 6-3, where should

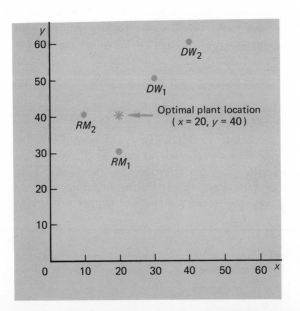

Figure 6-3 **Existing raw materials sources and distribution warehouses (locations shown on a coordinate system with arbitrary origin)**

TABLE 6-1

175

Chapter 6
Facility Location
Planning

LOCATIONS OF EXISTING FACILITIES AND NUMBER OF LOADS TO BE MOVED

Existing facility (i)	L_i Annual number of loads moved between i and new plant	Coordinate location of existing facility i	
		x_i	y_i
RM_1	700	20	30
RM_2	900	10	40
DW_1	400	30	50
DW_2	500	40	60
	2,500		

we locate the new plant so as to minimize annual transportation costs of the entire network of facilities?

The simple median model can help answer this question. This model considers the volume of loads transported on *rectangular* paths.[2] All movements are made in east-west and/or north-south directions; diagonal moves are not considered, although the simple median model can closely approximate the optimal location.

Table 6-1 shows the number of loads, L_i, to be shipped annually between each existing facility and the new plant; it also shows the x and y coordinates (location) of each existing facility.

The model   Since we assume that the transportation cost for a load is proportional to the distance it is moved, transportation cost is measured by adding the number of loads times the distance each is moved:

$$\text{Transportation cost} = \sum_{i=1}^{n} L_i D_i \qquad (6\text{–}1)$$

In equation 6-1, L_i is the number of loads to be moved between the new plant and existing facility i. In our example there are $i = 4$ existing facilities. D_i represents the distance between the new plant and facility i. This, the distance each load is to be moved, depends on our location choice. We then add together the number of loads times the distance they are moved from each existing site. The answer represents the cost of all movements in the system.

---

[2] See R. C. Vergin and J. D. Rogers, "An Algorithm and Computational Procedure for Locating Economic Facilities," *Management Science* 13, no. 6 (February 1967), pp. 240–54.

Since all loads must be moved on rectangular paths, total distance of a load is measured by its length of movement in the x direction and in the y direction:

$$D_i = |x - x_i| + |y - y_i| \qquad (6\text{--}2)$$

The variables x and y in equation 6-2 represent the coordinates of any proposed location for the new plant. Once a location is specified, the distance for all load movements (D_i) can be calculated. What we wish to do is find the values for x and y (new plant) that result in minimum transportation cost. We use these three steps:

1. identify the median value of the total number of loads moved,
2. find the x-coordinate value of the existing facility that sends (or receives) the median load, and
3. find the y-coordinate value of the existing facility that sends (or receives) the median load.

The x and y values found in steps 2 and 3 define the desired location for the new facility.

Application of the model

Let us apply these steps to the data in Table 6-1.
1. *Identify the median load.* Total number of loads moved to and from the new plant will be 2,500. The *median* number of loads is that value above which half the number of loads lie and below which the other half lie. If the total number of

---

TABLE 6-2

CALCULATION OF TOTAL COST FOR OPTIMAL PLANT LOCATION ($x = 20$, $y = 40$)

(1)	(2)	(3)	(4)	(5)	(6)
Existing facility *i*	x_i for existing facility	x for new plant	Distance loads move in x-direction $\|x - x_i\|$	y_i for existing facility	y for new plant
1	20	20	0	30	40
2	10	20	10	40	40
3	30	20	10	50	40
4	40	20	20	60	40

loads is odd, the median load will be the middle load. If the total number of loads is even (for example 2,500), the median loads will be the two middle loads. For 2,500 loads, the median loads are the 1,250th and 1,251st loads, since 1,249 loads lie above and below these amounts.

2. *Find x-coordinate of the median load.* First we consider movements of loads in the *x-* direction. Beginning at the origin of Figure 6-3 and moving to the right along the *x*-axis, observe the number of loads moved to or from existing facilities. Loads 1–900 are shipped by RM_2 from location $x = 10$. Loads 901–1,600 are shipped by RM_1 from location $x = 20$. *Since the median loads (1,250, 1,251) fall in the interval 901–1,600, x = 20 is the desired x-coordinate location for the new plant.*

3. *Find y-coordinate of the median load.* Now consider the y-direction of load movements. Begin at the origin of Figure 6-3 and move upward along the y-axis. Movements in the *y* direction begin with loads 1–700 being shipped by RM_1 from location $y = 30$. Loads 701–1,600 are shipped by RM_2 from location $y = 40$. *Since the median loads (1,250, 1,251) fall in the interval 701–1,600, y = 40 is the desired y-coordinate for the new plant.*

The optimal plant location, $x = 20$ and $y = 40$, results in minimizing annual transportation costs for this network of facilities. To calculate the resulting cost, we substitute equation 6-2 into equation 6-1:

$$TC = \sum_{i=1}^{n} L_i (|x - x_i| + |y - y_i|) \tag{6–3}$$

Total cost, $44,000, is shown in Table 6-2. Since distance was assumed

(7) Distance loads move in y-direction $\|y - y_i\|$	(8) Total distance (D_i) loads move (4) + (7) $\|x - x_i\| + \|y - y_i\|$	(9) Number of loads L_i	(10) Number of loads times distance moved (8) × (9) $D_i \times L_i$
10	$10	700	$7,000
0	10	900	9,000
10	20	400	8,000
20	40	500	20,000

$$\text{Total cost} = \sum_{i=1}^{4} L_i D_i = \$44,000$$

to be proportional to transportation costs, total distance loads can be viewed in dollar units ($44,000) rather than distance units (44,000).

Some concluding remarks are in order. First, we have considered the case in which only one new facility is to be added. The procedure for adding *multiple* new facilities is beyond the scope of this book.[3] Second, you should note an important assumption of this model: any point in the $x = y$ coordinate system is an eligible point for locating the new facility. The model assumes that the optimal point is a feasible plant site; it does not consider whether or not roads exist there, nor does it consider the physical terrain, population densities, or any other of the many important locational considerations.

Linear Programming

Linear programming may be helpful after the initial screening phase has narrowed the feasible alternative sites to a finite number. The remaining candidates can then be evaluated, one at a time, to determine how well each would fit in with existing facilities, and the alternative that leads to the best overall system (network) performance can be identified. Most often, overall transportation cost is the criterion used for performance evaluation. A special type of linear programming called the *distribution* or *transportation* method, has been found to be of particular usefulness in location planning. It has been applied in the simplified example that follows. The mechanics of this technique are omitted in the example but are demonstrated in the supplement to this chapter. Our example shows how to conceptualize and set up the problem in a linear programming framework. It also shows the end result, or optimal solution, of the analysis.

=== EXAMPLE ===

Alpha Processing Company has three Midwestern production plants located at Evansville, Indiana; Lexington, Kentucky; and Fort Wayne, Indiana. Plans being developed for operations five years hence will require that 200 shipments of raw materials be delivered annually to the Evansville plant, 300 shipments to Lexington, and 400 shipments to Fort Wayne. Currently, Alpha has two sources of raw materials, one at Chicago, Illinois, the other at Louisville, Kentucky. The Chicago source will be capable of supplying 300 shipments per year; Louisville has a 400 shipment capacity. An additional source of raw materials must therefore be opened to meet the anticipated raw material needs of the plants. Preliminary screening by Alpha has narrowed the choice to two attractive alternatives, Columbus, Ohio, and St. Louis, Missouri. Each of these sites would be capable of supplying 200 shipments annually. Alpha has decided to make its selection on the basis of minimizing transportation costs. Estimates of the cost per shipment from each source to destination are shown in the cells of the matrix in Table 6-3.

---

[3] For adding multiple facilities, see R. A. Johnson, W. T. Newell, and R. C. Vergin, *Operations Management: A Systems Concept* (Boston: Houghton Mifflin Co., 1972).

TABLE 6-3

SOURCES, DESTINATIONS, AND COSTS OF RAW MATERIAL SHIPMENTS

Source	Evansville	Lexington	Fort Wayne	Number of shipments available from source
Chicago	$200	$300	$200	300
Louisville	100	100	300	400
Columbus	300	200	100	200
St. Louis	100	300*	400	200
Number of shipments needed by destination	200	300	400	

*Cost to transport one shipment from St. Louis to Lexington

The cost analysis for Alpha Company proceeds in two stages. Stage one finds the lowest cost obtainable if the Columbus source were added to the existing network. Stage two determines the minimum cost possible if the St. Louis source were chosen. The results of these two analyses are compared, and the most favorable alternative is then selected. A final solution of this analysis for Alpha is shown in Figure 6-4.

If Columbus is selected, minimum annual shipping costs will be $120,000. This occurs if 100 shipments go from Chicago to Evansville

Figure 6-4 Evaluation of system transportation costs for two raw materials sources

(*a*)
If Columbus is selected destination

Source	Evans-ville	Lexing-ton	Fort Wayne	Shipments available
Chicago	$200 / 100	$300	$200 / 200	300
Louisville	$100 / 100	$100 / 300	$300	400
Columbus	$300	$200	$100 / 200	200
Shipments needed	200	300	400	

Minimum total annual cost = $120,000

(*b*)
If St. Louis is selected destination

Source	Evans-ville	Lexing-ton	Fort Wayne	Shipments available
Chicago	$200	$300	$200 / 300	300
Louisville	$100	$100 / 300	$300 / 100	400
St. Louis	$100 / 200	$300	$400	200
Shipments needed	200	300	400	

Minimum total annual cost = $140,000

(costing $200 each), 200 shipments from Chicago to Fort Wayne (costing $200 each), 100 from Louisville to Evansville ($100 each), 300 from Louisville to Lexington ($100 each), and 200 shipments from Columbus to Fort Wayne ($100 each). These optimal shipment quantities are shown beneath the diagonal lines in the appropriate cells in part (*a*) of Figure 6-4. This shipping plan satisfies the raw material needs of all three plants and fully uses the capacities of all three raw materials sources. Any different patterns of source-to-destination shipments will result in higher annual shipping costs.

Part (*b*) of Figure 6-4 shows that if St. Louis is selected, the minimum cost shipping pattern will incur $140,000 of annual costs. Columbus is therefore the preferred raw materials location site.

Simulation

Although several quantitative models like the ones we've discussed can handle location problems of limited scope, many real world problems are more complex than our examples. Some systems have multiple sources shipping to numerous plants; they in turn ship finished goods to warehouses from which further shipments are made to retailers. A multiechelon (multilevel) system such as this is shown in Figure 6-5. Even with the simplest revision of this system, adding or deleting one network component, the combinational aspects of the problem make it computationally difficult to evaluate. More realistically, we may wish to consider more drastic changes, such as a total revision of the warehousing network. With problems of this complexity, no optimal solution is possible. Instead, approximation techniques like computer simulation are used.

The grocery products division of Ralston Purina, for example, decided to evaluate the effects of deleting various warehouses in ten Midwestern

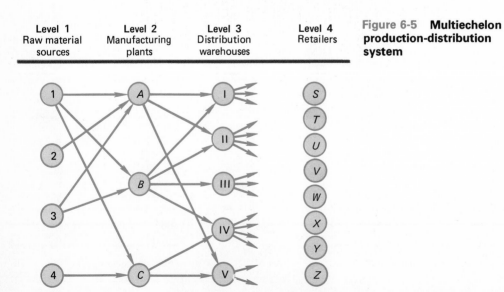

| Level 1 Raw material sources | Level 2 Manufacturing plants | Level 3 Distribution warehouses | Level 4 Retailers |

Figure 6-5 **Multiechelon production-distribution system**

states.[4] To do this, they built a simulation model of a system similar to the one we've shown in Figure 6-5. By examining many warehouse locational patterns, the simulation analysis showed that distribution costs could be lowered by reducing the existing five warehouses to a three warehouse configuration. Although the simulation model cost more than $50,000 to build, the company had made a good investment, because closing two warehouses produced an annual savings of $132,000, several times the cost of the simulation. The simulation was used for other analysis purposes as well.

Besides its industrial application, simulation can also be useful in locational problems in the service and public sectors. Recently, for example, simulation was applied to the problem of snow and ice removal in Tulsa, Oklahoma.[5] The city's salt spreader trucks are used to keep transportation networks open to traffic and to prevent accidents during winter snowstorms. The simulation model evaluated salt spreading times for alternative spreader truck routings and salt pile locations. Since trucks must go back to the salt pile for refills, salt pile location affects total spreading time. The simulation considered the existing salt pile and two additional locations. Results showed that although spreading time would be minimized using all three locations and decreased using some two-pile combinations, time reduction with any of those plans didn't warrant expanding.

Although simulation can handle complex problems, its application usually requires quantities and types of information inputs that may not be readily available. In the Ralston Purina simulation, computerizing existing freight rates between warehouses and all the grocery stores receiving products was a major data processing problem. Furthermore, as Ralston Purina found, extensive model development and validation can be difficult and expensive. We recommend the simulation approach for relatively large systems in which modifications resulting in small percentage savings can represent large dollar reductions in operating costs.

Because they can involve many different consequences for the organization, location decisions are difficult and complex.[6] Our previous discussions of models focused on the *cost* consequences. But costs are not the whole story, and models must be interpreted with caution because model results are deceptively precise. No matter how exact, models are inadequate; they simply don't consider any aspects of a problem that are nonquantifiable. New locations require that organizations establish relationships with new

[4]This simulation study is reported by R. E. Markland, "Analyzing Geographically Discrete Warehousing Networks by Computer Simulation," *Decision Sciences* 4, no. 2 (April 1973), pp. 216–36.

[5]The model is presented in T. M. Cook and B. S. Alprin, "Snow and Ice Removal in an Urban Environment," *Management Science* 23, no. 3 (November 1976), pp. 227–34.

[6]A substantial portion of this section is taken from R. J. Ebert and E. E. Adam, Jr., "Behavioral Dimensions of Facility Location Planning," *Business Horizons* (forthcoming December 1977). Copyright, 1977, by the Foundation for the School of Business at Indiana University. Reprinted by permission.

environments and employees, and adding or deleting facilities requires adjustments in the overall management system. As new components are added, the organization becomes more complex to manage. The organization structure and modes of making operating decisions must be modified to accommodate the change. These hidden "system costs" are usually excluded from quantitative models, and yet they are very real aspects of the location decision.

Our coverage of behavioral dimensions of location planning includes three considerations: cultural differences in the location decision, job satisfaction of employees, and consumer dimensions of location.

Cultural Differences

The decision to locate a new facility usually means that employees will be hired from within the new locale. It also means that the organization must establish appropriate community relations to "fit into" the locale as a good neighbor and citizen. To be successful at these endeavors, the organization must recognize the peculiar circumstances that can exist in different locations. Our country is huge and diverse. Not only are there regional subcultures; there are behavioral differences in the way people in ghettos, ethnic communities, and urban, suburban, and rural areas react to new businesses. Managerial style and organizational structure must be adapted to the economic, political, religious, and social differences at different locations. The facility must be aware of, and adapt to, the norms and customs of local subcultures. Although an authoritarian leadership and managerial style may be well suited to one location, it may be clearly inappropriate in another, where a democratic, participative approach may be more successful. You will be able to understand these differences better if you think about the factors that influence the development of the individual human personality. Each of us is an individual, of course; but part of what makes us the way we are is the subculture we belong to.

The individual personality results from a combination of inborn characteristics (heredity factors) and the environment. Our size, skin pigmentation, physical capabilities, and intellectual capacity affect our personality. Combining with these hereditary traits are environmental factors, customs, values, and standards that are transmitted from generation to generation. All these elements combine with those unique experiences everyone has to form an individual personality, and that personality, in turn, affects our behavior, attitudes, and ways of viewing our own lives as well as the lives of others.

At the heart of environmental influences are four social institutions that provide the individual's value systems: the family, religion, the school, and the state. Differences in subcultures are ultimately reflections of influences from these sources. The individual's disposition toward accepting responsibility, exercising independence of thought and initiative, style of interpersonal interaction with others, and lifelong goals and aspirations are tempered by environmental elements. Family structures and role relationships, for example, differ across subcultures. The family experience can mold one's views on the "proper" roles of men and women. These views are carried over into the workplace and affect employees' attitudes toward men or women occupying certain occupational roles. Employee acceptance of superior-subordinate relationships and varying degrees of authoritarianism may vary with subcultures in which family relationships are male-dominant, female-dominant, or egalitarian.

Within the United States, employees from different subcultures bring various value systems into the job setting. In a Midwestern rural setting, we are likely to find a high percentage of people adhering to a middle-class value system. Here we would expect to find a strong influence of the Protestant ethic, the belief that each person is responsible for his own situation instead of being compelled by forces beyond his control. Rural Midwesterners generally value hard work for its own sake and strive for occupational achievement by attaining responsible positions at work. In an urban setting, on the other hand, less uniformity exists. Various ethnic groups and social classes contribute to heterogeneous value systems. Members of a lower-class subculture are less likely to adhere to middle-class ideals than are rural workers. Their life goals, beliefs about the role of work, career aspirations, and perceptions of opportunity result in different on-the-job behaviors and talents. Such differences have implications not only for managerial style but for staffing, training, and job mobility as well.

Age distributions often vary from one geographical location to another, and workers' ages can affect on-the-job behavior too. When the Vega plant in Lordstown, Ohio, faced a pervasive labor problem a few years ago, management found that within the plant the general age of the work force determined the intensity of labor's protest—the lower the age, the likelier the outcries. During the dispute UAW vice-president Ken Bannon commented, "The traditional concept that hard work is a virtue and a duty, which older workers have adhered to, is not applicable to younger workers, and the concepts of the younger labor force must be taken into account."[7]

At the international level, even greater cultural differences are observed. The decision to locate in another country raises some questions that may not be apparent at first glance. An organization cannot change overnight centuries of custom and tradition; it must be prepared to adapt to existing cultural patterns. Compare, for example, the Japanese work tradition of a few years ago with Western industrial societies':

> Japanese workers are hired for life. They are practically never fired. Promotions go largely by seniority even at managerial levels. The incompetent executive moves up with advancing years to positions with titles appropriate to his age—even when this means devising types of duties that will keep him from interfering with the progress of the firm. The pay of workers bears no relation to their productivity. The pay envelope is the sum of a

[7] "The Spreading Lordstown Syndrome," *Business Week*, no. 2218 (March 4, 1972), pp. 69–70.

complex set of factors, in which length of service and number of dependents figure prominently. All management decisions are made on a group basis—at least normally. If an individual were credited with a certain decision that turned out to be unwise, then the individual would lose face. To spare management people from such humiliation, to all appearances the group as a whole shares responsibility in all decisions.[8]

Obviously operations managers in Japan face a very different set of managerial problems than their U.S. counterparts. Wage determination, employee turnover, hiring, and promotion practices are not at all the same.

The need for recognizing international differences in cultural and social systems is illustrated in one study contrasting experiences in the United States and Europe.[9] The European social system has resulted in more of a "managerial elite" in their organizations than in those in the United States. A gap in knowledge, skills, and value orientations exists between upper and lower managerial levels. Because of education, training, and the socialization process, including a lifelong exposure to a relatively rigid class system, lower subordinates have not been prepared to accept participative managerial styles. Further, higher management is not disposed toward creating and using such styles. Thus, social distance and lack of preparation have tended to result in organizational forms that are more authoritarian/centralized than participative/decentralized. Attitudes toward executive mobility in the U.S. and Europe have also differed. A manager's diverse employment and experience background is generally valued in the U.S. In Europe, however, employment diversity is often regarded as indicative of questionable competence or loyalty.

In managerial decision making too, cultural differences are apparent. Management decision processes depend on the decision maker's value system. Like everyone else, managers' cultural backgrounds determine their norms and values. Consequently, their backgrounds help determine what alternatives are acceptable to them in a decision situation. Several cross-cultural studies have revealed differences in managerial value systems. One study of the life goals of managers in several countries revealed striking contrasts between those in the U.S. and in Denmark. Danish managers ranked "service" highest and "leadership" eighth from among a list of life goals; U.S. managers expressed almost the opposite rank ordering of these factors.[10]

By recognizing these cultural differences, we can anticipate special problems if we decide to locate in another society. It is not simply a matter of duplicating a highly refined manufacturing process from the U.S. somewhere else, particularly in an underdeveloped country. In discussing the transfer of technology from developed to less developed countries, one

[8] William F. Whyte, *Men at Work* (Homewood, Ill.: Richard D. Irwin, Inc., 1961), p. 66.

[9] Fremont E. Kast, "Management Concepts and Practices: European Style," *Business Horizons* 7, no. 4 (Winter 1964), pp. 25–36.

[10] See R. A. Alexander, G. V. Barrett, B. M. Bass, and E. C. Ryterband, "Empathy Projection and Negation in Seven Countries," in *Clinical Psychology in Industrial Organizations*, L. E. Abt and B. F. Reiss, eds. (New York: Grune and Stratton, Inc., 1971), pp. 29–49.

researcher points out that ". . . the developed country's class structure, behavior and attitude are often implicitly built into its technology."[11] The productive tools and techniques that are workable and appropriate at home may be unworkable abroad:

> A familiar sight in any less developed economy is the half finished plant, abandoned and idle, or the broken down machine awaiting spare parts, or the huge factory producing at a tenth of its potential capacity. Where four men could do a job at home, twenty-five are required abroad, and often the job cannot be done at all.

Merely transferring tools and equipment is not adequate. To operate the physical facility, managerial techniques and skills, in proper mixture, must be borrowed from the culture, and so must the cultural assumptions that are needed to make them work. Consider the situation depicted in Figure 6-6. The triangle represents the hierarchical mixture of employees needed to operate a facility in an industrialized Western culture. Relatively few people are needed at the top levels of the organization, more in the middle, and even more at the bottom. The society (outlined by the dotted line) has a mixture of available human skills and orientations that are inconsistent with the needs of the technology. This society features a relatively large proportion of people possessing top-level skills (area a), few in the middle (area b), few at the bottom, and a large number of unemployable persons (area c). Where will the skills that are needed to operate the technology come from? It may be necessary to establish schools or training programs, or otherwise to try to change centuries of tradition in order to garner appropriate human resources for successful operation of the facility. Unanticipated disruptions might also arise if local governments put pressure on the organization to hire the unemployables so as to raise the local standard of living. Clearly, the economic, political, and cultural makeup of a society has far-reaching effects on the technological and economic success of multinational locational decisions.

Figure 6-6 Technological skill requirements compared to cultural skill availability

Source: Richard N. Farmer, "Organizational Transfer and Class Structure," *Academy of Management Journal* 9, no. 3 (September 1966), p. 211.

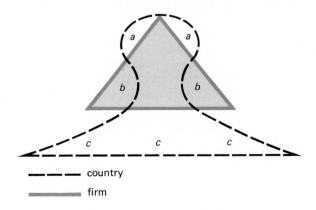

country

firm

[11] See Richard N. Farmer, "Organizational Transfer and Class Structure," *Academy of Management Journal* 9, no. 3 (September 1966), pp. 204–16.

Job Satisfaction

In recent years managers have been very concerned about employee job satisfaction. They are rightfully interested, because job satisfaction has an impact on how well the organization operates. A recent review of current research has led one writer to conclude that the work role most conducive to job satisfaction has participative supervision, an opportunity to interact with peers, varied duties, high pay, promotional opportunities, and finally, control over work methods and pace.[12] Although no consistent overall relationship between job satisfaction and *productivity* seems to exist, other important relationships have been found. As compared with employees with *low* job satisfaction, those expressing *high* job satisfaction exhibit the following characteristics:

1. lower labor turnover,
2. less absenteeism,
3. less tardiness, and
4. fewer grievances.

These four factors can have substantial impact on both costs and disruptions of operations. But how is job satisfaction related to facility location? There is some evidence that satisfaction is related to community characteristics. One study of female clerical workers, for example, found that job satisfaction was inversely related to community prosperity.[13] This was particularly true about pay (one aspect of overall job satisfaction). Employees in more prosperous communities were less satisfied with their work than those in less prosperous communities. Why? Perhaps because community characteristics provide a frame of reference; workers in prosperous settings may think more job opportunities are available and thus tend to be somewhat dissatisfied with their existing work.

In a similar vein, earlier research showed that employee morale tended to be lower in large industrialized metropolitan locations. Studies in other companies have found higher employee satisfaction in small town settings and where there is a lower degree of unionization. Unfortunately, however, all these results are not as clear and definitive as they at first appear. It seems that an important consideration, the type of job, has been neglected. A study of male blue-collar workers in urban and small town settings illustrated this point.[14] Urban workers tended to have higher overall satisfaction when their jobs placed low demands on their capabilities than when jobs were highly demanding. Workers in small town settings expressed higher job satisfaction in jobs that placed high demands on them. A later

[12]B. K. Scalan, "Determinants of Job Satisfaction and Productivity," *Personnel Journal* 55, no. 1 (January 1976), pp. 12–14.

[13]C. L. Hulin, "Effects of Community Characteristics on Measures of Job Satisfaction," *Journal of Applied Psychology* 50, no. 2 (1966), pp. 185–92.

[14]J. C. Worthy, "Organizational Structure and Employee Morale," *American Sociological Review* 15 (1950), pp. 169–79.

study of 2,500 female workers in England found similar opinions. Women from urban communities tended to accept systematized and paced work more readily than those from rural areas.[15] The studies to date, then, show that location is not the sole factor for predicting job satisfaction. Job design, the type of work being done, must also be considered. A careful matchup between type of job and people with the community orientation to do it is important.

Although we discuss job design more fully in Chapter 9, we must consider the locational aspect of it now. One method of job design is called *job enlargement*. Unlike rigidly paced, systematized work, job enlargement calls for jobs with varied work content. It attempts to reverse trends toward simplification and specialization of work. The idea is that by allowing more work variety and employee responsibility, workers will have higher job satisfaction. Can we predict that employees will be more satisfied with enlarged jobs than with routinized jobs? The answer depends on the value system of the employee.[16] Employees from communities having a high acceptance of middle-class value systems, such as rural and small communities, are more satisfied working at enlarged jobs. Employees from communities that are alienated from middle-class value systems, often large, industrialized urban areas, are less satisfied with enlarged jobs.

Figure 6-7 shows the interrelationships involved. The front surface (*a-b*) represents an alienated community. Satisfaction is higher for jobs with low levels of responsibility (routine jobs), and as responsibility increases, job satisfaction decreases. The rear face of the diagram (*c-d*) represents a community not alienated from middle-class values. Here, satisfaction is highest when jobs require greater responsibility (enlarged jobs).

In choosing a location, managers should consider the dominant value systems of the community and design jobs, when possible, to match up with these value systems. This may require that the originally planned conversion technology be revised to incorporate new job designs. If because of the nature of the product the technical requirements for conversion are fairly rigid, job redesign may not be feasible. In this case management may have to choose a different location. We attempt to balance all these considerations to attain suitable levels of job satisfaction.

Consumer Considerations

For many organizations, location planning must emphasize consumer behavior and proximity to customers. If your primary product is to provide a service to the public, locational convenience for the customer may be

---

[15] This study was reported by R. Wild and T. Kempner, "Influence of Community and Plant Characteristics on Job Attitudes of Manual Workers," *Journal of Applied Psychology* 56, no. 2 (April 1972), pp. 106–13.

[16] See C. L. Hulin and M. R. Blood, "Job Enlargement, Individual Differences, and Worker Responses," *Psychological Bulletin* 69, no. 1 (1968), pp. 41–55.

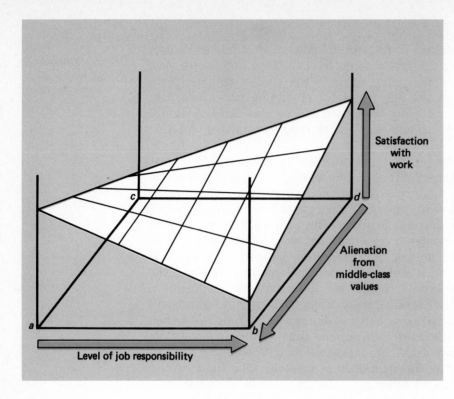

Satisfaction with work

Alienation from middle-class values

a *b* *c* *d*

Level of job responsibility

Figure 6-7 **Response surface depicting interrelationship among level of job responsibility, satisfaction with work, and alienation of blue-collar workers from middle-class work norms**

Source: Charles L. Hulin and Milton R. Blood, "Job Enlargement, Individual Differences, and Worker Responses," *Psychological Bulletin* 69, no. 1 (1968), p. 51. Copyright 1968 by the American Psychological Association. Reprinted by permission.

the prime consideration. Theaters, banks, supermarkets, and restaurants heavily emphasize customer convenience when choosing a location. In fact, convenience of location itself is often considered to be the product offered by some firms. For these reasons the location decision may be regarded as a marketing function instead of a production/operations responsibility, especially as it affects revenues rather than costs.

The operations manager is ultimately concerned with the efficiency and effectiveness of the facility, an end result that depends on the simultaneous effects of several factors, one of which is the location of the facility. The interrelationships among these factors is shown in Figure 6-8. From a systems viewpoint, these technology, human, and economic factors must all be considered in the planning process.

SUMMARY   The problems of planning for capacity and location of facilities are interrelated, because the decision to change capacity often involves the location of new facilities or the dislocation of existing ones. Problems of selecting a facility location require careful consideration of how costs and revenues will be affected. Preliminary studies are needed to gather information from many sources and to identify feasible sites. Detailed studies using models enable the operations manager to evaluate cost consequences of each locational alternative. Some of these models are simulation models, which can be constructed to include many types of costs in complex multilevel production-distribution systems, and simple median and linear programming models, which are particularly useful when there are substantial transportation costs among multiple facilities in a system.

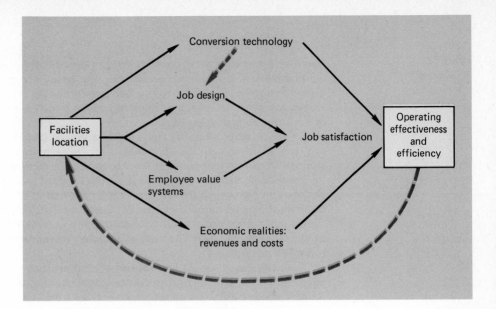

Figure 6-8
Technological, human, and economic impacts on facilities planning

Conversion technology

Job design

Facilities location

Job satisfaction

Operating effectiveness and efficiency

Employee value systems

Economic realities: revenues and costs

Throughout the process of identifying and evaluating alternatives, management must consider the behavioral implications of location. The revenues of many service organizations depend upon a location featuring customer convenience and accessibility. Organizations having less direct contact with the consuming public must recognize potential differences in employee behavior that can arise at various locations. In the various regions within a country, different life styles and value orientations are necessarily carried over into the work place, and these differences affect on-the-job behavior and overall organizational performance. Subcultural differences have implications for both job design (conversion technology) and managerial style.

At the international level, cultural differences limit locational alternatives in other countries. At the very least, production/operations managers must recognize that locating in another country usually involves more than a simple transplanting of technology, and they must try to uncover any "hidden" problems. The skills and environmental support required to operate may be scarce or nonexistent, or cultural differences may inhibit efficient operations—to name just a couple of potential difficulties.

Facilities location planning involves consideration of technology, behavior of potential employees, and the economic realities of increasing revenues and controlling costs. What initially appeared to be a rather simple cost minimization problem turns out to be quite a complex challenge to the operations manager.

Porta-Putt, Inc.   **CASE**

Porta-Putt, Inc., manufactures and distributes gasoline-powered outboard motors for boats. One of their three plants, the St. Louis assembly plant, is obsolete. The Los Angeles and Chicago assembly plants were recently renovated. Rather than continue operation in St. Louis, management is considering the possibility of finding a new location for the third plant.

This is an opportune time, because in two years the new Denver distribution warehouse will be opened. Since the new assembly plant could be the primary supplier of motors to the Denver warehouse, the new plant could be located so as to minimize shipping costs, which are a substantial part of Porta-Putt's operating costs.

Two types of shipping costs are incurred at the St. Louis plant. First, raw materials and subcomponents used in assembling the motors are shipped from Minneapolis and Seattle to the St. Louis facility. Then, after final assembly, the St. Louis plant ships the finished products to the Denver distribution center. Figure 6-9 shows the geographic locations of the three facilities that ship to or from the St. Louis facility. Table 6-4 summarizes the annual number of standard loads shipped between St. Louis and each of the other three sites. The cost of shipping a standard load is estimated to be 10¢ per mile.

Management would like to find a location that would minimize the potentially high annual transportation costs. At the same time, however, there is some hesitation about moving away from metropolitan St. Louis, the original assembly facility established thirty-five years ago. Porta-Putt's experienced work force has survived many work-methods and assembly-line changes. From these refinements had evolved an intricate assembly operation that efficiently produced quality motors—until recently, when the plant became technologically obsolete. The vice-president, who must make the relocation decision, feels that he should tell the St. Louis employees they might loose their jobs, but so far he has only discussed this possibility with several managers there. When the idea of relocation was introduced, these managers were dismayed at the prospect of leaving the St. Louis area. Present an analysis of the major factors in this decision.

TABLE 6-4

**SHIPMENTS BETWEEN THE ST. LOUIS PLANT
AND OTHER PORTA-PUTT FACILITIES**

Existing facilities	Annual number of standard loads	Coordinates of Existing facility	
		x	y
Denver	10,000	1,000	550
Seattle	8,000	100	1,100
Minneapolis	4,000	1,600	900

1. Although facility location is a planning decision, it has implications for decisions in the organizing and controlling subfunctions. Explain.

2. Outline the factors that should be considered in locating a nuclear generating plant. List these factors in order of priority to show each's importance to the decision.

3. Contrast the location problems of a manufacturing firm and a super-

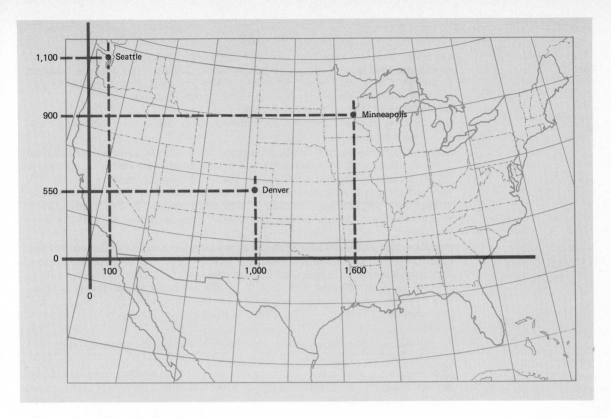

Figure 6-9   Porta-Putt, Inc.

market, showing the relevant considerations they share and those that differ.

4. Discuss the possible reasons for changing the location of an emergency services system, such as an urban fire fighting company.

5. Suppose for economic reasons you wish to locate your manufacturing facility in a small community that currently seems to be unfavorably disposed toward your industry. What strategies might you employ before making your decision?

6. Discuss the primary limitations of the simple median model. How important to the location problem are these limitations?

7. The simple median model is appropriate for some location problems; linear programming is appropriate for others. Identify the conditions of the location problem

that would lead you to select one model over the other.

8. In facility location analysis, under what circumstances would computer simulation be preferred over other models?

9. What aspects of different subcultures should be considered in locational analysis?

10. How might subcultural differences at alternative sites affect the organizing and controlling activities in a facility?

11. If you expand your existing company by opening a new division in a foreign country, should the new division be staffed by local personnel or by personnel imported from the parent organization? Explain.

12. Discuss the relationships among job satisfaction, personal value systems, facility location, and productivity.

1. Location *A* would result in annual fixed costs of $300,000, variable costs of $63 per unit, and revenues of $68 per unit. Annual fixed costs at location *B* are $800,000, with variable costs of $32 per unit, and revenue of $68 per unit. Sales volume is estimated to be 25,000 units per year.
   (a) Which location is most attractive?
   (b) Discuss possible reasons for differences in the cost structures at the two locations.

2. Bigtown is trying to find the best location for a master solid waste disposal station. At present, four substations are located at the following coordinate (*X, Y*) locations: station 1 (40, 120), station 2 (65, 40), station 3 (110, 90), and station 4 (10, 130). The number of loads hauled monthly to the master station will be 300 from station 1, 200 from station 2, 350 from station 3, and 400 from station 4. Use the simple median model to find the best location.

3. Bigtown public officials (see problem 2) are puzzled because of adverse public reaction to the proposed location of a master solid waste disposal station. The public works manager has determined that locations in the area from *X* = 30 to *X* = 140 and *Y* = 5 to *Y* = 120 are not feasible location sites. The city engineer proposes two new alternatives, one at (*X* = 25, *Y* = 25), the other at (*X* = 70, *Y* = 150). Which is the best site for the master disposal station?

4. Revise the simple median model to reflect differences in transportation cost rates for loads flowing between the new facility and several existing facilities.

5. Can Bigtown's problem of locating the solid waste station (problem 2) be set up in a linear programming framework? Explain.

6. Highline enterprises manufactures its product at plants in Los Angeles and Chicago. Shipments are then sent to customers in Denver, Seattle, and New York. The Los Angeles plant produces a maximum of 50 shipments annually, and the Chicago plant produces a maximum of 70 shipments. Costs per shipment from Los Angeles are $1,000 to Denver, $900 to Seattle and $1,600 to New York. A shipment from Chicago costs $800 to Denver, $1,300 to Seattle, and $1,000 to New York. Next year, demand is expected to be for 60 shipments at Denver, 40 at Seattle, and 80 at New York. Highline will build a new plant at either Dallas or Knoxville, and the plant will have an annual capacity of 60 shipments. At Dallas, manufacturing costs would average $100,000 per shipment; the manufacturing cost at Knoxville would be $80,000. Shipment cost from Dallas is $600 to Denver, $1,000 to Seattle, and $1,400 to New York. From Knoxville a shipment to Denver is $900, to Seattle $1,200, and to New York $700.
   (a) Set up this problem in a linear programming framework.
   (b) Outline the specific kinds of information you would expect from the linear programming model.
   (c) What relevant information for this decision would not be provided by the model?

7. A company has conducted a comprehensive study of five cities, one of which will be selected as the site for a new facility. Annual operating costs for each city are estimated as follows:

Annual Operating Costs ($millions)

City	Labor	Transportation	Local taxes	Power	Other
1	.90	.10	.17	.21	.16
2	1.10	.08	.20	.29	.11
3	1.20	.07	.25	.25	.12
4	.85	.12	.19	.18	.16
5	.75	.14	.17	.23	.18

For each community, the company compiled subjective ratings of several important attributes:

Attribute

City	Community receptivity	Labor availability	Transportation quality	Quality of life
1	very good	good	fair	acceptable
2	fair	very good	acceptable	fair
3	good	fair	outstanding	good
4	fair	outstanding	acceptable	very good
5	very good	acceptable	fair	outstanding

(a) On the basis of annual operating costs, which site is best?
(b) Devise a method for quantifying the intangible factors, and integrate them with the cost data into overall evaluation measures. Which site is best now?

GLOSSARY

Consumer behavior: the acts and decisions of individuals in obtaining and using goods and services

Culture: socially shared and transmitted knowledge, beliefs, customs, and morals

Job enlargement: procedure of redesigning jobs or modifying work content to provide varied work content, employee responsibility, and less routinization

Job satisfaction: employee perceptions of the extent to which their work fulfills or satisfies their needs

Job simplification: process of systematizing and subdividing work to form jobs with specialized work content

Labor turnover: a measure of the stability or change in the organization's work force; the net result of employee terminations and entrances

Location of a facility: geographic site at which a productive facility is situated

Subculture: regional or ethnic variations of a culture

Value system: individual's beliefs or conceptions of what is desirable, good, and bad

SELECTED READINGS

Ebert, R. J. and T. R. Mitchell. *Organizational Decision Making: Concepts and Analysis.* New York: Crane, Russak & Co. Inc., 1975.

Farmer, R. N. "Organizational Transfer and Class Structure." *Academy of Management Journal* 9, no. 3 (September 1966): 204–16.

Hulin, C. L. "Effects of Community Characteristics on Measures of Job Satisfaction." *Journal of Applied Psychology* 50, no. 2 (1966): 185–92.

Hulin, C. L. and M. R. Blood. "Job Enlargement, Individual Differences, and Worker Responses." *Psychological Bulletin* 69, no. 1 (1968): 41–55.

Kast, F. E. "Management Concepts and Practices: European Style." *Business Horizons* 7, no. 4 (Winter 1964): 25–36.

Sweeney, D. J. and R. L. Tatham. "An Improved Long-Run Model for Multiple Warehouse Location." *Management Science* 22, no. 7 (March 1976): 748–58.

Whyte, W. F. *Men at Work.* Homewood, Ill.: Richard D. Irwin, Inc., 1961.

Supplement to Chapter 6

LINEAR PROGRAMMING: THE TRANSPORTATION METHOD

The transportation (or distribution) method is a special form of the general linear programming problem and must meet the general characteristics noted in the supplement to Chapter 5. Additionally, the transportation method is applicable to problems with the following characteristics:

1. *Sources.* A quantity of resources exists at a finite number of "sources," and these resources are available for allocation.
2. *Destinations.* A finite number of "destinations" exists, each of which needs to be supplied with a specified quantity of resources that are available from the sources.
3. *Homogeneous units.* From the viewpoint of the destinations, the available resources are homogeneous; that is, a unit of resource supplied by one origin (source) is equivalent to a unit supplied by any other origin.
4. *Costs.* The cost of allocating a unit of resource from each origin to each destination is known and constant.

Although problems meeting the above conditions can be formulated and solved by the simplex method, the transportation method is less cumbersome. We'll first explain the procedure in general terms and then apply it to the Alpha Processing location problem from Chapter 6.

The transportation format consists of a source-destination matrix, as shown in Figure S6-1. There are *m* distinct sources (rows), each of which has RA_i units of resource available. The RA_i are usually not numerically equal. There are *n*

Destination (j)

Source (i)	A	B	-----	n	Units of resource available from source i
1	C_{1A}	C_{1B}		C_{1n}	RA_1
2	C_{2A}	C_{2B}		C_{2n}	RA_2
• • • • •					
m	C_{mA}	C_{mB}		C_{mn}	RA_m
Units of resource needed at destination j	RN_A	RN_B		RN_n	ΣRA_i / ΣRN_j

Figure S6-1 Transportation LP matrix

destinations, each in need of RN_j units of resource. The cost of allocating one unit of resource from source i to destination j is C_{ij}. The problem is to allocate resources from sources to destinations so that the total cost of allocations for the system is minimized. The restrictions are:

1. all destination needs must be met,
2. no source may allocate more units than it has available, and
3. negative quantities cannot be allocated.

The objective, then, is to minimize total cost

$$TC = C_{1A} X_{1A} + C_{1B} X_{1B} + \ldots + C_{2A} X_{2A}$$
$$+ C_{2B} X_{2B} + \ldots + C_{mA} X_{mA} + C_{mB} X_{mB}$$
$$+ \ldots + C_{mn} X_{mn}$$

where X_{ij} is the number of units allocated from i to j, subject to the above restrictions (constraints).

The Transportation Method

Here is the Alpha Processing Company example once again.

================ EXAMPLE ================

Alpha Processing Company has three Midwestern production plants located at Evansville, Indiana; Lexington, Kentucky; and Fort Wayne, Indiana. Plans being developed for operations five years hence will require that 200 shipments of raw materials be delivered annually to the Evansville plant, 300 shipments to Lexington, and 400 shipments to Fort Wayne. Currently, Alpha has two sources of raw materials, one at Chicago, Illinois, the other at Louisville, Kentucky. The Chicago source will be capable of supplying 300 shipments per year; Louisville has a 400 shipment capacity. An additional source of raw materials must therefore be opened to meet the anticipated raw material needs of the plants. Preliminary screening by Alpha has narrowed the choice to two attractive alternatives, Columbus, Ohio, and St. Louis, Missouri. Each of these sites would be capable of supplying 200 shipments annually. Alpha has decided to make its selection on the basis of minimizing transportation costs. Estimates of the cost per shipment from each source to destination are shown in the cells of the matrix in Table 6-3 (see text of chapter).

Alpha Processing's three manufacturing plants and two raw material sources send shipments as needed to the various plants. The addition of a new raw material source at Columbus, Ohio, is being considered. We will focus on that one alternative. Management would like to know how to allocate raw materials from the three sources to the plants so that annual transportation costs of the system are minimized. Shipment costs, plant requirements, and source availabilities are summarized in Figure S6-2.

Cost per shipment is the dollar amount in each cell

Plant (destination)

		P_1	P_2	P_3	Number of shipments available annually from source i
Raw material source	RMS_1	$200	$300	$200	300
	RMS_2	$100	$100	$300	400
	RMS_3	$300	$200	$100	200
Number of shipments needed annually at plant j		200	300	400	900
					900

Figure S6-2 **Transportation matrix for Alpha Processing Company, adding the Columbus raw materials source (RMS_3)**

A five step procedure will be used to find the set of allocations that minimize total shipment costs:

1. Frame the problem such that the total number of shipments available equals the number of shipments needed.
2. Create an initial feasible solution.
3. Evaluate the existing solution for possible improvement.
4. Modify the existing solution.
5. Repeat steps 3 and 4 until no further improvement is possible.

1. *Ensure that availability equals requirements.* In Figure S6-2, the number of shipments available at the three sources (900) is equal to the number needed by the destinations. Later we will show how to adjust the matrix when this equality does not exist.

2. *Create an initial feasible solution.* A *feasible* solution is one in which the needs of all destinations are filled and the capacities of all sources are fully used. Many initial solutions are possible. By convention, we will use the Northwest Corner Rule to create an initial solution here. Allocate as many shipments as possible into the northwest cell of the matrix. In this example, 200 units can be allocated from RMS_1 to P_1. Thereafter, allocations are made to adjacent cells to the east or south of the northwest corner. As shown in Figure S6-3, the next allocation would be 100 shipments from RMS_1 to P_2. At this stage the requirements of P_1 have been met and the shipping capacity of RMS_1 has been fully utilized. The third assignment will be 200 shipments from RMS_2 to P_2. Next, 200 shipments go from RMS_2 to P_3. Finally, 200 shipments are assigned from RMS_3 to P_3. These shipments are recorded beneath the diagonals in the appropriate cells. Overall, the pattern of shipments in the matrix flows generally from the northwest to southeast. All of this was done without regard to the costs involved. The resulting initial solution is feasible because all restrictions in the problem have been met. If this pattern of shipments was used, the annual cost would be

$$TC = (\$200) \times (200) + (\$300) \times (100) + (\$100) \times (200) + (\$300) \times (200) + (\$100) \times (200) = \$170,000$$

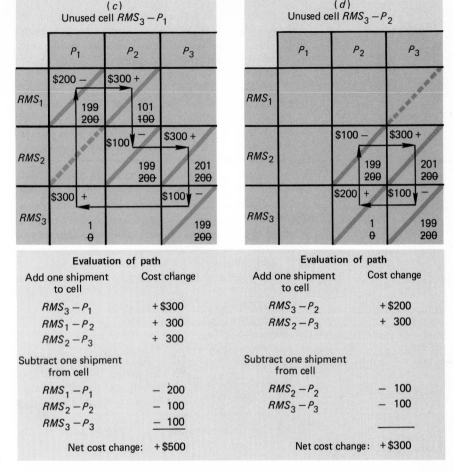

(c)
Unused cell $RMS_3 - P_1$

	P_1	P_2	P_3
RMS_1	$200 -$ 199 ~~200~~	$300 +$ 101 ~~100~~	
RMS_2		100 199 ~~200~~	$300 +$ 201 ~~200~~
RMS_3	$300 +$ 1 ~~0~~		100 199 ~~200~~

(d)
Unused cell $RMS_3 - P_2$

	P_1	P_2	P_3
RMS_1			
RMS_2		$100 -$ 199 ~~200~~	$300 +$ 201 ~~200~~
RMS_3		$200 +$ 1 ~~0~~	100 199 ~~200~~

Evaluation of path		Evaluation of path	
Add one shipment to cell	**Cost change**	**Add one shipment to cell**	**Cost change**
$RMS_3 - P_1$	$+ \$300$	$RMS_3 - P_2$	$+ \$200$
$RMS_1 - P_2$	$+ \ 300$	$RMS_2 - P_3$	$+ \ 300$
$RMS_2 - P_3$	$+ \ 300$		
Subtract one shipment from cell		**Subtract one shipment from cell**	
$RMS_1 - P_1$	$- \ 200$	$RMS_2 - P_2$	$- \ 100$
$RMS_2 - P_2$	$- \ 100$	$RMS_3 - P_3$	$- \ 100$
$RMS_3 - P_3$	$- \ 100$		
Net cost change:	$+ \$500$	**Net cost change:**	$+ \$300$

Figure S6-4 (cont.)

in part (a) of Figure S6-4, shows that this cell is unattractive and does not offer a desirable alternative solution. We now proceed to evaluate the other unused cells.

The stepping stone path for evaluating unused cell $RMS_1 - P_3$ consists of $(RMS_1 - P_3) \rightarrow (RMS_2 - P_3) \rightarrow (RMS_2 - P_2) \rightarrow (RMS_1 - P_2)$. The clockwise direction of movement on this path (part (b) of Figure S6-4) is irrelevant; it could just as well have been counterclockwise. This unique path shows that overall costs would be *reduced* by $300 if a shipment were made from RMS_1 to P_3. Instead of changing the existing solution to obtain this cost savings, we will first evaluate all other unused cells to see if even greater cost savings may be possible.

The stepping stone paths have been evaluated for each of the two remaining unused cells. Parts (c) and (d) show that costs would increase if shipments were made to either $RMS_3 - P_1$ or $RMS_3 - P_2$.

As you can see, only one of the four unused cells in the original solution, cell $RMS_1 - P_3$, offers any cost reduction.

4. *Modify the existing solution.* The original solution will be modified by allocating shipments into cell $RMS_1 - P_3$. Furthermore, since $300 of cost savings result for each shipment, we will allocate as many as possible. Examination of part (b) of Figure S6-4 reveals that 100 shipments, at most, can be allocated,

since no more than 100 can be removed from cell RMS_1-P_2. Therefore, 100 units will be added to RMS_1-P_3, and appropriate adjustments will be made in cell shipments on the rest of the evaluation path. This course of action will result in a cost savings of ($300/shipment) × (100 shipments) = $30,000. The modified solution is shown in Figure S6-5, part (a).

    5. *Reevaluate and modify.* The first revised solution is now treated as a new problem in which steps 3 and 4 are repeated. Applying the stepping stone procedure, we find that only one cell (RMS_2-P_1) offers any cost reduction. This desirable change is highlighted in Figure S6-5, part (b). Therefore, a second revised solution is created by allocating as many shipments as possible, 100, into RMS_2-P_1 (see Figure S6-6).

    Evaluation of the unused cells in Figure S6-6 shows that no further cost reduction is possible; adding shipments to any of the unused cells will cause total costs to increase (as shown by the positive cell evaluations shown in parentheses). The optimal solution has been found. If the Columbus, Ohio, raw material source is added to the existing network, the best shipping pattern is to send 100 shipments from RMS_1 to P_1, 200 from RMS_1 to P_3, 100 from RMS_2 to P_1, 300 from RMS_2 to P_2, and 200 from RMS_3 to P_3 when RMS's were respectively Chicago, Louisville, and Columbus, and P's were Evansville, Lexington, and Fort Wayne.

Some Additional Considerations

Inequality of availability and requirements

We said earlier that the transportation method can be applied only when the resources available equal the resources required. In the Alpha Company example, 900 shipments were needed and 900 were available. If the problem had originally stated that only 800 shipments were required by the destinations, an additional

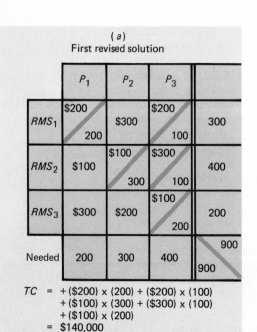

(a)
First revised solution

	P_1	P_2	P_3	
RMS_1	$200 \qquad 200	$300	$200 \qquad 100	300
RMS_2	$100 \qquad $100	$100 \qquad 300	$300 \qquad 100	400
RMS_3	$300	$200 \qquad 200	$100	200
				900
Needed	200	300	400	900

$$
\begin{aligned}
TC &= +(\$200) \times (200) + (\$200) \times (100) \\
   &\quad + (\$100) \times (300) + (\$300) \times (100) \\
   &\quad + (\$100) \times (200) \\
   &= \$140,000
\end{aligned}
$$

Figure S6-5 **Assignment revisions for Alpha Processing Company**

(b)
Evaluation of unused cells in first revised solution

	P_1	P_2	P_3
RMS_1		+$300	
RMS_2	−$200		
RMS_3	+$200	+$300	

	P_1	P_2	P_3	Available
RMS_1	$200 100	$300 (+$100)	$200 200	300
RMS_2	$100 100	$100 300	$300 (+$200)	400
RMS_3	$300 (+$200)	$200 (+$100)	$100 200	200
Needed	200	300	400	900 / 900

$$TC = (\$200) \times (100) + (\$200) \times (200) + (\$100)$$
$$\times (100) + (\$100) \times (300) + (\$100) \times (200)$$
$$= \$120,000$$

Figure S6-6 **Second revised (optimal) solution for Alpha Processing Company**

fictitious destination would be created and added to the matrix. This new dummy plant, P_4, would become a column with a requirement of 100 shipments, and the adjustment would provide the necessary equality. A zero cost coefficient would be inserted in each cell of the dummy column to reflect the fact that assignments in these cells are fictitious, having no real cost. The use of a dummy row or column, whichever is needed, is equivalent to the use of slack variables in the simplex method.

Degeneracy   A condition called degeneracy exists in a transportation problem when the number of used cells is less than ($m + n - 1$). Degeneracy can occur at the initial or at intermediate stages of the problem. When degeneracy exists, it means that a unique stepping stone path cannot be identified for evaluating an unused cell. A standard procedure for overcoming degeneracy calls for placing an arbitrarily small, fictitious assignment called *theta* (Θ) in one of the currently unused cells. The cell with *theta* is then treated as if it were a used cell during this stage of the problem. *Theta* is not, however, a real assignment, and it does not result in any real cost.

To illustrate the use of *theta,* suppose we had the intermediate solution shown in Figure S6-7(a). The four used cells are not adequate for evaluating the unused cells, since $(3 + 3 - 1) = 5$ used cells are needed. A *theta* must be added—but where? The choice is arbitrary, but time can be saved by adding *theta* to an empty cell that will allow as many unused cells as possible to be evaluated. In this example, *theta* is added to RMS_2-P_1 in part (b) of the figure. This cell then becomes one of the stepping stones for evaluating RMS_1-P_1, RMS_3-P_2, and RMS_3-P_3. The evaluation path for RMS_3-P_3 is traced out in the figure. *Theta* remains in the matrix until it is subtracted out, or until a real allocation is made into its cell. It then disappears from the problem.

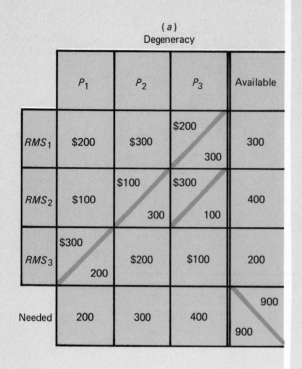

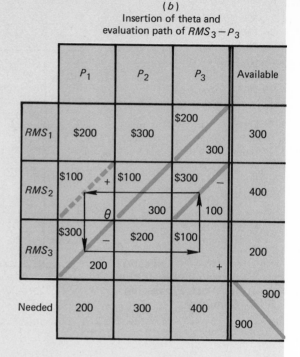

Figure S6-7 **Degenerate solution for Alpha Processing Company**

| | Maximization Problems | Sometimes the problem has a maximization rather than minimization objective. The same procedure is used in either case. In a maximization problem, the cell evaluations have |

Maximization Problems Sometimes the problem has a maximization rather than minimization objective. The same procedure is used in either case. In a maximization problem, the cell evaluations have a reverse interpretation. When maximizing, a positive cell evaluation indicates that further improvement is possible in that cell. A negative evaluation indicates that the cell offers an undesirable change.

Alternative optimal solutions The final optimal solution may not be unique. Alternative optimal solutions exist whenever any unused cells have zero cell evaluations. A zero evaluation means that although the existing solution mix can be changed, the criterion value will not change.

REVIEW AND DISCUSSION QUESTIONS

1. In general, how do you decide which cost elements to include in or exclude from the cells of a transportation LP problem?

2. What problem characteristics must exist to enable the use of the transportation method of LP?

3. Explain what is happening when you use the stepping stone procedure for cell evaluation.

4. What is meant by the property of "homogeneity"? Why is it important?

5. Identify the similarities and differences of the transportation and simplex methods of LP.

6. What is the significance of having $(m + n - 1)$ used cells in solution? Will an optimal solution have $(m + n - 1)$ used cells?

7. Describe the northwest corner rule as a method for obtaining an initial feasible solution. Are there other ways of getting an initial feasible solution? Explain.

8. What conditions must exist to enable you to know an optimal solution has been found? That an alternative optimal solution exists?

9. If total resources available are unequal to the total required, what adjustments must be made in formulating the problem?

10. Why are dummy cells assigned a cost coefficient of zero? Can non-zero cost coefficients be used? Explain.

11. For an optimal solution matrix, give an economic interpretation of the cell evaluations.

12. What is the significance of degeneracy in transportation LP problems?

13. What types of locational problems can be aided by the transportation method of LP?

PROBLEMS

1. Consider the following problem, in which costs are recorded for allocating one unit from each source to each destination:

Source	Destination A	B	C	Maximum units available
1	$1	$3	$2	275
2	2	4	1	325
3	3	2	3	300
Minimum units requested	350	400	150	

(a) Use the northwest corner rule to obtain an initial feasible solution.
(b) What is the cost of this initial solution?
(c) Find the minimum cost solution.
(d) What is the optimal allocation pattern, and what is its cost?
(e) Is there an alternative optimal solution?

2. Suppose the data matrix in problem 1 contained profit figures rather than costs. Find the profit maximizing solution.

3. Set up problem 1 in a simplex format.

4. The costs of shipping a unit from each source to each destination, along with the rim requirements, are shown below.

Source	Destination A	B	C	D	Source availability (units)
1	$7	$10	$8	$5	728
2	6	4	9	7	475
3	3	6	5	8	775
Destination requirements (units)	226	675	351	455	

(a) Develop an initial feasible solution using the northwest corner rule.
(b) Find the optimal solution.
(c) Interpret the optimal solution.

5. Following are the source availabilities, destination requirements, and the costs of assigning a unit from each source to each destination:

	Destination			
Source	A	B	C	Source availability (units)
1	$4	$7	$3	250
2	5	6	2	150
3	3	7	5	250
4	6	1	4	200
Destination requirements (units)	350	300	200	

Develop an initial feasible solution using the northwest corner rule, and find the optimal solution.

6. Refer to problem 6 at the end of Chapter 6. Solve the problem using the transportation method. Which site should be selected, Knoxville or Dallas? Explain.

7. A company has factories at cities V, W, and X. Management will add an additional plant at city Y or Z, with an annual capacity of 500,000 units of output. Capacities of existing plants are 722,000 at V, 510,000 at W, and 808,000 at X. City Y is attractive because labor costs will average only $5.10 per unit, compared to $5.40 at city Z. Unit labor costs are $5.25 at V, $6.30 at W, and $5.70 at X. The factories annually ship output to wholesalers in cities A (615,000 units), B (961,000 units), and C (914,000 units), with shipping costs as follows:

	Average Cost of Shipping One Unit To Wholesaler		
From factory	A	B	C
V	$1.00	$1.50	$1.25
W	1.25	1.30	1.10
X	.90	1.15	1.35
Y	1.05	.95	1.00
Z	.95	.80	1.10

Which site, Y or Z, is most attractive?

8. Bill's Gravel Company operates three gravel pits from which loads of gravel are shipped to various construction sites. Pit 1 has a monthly capacity of 100 loads; 85 loads can be delivered from pit 2, and pit 3 can supply 145 loads each month. Requests for deliveries next month have come from four construction sites, A (131 loads), B (77 loads), C (49 loads), and D (104 loads). Bill's profits depend on which pit is used to supply each construction site:

5000

Profit per Load of Gravel
Construction Site

From pit	A	B	C	D
1	$24	$30	$27	$32
2	29	19	21	36
3	26	29	20	18

What should Bill do?

Anderson, D. R., D. J. Sweeney, and T. A. Williams. *An Introduction to Management Science.* St. Paul, Minn.: West Publishing Co., 1976.

Bierman, H., Jr., C. P. Bonini, and W. H. Hausman. *Quantitative Analysis for Business Decisions*, 5th ed. Homewood, Ill.: Richard D. Irwin, Inc., 1977.

Dantzig, G. B. *Linear Programming & Extensions.* Princeton, N.J.: Princeton University Press, 1963.

Wagner, Harvey M. *Principles of Management Science, With Applications to Executive Decisions.* Englewood Cliffs, N.J.: Prentice-Hall, Inc., 1970.

SELECTED
READINGS

7 Layout Planning

So far in our discussions we have been emphasizing the importance of planning by the operations manager. In Chapter 4, you may recall, we discussed planning production/operations in advance of actual resource conversion; in Chapters 5 and 6, we focused on external aspects of conversion process design—establishing capacity and facility location. We continue our emphasis on planning now by considering the internal arrangement of the conversion facility. Figure 7-1 shows how layout planning fits into our production/operations model; it also emphasizes the importance of modeling and behavioral considerations in layout planning.

As you read this chapter, you should remember that layout planning will eventually influence both the organizing and the controlling activities of the operations manager. In Chapter 2 we presented a survey of major problems of operations managers. Among problems most frequently mentioned were cost, labor, quality and production control, labor/industrial relations, and production planning and scheduling. On the surface, these problems appear to arise from day-to-day difficulties. Many of these short-run problems, however, can largely be prevented by proper planning and design of the conversion process. Over long periods of time, good planning can effect savings in day-to-day operating costs. If we try to use quickly conceived, inexpensively developed plans, we may end up with much higher costs of operation and control in the long run. A good planning job now will pay for itself not once but many times, year after year. For these reasons, the "organizing" and "controlling" circles overlap "planning" in Figure 7-1. The planning that is done now is closely related to the organizing and controlling efforts that will be needed later.

Layout design interrelates with the capacity decision (Chapter 5) and the processing technology, both of which dictate some spatial requirements

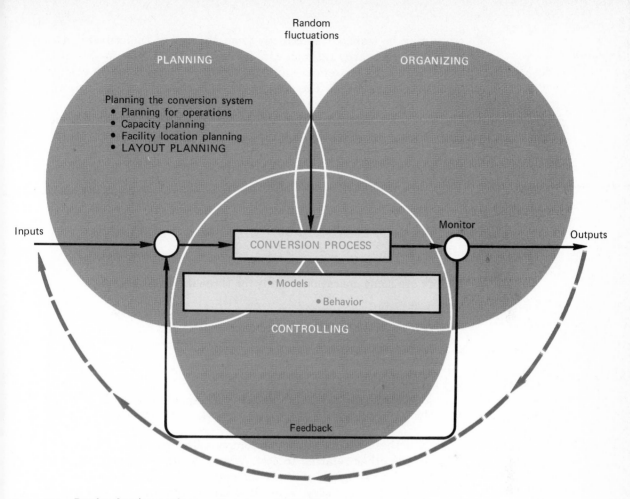

Random
fluctuations

PLANNING

ORGANIZING

Planning the conversion system
• Planning for operations
• Capacity planning
• Facility location planning
• LAYOUT PLANNING

Inputs

Monitor

Outputs

CONVERSION PROCESS

• Models

• Behavior

CONTROLLING

Feedback

Figure 7-1   Production/operations management activities

on the facility. On the input side of operations, for example, capacity and technology require that certain quantities of raw materials be on hand, stored in appropriate places, to allow subsequent operations to flow smoothly. The sizes and locations of these storage areas must be considered in layout. For some conversion processes, extra inventories of built-up products are needed between work stations to reduce the disruptions of delays or breakdowns at intermediate stages of conversion. Where should these inventory storage areas be located?

The locations of various departments must also be decided. Equipment maintenance departments may have to be located near some especially breakdown-prone departments to ensure continuous, uninterrupted work flows. At the output side of conversion, finished goods storage areas and the conveyances for getting finished products into storage must both be considered. The size of the product and the volume of output will dictate storage area requirements; but so will our shipping plans, which are part of the physical distribution system. Large volumes of output produced to order may be transported directly from the end of the conversion line and packed into nearby railroad cars for immediate shipment. Or outputs may go into a large warehouse area, to be loaded after a future customer order has been received. The design of the system will determine costs of storage and materials handling.

To see how layout planning affects operating costs and effectiveness, we will have to examine layout concepts, particularly different types of layout designs. Some modeling techniques are also useful for layout planning, and behavioral factors must be considered too. But let's begin by finding out just what layout planning is.

LAYOUT CONCEPTS

Identifying Planning Goals

Here are some operational goals for three different organizations:

- *for a manufacturer of power mowers:* To produce 500,000 mowers each year at a unit production cost of no more than $32.
- *for preparing patient meals in a hospital:* To prepare appropriate food trays for 500 patients within a one-hour interval at each of three serving times during the day. Preparation costs are not to exceed $3 per patient per day.
- *for a warehousing and distribution facility:* Annually to process (fill) 15,000 shipment requests while keeping operating costs at or below $200,000.

Each of these goals has two subcomponents, one relating to capacity or volume, the other relating to cost. Where did these goals come from? Actually they are subgoals that are supportive of higher level goals. For the manufacturing company, a profit-making organization, the decision to enter the power mower market required development of long-term plans using forecasts of market demand. After having assessed market potential and estimated a competitive selling price and required capital investment, management determined that unit production costs would need to be $32 or less, at a volume of 500,000 units, in order to achieve the desired level of profitability. But in order to meet that goal of $32 a unit, the operations manager is going to have to plan the layout of the facility very carefully. As you can see in Figure 7-2, a good layout will yield the desired profit, but a poor one will not.

Nonprofit organizations need to watch their costs just as closely as do profit-making companies. Today hospitals are experiencing ever-increasing costs of health care delivery. Pressures arise not only from patients (customers) but from government and other sources as well to cut these costs. Hospital administrators are faced with the task of simultaneously maintaining or improving services and reducing the costs of delivering them. Consequently, the reduction of food preparation costs, one of several subgoals of the hospital, may be a primary goal for the manager of the dietetics operation. Layout planning of the food preparation area can keep meal preparation costs down.

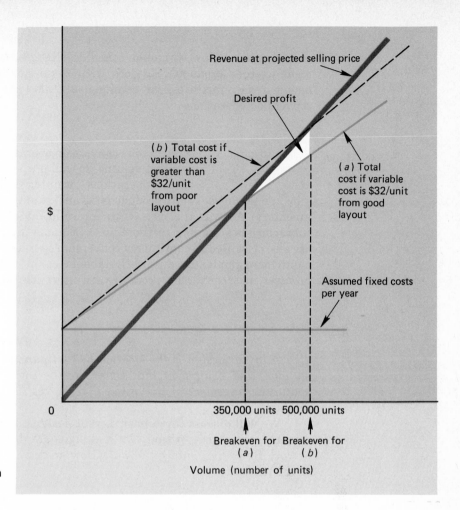

Revenue at projected selling price

Desired profit

(b) Total cost if variable cost is greater than $32/unit from poor layout

(a) Total cost if variable cost is $32/unit from good layout

$

Assumed fixed costs per year

0

350,000 units   500,000 units

Breakeven for   Breakeven for
(a)   (b)

Volume (number of units)

Figure 7-2 Facilities layout affects breakeven volume of operations

Warehouse/distribution operations exist in both the private and public sectors. Several U.S. Air Force supply depots, for example, operate daily at specific geographic locations. They package and ship materials and component parts requested by Air Force installations around the globe. As governmental budgets are slashed, operations managers must undertake programs to meet delivery schedules more efficiently without sacrificing delivery effectiveness. Layout planning can help.

Types of Manufacturing and Service Operations

The operations function in both manufacturing and service organizations can be divided into two basic types, intermittent and continuous, depending on the degree of product standardization and volume of output.

Intermittent operations

Intermittent manufacturing is conversion with production characteristics of low product volume, general purpose equipment, labor-intense operations, interrupted product flow, frequent schedule changes, large product mix, and made-to-order products. Services with these same characteristics (automobile repair facilities, for example) are also classified as intermittent conversion operations.

Continuous operations

Continuous conversion operations are featured by high product volume, special purpose equipment, capital-intense operations, uninterrupted product flow, few schedule changes, small product mix, and standardized products made to inventory. As was the case with intermittent operations, services with characteristics similar to those in continuous manufacturing operations are also classified as continuous conversion operations (a soft drink bottling plant, for example). Because of the labor intensity of most service operations, however, most conversion processes are intermittent rather than continuous.

Basic Layout Designs

A layout design is the location or configuration of departments, work stations, and equipment that constitute the conversion process. It is the spatial arrangement of the physical resources that are used to create the product.

We will discuss three basic layout designs: process-oriented, product-oriented, and fixed-position. These designs are differentiated by the types of work flows they entail; the work flow, in turn, is dictated by the nature of the product.

Process layout

Process-oriented layouts are appropriate when work flows are not standardized for all units of output, a condition that is found in intermittent manufacturing. Unstandardized work flows occur either when a variety of different products is produced, or when one basic type of product with many possible variations is made. *In a process layout, the processing components (work centers or departments) are grouped together according to the type of function they perform.* Distribution warehouses, hospitals and medical clinics, universities, office buildings, and job shop facilities are often designed in this manner. Figure 7-3 shows a process layout for a medical clinic. Another characteristic of process layouts is the grouping of similar types of machines so that the product can travel to the machines required by the operation (see Figure 7-4).

Product layout

Product-oriented layouts are used when one standardized product is being produced, usually in large volume (a characteristic of continuous manufacturing). Each of the units of output

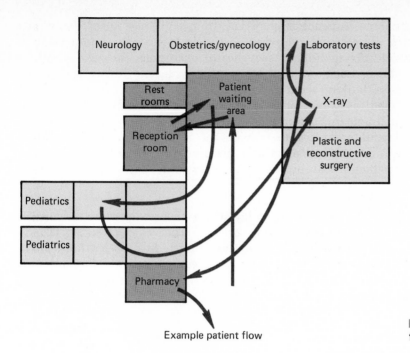

Example patient flow

Figure 7-3 **Process layout for medical clinic**

Figure 7-4 **Process layout in manufacturing**

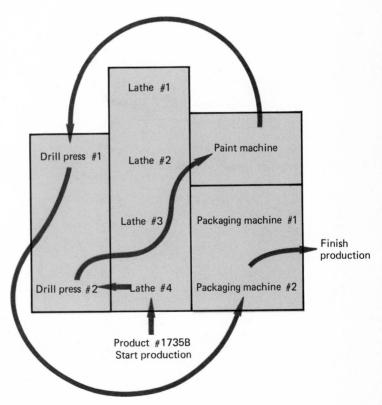

requires the same sequence of operations from beginning to end. *In product layout, work centers and equipment are therefore ideally arranged in a line to provide the specialized sequence of operations that will result in product buildup.* Each work center may provide one highly specialized part of the total buildup sequence. Automatic car washes, cafeteria serving lines, mass medical exams for military recruits, automobile assembly, and beverage bottling plants use product-oriented layouts. Figure 7-5 illustrates a product layout organized to provide the necessary sequence to build up, from beginning to end, a manufactured product. Figure 7-6 illustrates a familiar product layout, an automated carwash.

Fixed-position layout

Fixed-position layouts are necessary when, because of its size, shape, or any other characteristic, it isn't feasible to move the product. *In fixed-position layout, the product remains in one location; tools, equipment, and human skills are brought to it, as needed, to perform the appropriate stages of buildup.* Layouts for building ships, locomotives, and aircraft are often of this type,

Figure 7-5 Product layout in manufacturing

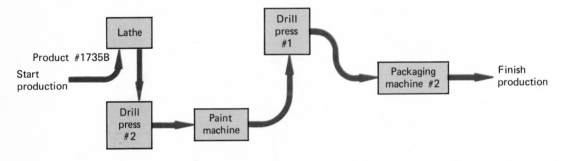

Figure 7-6 Product layout of carwash

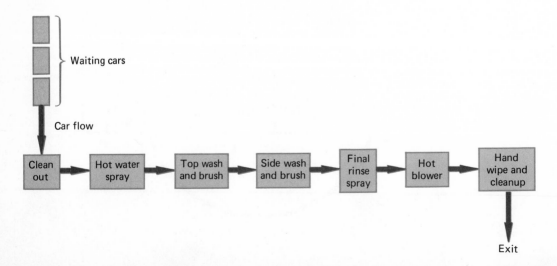

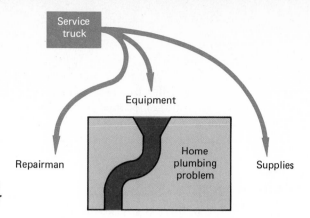

Figure 7-7 **Fixed position layout for plumbing repair service**

as are agricultural operations, in which plowing, planting, fertilizing, and harvesting are performed as needed in the fields. A home plumbing repair operation in which resources are brought to the service site is illustrated in Figure 7-7.

Combination layouts Often pure layouts do not exist, and a combination layout must be used. This is most common for process and product combinations. A process layout, for example, might be logical for a new product with modest volume, infrequent production runs, and equipment utilized only 5 to 10 percent of the time. If volume increases substantially, however, equipment may be tied up by the product much longer, perhaps as much as 75 to 80 percent of the time. It then makes economical sense to develop a product layout and use the idle equipment the remaining 20 to 25 percent of the time on jobs best suited for process layout. A similar situation might exist for process-fixed and product-fixed combination layouts.

EXAMPLE

Refrigerator manufacturers use a process-oriented arrangement to produce various parts and subcomponents. Metal stamping may be consolidated into one department, all types of welding in another, and various heat-treating processes grouped into yet a third work center. At the same time, all these components are brought together in assembly operations, especially for final assembly of the product. The final assembly operations are designed on a product flow or product-oriented basis.

Differences Among Basic Layout Designs

Does it really matter what type of basic design is selected? Yes, it does. The appropriate layout depends upon many factors: anticipated volume, degree of product standardization, physical characteristics of the product, available alternative technologies, and the availability of adequate long-term and short-term financial resources. Table 7-1 summarizes some ways in which basic layouts differ from one another.

For some products, only one type of conversion process may be technologically feasible. In those cases, the process will dictate the type of layout design. But sometimes several methods of conversion may exist. Then the choice of layout design should be based on relative economic advantages and the availability of financial resources.

TABLE 7-1

CHARACTERISTICS OF LAYOUT DESIGNS

Aspect of the conversion process	Product-oriented	Process-oriented	Fixed-position
Product characteristics	Layout geared to producing a standardized product, in large volume, at stable rates of output	Layout capable of processing diversified products requiring common fundamental operations, in large or small volume, at varying rates of output	Low volume, each unit often unique
Product flow pattern	Straight line flow of product; same sequence of standard operations on each unit	Diversified flow pattern; each order (product) may require unique sequence of operations	Little or no product flow; equipment and human resources brought to site as needed
Human skills requirements	Tolerance for performing routine, repetitive tasks at imposed pace; highly specialized work content	Primarily skilled craftsmen, capable of performing without close supervision and with moderate degree of adaptability	High degree of task flexibility often required; specific work assignments and location vary
Supporting staff	Large administrative and indirect support staff for scheduling inputs of materials and people, work analysis and maintenance	Must process skills for scheduling, materials handling, and production and inventory control	High degree of scheduling and coordinating skills required
Material handling	Material flows predictable, systematized and often automated	Type and volume of handling required is variable; duplication of handling often occurs due to intermittent storage (waiting time) before next operation facility is available	Type and volume of handling required is relatively variable, often low; may require heavy-duty general purpose handling equipment

Most of the production/operations management activities that are treated as chapters in this book are discussed in terms of concepts, models, and behavior. *The modeling and behavioral layout techniques and issues are distinctly different; they depend upon whether the layout is process or product.* For the most part, they are not interchangeable, so we will discuss them separately. Let's begin by examining modeling and behavioral techniques that are applicable to the process layout.

Aspect of the conversion process	Product-oriented	Process-oriented	Fixed-position
Inventory requirements	High turnover of raw material and work-in-process inventories	Low turnover of raw material and work-in-process inventories; high raw materials inventories needed on hand due to wide variety of product requests; work-in-process inventories arise from movement of materials	Low or high turnover of inventories due to duration of production cycle; lengthy cycle can result in inventory tie-ups for long periods; inventories ordered as needed.
Space utilization	Efficient utilization of space, high rate of product output per unit of space	Relatively low rate of output per unit of facility space; occurs due to large storage requirements (work-in-process) and frequent underutilization (low demand) in some operating areas	Not applicable when conversion occurs outside the facility; for conversion within the facility, a low rate of space utilization per unit of output may occur
Capital requirements	High capital investment in equipment and processes that perform very specialized functions	Equipment and processes are general purpose and feature flexibility for performing various functions	General purpose equipment and processes that are mobile to permit movement to job site
Product cost components	Relatively high fixed costs; low unit direct labor and materials costs	Relatively low fixed costs; high unit costs for direct labor, materials (inventory) and materials handling	High labor and materials costs; relatively low fixed costs

DEVELOPING THE PROCESS LAYOUT: MODELS AND BEHAVIOR

Process Layout Models

Many kinds of models are useful in layout planning. Mathematical analysis can help managers conceptualize the problem; computer models can provide quick approximations of good layouts; and physical models (templates and scale models, among others) can aid us in visualizing the physical aspects of layouts.

EXAMPLE

In designing and constructing a new manufacturing facility in Kentucky, an initial task was to list all equipment to be placed into a boiler room, which was to be attached to the main building. This task had to be done first, because only after the room had been sized could the price be negotiated with the general building contractor. First, the floor dimensions and heights of all boilers, air compressors, water pumps, and similar equipment were obtained. Second, templates were cut to scale. Third, alternative layouts were tried until a reasonable layout was found. Upon review, an experienced maintenance foreman pointed out that to "rod-out" (clean) the boilers, a wall would have to be knocked out. To avoid having to knock a wall out, the boilers were turned in another direction on the template; but this increased the space requirements. After review by several technical people, a reasonable layout and size were decided upon and the boiler room constructed accordingly.

Graphic and schematic analysis

Perhaps the most widely used layout technique is the use of templates, two-dimensional cutouts drawn to scale. In a trial and error fashion, analysts move these templates about on a surface until they find a reasonable layout. Typically, scaled cutouts for equipment are moved about within a scaled model of the walls and columns of the facility. This technique is used for all three types of layouts, process, product, and fixed. The state of the art in graphic and schematic analysis, which is not changing as rapidly as other techniques, has been summarized:

> The most familiar tools utilized for the solution of layout problems have been graphic and schematic models, particularly two- and three-dimensional templates, assembly charts, operation process charts, and product flow process charts.

> Recent improvements in graphic and schematic layout techniques include "link analysis," "travel charting" and "operations sequence analysis." These techniques utilize data collected on the amount of materials flowing from each department to every other department for some time period. The data are accumulated into a matrix form which is frequently referred to as a "from–to chart," "cross chart," or "flow matrix." The methodology for reducing materials flow is to locate departments in such a way as to minimize the volume of nonadjacent departmental flow.

Link analysis, travel charting, and operations sequence analysis, albeit great improvements over preceding methodology, become virtually unmanageable when the number of departments become at all large (say above 10) unless the flow has a dominant pattern.[1]

Although some of these techniques are beyond the scope of this book, we will be encountering some product and process charts in a future chapter on job design and work measurement.

A load-distance model

In a process-oriented facility, diversified products are processed, work flows in various day to day patterns, and a relatively high amount of material must be handled. The flow path of a typical product through successive stages of buildup reveals many movements from one work center to another. An outpatient of a medical clinic may move through as many as six different work centers for treatment. The manufacture of a special-order tool may require that it move through twenty different work centers as buildup progresses from raw materials to finished form. Although the flow path in each case depends upon the particular needs of the individual product, each product must be transferred or moved among many work centers. All this movement costs money. People and equipment must be on hand, and space must be available for storing the product while it awaits its turn in the next work center. Since transporting per se adds no direct value to the product, it is a wasteful expenditure. Managers of process-oriented facilities therefore seek layout designs that will reduce or minimize unnecessary flows among departments.

The most commonly used quantitative model for process layout considers not only the *number* of interdepartmental moves of a product but also the *distances* over which the moves are made. A long move is usually more costly than a short move. In this model, we try to minimize the criterion (C) that considers both the number of loads and distances moved. Minimize C where

$$C = \sum_{i=1}^{N} \sum_{j=1}^{N} L_{ij} D_{ij} \qquad (7\text{-}1)$$

where N = the number of work centers,

L_{ij} = the number of loads or movements of work between work centers i and j, and

$D_{i}oij$ = the distance between work centers i and j

We must begin by estimating the number of loads, L^{ij}, expected to be moved among all pairs of departments during an appropriate planning

[1]Thomas E. Vollmann and Elwood S. Buffa, "The Facilities Layout Problem in Perspective," *Management Science* 12, no. 10 (June 1966), pp. B451–52.

horizon, say one year. These estimated annual volumes of movements can be summarized in a flow matrix like that in Table 7-2.[2] Estimates can be obtained from past records in production control, work flow analysis, or aggregate production schedules.

The next step is to determine the distances, D^{ij}, among all pairs of departments. These will depend on the relative locations you assign to the departments in your layout design. You begin the design process by proposing an initial layout configuration; departments are assigned to available spaces. Then, using equation 7-1, you measure the effectiveness of the initial configuration. Finally, you modify the initial layout so that you can increase effectiveness by reducing transport costs. Repeat this process until you can find no further improvement. When you have completed this whole process, you will have found the spatial arrangement of work centers that will best minimize annual costs of product movement.

TABLE 7-2

FLOW MATRIX SHOWING ESTIMATED NUMBER OF LOADS, L_{ij}, PER PLANNING PERIOD AMONG ALL PAIRS OF DEPARTMENTS

		Department				
		1	2	3	4	5
Loads moved between departments 1 and 2	1	—	(220)	130	400	370
	2		—	0	400	470
	3			—	150	400
	4				—	100
	5					—

Actually, the cost effectiveness of each possible design need *not* be fully calculated with equation 7-1. Although many different designs are possible, many of them are equivalent, or nearly so, from a transport cost viewpoint, and they need not be calculated separately. Figure 7-8 shows four of the different ways that six work centers could be assigned to six available areas. From a geometric viewpoint, the four configurations are nearly equivalent. In each design, these pairs of departments are located as close to one another as is possible: 1-2, 2-3, 4-5, 5-6, 1-4, 2-5, 3-6. Further redesigns cannot reduce transport costs of flows between these

---

[2]The flow matrix in Table 7-2 is appropriate when the *direction* of flow between departments is immaterial. In some situations, however, a load from *i* to *j* may be more or less costly than a load moving from *j* to *i*. In those cases, an expanded flow matrix must be developed so as to identify the direction of flow. For a discussion of this expanded treatment, see Richard A. Johnson, William T. Newell, and Roger C. Vergin, *Operations Management: A Systems Concept* (Boston: Houghton Mifflin Co., 1972).

work centers. Therefore, the evaluation criterion needs to consider only the flows between *nonadjacent* departments: 1-3, 1-6, 3-4, 4-6. This means that the $L_{ij} D_{ij}$ computations following the initial evaluation for a layout design can be reduced just to those with nonadjacent flows. We will illustrate these concepts with a simplified example. After reading it, you should be able to do a simple layout analysis.

=== EXAMPLE ===

Greenwich Supply Company is a wholesale warehouse distribution facility. It receives orders from building contractors for kitchen cabinets and appliances. Inventories of various products are stored in the warehouse and retrieved, as needed, to fill each order. All products for an order are transported by forklift truck to a centralized packing area where they are packaged for shipment to the contractor. Each completed order is then moved by forklift from the packing area to the shipping and receiving dock. Can the warehouse layout be modified to reduce materials handling costs?

The existing facility layout is diagrammed in Figure 7-9. Section 1 is the shipping and receiving dock, and section 9 is the current packing area. The other fourteen sections are storage areas for different types of appliances and cabinets.

Materials handling flows occur between the packing area and the other fifteen sections. Loads are hauled to area 1 from only one source, section 9. All other loads flow from the remaining sections *into* section 9. The location of the shipping and receiving dock is fixed; it cannot be relocated. All other sections are eligible for relocation.

An examination of records for the last two years reveals the average annual load flows in Table 7-3. We now use equation 7-1 to calculate the effectiveness of the existing layout for this representative flow pattern. Table 7-4 shows the calculations for both adjacent and nonadjacent loads. The existing layout has a load distance rating of 12,300.

To improve the layout, we try to move those departments with heavy load flows closer together. Departments 8 and 9, for example, can be exchanged, thus moving the packing area closer to the shipping dock. We could also relocate department 16 closer to the packing area, and department 14 could be relocated to a more remote setting. A revised layout incorporating these and other changes is shown in Figure 7-10.

This process is then repeated to obtain a second revised layout. Overall, the layout analysis has reduced load movements by 34 percent. If the new layout is implemented, material handling costs are expected to be reduced by about this same amount. In addition to these direct cost savings, we expect that day to day congestion will be reduced in the order filling operation.

1	2	3
4	5	6

4	5	6
1	2	3

4	2	3
1	5	6

4	5	3
1	2	6

Figure 7-8 Four different but equivalent layout configurations

2	3	4	5	6
1 Shipping and receiving	7	8	9 Packing area	10	11
12	13	14	15	16

Figure 7-9 Existing layout of Greenwich Supply Company's relative locations of product storage areas (aisles omitted)

Some limitations   All models have limitations, and the one in our example is no exception. Since many vital aspects of the real layout problem are not considered in the model, it may not yield a realistic layout design. At best, our analysis provides a starting point, a layout that can be modified to account for additional complexities. Often the sizes and/or shapes of all departments cannot be uniform. Special restric-

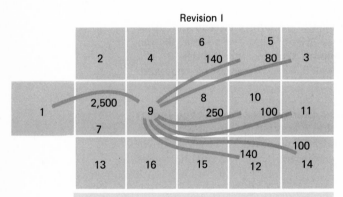

Figure 7-10 Two revised layouts with effectiveness ratings computed

Effectiveness			
Adjacent departments		Nonadjacent department	
Departments	$L_{ij}D_{ij}$	Departments	$L_{ij}D_{ij}$
2-9	500	3-9	240
4-9	320	5-9	280
6-9	150	10-9	500
7-9	160	11-9	300
8-9	330	12-9	280
13-9	240	14-9	300
15-9	240	9-1	5,000
16-9	500		
Subtotal = 2,440		Subtotal = 6,900	
Total effectiveness = 2,440 + 6,900 = 9,340			
Improvement over initial layout = 24%			

TABLE 7-3

AVERAGE NUMBER OF LOADS (ANNUALLY) FLOWING AMONG DEPARTMENTS

| From department | To department | | | | | | | | |
	1	2	3	4	5	6	7	8	9
1									
2									500
3									80
4									320
5									140
6									150
7									160
8									330
9	2,500								
10									250
11									100
12									140
13									240
14									100
15									240
16									500

Figure 7-10 **(cont.)**

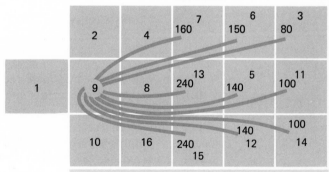

Revision II

Effectiveness			
Adjacent departments		**Nonadjacent departments**	
Departments	$L_{ij} D_{ij}$	Departments	$L_{ij} D_{ij}$
9-1	2,500	3-9	320
2-9	500	5-9	420
4-9	320	6-9	450
8-9	330	7-9	320
10-9	250	11-9	400
16-9	500	12-9	420
		13-9	480
		14-9	400
		15-9	480
Subtotal = 4,400		Subtotal = 3,690	

Total effectiveness = 4,400 + 3,690 = 8,090

Improvement over initial layout = 34.2%

Improvement over Revision I = 13.4%

══════ TABLE 7-4 ══════

CALCULATION OF EXISTING LAYOUT EFFECTIVENESS

	Adjacent departments		
Adjacent departments	Unit distance between departments	Number of loads between departments	Loads times distance
3–9	1	80	$1 \times 80 = 80$
4–9	1	320	$1 \times 320 = 320$
5–9	1	140	$1 \times 140 = 140$
8–9	1	330	$1 \times 330 = 330$
10–9	1	250	$1 \times 250 = 250$
13–9	1	240	$1 \times 240 = 240$
14–9	1	100	$1 \times 100 = 100$
15–9	1	240	$1 \times 240 = 240$

$$\sum_{i=1}^{N} \sum_{j=1}^{N} L_{ij} D_{ij} \quad \text{for}$$

movements between adjacent departments = 1,700

Total effectiveness for all departments = 1,700 + 10,600 = 12,300

tions may be imposed by aisle requirements, limited access to work areas, different types of materials handling methods (hand trucks, overhead cranes, conveyors, and so on), special electrical and plumbing requirements, and many other factors. In addition, the model we have used can require lengthy computational efforts, particularly when the number of departments and combinations of interdepartmental flows become large. For these reasons, alternative types of layout analysis are often used.

Computer models   Many computer based layout models have been developed in recent years. We will briefly discuss only one of them, CRAFT, the Computerized Relative Allocation of Facilities Technique.[3] CRAFT is a heuristic procedure (one in which a set of rules is systematically applied); it rearranges departmental locations in an attempt to find configurations that reduce the materials handling costs of the facility. The user has no assurance that the *best* (least cost) possible configuration will ever be found. Instead, the idea is to obtain a *satisfactory* layout

[3] Elwood S. Buffa, Gordon C. Armour, and Thomas Vollmann, "Allocating Facilities with CRAFT," *Harvard Business Review* 42, no. 2 (March–April 1964), pp. 136–58.

Nonadjacent departments

Nonadjacent departments	D_{ij} unit distance between departments	L_{ij} number of loads between departments	$L_{ij}D_{ij}$ loads times distance
2–9	2	500	$500 \times 2 = 1{,}000$
6–9	2	150	$150 \times 2 = 300$
7–9	2	160	$160 \times 2 = 320$
11–9	2	100	$100 \times 2 = 200$
12–9	2	140	$140 \times 2 = 280$
16–9	2	500	$500 \times 2 = 1{,}000$
9–1	3	2,500	$2{,}500 \times 3 = 7{,}500$

$$\sum_{i=1}^{N} \sum_{j=1}^{N} L_{ij}D_{ij} \quad \text{for}$$

movements between nonadjacent departments $= 10{,}600$

design, one that may not be optimal but is still acceptable. CRAFT can be helpful in avoiding many tedious hand calculations required by manual methods. Thousands of alternative layout patterns can be evaluated in a matter of minutes by the computer.

CRAFT can handle the layout problem for a facility consisting of up to forty work centers of different shapes and sizes, and individual work centers can be specified as either movable or immovable for purposes of relocation. This flexibility allows the user to take into account realistic restrictions imposed by the construction of buildings. CRAFT also considers differences in types and costs of materials handling among work centers. To use CRAFT, the analyst must provide certain types of input information:

1. an initial layout configuration showing the overall size (square feet) of the facility, and the number, location, and size of each department,
2. a load matrix identifying the volumes of materials flows among all departments,
3. a transport cost matrix identifying the cost of transporting a load for one unit distance between departments with interchanges of materials.

The evaluation procedure uses a criterion similar to equation 7-1. After calculating the effectiveness of the initial layout, CRAFT exchanges pairs of departments. The resulting effectiveness of each exchange is evaluated until all eligible exchanges have been considered. Then the best of these exchanges is made by the computer and the entire process is repeated. When total materials handling costs can be reduced no further or when a specified number of repetitions has been reached, the best solution to date can be printed out. The output consists of a layout in the form of a block diagram and a statement of the associated material handling costs.

Many of the limitations of our previous model also apply to the final design obtained from CRAFT. It provides a starting point, but further modification is required to get a realistic design. Human judgment, based on both future plans and knowledge of past difficulties, must be applied to the layout design.

Behavioral Aspects of Process Layout

Operations managers must consider individual and group behavior when planning a process-oriented layout. Why? For several reasons. The layout specialist's problem-solving ability, which is necessary for developing the final design, is a form of individual behavior. Also, the layout design, once implemented, can affect both employee relationships and group behavior and customer behavior and satisfaction.

Behavior in layout design From the designer's point of view, the task of creating a layout design is a complex problem. Many configurations are possible—but which is best? One new design may facilitate materials handling better, but another may require a less costly revision of existing facilities. Still other modifications may cost more now but offer more flexibility and lower cost for future expansion. While all these considerations are being mulled over, the designer may feel severe time pressures to get the final design completed. Under conditions like these, it is impossible to search out and evaluate every possible design alternative. Even if all possible designs could be identified, it is unlikely that everyone the designer consulted would agree that a single choice is best. Consequently, instead of seeking the optimal design, we usually look for a satisfactory suboptimal design (an example of satisficing behavior, which we discussed in Chapter 3). Such a design would offer an appropriate balance among all the various economic and technological factors we have mentioned.

Since resources and time for completing the design are limited, the information search to find design alternatives must be limited too. The designer usually begins searching locally within the internal workings of the organization itself for a familiarity with the product, existing processes, people, equipment, and facility. These efforts are assisted by process engineers, material handling specialists, cost accountants, and maintenance specialists. The designer's experience with these facets of operations leads to preliminary designs or redesigns. The search may then expand to external sources in an attempt to gather additional ideas. Trade associations and trade publications provide information about the layout experiences of similar organizations. Suppliers of materials and equipment often offer detailed information on layout characteristics needed for their equipment and materials. Eventually, cost estimates of contemplated changes are obtained from appropriate sources. These are revised throughout the design process. At some stage, management may determine that the original planning goals are infeasible from a cost/technology viewpoint. In that case, goals must be redefined, and redesign must be initiated accordingly. In this way the process continues until a suitable layout design emerges.

As the search for a satisfactory design progresses, the designer often accumulates large volumes of ideas and information. Somehow these data must be organized and synthesized. Often, experienced layout designers use models to help them keep track of all the information they've accumulated. Sometimes they use three-dimensional scale models showing the overall layout in precise detail. This layout is updated as changes are made. Graphs, drawings, and templates can also be helpful. Quantitative data are often recorded in charts, graphs, tables of numbers, and on computer printouts. All these devices help the designer preserve relevant data in an orderly fashion so that the full implications of a proposed layout change can be determined in a reasonable amount of time.

Until recently, the techniques we've described were used almost exclusively by layout designers. But within the last twenty years, the designer's role seems to have changed with the introduction and increasing use of computer heuristics. Several computerized layout routines similar to CRAFT systematically search and evaluate many alternative designs very rapidly. Contemporary writings seem to assume that these computer approaches are superior to the traditional designs that people developed. But are they? A recent study suggests that they may not be.[4] The study found that people developed more economical designs to reduce materials handling costs than did three of the more widely publicized computer-based design models. This was true for both large and small layout problems. Although modern technologists have assumed that computer models would be superior to humans' designs, especially as the size (number of departments or work centers) of the layout problem increases, the experimental results did not support this assumption. The researchers offer the following possible explanation of their findings:

> It may well be that in problems of larger size the ability of man to recognize and visualize complex patterns gives him an edge over the essentially mechanical procedures followed by the computer programs. Such an explanation is supported by experience in other types of problem solving . . . (179)

---

[4]Michael Scriabin and Roger C. Vergin, "Comparison of Computer Algorithms and Visual Based Methods for Plant Layout," *Management Science* (October 1975), pp. 172–81.

We can draw two conclusions from the results of this study. First, we must not be too hasty in adopting computer-based models at the expense of human experience and problem-solving skills until the question of relative superiority is answered. Second, some combination of human and computer interaction may lead to even better results. The researchers have stated the case for human involvement:

> If the computer algorithms do not afford a significant advantage in terms of results, that is, if certain persons can compete effectively with the computerized algorithms, then it stands to reason that those same persons could do even better in the overall layout problem, where they can apply their experience, concurrently taking into account other considerations (other than just materials handling costs) such as noise levels, ventilation, future expansion plans, and so on. (173)

Individual and interpersonal behavior of employees

We know that our environment affects how people feel about themselves and react toward others. Employees spend several hours a day in their places of work, and the layout design can either help or hinder their relationships with each other. We don't know enough about this phenomenon yet to give precise design guidelines, but the operations manager should be aware of the behavioral effects of layout changes. If the operations manager must deal with unions in the facility, as is the case when job specifications are set by contract, the job of planning layout is more complicated. To the extent that the layout affects jobs, the operations manager must consult shop stewards before making layout decisions.

Process layouts result in departmentalization of activities according to skills. Each skill or craft group establishes norms, agreements about behavior, that determine the kinds and amounts of productive effort its members make. Often these norms are compatible with official standards set by management, but at other times they are not. Group members often develop great pride in their craft specialties and strong feelings of group affiliation. Sometimes groups begin to compete with each other. These facts have two important implications. First, a redesigned layout may inadvertently disrupt existing group relationships. If the relayout causes a group to be disbanded and its members reassigned to newly formed work centers, some period of time will have to elapse before new group structures fully develop. Employee reactions to these changes may be adverse, and absenteeism, employee turnover, and labor relations problems may all increase.

Another implication that stems from strong group affiliations has to do with the types of managerial skills that will be needed. Physical proximity and occupational similarities among members in a work center result in group interest and loyalty that are more inner-directed than outer-directed. Group loyalties can lead to conflicts among groups. As a result, *the manager of the entire operation must be particularly skilled at intergroup coordination.* Customers don't know and don't care whether work centers are well staffed and harmoniously operated; they want a suitable product on time at a reasonable cost. Managers want the same things, but to get them, they must schedule and coordinate the overall efforts of a large network of work groups—not just one. Thus managers must both deal with loyalties within groups and at the same time coordinate efforts of many groups. This is a formidable task.

A different type of difficulty arises in the layout of facilities for service producing organizations. Consider a large insurance company office. Specific work centers can be identified: photocopying, records, typing, clerical, maintenance, legal contracts, and personnel departments. Although a specific insurance policy, for example, may flow among departments, materials handling per se is not the dominant layout design consideration. Instead, a less tangible criterion may be primary. Management may wish to locate departments so as to maximize professional interaction among specific types of employees. When interaction between two departments is necessary, perhaps they should be located side by side, even though overall interdepartmental movements of records, paperwork, and people would be increased. Recently office layout designers have been paying greater attention to this behavioral element. Employees provide information about their interaction with others, so that the layout design can encourage productive patterns of interaction.

Customer behavior Process layout is frequently used when orders are taken to customer specifications and most orders are slightly different from one another. For some organizations, this customer-producer interaction creates special problems, especially when the customer is present in the facility and takes part in the conversion process. In medical, dental, and legal facilities, welfare agencies, supermarkets, and banking businesses, individual customers (clients) have differing needs, and they may be "processed" through different departments accordingly. The layout can affect not only the quality and speed of service, but customer satisfaction as well. In these cases, layout is not just an operations problem, but also at least partially a marketing function. The layout of a full facility bank, for example, must be based on several criteria. Facilities for such daily transactions as withdrawals, deposits, and money orders must be conveniently located for quick processing of walk-in customers. At the same time, areas for loan applications must be both quickly accessible and private. Data processing facilities and maintenance and administrative offices can be placed in more remote locations. Overall, the facility must provide a balance between easy, quick service on the one hand and efficient flows of materials and information for internal operations on the other.

Materials handling efficiency, inventory minimization, and other such criteria, while of primary concern in warehousing and industrial facilities, may play very minor roles in deciding layout designs in some other organizations. Retail establishments like supermarkets and department stores rely on layout as a chief means of facilitating customer purchases. The decisions as to which products to group together and the amount of store space to allocate to each should be based on consumer behavior and preferences, not on internal operating measures like materials handling costs and so on. The data for determining good layouts often come from marketing research studies of consumer tastes, preferences, and expectations. Management determines locations of displays and products to aid the consumer; this may require duplication of inventories to achieve logical clusters of individual products. In a department store, for example, shovels may be found both in the hardware department and in the garden center. Although this duplication results in a higher inventory of shovels, it also provides greater convenience and makes sense from the customer's perspective.

Measuring subjective criteria One of the primary parameters of layout design is flexibility, especially for organizations with a recent history of growth and change. In large offices, for example, departmental space requirements change, and layouts are modified accordingly. Traditionally, this involved tearing down and reconstructing walls and modifying heating, lighting, and air distribution systems. In some organizations these changes occur frequently, and high costs of construction and reconstruction result. To offset these costs, in recent years open design strategies have been used increasingly. Basically, one massive room is subdivided into offices and work areas separated by movable panels, with special attention given to the acoustical properties throughout the structure. This arrangement retains a suitable degree of privacy and also provides flexibility at a reasonable cost.

Although a single effectiveness criterion sometimes may not apply, we may nevertheless be able to use a revision of our previous layout criterion. In equation 7-1, L_{ij} could be used as a subjective priority indicator instead of the number of loads between two departments. Early in the design phase of layout, management can use an arbitrary scale, say between 1 and 10, to rate the importance of having two departments located close together. A rating of 10 indicates the most importance, 1 the least importance. After rating the importance of proximity for all pairs of departments, management can summarize the resulting priorities in a matrix. This L_{ij} matrix can then be used in equation 7-1, and the layout procedure can proceed as we described it earlier. This procedure provides a systematic way of using subjective priorities, including behavioral phenomena, in layout analysis.

DEVELOPING THE PRODUCT LAYOUT: MODELS AND BEHAVIOR Organizations that produce large volumes of a single product can gain economic benefits from a product-oriented (assembly line) layout. An entire facility can be specially designed for this purpose. Early in the twentieth century, Henry Ford revolutionized an industry and the U.S. economy by mass producing automobiles. Since each car was identical, the entire buildup sequence could be studied in careful detail. All work requirements were subdivided into smaller and smaller tasks that, when performed in proper sequence on each car, resulted in a large volume of finished cars each day. At the beginning of the line, the basic framework of the car, the chassis, began its straightline flow through the sequence of work stations, each of which performed a different task. Each task was highly specialized, each just one very small part of the total work effort needed for a complete car. A worker would perform one single task again and again on every car that flowed down the line. Since the line was paced, the worker had only a short time to perform the task. Each task was minutely studied by engineers and managers to find ways to do it more quickly and at lower cost. (This is called *job analysis*.) Better work methods, specialized equipment and tools, and extensive employee training were used to reduce performance times. Because of its repetitive and specialized nature, each task was relatively easy to understand and learn, and workers became highly proficient. Although many workers were required for the entire line, each one did his job so well that large volumes of cars flowed off the end of the line at a price that millions of people could afford. This, then, was the basic concept of the Ford assembly line. By making a large investment in specialized equipment, materials, processes, and human skills, management could create a large volume of a product at a profit. These fundamental concepts, including the product layout, are as applicable today as they were in 1913. Later, we shall examine some contemporary behavioral considerations that were of minor concern at the beginning of the century.

Product Layout Models

Graphic and
schematic analysis
Assembly lines are most often designed and laid out by industrial engineers. Historically, they have used trial-and-error manual techniques and templates, drawings, and graphical procedures to develop initial designs and then improve them. Unfortunately, for large facilities with many tasks and work stations we have no mathematical procedures for insuring that the best possible design has been found. The quality of the design therefore depends upon the experience and judgment of qualified designers. Substantially the same graphic and schematic techniques are used as those we discussed for process layout.

Heuristics in
product layout
Mathematical and computer-based models can offer some assistance in obtaining a quality design. Using logical procedures known as *heuristics*, these models systematically create and evaluate assembly line designs. Applied to product layout, heuristics are logical sets of rules that help the layout analyst rapidly identify and evaluate many alternative designs, far more than could be evaluated manually or intuitively. These rules are developed as much by observation and experimentation as they are by theory, and they are often specially adapted to the specific problem at hand.

Defining the design problem

The fundamental problem of layout planning for assembly lines is to find the number of work stations (workers), and the tasks to be performed at each station, so that a desired level of output is achieved. All of this is to be accomplished in such a way that excessive input resources are minimized.

Notice several important points in this definition. First, the design focuses on achieving a desired level of productive capability (output capacity). The desired *capacity* is an important management decision, as we discussed in Chapter 5. Second, if tasks are to be assigned to work stations, the *sequence* of tasks must be considered. Which tasks must be done first, and which ones may follow? Usually some different sequences are possible, and others are prohibited by the nature of the product. Therefore, sequence restrictions must be identified and complied with in the design. Finally, the definition emphasizes our concern with attaining desired output *efficiently*, without using unnecessary input resources.

Capacity, Sequencing, and Efficiency

Let's illustrate these ideas by using an example.

EXAMPLE

A manufacturer is developing plans for a facility to make aluminum storm windows. The operations manager has obtained the tentative assembly line layout design shown in Table 7-5 and Figure 7-11. The manager wishes to know if this is a good design. Are better designs possible?

This is a good design if:

1. it meets the desired output capacity,
2. the sequence is properly established, and
3. it is an efficient line.

Figure 7-11 Diagram for storm window assembly line

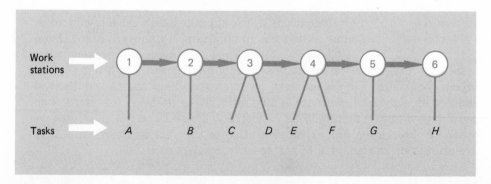

TABLE 7-5

INITIAL ASSEMBLY LINE DESIGN FOR ASSEMBLY OF ALUMINUM STORM WINDOWS
(Desired output capacity: 320 windows per day)

Work station	Preceding work station	Task to be performed at work station	Task definition	Task time (seconds)
1	—	A	Assemble and position frame	70
2	1	B	Install rubber molding	80
3	2	C	Insert frame screws	40
		D	Install frame latch	20
4	3	E	Install frame handle	40
		F	Install glass pane	30
5	4	G	Cover frame screws	50
6	5	H	Inspect and pack window unit	50
				380

1. Is capacity adequate? Capacity is determined by the longest time required from among all the work stations. From Table 7-5, we know that the work done at station 1 requires 70 seconds, and station 2 requires 80 seconds. Station 3 consists of two tasks, inserting frame screws (C) and installing the frame latch (D). Thus, the work done at station 3 requires 60 (40 + 20) seconds. The times required for stations 4, 5, and 6 are 70, 50, and 50 seconds. The longest time, then, is needed at station 2 (80 seconds), since a unit spends fewer than 80 seconds at every other station. Since every unit passes through all stations, and each must spend 80 seconds at station 2, station 2 is the *bottleneck* operation, the station that restricts the rate of flow off the line. A finished window assembly will flow off the end of the line every 80 seconds. This length of time is called the *minimum cycle time* of the line. It is the shortest elapsed time between successive units being completed by the entire line.

With a cycle time of 80 seconds, how many windows will be produced daily? It depends on the length of a working day. If the operation runs for one 8-hour shift each day, then the available productive time each day is 28,800 seconds (8 hours × 3,600 seconds per hour). Therefore, maximum daily output can be determined by calculating as follows:

$$\text{Maximum daily output (number of units)} = \frac{\text{Available time per day}}{\text{Cycle time required per unit}}$$

$$\text{Maximum daily output} = \frac{28,800 \text{ seconds/day}}{80 \text{ seconds/unit}}$$

$$= 360 \text{ units}$$

We see, then, that since it can generate more than the required 320 units daily, this assembly line design provides adequate output capacity.

There is an alternative method for determining whether capacity is adequate. We can calculate the *maximum allowable cycle time* if desired capacity (320 units per day) is to be achieved.

$$\text{Maximum allowable cycle time to meet desired capacity} = \frac{\text{Available time per day}}{\text{Desired number of units per day}}$$

$$= \frac{28{,}800 \text{ seconds/day}}{320 \text{ units/day}}$$

$$= 90 \text{ seconds/unit}$$

This calculation shows that any design with a cycle time of 90 seconds or less will provide the desired capacity. Designs with cycle times in excess of 90 seconds will not be of adequate capacity.

2. Is the sequence of tasks correct? For our simple example, we have stated one straightforward sequence. There are no alternatives available.

3. Is the line efficient? We find out by measuring the extent to which our human input resources are being utilized. The proposed design has six stations, each manned by one employee. All six workers are paid daily wages for eight hours. How wisely are we utilizing this available resource in the proposed design? How much of our employees' time is spent on productive effort assembling windows? How much on nonproductive efforts or idleness? It depends on the pace of the line that management selects. The pace can be set anywhere between the cycle times of 80 and 90 seconds. A pace greater than 90 seconds per cycle will slow the line so much that the line will not achieve desired capacity. A pace below 80 is not possible because of the bottleneck operation at station 2. In Table 7-6, we have calculated the effectiveness of labor utilization for cycle times of 90 and 80 seconds.

As you can see, idleness is higher for the 90-second cycle, and labor utilization is more effective for the 80-second cycle. We can further calculate the number of daily hours of idleness for each cycle.

$$\text{Daily labor hours idle} = \frac{(\text{Idle seconds/cycle})(\text{Cycles/day})}{(\text{Seconds/hour})}$$

$$\text{Daily labor hours idle} \atop (\text{90-second cycle}) = \frac{(160)\left(\dfrac{28{,}800}{90}\right)}{3{,}600} = 14.2 \text{ hours}$$

$$\text{Daily labor hours idle} \atop (\text{80-second cycle}) = \frac{(100)\left(\dfrac{28{,}800}{80}\right)}{3{,}600} = 10.0 \text{ hours}$$

If the hourly wage is $5, then $50 is paid each day for idleness on the 80-second line. On the 90-second line, $71 is paid daily for idleness.

TABLE 7-6

CALCULATION OF LABOR UTILIZATION EFFECTIVENESS FOR PROPOSED 80-AND 90-SECOND LINES

	1	2	Station 3	4	5	6	Total time per cycle	Utilization of employees (efficiency)
Effectiveness for 90-second cycle time (seconds)								
Productive time (task time) expended each cycle	70	80	60	70	50	50	380	$380/540 \times 100 = 70.4\%$
Available employee time each cycle (cycle time)	90	90	90	90	90	90	540	—
Idle time each cycle	20	10	30	20	40	40	160	$160/540 \times 100 = 29.6$
Effectiveness for 80-second cycle time (seconds)								
Productive time (task time) expended each cycle	70	80	60	70	50	50	380	$380/480 \times 100 = 79.2$
Available employee time each cycle (cycle time)	80	80	80	80	80	80	480	—
Idle time each cycle	10	0	20	10	30	30	100	$100/480 \times 100 = 20.8$

These excessive costs would eventually have to be passed on to the customer by appropriate price setting. Clearly, an efficient layout design has long-run importance for both the company and the consumer.

Balancing the line   How can the cost of idleness be reduced? The most common way is to redefine the work content at each station. Perhaps the eight elementary tasks (A to H in Table 7-5) can be reassigned in different ways, and we can come up with work assignments that are more evenly distributed in terms of time. If productive times required at all stations were equal, we could have no idle time, and the line would be perfectly balanced. *The design problem of finding ways to equalize performance times at all stations is called the line balancing problem.* In the process of solving a line balancing problem, we may even be able to identify and eliminate unnecessary work stations. Our procedure for improving the design uses six steps:

1. define elemental tasks,
2. identify precedence requirements,
3. calculate the minimum number of work stations needed,
4. apply an assignment heuristic for specifying the work content at each station,
5. calculate effectiveness and efficiency, and
6. seek further improvement.

We have already done the first step, defining elemental tasks, and shown them in Table 7-5. In general, we use job analysis (also called work content analysis) to subdivide the total work into subtasks. There is a limit, however, to how far this subdividing can go. Beyond it, further subdivision of an element creates a total time greater than that of the original element. An elemental task, then, is the smallest work task that can reasonably be assigned to a work station. Tasks *A* through *H* are examples.

The second step tells us that elemental tasks cannot be done in just any order. The nature of the product and the processes for producing it require that some tasks be done before others. Certainly the window units, for example, cannot be packed until they are completely assembled. Production designers must specify which tasks must precede other tasks.

These precedence relationships can be summarized in a diagram like the one in Figure 7-12. Arrows are used to show only the required *direction* of flow; arrow length has no meaning. The nodes are the tasks. The diagram shows that task *A* must be done *before* we can do tasks *B, C, D,* or *E*. *F* cannot be done until *B and C* are completed. *G* cannot be done before *C* is completed, and *D, E, F,* and *G* must precede *H*. The diagram also implies that *B, C, D,* and *E* can be done in any order. *F* and *G* may either precede or follow *D* and *E*.

It is usually helpful to know how many work stations will be needed. Once the desired line output is specified, we can calculate the *theoretical minimum number of stations* that will be required, the third step in our

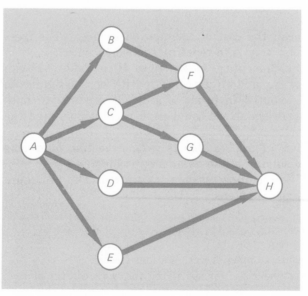

Figure 7-12 **Precedence relationships for window assembly**

procedure. From this calculation the planner has an idea as to the *least* number of stations needed:

$$\text{Theoretical minimum number of stations} = \frac{\left(\begin{array}{c}\text{Total work content}\\\text{(time) per unit}\end{array}\right)\left(\begin{array}{c}\text{Desired number of}\\\text{units per day}\end{array}\right)}{\left(\begin{array}{c}\text{Total productive time available}\\\text{per day}\end{array}\right)}$$

$$= \frac{(380 \text{ seconds/unit})(320 \text{ units/day})}{(28{,}800 \text{ seconds/day})}$$

$$= 4.22 \text{ stations}$$

The total work content (time) that goes into the manufacture of one window is the sum of the task times for tasks *A* through *H*. Thus, each finished unit has $70 + 80 + 40 + 20 + 40 + 30 + 50 + 50 = 380$ seconds of labor content. A minimum of 4.22 stations will be required. Since we are dealing in whole stations, at least five stations will be needed. The *actual* design may use more than the minimum number of stations; it depends on the types of precedence relationships that exist in the problem. The initial design in Table 7-5 used six stations.

The fourth step involves applying an assignment heuristic. The designer must now assign eight tasks to five or more stations. The performance times for tasks assigned to each station cannot exceed the 90-second maximum cycle time. Furthermore, tasks must be assigned in compliance with the precedence relationships. Several combinations of task-to-station assignments meet these requirements. For larger problems with thousands of tasks and hundreds of stations, there are enormous numbers of feasible designs. To trim such problems down to reasonable size, we often use heuristics. Although heuristics do not guarantee that the best solution to a problem will be found, they do help simplify complex problems and may lead to satisfactory solutions. We will apply a "longest-operation-time" rule to the line balancing problem. First we will find a balance to achieve the maximum allowable cycle time (90 seconds), and then we will balance to achieve the minimum possible cycle time (80 seconds).

The steps in the longest-operation-time (LOT) rule are:

LOT 1. Assign remaining tasks to the next station according to the length of task operation time; the eligible task with the longest time is assigned first. Maintain precedence relationships.

LOT 2. After assigning a task to a station, determine how much unassigned time remains at the station.

LOT 3. Determine whether other eligible tasks can be assigned to the station. If so, make the assignment. Maintain precedence relationships. If not, return to step 1 and add a new station. Continue until all tasks have been assigned to stations.

To apply the rule, we first array the tasks in descending order of operation time.

Task	Operation time (seconds)
B	80
A	70
G	50
H	50
C	40
E	40
F	30
D	20

In step LOT 1 we try to assign B to station 1, since B has the longest time. However, B is ineligible because it must follow A (precedence requirement). In fact, A *must* be assigned to station 1 before any other task becomes eligible for assignment. After A is assigned to station 1, 20 seconds of unassigned time remains (LOT 2). Using LOT 3, we see that D is the only eligible task that can be assigned to this station. B, C, and D all meet the precedence requirements, but their operation times exceed the unassigned time (20 seconds) at station 1. Therefore, station 1 consists of tasks A and D for a total of 90 seconds operation time.

Now we add station 2. B has the longest operation time (80 seconds) among the eligible unassigned tasks. B is therefore assigned to station 2. Using LOT 2, we find that 10 seconds ($90 - 80 = 10$) of unassigned time remain at this station. Since all other tasks require more than 10 seconds, none is eligible to be added to station 2.

To the third station we may assign C or E. We arbitrarily select C, with an operation time of 40 seconds. Remaining unassigned time at station 3 is therefore 50 seconds ($90 - 40 = 50$). Then E and G become eligible at this station. Since G has the longest operation time, it is assigned. Thus station 3 consists of tasks C and G with a total performance time of 90 seconds ($40 + 50 = 90$).

This entire process, carried to completion, is summarized in Table 7-7. The procedure has resulted in a five-station assembly line consisting of the work elements shown in Figure 7-13.

The design is *effective* if it meets the desired capacity—if the output goal is accomplished. Its *efficiency* is measured by the labor utilization measure we described earlier. In the fifth step, we want to check both measures of performance. In the previous section, we balanced to achieve the maximum allowable cycle time (90 seconds). We have also obtained a balance to achieve the minimum possible cycle time (80 seconds), although the analysis is not shown here. Both designs are shown in Figure 7-14, along with calculations of efficiency and effectiveness. Both of these designs are more efficient than the ones presented to the operations manager in our example earlier in this chapter.

At this stage, we may be able to improve a design by trial and error, step 6 of our procedure. In addition, many other heuristics may be used instead of the longest-operation-time approach. Several computerized heuristics are available, and since different heuristics can lead to different designs, you may wish to try more than one approach.

TABLE 7-7

ASSIGNING TASKS TO STATIONS USING THE LONGEST-OPERATION-TIME HEURISTIC ACHIEVING A 90-SECOND CYCLE TIME

Heuristic steps	Station	Eligible tasks	Task selected for assignment	Task operation time (seconds)	Unassigned time remaining at station (seconds)	Remaining eligible tasks for this station
1	1	A	A	70	20	D
2	1	D	D	20	0	none
3	2	B,C,E	B	80	10	none
4	3	C,E	C	40	50	E,F,G
5	3	E,F,G	G	50	0	none
6	4	E,F	E	40	50	F
7	4	F	F	30	20	none
8	5	H	H	50	40	none

There are occasions when output capacity and efficiency can be increased by deviating from the procedures we have presented. "Task sharing," for example, occurs when there are three stations, each manned by one operator, all of which have some idleness each cycle. By eliminating one operator, we can reduce idleness by letting the remaining two take turns doing the task at the third station. Other improvements are possible if more than one person can be assigned to a single work station. Finally, if the desired output level exceeds the line capability, further work analysis may be helpful. Bottleneck operations may be reexamined by time study, or methods improvements may be sought to reduce task time. These topics are covered more fully in a future chapter.

Figure 7-13   Revised diagram for storm window assembly

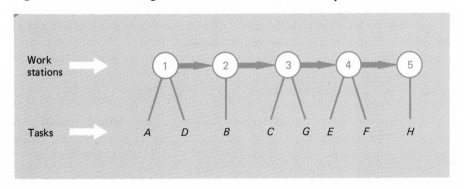

237

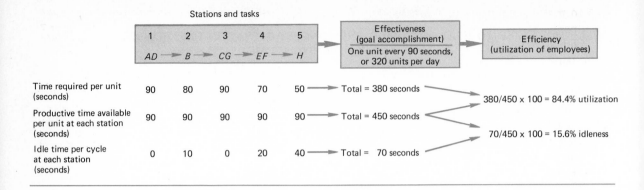

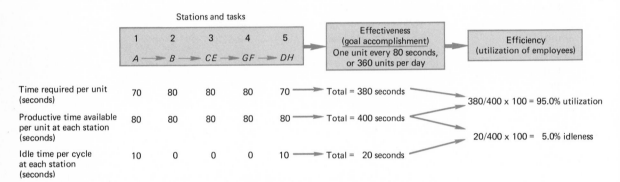

Figure 7-14 **Assembly line designs for 90-second and 80-second cycles**

Behavioral Aspects of Product Layout

It is not suprising that the major behavioral issues in product-oriented layouts revolve around employee satisfaction, motivation, and potential boredom. These topics will be touched upon only briefly here; they are covered more thoroughly in Chapter 9.

Historically, the assumption has been that ever-increasing job specialization would lead to increased labor productivity. Experience has shown this assumption to be true up to a point. In some cases in which productivity has increased, however, there have also been some unexpected costs. Sometimes routinization leads to job dissatisfaction, absenteeism, and higher employee turnover. Often employees feel that as jobs become more highly specified, something gets "lost"; the work tends to become meaningless. When this happens, productivity may decrease. Recently, some behavioral concepts for overcoming these problems have been proposed.

Job enrichment is an approach to job design that tries to make jobs meaningful to employees. Using various methods, management helps employees understand that although their own small tasks may seem unimportant, they are really all vital; otherwise they wouldn't exist. One way to make employees feel involved is to give them information about daily performance on output, quality, and costs.

Job enlargement involves redesigning job content to overcome monotony, boredom, and routinization. Perhaps new tasks or tasks requiring a variety of movements and skills can be added to workers' jobs so that routinized work patterns can be broken up. Although job enlargement is not always successful, it has been helpful in jobs with routine, repetitive tasks with low cycle times (two minutes or less).

Job rotation does not involve redesigning work tasks but merely rotating employees periodically from job to job. Rotation provides a change of pace, which can reduce the boredom of routine tasks.

Theories and suggestions for implementing job enlargement/ enrichment programs abound. The operations manager, however, should exercise caution in arriving at firm conclusions about their potential. Sometimes managers feel that all routine, repetitive tasks are undesirable and should be eliminated. This is not necessarily true. For *some* employees, routine tasks may be disagreeable, but others acutally prefer them. This issue emphasizes once again that the ability to find a good match-up between employees and work assignments is a vital skill for a manager of a product-oriented facility. If you decide to incorporate some enlargement/enrichment ideas in the design of an assembly line, you may want to remember these suggestions:

1. Try to avoid rigid pacing lines.
2. Use short lines (few people) where possible.
3. Try to use single-product lines rather than mixed-product lines.
4. Achieve task variety by rotating workers.
5. Give consideration to allowing workers to determine work content at each station.
6. Develop selection procedures for finding and employing people who like repetitive work.
7. Develop ways to help managers and engineering specialists understand each others' technical and personnel problems in designing and using assembly lines.[5]

SUMMARY

Layout decisions are made only periodically. Since they have long-run consequences, they must be planned carefully. The layout design ultimately affects the cost of producing goods and delivering services for many years into the future. As plans are developed, we must consider their implications for organizing and controlling.

We have discussed three basic layout formats: process, product, and fixed-position. Process layouts are arranged in such a way that work centers or departments are grouped together according to the type of function they perform. Product layouts arrange work centers and equipment in a line so that

[5]These and other guidelines appear in Richard B. Chase, "Strategic Considerations in Assembly-Line Selection," *California Management Review* (Fall 1975), pp. 17–23.

a specialized sequence of operations will result in product buildup. In a fixed-position layout, the product remains in one location, and resources are brought to it.

For process and product layouts, the design begins with a statement of the goals of the facility. Layouts are designed to meet these goals. After initial designs have been developed, improved designs are sought. This can be a cumbersome and tedious task because the number of possible designs is so large. For this reason, quantitative and computer-based models are often used to assist the designer. The models for process and product layouts are distinctly different: process models generally minimize load (volume)-distance moved relationships, and product models generally focus on minimizing idle labor time through line-balancing techniques.

The planner must not become too enamored with quantitative considerations; behavioral factors may be equally or more important. The behavioral aspects of layout provide some useful guides for planning, and the operations manager must remember to consider the needs of employees in the planning process. Such approaches as job enrichment, job enlargement, and job rotation can help employees understand their role in the organization and minimize boredom.

CASE

Sonographic Sound Systems, Inc.

SSS is a small local manufacturer of high quality phonographs. For two years, SSS has produced its most popular portable phonograph on an eight-hour shift at a rate of 84 units per day. Management is satisfied with existing plant capacity but is concerned about the labor efficiency of its main assembly line. Fred Regos, operations manager, has asked his industrial engineer to recommend a redesign of the existing assembly line, because the vice-president has established a goal of increasing labor utilization without decreasing output rate. This goal is consistent with the broader goal of a cost reduction of 10 percent for the production facility.

The assembly line currently has seven stations in which a total of ten tasks are performed. The task descriptions, times, and precedence relations are as follows:

Task	Description	Must follow (predecessor)	Task time (minutes)
A	Load chassis frame	—	1
B	Insert gear assembly on frame	A	2
C	Install electric motor on frame	A	4
D	Assemble turntable stem to gear assembly	B	2
E	Install rubber bearing assembly onto gear assembly	B	1
F	Mount, fit, and fasten turntable mechanism to stem	D	5
G	Interconnect gear and motor assemblies	C and E	1
H	Install turntable	F and G	3
I	Install tone arm assembly	G	4
J	Install and fasten cover	H and I	3

The existing assembly line and personnel are:

Station	1	2	3	4	5	6	7
Work content	*A* and *B*	*D* and *E*	*C* and *G*	*F*	*H*	*I*	*J*
Worker	Alice	Tom	Bill	Debbie	Sam	Clorice	Ike

All employees have been with SSS two years or more. Tom finds that he has time on his hands and enjoys chatting with Alice. In all his time at SSS, Sam has never worked at another station. Although Bill doesn't like to perform task *G*, he takes great pride in his skill at doing *C*. Clorice and Ike agree that their jobs tend to get boring.

What changes would you recommend to Fred Regos? What reactions to these changes would you expect from the line employees?

1. What important organizational goals should one consider before developing a layout design?

2. Describe and illustrate the significant relationships among the capacity and layout decisions.

3. What relationships exist between the layout and location decisions?

4. What are some examples of organizations in which layout is of major significance? Minor significance?

5. Compare and contrast the characteristics of intermittent and continuous conversion operations.

6. Give examples of organizations that have predominantly product, process, and fixed-position layouts.

7. Identify and describe the different models used to assist the layout designer.

8. Compare the manual and quantitative models for process layout design. What are the advantages of each kind of model?

9. Compare the manual and quantitative models for product-oriented layout design. What are the advantages of each kind of model?

10. To what extent do the quantitative layout models consider behavioral factors?

11. Identify the primary behavioral factors involved in process-oriented layout design. Give examples.

12. Identify the primary behavioral factors involved in product-oriented layout design. Give examples.

13. What are some organizations in which behavioral considerations might be a major layout concern? In what kinds of organizations would they be of minor concern?

14. Some would contend that employees generally should not have a major voice in layout design. Others argue that the layout should be developed in a participative manner, with major involvement by employees. Discuss this issue.

15. Compare differences in design strategies for developing an initial layout design (for a new facility) and for developing a revised layout design (for an existing facility).

16. (a) Give an example of a situation in which behavioral factors are a major consideration in layout design.

    (b) What types of behaviors must be considered?

    (c) What strategy would you use for incorporating these factors into your design?

PROBLEMS

1. A manufacturing company incurs a variable cost of $40 per unit produced and receives revenues of $60 per unit. Two alternative layout designs are being considered for finished goods storage and shipment. The first alternative would involve loading the products directly into trucks for shipment at a large loading facility near the end of the assembly lines. Annual fixed costs of operation of the large truck fleet would be $300,000; materials handling costs would be $150,000.

   The second alternative, a large warehouse near the assembly area, would result in a truck fleet costing $170,000 annually, average additional inventory carrying costs annually of $100,000, $45,000 each year to manage and maintain inventories, $10,000 damage to products annually, and $20,000 per year to load, operate, and maintain the conveyance equipment from the assembly area to the warehouse.

   Existing fixed costs of operation (in addition to the two layout alternatives) are $600,000 per year. What impact, if any, do the layout designs have on the company's breakeven volume of operation?

2. A custom packaging company is designing a one-floor facility that is 60 units long on each side in overall dimensions. Nine processing departments, each 20 × 20 units, are to be located within the structure. The number of loads to be transported among departments is:

ANNUAL NUMBER OF LOADS AMONG DEPARTMENTS

Depart-ment	Fabri-cation	Packing	Paper	Leather	Wood	Glass	Sheet metal	Forming	Assembly
Fabri-cation	—	200	100	100	50	—	50	—	200
Packing	—	—	300	50	100	50	—	—	600
Paper	—	—	—	—	200	—	—	100	—
Leather	—	—	—	—	100	—	50	—	200
Wood	—	—	—	—	—	200	—	—	400
Glass	—	—	—	—	—	—	—	—	300
Sheet metal	—	—	—	—	—	—	—	400	300
Forming	—	—	—	—	—	—	—	—	500

What is your recommended layout?

3. A small printing shop wishes to locate its seven departments in a one-floor building that is 40 units wide and 50 units long. Department sizes are:

Department	Length (units)	Width (units)
Layout	10	10
Cutting	20	10
Shipping	10	10
Supply storage	20	15
Printing	25	20
Binding	20	20
Art	20	20

The average annual number of loads flowing between departments is expected to be:

ANNUAL NUMBER OF LOADS AMONG DEPARTMENTS

To department

From department	Layout	Cutting	Shipping	Supply storage	Printing	Binding	Art
Layout	—	—	—	—	—	—	—
Cutting	—	—	—	100	—	400	—
Shipping	—	—	—	500	—	—	—
Supply storage	—	600	100	—	400	100	—
Printing	—	—	—	—	—	1,200	100
Binding	—	100	1,000	—	200	—	—
Art	—	100	—	—	100	—	—

What is your layout recommendation?

4. Reconsider problem 2. Suppose the costs of transporting each shipment were:

COST PER SHIPMENT ($ PER UNIT DISTANCE OF MOVEMENT)

Department	Fabrication	Packing	Paper	Leather	Wood	Glass	Sheet metal	Forming	Assembly
Fabrication	—	$2.00	1.00	1.00	1.00	—	2.00	—	1.50
Packing	—	—	1.00	1.00	1.00	1.00	—	—	1.00
Paper	—	—	—	—	1.00	—	—	1.00	—
Leather	—	—	—	—	1.00	—	1.00	—	1.00
Wood	—	—	—	—	—	1.00	—	—	2.50
Glass	—	—	—	—	—	—	—	—	4.00
Sheet metal	—	—	—	—	—	—	—	3.00	1.00
Forming	—	—	—	—	—	—	—	—	2.00

(a) What is your recommended layout?

(b) Compare your new layout with your previous recommendation and explain any differences.

5. A group of physicians is considering forming a new medical clinic in a single-story facility in a suburban area. Although design plans are just underway, they have decided to have service departments with these relative sizes (space requirements):

Service department	Size (sq ft)
Laboratory	600
Plastic surgery	600
Patient waiting area	600
Ob./gyn.	800
Neurology	600
Pediatrics	1,800
Pharmacy	400
X-ray	600

The number of patients flowing among pairs of departments during each month are expected to be:

NUMBER OF PATIENTS FLOWING BETWEEN DEPARTMENTS

Department	Lab	Plastic surgery	Waiting	Ob./gyn.	Neurology	Pediatrics	Pharmacy	X-ray
Lab	—	20	50	100	80	200	—	200
Plastic surgery	—	—	70	—	10	—	20	5
Waiting	—	—	—	400	100	900	—	50
Ob./gyn.	—	—	—	—	—	50	40	50
Neurology	—	—	—	—	—	10	20	80
Pediatrics	—	—	—	—	—	—	150	200
Pharmacy	—	—	—	—	—	—	—	30

The physicians are not yet concerned with the overall configuration of the building, just so all departments are on one floor. There is a direct relationship between number of patients and patient walking distances. What relative department locations do you recommend for minimizing patient flows (walking distances)?

6. In considering a new office layout, a designer obtained importance ratings for locating service groups near one another. On a scale of 1 (low importance) to 10 (high importance), service group proximity ratings were:

IMPORTANCE OF CLOSE PROXIMITY AMONG SERVICE GROUPS

Service group	Maintenance	Library	Design	Estimating	Accounting	Computer	Records	Sales engineers	Management
Maintenance	—	—	—	—	—	—	—	—	—
Library	—	—	9	—	—	—	—	2	—
Design	—	—	—	8	—	8	7	10	7
Estimating	—	—	—	—	4	—	2	10	4
Accounting	—	—	—	—	—	6	10	5	3
Computer	—	—	—	—	—	—	2	6	3
Records	—	—	—	—	—	—	—	5	—
Sales engineers	—	—	—	—	—	—	—	—	8

Assume the overall space is 3 units wide and 3 units long; all service group areas are of equal size, 1 unit by 1 unit. What is your recommended layout design?

7. Consider the following production line in which work elements A-H must be performed in alphabetical order:

Work station:	1	2	3	4	5	6
Work elements:	A, B	C	D, E	F	G	H
Element time (minutes):	2, 1.5	4	2, 2	3	2.5	3

(a) Identify the bottleneck operation.
(b) What is the minimum cycle time?
(c) Assuming an eight-hour work day, what is the maximum daily output?
(d) If the line uses one employee per station, how many hours of idle time exist daily? How many hours of productive time?
(e) Calculate the efficiency of the line.

8. An assembly line must be established to include these tasks:

Task	Time (seconds)	Must follow
A	120	—
B	50	A
C	40	B
D	80	C, F
E	100	A
F	20	E
G	90	H
H	60	A
I	30	A
J	60	D, G, I

(a) Construct a precedence diagram for the tasks.
(b) To balance the line to a 120-second minimum cycle time, what is the theoretical minimum number of work stations?
(c) Use the longest-operation-time rule to balance the line to a 120-second cycle.
(d) What is the efficiency of the line?

9. For the data in problem 8, suppose that management desires 200 units of output daily; balance the line to achieve this goal. What is the theoretical minimum number of work stations? Calculate the efficiency of the line. Assume an eight-hour work day.

GLOSSARY

Adjacent loads: movements or flows of products between adjacent departments

Bottleneck operation: of all assembly line work stations, the one that requires the longest operation time

Cycle time: elapsed time between completed units coming off the end of an assembly line

Elemental task: the smallest work task that can be assigned to a work station

Fixed-position layout: facility arrangement in which the product remains in one location; resources are brought to the product location to perform the appropriate stages of buildup

Heuristic: simplification procedure in which a set of rules is systematically applied; results in the discovery of a satisfactory problem solution

Job analysis: minute study of a task in an effort to eliminate unnecessary activity and find ways to do the task faster and cheaper

Job enlargement: redesigning jobs or modifying work content to overcome monotony, boredom, and routinization

Job enrichment: procedure of redesigning work content to make jobs more meaningful by involving employees in planning, organizing, and controlling work

Layout design: location or configuration of departments, work stations, and equipment that constitute the conversion process; spatial arrangement of the physical resources used to create the product

Line balancing: assigning tasks to assembly line stations so that performance times are equalized as much as possible

Load-distance rating: measure of effectiveness of a process-oriented layout; calculated by summing the product of load X distance for all departments

Norms: agreements as to how group members should behave

Precedence requirement: restriction on the order or sequence in which tasks must be performed

Process layout: arrangement of facility so that work centers or departments are grouped together according to the type of function they perform

Product layout: arrangement of facility so that work centers and equipment are in a line; provides specialized sequence of operations that will result in product buildup

SELECTED READINGS

Buffa, Elwood S., Gordon C. Armour, and Thomas Vollmann, "Allocating Facilities with CRAFT," *Harvard Business Review* (March–April 1964): 136–58.

Chase, Richard B. "Strategic Considerations in Assembly-Line Selection." *California Management Review* (Fall 1975): 17–23.

Ignall, Edward J. "A Review of Assembly Line Balancing." *Journal of Industrial Engineering* (July–August 1965): 244–54.

"In McDonald's Offices, Everyone is Out in the Open." *The Office* 84, no. 3 (September 1976): 115–19.

Johnson, Richard A., William T. Newell, and Roger C. Vergin. *Operations Management: A Systems Concept.* Boston: Houghton Mifflin Co., 1972.

Lee, Robert C. and James M. Moore. "CORELAP—Computerized Relationship Layout Planning." *Journal of Industrial Engineering* (March 1967): 195–200.

Mariotti, John. "Four Approaches to Manual Assembly Line Balancing." *Journal of Industrial Engineering* (June 1970): 35–40.

Mastor, Anthony A. "An Experimental Investigation and Comparative Evaluation of Production Line Balancing Techniques." *Management Science* (July 1970): 728–46.

Parsons, J. A. "A Technique for Suboptimal Solutions to the Facilities Layout Problem." *Journal of Systems Management* 25, no. 7 (July 1974): 42–43.

Scriabin, Michael and Roger C. Vergin. "Comparison of Computer Algorithms and Visual Based Methods for Plant Layout." *Management Science* (October 1975): 172–81.

Sommers, M. S. and J. B. Kernan. "A Behavioral Approach to Planning, Layout, and Display." *Journal of Retailing* 41, no. 4 (Winter 1965–66): 21–26.

Terry, George R. *Office Management and Control.* 7th ed. Homewood, Ill: Richard D. Irwin, Inc., 1975.

Tonge, F. M. "Assembly Line Balancing Using Probabilistic Combinations of Heuristics." *Management Science* 11, no. 7 (May 1965): 727–35.

Vollmann, Thomas E. and Elwood S. Buffa. "The Facilities Layout Problem in Perspective." *Management Science* 12, no. 10 (June 1966): B450–58.

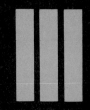

Part

ORGANIZING
FOR
CONVERSION

8

Organizing and Staffing for Operations

As we have said before, production/operations managers plan, organize, and control the conversion of resources into outputs of goods and services. In an earlier chapter, we set forth planning fundamentals; in this one, we present the basics of organizing for operations. Since staffing the organization goes hand in hand with the organizing effort, we'll also discuss that aspect of organizing. For those with a management background, and for those who have studied management fundamentals, this chapter will primarily provide a review.

ORGANIZING FOR OPERATIONS

Organizing Defined

Organizing is the means by which individuals, groups, and facilities are combined in a formal structure of tasks and authority. Through its structure, the organization provides a means for people, equipment, and facility to work together so that they can achieve the organization's goals. In organizations, jobs that are similar in function and use of equipment are grouped into departments. The departments are then related to one another. Thus the organization is built from the job up, not from the top down.

In one sense, an organization can be likened to a machine. A properly designed, functional, finely tuned, well-lubricated machine can be used to achieve output—and achieve it efficiently. Similarly, the organization, if it is well designed, functional, finely tuned, and lubricated with communication channels can be used to achieve output efficiently too. Another

248

analogy may help you understand the role good organization can play. If you were going to travel across the country, you would probably prefer to use a car or a plane instead of a horse or your own feet. Going by foot or on horseback wouldn't be impossible, but it would be difficult and slow. Similarly, a business can be run without effective organization, but it's a difficult task. Good organization can assist operations managers in achieving output goals, just as cars and planes can get you across the country, faster and easier than those goals can be achieved without it. And like cars and planes, organization is a *means* to an end, not the end in itself. The "end" in operations is the output goal: output is delivered on time, of desired quality, and with efficient use of resources. Proper organization can help get you there.

Planning, Organizing and Controlling

You may remember that in Chapter 1, we advocated a functional approach to management that focuses on planning, organizing, and controlling. Although in this chapter we focus on organizing, you should keep in mind that all the functions are interrelated, as we show in Figure 8-1. Coordinating, directing, motivating, and staffing, although they are not shown on the figure, are also related to organizing. The organizing function provides a structure of tasks and authority. This structure specifies formal relationships among individuals and groups. In the planning process, these formal relationships are used to develop courses of action, and in the control process, they are used to communicate feedback. Obviously, if organization is poor, both planning and control suffer considerably, and so do all the other functions related to organizing.

EXAMPLE

At Trinity Lutheran Church, democracy is emphasized in decision making. Because Trinity was growing rapidly, it was becoming exceedingly difficult to plan and control church operations through the various boards and the Voters Assembly. The Board of Education and the Boards of Finance and Stewardship referred most decisions directly to the Voters Assembly, where meetings were long, and ultimate decision making was slowed considerably. Planning was difficult and untimely. Realizing there was a deficiency in organizing, the Voters Assembly directed a charter study to examine reorganization and delegation of authority to lower levels. Subsequent reorganization placed more decision making in the hands of the individual boards and a new Board of Directors, which consisted of board chairpersons and other officers. Voters Assembly meetings, now fewer, focus on critical policy issues of the church. An organization that allows improved planning and control within the church operations was developed.

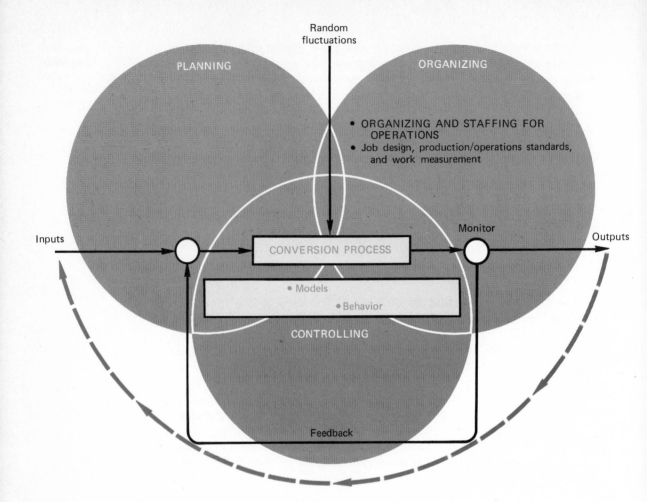

Random
fluctuations

PLANNING

ORGANIZING

- ORGANIZING AND STAFFING FOR OPERATIONS
- Job design, production/operations standards, and work measurement

Inputs

Monitor

Outputs

CONVERSION PROCESS

- Models
  - Behavior

CONTROLLING

Feedback

Figure 8-1 **Production / operations management activities**

Organization Charts

Line and staff   A line function in an organization is generally responsible for attaining the primary goals of creation,
distribution, and financing the output of goods or services. Thus, produc-
tion/operations, marketing, and finance are usually considered line functions. They derive directly from operational activities. Staff functions, on
the other hand, are supportive; they assist the line functions. They advise,
support, analyze, and recommend to line functions. Consequently, line
functions contribute directly to reaching the organization's goals, and staff
functions contribute more indirectly. Sometimes the roles of these two
functions are hard to distinguish, and the degree to which a function
is line or staff becomes a matter of judgment. How much does the function
directly contribute to the attainment of the organization's primary goals?
If the degree is high, it is probably a line function; if the degree is low,
it's probably a staff function. Within each overall line function, there

can be, and usually are, staff functions as well. To assist the line production manager, for example, production control is often organized in a staff capacity. To keep these functional relationships straight, management often constructs an organization chart.

Constructing the organization chart An organization chart is a graphical model of the formal structure of an organization. In such a chart, the boxes represent formal organization positions, and the lines between the boxes represent lines of authority among positions.

Figure 8-2 shows a typical organization chart for an insurance company. The chart has been simplified to illustrate the basic line functions of this company: underwriting, claims, marketing, and finance. The vertical line from the president to these functions designates them as line activities and indicates the authority hierarchy. The production/operations functions in the insurance service take place in underwriting and claims, the activities that create insurance. The horizontal line from the president to administrative services designates administrative services as a staff function. Administrative services, including personnel, legal, and computer services, assist the president in meeting the primary goals of the insurance company. This chart illustrates the formal chain of command. Note that the key elements of the organization chart are the boxes, which designate functions, and the lines, which designate authority, in this case line and staff authority. The organization chart is a straightforward schematic model that pictorially depicts relationships among variables.

How useful is an organization chart? It depends on the needs and knowledge of the user. Just as such other schematic models as toy assembly sketches and road maps are useful only if the person who has them understands the lines and symbols, an organization chart is helpful only if its symbols and relationships are clearly understood. A good chart can assist in clarifying lines of authority, or it can be used to explain organizational relationships to new employees. But the mere existence of the chart doesn't guarantee its usefulness.

If you have an outdated road map or a map of Indiana when you are traveling through California, it doesn't do you much good. Neither does an outdated or inappropriate organization chart. To be effective, the

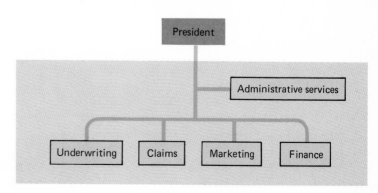

Figure 8-2 Insurance company organization chart

organization chart doesn't need to be widely distributed. Sometimes detailed, current charts are kept in a desk in the chief operating office, and lines of authority are communicated verbally. This is perfectly all right; it's better not to distribute a chart at all than to distribute one that is dysfunctional. In practice, most charts are used to keep track of changes in the organization as they are made rather than for specifying the organization in advance. It's more important for operations managers to keep track of authority changes as they take place than it is to specify those changes on a revised, distributed chart.

Approaches to Organizing

Five basic approaches to organizing are useful to the production/operations manager: organizing by product, by customer, by geographical area, by function, and by project. Most organizations use some combination of these basic approaches.

Product

In many firms, the product or service is the focus of the organizing effort. In city government, work units are created for street and road service, utility services, and social services. Production in conglomerate companies is often organized by product, with managers in charge of chemicals, metal fabrication, drugs, and so on. If an insurance company were organized by product, life, health, automobile, and home insurance services might be handled separately, as shown in Figure 8-3.

Customer

Jobs may be grouped according to the type of customer being served. For a metal fabrication company, customers might be automobile or appliance manufacturers. In our insurance company example, two types of clients could be identified: industrial and general consumers. (See Figure 8-4.) Below the customer level is product

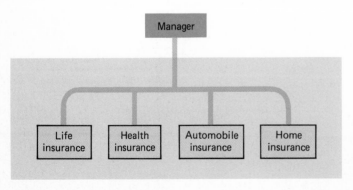

Figure 8-3 **Organization by product in an insurance company**

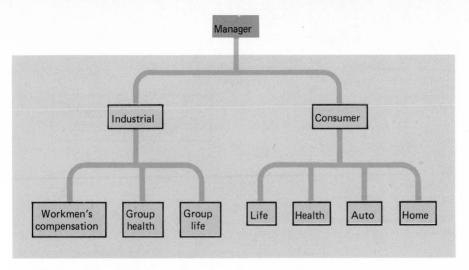

Figure 8-4   **Organization by customer in an insurance company**

organization; life, health, auto, and home insurance for consumers are handled separately from workmen's compensation, group health, and group life insurance for industrial clients. If you compare Figures 8-3 and 8-4, you'll see that the same company can use more than one form of organization, depending on its individual situation.

Geographical area   Often production/operations are organized on a geo-graphical basis. In our discussion of facility location, we found that locations close to customers were often chosen for many products and services. In these instances production and operations are usually grouped within a firm by geographical areas. Commonly, firms are organized first by country or international region (United States, Canadian, and European operations, for example) and then further organized within those regions (northern, southern, eastern, and western operations). Our insurance company has the marketing and claims functions divided into the western and eastern United States; these are further divided by states within these major geographical areas.

Function   The most common basis for oganizing is according to the functions being performed by people in the unit, the work being carried out. (This was illustrated in Figure 8-2.) In Figure 8-5 we have shown the production function in a manufacturing setting, the Columbia, South Carolina, works of a paper company. Notice that the primary line activity under the production manager is divided into two product groups, (1) corrugated boxes and (2) noncorrugated boxes and papers. Managers of staff activities who report to the works manager include those in charge of production control, technical services, quality assurance, and plant personnel. As they are drawn on the organization

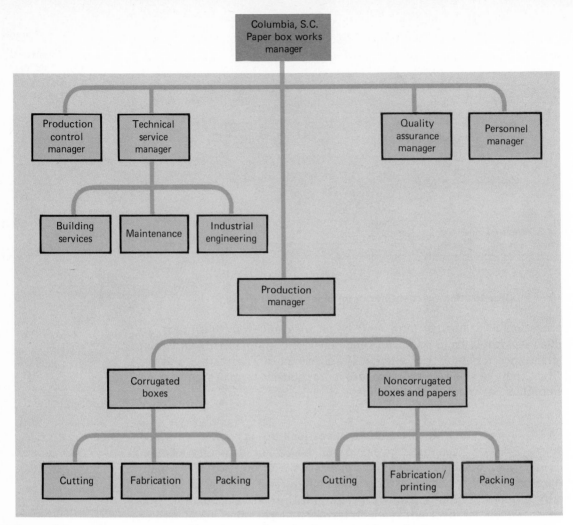

Figure 8-5 **Organization chart of production function in a paper box plant**

chart, these staff functions appear to be designated as line functions. The actual functions provide analysis, support, and recommendations to the works manager concerning production. In actual organization charts, one must be cautious; downward flowing functions are not always line functions, as organization theory would lead us to believe. This paper company is a typical manufacturing organization in that the primary function, production, is divided into two subfunctions and secondary (support, staff) functions.

Figure 8-6 allows us to illustrate a point we have been stressing in this book, that some operations functions in service organizations correspond to production functions in manufacturing companies. The managers of the primary functions of accounting, customer relations, bonds and collections, and internal operations all report to the vice-president of operations at a commercial bank. Staff functions of personnel and the support staff (switchboard, custodians, etc.) also support operations.

How can we tell whether the downward flowing activities are line or staff functions? Strict interpretation of the organization chart says that all the functions at both the paper company and the commercial bank *are shown as line.* Interpreting some, bank personnel, for example, as staff is purely subjective on our part. There can be little argument about the importance of the personnel function to production/operations. The extent to which this function "contributes to the primary production goals" or is "supportive" determines whether the function is line or staff. From experience and visits with managers in many such organizations, we *judged* certain activities to be staff, even though they are shown as line.

Again, we caution you to not assume that a function that is supportive and clearly staff in nature will always flow horizontally. Those managers who construct organization charts often block out major functions without regard to their line or staff designation. Such was the case at the paper company and the commercial bank.

Project

A convenient way to organize operations is by the product mission concept. A project, one short set of

Figure 8-6   **Organization chart of operations function in a commercial bank**

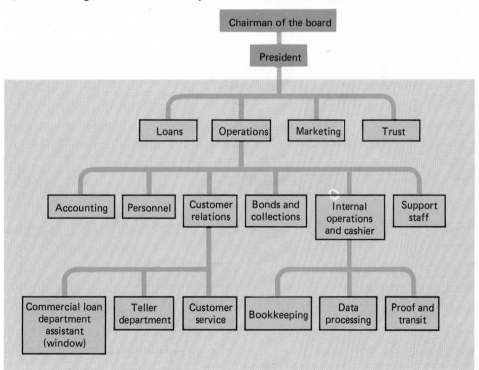

activities, often consists of products designed to accomplish one specific mission. Project (program) organization, a modification of the product and functional organization approaches, is quite useful in government, research and development, and large-scale construction projects like the Alaskan pipeline.

Figure 8-7 illustrates project organization within the National Aeronautics and Space Administration (NASA). The project (program) level of NASA is illustrated by the various offices shown. Such individual projects as APOLLO and its subprojects would appear at lower levels in the organization chart. It is difficult, at the general level illustrated here, to see very much difference between function and project management. The main difference has to do with the expected duration of the functional unit or group. In project organizations, the work units know in advance that the group may be disbanded upon termination of the project.

Classical Organization Concepts for Operations Managers

Several concepts regarding organization need to be clearly understood by the production/operations manager. As an operations manager, you will be required to organize and reorganize operations, since in the conversion process, part of the business is often capital and labor intense. Once you master these ideas, other managerial functions will be much easier.

Goals

It is difficult, if not impossible, to organize without clear goals. Without clear, concise goals, it is difficult to group jobs into departments, relate departments to one another, and delineate line and staff activities. Goal formation is a phase of planning, a phase that should be accomplished before, or at least concurrent with, the organizing effort.

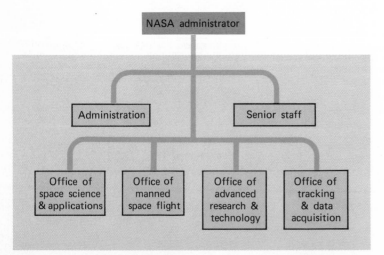

Figure 8-7 **Project organization within NASA**

Authority and responsibility
Authority is the right to give orders (to command); responsibility is the duty to be accountable. Authority is delegated from superiors to subordinates; then the subordinate assumes responsibility. Authority flows from the top of the organization downward, and responsibility flows back up the organization. The delegation of authority does not relieve the delegator of the responsibility for performance. You cannot delegate away responsibility; you delegate only the right to command or direct. When a manager delegates, he or she shares responsibility.

Unfortunately, to be an effective delegator of authority, one has to overcome some barriers. One of these is fear. Sometimes supervisors, afraid that subordinates will fail, try to do everything themselves. Sometimes they're afraid that giving up part of their jobs to someone else will result in a loss of their own job security, so they hesitate to delegate authority to anyone else. Another barrier is a lack of communication and planning. To delegate, a supervisor must plan ahead, decide whom to delegate to, communicate with that person, and follow up to assure that the task is being performed. (This follow up is part of the control function.) Although many managers find it difficult to delegate authority, it is an essential part of managing, and with training, barriers like these can be overcome. Perhaps someone will coach you in delegating a little at a time. Like any other skill, this one can be learned, and it's important for you to learn it.

Span of control
Span of control reflects the number of subordinates who report directly to the supervisor. Some classical theorists suggested specific numbers for proper span of control—four for top management and eight to twelve for lower management, for example. We have since abandoned the search for a single span of control that would be "best" for all situations. Rather, behavioral and organizational research studies have identified three factors that directly affect the span of control, the characteristics of the supervisor, the subordinate, and the job itself.

===== EXAMPLE =====

A recent business school graduate was working as a line foreman in his father's construction company. The company's principal operations involved laying telephone cables cross-country for major utilities. The company operated in some twenty midwestern and southwestern states. The new foreman had experimented with several different numbers of employees and found that a crew of eight was ideal. Usually, these eight were spread out in at least two physical locations; some control and direction had to be exercised hourly over their work. The new foreman wondered why his professors in business school had not pointed out to him that eight was the proper span of control.

Probably the new line foreman's professors had told him that the span of control varies with the situation. The characteristics of this particular situation—a new foreman, workers in several locations, and backhoe and manual labor tasks—demanded a span of control of eight. But different characteristics—say an experienced foreman, a single location, and more group tasks—might call for a larger span of control.

Unity of command   The flow of authority in an organization is often called a chain of command. If you look again at Figure 8-4, you'll see that one flow of authority is from the manager to the industrial division supervisor to the workmen's compensation supervisor. The chain of command follows this same path. Unity of command is somewhat different. A classical concept that is still valid for production and operations, it requires that a subordinate shall have one and only one supervisor. In Figure 8-4, the industrial division supervisor has only one supervisor, the manager. Unity of command does *not* imply that the supervisor has only one subordinate. There will be occasions when the unity of command principle will be violated, temporary assignments to committees or special assignments under another supervisor, for example. We have found, however, that employees like the idea of having one supervisor who disciplines, evaluates performance, approves vacations, and oversees their overall job-related activities.

At times in production, under pressure to meet delivery dates and produce output, supervisors have a tendency to jump the chain of command. A first-line supervisor might skip the shift foreman and give information to and receive instructions from the plant manager or works manager. This undercuts the authority of the shift foreman and makes his job very difficult. If it continues, why have the shift foreman at all? From a human relations standpoint especially, jumping the chain of command must be stopped. The best person to stop it is the highest level supervisor involved; he or she has the authority to insist on following proper procedure. If the supervisor who is caught in the middle, like our shift foreman, can confront his supervisor with specific complaints, perhaps the problem can be resolved. But don't count on it. If you're the production/operations manager and someone beneath you has a complaint, he'll probably come to you, and it'll be your responsibility to enforce the chain of command.

Models of Organizational Structure

Several models suggest ways to organize group effort. It is beyond the scope of this book to present these models in detail, so we'll briefly mention them here. If someday you face major organizational problems, or if you are interested in these models now, you can find in the selected readings at the end of this chapter several excellent books on the subject.

1. *Bureaucratic Model.* Max Weber's bureaucratic model consists of characteristics such as fixed official duties, hierarchy in organizations,

a complete set of abstract rules for every event, impersonality, and technical qualifications for positions in the organization. It is rigid and not subject to change.

2. *McGregor's Theory X and Theory Y.* These theories of organizational structure contrast the essentials of the bureaucratic model (Theory X) with the essentials of human relations (Theory Y). McGregor is making a case for more personalization of relationships in organizing as he supports Theory Y.

3. *Matrix Approach.* Andre L. Delbecq and others developed this approach to organizing. It considers the nature of the task, the personality of the personnel, and the historical circumstances associated with each unit.

4. *Technology.* Joan Woodward, after ten years of research in Great Britain, classifies firms according to the complexity of technology: small batch production, large batch and mass production, and long-run continuous process production. Successful firms in each of these classes tend to have similar organizational structures.

5. *Open System Organizations.* James D. Thompson describes this approach to organizing, which emphasizes reactions to changes in goals, the environment, and other key elements that make up the organization. Policies and rules must be flexible so that the organization can be changed as environmental circumstances change.

In production/operations it is rare to see any one model used alone, but it is not so unusual to find a dominant model in any one situation.

Building the Organization

The bottoms-up approach

Often students involved in case exercises tend to focus their reorganizing efforts on the higher levels of the organization, assigning various functions to vice-presidents, regrouping major divisions, and so on. This view, which we will call tops-down reorganization, is often encouraged by the available data in the case. Unfortunately, first-level and middle-level managers also tend to look for tops-down reorganization, often complaining about how their jobs are hampered by managers above them. Our answer to this is to encourage you, as potential first-line and middle-line managers, to take a bottoms-up approach to organizational change. Get involved. Start with examining the job content of those jobs for which you are responsible. Many managers do not know what their own subordinates are doing on a daily basis. Once your own work area and jobs have been properly analyzed and tasks grouped into logical, meaningful, productive jobs, you will be in a position to exert influence upward concerning reorganization of parallel or superior jobs and work units.

We are not suggesting that organizations cannot be designed from the top down. All good architects and builders have an idea about how the final buildings will look, even though they design or build the footings and foundations before they do the roofs. Likewise, although an overall view of the final production/operations organization is helpful, we suggest that organization change can most effectively be brought about by focusing first on individual jobs, the building blocks of any organization. Let's examine some useful techniques for job analysis.

Job analysis   Job analysis, the study of similar tasks performed by one or more people, is aimed at discovering the responsibilities, duties, and educational and skill requirements necessary for doing a particular job. It is similar to work measurement and job design, which are covered elsewhere in this book. All three have one requirement in common: before you can improve them, you must know the existing job content.

Job descriptions   Job analysis results in job descriptions and job specifications. Job descriptions are used for organizing, job evaluation, selection and placement, training and development, safety, labor relations, methods improvement, wage and salary surveys, and counseling. Our primary concern here is the use of the job description in organizing.

There are several approaches to job analysis, including the personal interviews, direct observation, and written questionnaires. We prefer an approach that begins with a questionnaire, so that we can get information from employees. Then, from a personal interview of from 30 to 60 minutes at the work station, we can get a good audit of the job and assure that our analysis is complete. After the job analysis has been completed, the job description is prepared. It can be used as written documentation of the responsibilities, duties, and requirements involved in the job. The job description provides a good basis for reassignment of duties and responsibilities, and can result in a change in the organization.

EXAMPLE

A large metropolitan public library had existed for decades and prided itself in its extensive collection and services. Jobs in the library, which employed 235 people, had never been documented. A new director, hired from another geographical region, wanted to make some organizational changes, but he needed specific job information that was available only to experienced personnel. After discussion of needs and approaches with us, he decided to hire a recent college graduate, have us train him in job analysis and preparing job descriptions, and postpone the reorganization effort until all jobs were documented as they currently existed. We assisted in developing job analysis procedures and training the new employee. The procedure involved two steps; all the employees documented their jobs, and then the job analyst (the new employee) verified these documentations with the employees and their supervisors. After six months, a complete set of job descriptions was ready and the reorganization study began.

Departmentalization Jobs are grouped by some characteristic similarities into homogeneous units called departments. Departments differ, of course, from one type of organization to another. In a Sears store, household, men's wear, and women's wear make up some of the departments; in a Chevrolet assembly plant, painting, assembly, and maintenance units form departments; and in the Army, infantry, supply, and engineering are separately grouped. At a higher level in the organization, departments are grouped by function, geographic location, or other criteria. The groupings may result in operating divisions, plants, works, or similar organizational units in conversion processes. The grouping of departments is basically a matter of weighting and balancing the advantages and disadvantages of alternative approaches.

Developing an Some people feel that although the classical concepts
organization that we've discussed are important to understand, they leave us a bit in the dark as to how to proceed in developing a new organization on a step by step basis. One expert suggests that these steps might be helpful:

1. Clearly determine the objective of the enterprise.
2. List the areas of activity by main division and subdivision. This listing of activities should be complete. It should include tools, products, and processes and will suggest some natural divisions.
3. Determine the ideal structure to accomplish the desired activities regardless of availability of funds or personnel. Because this structure is ideal and no regard has been given to funds or personnel, it might never be implemented.
4. Make a detailed survey of available personnel from the point of view of capacities and abilities. List all personnel currently in the organization and those available from outside the organization. Clearly indicate their capabilities and abilities.
5. Revise the "ideal" organization in light of the available personnel and funds. This will result in the current working organization.[1]

This list is not out of line with the bottoms-up concept. Although the procedure applies to new organizations and the bottoms-up concept applies more to reorganization and improvements, both aim at a realistic approach to bringing about a good organization for production or operations.

The Informal Organization

The organization chart delineates formal relationships among supervisors and subordinates. These relationships do not necessarily exist in reality. Often within the formal organization is an informal one with its own

[1]Claude S. George, Jr., *Management for Business and Industry*, rev. ed. (Englewood Cliffs, N.J.: Prentice-Hall, Inc., 1970), pp. 108–109.

authority, responsibility, and communication channels. Such an informal organization is not necessarily either good or bad, but you should be aware of its frequent existence. If there is an informal organization substantially different from the formal organization, often it's the result of poor management. Sometimes ineffective supervisors do not clearly delegate authority. As a result, responsibility is sometimes assumed by people other than those who should be assuming it. If subordinates are accomplishing tasks and meeting organizational goals beyond their responsibilities, they are often elevated in the informal organization to positions of importance far beyond their official positions. When management is poor, a situation like this can exist throughout the whole organization. Since the wage and salary structure is designed for the formal organization, exceptional performance is not systematically recognized, evaluated, and rewarded.

Subordinates as well as supervisors can encourage an informal organization. Often at lower levels in the organization, employees who have limited group work experience and education just cannot perceive formal organization relationships. They tend to go to people whom they know will get things done rather than those who should be getting things done. Employees at these lower levels can provide some interesting insights into the informal organization, and the effective operations manager makes use of their information.

Simply because managers have formal power does not necessarily mean that they exercise actual power. Often a dominant coalition, a powerful group of perhaps half a dozen people across several levels within the organization, emerges informally. People who make up these coalitions rely on informal communication networks, and they can dominate the entire organization in establishing and accomplishing goals. Within a complex organization, informal power groups can exist at various levels and within many functions, including operations.

Organization Fallacies

In stressing organizational concepts, we don't mean to imply that they're the answer to every problem you may face. For one thing, if they're not clearly understood, they may be misapplied. No concept, no matter how useful, is without fallacies. In the hope that you'll be able to avoid them, let's look at some mistaken ideas about organizing.

Organization/
reorganization

How much effort should be expended on organizing and reorganizing? There is a limit to how much effort should be spent on organizing and reorganizing to gain efficiency and effectiveness. Continued emphasis on reorganization can impede the conversion process. An inordinate amount of time spent in reorganizing and again reorganizing steals time that should be spent on planning, directing, controlling, and other managerial activities. The result can be an overall decrease in organization productivity.

The employee and the organization

In the long run, the keys to an effective organization are the employees who hold the positions. If the organization provides the machinery for accomplishing goals, the people provide the fuel for performance. It is a mistake to believe that the organizational structure can accomplish organizational goals. Goal accomplishment is aided by effective organizing, but it is accomplished by people working together toward a common end.

The systems approach

The systems approach has been and will continue to be stressed in this book. We do not suggest, however, that a systems approach should be allowed to dominate organizing efforts. It isn't necessary for the entire marketing, finance, and production systems to be organized at once. If waiting for a general reorganization would inhibit job analysis, job design, and job regrouping at the grass roots level, then reorganization can and should be piecemeal. Often, for example, as key staff are changed, job regrouping becomes necessary. Operations managers' characteristics may have to be reexamined if new employees and new jobs become their responsibilities.

Job regrouping concepts, based on situational leadership theory, allow for matching jobs with managers and subordinates. Regrouping at a specific level within the organization can often take place without waiting for a total system reorganization.

Constraints in Personnel Decisions

Once production and operations have been established, staff must be acquired to fill the positions in the organization. Traditionally, personnel management has not been treated in books on production/operations management. Although we will not consider staffing problems and solution techniques in depth, we think it will be helpful to present an overview. Our reasoning is simple: it is not practical to assume that labor and management skills are readily available; they must be acquired. Since staffing for production/operations is often assigned to production/operations managers, they must either handle staffing themselves or organize a personnel management staff to assist them (see Figures 8-5 and 8-6). Let's examine some constraints that the production/operations manager must consider when staffing the organization.

Individual differences

Individuals differ in their abilities to perform different tasks, and these differences must be considered when staffing decisions are made. In verbal and intellectual capacities, you must assume no differences between men and women, younger and older workers, and people of all geographical and racial backgrounds. Of course, people have varying educational backgrounds, skill and experience levels, and personalities, and you should take these into account when you hire people for specific jobs. It's also a good idea to have a wide age distribution, so that when some workers retire, others have been trained to take their places.

Cultural
differences

If your organization has facilities in other countries, cultural variations may require some adaptation. Many studies illustrate the worker and managerial differences attributable to cultures. Managers in Nordic-European countries, Latin-European countries, the United States, Great Britain, developing countries, and Japan all show similar attitudes on some dimensions and distinctly different attitudes on others. These cultural differences are extremely important when decisions are made concerning the design of jobs and the selection of managers to supervise facilities. Consider the modification of quality control procedures due to cultural differences in the following example.

=== EXAMPLE ===

Quality control in the United States and Canada is a job concept that focuses on statistical analysis and error detection with correction on the job. Often quality control departments are established in manufacturing with the staff authority to monitor quality. In Japan, there is a unique concept of Quality Circles (QC) that is culturally based. Japanese workers are employed by a company for life. Within a company, the operative workers form small circles (4 to 12 members) in which quality improvement is studied and discussed. These QC groups meet frequently in a social setting and discuss job quality and methods for improvement. Quality control is not a staff function kept at work but rather an intregral part of the life style of the operative worker. QC circles have been extremely effective in Japan and are widely recognized and discussed at international meetings of such groups as the American Society for Quality Control.

Geographical
differences

Consideration should be given to the geographical area within a country when operations are being located and subsequently staffed. In attitudes, work efficiency, and the availability of professional personnel, there are some differences among urban, rural, and underdeveloped areas. Because suburban and rural areas offer improved productivity and labor availability, there seems to be a trend toward locating facilities there. If you plan to build a facility in a new location, you might keep in mind that many professionals prefer to live in a small community near a major city, but that underdeveloped areas are often a source of eager, although sometimes unskilled, workers. All employees want to live and work in areas with good health care, a pleasant climate, and low taxes. Although facility location involves many more considerations than these (see Chapter 6), the needs of both professional and nonprofessional workers should be a factor in the final decision.

It is more difficult to staff in some industries than in others. Some reasons for these difficulties are:

- selected industries must locate near raw material sources in remote areas;
- some industries have a high propensity for strikes;
- traditionally, low wages prevail in some industries because of the economic nature of the product or service;
- cyclical characteristics of an industry may lead to unstable employment; and
- a high degree of government regulation may pose staffing difficulties.

In the 1960s and 1970s, many college graduates have shown a willingness to trade financial rewards for jobs, like those in environmental and pollution control, that they consider meaningful and socially responsible. When trends like this occur, staffing in currently preferred industries is easier than it is in others. Recently, for example, industries dealing with noise, water, and air pollution control have had an advantage in staffing over such traditional industries as steel, automotive, and mining.

Legal framework:
EEOC

Perhaps the most significant legislation affecting staffing patterns of the last several decades consists of the set of laws administered by the Equal Employment Opportunity Commission (EEOC). The EEOC requires equal opportunity for employment and advancement regardless of sex, age, race, or national origin. Initially, the EEOC focused voluntary employer compliance, but more and more the agency is turning to the courts when the laws have been violated.

From the operations manager's viewpoint, one of the more significant developments is the class action suit. In a class action suit, an individual who feels he or she has been discriminated against may sue an employer on behalf of all those who are being, or might have been, similarly mistreated. Once the suit process has begun, the employer may not attempt to talk the plaintiffs into a settlement. The employer can be sued for lost past pay and benefits and mental anguish suffered while the discrimination was taking place. The class action suit (the individual is a member of a class) must come to trial. These suits are very costly for employers since they must gather data, pay legal fees, and possibly make class payments. Attorneys representing those who bring class action suits find these cases attractive, both because their fees are usually a percentage of the class settlement and because many lawyers feel that discrimination has actually taken place. Consequently, there is no shortage of attorneys willing to help their clients bring a class action suit.

The best way to avoid a class action suit in production/operations is to become informed about the law—and enforce it. Take seminars; read government publications; talk to your company's personnel staff specialists. Since the law applies to all employers except small companies that do not engage in interstate commerce, most production/operations managers must see to it that the law is obeyed. Many organizations have already established Affirmative Action programs designed to bring themselves into compliance within a specified time frame.

Legal framework: collective bargaining

When staffing, operations managers must be aware of the implications of unionization. In one twelve-month period, we were directly involved in staffing a new manufacturing facility, observed a National Labor Relations Board election for representation, saw the United Auto Workers elected as the bargaining unit, bargained collectively, experienced a labor strike, operated the plant during the strike, and settled the strike. (We then had three years of labor peace.) During this year-long process, operating management found two things very difficult: the overwhelmingly favorable vote for union representation (about 90 percent) and the pressures on themselves and their families during the strike. Unionization and collective bargaining are not all bad, by any means; but when you are staffing a facility, you should be aware that you may have to deal with them whether you want to or not.

Because the legal framework for collective bargaining is complex, most organizations seek legal assistance in their labor-union negotiations. Basically, the National Labor Relations Act (the Wagner Act) and the Labor-Management Relations Act of 1947 (the Taft-Hartley Act) provide the legal framework for the United States. There are specific laws for organizing, bargaining collectively in good faith, and operating continuously (without strikes) during the length of the contract. In Canada, individual provinces have adopted their own labor laws, most of which are similar to those in the United States. Collective bargaining laws affecting Canadian public-sector employees, however, are more well-developed than ours and provide much more efficient machinery for negotiation.

Unions often place new restrictions on management. To owners, the erosion of "management rights" is often more critical than the more direct economic impact of unionization. Although unionism is often viewed negatively by management, sometimes unions can benefit employers by providing a framework for labor-management relations.

EXAMPLE

After the loss of the election we described before, the company president told us not to be discouraged by the defeat. At one of his plants, he told us, management was so ineffective that without the guidance of the labor contract, the plant would have operated at even less operating efficiency.

Union spokesmen argue that increased wages and fringe benefits, improved working conditions, and job security through seniority systems benefit the workers. We would like to stress that unionization need not be a two-person zero sum game, with a loser for every winner. Perhaps both sides can gain from a mature labor policy. So become informed about the legal aspects of collective bargaining and make up your mind to establish or accept your firm's relations with unions with a positive attitude.

Manpower Planning

Manpower planning attempts to ensure that to meet the organization's goals, the correct number and kinds of human skills will be at the right places when they are needed. To accomplish this, planning forecasts must be made, and a skills inventory must be kept. The forecasted needs can be compared with actual manpower, and courses of action can then be established to meet these needs.

Manpower forecasts
The key to effective manpower forecasts is the validity of the basic business forecast, which is part of the general management planning effort. Virtually all organizations do short-term manpower forecasting. It is not difficult to project manpower needs over the next several weeks and months based on orders in hand or service levels required. Intermediate needs for one to four years are more difficult; manpower planning depends upon actual decisions, such as new plants and facilities locations, that have already been made. Because so many goals of management hinge on this intermediate time period, it is probably the most critical manpower planning time horizon. If a high percentage of their intermediate plans are not effective, managers may not be around to evaluate long-range plans (from 5 to 10 years). The degree to which long-range manpower planning succeeds depends substantially upon long-term planning and forecasting and the subsequent business strategies that attempt to implement those plans.

Typically, forecasts for products and services in operations are converted into the labor levels needed to support the forecasted output. Labor is classified by skill requirements and correlated with projected output volume.

Skills inventory
Personnel records constitute the major source of data for current skills inventories. Such demographic data as education, training, age, and job experience are available in the personnel office, especially if your company has a computerized data base. More subjective factors—willingness to change locations, performance evaluations, and test scores—can also be included in the skills inventory, as can information on voluntary quits, retirements, dismissals, promotions, transfers, layoffs, and deaths. Since the skills inventory and the manpower forecast must be compared, they should have the same general form, at least in part. Normally, however, the skills inventory is more complete than the manpower forecast.

One relatively new inclusion on skills inventories is human asset accounting. In this category, dollar values are placed on various occupations within the organization. Determining and measuring human assets is very difficult, however. Of what dollar value is a custodian? A tool and die maker? A shift foreman? A vice-president of manufacturing? Because of the complexities and difficulties involved in human asset accounting, it is still more conceptual than practical.

The learning phenomenon

Generally, the marketplace does not provide the exact skills necessary for the job you want to fill. Although we believe that operations management, for example, can be learned and transferred across industries, a particular operations management job usually has critical aspects that are technologically related to the position at hand. Furthermore, becoming an operations manager requires learning a set of behaviors, and at the time you're hiring, different applicants will have acquired different levels of expertise. It takes time to learn to be a production/operations manager, a fact of life you must consider in manpower planning. Figure 8-8 illustrates the way learning might progress for a hypothetical production/operations manager over his or her career. If our hypothetical manager transferred from one technology to a new one, the curve's smooth flow might be interrupted for a time. But if the new environment were conducive to mastering skills, the manager's previous experience would help him or her learn the new technology quickly. Learning curves can be constructed more precisely for routine, repetitive jobs; we'll discuss them in more detail elsewhere.

Figure 8-9 shows one model of a manpower planning system. The keys to the planning system are data on the current work force (the skills

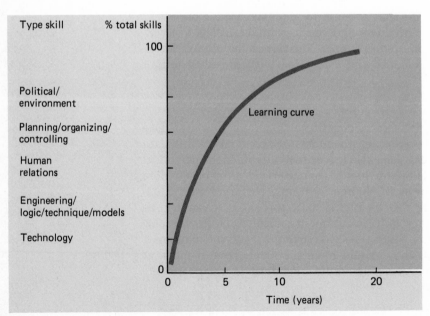

Figure 8-8 **Hypothetical learning curve for an operations manager**

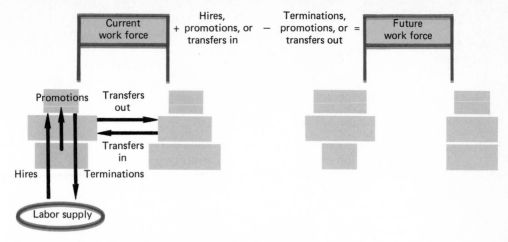

Figure 8-9 **Overview of a manpower planning system**
Source: R. H. Fulton, "A Company Technique for Estimating Future Manpower Requirements," in R. A. Beaumont, ed., *Manpower Planning* (New York: Industrial Relations Counselors, 1970), p. 42.

inventory), projected hires and promotions (from the manpower forecast), and termination, promotions, and transfers out. The result of the manpower planning system is a future work force plan.

Staffing the New Facility

Labor surveys   Before locating a facility, management usually gathers preliminary information about the availability of various labor skills and the prevailing wage rates in the area. Once the decision to locate a new facility has been made, operating management undertakes a more detailed wage survey. The wage survey is an attempt to obtain information on wage rates from employers with similar jobs in the competitive labor market, which varies for professionals, semiskilled, and skilled labor.

=== EXAMPLE ===

An existing regional library conducted a labor survey by examining state and national salary levels of professional librarians. The researcher felt that the home state and, to a lesser extent, the geographic part of the United States where this state was located, constituted the librarians' main labor market. On the other hand, wages of clerical staff, bookmobile drivers, maintenance people, and guards were compared against those in the local community and other communities within driving range.

It is impossible to obtain exactly comparable data in a wage survey because jobs vary from one organization to another. Usually, you need to ask respondents for job descriptions, wage rates, and, if possible, the average wage for jobs you are surveying. You don't necessarily have to survey *all* jobs in your organization, but do survey those that are representative.

In a unionized area, the wage survey is relatively easy; union contracts can be collected and examined. Even in nonunionized areas, there is often a personnel managers' association of some type that coordinates the exchange of wage and salary data among organizations, both private and public.

Wage survey data should be summarized with highs, lows, and midpoints identified in a summary table. Typically, you will find a range of wages for the same job, depending upon organizations' abilities to pay, awareness of competition, and wage strategies. As an operations manager, your wage strategy should be set with one eye on the competitive wage market; job turnover and inability to attract quality employees often result from poor wages.

The employee   Obviously, employees in the new facility will be either transfers from within your organization or new employees. In management and such technical areas as engineering, accounting, and maintenance, transfers often provide the key employees. Depending upon the size of the facility, various numbers of employees might be transferred into a new facility to form the technical and managerial core around which the facility is staffed.

Although new facilities are partially staffed by transferring employees from within, some new employees will have to be hired too. Usually some new employees are sent to old facilities for training, and others are trained as the new facility comes on stream. This procedure is similar in both private and public organizations, for expanding department stores, utility companies, appliance manufacturers, and veterans' hospitals.

Performance Appraisal and Employee Evaluation

Once the facility is organized and staffed, management must arrange ways to appraise performance and evaluate employees. Appraisal can be judgmental, objective, or a combination of the two. Superiors, peers, subordinates, one's self, or assessment specialists can all form a judgmental appraisal of a manager's performance. By far the most prevalent judgmental appraisal is made by a manager's supervisor. Most managers continually appraise their own performance, too, although their judgment is not usually recorded by the organization.

The most commonly used objective measures of an operations manager's performance are related to productivity and cost control in the operating facility. Efficiency in the use of resources can be measured at the plant, department, and group levels. Other key operating variables that are indicative of performance and that can be objectively measured are scrap and rework costs, labor inefficiency, job turnover, absenteeism, safety records, grievances, disciplinary actions, and control of overhead costs.

Since most of the measures we've described are appropriate only for managers, employees at lower levels in the organization are usually evaluated in other ways. Often, a rating method incorporating detailed descriptions of job behavior is used to evaluate operative employees. Rating techniques vary from simple rating scales to employee comparison systems, checklists, critical incident techniques, and essay evaluations. Although the rating technique is generally developed by someone else, operations managers do have to use it, and they have to train others to use it too. In any rating process, errors and biases can easily creep into the procedure. Since appraisal and evaluation are critical to an organization's long-run performance, operations managers should take the task seriously and guard against any errors and personal biases that could undermine objectivity.

The strengths and weaknesses of appraisal techniques are detailed in special books and courses that train personnel managers to develop performance appraisal and employee evaluation systems.

Compensation

Anyone who takes pride in his work knows that the intrinsic rewards of a job well done are one kind of compensation. Although much of the management literature in the 1960s placed great importance on the motivational aspects of intrinsic rewards, in the 1970s there has been a turn toward stressing extrinsic compensation, the monetary rewards that are primary to most workers. This is the form of compensation we'll discuss here.

Job evaluation and wage structure Apart from the workers who are doing them, jobs themselves must be ranked according to difficulty before wages can be set. The comparison of one job to other jobs is the basis of job evaluation, which uses the job description in the comparison. Evaluation techniques vary from judgmental ranking to more detailed and expensive point ranking schemes. The result is a progression of jobs from those requiring the least skill, experience, and abilities to those jobs requiring the most. In a bank, the custodians' and groundskeepers' jobs would appear closer together and at a lower level than would those of the auditor or manager of customer relations. After all the jobs have been evaluated, a comparative ranking provides the basis for compensation.

The wage structure is the relative wage of one job as compared to others. Organizations often prefer an overlapping wage structure in which a person in a lower job classification can be compensated more for performance and experience than the new employee in the next higher job classification. Figure 8-10 shows an overlapping wage structure. In class 3, for example, there might be four bank jobs: drive-in bank teller, walk-up window teller, accounting clerk I, and customer relations clerk II. These jobs all earn wages ranging from $2.90 to $3.85 per hour, but

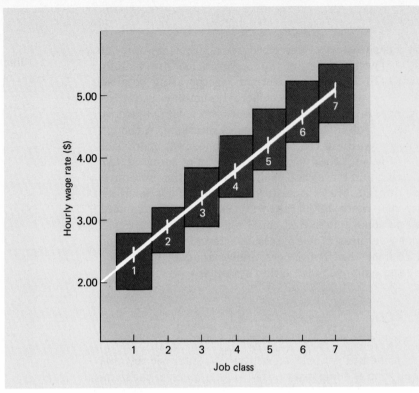

Figure 8-10 **Typical wage structure**

all the employees in these jobs do not necessarily earn the same hourly rate. Similarly, a new employee in class 3 might earn less than an experienced employee in class 2.

Pay systems   Pay systems are fundamentally hourly or incentive compensation programs. Hourly payment plans are straightforward, the worker receiving an hourly wage with overtime payment, which varies depending upon federal and state law, company policy, and negotiated union contracts. There are many different incentive payment plans. Individual incentive plans can be computed a number of ways, but most vary wages directly with the quantity of work produced; they are called piece-rate plans. In some plans, a quality penalty is imposed for excessive errors. Incentive plans were initially developed for manufacturing jobs, but they have subsequently been applied to a variety of occupations, including motel maids, painters, inspectors, mechanics, and clerical workers. In marketing, individual incentive plans are as prevalent as are the operations incentive plans.

A major problem with incentive plans has arisen from job changes caused by automation. Often when jobs become automated, productivity increases and labor content decreases. It is difficult to determine how much of the productivity gains are due to changes in capital (automation), and how much can be attributed to labor (the worker). As we will learn, job measurement is not so precise as to provide definitive answers to this question. Another problem with incentive plans and automation is that when jobs are automated, management often discards the old incentive plans in favor of new ones with higher output standards. Workers tend to react negatively to new incentive systems, even though new equipment can help them achieve the higher standard. To avoid this problem, many organizations have turned from incentive systems toward hourly wage systems. Other organizations have also implemented hourly wage plans because unions exert pressure for wage equality, a situation not in harmony with incentive plans.

Another kind of incentive plan is the group incentive plan. It offers lower industrial engineering and payroll costs than do individual incentive plans. Two such group plans are the Scanlon and Lincoln plans, both of which stress substantial sharing of productivity gains with employees. The president of Lincoln Electric, where the Lincoln plan is used, feels that it works very well. Lincoln has been able to reduce the unit cost of its basic product during the past fifteen years, a time when competitors' unit prices have more than doubled because of increased labor and material costs. The results for Lincoln Electric have been significant increases in market share and profitability; the results for Lincoln employees have been wage gains unequaled in most firms throughout the United States and Canada. An impressive record indeed.

Even those group incentive plans that are successful, however, involve some problems. Because of group pressure, output may be restricted. Sometimes workers attempt to lower the standard over time. And the cost of maintaining the incentive program is high.

Generally, management and professionals are paid an agreed-upon monthly or annual wage. Salaries are typically reviewed at least annually and adjusted according to performance, cost of living, comparative wages within the firm and in the marketplace, and the overall worth of the employee to the organization. Frequently, all salaried employees participate in a profit-sharing program in which a percentage of profits is distributed to employees. In addition, top management often benefits from various bonus plans that relate to overall organization performance. Bonus plans for production/operations managers can be based upon profitability or cost control, the areas of their greatest contributions.

Compensation plans are policy issues that must be addressed by operations managers. In a market economy, labor must be attracted and retained, or output cannot be produced. On the other hand, cost control is a primary goal in operations. Caught in the squeeze between retaining labor and controlling costs, the operations manager must continually evaluate compensation programs to maintain effective staffing for operations.

Planning, Organizing, and Controlling Activities

As we have said so many times, production and operations managers are involved in planning, organizing, and controlling activities. Since both planning and organizing activities precede the actual conversion process, it is difficult at times to distinguish between them. After the initial organizing and planning activities, operations control activities interact with other organizing functions. Table 8-1 shows the interaction between

INTEGRATING ORGANIZATION AND STAFFING INTO OPERATIONS MANAGEMENT ACTIVITIES

TABLE 8-1

ORGANIZING INTEGRATED WITH PLANNING AND CONTROLLING IN OPERATIONS

Planning and controlling activities	Primarily line activity	Primarily staff activity	Project organization	Job analysis and description	Organizing — Manpower planning
Planning					
Capacity planning	●*				●
Facilities location	●				●
Facilities layout		●			
Aggregate output planning	●				●
Supplementary planning for operations	●				●
Scheduling operations		●			
Project scheduling		●	●		
Controlling					
Evaluating					
Overall output	●				
Departments	●				
Employees	●			●	
Feedback for correction	●				
Cost control	●				
Inventory control		●			
Quality control		●			

*● denotes an interaction between the row and the column.

organizing and staffing activities and typical planning and control activities. You can see that some activities (new employee learning, job standards, work measurement) interact with both planning and control activities, whereas others (manpower planning, performance appraisal) interact pri-

Labor surveys	New employee learning	Skill inventory	Performance appraisal & evaluation	Compensation	Job standards	Work measurement	Job design
					•	•	
•		•					
	•				•	•	•
	•				•	•	
	•	•			•	•	•
	•				•	•	•
	•						•
	•		•	•	•	•	
	•		•	•	•	•	
	•		•	•	•	•	•
			•	•	•	•	
	•		•	•	•	•	•
			•	•	•	•	•
	•						

marily with one or the other. As we noted in Chapter 2, the emphasis in operations management is more on planning and control than on organizing. Effective organizing can enhance overall planning and control objectives, however, so the activity should not be ignored altogether.

Models and Behavior

If you look again at our familiar framework for analysis in Figure 8-1, you'll see that organizing has both modeling and behavioral dimensions. We haven't stressed these, but as we look back over some of the topics we've discussed in this chapter, we can see some important modeling and behavioral aspects in organizing.

Models

The organization chart is a schematic model; it shows a pictorial relationship among variables. The pictures we get from an organization chart are the flow of authority and responsibility among individuals and departments, different levels of authority, and the relationships among all the different functions.

Both communications networks, which are parts of unity of command and span of control, and organizational structure can be modeled, either pictorially or verbally. When we make up job descriptions, we are using descriptive models as an approach to job analysis. Forecasting for manpower planning, learning curves, and monetary compensation can all be modeled, some mathematically.

Behavior

Maintaining parity of authority and responsibility is a behavioral problem. It is a common error to expect subordinates to accept responsibilities without delegating commensurate authority. If a subordinate is required to obtain something from a worker over whom he has no authority, an uncomfortable and improper situation often results. This sometimes happens when staff positions are given line responsibilities. Managers must not allow a lack of parity between authority and responsibility.

Several organization fallacies have an essentially behavioral base. If managers expect reorganization to accomplish everything, or if they think the organization structure ensures performance, they are guilty of forgetting that *people* are responsible for the success of the organization.

Staffing can present behavioral problems for both employers and employees. Legally, an employer must bargain collectively with his or her employees if they vote for union representation. Some self-made owners find this a difficult procedure. Legally, too, employers must hire and promote people regardless of race, sex, age, or ethnic background. If an employer has prejudicial feelings, he or she may object to or try to circumvent the law (employees who are discriminated against object, too!). Staffing situations involving transfers and hiring can present behavioral problems as well. If promotions involving transfers are refused, management sometimes fails to understand the reasons for the refusal, and friction can develop. Friction can also develop with the entry of new employees, who may bring with them new personalities, job habits, and ideas that are upsetting to existing staff. (Behavioral change and resistance to change will be discussed in some detail later.)

Compensation involves wage and salary plans that are behaviorally specific; that is, they rely primarily on behaviors exhibited on the job. Group pressures in incentive plans make these plans not so straightforward and economically based as they would first appear. Sometimes pressures are brought on industrial engineering to reduce standards; payroll has a more difficult job than on an hourly system when people become upset at not being paid properly for their performance; and there can be considerable group pressures on fellow workers not to be "rate busters."

The organizing process focuses on the job itself as the fundamental building block. Some useful tools have been developed in industrial engineering and the applied behavioral sciences to assist the operations manager in understanding more about this basic building block. It is to these concepts, establishing performance standards, job measurement, and job design, that we turn in Chapter 9.

SUMMARY

Organizing is the means by which individuals, groups, and facilities are combined in a formal structure of tasks and authority. The organization structure, the organization's frame, can be viewed as the machine through which people function to achieve the organization's goals. The structure specifies formal relationships among individuals and groups that the planning process accepts for developing courses of action and the control process accepts when feedback is communicated through the organization.

An organization chart illustrates line and staff relationships, designates the flow of responsibililty and authority, and shows relative levels of authority. Production/operations managers often organize according to product, customer, geographical area, function, and project.

To function effectively, the operations manager must understand the organization's goals and subgoals, its channels of authority and responsibility, its span of control. He or she must insist on unity of command, so that employees report to only one supervisor.

If reorganization is considered, job analysis can be helpful. After duties, responsibilities, and requirements for all the organization's jobs have been studied, a job description can document the existing organization. Reorganization, either total or piecemeal, can then regroup jobs logically.

As a means of keeping up with changes in personnel and position, an organization chart is useful, although it does not necessarily reflect the real power sources in the company. Often an informal organization of powerful employees has more to do with accomplishing and establishing goals than does the formal organization reflected in the organization chart. A good production/operations manager should be aware of both the formal and informal power structures in the organization and use them both, if possible, to accomplish the organization's goals.

Once the organization of production and operations has been established, staff must be acquired to fill the positions. The manager must see to it that EEOC regulations are obeyed; people must be hired according to their abilities, not according to age, sex, race, or ethnic background. Wage structures, rating techniques, and unions must all be considered carefully in staffing decisions.

Manpower planning assists in staffing through planning forecasts, skills inventories, and data collection on transfers and terminations. To staff the new facility, managers must consider both the labor market, through the use of labor surveys, and whether new employees will be transfers or new hires. Once employees' services are attained, their performance must be appraised and evaluated. Whatever compensation plan is used, it should encourage desirable behaviors and discourage undesirable ones.

Organizing interrelates with planning and controlling activities in many different ways, some of which are shown in Table 8-1. These specific interactions illustrate the usefulness of the process approach to production/operations management in framing specific production/operation management activities, many of which involve organizing for operations.

CASE

Goldview Dishware

Goldview Dishware is a New England-based company that manufactures moderately priced household dishes. Since its founding in 1947 the company has been very profitable and has experienced moderate growth. The owners have adopted conservative financial and marketing policies but moderately progressive manufacturing policies. Figure 8-11 illustrates the manufacturing organization, providing details for plant 3, located in Dover, Delaware, which is considered to be a typical facility.

The plant manager of plant 3, Bill Cravens, has resigned to accept another position. In an exit interview conducted by Ned Mayer, the vice-president of manufacturing, several points were uncovered. Bill stated, "Tom Wilson, my engineering manager, is involved in scheduling production and frequently reassigns hourly production workers without my authorization. Tom is a hard worker, but my line foreman just can't stand having him around. I've taken the problem to Jan (the eastern works manager), but she knows Tom and I don't see eye-to-eye, so she supports Tom. In one case, Tom had Jan's verbal approval for a major scheduling change. The change wrecked a weekend of planning by our production control group."

Ned Mayer has asked Jan to start recruiting for a new plant manager. Looking through her files, Jan realizes that there never has been a job description developed for a plant manager position. She is at a loss as to how to proceed, so she is thinking of recommending Tom Wilson for the job.

Case questions:

1. What different types of organization are used in manufacturing by Goldview? Explain.
2. Based on plant 3's experience, would you recommend any organization changes within plants?
3. How can Tom Wilson be effectively utilized? What classical organization concepts are being violated?
4. How should Jan proceed in her recruitment dilemma?

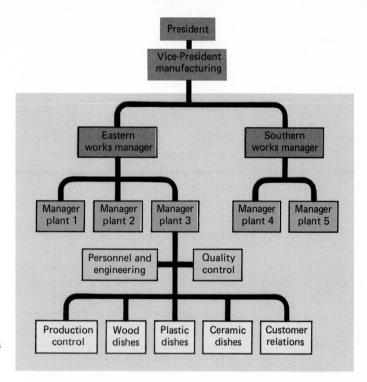

Figure 8-11 **Goldview Dishware's manufacturing organization**

1. Explain how an organization chart works and of what benefit it might be to operations management.

2. Describe the basic approaches to organizing. Give an example of each for a state licensing bureau office.

3. Explain how organization by project might be useful in the construction industry.

4. Contrast the bureaucratic and technology models of organizational structure.

5. If you were assigned a task to build a production organization for assembling corn cob pipes, how might you proceed? What tools or techniques might you use for assistance?

6. What problems can occur when an informal organization differs from the formal organization structure?

7. Discuss at least three constraints the production/operations manager might confront in staffing the organization.

8. Explain how manpower forecasts and skills inventories relate to manpower planning decisions.

9. A new household cleaner bottling plant is to be located near a multi-plant corporation in an expanding market area. What alternatives exist for staffing professionals in this facility?

10. How might formalized performance appraisal and performance evaluation systems assist production/operations managers achieve their goals?

11. Provide three examples of planning and control activities that relate to organizing and staffing activities. Explain the relationships.

12. Using examples, explain the modeling and behavioral dimensions of organizing for operations.

13. Distinguish between line and staff positions in an organization.

14. Why should a production/operations manager be concerned with EEO and labor laws? Isn't this the job of attorneys and personnel specialists?

GLOSSARY

Authority: the right to give orders

Chain of command: flow of authority

Departments: homogeneous units of jobs grouped together by characteristic similarities

Employee evaluation: measuring actual job performance and comparing it with standard performance

Informal organization: authority, responsibility, and communication channels that circumvent the formal organization

Job analysis: the study of similar tasks performed by one or more people to determine responsibilities, duties, and educational and skill requirements necessary for doing a particular job

Job description: a written documentation of a job prepared from the job analysis; focuses on duties and responsibilities

Labor surveys: information on availability of various labor skills and prevailing wage rates for an area

Line function: typically finance, marketing, and production; derives directly from operational activities and contributes to attainment of primary goals

Manpower planning: assuring that to meet the organization's goals the correct number and kinds of human skills will be at the right places when they are needed

Organizing: means by which individuals, groups, and facilities are combined in a formal structure of tasks and authority

Pay systems: monetary compensation procedures that normally are (1) incentive or hourly for lower level employees and (2) monthly with or without incentives for higher level employees

Project: one short set of activities

Responsibility: the duty to be accountable for a specific set of events

Span of control: number of subordinates who report directly to the supervisor

Staff function: supports, advises, analyzes, and recommends to line function; contributes indirectly to attainment of primary goals

Unity of command: flow of authority allowing a subordinate to have one and only one supervisor

Wage structure: relative wage of one job as compared to others

SELECTED
READINGS

Beach, Dale S. *Personnel: The Management of People at Work.* 2nd ed. New York: Macmillan Pub. Co., Inc., 1970.

Delbecq, Andre L. and others. *Matrix Organization: A Conceptual Guide to Organization Variation.* Madison, Wisconsin: Bureau of Business Research and Service, Graduate School of Business, The University of Wisconsin, 1969.

George, Claude S. *Management for Business and Industry.* Englewood Cliffs, N.J.: Prentice-Hall, Inc., 1970.

Glueck, William F. *Personnel: A Diagnostic Approach*. Dallas: Business Publications, Inc., 1974.

Massie, Joseph L. and John Douglas. *Managing: A Contemporary Introduction*. Englewood Cliffs, N.J.: Prentice-Hall, Inc., 1973.

McGregor, Douglas. *The Human Side of Enterprise*. New York: McGraw-Hill Book Co., 1960.

Michael, Stephen R. and Halsey R. Jones. *Organizational Management: Concepts and Practice*. New York: Intext Educational Publishers, 1973.

Miner, John B. and Mary Green Miner. *Personnel and Industrial Relations: A Managerial Approach*. 2nd ed. New York: Macmillan Pub. Co, Inc.,1973.

Thompson, James D. *Organizations in Action*. New York: McGraw-Hill Book Co., 1967.

Weber, Max. "The Essentials of Bureaucratic Organization: An Ideal-Type Construction." In Robert K. Merton, et al., eds. *A Reader in Bureaucracy*, Glencoe, Ill: The Free Press, 1952.

Woodward, Joan. *Industrial Organization: Theory and Practice*. London: Oxford University Press, 1965.

9

Job Design, Production/Operations Standards, and Work Measurement

The framework for production/operations management shown in Figure 9-1 reviews for us the relationship of organizing to the planning and control functions and reminds us that models and behavior are also vital in organizing for conversion. As we employ this framework in studying the concepts and techniques relating to jobs in an organization, we'll discuss the traditional systematic approaches for establishing job standards, work measurement, and job design and examine some contemporary behavioral contributions directed at improving jobs.

This chapter focuses on people at work. The basic building block in a manufacturing or service organization is the job, a group of related tasks or activities that need to be performed to meet organizational objectives. Jobs are then grouped into larger units called departments, and departments are grouped into such basic functions as marketing, engineering, and production. Consider an example. The elements of placing a washer on a bolt, placing a nut on a bolt, and tightening the nut firmly with an automatic wrench constitute a *task*. Repeating this and similar tasks constitutes a *job* in the motor assembly *department*, which is in the *production function* of an organization that finances, markets, and produces washing machines. As we focus on people at work in this chapter, we'll use a narrow approach, examining in detail tasks and jobs in production and operations management. Learning a new job is an important part of people at work. Learning curve analysis, which has to do with job standards, is discussed in Chapter 19, in which we consider rational approaches to change. It could just as easily have been presented here, however.

Two basic developments have characterized organizations in modern industrialized societies. First and most significant was scientific manage-

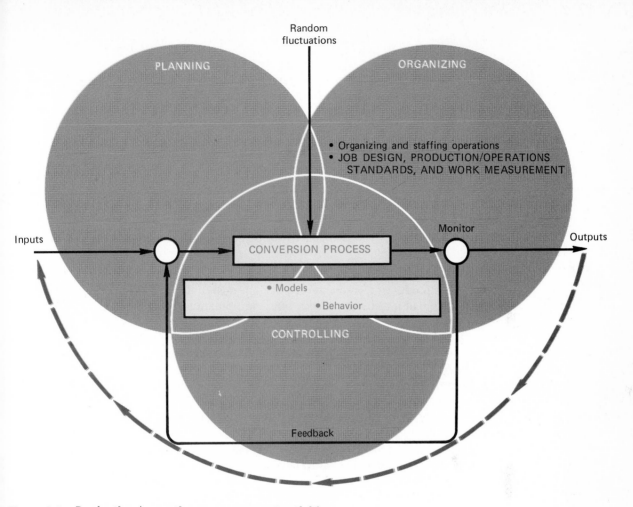

Figure 9-1 **Production/operations management activities**

ment's focus on the logic of the production process, particularly people and machines at work on a job. This follow-up of Adam Smith's concept of labor specialization has led to establishment of logical approaches to job design, individual and group standards for performance, and techniques for measurement of work. A good bit of the development in industrial engineering over the last century has been devoted to this rational, scientific, logical approach to job analysis.

More recently, human relations and behavioral science studies of jobs have come about. The development of the behavioral approach has tended to moderate scientific management's rational approach to jobs. The behavioral approach has provided clear evidence that people have multiple needs, feelings, and personal goals that are not always consistent with job designs, standards, and performance measures obtained from using traditional rational techniques. Clearly, the modern production and operations manager must be aware of and respond to the worker as an individual. The manager must moderate logical approaches and consider such alternatives as worker participation in job decisions. Sometimes workers can become involved through job redesign, job enlargement, and job enrichment.

In job design, we use methods analysis to establish the general work flow in the facility. Once the general work flow has been established, specific jobs can be detailed. After the jobs have been designed, a standard needs to be established to assure that the jobs are being performed properly. Establishing a standard, however, requires an understanding of work measurement. We want to emphasize that work measurement *follows* methods analysis. Only after we have established the proper method for getting the job done (job design) can we be concerned about measuring it (setting the standard through measurement). Obviously, setting a standard for an existing job and then redesigning it constitutes wasted effort. Let's begin our discussion of these three related areas with the one that comes first, job design.

JOB DESIGN

In production and operations, job design follows the planning and designing of product, process, and equipment. Job design specifies the content of each job and determines the distribution of work within the organization. Just as an architect can build (design) a house many different ways with many different materials, so can a manager build (design) a job with many different parts (elements). A combination of creativity and adherence to basic goals is critical to both the architect and the manager.

Although the two basic approaches to job design were developed separately, they are not mutually exclusive. The first, the micro approach, scientifically examines each detail of the job so that wasted effort is eliminated and output is raised. The second, more recent, approach to job design is behavioral. In it, psychological and socio-psychological considerations encourage job enlargement, job enrichment, and employee participation in job design. Under certain conditions, it too can result in improved output.

Traditional Job Design

Often managers, responsible for many subordinates and equipment, feel overwhelmed by details. Couldn't we be more efficient if we improved our jobs? But how can we improve them when we hardly know what the jobs consist of? One answer to the managers' dilemma is offered by the scientific approach. It urges managers to:

1. Identify the general operations problem area and the jobs that seem to be contributing to or causing the problem.
2. Carefully analyze and document how the work is currently being performed. (Established industrial engineering techniques are available to assist in analysis and documentation.)
3. Analyze the content of individual jobs and job elements.
4. Develop and implement new work methods.

Often jobs can be broken apart, separated into elements. If the elements are assigned to different workers, each worker can perform fewer elements, but he can perform them faster and perhaps under more specialized conditions (with special tools or work benches, for example). This is the basic concept of *specialization* that Adam Smith proposed in 1776. Specialization of labor has been very effective in increasing operating efficiency in manufacturing; it has been less effective, however, in the service industries.

To help the manager or a staff analyst study a job once a problem has been identified, certain techniques have been developed. One of these uses *operation charts* to analyze the job into elementary motions of the right and left hands—reaching, carrying, grasping, lifting, positioning and releasing, for example. Often a time scale is placed in the middle of the operation chart so that it is clear how much time is taken by each hand to perform the associated motion. Operation charts are appropriate for routine, repetitive, short cycle tasks performed on low to moderate production volumes. Figure 9-2 shows a right hand-left hand operation chart for assembling two mild steel (M.S.) plates. In this chart, there is no time scale, but you can see the standard process chart symbols.

Activity charts divide operations into the major task segments performed by the worker and the machine and separate them by a vertical

Figure 9-2 **Left-hand right-hand operations chart**

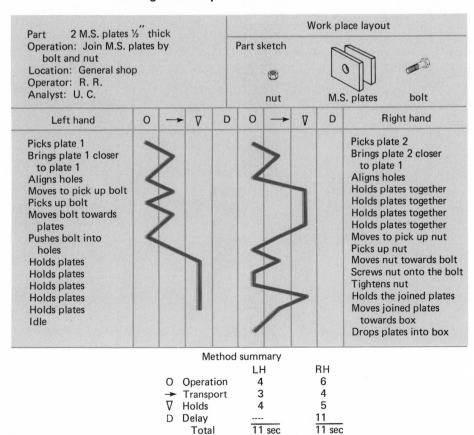

Method summary

		LH	RH
O	Operation	4	6
→	Transport	3	4
▽	Holds	4	5
D	Delay	----	11
	Total	11 sec	11 sec

time scale. In this way, the analyst can easily compute the percentages of productive and idle time and concentrate on methods of reducing idle time for the worker and/or the machine. Activity charts are appropriate for routine, repetitive tasks with worker-machine interaction. The activity chart in Figure 9-3 illustrates how a punched deck of computer cards is loaded and unloaded by a card reader. In this example, the analyst might improve efficiency by focusing on the first 10 seconds of idle machine time, the second 10 seconds of idle worker time, and the last 3 seconds of idle machine time.

Flow process charts analyze interstation activities, attempting to portray the flows of the overall production process. To capture this flow, analysts classify each movement of the product through the conversion process into one of five standard categories, operation, transportation, storage, inspection, or delay. Flow process charts are appropriate for visualizing the sequential stages of the conversion process. They help reveal

Figure 9-3 **Employee-machine activity chart**

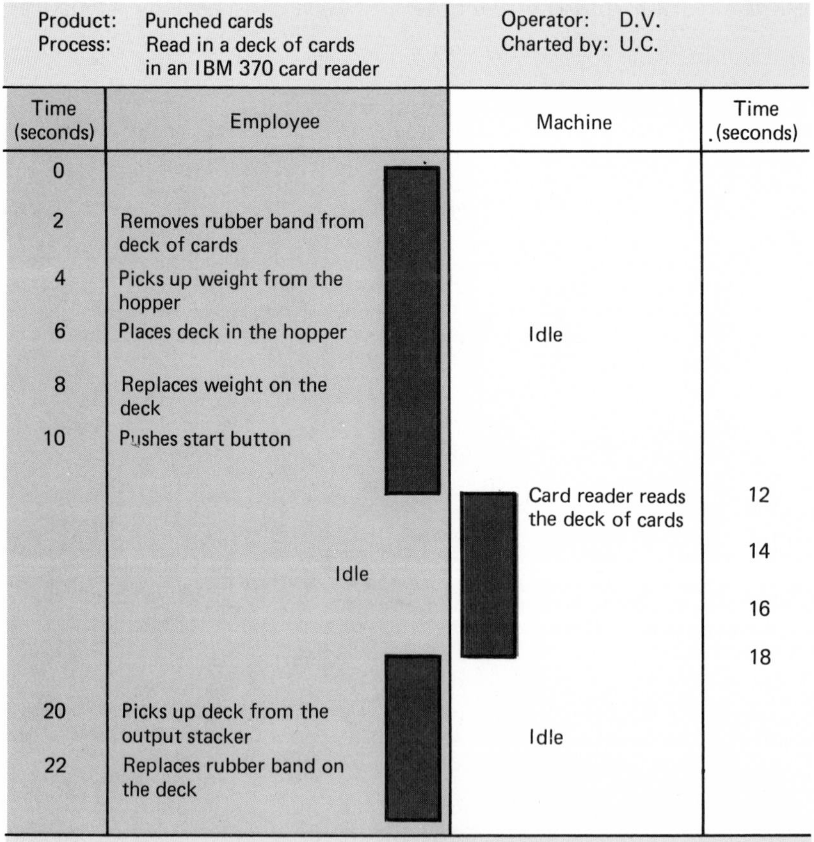

Product: Punched cards Process: Read in a deck of cards in an IBM 370 card reader		Operator: D.V. Charted by: U.C.	
Time (seconds)	Employee	Machine	Time .(seconds)
0			
2	Removes rubber band from deck of cards		
4	Picks up weight from the hopper		
6	Places deck in the hopper	Idle	
8	Replaces weight on the deck		
10	Pushes start button		
		Card reader reads the deck of cards	12
			14
	Idle		16
			18
20	Picks up deck from the output stacker	Idle	
22	Replaces rubber band on the deck		

Summary				
	Employee		Machine	
	Time (sec)	%	Time	%
Work	14	63.6	8	36.4
Idle	8	36.4	14	63.6

unnecessary product movements or duplication of effort whose elimination would improve efficiency. Flow process charts provide a broader level of analysis than the preceding methods; many jobs are examined, but none in depth. The five categories of product movement are:

○ *Operation:* the work performed in manufacturing the product; usually assigned to a single work station.

⇨ *Transportation:* any movement of the product, or any of its parts, among various locations in the production process.

▽ *Storage:* intervals during which the product, or any part of it, waits or is at rest. Often the symbol △T is used to designate temporary storage, when the product is stored for a short time before the conversion process has been completed, and △P is used to indicate permanent storage, when the completed product waits in a storage facility more than a day or two.

▢ *Inspection:* all activities performed to verify that the product meets mechanical, dimensional, and operational requirements.

D *Delay:* temporary storage before or after a production operation. When the temporary storage symbol is used, this category is often omitted.

━━━ EXAMPLE ━━━

A study was conducted to document current library operations in the technical processing function of a major resource library.[1] The purpose of the study was to provide a basis for specification of computer automation systems in technical processing. Figure 9-4 is a typical product process chart. Figure 9-5 is the flow diagram from which Figure 9-4 was developed. The following excerpt from the report illustrates this service sector application of traditional job design techniques.

Materials Flows and Procedures. **This section presents the operations of the University of Missouri-Columbia Elmer Ellis Library's Technical Services Division in considerable detail. Because of the extensiveness of this description, a summary of the processing of materials is presented. . . . The summary takes the form of "product process charts" and "floor diagrams" describing the general operations and movements undergone by the broader categories of library materials. The "station" identifiers heading each column of the process charts refer to desk locations as marked on the accompanying floor diagrams.**

Product process charts are in common use for describing processing of industrial materials, and they provide a convenient means of summarizing the numerous flow diagrams. . . . The charts are easy to read once the following symbols and corresponding meanings are understood:

[1]S. Craig Moore, Everett E. Adam, Jr., Edward P. Miller, Daniel W. Doell, and Louis E. Fruend, *Library Studies Project:* Volume I, *Project Summary,* and Volume II, *Technical Services in the UMC Library System* (Columbia: University of Missouri, 1973). See pp. 12–15, Vol. II.

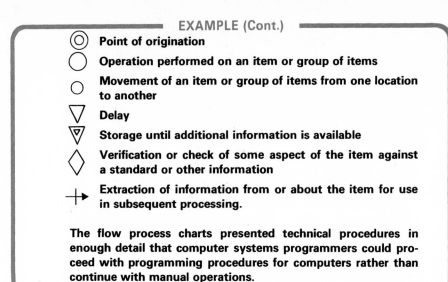

EXAMPLE (Cont.)

◎ **Point of origination**

○ **Operation performed on an item or group of items**

○ **Movement of an item or group of items from one location to another**

▽ **Delay**

▽ **Storage until additional information is available**

◇ **Verification or check of some aspect of the item against a standard or other information**

⊢→ **Extraction of information from or about the item for use in subsequent processing.**

The flow process charts presented technical procedures in enough detail that computer systems programmers could proceed with programming procedures for computers rather than continue with manual operations.

Figure 9-4 Product process chart of library operations

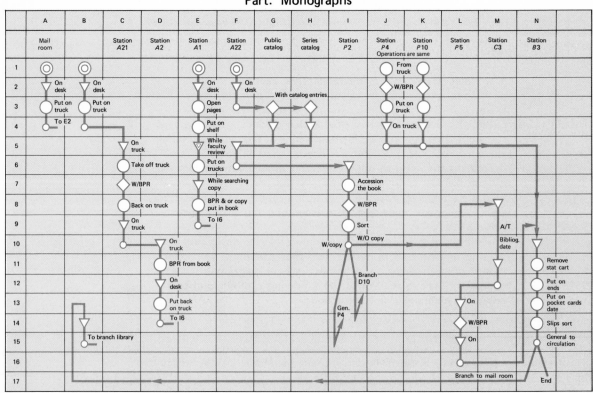

Product Process Chart
Part: Monographs

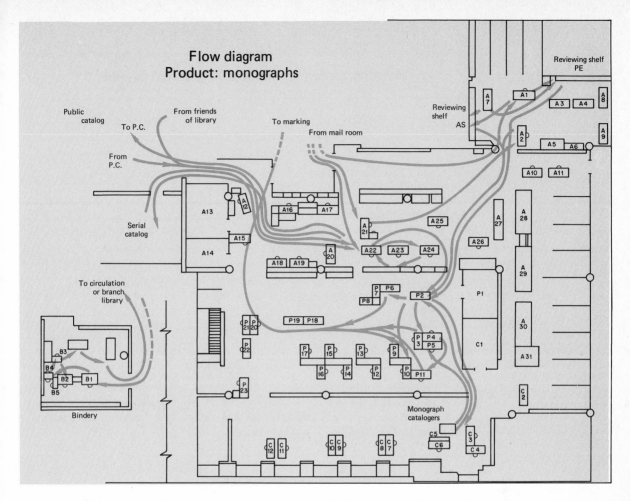

Figure 9-5 **Flow diagram of library product**

These three traditional techniques, operation charts, activity charts, and flow process charts, facilitate intrajob analysis (at the individual job station) and interjob analysis (between job stations). After systematically studying existing job content, engineers and technicians can often find means of improving jobs that have been overlooked by foremen and managers. To reduce idle time, they may recommend eliminating unnecessary elements or modifying the sequence of elements. We don't mean to imply that these techniques are the only ways to design jobs; excellent improvements are often brought about without them. But these charts have proven useful to many organizations, and they can help bring about efficiencies when they are used as aids in decision making.

In Table 9-1, we summarize the application of these traditional work methods techniques to various kinds of work activities. In the table, two terms are mentioned for the first time: gang process charts, which trace the interaction of several workers and one machine, and principles of

━━━━━━━━━━━━━━━ TABLE 9-1 ━━━━━━━━━━━━━━━

TRADITIONAL WORK METHODS AIDS IN JOB DESIGN

Activity	Analysis method
Routine, repetitive tasks with short cycle times and low to moderate production volumes; stationary worker at a fixed work place	Operations charts, principles of motion economy
Routine, repetitive tasks with long cycle times and moderate to high production volumes; worker interacts with equipment or other workers	Activity charts, worker-machine charts, gang process charts
Overall conversion process; interactions of workers, work stations and work units; flow of work	Process charts, flow diagrams

motion economy. *Principles of motion economy are general guidelines for analyzing and improving work arrangements, the use of human hands and body, or the use of tools to increase efficiency and reduce fatigue.* Table 9-2 lists several principles of motion economy, many of which can be applied to both shop and office work.

Worker physiology
Over the years considerable effort has been devoted to studying people's physiology as it relates to their work. Statistics on reaching range, grip strength, lifting ability, and many other physiological factors have been reasonably well documented. Work place arrangements, job design, and equipment design all require consideration of physiological factors. If you're interested, an industrial engineering handbook is a good source of information on the physiological capabilities of workers.

Working
environment
The working environment is extremely important in designing jobs. Temperature, humidity, and air flow all affect work. One classic study in Britain illustrates the effects of temperature on performance.[2] Before the experiment began, testing identified "good" and "average" performers. High and low incentives

[2]N. H. Mackworth, "High Incentives versus Hot and Humid Atmospheres in a Physical Effort Task," *British Journal of Psychology* 38 (1947), pp. 90–102.

were used with each group, and temperatures of the workers' rooms were changed from day to day. The results of this study are shown in Figure 9-6. As you can see, performance (amount of work done) decreased for

---

TABLE 9-2

PRINCIPLES OF MOTION ECONOMY

Use of the human body	Arrangement of the work place	Design of tools and equipment
The two hands should begin as well as complete their motions at the same time.	There should be a definite and fixed place for all tools and materials.	The hands should be relieved of all work that can be done more advantageously by a jig, a fixture, or a foot-operated device.
The two hands should not be idle at the same time except during rest periods.	Tools, materials, and controls should be located close in and directly in front of the operator.	Two or more tools should be combined whenever possible.
Motions of the arms should be made in opposite and symmetrical directions and should be made simultaneously.	Gravity feedbins and containers should be used to deliver materials close to the point of use.	Tools and materials should be prepositioned whenever possible.
Hand motions should be confined to the lowest classification with which it is possible to perform the work satisfactorily.	Drop deliveries should be used wherever possible.	Where each finger performs some specific movement, such as in typewriting, the load should be distributed in accordance with the inherent capacities of the fingers.
Momentum should be employed to assist the worker wherever possible, and it should be reduced to a minimum if it must be overcome by muscular effort.	Materials and tools should be located to permit the best sequence of motions.	Handles, such as those used on cranks and large screwdrivers, should be designed to permit as much of the surface of the hand to come in contact with the handle as possible. This is particularly true when considerable force is exerted in using the handle. For light assembly work the screwdriver handle should be so shaped that it is smaller at the bottom than at the top.
Smooth continuous motions of the hands are preferable to zigzag motions or straight-line motions involving sudden and sharp changes in direction.	Provisions should be made for adequate conditions for seeing. Good illumination is the first requirement for satisfactory visual perception.	
Ballistic movements are faster, easier, and more accurate than restricted (fixation) or "controlled" movements.	The height of the workplace and the chair should preferably be arranged so that alternate sitting and standing at work are easily possible.	Levers, crossbars, and handwheels should be located in such positions that the operator can manipulate them with the least change in body position and with the greatest mechanical advantage.
Rhythm is essential to the smooth and automatic performance of an operation, and the work should be arranged to permit easy and natural rhythm wherever possible.	A chair of the type and height to permit good posture should be provided for every worker.	

From R. M. Barnes, *Motion and Time Study: Design and Measurement of Work*, 6th ed. (New York: John Wiley & Sons, Inc., 1968), p. 220.

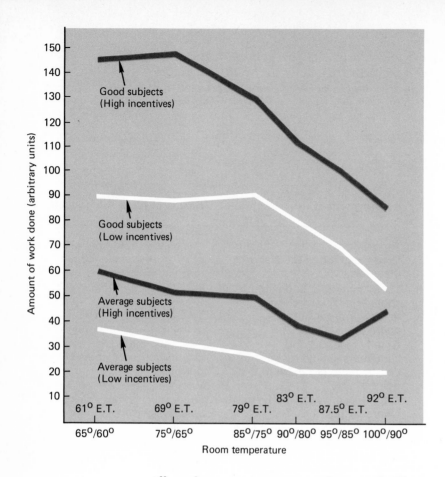

Figure 9-6 **Level of ability and the effects of stronger incentives in hot and humid atmospheres**

Source: N. H. Mackworth, "High Incentives versus Hot and Humid Atmospheres in a Physical Effort Task," *British Journal of Psychology* 38 (1947), pp. 90–102. Reprinted by permission of Cambridge University Press © The British Psychological Society, 1947.

all workers as temperatures increased. The most work was performed at temperatures of about 60 degrees Fahrenheit; as temperatures increased to 80, 85, and 90 degrees, work accomplishment dropped off substantially. Although this study concentrated on workers performing physical tasks, the same principle holds for clerical workers. Optimal temperatures for work that is not physically demanding varies from 68 to 72 degrees; as temperatures increase, performance decreases.

If you've ever tried to mow grass or move furniture on a hot, humid day, you know how much harder high temperatures make your job. The same is true for less physically demanding work: typing, writing, and studying, while easier at temperatures a little warmer than those that are best for manual tasks, are harder when temperatures are very high than when they are moderate.

The Occupational Safety and Health Act

Just as noise, airflow, light intensity, and many other environmental variables affect productivity, they also affect health and safety. Recognizing the lack of national uniformity in working conditions, Congress passed the Williams-Steiger Occupational Safety and Health Act of 1970 (OSHA). The Act, which covers every employer with one or more employees in a business concerned with commerce, establishes strict health and safety standards by encompassing existing codes and adding to them. Publications describing the program are available from local OSHA area directors; they describe the Act's purpose like this:

> . . . to assure as far as possible every working man and woman in the Nation safe and healthful working conditions and to preserve our human resources . . .

How is OSHA to implement this mandate? Congress was specific:

- by encouraging employers and employees to reduce hazards in the workplace, and start or improve existing safety and health programs;
- by establishing employer and employee responsibilities;
- by authorizing OSHA to set mandatory job safety and health standards;
- by providing an effective enforcement program;
- by encouraging the states to assume the fullest responsibility for administering and enforcing their own occupational safety and health programs that are to be at least as effective as the federal program; and
- by providing for reporting procedures on job injuries, illnesses, and fatalities.[3]

Although the program's success depends mostly on voluntary compliance, OSHA does provide enforcement measures and information to employers to help them understand and obey the law.

Behavioral Dimensions of Job Design

In the past, industrialized societies have used economic criteria as their primary guides in designing jobs. Traditional job design emphasizes specialization, task repetition, and reduction of skill requirements to minimize the impact of the individual worker on the production process. Jobs have been designed to minimize immediate cost and maximize immediate productivity. We agree that economic criteria are still paramount. We mustn't forget, though, that behavioral implications in job design can and do influence performance. To ignore these concepts is to bypass the opportunity to add further economic benefits to those we obtain through traditional approaches. With that goal in mind, let's examine the behavioral ideas of job enlargement, job enrichment, job rotation, and participative job design.

Job enlargement   We can think in terms of jobs being composed of tasks, each of which is performed by a worker. Each task has associated with it a set of stimuli, auditory, visual, and/or tactile.

[3]U.S., Department of Labor, Occupational Health and Safety Administration, *All About OSHA*, OSHA publication No. 2056, p. 3.

As the worker performs the tasks, he or she receives various stimuli, cues. The number and kinds of stimuli depend on the nature of the tasks. A job consisting of many varied tasks provides varied stimuli; a job with routine, repetitive tasks usually provides few stimuli.

Job enlargement argues that we have simplified and routinized jobs to the point where they are so specialized that workers perceive them to be monotonous; workers are bored and dissatisfied. Because of boredom and job dissatisfaction, many workers withdraw from the organization, which has high levels of tardiness, absenteeism, and turnover. If managers would enlarge jobs by adding tasks, additional stimuli would reduce the ill effects of too simplified, too specialized jobs. Figure 9-7 illustrates the assumptions behind job enlargement.

One conceptualization of an enlarged job offers the employee four opportunities:

1. variety, the opportunity to use a variety of skills,
2. autonomy, the opportunity to exercise control over how and when the work is completed,
3. task identity, the opportunity to be responsible for an entire piece or program of work, and
4. feedback, the opportunity to receive on-line information.[4]

Thus job enlargement is the procedure of redesigning jobs or modifying work so that employees can feel more involved in and responsible for what they do.

The nature and content of a job may be changed through job enlargement in two basic ways. First, more tasks of a similar nature and skill level can be added. If a job consists of tightening one nut on one bolt, for example, it could be redesigned to consist of tightening four different nuts on four different bolts. The job would then be enlarged horizontally. Second, other tasks of a different nature but similar skill level may be added. Instead of tightening one nut on one bolt, the worker could assemble two pieces of metal and a piece of plastic, tighten a nut and bolt to hold the assembly together, and walk to a storage area to get more nuts and bolts. The job would then be enlarged vertically.

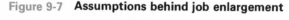

Figure 9-7   **Assumptions behind job enlargement**

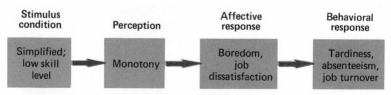

[4]J. R. Hackman and E. E. Lawler, "Employee Reactions to Job Characteristics," *Journal of Applied Psychology,* Monograph 55 (1971), pp. 259–86.

━━━━━━━━━━ **EXAMPLE** ━━━━━━━━━━

Recently, a job analysis was performed on all the positions in a regional library. The five circulation clerks' duties included working at the circulation desk, shelving books, and maintaining a particular part of the general collection (records, films, or young adult periodicals). The analyst discovered that the clerks found maintaining part of the collection the most rewarding and important part of their jobs. The routine, repetitive circulation duties included merely receiving and checking out books.

After their jobs had been redesigned, circulation clerks continued to perform their old duties of shelving books and maintaining a special part of the general collection, but they also began to perform some of the duties formerly done by a page. Time at the circulation desk was not allowed to exceed two hours at any one time, and total time at the desk was normally no more than four hours a day. This essentially vertical redesign resulted in increased job satisfaction and reduced job turnover.

Some empirical evidence suggests that jobs with cycle times of less than one and one-half minutes can be enlarged to obtain increases in output. One economic model shows that four different kinds of costs are incurred when a job is either too small or too large:

1. The imbalance-of-work cost. This cost results from the imperfect divisibility of productive tasks. In extending the division of labor concept, productive jobs must be subdivided into smaller and smaller tasks. These jobs and the subsequent tasks are *not* perfectly divisible.

2. Nonproductive work cost. This cost is incurred in operations that do not contribute *directly* to the value added to the product or service. Nonproductive costs are material handling, sweeping and cleaning, necessary visits to rest rooms, and start-up time.

3. Learning costs. Learning costs include those for initially learning the job, those for recurring learning, and the pace-achievable cost. The pace-achievable cost is not precisely related to learning costs; it is the relationship between the length of the task and worker dexterity. Within limits, the shorter the task and the less dexterity required, the quicker a worker can achieve the desired pace and the lower this part of learning cost.

4. The wage cost of skill. The wage cost of skill is related to the deskilling of work. The more specialized the tasks, the narrower the range of specialized skills, and the easier it is to assign tasks to the highest skill level required. Accordingly, the more refined the task, skill level, and wage rates, the more likely that costs will tend to be minimized.[5]

As Figure 9-8 shows, if these four costs are combined, the cost of a typical task is minimized at some point.

[5] Maurice Kilbridge and Leon Webster, "An Economic Model for the Division of Labor," *Management Science* 12, no. 6 (February 1966), pp. B255–69.

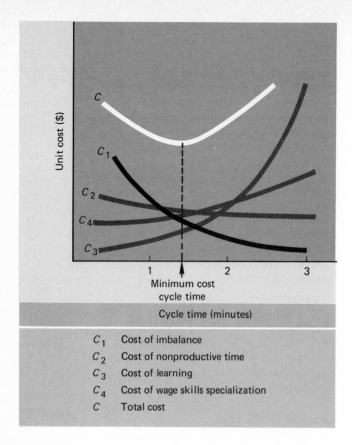

Figure 9-8 **Typical cost relationships for enlarged tasks**

Source: Maurice Kilbridge and Leon Webster, "An Economic Model for the Division of Labor," *Management Science* 12, no. 6 (February 1966), pp. B255–69.

The shape of the curve varies from job to job, and determining the minimum cost point for different jobs is more an empirical, trial-and-error procedure than it is a mathematical or graphical modeling procedure. The point is that by enlarging or reducing (further specializing) a job, managers can reach a minimum cost point.

Much research has been done on job enlargement.[6] We will discuss one of the broader studies, which reports on job enlargement programs within AT&T.[7] To date, there have been some eighteen studies in AT&T contrasting enlarged jobs with control groups in which jobs were unchanged. Table 9-3 shows the extensiveness of the enlargement studies. The study found that the jobs that were most successfully enlarged were in the treasury and commercial departments; improvements in traffic, plant, and engineering jobs were modest, and in one job enlargement group there was no change at all in performance. Table 9-4 shows the savings resulting from one of the more successful attempts at job enlargement, the shareholder correspondents' jobs.

Some cautionary words are in order, however. Although the Bell System reported much success with job enlargement, even in that extensive program

---

[6]An excellent review of the literature of job enlargement can be found in C. C. Hulin and M. R. Blood, "Job Enlargement, Individual Differences, and Worker Responses," *Psychological Bulletin* 69 (1968), pp. 41–55.

[7]R. N. Ford, *Motivation Through the Work Itself* (New York: American Management Association, 1969).

TABLE 9–3

BELL SYSTEM JOB ENLARGEMENT STUDIES*

Department	Job	Location	Enlarged jobs
Treasury	Shareholder correspondent	New York City	28
Commercial	Service representative	Toronto	50
		Montreal	75
		Chicago	40
		Illinois—suburban	25
		Illinois—suburban	25
		Northern Massachusetts	70
		Rhode Island	60
		Maryland	65
Traffic	Toll operator	Saginaw, Michigan	250
		New York City	350
Plant	Installer	California—large urban	45
		Chicago	30
	Frame cross-connection	New York City	40
Comptroller's	Service order reentry clerk	Los Angeles	30
	Service order transcription clerk	Atlanta	20
	Key puncher	Minnesota	13
Engineering	Equipment engineer	Detroit	30

*Reprinted by permission of the publisher from *Motivation Through the Work Itself* by R. N. Ford, © 1969 by American Management Association, pp. 48–49.

TABLE 9-4

SAVING OVER AN 18-MONTH PERIOD FROM ENLARGING SHAREHOLDER CORRESPONDENT JOB*

Activity	Reduction
Twenty seven percent drop, turnover, nonsupervisory specialists	$245,000
Investigation and file clerks—salaries, annual (force reduced from 46 to 24 clerks, three management jobs eliminated)	135,000
Correspondents' group—salaries (five management, four verifier jobs eliminated)	76,000
Stock transfer group—salaries eliminated	40,000
Merger of employee stock—pension unit and dividend reconciliation unit—salaries eliminated	100,000
Improved productivity (not priced)	
Improved service indexes (not priced)	
Improved tone of exit interviews (not priced)	
Personnel section, job rearrangements (not priced)	
Offset—half salary, six employees working on job enlargement program part-time	(38,000)
Total cost reduction	$558,000

*Reprinted by permission of the publisher from *Motivation Through the Work Itself* by R. N. Ford, © 1969 by American Management Association, p. 44.

not every enlargement resulted in increased performance. Further, the jobs selected for enlargement in these studies were routine, repetitive jobs with high probabilities of success. The Bell System found limited success with enlarging the jobs of managers and professionals. In general, it appears that jobs performed by some blue-collar workers offer maximum potential for performance gains from enlargement.

It is very difficult to make a strong generalization about applying job enlargement. We do know that managers and professionals tend to respond favorably to more responsibility and are likely to accept jobs that are even broader than we might think. Attempts to enlarge blue-collar jobs, however, provide mixed results. It seems clear that for routine, repetitive jobs with total job cycle times below one and one-half to two minutes, there is some chance of improved performance through job enlargement. One study reported that when foremen were given broader responsibilities, quality increased, cost decreased, and there was no change in organizational withdrawal. Other studies have reported improved satisfaction from job enlargement without performance changes. Perhaps these job satisfaction gains, which quite frequently result in decreased organization withdrawal, will turn out to be the primary, or at least the most consistent, benefit that can be attained from systematic job enlargement programs.

Job enrichment Job enrichment presumes that many jobs are so highly specialized that operative workers can no longer visualize how their work contributes to the organization goals. The worker tightening a nut on a bolt all day long loses sight of the fact that this nut helps hold a wheel on a new automobile and thereby provides safety for some new owner. The worker loses sight of the fact that the safety of a family might well depend upon how diligently he tightens every nut on each automobile.

EXAMPLE

A manufacturing vice-president for a leading foods manufacturer visited a class in beginning operations management and explained how job enrichment worked at his organization. The company was brand labeling corn flakes for a larger grocery chain, and the buyers were at the corn flakes plant for the day. Two production workers were selected and brought directly into a conference room where boxes of both competitors' and the company's corn flakes were available. These workers were asked, "Why are our corn flakes as good or better than others?" They answered by crunching various brands on the table and explaining in detail their jobs and quality control. Two benefits resulted from this. First, the buyers were impressed with the workers' knowledge. Second, and most important, the workers returned to the work place enthused about their contribution, and they spread this enthusiasm to other workers in their group. They related their contribution in "selling the product." The operative workers' jobs were more meaningful to them, and their attitudes toward their jobs were improved.

Job enrichment not only provides satisfaction, however; it also makes the organization more efficient. Many managers feel that the goals of job enrichment and increased efficiency are not only compatible; they are necessary partners. They argue that it's impossible to sustain productivity without the conscious satisfaction that job enrichment helps create.

Two conditions need to be established for effective job enrichment:

1. Management must supply information on goals and performance that previously was not available to the workers.
2. A proper *organizational climate* has to be established for success. Primarily, this climate does not imply excessive control of individual behavior in the organization.

These two conditions can be met by reorienting traditional management thinking:

1. Every employee must be viewed as a manager. Each must get involved in the management activities of planning, organizing, and controlling his or her own job. This is the basic goal of job enrichment.
2. The organization should strive to make work like play. Fun should be returned to the job. If a worker's job can be designed so that it offers the rewards that a game does—visible and meaningful goals, immediate feedback, group cohesiveness, and people who are there because they want to be—then workers will enjoy their jobs. We've designed too many of these rewards out of jobs; we can design them back in.[8]

Job enrichment is the procedure of redesigning work content to give more meaning and enjoyment to the job by involving employees in planning, organizing, and controlling their work.

Although not every job can be enriched, there are many partial solutions for jobs that are hard to enrich, particularly routine, boring, and otherwise undesirable jobs. Table 9-5 offers a few suggestions.

As is true with job enlargement, studies of job enrichment aren't conclusive, and not every job can be enriched. Studies that have been done have generally concentrated on jobs lending themselves to enrichment. Some workers don't accept the middle-class values and goals inherent in job enrichment; they "don't want to be a manager." For some workers, enrichment might reduce social interaction, a result many workers would find undesirable. And many employees prefer a low level of required competency, high security, and relative independence to the increased responsibility and growth that job enrichment implies.

Job enrichment does have promise, though, and has been successful in some situations. We simply want to caution you against accepting this behavioral technique *in place of* sound work measurement and traditional job design procedures. A possible supplement? Yes. A replacement? We think not.

[8]M. Scott Myers, *Every Employer a Manager* (New York: McGraw-Hill Book Co., 1970), pp. 47–49 and 70.

TABLE 9-5

PARTIAL JOB DESIGN SOLUTIONS FOR JOBS THAT CANNOT BE ENLARGED OR ENRICHED

Job characteristics	Partial solutions to job design
Routine, repetitive, boring, hot, noisy, generally undesirable	Use the job as an entry job in the organization, with the understanding that the employee will be there only a short time. Occasionally a worker might even want to remain in the job.
	Post the job daily. Often you will get a few daily volunteers who are looking for a change but don't want the job permanently.
	Employ the mentally handicapped, fitting them carefully to these types of jobs. They often make excellent employees when adequately trained and properly matched to a job.
	Employ part-time workers. Especially if full-time work is not available, part-time workers are often happy to do work that they would dislike on a full-time basis.

Job rotation

An excellent way to approach jobs that cannot be redesigned or automated to eliminate undesirable features is to move employees into the job for a short period of time and then move them out again.

Have you ever worked the graveyard shift (from midnight until 8:00 A.M.)? Many people find it undesirable. In such service organizations as police and fire departments and hospitals, however, the graveyard shift is necessary, and workers are rotated into and out of it. Just as employees can rotate in and out of a shift that is undesirable, they can be rotated in and out of jobs that are undesirable. This rotation technique modifies the impact of incomplete job design solutions. Although its use is often restricted by the seniority system in both union and nonunion shops, it's a technique that has been successful in many situations, and we suspect that it will continue to be used.

Participation in job design

There is very little in life that people feel more strongly and possessive about than their jobs. In later chapters, we will discuss change and resistance to change in detail; we'd like to point out now, however, that when jobs are redesigned, you should expect resistance to change of some magnitude and intensity. Employees have seen far too many changes for the sake of change in their organizations. It sometimes seems to them that every new manager brings new procedures and programs that upset their established patterns and, at least in the short run, make their jobs more difficult. The general feeling is, "I know this job better than you do; who are you to be changing it?" It is much easier to bring about meaningful change in jobs if you involve the workers, or at least give them the opportunity to participate, in the change process. If they're involved, they can learn the changed job more easily than they could otherwise because they have a positive attitude. It really doesn't take much effort or time to explain the goals of the new job and ask for suggestions. We suggest you try it.

Let's say that you've used the available charts, examined environmental impacts and followed the guidelines established in OSHA, made changes through enlargement or enrichment, and finally completed the job design. Now you need a performance standard to be sure the job is being done properly. Let's see how standards are established in production and operations.

PRODUCTION AND OPERATIONS STANDARDS

In the conversion process, a product or service is produced as output. To produce this good or service effectively and efficiently, management must establish goals for evaluating actual performance before the conversion process begins. These goals are translated into standards. A production and operations standard is a criterion established as a basis for comparison in measuring or judging output. The standard can be set for quantity, quality, cost, or any other attribute of output, and it is the basis for control. Without established, measurable standards, there is no way to compare actual performance with planned performance and, therefore, no way to take corrective action through the control function if necessary.

At what levels in the organization should standards be set? Are standards static or dynamic? What are the uses of standards? How are they actually established? It is to these and similar questions that we turn now.

Standards at Various Levels in the Organization

Individual job standards   The terms *standard, labor standard, production standard,* and *time standard* are used interchangeably in operations management. A labor standard is simply what is expected from an average worker under average working conditions for a given time period. It is the concept of a "fair day's work." A standard set at the lowest level within the organization is expressed in terms of production time required per unit of output or, conversely, output per unit of time. A candy-making operation, for example, in which coconut is sprinkled on soft chocolate might have a standard of .01 minutes per piece or 100 pieces per minute.

Departmental standards   Several workers may perform as a unit, thus forming a team assembly operation. These teams and the equipment they utilize may have one group standard for the team output. By adding all the individuals and teams together, managers can set department standards for quality, quantity, costs, and delivery dates. A department may be expected to produce a given volume of parts, a given volume per unit of time, a given volume per actual labor hour incurred, or any similar quantity standard, for example.

In production/operations, one of the basic units of accountability is the department; the foreman or supervisor of the department is often evaluated in terms of his or her ability to manage the department efficiently. Frequently this evaluation is made against an expectation to operate at or near a 100 percent labor efficiency. (Labor efficiency is the comparison of "actual" labor hours to "standard" labor hours.) In other words, for every actual labor hour used directly in operations, an expected number of pieces should be produced; this expected number is the standard. If the expected number is attained, 100 percent of standard is earned. If more pieces are produced, a greater than 100 percent efficiency occurs, and if fewer pieces are produced, a less than 100 percent efficiency is earned.

Plant standards   At the plant, works, or comparable service level unit (such as a hospital or a school), quantity and labor standards are maintained as a goal just as they are at the department level. At this level, however, more standards are added, and some of them conflict. Cost standards, for example, are critical at this level. Operations managers have very little control over the pricing, marketing, and financial decisions that affect organization profitability. They can control costs, however, and operations managers are expected to be cost minimizers. The problem is that they face certain conflicting constraints. A specified volume of goods or services must be produced; labor, materials, and overhead standards must be maintained, and at the same time their costs must be controlled. If you are familiar with cost accounting systems, you realize the need for accurate cost systems for labor, materials, and overhead. Likewise, quality levels must be maintained commensurate with product objectives. The point is clear—operations managers have multiple goals, and they must react to them with multiple standards.

Surprisingly, labor time standards are used much less uniformly in the service sector than they are in hard goods manufacturing. Since the service sector is generally more labor intense, it could benefit most from labor time standards. If you, as an emerging operations manager, find yourself employed in the service sector, you have an opportunity to bring great benefits to the largest labor sector of the economy by applying these scientific management techniques.

The Dynamic Nature of Standards

Technologies change; materials change; over generations, physical characteristics of workers change; and products or services change. So do work methods. As work methods change, standards must be revised. They are dynamic, not static, and they must be realistic and contemporary.

Reviewing and auditing standards so that integrity is maintained should be routine procedures. For new products and services, standards should be set carefully and added to the current set.

EXAMPLE

One actual manufacturing facility, which is now out of business, had unrealistically low production standards. With modest effort, both employees and departments consistently performed 100 to 150 percent of standard. Upon investigation, analysts found that over the decades, workers, especially supervisors, had successfully reduced the standard number of pieces per hour. This reduced standard, accompanied by modestly increased automation, resulted in unrealistic and irregular engineering standards, mainly because supervisors interfered when new standards were attempted. Inefficiency affected standard costing, product price, and eventually the customers; the division's prices became noncompetitive, and general management forced the plant to close down. The supervisors' efforts to keep standards low so that their group performance appeared good ("beating down" the standards) was disastrous for the facility.

Uses of Standards

At the plant level, standards are used to measure overall plant performance and assure effective resource utilization. At the worker or department level, in hospitals, cafeterias, sheet metal shops, and automobile manufacturing facilities, time (labor) standards find varied and important uses. As a basis for making operating decisions, time standards are used to evaluate the performance of workers and facilities and for predicting, planning, and controlling operations. (See Table 9-6.) Standards established by industrial engineering are used in production control, cost accounting, and many other departments or work units. They play an important overall role in the product pricing decision. The time standard is a key communication device between those involved in the actual conversion activities and those planning, organizing, and controlling those activities.

Consider two uses of time standards in Table 9-6, formulating standard costs and cost estimating. Standard costs are computed in accounting as:

$$\text{Standard cost} = \text{Standard usage} \times \text{Standard labor rate}$$

The standard usage is the industrial engineering established time (labor) standard; the standard labor rate is the accepted labor rate for the labor force that will be performing the work. If the standard usage, the labor standard, is incorrectly established, the standard cost will be in error.

TABLE 9-6

USES OF TIME (LABOR) STANDARDS

Evaluating performance	Predicting, planning, and controlling operations
Evaluating individual performance; subsequent compensation	Aggregate planning of work force levels and production rates
Evaluating department performance; subsequent supervisor compensation	Capacity planning and utilization
	Scheduling operations; time sequencing jobs
Evaluating process design, layout, and work methods	Cost estimating of products and production lots
Estimating expense and revenue streams in equipment evaluation as alternatives are compared	Planning types of labor skills necessary and budgeting labor expenses
Formulating standard costs	

Standard costs are compared to actual costs giving a labor efficiency variance where:

$$\text{Actual costs} = \text{Actual usage} \times \text{Standard labor rate}$$

and

$$\text{Labor efficiency variance} = \text{Standard costs} - \text{Actual costs}$$

Key operation management performance evaluation decisions are based on labor efficiency variances, so it is important for data in calculating the variance to be correct. The following example illustrates how an error in establishing the labor standard carries through to the labor efficiency variance.

EXAMPLE

A manufacturing firm introducing a new product set a preliminary labor standard at 10 units per hour. The standard labor rate is $4 per hour in the plant where the part is to be produced. During the third month of production, 800 units were produced using 90 labor hours. The labor efficiency variance is calculated as

$$\text{Standard cost} = (.10 \text{ hr/unit}) (800 \text{ units}) (\$4/\text{hr})$$
$$= \$320$$
$$\text{Actual cost} = (90 \text{ hrs}) (\$4/\text{hr})$$
$$= \$360$$
$$\text{Variance labor efficiency} = \$320 - \$360 = \$-40$$

One approach to cost estimation for products and services is to use the standard usage (the labor standard) and standard labor rate to compute a standard labor cost. In costing the product or service, the standard labor cost can be used directly, or it can be adjusted to reflect historical performance. The ultimate cost estimate will incorporate the standard labor cost with material and overhead costs. This cost estimate is used in the product or service pricing decision. If the labor standard is in error, the standard labor cost, the cost estimate, and the ultimate product or service price will all be in error.

Formal and Informal Standards

The actual work standard may vary considerably from the scientifically established industrial engineering standard. There is no escaping the impact of the informal organization, with its own communication network, system of authority, leaders, and work standards. Operations managers should not ignore the informal organization. Rather, they must attempt to influence the informal organization to communicate its work standards and at the same time attempt to influence the acceptance of formal standards by the informal work group. A classic example of how to use the informal work group is found in the Harwood Manufacturing "participation" studies (to be discussed in detail in Chapter 20). Job standards for a job redesign were set informally by participating workers. When checked against previous performances and industrial engineering standards, the informal standards were perfectly acceptable. Management received an unexpected side benefit from operative workers' participation in change: quickly established, acceptable standards.

The message is clear. If you make yourself aware of informal standards and try to bring them into accord with formal standards, your chances of having actual performance correspond with formal standards are greatly increased.

Management was somewhat concerned about the negative variance but decided to have industrial engineering thoroughly check the labor standard. Engineering recommended the standard be established at 12 units per hour; this was done. The labor efficiency variance was recalculated as:

$$\text{Standard cost} = (0.0833 \text{ hr/unit})(800 \text{ units})(\$4/\text{hr})$$
$$= \$266.56$$
$$\text{Variance labor efficiency} = \$266.56 - \$360 = \$-93.44$$

The labor standard was in error by 20 percent (from 10 to 12 units per hour). This resulted in more than doubling the unfavorable variance (from $-40 to $-93.44). Management now set out to find causes for the more unfavorable variance.

A labor standard tells what is expected of an average worker performing under average job conditions. The critical questions in establishing a labor standard are:

1. How do we determine who is an "average" worker?
2. What is the appropriate performance dimension to be measured?
3. What scale of measurement should be used?

After answering these questions, you can use work measurement techniques to establish labor time standards. *Work measurement is the determination of the degree and quantity of labor in production/operations tasks.*

The Average Worker

People vary not only in such physical characteristics as height, arm span, and strength, but in their working pace as well. To determine a labor standard, we need to find an "average worker"—but how do we do that? If we choose one typical worker, he or she may not be typical in every respect. Usually, the best thing to do is observe several workers and estimate their average performance. As Figure 9-9 shows, we need to trade off the costs of sampling and the costs of inaccurate standards. The total cost of establishing a standard is increased by the number of workers sampled and studied in depth. If we study each of seven workers one hour rather than each of three workers for an hour, the cost of studying

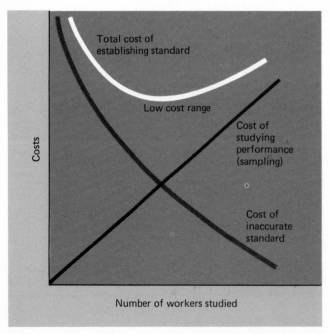

Figure 9-9 Costs in establishing standards for differing numbers of workers

performance (the sampling cost) more than doubles. The tradeoff is that the more workers sampled and studied, the closer the performance standard should be to true "average" performance. There are also costs associated with inaccurate standards; they can lead to tolerating inefficiencies, result in distorted product costs, and affect all the uses of standards we listed in Table 9-6. We can't guarantee an accurate standard, but if we increase the number of workers studied, we can reduce the total costs of inaccuracy. In trading off the costs of sample size and the costs of inaccuracy, we can find a range of reasonably low total costs (see Figure 9-9). Within this range, as close as possible to the lowest cost is where the sample size should be set.

The concept of an average worker brings up yet another point. Once average performance rates have been determined, the performance standard remains to be set. Should the standard be set at the average of total performances for the group, or at a level at which almost all the group can be expected to reach the standard? Table 9-7 and Figure 9-10 show a hypothetical situation in which workers are divided into five performance categories. Should the standard be set at 22.25 units per hour, the mean, or at 14 units per hour, a number that 95 percent of the workers can be expected to reach? Arguments for both sides are obvious. Some engineers feel that quoting a minimum standard, the second choice, encourages poor performance. They prefer to have about one-half the workers seeking but not attaining 100 percent of the standard; that is, they suggest setting the standard at the mean performance. Others feel that standards should be attainable by 90 to 95 percent of the workers. Both approaches can be used effectively.

Figure 9-10 **Frequency distribution of workers sampled**

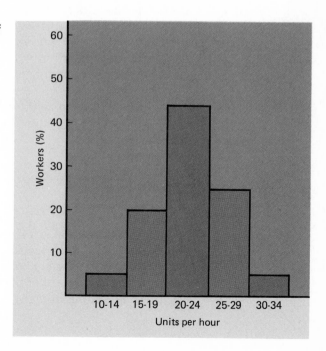

TABLE 9-7

DISTRIBUTION OF 100 WORKERS SAMPLED

Number of workers sampled	Performance in units per hour	Frequency of total workers	Cumulative frequency of workers	Complimentary cumulative frequency of workers
5	10–14	0.05	0.05	0.95
20	15–19	0.20	0.25	0.75
45	20–24	0.45	0.70	0.30
25	25–29	0.25	0.95	0.05
5	30–34	0.05	1.00	0.00

Performance Dimensions

When establishing work standards, management generally considers quantity to be the primary performance to be measured and quality the secondary standard. Quantity is usually measured as pieces per time period in manufacturing and service units per time period in service industries. A lumber sawing operation, for example, might have standard performance set at 1,200 pieces sawed per hour; a bank teller might have standard performance measured and set at 24 customers served per hour. Quality standards are often set as a percent defective—defective units divided by total units, all multiplied by 100. The sawing operation might have a quality standard of 1.0 percent allowable defective units, and the teller operation might allow a 0.05 percent error in counting coins. The key points in determining dimensions of performance are:

1. The dimension must be specified before the standard is set.
2. The standard and subsequent actual performance dimension must both be measurable.

Measurement Scales

Our discussion of work measurement will use a scale in which the normal performance is scaled at 100 percent. This scale is illustrated in Figure 9-11. If performance is 25 percent above normal, the worker is producing at 125 percent of the normal scale. You can find a more detailed discussion of scaling in many industrial engineering texts.

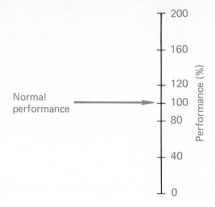

Figure 9-11 **Most common work measurement scale**

Accuracy

How accurately can a work standard be set? Obviously, experienced raters can set a standard more accurately than can inexperienced raters. Although even experienced raters make errors, the standards they set are generally found to have lower variability than standards set using only historical data. We recommend that you use raters for work measurement, although you must be aware that because setting a standard is not a finely developed scientific procedure, there are bound to be some errors.

Work Measurement Techniques

There are six basic ways of establishing a time (work) standard:

1. Ignoring formal work measurement.
2. Using the historical data approach.
3. Using the direct time study approach.
4. Using the predetermined time study approach.
5. Using the work sampling approach.
6. Combining approaches 2 through 5.

Ignoring formal work measurement   For many jobs in many organizations, especially in the labor-intense service sector, formal labor standards are simply not set at all. The issue of a fair day's work for a fair day's pay is ignored. The result is poor management or ineffective administration. Even though there is no explicit basis for criticism, workers may be blamed for poor performance and inefficiency. If workers are given no specific, understandable goals, poor labor efficiency can easily result. Often because management has not established a work (time) standard, some informal standard is established by default. Since this informal standard generally compares unfavorably with those set by other techniques, we do not recommend ignoring formal work measurement.

Historical data
approach

This method assumes that past performance represents normal performance. In the absence of other formal techniques, some managers use past performance as their main guide in setting standards. But what happens if past performance is unacceptable? Performance evaluation, planning, and control of operations turn out to be based on inefficiencies; and these inefficiencies are now built into the standard for future performance.

What are the advantages of this method? Basically, it is quick, simple, inexpensive, and probably better than ignoring the questions of establishing a work standard at all. The major disadvantage, as you have observed, is that the past might not at all represent what an average worker could perform under average working conditions. Some of the historical data may reflect unusual working conditions or the performances of unusually capable or incapable workers. Unless management intuitively adjusts past performance data upward or downward before applying it as a standard, the historical approach may misrepresent average performance. In spite of these weaknesses, however, many companies and government agencies have used the method successfully to achieve goals of profitability, growth, and survival over extended periods of time.

Direct time study
approach

Often called a time study, a stopwatch study, or "clocking the job," this technique is certainly the most widely used method for establishing work standards in manufacturing. Perhaps you have observed a job being studied by an industrial engineer, clipboard and stopwatch in hand.

How does direct time study work? We won't go into the fine points here, but basically there are six steps in the procedure:

1. Observe the job being timed. This technique depends upon direct observation and is therefore limited to jobs that already exist. The job selected should be standardized, in terms of equipment and materials, and the operator should be representative of all operators.
2. Select a job cycle. Identify the work elements that constitute a complete cycle. Decide how many cycles you want to time with a stopwatch.
3. Time the job for all cycles. Workers behave in varying ways when their performances are being recorded; common reactions are resentment, nervousness, and slowing the work pace. To minimize these effects, repeated study, study across several workers, and standing by one worker while studying a job somewhere nearby, perhaps in another department, can be helpful.
4. Compute the normal time based on the cycle times.
5. Determine allowances for personal time, delays, and fatigue.
6. Set the performance standard as the sum of observed normal time and determined allowances (the sums of steps 4 and 5).

EXAMPLE

311
Chapter 9
Job Design,
P/O Standards,
Work Measurement

A laboratory research study required that a routine, repetitive task be designed so that quantity and quality could easily be measured.[9] A collating task similar to such industrial jobs as collating sheets of paper for marketing mailing, interleaving ash trays and paper in a packing operation, or collating papers for filing by an office file clerk was devised. For this collating task, a worker took an IBM data processing card from each of six boxes, examined each card for keypunching errors, and sequenced the cards in order, one from each box. A sequence of six good cards made one good unit. The worker then stepped to another table and placed the unit in a box of good units. If an error card was found, the worker placed the error card in an error box and returned to obtain a good card from the box in which he had found the error card. The study required that he repeatedly collate good units of six cards for several hours.

A time study was made by observing five different workers for twenty cycles each. A cycle consisted of starting at box one, completing a unit, and returning to box one. The average time for each worker is expressed as an observation and shown in the table. Workers were observed without their knowledge; the average overall cycle time was 0.2247 minutes per cylce. (Another way of stating the standard would be at 4.4503 units per minute or, more commonly, 267 units per hour.)

Direct Time Study for the Quantity Standard
(expressed in minutes per cycle)

Observation	Single card	Six cards	Average time
1	.0286	.1610	.1966*
2	.0255	.0154	.2287
3	.0166	.2089	.2804
4	.0276	.1616	.1831
5	.0292	.2096	.2345
Average	.2550	.1790	.2247

*Average of performance times for twenty cycles.

One question arises from this example. Why was the sample made up of five workers and twenty cycles? It was judged that this sample was of sufficient size to give a reasonably accurate estimate of average time at a reasonable cost; in direct time study there is an accuracy/cost tradeoff.

Predetermined time study approach

For jobs that are not currently being performed but are being planned, the predetermined time study approach is helpful in setting standards. Predetermined time studies can also be applied to existing jobs as

[9]Everett E. Adam, Jr. "An Analysis of the Change in Performance Quality Employing Operant Conditioning Procedures," *Journal of Applied Psychology* (December 1972).

an alternative to using direct time study methods. The bases of this technique are the stopwatch time study and time study from films. Historical data for tens of thousands of people making such basic motions as reaching, grasping, stepping, lifting, and standing have been accumulated. These motions have been broken down into elemental actual times, averaged by industrial engineers into predetermined standards, and published in table form. The procedure for setting a predetermined time standard is:

1. Observe the job or think it through if it is yet to be established. If you are observing the job, it is best to use a typical machine, representative materials, and an average worker performing the job correctly.
2. Record each job element. Do not be concerned about elemental times; just thoroughly document all the motions performed by the worker.
3. Obtain a table of predetermined times for various elements and record the motion units for the various elements. Motion units are expressed in some basic scale (a Therblig scale is often used) that corresponds to time units.
4. Add the total motion units for all elements.
5. Estimate an allowance for personal time, delays, and fatigue in motion units.
6. Add the performance motion units and allowance units for a standard job motion unit together and convert these motion units to actual time in minutes or hours. This total time is the resulting predetermined time standard.

This procedure is illustrated by reexamining the collating task we discussed earlier.

=== EXAMPLE ===

For the collating job, a predetermined time standard was set. Table 9-8 shows the motions of the right and left hands, provides a code, and shows the TMU (Time Measurement Unit) motion units. This technique is called **Methods Time Measurement (MTM)** and is a widely accepted predetermined time study approach. The MTM procedure allows one to observe the task, breaking it down into movements that have been studied in depth and that have a predetermined average time. The MTM chart in Table 9-8 was broken into several blocks for clarity.

If a worker were in front of box number one, he would reach to the box, grasp a card, apply pressure to separate, turn the card to an observable angle, move to a focus point, and transfer the card to the left hand. At this point, a subtotal of Time Measurement Units (TMU) can be obtained; this subtotal is multiplied by 6 to get the total time required to gather six cards. (You may ignore the numbers on the cards.)

The next explainable block begins after six cards have been obtained and observed. Here the worker transfers the block of cards to his right hand,

TABLE 9-8

METHODS TIME MEASUREMENT CHART FOR THE QUANTITY STANDARD

Right hand	Code	TMU	Code	Left hand
		14.2	R12D	Reach to cards
		3.5	G1B	Grasp a card
		10.6	AP2	Apply pressure to separate
		3.5	T45S	Turn card
		13.4	M12B	Move to focus eyes
Transfer card from other hand	G3	5.6		
Subtotal		50.8		Subtotal
Multiplied by 6		304.8		Multiplied by 6
		5.6	G3	Transfer cards from other hand
		13.4	M12B	Move to final box
		4.0	D1E	Disengage cards
		15.0	WP(1)	Walk to start again
Subtotal		342.8		Subtotal
Error allowance		3.2		Error allowance
Subtotal		346.0		Subtotal
		51.9		15 percent personal, fatigue, and delay allowance
Total TMU		397.9		Total TMU

moves them to the storage box, and disengages the cards. (Cards were "disengaged" rather than "released" because they had to be stacked in the box with some care.) The worker now takes a step back to the starting position. Since walking is done while collating the cards, no other walking allowance is given.

The final two explainable blocks are for error allowance (placing an error card in the error box) and for personal needs (fatigue and unavoidable delay). The error allowance is calculated in Table 9-9. The last line in the table shows that only 3 1/2 percent of the total cards are error cards. Actually 4 percent are error cards, but historical data indicate that only seven of the eight error cards are removed from the boxes by the worker. The time allowance for personal needs, fatigue, and unavoidable delays is a standard industrial engineering allowance. Fifteen percent, a widely used allowance, is assumed for this task.

The total MTM time per cycle, 397.9 TMU, is converted directly to .23838 minutes per cycle. This is 4.195 units per minute, or 252 units per hour.

TABLE 9-9

ERROR ALLOWANCE FOR METHODS TIME MEASUREMENT QUANTITY STANDARD

Right hand	Code	TMU	Code	Left hand
Total time for		50.8		Total time for one card
one card		30.0	WP(2)	Walk to discard box (and return)
		10.6	M6B	Move error card to box
Subtotal		91.4		Subtotal
Multiplied by .035 (error percentage)		3.2		Multiplied by .035 (error percentage)

The primary advantage of predetermined time studies is that they eliminate nonrepresentative worker reactions to direct time studies. Workers don't slow the pace or get nervous because the standard is set away from the workplace in a logical, systematic manner. Since the workers aren't anxious, disruptions on the shop floor are less severe with this technique than with direct time studies. The basic disadvantage of this technique is encountered early in its use. If some job elements are not recorded, or if they are recorded improperly, future timing won't be accurate. If job elements can't be properly identified and set forth in a table, they must be evaluated with the direct time study approach.

Work sampling approach Work sampling, which was pioneered in the 1930s, is the most recently developed technique of those discussed here. Work sampling does not involve stopwatch measurement, as do many of the other techniques; instead, it is based on simple random sampling techniques derived from statistical sampling theory. Its purpose is to estimate what proportion of a worker's time is devoted to work activities. It proceeds along these steps:

1. Decide what conditions you want to define as "working" and what conditions you want to define as "not working." Not working consists of all activities not specifically defined as working.
2. Observe the activity at selected intervals, recording whether a person is working or not.
3. Calculate the proportion of the time a worker is engaged in work (P) with this formula:

$$P = \frac{x}{n} = \frac{\text{Number of observations in which working occurred}}{\text{Total number of observations}}$$

With this calculation the manager can measure the proportion of time a worker is engaged in work activity; this proportion can then be used as a performance standard.

EXAMPLE

A library administrator was concerned about the percent of time that a circulation clerk spent with patrons at the desk. Circulation activity included only those times when a clerk was engaged in assisting a patron at the circulation desk. The information clerk working at a nearby desk was asked to record every half-hour for a week whether or not the circulation clerk was "working." Results were as follows:

Day	Number of observations	Number of circulation (working) observations
Monday	16	8
Tuesday	15	8
Wednesday	20	12
Thursday	16	10
Friday	16	10
Total	83	48

The proportion of the time spent in the cirulation activity, as defined by the administrator, was

$$P = \frac{x}{n} = \frac{48}{83} = .578$$

The administrator concluded that the proportion was low enough to add other clerical activities to this job.

The work sampling approach to job measurement is particularly adaptive to service sector jobs—jobs like those in libraries, banking, health care, insurance companies, and government. Rather than setting a standard in pieces per hour, management can define work in such a way that it can be measured.

A good deal of the accuracy of this technique depends upon sample size. As is the case with any sampling procedure, there is a tradeoff between larger sample size and increased accuracy versus the cost of increasing the sample size. Reliability and precision are the key statistical concepts; if you're interested, a basic statistics book can assist you in setting the sample size for various reliability levels.

By including a concept called *rating* or *leveling performance,* you can extend work sampling to include output standards. Once a job has been studied, the analyst must decide whether the worker's performance was average, above average, or below average. If the analyst decides performance was average, no adjustment is made. If the analyst decides the worker is above average, his or her rate is multiplied by a factor less than one; if the employee was working below average, the rate is leveled to average by multiplying the observed performance by a factor greater than one.

The accuracy of performance leveling depends, in large part, upon the industrial engineer's judgment and talent. Thus, the technique may lack objectivity, and results may be uneven from study to study. Another disadvantage is that the study must be limited to few workers. Further, "working" is a broad concept, not easily defined with precision. There are, however, some obvious advantages with work sampling. It is simple, easily adapted to service sector and indirect labor jobs, and an economical way to measure job performance. In short, work sampling is a useful work measurement technique if it is used with discretion.

Combining work measurement techniques

Which work measurement technique should you use? In practice, they are used in combination, as cross-checks. One common practice is to observe a job, write down in detail all the job elements, and set a predetermined time standard. Then one can check the history of performance on this or similar jobs to verify that the predetermined standard is reasonable. To provide a further check, the job by elements and in total can be time studied. The point is clear; no one work measurement technique is totally reliable. Because of the high skill level required in setting the standard, a cross-check is recommended wherever possible.

EXAMPLE

For the collating task we discussed earlier, the predetermined time standard was .2383 minutes per collation cycle. This was cross-validated by direct time study, which provided a standard of .2247 minutes per cycle. Finally, according to a previous study that used this task but under slightly different working conditions, actual historical times in the similar task were .1954 minutes per cycle. The first two times cross-validated quite closely, and the historical standard was reasonably close, so the predetermined time standard was adopted.

Work measurement for white-collar workers

Among the work measurement techniques presented, which appear most suitable for white-collar workers? Since white-collar jobs are typically labor intense and minimally automated, the same measurement techniques employed in the service sector would seem appropriate. We suggest a combination of historical data and work sampling. When predetermined time study can be used—on more routine white-collar jobs—it can be a useful approach too.

Organizational Impact of Work Measurement

Work measurement is the key to developing work standards, and work standards are a very important part of the total information system

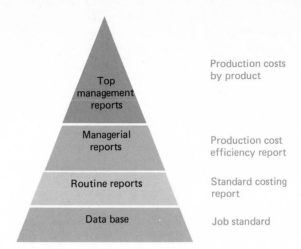

Figure 9-12 **Job standards in data base of management information system**

Production costs by product

Production cost efficiency report

Standard costing report

Job standard

used throughout the organization. Figure 9-12 illustrates one application of work measurement as it filters up the total information system into the highest level of managerial reporting. Unfortunately, erroneous work measurement affects key operating reports and decision making at the highest levels in the organization. As you can see, the work or job standard affects standard costing, and standard costing affects production cost efficiency reports. Since general management decisions about profitability are based on production costs, the production cost efficiency reports are crucial to general management. Stated a little differently, the job standard is used to cost out a product in cost accounting. Production management is judged against this cost standard, and top management sets key decisions on prices and products on the basis of standard cost and efficiency information. To have reliable data at each of these levels, accurate job measurement is absolutely necessary. Obviously, errors at the data base are rapidly compounded.

Models and Behavior

Traditional techniques of job design, setting job standards, and work measurement can be supplemented by the more recent behavioral science findings we discussed earlier in this chapter. Although the traditional view of employees as economically motivated, machinelike beings has been modified by the behavioral approach's demonstration of people's complex needs and feelings, we need not entirely discard traditional, established techniques for analyzing people at work just because our concept of human beings has changed. Rather, we need to explore further the possibility of integrating job enlargement, job enrichment, and participation techniques into the organization as we seek greater productivity gains from employees. Combining traditional models with behavioral considerations should provide positive results impossible with either concept by itself.

A key function in production/operations management is organizing work. This requires the manager to design jobs, establish job standards, and perform work measurement. In practice, methods analysis (job design) is followed by work measurement (establishing the job standard through measurement).

Traditional approaches to job design have emphasized the use of operation charts, activity charts, flow process charts, and principles of motion economy. Consideration must also be given to worker physiology and environmental conditions as these affect job design. Such behavioral concepts as job enlargement, enrichment, rotation, and design participation can enhance productivity and satisfaction. If managers use both traditional modeling and contemporary behavioral concepts in designing jobs, the results may be more efficient and effective performance than could be provided by either alone.

After the job has been designed, individual, department, and plant job standards must be established. Standards are used for evaluating the performance of employees and facilities and predicting, planning, and controlling operations. The successful manager will realize that informal job standards exist in the organization and attempt to align them with the organization's formal standards.

Although work measurement techniques do not provide perfect accuracy, they are considerably more accurate than other alternatives, including total reliance on management's judgment. Methods of work measurement vary from ignoring the problem altogether to techniques using historical data, direct time study, predetermined time study, and work sampling. In practice, several techniques are used in combination to cross-validate the work that is measured.

CASE

Sediment Oil Company

Sediment Oil Company is a regional independent company that distributes gasoline and oil products in sixteen western states. Distribution is divided by market area, and an operations manager is responsible for about twenty-two retail service stations, all of which are company owned and operated. Each station has a manager, an assistant manager, and from one to six additional employees.

Todd Smith is a new operations manager with six year's experience in retail clothing. He has been assigned a district that has nineteen service stations. The district is not profitable as a whole and is experiencing high job turnover. Upon investigation, Todd finds the high job turnover to be in the job performed at the pump, the attendant position. Further, when reviewing profitability overall and at individual stations, Todd finds that labor costs are excessive compared to more profitable company operations.

Todd is determined to focus on the attendant position for improvement. He remembers the typical attendant pumping gasoline, servicing vehicles at pump islands, and waiting for vehicles when doing neither of these tasks. Todd has noticed that both credit card and cash sales are handled by either the manager or the assistant manager. This seems unusual to him; it is unlike his experience in retail clothing. Likewise, the manager, assistant manager, or a mechanic do all the mechanical work, from repairing tires to tuning engines. Stations are not equipped for full-line auto mechanic work, but they do provide limited services with proven profitability.

Todd has decided to analyze closely the work of the station attendant, but he is not sure how to document or measure the current situation. Todd believes that he can redesign the job to cut down on labor and decrease job turnover. The state manager, to whom Todd reports, will be spending two days traveling with Todd at the end of next week. Todd hopes to have a detailed plan for measuring and redesigning the attendant's job for approval by the state manager, but he is having problems preparing a plan.

REVIEW AND
DISCUSSION
QUESTIONS

1. Explain the difference between job design and production/operations standards.

2. Discuss the relationship between work measurement and methods analysis. Which typically follows the other? Why?

3. Contrast operation charts, activity charts, and flow process charts.

4. Each of us realizes that such environmental variables as temperature and noise affect our work. What empirical evidence can you cite that supports the impact such environmental variables have on output?

5. What is OSHA? What might the Act do for the employer and employee?

6. Contrast job enlargement and job enrichment. Are they mutually exclusive?

7. Discuss the assumptions behind job enlargement.

8. Explain how departmental and plant standards differ from individual job standards. Provide an example of each from an organization of your choice.

9. Select two uses of time (labor) standards. Explain how the time standard could help a municipal police department in a city of 40,000 persons for the two uses you have selected.

10. It seems that the more workers studied in establishing a labor standard, the more accurate the standard. Therefore, every worker should be studied. True or false? Explain your answer.

11. Explain the predetermined time study approach to work measurements.

12. Why would combinations of work measurement approaches be a good strategy in establishing a standard?

13. Explain how you would proceed to set a standard for a group of seven draftsmen in a large architectural firm.

14. Why are production/operations standards important?

PROBLEMS

1. A large dairy farm expects the hay crew to place 1,200 bales of hay in the barn daily during harvest. The contract costs for labor only are $140 per day (for a crew of four). In the past four days 5,200 bales have been harvested. What is the farm manager's labor efficiency variance for the hay crew? Would you suggest any action based on this figure?

2. American Commerce's labor standard for over-the-road truck drivers is 320 miles per eight-hour shift. Current wages are $8 per hour under a nationwide contract. The assigned drivers from the Cleveland terminal logged 31,525 miles the first week of April and recorded 822 hours of work. A no overtime policy is in existence for Cleveland-based drivers.
   (a) What is the labor efficiency variance for the first week of April?
   (b) The American Commerce shop steward (driver union representative) contends that since the drivers log primarily noninterstate miles, the standard should be 10 percent less, or 288 miles per day. Operating management would like a comparative labor variance for the first week in April. What do these labor variances actually mean to management?

3. Direct time study for a task resulted in the following times, expressed in minutes per cycle.

Observation	Average time
1	1.231
2	1.302
3	1.754
4	1.272

A predetermined time standard was set at 2,128 TMU per cycle, which converts to 1.275 minutes per cycle. What time standard would you recommend? Justify your choice.

4. A student is facing midterm exams and decides to start the semester's first real studying. After one day in the library the student is dismayed to find that at the rate of present studying, completion of preparation will be four days after midterms are over. A friend volunteers to do a work sampling study and finds the following:

Two-hour time period	Number of observations	Number of studying observations
1	12	9
2	21	10
3	9	4

As a percentage, what is the proportion of time spent studying?

5. Filing clerks in a state department of welfare were considered to be filing any time they had a paper in their hands. The following seven days of observations were selected at random over the past month. What proportion of the time is spent in filing? What work measurement approach is this? How might one alternatively define filing?

Day	Number of observations	Number of filing observations
1	12	8
2	19	12
3	10	5
4	23	14
5	15	10
6	12	9
7	17	11

GLOSSARY **Activity chart:** divides operations into major task segments performed by workers and machines; times them to determine idle and productive times; appropriate for routine, repetitive tasks with worker-machine interaction

Direct time study: a work measurement technique that involves observing the job, determining the job cycle, stopwatch timing the job cycle, and computing a performance standard

Flow process chart: analyzes interstation activities to capture the flows of products through the overall production process

Gang process chart: traces interaction of several workers and one machine

Job: group of related tasks or activities that need to be performed to meet organizational objectives

Job design: specifies the content of each job and determines the distribution of work within the organization

Job enlargement: procedure of redesigning jobs or modifying work content to provide greater stimulus variety, autonomy, task identity, and feedback for the worker

Job enrichment: procedure of redesigning work content to give more meaning and enjoyment to the job by involving employees in planning, organizing, and controlling their work

Job rotation: movement of employees into a job for a short period of time and then out again

Operation chart: analyzes and separates the motions of the right and left hands to determine how much time is taken by each hand for a job; appropriate for routine, repetitive, short cycle tasks

OSHA: Williams-Steiger Occupational Safety and Health Act of 1970; develops standards, penalties and enforcement procedures for job-related safety and health

Predetermined time study: a work measurement technique that involves observing or thinking through a job, recording job elements, recording preestablished motion units, and computing a performance standard

Principles of motion economy: general statements focusing on work arrangements, the use of human hands and body, and the use of tools

Standard: a criterion established as a basis for comparison in measuring or judging output

Work measurement: the determination of the degree and quantity of labor in production tasks

Work sampling: work measurement technique that involves defining the condition "working," sampling the activity over time, and computing proportion of time the worker is engaged in "work"

Adams and Slocum. "Work Groups and Employee Satisfaction." *Personnel Administration* (March–April 1971): 37–43.

Barnes, R. M. *Motion and Time Study: Design and Measurement of Work.* 6th ed. New York: John Wiley & Sons, Inc., 1968.

Ford, R. N. *Motivation Through the Work Itself.* New York: American Management Association, Inc., 1969.

Hackman, J. R. and E. E. Lawler. "Employee Reactions to Job Characteristics." *Journal of Applied Psychology.* Monograph 55 (1971): 259–86.

Hulin, C. C. and M. R. Blood. "Job Enlargement, Individual Differences, and Worker Responses." *Psychological Bulletin* 69 (1968): 41–55.

Kilbridge, Maurice and Leon Webster. "An Economic Model for the Division of Labor." *Management Science* 12, no. 6 (February 1966): B255–69.

Mackworth, N. H. "High Incentives Versus Hot and Humid Atmospheres in a Physical Effort Task." *British Journal of Psychology* 38 (1947): 90–102.

Nadler, Gerald. *Work Design: A Systems Concept.* Rev. ed. Homewood, Ill.: Richard D. Irwin, Inc., 1970.

U.S. Department of Labor. Occupational Health and Safety Administration. *All About OSHA.* OSHA publication No. 2056.

Walker, G. R. and R. H. Guest. *The Man on the Assembly Line.* Cambridge, Mass.: Harvard University Press, 1952.

SELECTED READINGS

PLANNING THE USE OF THE CONVERSION SYSTEM

Forecasting

10

In operations management, it is necessary to consider future events that might be critical to production or operations. As Figure 10-1 shows, forecasting is a subphase of planning. To understand some of the dimensions of forecasting, you have to consider human behavior.

In this book, we have divided planning into two subsegments, both of which require information obtained from forecasts. We have already examined planning *of* the conversion system, its capacity, location, and layout. Now we consider the second subsegment, planning the *use of* the conversion system.

We know that in the management process, planning, organizing, and controlling are not independent processes; they interrelate and overlap. If operations have been properly planned and organized, control is easier and smoother. This is where forecasting comes in. It can reduce the costs of readjusting operations in response to unexpected deviations by specifying future demand. Clearly, if future demand for goods and services is accurately estimated, operating efficiency increases.

In a broad sense, forecasting presents a philosophical dilemma. "You can never plan the future by the past," said Edmund Burke; but Patrick Henry disagreed: "I know of no way of judging the future but by the past." Whether and how to use the past to predict the future is a dilemma managers and leaders have confronted for centuries, and it is still unresolved. In operations management, we try to forecast a wide range of future events that could potentially affect success. Most often the basic concern is with forecasting customer demand for our products or services. We may want long-run estimates of overall demand or shorter-run estimates of demand for each individual product. Even more detailed estimates are

FORECASTING IN OPERATIONS

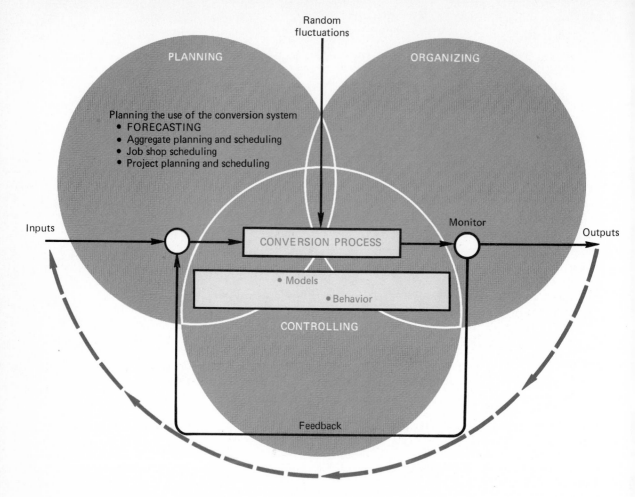

Figure 10-1 **Forecasting in operations**

needed for specific items or subcomponents that go into each product. We want to know, for example, how many subassemblies we'll need, and within the subassemblies, how many screws, nuts, and washers.

We can distinguish among these different kinds of forecasting needs by considering how far into the future they focus. Detailed forecasts for individual items are used to plan the short-run *use of* the conversion system. At the other extreme, overall product demand forecasts are needed for planning capacity, location, and layout on a much longer time horizon. Different forecasting time horizons must be used to obtain information needed for various types of planning decisions, as Figure 10-2 shows.

Forecasting Defined

In business, economic, and political communities *forecasting* has various meanings. In operations management, we adopt a rather specific definition of *forecasting*, and we distinguish it from the broader concept of "prediction."

Forecasting is a process of estimating a future event by casting forward past data. The past data are systematically combined in a predetermined way to obtain the estimate of the future.

Prediction is a process of estimating a future event based on subjective considerations other than just past data; these subjective considerations need not be combined in a predetermined way.[1]

As these definitions make clear, forecasts can only be made when a history of past data exists. An established TV manufacturer, for example, can use past data to forecast the number of coasters required for next week's TV assembly schedule. A fast food restaurant can use past data to forecast the number of hamburger buns required for this weekend's operations. But suppose the manufacturer offers a new TV model or the restaurant decides to offer a new food service. Since no past data exist to estimate first year sales of the new products, prediction, not forecasting, is required. For predicting, good subjective estimates can be based on the manager's skill, experience, and judgment; but forecasting requires statistical and management science techniques.

In business in general, when people speak of forecasts, they usually mean some combination of both forecasting and prediction. Commonly, forecasting is substituted freely for "economic forecasting," which implies some combination of objective calculations and subjective judgments. We caution students and operations managers to avoid misunderstandings by clarifying what they mean by "forecasting" when they are discussing perceived problems, solution methods, and subsequent actions based on forecasts.

[1]R.G. Brown, *Smoothing Forecasting and Prediction of Direct Time Series* (Englewood Cliffs, N.J.: Prentice-Hall, Inc., 1963), p. 2.

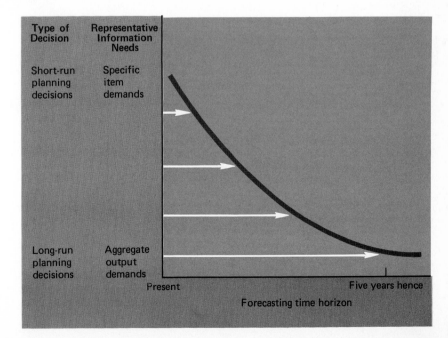

Figure 10-2 Forecasting requirements in production/operations

326
Part IV
Planning Use
of Conversion
System

Forecasting and Operations Subsystems

The aggregate demand forecast is normally obtained by estimating expected volumes of sales, expressed in dollars, and then converting these estimates from sales dollars into homogeneous production units. Production units, such items as number of televisions in a plant, number of patients fed in a hospital, number of books circulated in a library, or lots of common stock sold in a brokerage house, can then be subdivided into component parts and converted into estimates of direct labor hours or material requirements. The resulting product forecasts are used as a basis for planning and controlling production subsystems, as shown in Figure 10-3.

In studying forecasting, we must be careful not to immerse ourselves in techniques and lose track of the reasons for forecasting. Future estimates are necessary for planning the system, planning the use of the system, and controlling the system to facilitate effective and efficient output of goods and services.

Planning the
system

As Figure 10-3 shows, in planning the system we need to know future aggregated demands so that processes can be designed or redesigned to create the product flows necessary to meet demand. The degree to which we automate, for

Figure 10-3   Demand forecasting and production/operations subsystems

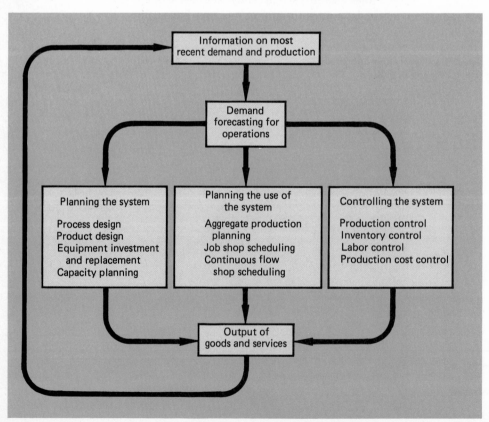

example, depends a great deal upon future product demand. Automated, continuous flows facilitate high production volumes; manual or semiautomated, intermittent flows are generally more economical for smaller production volumes. The demand estimate is critical to this design decision. Once process design, product design, and equipment investment decisions have been made for an anticipated volume, we are locked into a facility of specified capacity. Thereafter wide variations between anticipated demand and actual demand can result in excessive production and operating costs.

These long-run planning decisions require consideration of many factors—general economic conditions, industry trends, likely competitor actions, and overall political climate, among others. Therefore it is not surprising that prediction is used at least as frequently as forecasting in obtaining estimates of long-run future demand.

Capacity planning, which makes use of long-run estimation, is one of the areas in production/operations that is both critical and underutilized. In steel, power generation, and other basic industries, if capacity is not expanded fast enough, both individual firms and the national economy suffer. Particularly during periods of recession, when there is excess current capacity, operations managers tend to become overcautious in forecasting and planning additional future capacity. With the costs of excess capacity fresh in their minds, they tend to underestimate future demand.

Planning the use of the system

For deciding how best to use the existing conversion system, accurate demand forecasts are very important. Management needs short-run capacity forecasts— demand forecasts for three months, six months, and a year into the future. Both current and future work force levels and production rates must be established from these forecasts. Job scheduling in intermittent and continuous operations is more stable if future demand is accurately specified.

Controlling the system

As a *production unit basis* for control, forecasting is a short-term problem. Managers need forecasts of demand for operating decisions in production scheduling in job shops and continuous flow shops, for inventory control, production control, labor control, and overall production cost control. Accurate forecasts are needed for the immediate future—hours, days, and weeks ahead. No longer acceptable is an earlier generations' assumption that "all that is produced can be sold." Think about the costs of overproduction of some products and underproduction of others in steel mills, auto manufacturing, and clothing industries. Clearly, survival may depend on production nearing demand in the short run as well as in the long run.

Output of goods and services

Because of uncertainties in both the environment and the production process, output does not always reach the planned amount, nor does it always correspond with actual demand—even when plans are implemented. Actual demand and output must be monitored, compared with previous plans, and fed back into the demand forecasting decision system so that replanning can be done. As Figure 10-3 shows, the forecasting subsystem is a critical part of the production/operations system. It assists in the interaction among the planning, organizing, and controlling functions so that all the elements can work together for an efficient and effective conversion system.

Characteristics of Demand Over Time

For the systematic analysis of historical data that forecasting problems require, managers commonly use a time series analysis. Analysts plot demand data on a time scale, study the plots, and often discover consistent shapes or patterns. A time series of demand might have, for example, a constant, trend, or seasonal *pattern* (Figure 10-4) or some combination of these patterns (Figure 10-5). A pattern is the general shape of the time series, the general form of its central tendency. Although some individual data points do not fall in the pattern, they tend to cluster around it. To describe the dispersion of individual demands about a pattern, we use the term *noise*. A condition of low noise exists when the points are tightly clustered around the pattern. High noise means the points are highly dispersed. Figure 10-5 shows both high and low noise levels. If you tried to envision the data in Figure 10-5 without the solid line showing the pattern, you might find it difficult to identify the general pattern. Because noise in the demand can effectively disguise the pattern, manual forecasting, and computer modeling as well, can be very difficult; the result can be high forecast errors.

Analysts use the term *stability* to describe a time series's tendency to retain the same general shape over time. The shapes of demand patterns for some products or services change over a period of time, and the shapes for others do not. Future demands are easier to forecast when the pattern

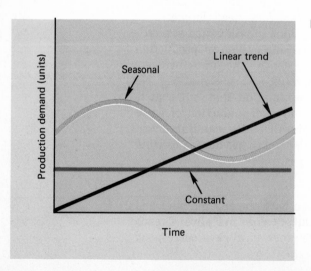

Figure 10-4 **Demand patterns**

Production demand (units)

Seasonal

Linear trend

Constant

Time

is *stationary* (stable) than when it is *dynamic* (unstable). Figure 10-6, taken from a study of demand for frosted microscope slides in a large medical center, shows an example of shifting demand. Examination of the dots reveals noticeable upward shifts beginning at about period (week) 150. Later, these shifts become more pronounced. In the study, two forecasting models, simple exponential smoothing and adaptive exponential smoothing, were used to forecast actual demand. These models will be discussed later in this chapter; here we will just observe that one model, the adaptive, responded more quickly to the demand shifts than did the other model.

Figure 10-5 **Noise in demand**

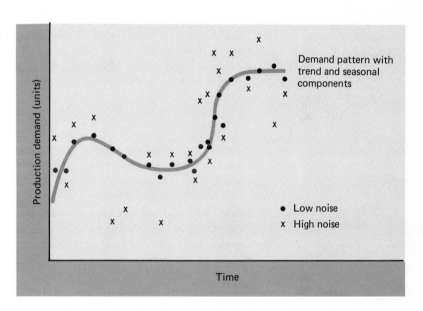

Figure 10-6 **Frosted microscope slide demand**

Source: Everett E. Adam, Jr., William L. Berry, and D. Clay Whybark, "The Hospital Administrator and Management Science," *Hospital & Health Services Administration* 19, no. 1 (Winter 1974), p. 38.

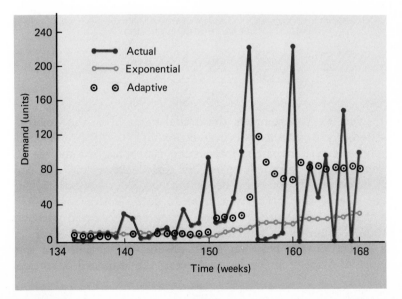

**Dependent versus
independent
demand**

Demand for a product or service is *independent* when it is unrelated to demand for any other product or service. Conversely, *dependent* demand for a product or service occurs when the demand for two or more items interrelates. The dependency may occur when one item demand is derived from a second item (verticle dependency) or when one item relates in another manner to the second item (horizontal dependency). In a movie theater, for example, demand for film postage is independent of demand for popcorn. Verticle dependency might be the relationship between popcorn and theater ticket (patron) demand. Horizontal dependency might be the relationship between popcorn demand and popcorn box demand.

When dependent demand exists in operations management, only the parent item need be forecast; all dependent items can be related to that forecast. If items are independent, there needs to be a forecast for each item. Our discussion in Chapter 16 on material requirements planning (MRP) will further develop this concept.

Forecast Error

Later, when we evaluate different forecasting methods, we'll need a measure of effectiveness. Forecast error is the scorekeeping mechanism most commonly used. *Forecast error is the numeric difference between forecasted and actual demand.* Obviously, a method that results in large forecast errors is less desirable than one yielding fewer errors. We'll discuss two measures of error, MAD and Bias.

MAD

Equation 10-1 defines the most important error measure, Mean Absolute Deviation (MAD):

$$MAD = \frac{\text{Sum of absolute deviations for all periods}}{\text{Total number of periods evaluated}} \tag{10-1}$$

$$= \frac{\sum_{i=1}^{n} |\text{Forecasted demand} - \text{Actual demand}|_i}{n}$$

In each period (i), you compare the actual demand to the amount you had forecasted. If your forecast was perfect, actual equals the forecasted amount, and there is zero error. As forecasting continues, the degree of error is accumulated and recorded, period by period. After any number of periods (n) has elapsed, you may use equation 10-1 to calculate the average (mean) size of the forecasting error to date. Notice that MAD is an average of several *absolute deviations;* errors are measured without regard to sign. MAD expresses the extent but not the *direction* of error.

There is a relationship between mean absolute deviation and the classical measure of dispersion for forecast error, the standard deviation

(σ_e). If the forecast is working properly, forecast errors are normally distributed. When this is so, the smoothed mean absolute deviation (SMAD) is used to estimate the standard deviation. The relationship is:

$$\sigma_e = 1.25\ SMAD$$

Exponential smoothing will be explained later in this chapter; for now you may think of exponentially smoothed MAD as an average MAD over time.

Bias

Equation 10-2 is a less commonly used error measure called Bias:

$$Bias = \frac{\text{Sum of algebraic errors for all periods}}{\text{Total number of periods evaluated}} \quad (10\text{-}2)$$

$$= \frac{\sum_{i=1}^{n} (\text{Forecasted demand} - \text{Actual demand})_i}{n}$$

Unlike MAD, Bias indicates the *directional* tendency of forecast errors. If the forecasting procedure repeatedly overestimates actual demand, Bias will have a positive value; consistent underestimation tendencies will be indicated by a negative value.

=== EXAMPLE ===

An aluminum extruder estimated demand for a shower stall extrusion to be 500 per month for each of three future months. Later the actual demands turned out to be 400, 560, and 700. His forecast errors, MAD and Bias, are calculated here.

$$MAD = \frac{|500 - 400| + |500 - 560| + |500 - 700|}{3}$$

$$= \frac{100 + 60 + 200}{3}$$

$$= 120 \text{ units}$$

$$Bias = \frac{(500 - 400) + (500 - 560) + (500 - 700)}{3}$$

$$= \frac{100 - 60 - 200}{3}$$

$$= -53 \text{ units}$$

As you can see, MAD is 120 units, and Bias is -53 units. Since MAD measures the overall accuracy of the forecasting method, we would conclude that this aluminum extruder does not have a very accurate model. He has a high average absolute error, 24 percent of the forecasted number of shower stall extrusions. The Bias measures *the tendency consistently to over- or underforecast.* In this example, the extrusion forecaster has a tendency to underestimate by 53 units; since actual demand averages 553 units, Bias is, on the average, a 9.6 percent underforecast.

An ideal forecast would have zero MAD and Bias. We find in practice, however, that there is usually a tradeoff between MAD and Bias; in some situations, one must be held low at the expense of the other.

Costs of errors   How important is forecast accuracy? It depends on the situation. Often important decisions are based on forecasted information, and large errors can result in very costly mistakes. Some kinds of estimation errors are more costly than others. In some settings the *direction* of error is critical; in other cases the *magnitude* of error is most important. Although the exact costs of errors are often difficult to determine, forecast errors can and should be converted into costs, even though such a conversion may have to be approximated intuitively.

Equation 10-3 is a general expression showing that operating cost is a function of forecast error:

$$\text{Operating cost} = \text{Function of forecast error} \qquad (10\text{-}3)$$
$$= [C_1][f(\text{MAD})] + [C_2][f(\text{Bias})]$$

where:

$$C_1 = \text{relative importance of MAD errors as cost}$$
$$C_2 = \text{relative importance of Bias errors as cost}$$

The relative costs of errors of magnitude and direction are not always equal. In the hospital setting in the following example, a slight positive Bias (overproduction) was more acceptable than a negative Bias (underproduction), and it was further desired that MAD be held as near zero as this Bias would allow.

Forecasting in the Service Sector

As we mentioned in Chapter 2, traditional production applications are beginning to appear in service sector operations. In 1974 and 1975, the Production/Operations Management Division of the Academy of Management commissioned a study of service sector operations.[2] A questionnaire was distributed to 251 P/OM Division members, primarily to management professors. Responses indicated that of all the traditional P/OM techniques,

[2]Everett E. Adam, Jr., John S. Bachman, John S. Fryer, Art Laufer, and Jonathan Rachik, "P/OM Service Sector Study Group Report" (Paper presented at the Academy of Management Conference, New Orleans, Louisiana, August 1975).

EXAMPLE

In a study in which food service demand was being forecasted at a medical center, dieticians estimated that the cost of underproduction was twice that of overproduction. This was true because the nutritional value of food for patients was important, and the physicians became quite upset when shortages affected their patients. The situation was expressed:

Forecast error cost = C_1 (Overproduction) + $2C_2$ (Underproduction)

where:

Overproduction occurs when forecast > actual demand

Underproduction occurs when actual demand > forecast

The amount of over- or underproduction is calculated for *n* periods as follows:

$$\text{Overproduction} = \sum_{i=1}^{n} (\text{Forecast} - \text{actual})_i$$

$$\text{Underproduction} = \sum_{i=1}^{n} (\text{Actual} - \text{forecast})_i$$

This set of cost and forecasting relationships was used to select a forecasting model from among several different forecasting models in a 400-bed hospital environment. Since the menu allowed substantial patient selection, 18 different diets and hundreds of different menu items had to be forecasted daily.[3]

---

forecasting is the most frequently applied technique in the service sector. It ranked ahead of many of the other important techniques—systems theory and modeling, job design and work measurement, inventory models, and human behavior models. These results, paired with increased economic activity in the service sector, suggest that the importance of forecasting will continue to increase in the future.

Intuitive or Formal Approaches?

In the practice of operations management today, two fundamental approaches to forecasting are dominant, intuitive estimates of the future and formal statistical modeling. The intuitive approach, which is based on experience, is essentially a summary of a manager's guesses, hunches, and judgments concerning future events. This approach is as much prediction as it is forecasting. The statistical modeling approach systematically combines specific numerical data into a summary value that is then used as a forecast. Within the statistical approach are two basic types of models,

[3] Ann Messersmith, "A Multi-Echelon Menu Item Forecasting System" (Ph.D. diss., University of Missouri—Columbia, 1975).

which are distinguished by the type of data they use. *Demand-based* models rely solely on historical data about the item that is being forecasted. If we desire a forecast of monthly demand for a lounge chair, for example, our model requires historic monthly demand data for lounge chairs. *Causal* models, on the other hand, may use additional types of data as well. These models might formally relate lounge chair demand to other variables believed to influence demand, such as the number of new housing starts.

A manager must ask several questions when selecting a forecasting approach. First, what is the purpose of the forecast—how is it to be used? Exactly what is being forecasted? Demand for a new product? Completion time on a research and development project? Will the forecast be used to schedule the day to day use of machinery and equipment? Obviously, the approach that should be selected depends upon what the forecast will be used for.

Second, the operations manager must ask about the conversion system in which the forecasts will be used. Is this system stable or dynamic, large or small, technologically simple or complex? Both the costs of obtaining better forecasts and the accuracy that is possible should be carefully considered.

Finally, the manager must ask how well the past represents the future. For a new product, the situation may be very dynamic, and the best forecast might be the preceding period's demand. For very stable products and production processes, an average of the preceding six periods might be a better estimate. What past period to use for future estimates is a difficult decision, and it's the crux of the forecasting dilemma.

Costs and accuracy   There is clearly a cost/accuracy tradeoff in selecting a forecasting approach. The more sophisticated approaches tend to have relatively high costs of implementation and maintenance, but they often provide more accurate forecasts with resulting lower operating costs. Figure 10-7 illustrates one hypothetical cost situation. Note that for any forecasting situation there is an optimal cost region where reasonable accuracy is obtained. Our goal in forecasting for operations is to operate somewhere in this optimal region.

An Overview of Specific Forecasting Methods

Tables 10-1, 10-2, and 10-3 summarize modern forecasting techniques. The techniques have been grouped into qualitative methods (Table 10-1), time series analysis and projection methods (Table 10-2), and causal models (Table 10-3). You may find it helpful to compare methods within and among the tables. The most frequently used techniques for operations management situations are the qualitative and time series models. The causal models are often more costly to implement and do not offer increased accuracy for short-term item forecasting problems typically faced by the production/operations manager. Even though the qualitative techniques

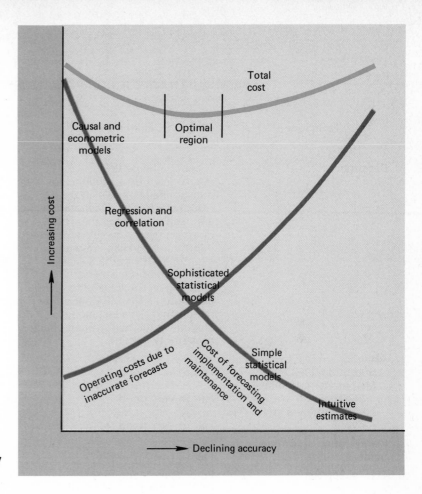

Figure 10-7 **Cost/accuracy tradeoffs in forecasting**

are very popular, they have definite accuracy limitations. We'll limit ourselves to a brief discussion of two qualitative methods and then proceed to some useful time-series models.

Qualitative Techniques

Delphi   The Delphi technique is a group process intended to achieve a consensus forecast, often a technological forecast. The process asks a panel of experts from either within or without the organization to provide written comments on the point in question.

The procedure works like this:

1. A question, the situation needing a forecast, is provided in writing to each expert in a general form. Each expert makes a brief prediction.
2. The coordinator who provided the original question brings the statements together, clarifies them, and edits them.
3. The summaries of the experts provide the basis for a set of questions the coordinator now gives to the experts. These are answered.
4. The written responses are brought together by the coordinator and the process repeated until he or she is satisfied with the overall prediction that can be synthesized from the experts.

TABLE 10-1

BASIC QUALITATIVE FORECASTING TECHNIQUES*

Technique	Delphi method	Market research
Description	A panel of experts is interrogated by a sequence of questionnaires in which the responses to one questionnaire are used to produce the next questionnaire. Any set of information available to some experts and not others is thus passed on to the others, enabling all the experts to have access to all the information for forecasting. This technique eliminates the bandwagon effect of majority opinion.	The systematic, formal, and conscious procedure for evolving and testing hypotheses about real markets.
Accuracy		
Short-term (0–3 mon)	Fair to very good	Excellent
Medium-term (3 mon–2 yrs)	Fair to very good	Good
Long-term (2 yrs and over)	Fair to very good	Fair to good
Identification of turning point	Fair to good	Fair to very good
Typical application	Forecasts of long-range and new product sales, forecasts of margins.	Forecasts of long-range and new product sales, forecasts of margins.
Data required	A coordinator issues the sequence of questionnaires, editing and consolidating the responses.	A minimum of two sets of reports over time. A considerable collection of market data from questionnaires, surveys, and time series analyses of market variables are necessary.
Cost of forecasting with a computer	$2,000+	$5,000+
Is calculation possible without a computer?	Yes	Yes
Time required to develop an application and make forecasts	2 months+	3 months+

*Source: From John S. Chambers, Satinder K. Mullick, and Donald D. Smith, "How to Choose the Right Forecasting Technique," *Harvard Business Review* 49, no. 4 (July–August 1971), pp. 55–64. Copyright © 1971 by the President and Fellows of Harvard College; all rights reserved.

Panel consensus	Visionary forecast	Historical analogy
Based on the assumption that several experts can arrive at a better forecast than can one person. There is no secrecy, and communication is encouraged. Forecasts are sometimes influenced by social factors and may not reflect a true consensus.	A prophecy that uses personal insights, judgments, and, when possible, facts about different scenarios of the future. It is characterized by subjective guesswork and imagination; in general, the methods used are nonscientific.	A comparative analysis of the introductions and growth of similar new products; bases the forecast on similarity patterns.
Poor to fair	Poor	Poor
Poor to fair	Poor	Good to fair
Poor	Poor	Good to fair
Poor to fair	Poor	Poor to fair
Forecasts of long-range and new product sales, forecasts of margins.	Forecasts of long-range and new product sales, forecasts of margins.	Forecasts of long-range and new product sales, forecasts of margins.
Information from a panel of experts is presented openly in group meetings to arrive at a consensus forecast. Minimum is two sets of reports over time.	A set of possible scenarios about the future prepared by a few experts in light of past events.	Several years' history of one or more products.
$1,000+	$100+	$1,000+
Yes	Yes	Yes
2 weeks+	1 week+	1 month+

TABLE 10-2

BASIC TIME SERIES ANALYSIS AND PROJECTION FORECASTING TECHNIQUES*

Technique	Moving Average	Exponential smoothing
Description	Each point of a moving average of a time series is the arithmetic or weighted average of a number of consecutive points of the series, where the number of data points is chosen so that the effects of seasonals or irregularity or both are eliminated.	Similar to moving average, except that more recent data points are given more weight. Descriptively, the new forecast is equal to the old one plus some proportion of the past forecasting error. Adaptive forecasting is somewhat the same except that seasonals are also computed. There are many variations of exponential smoothing: some are more versatile than others; some are computationally more complex; some require more computer time.
Accuracy		
Short-term (0–3 mon)	Poor to good	Fair to very good
Medium-term (3 mon–2 yrs)	Poor	Poor to good
Long-term (2 yrs and over)	Very poor	Very poor
Identification of turning point	Poor	Poor
Typical application	Inventory control for low volume items	Production and inventory control, forecasts of margins and other financial data.
Data required	A minimum of two years of sales history, if seasonals are present. Otherwise, fewer data. (Of course, the more history the better.) The moving average must be specified.	The same as for a moving average.
Cost of forecasting with a computer	$.005	$.005
Is calculation possible without a computer?	Yes	Yes
Time required to develop an application and make forecasts	1 day	1 day

*Source: From Chambers, Mullick, and Smith, "How to Choose the Right Forecasting Technique," *Harvard Business Review* 49, no. 4 (July–August 1971), pp. 55–64. Copyright © 1971 by the President and Fellows of Harvard College; all rights reserved.

Box-Jenkins	X-11	Trend projections
Exponential smoothing is a special case of the Box-Jenkins technique. The time series is fitted with a mathematical model that is optimal in that it assigns smaller errors to history than any other model. The type of model must be identified and the parameters then estimated. Apparently the most accurate statistical routine presently available but also one of the most costly and time-consuming.	Decomposes a time series into seasonals, trend cycles, and irregular elements. Primarily used for detailed time series analysis (including estimating seasonals); but its uses have been extended to forecasting and tracking and warning by incorporating other analytical methods. Used with special knowledge, it is perhaps the most effective technique for medium-range forecasting allowing one to predict turning points and to time special events.	Fits a trend line to a mathematical equation and then projects it into the future by means of this equation. There are several variations: the slope-characteristic method, polynomials, logarithms, and so on.
Very good to excellent	Very good to excellent	Very good
Poor to good	Good	Good
Very poor	Very poor	Good
Fair	Very good	Poor
Production and inventory control for large volume items, forecasts of cash balances.	Tracking and warning, forecasts of company, division, or department sales.	New product forecasts (particularly intermediate and long-term).
The same as for a moving average. However, in this case more history is very advantageous in model identification.	A minimum of three years' history to start. Thereafter, the complete history.	Varies with the technique used. However, a good rule of thumb is to use a minimum of five years' annual data to start. Thereafter, the complete history.
$10.00	$10.00	Varies with application
Yes	No	Yes
1–2 days	1 day	1 day

TABLE 10-3

BASIC CAUSAL FORECASTING TECHNIQUES*

Technique	Regression model	Econometric model	Intention-to-buy anticipations surveys
Description	Functionally relates sales to other economic, competitive, or internal variables and estimates an equation using the least-squares technique. Relationships are primarily analyzed statistically, although any relationship could be selected for testing on a rational ground.	A system of interdependent regression equations that describes some sector of economic sales or profit activity. The parameters of the regression equations are usually estimated simultaneously. As a rule, these models are relatively expensive to develop and can easily cost between $5,000 and $10,000, depending on detail. However, due to the system of equations inherent in such models, they will better express the causalities involved than an ordinary regression equation and hence will predict turning points more accurately.	Surveys of the general public determine intentions to buy certain products or derive an index that measures general feeling about the present and the future and estimates how this feeling will affect buying habits. More useful for tracking and warning than forecasting. The basic problem in using them is that a turning point may be signaled incorrectly (and hence never occur).
Accuracy Short-term (0—3 mon)	Good to very good	Good to very good	Poor to good

Technique	Input-output model	Economic input-output model	Leading indicator	Lifecycle analysis
Description	A method of analysis concerned with the interindustry or interdepartmental	Sometimes combined with econometric models for	Time series of an economic activity whose movement in a	Analysis and forecasting a new product growth rates based on

*Source: From Chambers, Mullick, and Smith, "How to Choose the Right Forecasting Technique," *Harvard Business Review* 49, no. 4 (July–August 1971), pp. 55–64. Copyright © 1971 by the President and Fellows of Harvard College; all rights reserved. (Adapted)

Technique	Regression model	Econometric model	Intention-to-buy anticipations surveys
Accuracy (cont)			
Medium-term (3 mon–2 yr)	Good to very good	Very good to excellent	Poor to good
Long-term (2 yrs and over)	Good	Very poor	Good to very good
Identification of turning point	Very good	Excellent	Good
Typical application	Forecasts of sales by product classes, forecasts of margins.	Forecasts of sales by product classes, forecasts of margins.	Forecasts of sales by product class.
Data required	Several years' quarterly history to obtain good, meaningful relationships. Mathematically necessary to have two more observations than there are independent variables.	The same as for regression.	Several years' data are usually required to relate such indexes to company sales.
Cost of forecasting with a computer	$100	$5,000+	$5,000
Is calculation possible without a computer?	Yes	Yes	Yes
Time required to develop an application and make forecasts	Depends on ability to identify relationships	2 months+	Several weeks

Technique	Input-output model	Economic input-output model	Leading indicator	Lifecycle analysis
Description	flow of goods or services in the economy or a company and its markets. It shows what flow of inputs must occur to obtain outputs. Considerable	forecasting. The input-output model is used to provide long-term trends for the econometric model; it also	given direction precedes the movement of some other time series in the same direction.	S-curves. The phases of product acceptance by the various groups such as innovators, early adapters, early majority, late majority, and

TABLE 10-3 (cont.)

Technique	Input-output model	Economic input-output model	Leading indicator	Lifecycle analysis
Description	effort must be expended to use these models properly, and additional detail, not normally available, must be obtained if they are to be applied to specific businesses. Corporations using input-output models have expended as much as $100,000 and more annually to develop useful applications.	stabilizes the econometric model.		laggards are central to the analysis.
Accuracy				
Short-term	Not applicable	Not applicable	Poor to good	Poor
Medium-term	Good to very good	Good to very good	Poor to good	Poor to good
Long-term	Good to excellent	Very poor	Very poor	Poor to good
Identification of turning point	Fair	Good	Good	Poor to good
Typical application	Forecasts of company sales and division sales for industrial sectors and subsectors.	Company sales for industrial sectors and subsectors.	Forecasts of sales by product class.	Forecasts of new product sales.
Data required	Ten or fifteen years' history. Considerable amounts of information on product and service flows within a corporation (or economy) for each year for which an input-output analysis is desired.	The same as for a moving average and X-11.	The same as an intention-to-buy survey + five to ten years' history.	As a minimum, the annual sales of the product being considered or of a similar product. It is often necessary to do market surveys.
Cost of forecasting without a computer	$50,000+	$100,000	$1,000	$1,500
Is calculation possible without a computer?	No	No	Yes	Yes
Time required	6 months+	6 months+	1 month+	1 month+

The key to the Delphi technique lies in the personnel involved. The panel members frequently have diverse backgrounds; two physicists, a chemist, an electrical engineer, and an economist might make up a panel. The coordinator must be talented enough to synethesize diverse and wide-ranging statements and arrive at both a structured set of questions and a forecast.

An advantage of this method is that since direct interpersonal relations are avoided, there are no personality conflicts or dominance by one strong-willed member of the group. The Delphi method has worked successfully for those involved with technological forecasting.

Nominal group technique   The basic assumption behind the nominal group technique is that a structured group of knowledgeable people will be able to arrive at a consensus forecast. The process works like this. Seven to ten people are asked to come to a meeting room and sit around a table in full view of each other, but they are asked not to speak to each other. The group facilitator hands out copies of or writes on a blackboard the question needing a forecast. Each group member is asked to write down ideas about the question. After a few minutes, the group facilitator asks each individual in turn to present to the group one idea from his or her list. A recorder writes each idea on a flip chart so that everyone can see it. No discussion takes place in this phase of the meeting; members continue to give their ideas in a round robin manner until all the ideas have been written on the flip chart.

Usually somewhere between fifteen and twenty-five propositional statements result from the round robin, depending upon the question and group composition. During the next phase of the meeting, the members of the group discuss the ideas that have been presented. The facilitator makes sure that all the ideas are discussed; members may ask for clarification of the ideas on the chart. Often similar ideas are combined, and the total number of propositions is reduced. When all discussion has ended, members are asked to vote independently by ranking the ideas, in writing, according to priority. The group decision is the mathematically pooled outcome of the individual votes.

The objectives of the process are:

1. To assure different processes for each phase of creativity.
2. To balance participation among members.
3. To incorporate mathematical voting techniques in the aggregation of group judgment.

The nominal group technique arrives at a forecast, which is the alternative receiving the most votes from the group. Sometimes after the group has been dismissed, several of the high ranking forecasts can be combined into a broader consensus forecast. The keys to the nominal group process are clearly identifying the question to be addressed, allowing creativity, encouraging limited, directed discussion, and ultimately voting.

The nominal group technique can be used for a number of questions besides technological and qualitative forecasting. We have observed, participated in, and conducted nominal group sessions aimed at identifying goals of a computer center, arriving at a ranking of future scientific research needs, and identifying key quality variables in a quasi-manufacturing and in a service conversion process. The process is not sophisticated; it works; and it leaves group members with a true sense of participation and the organization with tangible outputs.

USEFUL FORECASTING MODELS FOR OPERATIONS

Basic Averaging Models

Many models use historical data to calculate an average of past demand. This average is then used as a forecast. There are several ways of calculating an average; here are a few.

Simple average

A simple average is an average of past data in which the demands of all previous periods are equally weighted. It is calculated as follows:

$$\text{Simple Average } (SA) = \frac{\text{Sum of demands for all past periods}}{\text{Number of demand periods}}$$

$$SA = \frac{D_1 + D_2 + \ldots + D_n}{n} \tag{10-4}$$

where:

D_1 = the demand in the most recent period

D_2 = the demand that occurred two periods ago

D_n = the demand that occurred n periods ago

When simple averaging is used to create a forecast, the demands from all previous periods are equally influential (equally weighted) in determining the average. In fact, a weighting of $1/n$ is applied to each past demand:

$$SA = \frac{D_1 + D_2 + \ldots + D_n}{n} = \frac{1}{n} D_1 + \frac{1}{n} D_2 + \ldots \frac{1}{n} D_n$$

Before proceding further, perhaps we should consider why we are averaging at all. As you may remember from our earlier discussion of "noise" in the demand data, we are trying to detect the underlying general pattern or central tendency of demand. The demand for any one period will probably be above or below the underlying pattern, and the demands for several periods will be dispersed or scattered around the underlying pattern. Therefore, if we average all past demands, the high demands

=== EXAMPLE ===

At Welds Supplies, total demand for a new welding rod has been 50, 60, and 40 dozen each of the last quarters. The average demand has been:

$$SA = \frac{D_1 + D_2 + D_3}{3}$$

$$= \frac{50 + 60 + 40}{3}$$

$$= 50$$

A forecast for all future periods could be based on this simple average and would be 50 dozen welding rods per quarter.

that occurred in several periods will tend to be offset by the low demands in the other periods. The result will be an average that is representative of the true underlying pattern, particularly as the number of periods used in the average increases. Averaging reduces the chances of being misled by a random deviation occurring in any single period.

One advantage of the simple average method is that all past periods' demands enter into the calculation, and thus the effects of randomness are minimized. There is also a major disadvantage, however. If the underlying demand pattern changes over time, the estimate may not be representative of the future. Why? Because although the demands from many periods ago may not be indicative of recent trends, they are still given as much weight as the more recent demands. This difficulty is overcome to some degree by using a simple moving average.

Simple moving average

A simple moving average combines the demand data from several of the most recent periods, their average being the forecast for the next period. Once the number of past periods to be used in the calculations has been selected, it is held constant. We may use a three-period moving average or a twenty-period moving average, but once we decide, we must continue to use the same number of periods. After selecting the number of periods to be used, we weight the demands for each equally to determine the average. The average "moves" over time in that after each period elapses, the demand for the oldest period is discarded, and the demand for the newest period is added for the next calculation.

A simple n-period moving average is:

$$\text{Moving average } (MA) = \frac{\text{Sum of old demands for last } n \text{ periods}}{\text{Number of periods used in the moving average}}$$

$$MA = \frac{\sum_{t=1}^{n} D_t}{n} = \frac{1}{n}D_1 + \frac{1}{n}D_2 + \ldots \frac{1}{n}D_n \qquad (10\text{-}5)$$

where:

$t = 1$ is the oldest period in the n-period average

$t = n$ is the most recent time period

═══════════════ EXAMPLE ═══════════════

Frigerware has experienced the following product demand for ice coolers this past six months:

Time	Number of ice coolers demanded
January	200
February	300
March	200
April	400
May	500
June	600

The plant manager has requested that you prepare a forecast using a six-period moving average to forecast July sales. It is now July 2nd, and we are to begin our production run on ice coolers July 6th.

$$MA = \frac{\sum_{t=1}^{6} D_t}{6} = \frac{200 + 300 + 200 + 400 + 500 + 600}{6}$$

$$= 367$$

Using a six-month moving average, the July forecast is 367. Now examine the data. Perhaps a three-month moving average might be better than a six-month. If we use three months:

$$MA = \frac{\sum_{t=1}^{3} D_t}{3} = \frac{400 + 500 + 600}{3}$$

$$= 500$$

If we used a one-month moving average, next month's sales is last month's actual demand, and the July forecast is 600.

We must make some recommendation to the plant manager for Frigerware. For now, let's recommend using a three-month moving average of 500 ice coolers for July, since that number looks more representative of the time series than a six-month moving average, and it is based on more data than is the case with a one-month moving average.

Weighted moving average

Sometimes the forecaster wishes to use a moving average but does not want all n periods equally weighted. *A weighted moving average model is a moving average model that incorporates some weighting of old demand other than an equal weight for all past periods under consideration.* The model is simply:

Weighted moving average (*WMA*) = Each periods' demand times a weight, summed over all periods in the moving average

$$WMA = \sum_{t=1}^{n} C_t D_t \qquad (10\text{-}6)$$

where:

$$0 \leq C_t \leq 1.0$$

$$\sum_{t=1}^{n} C_t = 1.0$$

This model allows uneven weighting of demand. If n is three periods, for example, we could weight the most recent period twice as heavily as the other periods by setting $C_1 = 0.25$, $C_2 = 0.25$, and $C_3 = 0.50$.

EXAMPLE

For Frigerware, a forecast of demand for July using a three-period model with the most recent period's demand weighted twice as heavily as each of the previous two periods' demands is:

$$WMA = \sum_{t=1}^{3} C_t D_t = .25(400) + .25(500) + .50(600)$$

$$WMA = 525$$

An advantage of this model is that it allows you to compensate for some trend or for some seasonality by carefully fitting the coefficients, C_t. If you want to, you can weight recent months most heavily and still dampen somewhat the effects of noise by placing small weightings on older demands. Of course, the modeler or manager still has to choose the coefficients, and this choice will be critical to model success or failure.

Regression

Linear regression   Although linear regression methods are computationally more complex than the others we've discussed, they have been found useful in some situations. They may be applied, for example, when a plot of the data suggests that the underlying pattern is a straight line, or nearly so. Since linear regression isn't widely applied in individual item forecasting, we won't dwell on it here; but we should recognize that regression is often useful in representing economic relationships and as such is useful in many other business applications. When data are linear and stable, linear regression can sometimes be used. It requires much data, however, and they can be cumbersome and costly to store. It's also costly to perform the required calculations period by period, often weekly, for thousands of production or operations supply items.

Exponential Smoothing

Exponential smoothing models are well known and often used in operations management. The reasons for their popularity are two: they are readily available in standard computer software packages, and the models require relatively little data storage and computation, an important consideration when forecasts are needed for each of many individual items. Many computer companies have spent considerable time developing and marketing forecasting software and educating managers in how to use it. In addition, some major professional and trade associations, among them the American Production and Inventory Control Society (APICS), have introduced their members to these techniques.

Exponential smoothing is a specific averaging technique. It is distinguishable by the special way it weights each of the past demands in calculating an average. The pattern of weights is *exponential* in form. Demand for the most recent period is weighted most heavily; the weights placed on successively older periods decay exponentially. In other words, the weights decrease in magnitude the further back in time the data is weighted; the decrease is nonlinear (exponential).

First order exponential smoothing

To begin, let's examine the computational aspects of first order exponential smoothing. The equation for creating a new or updated forecast uses two pieces of information: actual demand for the most recent period and the previous (most recent) forecast. As each time period expires, a new forecast is made:

$$\text{Forecast of next period's demand} = \alpha \left(\begin{array}{c} \text{Most} \\ \text{recent} \\ \text{demand} \end{array} \right) + (1 - \alpha) \left(\begin{array}{c} \text{Most} \\ \text{recent} \\ \text{forecast} \end{array} \right)$$

$$F_t = \alpha D_{t-1} + (1 - \alpha) F_{t-1} \qquad (10\text{-}7)$$

where:

$$0 \leq \alpha \leq 1.0, \text{ and } t \text{ is the time period}$$

After time period $t - 1$ *ends,* you know the actual demand that occurred (D_{t-1}). At the *beginning* of period $t-1$ you had made a forecast (F_{t-1}) of what would be demanded during $t-1$. Therefore, at the *end* of $t-1$ you have both pieces of information needed for calculating a forecast of demand for the upcoming time period, F_t.

Why is this model called *exponential* smoothing? An expansion of equation 10-7 shows:

Since:

$$F_t = \alpha D_{t-1} + (1 - \alpha)F_{t-1} \qquad (10\text{-}8)$$

then:

$$F_{t-1} = \alpha D_{t-2} + (1 - \alpha)F_{t-2} \qquad (10\text{-}9)$$

and similarly:

$$F_{t-2} = \alpha D_{t-3} + (1 - \alpha)F_{t-3} \qquad (10\text{-}10)$$

We begin expanding by replacing F_{t-1} in equation 10-8 with its equivalent, the right side of equation 10-9:

$$F_t = \alpha D_{t-1} + (1 - \alpha) \left[\alpha D_{t-2} + (1 - \alpha)F_{t-2} \right]$$

$$F_t = \alpha D_{t-1} + \alpha(1 - \alpha)D_{t-2} + (1 - \alpha)^2 F_{t-2} \qquad (10\text{-}11)$$

We continue expanding by replacing F_{t-2} in equation 10-11 with its equivalent, the right side of equation 10-10:

$$F_t = \alpha D_{t-1} + \alpha(1 - \alpha)D_{t-2} + (1 - \alpha)^2 \left[\alpha D_{t-3} + (1 - \alpha)F_{t-3} \right]$$

$$F_t = \alpha D_{t-1} + \alpha(1 - \alpha)D_{t-2} + \alpha(1 - \alpha)^2 D_{t-3} + (1 - \alpha)^3 F_{t-3} \qquad (10\text{-}12)$$

Equation 10-12 can be rewritten as:

$$F_t = \alpha(1 - \alpha)^0 D_{t-1} + \alpha(1 - \alpha)^1 D_{t-2} + \alpha(1 - \alpha)^2 D_{t-3} + (1 - \alpha)^3 F_{t-3} \quad (10\text{-}13)$$

We have now expanded equation 10-8 to obtain equation 10-13. The expansion could be continued further, but it is not necessary for illustrating our point; equation 10-13 shows the relative weight that is placed on each past period's demand in arriving at a new forecast.

Since $0 \le \alpha \le 1.0$, the terms $\alpha(1 - \alpha)^0$, $\alpha(1 - \alpha)^1$, $\alpha(1 - \alpha)^2$ . . . are successively smaller in equation 10-13. More specifically, these weights are exponentially distributed; the most recent demand, D_{t-1}, is given the most weight, while the older data are weighted less and less heavily. Suppose, for example, we are using $\alpha = .2$. Then $\alpha(1 - \alpha)^0 = .2$, $\alpha(1 - \alpha)^1 = .16$, $\alpha(1 - \alpha)^2 = .128$, etc., and these are the relative weightings being placed on D_{t-1}, D_{t-2}, D_{t-3}, etc., respectively. Remember, all of this is being accomplished automatically when you use the simple forecasting equation 10-8.

As with other statistical forecasting models, in exponential smoothing we have the problem of parameter selection; that is, we must fit the model to the data. To begin forecasting, some reasonable estimate for an old beginning forecast is necessary. Likewise, a smoothing coefficient, α, must be selected. This choice is critical. As equation 10-7 shows, a high α places heavy weight on the most recent demand, and a low α weights recent demand less heavily. A high smoothing coefficient is more appropriate for new products or items for which the underlying demand is shifting about, or unstable. An α of 0.7, 0.8, or 0.9 might be best for these conditions. If demand is very stable and believed to be representative of the future, the forecaster wants to select a low α value to smooth out any sudden noise that might have occurred. The forecasting procedure, then, does not overreact to the most recent demand. Under these stable conditions, an appropriate smoothing coefficient might be 0.1, 0.2, or 0.3. When demand is slightly unstable, smoothing coefficients of 0.4, 0.5, or 0.6 might provide the most accurate forecasts.

EXAMPLE

Phoenix General Hospital has experienced irregular, and usually increasing, demand for disposable kits throughout the hospital. The demand for a disposable plastic tubing in pediatrics for the last two months has been: September: 300 units and October: 350 units. The old forecasting procedure was to use last year's average monthly demand as the forecast for each month this year. Last year's monthly demand was 200 units. Using 200 units as the September forecast and a smoothing coefficient of 0.7 to weight recent demand most heavily, the forecast for *this* month, October, would have been (t = October):

$$F_t = \alpha D_{t-1} + (1 - \alpha)F_{t-1}$$
$$= 0.7(300) + (1 - .7)200$$
$$= 210 + 60$$
$$= 270$$

The forecast for November would be (t = November):

$$F_t = \alpha D_{t-1} + (1 - \alpha)F_{t-1}$$
$$= 0.7(350) + (1 - .7)270$$
$$= 245 + 81$$
$$= 326$$

Instead of last year's demand for 200 units, November's forecast is for 326 units. The old forecasting method, the heuristic based on a simple average, provided a considerably different forecast from the exponential smoothing model.

Selecting forecasting parameters and comparing models

The procedure for selecting forecasting parameters is given in the first four steps that follow; the fifth step is used for comparing and selecting models:

1. Partition the available data into two subsets, one for fitting parameters (the "test" set) and the other for forecasting.

2. Select an error measure to evaluate forecast accuracy of the parameters to be tried. MAD and/or Bias are useful error measures.

3. Select a range of α values to be evaluated. Using one of the α values, apply the forecasting model to the test set of data, recording the resulting forecast errors. Then, selecting a new value for α, repeat the process. Continue this process until representative α values in the selected range have been tested.

4. Select the α value that resulted in the lowest forecast error when applied to the test data. Your model is now fit to the demand data.

5. Forecast with the exponential (or moving average) model that you have fit to test data on the balance of the data. You can also use these data to compare alternative models that have previously been fit to representative demand data.

If you do not intend to compare models, there is no need to partition the data; *all* the data can be used as the test data in steps 1 through 4.

Figure 10-8 illustrates forecasting performance for two different smoothing coefficients for an unstable demand series. The exponential smoothing model with the higher α value performed best; it adapted more quickly to the shift in demand in period 6 than did the lower α value.

Simple exponential smoothing and the other exponential smoothing models share the advantages of requiring that very few data points be stored. To update the forecast from period to period, you need only α, last period's demand, and last period's forecast. Remember, this model incorporates in the new forecast *all past demands.* The model is easy to understand and easily computerized for thousands of part numbers, supply items, or inventory items. The smoothing coefficient can be set for classes or families of items to minimize the cost of parameter selection. We have observed use of the model in both the manufacturing and service sectors. The model's operating simplicity and efficiency for economically obtaining "quick and easy" forecasts are its main advantages.

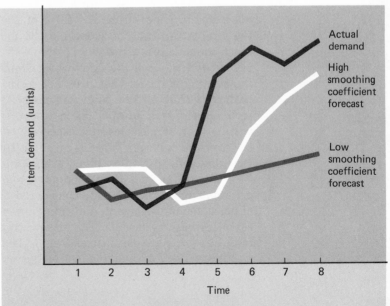

Figure 10-8 Selection of smoothing coefficients

If the modeler or manager is unsure about the stability or form of the underlying demand pattern, adaptive exponential smoothing provides a good forecasting alternative. In adaptive exponential smoothing, the smoothing coefficient, α, is not fixed; it is set initially and then allowed to fluctuate over time based upon changes in the underlying demand pattern. This method is discussed in the supplement at the end of this chapter.

SELECTION OF THE FORECASTING MODEL

We've discussed several statistical forecasting models for demand estimation in planning and control. As a manager, you now have the task of selecting the best model for your needs. Which one should you choose, and what criteria should you use to make the decision?

As we've said before, criteria that influence model selection are *cost* and *accuracy*. Accuracy (forecast error), as measured by MAD and Bias, can be converted into cost (dollars). *Costs to be considered in model selection are implementation costs, systemic costs, and forecast error costs.* Implementation costs include costs of programming and costs of initiating forecasting parameters, training users, and the initial dysfunctional effects of changing from an old forecasting procedure. Systemic costs include costs of monitoring the forecasting system, computer run time or manual computation time, and other costs of maintaining the forecasting system.

The moving average, exponential smoothing, and adaptive models can each be evaluated as to implementation and systemic costs. A simple moving average model, for example, would have low costs of programming training and moderate parameter initialization costs. Computer run time costs might be low, but manual computational costs and costs of monitoring the system could be high. Actual dollar estimates depend upon the number of items to be forecasted and the completeness of the data base.

Forecast error costs are more complex to evaluate. They depend upon noise in the time series, the form of the demand pattern, the length of the forecasting time horizon, and the measure of forecast error. We can reach one conclusion, however: *forecast error and subsequent model selection are dependent upon the underlying demand pattern.* There is little value in selecting a model that does not correspond to the underlying demand pattern. Errors will be high and costly. A simple moving average model, for example, will always lag a linear trend component, and the result will be high forecast errors, especially if the number of periods used in the average is large. There is no substitute for careful analysis of typical item demands, including plots, when a model is being selected.

Several studies have evaluated and compared the performances of different models. One study considered the effects of differences in level of noise, demand pattern, and time horizon on forecast errors for a limited set of forecasting models. The intent was to identify the better forecasting model under these various conditions. The summary of results is presented as Figure 10-9. Although some of the models that were found to be best

Length of forecast period	1 period ahead					12 periods ahead				
Across all demand patterns and noise levels: best models*	(5)					(6)				
Demand pattern* across all noise levels	1	2	3	4	5	1	2	3	4	5
Best model(s)*	(2),(4) (6),(7)	(5), (6)	(5)	(1), (5)	(1),(5)	(2),(4) (6)	(6)	(1),(5) (7)	(6)	(3)
Noise level across all demand patterns	Low		High			Low		High		
Best model(s)*	(5)		(4),(6)			(3),(6)		(3),(6)		

*Variable descriptions

Independent variable	Level	Description
Demand pattern	1	Constant
	2	Linear trend
	3	Seasonal
	4	Permanent, seasonal and trend
	5	Linear trend and step function
Forecast model	(1)	Moving average (1 period)
	(2)	Moving average (2 period)
	(3)	Winters' model
	(4)	First order exponential smoothing
	(5)	Second order exponential smoothing
	(6)	Exponential double smoothing
	(7)	Adaptive exponential smoothing

Figure 10-9 Forecast model selection based on forecast errors

Source: Adapted from Everett E. Adam, Jr., "Individual Item Forecasting Model Evaluation," *Decision Sciences* 4, no. 4 (October 1973), p. 468.

are too complex for our introductory treatment (except for exponential double smoothing, which is presented in the supplement to this chapter), you should notice that different models were best, depending on the type of demand pattern and noise level, and that several models were usually equally good. It is typical in forecasting to have a choice of several good models for any one demand pattern when the choice is based only on forecast error. *Notice also that there is no one model that is best for all demand patterns.* This is the study's most significant conclusion.

Forecasts are not always made with statistical models. Individuals can and do forecast by intuitively casting forth past data, and they often intervene in other ways in the statistical forecasting procedure as well. A manager may feel that item forecasts generated by models must be checked for reasonableness by qualified operating decision makers. Forecasts generated by models should not be followed blindly; potential cost consequences must be carefully considered. Sometimes the model forecasts

BEHAVIORAL DIMENSIONS OF FORECASTING

will not be changed after review; sometimes they will be adjusted. In making these adjustments, decision makers can take into account qualitative data that are not in the model. (When a change based on other data is made, the forecast becomes a prediction.) Decision makers should use the forecasting model as an *aid* in decision making; they should not rely totally on the forecasting model for all decisions.

Individual Versus Model Forecasting

Many, perhaps most, forecasts for production/operations are individual intuitive forecasts. We have observed intuitive forecasts, for example, in large firebrick manufacturing facilities and hospitals. One of the problems in implementing item forecasting models lies in convincing the intuitive forecaster that he or she is not doing as good a job as could be done by a model.

EXAMPLE

For a 400-bed hospital, forecasts of the daily patient load for food services, the daily census, were being made manually. (See Fig. 10-10.) An experienced dietician was making these forecasts, but they incorporated considerable bias, partly because she feared the medical staff if shortages occurred. An adaptive exponential smoothing model improved considerably on the manual procedure, and the resulting implementation considerably reduced food costs from overproduction.

Figure 10-10 **Forecasting daily patient census in a hospital: exponential smoothing with tracking vs. manual procedures**

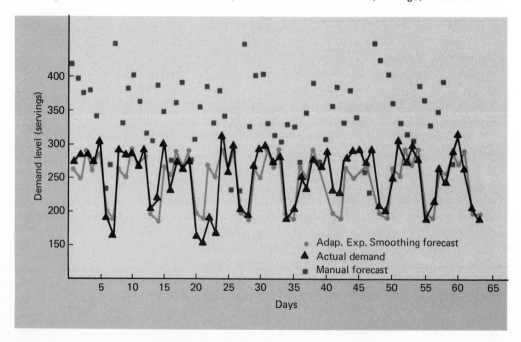

Currently, little is known about the relative effectiveness of intuitive forecasting. We can, however, provide a structured approach for examining this area of human behavior by analyzing some of the mental processes involved. A forecast may be regarded as the culmination of a process consisting of several stages, including information search and information processing. It results in human inferences about the future that are based on particular patterns of historical data presented to the forecaster. We can speculate about a number of environmental factors that may affect these mental processes and thereby affect intuitive forecasting performance.

Meaningfulness   The forecasting task itself requires the consideration of a restricted set of information cues about historical demand. Although the manner in which these data are utilized to make a "good" forecast may be complex, usually the form and type of information encountered are repetitive. As you may remember from our discussion of job enrichment and job design, if repetitive tasks can be made meaningful to the person performing them, positive effects usually result. Therefore, management should make the forecaster aware that his or her efforts are important to the company. If forecasts are accurate, the forecasters should be told that they are, so their behavior is reinforced. Furthermore, the forecaster should know that his or her information will contribute substantially to subsequent decisions affecting the entire organization. Imparting meaningfulness, then, may be expected to affect intuitive forecasting performance; the more meaningful the forecasting task, the more accurate the intuitive forecast.

Pattern complexity   The forecaster may be confronted with any of a variety of demand-generating functions. Previously we have examined constant, trend, and seasonal effects. Adding two or more components together (adding trend and seasonal components, for example) results in a more complex data generating function than either separately. Pattern complexity, the shape of the demand function, is a critical variable in intuitive forecasting, just as it is in model forecasting.

Some behavioral studies lead us to suggest that intuitive forecasters may perform better on linear than on nonlinear demand patterns. In many instances, when people try to make inferences based on nonlinear data their performance is less accurate than when linear data are present. In addition, people apparently try to use nonlinear data in a linear manner. Intuitive forecasting accuracy is probably lower for nonlinear than for linear demand patterns.

Degree of noise   Given sufficient historical data, the forecasting problems are trivial for most cases without noise. Introducing random variations, however, often brings about a condition psychologists call "cue uncertainty." Cue uncertainty results when noise in the old demand (the cue) hides or masks the basic demand pattern. At one extreme are demand patterns with zero random variability (no noise). Since no randomness is present, the past data provide a clear picture of the basic demand pattern. In other instances, however, the degree of noise is larger, and intuitive forecasting variability increases. Very large noise levels obscure the basis for accurate forecasting, and often the result is lower forecast accuracy.

Meaningfulness, pattern complexity, and degree of noise are three environmental factors that may affect human forecasting. These three factors were examined in a laboratory study of intuitive forecasting (see Table 10-4). The results indicated that pattern complexity and noise level did significantly affect forecast errors. The lower the mean error, the better that group's forecasting performance. Meaningfulness, as defined in this study, had no effect on forecast error. This result is inconsistent with many other job enrichment studies but concurs with some of the critics of the meaningfulness concept who question whether meaningfulness always uniformly increases performance.

TABLE 10-4

INTUITIVE FORECASTING MEAN ERRORS*

Factor	Level (mean error)		
Demand pattern, *A* (pattern complexity)	Trend (18.73)	Trend, low seasonal (17.77)	Trend, high seasonal (24.86)
Meaningfulness, *B*	Meaningful (20.00)	Nonmeaningful (20.91)	
Noise in demand, *C* (cue uncertainty)	High (27.66)	Low (13.25)	

*Source: Everett E. Adam, Jr. and Ronald J. Ebert, "A Comparison of Human and Statistical Forecasting," *AIIE Transactions* 8, no. 1 (March 1976), pp. 120–27. Copyright American Institute of Industrial Engineers, 25 Technology Park/Atlanta, Norcross, Georgia 30092.

Individual
variability

Another important finding in this study of intuitive forecasting was the wide variability of performance among the 240 forecasters. There were a few very good forecasters, but there were even more very poor forecasters. If planning and directing production and operations are based on poor intuitive forecasts, these variations in performance can be very expensive.

Individual versus
model
performance

In this same study, one-period-ahead forecasts were made for sixty consecutive periods by both human forecasters and several models. The exponential smoothing models, which were fit to the historical demands given to the intuitive forecasters, significantly outperformed group average performance on both period-by-period and overall bases. The findings are illustrated in Table 10-5. Again, the poor forecasters experienced especially high errors compared to the models. Only a few very good intuitive forecasters outperformed the models.

We know that intuitive forecasting and prediction are commonplace. Although models seem to compare favorably to intuitive forecasts, field studies (well documented real world experiences) are needed to support this contention. Again, as was the case with model selection, the complexity of demand patterns and the noise in the demand patterns are critical to intuitive forecasting performance. The operations manager would be wise to consider models as an alternative to individuals. Models generally are more accurate, and if a large number of items must be forecast, the models are more economical.

TABLE 10-5

FORECASTING MODELS VS. HUMAN PERFORMANCE*

Experimental condition	Forecast model mean error	Human performance mean error
Across patterns and noise		
First order[1]	17.306	20.460
Winters[2]	14.111	20.460
Patterns (across noise)		
First order		
Trend	12.083	18.737
Trend, low seas.	14.416	17.777
Trend, high seas.[3]	25.416	24.866
Winters		
Trend	11.250	18.737
Trend, low seas.[3]	16.250	17.777
Trend, high seas.	14.833	24.866
Noise (across patterns)		
High Noise		
First order	22.500	27.660
Winters	18.444	27.660
Low noise		
First order[3]	12.111	13.259
Winters	9.777	13.259

*Source: Adam and Ebert, pp. 120–27. Copyright American Institute of Industrial Engineers, 25 Technology Park/Atlanta, Norcross, Georgia 30092.
[1]First order exponential smoothing model.
[2]Winters three factor exponential smoothing with constant, trend, and seasonal factors.
[3]No significant differences between means. All other means were significantly different at $p < 0.001$.

SUMMARY   In operations management, we deviate from the general business concept of business forecasting and define forecasting as the use of past data to determine future events. Prediction, on the other hand, is used to refer to subjective estimates of the future. The skill, experience, and sound judgment of a manager are required for good predictions; often statistical and management science techniques must be used to make reasonable forecasts. Forecasts are a part of planning and subsequently become an input in operations for design, additional planning phases, and control.

Such characteristics of demand as pattern, stability, and noise affect the forecasting procedure. Forecast error, the difference between forecasted demand and actual demand, is the basic scorekeeping device for evaluating forecasting procedures.

There is a cost/accuracy tradeoff in selecting a forecasting approach. Generally, the less expensive the forecasting procedure, the less accurate the results. There are three basic groupings of forecasting techniques: qualitative models, time series analysis, and causal models. The individual item forecasting situation most frequently encountered in production/operations is best approached with time series models.

Before forecasting, one must fit such model parameters as initial forecasts and coefficients to the historical demand pattern data. If the demand pattern is unstable, shifting about, adaptive forecasting models are appropriate. In adaptive models, the parameters change over time as the demand pattern changes.

The key to selecting a forecasting model is the tradeoff between forecasting costs and accuracy. Implementation, systemic, and forecast error costs must all be considered forecast error costs. Research results show that the best forecasting model to use depends upon the forecast time horizon, noise, the measure of forecast error, and, most importantly, the demand pattern. There appears to be no one forecasting model that is best for all demand patterns, although double exponential smoothing does as well as any other.

Often, forecasts are not made with statistical models; individuals can and do intuitively use past data to forecast future events. Generally, individual forecasting performance *decreases* with lack of meaningfulness, increased pattern complexity, and increased cue uncertainty. There is considerable individual variability; some individuals are "good" forecasters, and some are "poor" forecasters compared to group averages.

Generally, forecasting models tend to outperform most intuitive forecasts. There are, however, a few individuals who seem consistently to outperform the models. Since models are generally more accurate and, if a large number of items must be forecasted, more economical than individuals, operations managers would be wise to consider their use.

CASE

Spradling Enterprises

Spradling Enterprises manufactures household cleaning products. One product, Stain-Re-Mover, product number SRM-10, has been difficult to produce in enough volume to sustain inventory between production batches. The table illustrates monthly demand in 24-case lots for the last 15 months, essentially the total life of SRM-10.

Monthly Demand for SRM-10 in 24 Case Lots

Month	Demand	Month	Demand
December 1976	22	August	57
January 1977	40	September	55
February	32	October	65
March	55	November	73
April	67	December	90
May	53	January 1978	81
June	90	February	93
July	62		

The production manager has asked production control to reexamine the item forecasting procedure for this product. In production control, the initial 12-month forecast from marketing is always used for a new product. In the absence of other instructions, their forecast of 50 lots per month has been used to date for SRM-10.

Spradling Enterprises uses first order exponential smoothing for forecasting item demand for all items after one year of product experience has occurred. Either a slow smoothing (smoothing coefficient of 0.2) or a fast smoothing (smoothing coefficient of 0.7) model is used for each product. The choice of fast or slow smoothing is based primarily on Mean Absolute Deviation (MAD) over the last six periods of data, with some consideration given secondarily to Bias. The initial forecast needed to evaluate fast or slow smoothing for a new product is always the marketing forecast.

The production control manager is concerned about the specific problem of changing the SRM-10 forecast to correspond with current procedures and the more general problem of developing a check list for reviewing the existing forecasting procedure for possible improvement.

1. Contrast forecasting and prediction and give an example of each.

2. Forecasting is an important information input for operations subsystem decisions. Explain what might be forecasted for a supermarket operation and relate that information to Figure 10-3.

3. Explain what the demand noise pattern and stability are in time series analysis.

4. Which would you use in evaluating a forecast, MAD or Bias? Why?

5. Present any evidence that suggests forecasting is an important problem in the service sector.

6. Examine Tables 10-1, 10-2, and 10-3, which summarize modern forecasting techniques. Is there any one best technique? What can be concluded from these tables?

7. Contrast the cost/accuracy trade-offs in forecasting model selection between sophisticated statistical models and intuitive estimates.

8. Explain how the nominal group technique would arrive at a consensus forecast.

9. Explain how the Delphi technique would arrive at a consensus forecast.

10. Individuals forecast intuitively. What are some of the variables that affect the relative effectiveness of those intuitive forecasts?

11. Compare intuitive forecasting to naive statistical forecasting models, citing any relevant research.

PROBLEMS

1. An ice cream parlor experienced the following demand for ice cream last month. The current forecasting procedure is to use last year's corresponding weekly sales as this year's forecast.

Week	Forecasted demand (gallons)	Actual demand (gallons)
June 1	210	200
June 8	235	225
June 15	225	200
June 22	270	260

Calculate MAD and Bias and interpret each.

2. The monthly cost of overstocking crates of lettuce in a grocery chain is estimated to be $5.50 times the average daily Bias for any one month.
   (a) Express this relationship as a cost function.
   (b) If daily Bias was a positive 137 crates last month, what was the total cost for that error?
   (c) How much should management be willing to spend for a perfect forecast?

3. A mole and gopher poison manufacturer has experienced the following monthly demand for an environmentally improved pesticide poison.

Month	Demand item #P107 (cases)
February	620
March	840
April	770
May	950
June	1,000

   (a) Using a three month simple average, what would the forecast have been for May and June?
   (b) What would the three month simple moving average have been for May and June?
   (c) Which forecasting method would you recommend? Why?

4. In finished goods, B&G Motors stocks three horsepower motors. Weekly demand for seven typical weeks is:

Week	Demand for 3-hp motor
42	10
43	12
44	8
45	10
46	9
47	6
48	4

(a) Calculate a weighted moving average forecast for weeks 49 and 50 using a three-period model with the most recent periods demand weighted three times as heavily as each of the previous two periods demands. After forecasting period 49, actual demand was 10 motors for the period.

(b) Examining the data visually, what would you suggest as a possible alternative weighted moving average model? Why?

5. Demand for part number 2710 has been as shown below. Our forecast for April was 100 units. With a smoothing constant of 0.20 and using first order exponential smoothing, what is the July forecast? What do you think about a 0.20 smoothing constant?

Time	Actual demand
April	200
May	50
June	150

6. A small electronic company produces pocket calculators and keeps item demand monthly. The following demand data are for a representative calculator: November, 45; December, 57; January, 60. Using 50 as the first order exponential smoothing forecast for November, forecast February sales.

7. A lumber company forecasts demand based on the last two months simple moving average. What would the forecast be for the following items for May? Specify any assumptions you make.

Month	Exterior plywood sheets		B&D saws		Craft paper rolls	
	Demand	Forecast	Demand	Forecast	Demand	Forecast
January	20	25	10	15	2	0
February	missing data	20	10	10	0	1
March	50	—	10	10	1	1
April	60	—	12	10	missing data	1

Does the company need to continue to carry four months of past data for this forecasting model?

8. **Wilson Meat Packing Co. forecasts hamburger demand with a five day moving average. Mr. Wilson has heard of exponential smoothing and has asked you to compare this to his method. You have selected a smoothing coefficient of 0.2, an arbitrary starting forecast for Tuesday of 200 pounds, and an error measure of MAD (mean absolute deviation). Based on Wednesday and Thursday, which model is best? Justify your choice based on MAD.**

Day	Hamburger demand	Mr. Wilson's forecast	Exponential smoothing forecast
Monday	"150"	120	–
Tuesday	"150"	150	200
Wednesday	"200"	175	
Thursday	"300"	200	

(Note: " " denotes actual at end of day, after that day's forecast.)

9. **The production manager estimates the cost of forecast error to be the absolute value of the multiple; $.50 times the product of Bias and MAD. Using his cost estimate for the item demand below, would you recommend a one or a two month simple moving average model? Conduct your analysis forecasting March and April only.**

Month	Actual demand
January	100
February	200
March	100
April	300

10. **For an office supply house, the demand for staplers appears to follow this distribution:**

Time period	Staplers demanded	Time period	Staplers demanded
10	103	15	138
11	95	16	"182"
12	100	17	"187"
13	140	18	"180"
14	139	19	"202"

We have a forecast of 145 units for period 16. The quotes (" ") mean actual demand is known at the end of that period. Using first order exponential smoothing with a moderately responsive smoothing coefficient of 0.2, forecast demand for periods 17 through 20. Now plot the actual and forecasted values for all periods for which you have data. Recommend to management an improved forecasting method, supporting your recommendation.

11. You are given the following demand for streaker sneakers:

Date	Demand
March 1	20
8	120
15	150
22	75
April 1	50

As a buyer for Knoxville's largest sneaker outlet, you have been told to forecast streaker sneaker demand weekly in April using first order exponential smoothing.
(a) What smoothing coefficient would you choose? Why?
(b) If the manager's forecast for April 1st was 75, using that as your starting value, what is your forecast for April 8th?

12. Northeastern Electric Company has experienced demand for a transistor, part #7513, as follows:

Period (weeks)	Demand	Forecasted demand
10	200	300
11	300	
12	500	
13	400	
14	300	

(a) Would you recommend first order exponential smoothing with a coefficient of 0.2 or 0.7? Justify your choice based on consideration of MAD.
(b) The inventory control manager of Northeastern Electric believes the most important cost consideration is not to have a stockout of this part. He estimates the cost of forecast error to be equal to the mean absolute deviation of forecast error plus three times the Bias. Considering this, would you change your recommendation in (a)? Justify your choice.
(c) If you could direct further study into an overall item forecasting procedure for Northeastern Electric parts, what would you suggest?

GLOSSARY

Adaptive exponential smoothing: models in which smoothing coefficient is not fixed but is set initially and then allowed to fluctuate over time based upon changes in the underlying demand pattern

Bias: forecast error measure that is the sum of actual errors for all periods divided by the total number of periods evaluated; gives the average of the forecast errors with regard to direction; shows any tendency consistently to over- or underforecast

Causal forecasting models: in a formal manner these relate demand to variables that are believed to influence demand

Demand pattern: general shape of the time series; usually constant, trend, seasonal, or some combination of these shapes

Demand stability: tendency for a time series to retain the same general shape over time

Exponential smoothing models: averaging method that exponentially decays the weight of an old demand on the current forecast

Forecast: use of past data to determine future events; an objective computation

Forecast error: the difference between forecasted demand and actual demand

Intuitive forecasts: general approach to forecasting that is essentially the manager's guesses and judgment concerning future events; qualitative forecasting methods

Mean Absolute Deviation (MAD): forecast error measure that is the sum of the absolute deviation of actual demand and forecast for all periods divided by the total number of periods evaluated; gives the average of forecast errors without regard to direction

Noise: dispersion of individual demands about a demand pattern

Prediction: subjective estimates of the future

Simple average: average of past data in which the demands of all previous periods are equally weighted

Simple moving average: average of several of the most recent periods' demand; most recent time periods are added and oldest ones dropped to keep calculations current

Statistical forecasting models: casting forward past data in some systematic method used in time series analysis and projection

Time series analysis: in forecasting problems, demand data are plotted on a time scale to reveal patterns of demand

Weighted moving average: moving average model that incorporates some weighting of old demand other than an equal weight for all past periods under consideration

SELECTED READINGS

Adam, Everett E., Jr. "Individual Item Forecasting Model Evaluation." *Decision Sciences* 4, no. 4 (October 1973): 458–70.

————, John S. Bachman, John S. Fryer, Art Laufer, Jonathan Rachik. "P/OM Service Sector Study Group Report." Paper delivered at the Academy of Management Conference (New Orleans, 1975).

————, William L. Berry, and D. Clay Whybark. "The Hospital Administrator and Management Science." *Hospital Administration* 19, no. 1 (Winter 1974): 30–41.

————, J.M. Berthot, and H.E. Riley, Jr. "Individual Item Forecasting Models: A Comparative Evaluation Based on Demand for Supplies in a Medical Complex." *Proceedings, Fourteenth International Conference of the American Production and Inventory Control Society* (November 1971).

————, and Ronald J. Ebert. "A Comparison of Human and Statistical Forecasting." *AIIE Transaction* 8, no. 1 (March 1976): 120–27.

Beach, L.R. and C.R. Peterson. "Man as an Intuitive Statistician." *Psychological Bulletin* 67, no. 7 (July 1967): 29–46.

Brown, R.G. *Smoothing, Forecasting and Prediction of Discrete Time Series.* (Englewood Cliffs, N.J.: Prentice-Hall, Inc., 1963).

Chambers, John S., Satinder K. Mullick, and Donald D. Smith. "How to Choose the Right Forecasting Technique." *Harvard Business Review* 49, no. 4 (July–August 1971): 55–64.

Costello, T.W. and S.S. Zalkind. *Psychology in Administration: A Research Orientation* (Englewood Cliffs, N.J.: Prentice-Hall, Inc., 1968): 225–26.

Delbecq, Andre, Andrew Van deVen and David Gustafson. *Group Techniques for Program Planning* (Glenview, Ill.: Scott, Foresman and Company, 1975).

Hammond, K.R. and D.A. Summers. "Cognitive Dependence on Linear and Nonlinear Cues." *Psychological Review* 72, no. 3 (1965): 215–24.

Harris, Ronald J. and Everett E. Adam, Jr. "Forecasting Patient Tray Census for Hospital Food Service." *Health Services Research* (Winter 1975): 384–93.

———, Aimee N. Moore, Everett E. Adam, Jr., and Ellen A. Scheer. "Evaluation of Statistical Forecasting Techniques for Patient Tray Census." Paper delivered at the Annual Conference of American Dietetic Association (Denver: October 1973).

Messersmith, Ann M., Aimee N. Moore, and Everett E. Adam, Jr. "A Multi-Echelon Model to Forecast Menu Item Demand in a Medical Center." *Proceedings, Sixth American Institute for Decision Sciences Conferences* (Atlanta: November 1974).

———, "A Multi-Echelon Menu Item Forecasting System." (Ph.D. diss.: University of Missouri-Columbia, 1975).

Muth, J.F. "Optimal Properties of Exponentially Weighted Forecasts." *Journal of the American Statistical Association* 55, no. 290 (June 1960): 297–306.

Raine, J.E. "Self Adaptive Forecasting Reconsidered." *Decision Sciences* 2, no. 2 (April 1971).

Swets, J.A. *Signal Detection and Recognition by Human Observers*. New York: John Wiley & Sons, Inc., 1964.

Whybark, D. Clay. "A Comparison of Adaptive Forecasting Techniques." *The Logistics and Transportation Review* 8, no. 3 (1972).

Supplement to Chapter 10

ADDITIONAL
FORECASTING
MODELS

There are many forecasting models other than those discussed in this chapter. We present three models of varying complexity in this supplement. Two models, a linear weighted moving average and double exponential smoothing, are moderately complex, and examples are included. The other model, an adaptive exponential smoothing model, is presented in summary form.

Linear Weighted Moving Average

Another weighted moving average model incorporates linear trends. The model is:

$$\text{Linear moving average } (LMA) = \frac{\sum\limits_{t=1}^{n} D_t}{n} + S(N) \qquad \text{(S10-1)}$$

where:

$$S = \text{slope} = \frac{\text{Sum weighted demand}}{\text{Squared weights}} = \frac{\sum\limits_{t=1}^{n} WD}{\sum\limits_{t=1}^{n} SW} \qquad \text{(S10-2)}$$

N_t = number of periods from the base period

EXAMPLE

For the Frigerware ice coolers in the two examples in the chapter, it is clear that there is trend in the data. The plant manager realizes this and asks you to compare some trend model to the three-month average model in which you forecasted the July demand of 500, based on a three-month moving average. First, we require an odd number of periods demand; we'll use the most recent five months.

Month	Number of ice coolers demanded	Weighting factor	Weighted demand	Square of weight factor
February	300	−2	−600	4
March	200	−1	−200	1
April	400	0	0	0
May	500	1	500	1
June	600	2	1200	4
	$\Sigma D = 2{,}000$		$\Sigma WD = 900$	$\Sigma SW = 10$

=== EXAMPLE (cont.) ===

$$\text{Slope } (S) = \frac{\Sigma WD}{\Sigma SW} = \frac{900}{10} = 90$$

$$N_t = \text{Number of months from base, April}$$

$$= 3$$

$$LMA = \frac{\Sigma D}{n} + S(N_t)$$

$$= \frac{2{,}000}{5} + 90(3)$$

$$= 400 + 270$$

$$LMA = 670$$

The linear moving average forecast for July is 670 ice coolers. When compared with a three-month average forecast of 500, this forecast has picked up the trend in the data and cast it forward.

The model calculates the slope of the trend (S); then it updates the simple moving average (the first term in the model) by multiplying the slope times the number of periods since the base month and adding this result to the base or simple moving average. You must use an odd number of periods for the model to work most effectively; that is, n must be an odd number.

By now, you are probably wondering what will happen to the LMA model when ice cooler demand falls off in the fall. That is a good question, and if the trend we've identified is really a seasonal phenomenon, our model will perform poorly. In that case, another moving average model might be best; a one- or two-month simple moving average might be reasonable, for example.

Double Exponential Smoothing

Double exponential smoothing is normally not included in an introduction to operations management. The model does, however, appear to smooth out noise in stable demand series. We are aware of one large drug manufacturer who uses this model to forecast item demand for the thousands of drugs produced.

The model is straightforward; it smooths the first order exponential smoothing forecast and the old double exponential smoothing forecast.

$$\text{Forecast next period} = (\alpha) \begin{array}{l} \text{First order} \\ \text{exponential} \\ \text{smoothing} \\ \text{forecast next} \\ \text{period} \end{array} + (1 - \alpha) \begin{array}{l} \text{Most recent} \\ \text{double} \\ \text{exponential} \\ \text{smoothing} \\ \text{forecast} \end{array}$$

$$FD_t = \alpha F_t + (1 - \alpha)FD_{t-1} \tag{S10-3}$$

where:

$$0 \le \alpha \le 1.0$$

Notice that F_t is the first order exponential smoothing model set forth as equation 10-7 in Chapter 10.

=== **EXAMPLE** ===

Milo, Inc., has a first order exponential smoothing model that has provided a forecast of 103,500 bushels for #3 grade wheat in Boone County in July. Last year's June production of #3 grade wheat was 70,500 bushels. We will use that figure as an estimate of the most recent double exponential smoothing forecast. Given that $\alpha = 0.20$ appears to be a good smoothing coefficient for Milo, Inc., calculate a double exponential smoothed forecast for July.

$$\text{Let } t = \text{July; then:}$$
$$FD_t = \alpha F_t + (1 - \alpha)FD_{t-1}$$
$$= 0.2(103{,}500) + (1 - .2)(70{,}500)$$
$$= 20{,}700 + 56{,}400$$
$$= 77{,}100$$

Our forecast for July is 77,100 bushels.

In this example, we see that the difference between first order exponential smoothing and double exponential smoothing is that the appropriate old forecast is smoothed with the *actual demand* in first order and smoothed with the *first order forecast* for this period in double smoothing. Actual demand is in the first order forecast, so that actual demand is in essence smoothed again, or double smoothed. The 103,500 first order forecast was smoothed again with the old second order forecast of 70,500; this resulted in a double exponential smoothing forecast of 77,100 bushels. If the 70,500 were an ongoing forecast, rather than an estimate, it would incorporate all old demand when expanded, just as is the case in first order smoothing.

The strength of double exponential smoothing is to dampen noise by double smoothing old demands. This strength makes the model conservative regarding change; the model is very slow to react to changes in underlying demand patterns.

Adaptive Exponential Smoothing

A simple adaptive model has been developed[1] in which alpha, the smoothing coefficient, is allowed to change plus or minus 0.05 in any one period toward a maximum (say, 0.95) or a minimum (say, 0.05). The decision as to whether

---

[1] See W.M. Chow, "Adaptive Control of the Exponential Smoothing Constant," *Journal of Industrial Engineering* 16, no. 5 (1965).

or not to change alpha is made *each period* based on a comparison of forecast error. Three forecast errors are calculated; forecast error is calculated for the current forecast using α; an error is calculated for a current forecast for (α + 0.05); and an error is calculated for a current forecast for (α − 0.05). The errors for all three forecasts are compared, and the new alpha is set by selecting the current forecast with the lowest error and setting alpha appropriately as α, α + 0.05, or α − 0.05. There are many more adaptive models and studies comparing adaptive to nonadaptive models; these studies indicate that some adaptive models are superior to other adaptive and nonadaptive models, especially for unstable demand patterns. The Trigg and Leach adaptive exponential smoothing model shown in Figure 10-6 adapted more quickly to demand for frosted microscope slides in a hospital than did simple exponential smoothing. Note the response of the models about period 150 as demand becomes unstable. A further comparison of the models based on MAD, Bias, and computer time in seconds gave results for simple exponential smoothing of 26.11, −6.58, 3.33 and for adaptive exponential smoothing of 27.40, 1.41, and 3.84. The significant difference was in Bias, favoring the adaptive model.

One should be cautioned that adaptive models react to any change in demand, whether it is a change in *pattern* or *noise*. We like the adaptive feature of changing to changing demand patterns but dislike the feature of "chasing noise around" that adaptive models tend to have. Weaknesses in this concept include the chasing of noise in the series, cost of modeling, and unwillingness by many managers and administrators to accept reasonably sophisticated models of operating systems. The strengths certainly outweigh the weaknesses for progressive businesses who can overcome most of these weaknesses and apply adaptive models for unstable demand patterns.

PROBLEMS

1. A telephone company is changing its forecasting method to the linear moving average model. Data for a recent period are shown here. What is the forecast for week 18? The company has decided to use five weeks from the base period in its forecast.

Week	Number of telephone installations
11	560
12	580
13	450
14	410
15	580
16	590
17	600

2. Carr Corporation uses a first order exponential smoothing model. For one item, the model provided a demand forecast of 65,500 units. This was used as November's production requirement. Although demand was actually 62,700 units during November, 65,500 units were produced. Calculate a double exponential smoothed forecast for December using 60,000 units as November's double exponential smoothed forecast. All smoothing coefficients are 0.3.

11 Aggregate Planning and Scheduling

Imagine yourself in charge of a large facility that houses many types of equipment and people. You are faced with some important questions. How should I use these potentially productive resources during the next six months, year, or even longer? The resources are here, but what is the best way to use them? Your answers to these questions will directly affect the success of your organization. One extreme approach is to ignore the questions, let nature take its course, and hope for the best. Or you may systematically establish a program of action for guiding the overall utilization of these productive resources. Aggregate output planning, the process by which we plan the overall use of conversion resources, is one way of doing this. In this chapter we identify and describe the aggregate planning problem, discuss some methods for developing aggregate plans, and consider the implementation of the aggregate plans once they've been made.

Keep in mind that our major focus is on the planning function of operations management. We are *planning* the use of existing conversion processes. Aggregate planning, together with organizing, is the basis for subsequent process control, as we show in Figure 11-1. In this chapter we will also examine the modeling and behavioral dimensions of the aggregate planning problem.

Scheduling is simply the time sequencing of events. Scheduling is a subphase of planning, in that once alternative programs of action are identified, a course can be established and time sequenced. Aggregate scheduling derives from the aggregate planning concept, and we will use the terms somewhat synonymously.

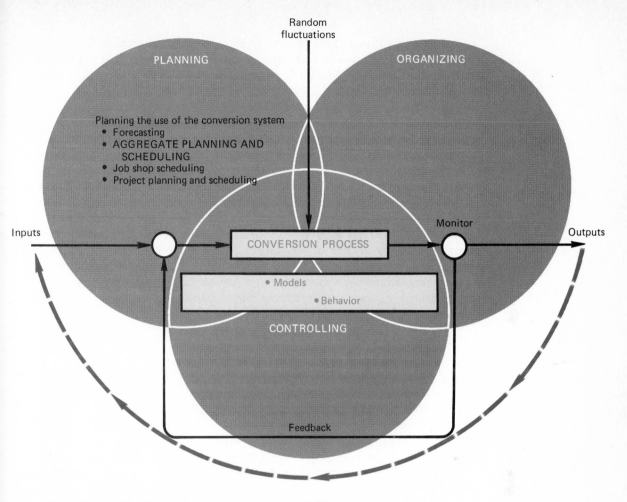

Figure 11-1 **Production/operations management activities**

Establishing Goals and Assessing Resources

THE
AGGREGATE
PLANNING
SITUATION

Concept of
aggregation

The operations manager usually finds it convenient to plan at different levels of abstraction. At one extreme is the broad overall level; planning on this level considers total output capabilities of all existing production resources without regard to specific products that could be produced. A brewery manager, for example, may plan in terms of gallons of beer-producing capacity of his or her facility, ignoring for the moment how that capacity will be subdivided among various types of beer and packaging alternatives. What overall level of output do you want? Once this question is answered, you have a sound basis for switching to a second, more detailed level of abstraction: how much of each individual product should be produced and in what sequence. Aggregate output planning deals with the first, and broader, of these two levels of abstraction.

371

The aggregate output question is extremely important for many reasons. First of all, productive resources are limited; resources are scarce. Thus, the manager is interested in using these limited resources in such a way that they produce the greatest possible benefits. If you do not think in terms of the "aggregate" output capabilities of available resources, you really have little basis for evaluating the overall effectiveness of current productive efforts. Second, the overall output of most organizations is not constant but varies from week to week, month to month, and year to year. The manager can have control over when and how these variations occur. By adopting an *aggregate* planning perspective, you can more effectively manage the *overall* costs of changing output levels. Third, coordination from an overall perspective can have important economic consequences. Without such coordination, for example, department *A* might experience costly layoffs of employees just before department *B* begins hiring new people. A coordinated effort could avoid such a situation by transferring employees departmentally. As a result, advertising, interviewing, physical exams, and unemployment benefit costs—all caused by fluctuating employment levels—could be avoided.

To develop a plan for aggregate output, you must identify a common unit for measuring quantities of different products. This is not a problem for organizations with a single product. Most organizations, however, have several products, and a "common denominator" for measuring total output may be difficult to find. A steel producer may use "tons of steel," and a paint producer may use "gallons of paint." But what about the appliance manufacturer whose products include toasters, waffle irons, and other small appliances? What about organizations whose outputs are services rather than physical goods? In cases like these, measures have to be determined to fit each organization individually. Urban transit systems, for example, may use "passenger miles" as a common measure of productive output; health care facilities may use "patient visits"; educational institutions may use "faculty-to-student contact hours" as the common measure of output. You can see, then, that each organization must exercise great care in determining a meaningful measure of organizational output if it wishes to develop plans for aggregate output.

Goals for aggregate output

Aggregate plans are developed with particular goals in mind. For a specific time frame or planning horizon, estimates of the aggregate demand for goods and/or services are made. Typically, *the goal is to develop a plan that will satisfy or meet demand, within the limits of available resources, at the least cost to the organization.* Such other goals as maintaining stable work force levels may also be planned for.

Assessing resources

What primary resources do we use to generate output? Can any of these resources be altered, so we can be more flexible in output rates? Since the overall capacity of operations is largely fixed, there are some constraints on output plans for the near future. Possibly, however, some short-term resources (work force and inventories of finished goods, for example) can be varied. Or perhaps capacity can be expanded temporarily by leasing or renting more facilities and equipment. It's the operations manager's job not only to identify resources but to determine which resources can be varied or manipulated to achieve various output rates. This determination identifies aggregate output *decision variables.* Alternative output *plans* can then be generated by using different combinations of these variables.

Planning Horizon and Demand Forecasts

Selecting a
planning horizon

Often plans for aggregate output are developed for periods of six months to one year into the future. As we shall see later, however, these plans are generally put into action much more frequently than this, on a weekly or monthly basis. If the implementation occurs over such short time intervals, why does the plan cover such a long time span? Because week-to-week and month-to-month actions are not independent of one another. In fact, they are closely interrelated, since management actions and decisions in one month determine which alternatives will be available in subsequent months. This is what happens with a multistage, or sequential, decision problem. If monthly decisions are evaluated as if they were simply a sequence of independent, single-stage decisions, very costly consequences can result. Managers must consider the future consequences of current decisions.

EXAMPLE

As manager of a refrigerator manufacturing facility, you wish to plan the level of output for February. At the end of January you observe 100 finished refrigerators left over in inventory. Twenty assemblers were on the payroll in January, each earning a salary of $800 per month. On average, each assembler is capable of producing 10 refrigerators per month. You have just been informed that 200 refrigerators will be demanded by customers during February. Since you already have 100 units in inventory, you decide to produce exactly 100 more units during February so you can meet the February demand of 200 units. Since only 10 assemblers will be required to produce February's planned output, you lay off 10 assemblers at an average layoff cost of $400 per worker. One month later you face a similar decision. Consumer demand for refrigerators in March is estimated to be 300 units. Since no refrigerators are left in inventory from February, the entire 300 units for March must be produced during March. To accomplish this, you must hire 20 additional assemblers at the beginning of March so that the work force (30 assemblers) can produce the required 300 units. The cost of hiring and training assemblers averages $300/assembler, and inventory costs are assumed to be negligible.

This is an example of planning with a one-month time horizon. If each month is treated separately and independently for planning purposes, what costs would result? Table 11-1 shows us.

Now suppose you had used a two-month planning horizon. At the end of January you find out that demand is expected to be 200 units in February and 300 units in March. With this information you develop the plan in Table 11-2 for both February and March. This plan calls for retaining all 20 assemblers for February and March and thereby avoiding the layoff and hiring costs of the first plan. This cost savings was accomplished by looking into the future and considering not only next month's expected demand but the demand for the following month as well. Now compare the February costs for the two plans. In the best plan (using a two-month horizon) we intentionally incur more costs in February than we would had we used the one-month horizon plan! But by so doing, we reduce the total cost for the entire planning horizon. This type of sacrificing strategy is a common phenomenon in multistage decision problems. As you can see, selecting an appropriate time horizon is very important for planning. Aggregate plans should be developed not to minimize costs in each individual period but overall, since minimizing costs in the short run can turn out to be a *suboptimal* plan in the long run.

We have seen that short time horizons can be undesirable. Can we select a horizon that is too long? From a practical standpoint, the answer is yes. By enlarging the planning horizon, we increase dramatically the number of possible alternative plans. If each of these many plans is evaluated so that the best plan can be selected, the costs of computation (and the time required) can become prohibitive. Also, forecasts of future demand usually become less accurate as we look farther into the future, and plans based on highly inaccurate forecasts are often of little value.

─────── TABLE 11-1 ───────

TOTAL COST USING A ONE-MONTH PLANNING HORIZON

Planned decisions and costs	February	March	Total
Number of employees	10	30	40
Units of output	100	300	400
Wages (costs)	10 × $800 = $8,000	30 × $800 = $24,000	$32,000
Layoff (costs)	10 × 400 = 4,000	0	4,000
Hiring (costs)	0	20 × 300 = 6,000	6,000
Total (costs)	$12,000	$30,000	$42,000

TABLE 11-2

TOTAL COST USING A TWO-MONTH PLANNING HORIZON

Planned decisions and costs	February	March	Total
Number of employees	20	20	40
Units of output	200	200	400
Wages (costs)	20 × $800 = $16,000	20 × $800 = $16,000	$32,000
Layoff (costs)	0	0	0
Hiring (costs)	0	0	0
Total (costs)	$16,000	$16,000	$32,000

Forecasts of aggregate demand   The benefits to be gained from aggregate planning efforts depend on forecasting capabilities. You may remember that in Chapter 10, we presented various models that can be used to forecast demand for individual products (outputs) for the planning horizon. These individual product demands can be converted

Figure 11-2   **Aggregate demand forecasts for an organization offering three products**

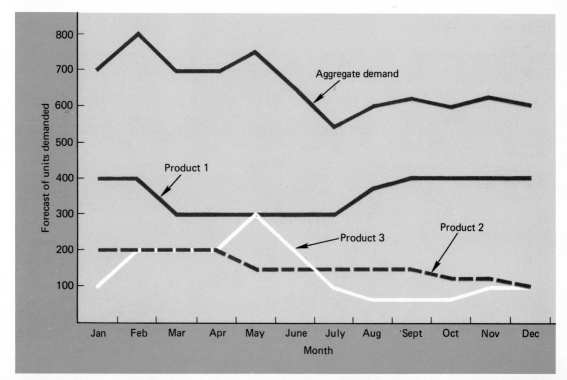

into a common unit and aggregate demand estimates arrived at.[1] Figure 11-2 shows aggregate demand forecasts for three products. These forecasts of the pattern of aggregate demand are necessary information inputs to aggregate planning. It is the month-to-month demand *fluctuations* that really create the output planning problem. If monthly demand did not fluctuate, if it were constant, the difficulties of output planning would be substantially reduced.

METHODS FOR DEVELOPING AGGREGATE PLANS

An Aggregate Plan for a Manufacturer

Let's apply these basic concepts to develop an aggregate output plan using a graphical approach. The goal is to find a plan that meets expected demand at minimum operating costs over a twelve-month horizon.

=== EXAMPLE ===

The company is a large volume producer of a standard size wheelbarrow called a wagon. Forecasts of demand for the coming year (Figure 11-3) reflect a major peak in the spring and a minor peak in the fall. Lowest demand occurs during the winter months. Output capability averages 10 wagons per month for each employee.

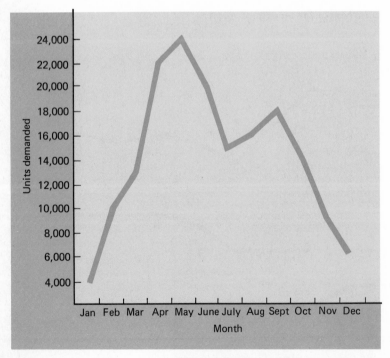

Figure 11-3 **Demand forecasts for the coming year**

---

[1]This method of aggregating demand forecasts has been presented by Martin K. Starr, *Production Management: Systems and Synthesis*, 2nd ed. (Englewood Cliffs: Prentice-Hall, Inc., 1972). See Chapter 8.

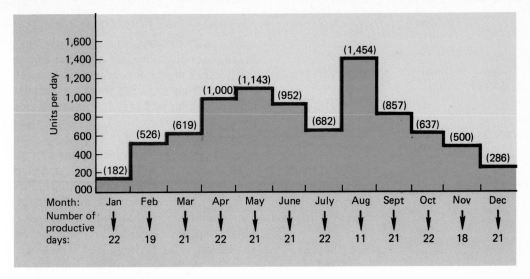

Figure 11-4 **Output rate per productive day when monthly production meets monthly demand**

The first step in the analysis is to examine carefully the productive requirements this demand pattern places on the facility. At first glance, May appears to be the peak month, with 24,000 units demanded. The actual number of available productive days must also be considered, however. Because of an annual vacation shutdown, for example, August has only eleven productive days. If our plan were to produce each month the number of wagons demanded, considerable fluctuation in output rate would result. This fluctuation is shown in Figure 11-4, where output rate is measured in units per available productive day.

Were it to produce the indicated number of units daily, the company would just meet its anticipated monthly demand. But the changes in output rate from month to month are large and can be very costly. Let's examine three "pure strategies" that the planner could use to cope with the wide swings in monthly demand.

Three Pure Planning Strategies

Several resources can be used to absorb monthly demand fluctuations. Common in manufacturing organizations are three of these resources: work force size, inventories, and work force utilization. Any one of these can be varied to meet demand variations without consideration of the other two (thus they can be called "pure" strategies). Usually, however, some combination of the three is better than using just one. In addition to these three internal resources, manufacturers often have opportunities to employ additional external resources. The use of subcontractors, rented or leased equipment, and other external resources is useful for responding to periods of heavy demand. Our discussion, however, will be limited to internal resources.

Strategy 1: Vary the number of productive employees in direct relation to monthly output requirements

From past history, management can estimate the average productivity per employee and thus determine the number of employees needed to meet each month's output. When required monthly output declines, employees can be laid off. As monthly demand increases, the size of the work force can be increased accordingly. In our example, output average per employee is 10 wagons per day. Therefore about 18 employees would be needed in January, 53 in February, 62 in March, and so on.

Several disadvantages are inherent in this strategy. First, direct costs of hiring and layoffs are very high. Second, indirect costs of training new employees, decreases in employee morale during periods of layoff, and the like are common. Third, required work skills may not be readily available when they are needed. Because fairly long lead times are often needed to procure special employee skills, these hiring lead times and training periods must be accounted for in the planning horizon. Fourth, sometimes community reactions to such a strategy are negative. Companies are known in the community by the employment practices they follow. Some industries are well-known for long histories of wide employment fluctuations. Usually, local workers prefer to obtain employment with companies having more stable employment practices. Finally, this strategy is not feasible for companies with guaranteed wage and other hiring and layoff agreements with unions.

Strategy 2: Maintain a constant work force size but vary the rate of work force utilization

Suppose for our example we chose the strategy of employing 70 workers per month throughout the year. On an average, this work force would be capable of producing 700 wagons each day. During the lean months (January, February, March, July, October, November, December) the work force would be scheduled to produce only the amount forecasted. Since the employees are capable of producing more than the forecasted amount, they would therefore be idle during some working hours. During high-demand months (April, May, June, August, September), overtime operations would be needed to meet demand. The work force would therefore be intensely utilized during some months and underutilized in other months.

A big advantage of this strategy is its avoidance of the hiring and layoff costs associated with strategy 1. But other costs are incurred instead. Overtime, for example, can be very expensive, commonly 50 percent higher than regular time wage rates. If overtime requires working on weekends or holidays, wage rates may be as much as 200 percent above regular rates. Furthermore, there are both legal and behavioral limits to the amount of overtime that can be required. When employees work extensive amounts of overtime, they tend to become inefficient, and productivity diminishes.

Idle time also has some subtle drawbacks. During slack periods, employee morale can diminish and employment uncertainties increase, especially if the idle time is perceived to be a prelude to future layoffs.

Opportunity costs also result from idle time. When employees are forced to be idle, the company foregoes the opportunity of getting units of output that could have been produced. Although wages are paid, output is not received. Some potential output has been lost forever.

Strategy 3: Allow inventories to fluctuate in response to demand variations

Finished goods inventories can be used to cushion the company's response to demand fluctuations. A fixed number of employees, selected so that little or no overtime or idle time is incurred, can be maintained throughout the planning horizon. Having been produced at a constant rate, output will exceed demand during slack demand periods, and finished goods inventories will accumulate. During peak periods, when demand is greater than productive capabilities, the demand can be supplied from inventory. This planning strategy results in fluctuating inventory levels throughout the planning horizon.

=== EXAMPLE ===

In Figure 11-4, there are 241 available productive days in which to produce 171,000 wagons. Therefore we must produce an average of about 710 wagons per day throughout the year to meet this total demand. This can be done during regular working hours by employing 71 workers (each producing an average of 10 wagons per day).

By following this strategy, we can determine how our inventory of finished goods will fluctuate during the year. We have done this in Table 11–3 and Figure 11-5. If we use strategy 3, inventories accumulate during the first three months of the year. After that, April demand exceeds productive capabilities. Part of April's demand must therefore be supplied from accumulated inventories. Similarly, inventories are further depleted in May. During June, finished goods inventories are totally depleted, and customer backorders (unfilled demand) result. Backorders accumulate to a maximum of 14,200 wagons as of the end of September. In October and November, expected demand is less than productive capabilities, and backorders are "worked off" (reduced). Finally, December planned production is sufficiently larger than demand, and inventory returns to near zero at the end of the planning horizon.

The comparative advantages of strategy 3 are obvious: stable employment, no idle time, and no expensive overtime. What about disadvantages? First, inventories of finished goods (and other types of inventories) are not cost-free. Inventories tie up working capital that could otherwise be earning a return on investment. Materials-handling costs, storage space requirements, risk of damage and obsolescence, clerical efforts, and taxes can all increase with larger inventories. Backorders can also be costly.

Customers may not be willing to tolerate backordering, particularly if alternative sources of supply are available; sales may be lost, and customer ill will may negatively affect future sales potential. In short, there are costs for carrying too much or too little inventory.

TABLE 11-3

PRODUCTION PLAN FOR STRATEGY 3

Month	Productive days	Planned output (units)	Expected demand (units)	Net additions (subtractions) to inventory (units)	End-of-month cumulative inventory to date (units)
Jan	22	15,620	4,000	11,620	11,620
Feb	19	13,490	10,000	3,490	15,110
Mar	21	14,910	13,000	1,910	17,020
Apr	22	15,620	22,000	(6,380)	10,640
May	21	14,910	24,000	(9,090)	1,550
June	21	14,910	20,000	(5,090)	(3,540)
July	22	15,620	15,000	620	(2,920)
Aug	11	7,910	16,000	(8,190)	(11,110)
Sept	21	14,910	18,000	(3,090)	(14,200)
Oct	22	15,620	14,000	1,620	(12,580)
Nov	18	12,780	9,000	3,780	(8,800)
Dec	21	14,910	6,000	8,910	110

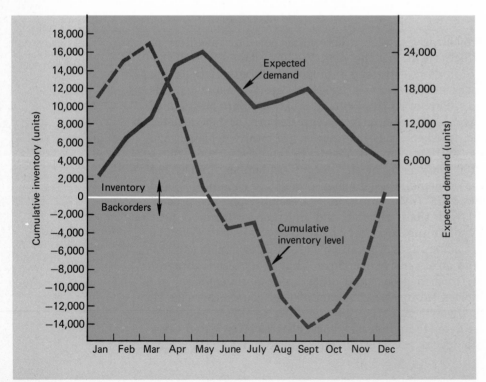

Figure 11-5
Cumulative inventory for strategy 3

Usually, none of the pure strategies is best by itself; a mixture of two or three is better. There is a large number of alternative plans or "mixtures" to choose from. One way to develop and evaluate these alternatives is by using a *graphical* planning procedure. The graphical method is convenient and relatively simple to understand, and it requires only minor computational effort. The graphical method follows these steps:

1. Develop a graph showing cumulative production days for the entire planning horizon on the horizontal axis and cumulative units of product on the vertical axis. Plot the cumulative demand data (forecasts) for the entire planning horizon.
2. Select a planning strategy, and determine the proposed production output for each period in the planning horizon. Calculate and plot on the graph the cumulative output for this tentative plan.
3. Compare expected demand and proposed output; plot both on the same graph. This comparison identifies periods of excess inventories and periods of inventory shortages, and it essentially evaluates the tentative plan.
4. Calculate the costs for this plan.
5. Modify the plan, attempting to reduce costs by repeating steps 2 through 4 until a satisfactory plan is established.

We will demonstrate steps 1 through 4 for three different aggregate plans. The fifth step, additional modification, is left for you to do as an exercise. Since step 4 requires cost data, the following cost estimates have been obtained for the wheelbarrow (wagon) manufacturer:

EXAMPLE

Inventory carrying costs are 50¢ per unit for each month that the wagon is carried in inventory. Inventory costs are based on the average level of inventory for the month. Costs are incurred for changing the company's production rate. When the production rate is increased, additional employees must be hired and trained, and some overtime work is required. When the production rate is reduced, some employees must be laid off and/or idle time occurs. The larger the change in production rate (increase or decrease), the greater the cost incurred. Table 11-4 shows the costs of changing production rates by different amounts. Production rates are expressed in terms of units (wagons) per *day*. It is assumed that daily production rate, once selected, will be used every day for the entire month. Production rates can be changed only from month to month, not during any one month. The company places a high cost on backorders and lost sales, a cost so high that management wants a plan in which output at least meets expected demand throughout the planning horizon.

A plan with level
production

We'll develop a plan that meets all the above requirements and that does so by using a constant output (production) rate. Step 1 of our procedure, plotting cumulative forecasted demand, is done in Figure 11-6.

TABLE 11-4

ESTIMATED COST FOR CHANGING PRODUCTION RATES FROM MONTH TO MONTH

Change in daily production rate from previous month in units (increase or decrease)	Estimated cost of changing production rate
1–200	$ 2,000
201–400	5,000
401–600	9,000
601–800	14,000

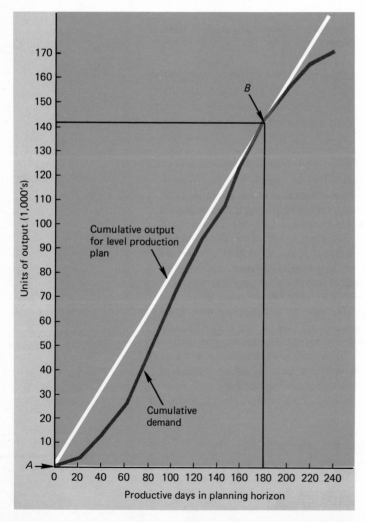

Figure 11-6 **Aggregate output plan and forecasted demand**

For step 2, we have specified a planning strategy consisting of a constant production rate for each day. If we were to plot cumulative production day by day for this strategy, it would appear as a straight line on the graph in Figure 11-6. The line would begin at the origin (zero units of output) and rise steadily to the right as cumulative output increases. The higher the production rates, the steeper the line would be (see Figure 11-7). What slope should be selected? The cumulative output line should be steep enough always to meet or exceed cumulative demand throughout the entire range of the cumulative demand curve. In this way, the plan avoids lost sales and backorders. If the production curve is too steep, however, excessive inventories are accumulated. The desired production is found by using a straight edge to pass a line through the origin (point *A*) and the outlying point (point *B*) on the cumulative demand curve. The cumulative production output described by this line meets our planning requirements: no units are produced at time zero; production commences at a constant daily rate; and total output exceeds total demand until the end of September (point *B*). At the end of September, units produced to date equal the total demanded to date. Thereafter, output exceeds expected demand for the remainder of the planning horizon. What is the daily production rate? Point *B* represents 180 cumulative days of production and 142,000 cumulative units of output. Thus:

$$\frac{142,000 \text{ units}}{180 \text{ days}} = 790 \text{ units/day (approximately)}$$

Since we know the daily production rate, we can now develop a detailed plan for each month. The plans are shown in Table 11-5. Since 790 units are produced each day, and since each employee can average 10 units per day, 79 employees will be needed.

Finally we can determine the cost of this plan. Since the daily production rate is unchanged from month to month, there are no production rate change costs. Table 11-5 shows average monthly inventories totaling 120,405 units for the year. Therefore, inventory costs will be about $60,202 (50¢ per unit per month).

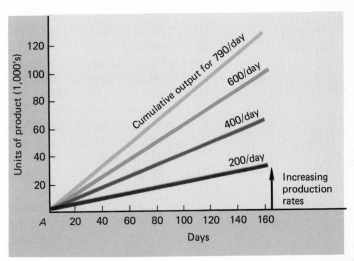

Figure 11-7 **Constant production rate lines**

TABLE 11-5

MONTHLY PLAN FOR LEVEL PRODUCTION RATE

Month	Days	Output rate/day	Output	Demand
Jan	22	790	17,380	4,000
Feb	19	790	15,010	10,000
Mar	21	790	16,590	13,000
Apr	22	790	17,380	22,000
May	21	790	16,590	24,000
June	21	790	16,590	20,000
July	22	790	17,380	15,000
Aug	11	790	8,690	16,000
Sept	21	790	16,590	18,000
Oct	22	790	17,380	14,000
Nov	18	790	14,220	9,000
Dec	21	790	16,590	6,000

A plan that closely follows demand

One alternative to producing at a constant rate is a plan in which monthly output is geared to meeting expected monthly demand. In this case, the cumulative output curve coincides with the cumulative demand curve. Therefore, we plan to produce 4,000 units in January, 10,000 in February, 13,000 in March, and so on. Since the number of days per month is known, the daily output rate for each month is easily approximated. In January, for example, 22 productive days are available. Since we propose producing 4,000 units in January, the daily production rate is:

$$\frac{4,000 \text{ units}}{22 \text{ days}} = 182 \text{ units/day (approximately)}$$

Using this procedure for each month results in the plan shown in Table 11-6. Since almost no excess inventories are on hand each month, inventory costs for this plan are very low. The monthly production rates differ slightly from those shown in Figure 11-2 because a positive net inventory is retained for each time period; that is, backorders or stockouts are not permitted. The daily production rate is changed each month. February's rate is 345 units per day greater than January's; from Table 11-4, we know that the cost of this increase is approximately $5,000. Similarly, we can calculate the cost of changing output rates for all the months in the planning horizon (see Table 11-7).

An intermediate plan

As we have seen, excessive inventories and changes in production rates can be costly. Let's develop a plan that changes production rates only occasionally instead

Beginning inventory	Net additions (subtractions) to inventory	Ending inventory	Average monthly inventory (beginning and ending)/2
0	13,380	13,380	6,690
13,380	5,010	18,390	15,885
18,390	3,590	21,980	20,185
21,980	(4,620)	17,360	19,670
17,360	(7,410)	9,950	13,655
9,950	(3,410)	6,540	8,245
6,540	2,380	8,920	7,730
8,920	(7,310)	1,610	5,265
1,610	(1,410)	200	905
200	3,380	3,580	1,890
3,580	5,220	8,800	6,190
8,800	10,590	19,390	14,095
			120,405

of every month. The plan in Table 11-8 calls for a constant production rate of 436 units per day during January, February, and March. This rate is boosted to 1,081 units per day from April through July. Output is then decreased to 688 units per day for the remainder of the year. The inventory cost of this plan would be 50¢ per unit inventoried, or $21,399. Production rate changes would cost $14,000 for the March–April change and $5,000 for the July–August change, for a total of $19,000.

Comparing the plans

Now we can evaluate the three plans on the basis of total cost for the planning horizon. We have done this in Table 11-9. The level production plan has high inventory costs and no rate change costs. The plan that varies production rate to meet demand has negligible inventory costs and high rate change costs. These plans exemplify two of the pure strategies discussed earlier. The third (intermediate) plan incurs substantial costs in both categories but has the lowest total cost. This plan reflects a mixed strategy, using moderate (not extreme) amounts of inventory and production rate changes to absorb demand fluctuations. Moderate inventories are accumulated in January, February, July, August, and December. Average inventories for the year are far lower in this plan than in the level production plan. These moderate inventory levels allow us to be selective in changing the production rate, and we can avoid the high costs of frequent and extreme changes.

In our example, we "smoothed" production fluctuations. This is why the aggregate planning process is sometimes called "production smoothing."

TABLE 11-6

MONTHLY PLAN FOR VARIABLE PRODUCTION RATE

Month	Days	Change in production rate	Output rate/day	Output
Jan	22		182	4,004
Feb	19	+345	527	10,013
Mar	21	+ 92	619	12,999
Apr	22	+381	1,000	22,000
May	21	+143	1,143	24,003
June	21	−191	952	19,992
July	22	−270	682	15,004
Aug	11	+772	1,454	15,994
Sept	21	−597	857	17,997
Oct	22	−220	637	14,014
Nov	18	−138	499	8,982
Dec	21	−213	286	6,006

As demand decreases to lower levels, it is cheaper to decrease production rates (occasionally) than to continue to build up excessive inventories. If there is any one generalization that can be made about aggregate planning, it is this: *when planning production, smooth out the peaks and valleys to meet uneven demand because extreme fluctuations in production are generally very costly.*

An Aggregate Plan For a Service Organization

Service organizations can also use aggregate planning. With service organizations, however, inventories of finished goods are not available for responding to demand fluctuations. Consider a city government's public works department, which is responsible for maintaining streets and roads throughout the year. Its "products" are:

1. repairing existing streets and roads (gravel, asphalt, concrete) and drainage systems,
2. build new roads, and
3. removing snow and ice.

The department cannot build up inventories of these finished products. It can, however, retain the resources that are necessary for providing the products. The proper mixtures of skilled labor, unskilled labor, equipment, supplies, and the use of subcontractors must all be selected to meet the demand for various "products" (services).

Demand	Beginning inventory	Net additions (subtractions) to inventory	Ending inventory	Average inventory
4,000	0	4	4	2.0
10,000	4	13	17	10.5
13,000	17	(1)	16	16.5
22,000	16	0	16	16.0
24,000	16	3	19	17.5
20,000	19	(8)	11	15.0
15,000	11	4	15	13.0
16,000	15	(6)	9	12.0
18,000	9	(3)	6	7.5
14,000	6	14	20	13.0
9,000	20	(18)	2	11.0
6,000	2	6	8	5.0
				139.0

TABLE 11-7

COSTS OF CHANGING PRODUCTION RATES FOR PLAN THAT CLOSELY FOLLOWS DEMAND

Months	Change in daily production rate (from previous month)	Estimated cost of change
Jan to Feb	+345	$ 5,000
Feb to Mar	+ 92	2,000
Mar to Apr	+381	5,000
Apr to May	+143	2,000
May to June	−191	2,000
June to July	−270	5,000
July to Aug	+772	14,000
Aug to Sept	−597	9,000
Sept to Oct	−220	5,000
Oct to Nov	−138	2,000
Nov to Dec	−213	5,000
Total		$56,000

TABLE 11-8

INTERMEDIATE PLAN

Month	Days	Change in production rate	Output rate/day	Output
Jan	22		436	9,592
Feb	19		436	8,284
Mar	21	+645	436	9,156
Apr	22		1,081	23,782
May	21		1,081	22,701
June	21		1,081	22,701
July	22	−393	1,081	23,782
Aug	11		688	7,568
Sept	21		688	14,448
Oct	22		688	15,136
Nov	18		688	12,384
Dec	21		688	14,448

TABLE 11-9

OPERATING COSTS FOR THREE PLANS

	Plan		
Type of cost	Level production rate	Variable production rate	Intermediate
Inventory	$60,202	$ 70	$21,399
Production rate change	0	56,000	19,000
Total cost	$60,202	$56,070	$40,399

Using "road miles" as the common unit for measuring aggregate demand and output, we have shown in Figure 11-8 the expected demand for a one-year planning horizon. The objective is to develop a plan for meeting demand at minimum cost. The plan includes determining an appropriate full-time, base work force for the year. We'll use the following example as our basis for discussing this public works department.

Demand	Beginning inventory	Net additions (subtractions) to inventory	Ending inventory	Average inventory
4,000	0	5,592	5,592	2,746
10,000	5,592	(1,716)	3,876	4,734
13,000	3,876	(3,844)	32	1,954
22,000	32	1,782	1,814	923
24,000	1,814	(1,299)	515	1,165
20,000	515	2,701	3,216	1,865
15,000	3,216	8,782	11,998	7,607
16,000	11,998	(8,432)	3,566	7,782
18,000	3,566	(3,552)	14	1,790
14,000	14	1,136	1,150	582
9,000	1,150	3,384	4,534	2,842
6,000	4,534	8,448	12,982	8,758
				42,798

EXAMPLE

In the past, the public works department has had an experienced work force of about 400 people averaging 2,000 road miles of service per month.

This figure is used to estimate the expected productivity of 5 road miles per employee per month, or .24 miles per employee per day. Three options are available for meeting excess demand:

1. The regular work force can work overtime. The overtime premium is 50 percent of the regular $900 monthly wage.

2. Subcontracting to private firms is available at an average cost of $240 per road mile. Contracts for these services must be arranged several months in advance.

3. Supplementary labor is available from May to September. Hiring and layoff costs average $100 per supplementary employee.

Let's evaluate a plan that employs 400 full-time employees throughout the year. Begin by plotting monthly output capability versus monthly demand. Assuming a workforce of 400 people, output capability averages 96 road miles per working day. Regular time output capability for each month is shown in Figure 11-9. For the public works department, cumulative demand is not a very meaningful measurement; it is more desirable to consider meeting each month's needs individually. If snow removal is needed in December, after all, the public works department has to remove the snow in December, not in February. The department has to ask, "Given a proposed work force size, how well can we respond to immediate needs?" Figure 11-9 shows that for a work force of 400, March, April, and December present periods of slack demand. In January and February, and from May through October, however, demands are far in excess of department output capabilities.

The current plan calls for using the regular work force throughout the year and meeting excess demand by subcontracting. The total costs of wages and subcontracting for this plan are shown in Table 11-10(a).

A second plan, very similar to the first, is also being considered. It calls for obtaining 100 supplementary employees from May through September. Thus, the monthly output capabilities of the deparmtent would be raised to 2,420; 2,520; 2,640; 2,640; and 2,520 road miles for these months. All additional demand will be met by subcontracting. The costs of this plan appear as part (b) in Table 11-10. The second plan offers a cost savings of $127,520 compared to the first plan. Various other combinations of overtime, subcontracting, and supplementary labor can be used in an attempt to gain further cost savings.

Figure 11-8 Aggregate demand for road and street services

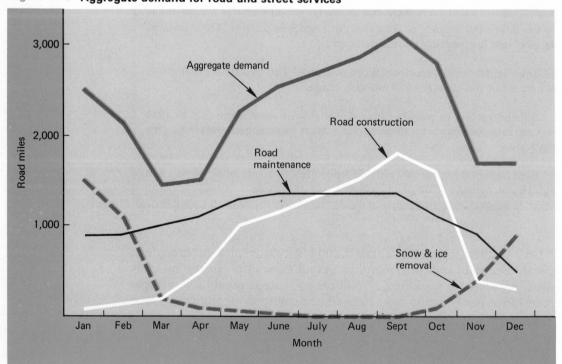

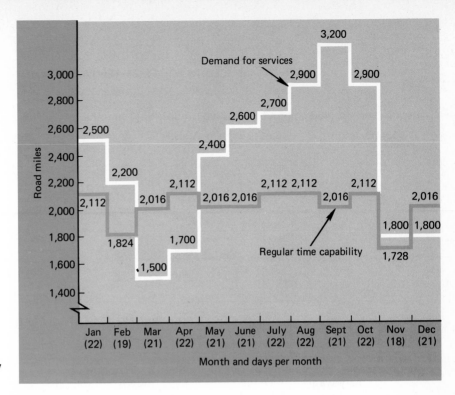

Figure 11-9 **Monthly demand and capability for road services**

What would be the effect of increasing the permanent work force size to 480 employees? Monthly regular-time capabilities would then become 2,534; 2,189; 2,419; 2,534; 2,419; 2,419; 2,534; 2,534; 2,419; 2,534; 2,074; and 2,419. If all other excess demand is met by subcontracting, the resulting costs would be those shown in part (c) in Table 11-10. This plan, compared to the first plan, suggests that increasing the permanent work force to 480 would be more costly than keeping the work force small. By now the fundamental considerations of the graphical technique should be clear. See if you can find a good aggregate plan for the public works department, and develop an alternative plan to assure yourself that you understand this planning procedure.

Additional Models for Aggregate Planning

The graphical technique (model) has the advantages of simplicity, understandability, and no requirement of any such special equipment as a computer. Its primary drawback is that the planner has no assurance that a "best" plan has been developed. How good is the plan we come up with? Experience and judgment are the only bases for answering this question. Some models, many beyond the scope of this book, have also been developed to judge aggregate plans. Sophisticated or simple, all these models share several features. First, they all require the user to specify a planning horizon and obtain aggregate demand forecasts. Second, in

TABLE 11-10

(a) COSTS FOR FIRST TENTATIVE PLAN

Regular wages: 400 employees @ $900/month × 12 months = $4,320,000

Subcontracting:

Month	Road miles
Jan	388
Feb	376
May	384
June	584
July	588
Aug	788
Sept	1,184
Oct	788
Nov	73
Total	5,152 × $240/mile = $1,236,480

Total cost = $5,556,480

(b) COSTS FOR SECOND TENTATIVE PLAN

Regular wages: 400 employees @ $900/month × 12 months = $4,320,000
Supplementary wages: 100 employees @ $900/month × 5 months = 450,000
Supplementary hiring and layoff: 100 employees @ $100 = 10,000

Subcontracting:

Month	Road miles
Jan	388
Feb	376
June	80
July	60
Aug	260
Sept	680
Oct	788
Nov	72
Total	2,704 × $240/mile = $ 648,960

Total cost = $5,428,960

(c) COSTS FOR THIRD TENTATIVE PLAN

Regular wages: 480 employees @ $900/month × 12 months = $5,184,000

Subcontracting:

Month	Road miles
Feb	11
June	181
July	166
Aug	366
Sept	781
Oct	366
Total	1,871 × $240/mile = 449,040

Total cost (exclusive of hiring costs) = $5,633,040

every model the decision variables must be explicitly identified. (Decision variables are the factors that can be varied to generate alternative plans—size of work force, production rate, overtime/idle time, inventory level, subcontracting, etc.) Third, the relevant costs must be identified. When decision variables are varied, some costs increase; others decrease. Those costs that change for different plans are called relevant costs; they include costs of wages, hiring/layoff, overtime, inventory, subcontracting, and so on.

Optimal Models

Linear programming
It is possible to formulate aggregate planning in a linear programming framework.[2] The linear programming procedure then identifies the *optimal* plan for minimizing costs. Not a trial-and-error procedure like the graphical method, this plan specifies the number of units of output to produce in each time period, how many shifts the manufacturing facility should operate each time period, and how many units of inventory should be carried each period. It does all of this by taking into account the operating capacity of the facility. One limitation of linear programming is its assumption of linear costs. As we shall see later, linear cost relationships are not always accurate representations of actual costs.

Linear decision rules
A well-known mathematical modeling approach identifying the *optimal* aggregate plan can be applied to various organizations. This procedure results in a set of equations that can be used to calculate the best work force size, production rate, and inventory level for each time period in the planning horizon. This set of equations has become known as the Linear Decision Rules (LDRs).[3] The advantages of this procedure are that, like linear programming, it guarantees an optimal solution and saves trial and error computations. In addition, it recognizes that some cost relationships may be nonlinear rather than linear. Examples of some of these nonlinear costs are shown in Figure 11-10. Notice that regular wage costs are linear; each additional unit of work force costs a constant amount. The other three cost functions are *non*linear; they are quadratic in form. The overtime cost, for example, rises much faster than do linear costs. Ten hours of overtime cost far more than ten times the cost of one hour of overtime. You may remember

[2]The application of linear programming to aggregate planning was pioneered by E. H. Bowman, "Production Scheduling by the Transportation Method of Linear Programming," *Operations Research* 4, no. 1 (February 1956), pp. 100–103.

[3]The procedure for developing the LDRs is demonstrated by C. C. Holt, F. Modigliani, J. F. Muth, and H. A. Simon, *Planning Production, Inventories, and Work Force* (Englewood Cliffs, N.J.: Prentice-Hall, Inc., 1960).

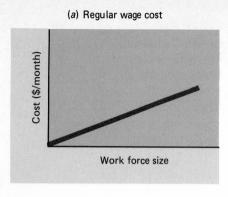

(a) Regular wage cost

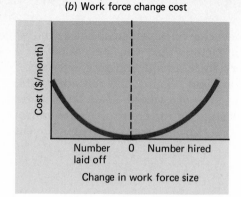

(b) Work force change cost

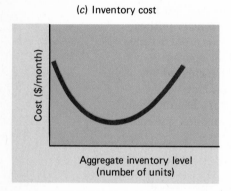

(c) Inventory cost

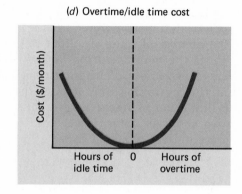

(d) Overtime/idle time cost

Figure 11-10 **Example cost relationships used in linear decision rules**

that linear programming uses only linear cost functions. The LDR model has an advantage, then, since it can use both linear and quadratic (nonlinear) cost relationships.

A disadvantage of the LDR model is that it must be tailor made for each organization. The procedure requires a careful study of a company's cost structure, which must then be expressed in mathematical form. Next, a rather extensive mathematical analysis must be made to come up with the proper Linear Decision Rules for that particular company. Whenever the company's cost relationships change, for example when salaries increase, the mathematical derivation of the LDRs must be redone.

Heuristic Approaches

A final class of aggregate planning models has evolved in recent years. These methods apply in situations in which management has done aggregate output planning on an intuitive basis.

Management
coefficient model
This procedure requires obtaining records of past work force, production, and inventory decisions. These data are analyzed by multiple regression techniques to find those regression equations that best fit the historical data. These regression equations are then used to make *future* planning decisions in much the same way that the LDRs are used.

Parametric
production
planning
In this heuristic approach, a rough estimation is made of four variables. These four variables are searched in combination to provide a least-cost decision combination. Since the four variables are inserted into work force and production rate decision rules for actual planning, this approach approximates the firm's aggregate planning environment.[4]

The advantages of these intuitive models are that they are easy to obtain if sufficient historical data are available and that by reducing the variability in decision making, they can reduce costs. They must be applied, however, with great caution. The fact that *past* decision-making tendencies have been successful does not necessarily mean they will be successful when they are applied mechanically to *future* circumstances. Furthermore, this procedure may provide plans that are nowhere near optimal.

Search Procedures

Often it is possible to have a computer search for optimal aggregate plans. The computer does this by trying many combinations of work force and production rate for each period in the planning horizon. Although it explores many possible combinations of these variables, it does not do so randomly. Very specific rules are built into the search procedure to guide the search in a systematic way. Work force and production rate, in combination, are increased and/or decreased. These variations result in cost changes. When a cost improvement is found, the computer attempts to make further improvements. The search continues until no further improvement results or until a specified amount of search has been reached.

A disadvantage of computer search is the possibility of obtaining a nonoptimal plan. The search guidelines, heuristics, are fallible. Although they explore and evaluate a large number of plans, they do not examine *all* possible plans. Thus unlike the mathematical optimization models, the best plan may not be discovered by computer search.

Computer search is probably the most flexible of the optimum-seeking aggregate planning models. Cost functions need not be linear or quadratic, nor do they need to be unchanging over time. Various types of costs and operating constraints can be incorporated in the model. When the tradeoffs for cost and accuracy are considered, the computer search procedures are very attractive approaches to aggregate planning.

[4]E. S. Buffa and W. H. Taubert, *Production-Inventory Systems: Planning and Control,* rev. ed. (Homewood, Ill.: Richard D. Irwin, Inc., 1974). See Chapters 5 and 7.

Unplanned Events

Once the aggregate plan is developed, it serves as a guide for making operating decisions. The plan must be continually updated as time elapses. Furthermore, it must be revised to take into account unplanned occurrences. Although January's *forecasted* demand may have been 4,000 units, at the end of January we may find that *actual* demand was above or below the forecasted amount, and ending inventory for the month may be at some level other than what we expected. Therefore, the original plan must be modified. Other unexpected events can also disrupt plans. Perhaps the planned output level for the month was not achieved, or perhaps the work force did not produce at its average capability. In any event, unplanned events must be taken into account by replanning for subsequent time periods. To replan, we simply reuse the planning methods or models we used before, except that we now use actual conditions instead of planned conditions.

Selection of an Aggregate Planning Technique

Few studies have compared the various solution techniques that range from simple graphical techniques to more complex mathematical models. The primary reason for a lack of comparative studies is the modeling costs involved in collecting data, fitting models, and comparing the models over time in the context of a real firm. A notable exception is the work of Lee and Khumawala.[5]

Lee and Khumawala compared four models with company decisions for an aggregate planning situation in a capital goods firm having an $11 million annual sales volume. The plant was a typical job shop

TABLE 11-11

COMPARATIVE PROFIT PERFORMANCE OF SELECTED AGGREGATE PLANNING MODELS*

Aggregate planning model	Annual profit
Company decisions	$4,420,000
Management Coefficients Model	4,607,000
Linear Decision Rule	4,821,000
Parametric Production Planning	4,900,000
Search Decision Rule	5,021,000

*Source: William B. Lee and Basheer M. Khumawala, "Simulation Testing of Aggregate Production Planning Models in an Implementation Methodology," *Management Science* 20, no. 6 (February 1974), p. 906.

[5]W. B. Lee and B. M. Khumawala, "Simulation Testing of Aggregate Production Planning Models in an Implementation Methodology," *Management Science* 20, no. 6 (February 1974), pp. 903–11.

manufacturing facility in which parts were produced for inventory and then assembled into the final product. A computer simulation was developed that closely followed the firm's operations and allowed the models to be compared. Models compared in the study are listed in Table 11-11. As you can see, comparative profits clearly favor each model over the existing company decisions. The Management Coefficients Model showed the least improvement, $187,000 (4 percent); the Search Decision Rule showed the greatest improvement, $601,000 (14 percent).

This comparative study illustrates that considerable absolute dollars can be turned into profits through effective aggregate planning. We recommend that graphical techniques be used, at least as an aid in aggregate planning. If the firm in this study used some graphical approach (a reasonable assumption), more complex and costly models might improve performance even further.

Behavioral Considerations

Behavioral considerations enter into aggregate planning both in the planning process itself and in attempting to implement the plan.

Behavior in the planning process
Some important behavioral factors arise from the combination of the extreme complexity of the planning problem and the capacity limitations of the person who must resolve the planning problem. Theoretically, the number of possible planning alternatives is infinite. But people do not possess sufficient mental capacity to deal with such vast ideas. Our integrative abilities, memory, and objectivity are limited.[6] Consider the time horizon that should be used for optimal planning. In some situations a long horizon is required, and problem complexities increase accordingly. Do planners adopt a long enough horizon? Some experimental research reveals that they do not.[7] Although "short-sighted" plans based on judgment and experience result in operating costs that are higher than they need to be, the use of longer horizons apparently poses a difficult mental task. Studies suggest two things: that training is needed to help planners learn how to incorporate longer time horizons, and that since formal models can be constructed to include longer time horizons, they should be used to supplement the human elements of the planning process.

Another behavioral consideration arises from the possible existence of irrelevant information. You may remember that in Chapter 3 we discussed benefits of formal modeling, particularly from the analyst who conducts the modeling effort. In doing the detailed work involved in modeling, the

---

[6]Human capacity limitations are analyzed in R. J. Ebert and T. R. Mitchell, *Organizational Decision Processes: Concepts and Analysis* (New York: Crane, Russak & Company, Inc., 1975).

[7]Time horizon and the effects of irrelevant information in intuitive planning are presented in the study by R. J. Ebert, "Environmental Structure and Programmed Decision Effectiveness," *Management Science* 19, no. 4 (December 1972), pp. 435–45.

analyst is in a position to act as an information filter for the planner; he or she can screen out irrelevant considerations in a decision problem. This is a significant consideration in aggregate planning, because the presence of irrelevant information can lead to inferior intuitive planning decisions. If planners are presented with irrelevant cost information, for example, they use that information for planning. On the surface, the irrelevant information may appear to be relevant and appropriate; the fact that the selected information is irrelevant may not be noticed by planners. Analysts, on the other hand, usually have more awareness of information relevancy because of their greater familiarity with the details of the problem.

These difficulties show why formal planning models are of such great potential value. The graphical procedure serves as a convenient way of providing orderliness in examining and evaluating alternative plans. It is a data organizer. It helps the planner keep track of the month-to-month implications of a proposed course of action. The more elaborate models (optimization models) develop good plans without requiring the strenuous information search and processing necessary for human intuitive planning procedures. At the same time, however, the operations manager must recognize the plan for what it is—a *guide* to action. Whatever the procedure used to generate the plan, the plan per se need not be implemented. The planning model is unlikely to have considered every relevant factor. The experience and judgment of the operations manager must be used to temper and modify any plan prior to its implementation.

Behavioral
considerations in
implementation

The implementation of a plan can affect organizational behavior in several ways. It signals the need for actions by other parts of the organization. Purchasing must undertake plans to acquire necessary materials and resources. Arrangements may have to be made for retaining the services of subcontractors. Changes in work force must be closely coordinated with the personnel department so that appropriate human resources are available when needed. In short, the adoption of an aggregate plan initiates decision-making activities throughout the organization.

Implementation of a plan may also affect the organizational climate. Both motivation and job satisfaction can be affected. If the work force is decreased in successive time periods, morale can diminish, and productivity may decrease. Suppose an aggregate plan calls for fluctuating work force levels in response to demand variations. Such a plan often calls for periods of high employee layoffs. When layoffs occur, or are anticipated, job security is threatened, and both morale and job satisfaction decrease. This is true not only for operative employees but on all levels throughout the organization.

In concluding this section we wish to emphasize the interdependence of the planning and organizing functions in P/OM. Consider the seemingly unrelated areas of job design (Chapter 9) and aggregate planning. If job design decisions are made independently of aggregate planning decisions, the result can be conflict and contradiction. Suppose that specific job design goals include both meeting output requirements and enhancing job satisfaction. At the same time an aggregate planning strategy might call for high layoff levels, a strategy that could lead to deterioration of job satisfaction. In a situation like this, different parts of the organization could be working at cross-purposes. Coordinating the efforts of organizational subunits and activities is a difficult but necessary part of the operations manager's job.

SUMMARY

Aggregate planning is helpful in coordinating the overall use of the conversion facilities. An aggregate plan requires that goals be established, resources be assessed, and forecasts of demand be obtained for a specified planning horizon. Various strategies are available for meeting demand by using combinations of resources in different ways.

Since there is such a large number of possible plans, several models have been developed for identifying and evaluating alternative plans. Although the graphical method is frequently used, other methods may also be useful. The approaches to aggregate planning are summarized in Table 11-12.

These planning methods have been developed most extensively for application in manufacturing organizations. The basic concepts, however, apply equally as well to service-oriented organizations. For manufacturing and service organizations, the graphical approach should be utilized for production planning so that the high costs of peaks and valleys in the production plan may be smoothed out over the planning horizon.

TABLE 11-12

SUMMARY OF AGGREGATE PLANNING METHODS

General solution approach	Method	Features
Trial and error	Graphical technique	Nonoptimal; balances demand and production with reasonable costs; relies on judgement of analyst; intuitively appealing to managers because of ease of understanding
Optimal models	Linear programming	Optimal solution to model guaranteed; linear constraints and objective function often not realistic
	Linear Decision Rules (LDR)	Optimal solution to model guaranteed; allows realistic nonlinear objective function; mathematically complex
Heuristic approaches	Managerial coefficients	Nonoptimal; models decision makers' past performance; reduces variability in decision making and therefore reduces costs; uses multiple regression
	Parametric production planning	Nonoptimal; searches four parameters input for work force and production rate decisions
Computer search	Search Decision Rule (SDR)	Nonoptimal; approximates low points in total cost curves; allows realistic total cost functions

1. Define aggregate planning; identify the relevant costs that should be considered in developing a plan for aggregate output.

2. What role does forecasting play in the aggregate planning process?

3. Demonstrate how aggregate planning and scheduling costs are affected by forecast errors.

4. Figure 11-2 showed an aggregate demand forecast that was derived from individual forecasts for three different products. What difficulties would you encounter in attempting to calculate such an aggregate forecast?

5. What factors should be considered in selecting a planning horizon? Explain.

6. Outline the advantages and disadvantages of the three pure strategies of aggregate planning.

7. Discuss similarities and differences in the aggregate planning problems facing service organizations and goods-producing organizations.

8. Compare and contrast three different methods of aggregate planning: graphical, linear programming, and a heuristic approach.

9. Aggregate plans are developed on the basis of demand forecasts. But after the forecasts have been made, actual demand often deviates from the forecasted amount. Explain how the aggregate planning process continues when this happens.

10. How frequently should previously developed aggregate plans be updated?

11. What problem characteristics cause the aggregate planning problem to be so complex?

12. The management coefficients approach is a combination of modeling and behavioral elements. Explain.

13. Explain how aggregate plans serve as initiators of action in other functional activities of the organization.

14. How might aggregate planning affect job satisfaction?

15. How is aggregate planning interrelated with organizing and controlling?

1. Refer to the data in Figures 11-3 and 11-4 and Tables 11-4 and 11-9. Develop an improved aggregate plan for wagon production.

2. Refer to the data in Table 11-10; develop an improved aggregate plan for the public works department.

3. Suppose for problem 1 an initial inventory of 10,000 wagons is on hand. Use the graphical method to find a good aggregate plan under these conditions.

4. For problem 1, assume that customer backorders (unfilled orders) are now allowed. The cost of a backorder is estimated to be $1 per unit per month. Use the graphical method to develop a good aggregate plan for wagon production.

5. Reconsider problem 1. Suppose three months have elapsed since initial planning, and during that time actual demand was 5,000 units in January, 12,000 in February, and 14,000 in March. New sales forecasts for April through December are 24,000; 25,000; 21,000; 16,000; 16,000; 18,000; 14,000; 10,000; and 7,000.
   (a) Revise your previous plan to take into account this recent information.
   (b) How do the costs compare to those of your original plan? Explain.

6. Referring to the data in problem 1, do the following:
   (a) Develop a good plan for the first three months of the year, ignoring the remaining months.

(b) Develop a good plan for the first six months of the year, ignoring the last six months.

(c) Assuming your six-month plan in part (b) is fully implemented, develop a good plan for the final six months of the year.

(d) Compare the costs of the three-month, six-month, and twelve-month plans. Explain any differences among them.

7. Randolf Corporation has estimated its production requirements for the coming year as follows:

Month	Productive days	Demand (units)
Jan	22	8,000
Feb	19	12,000
Mar	21	18,000
Apr	22	20,000
May	21	28,000
June	21	25,000
July	22	26,000
Aug	11	16,000
Sept	21	18,000
Oct	22	14,000
Nov	18	9,000
Dec	21	7,000

Currently, there are 100 employees with normal productivity of 12 units daily per employee. Daily capacity can be increased by up to 30 percent by working overtime at an additional cost of $2 per unit. Regular time salaries average $30 daily per employee. Costs of storing units in inventory are $2 per unit each month. Inventory shortages cost $10 per unit short. Costs of hiring and training a new employee are $300, and a layoff of an employee costs $200. Additional capacity is available by subcontracting to a local manufacturer at a cost of $8 per unit. Currently, Randolf has 5,000 units in inventory. Develop a good plan for next year's aggregate output.

Aggregate planning: process of determining courses of action for the overall levels of output and resources during each period of a planning horizon

Aggregate scheduling: time sequencing of selected levels of output; a subphase of aggregate planning

Backorders: outstanding or unfilled customer requests for output

Graphical method of aggregate planning: two-dimensional model showing the time phasing of demand and aggregate output rates

Human capacity limitations: restrictions on the amount and complexity of thought processes possible by the individual

Idle time: time that is available for, but is not devoted to, productive endeavor

Intuitive problem solving: process of solving problems on the basis of experience and judgment without assistance from formal models

Linear Decision Rules (LDRs): set of equations determining optimal work force and production decisions

Mixed strategy: aggregate scheduling strategy that incorporates or combines some elements from each of the "pure" aggregate planning strategies

Overtime: working hours that extend beyond the normal or regular hours of operation

Pure strategy: aggregate planning strategy using just one of several possible means to respond to demand fluctuations

Regular time: normal working hours; the standard weekly or monthly time commitment agreed upon between employer and employee

Relevant costs: those costs that change, or potentially change, depending upon the decision alternative selected

Search procedures: systematic methods for identifying and evaluating decision alternatives

Work force utilization: extent to which existing work force resources are over- or underutilized relative to their regular time availabilities

SELECTED
READINGS

Armstrong, T. B. "Job Content and Content Factors Related to Satisfaction for Different Occupational Levels." *Journal of Applied Psychology* 54, no. 1 (February 1971): 57–65.

Bowman, E. H. "Consistency and Optimality in Managerial Decision Making." *Management Science* 9, no. 2 (January 1963): 310–21.

Buffa, E. S. "Aggregate Planning for Production." *Business Horizons* 10, no. 3 (Fall 1967): 87–97.

———— and W. H. Taubert. *Production-Inventory Systems: Planning and Control*. Rev. ed. Homewood, Ill.: Richard D. Irwin, Inc., 1974.

Ebert, R. J. "Environmental Structure and Programmed Decision Effectiveness." *Management Science* 19, no. 4 (December 1972):435–45.

————. "Time Horizon: Implications for Aggregate Scheduling Effectiveness." *AIIE Transactions* 4, no. 4 (December 1972): 298–307.

———— and T. R. Mitchell. *Organizational Decision Processes: Concepts and Analysis*. New York: Crane, Russak & Co., Inc., 1975.

———— and D. Piehl. "Time Horizon: A Concept for Management." *California Management Review* 15, no. 4 (Summer 1973): 35–41.

Henderson, W. B. and W. L. Berry. "Heuristic Methods for Telephone Operator Shift Scheduling: An Experimental Analysis." *Management Science* 22, no. 12 (August 1976): 1372–80.

Holt, C. C., F. Modigliani, J. F. Muth, and H. A. Simon. *Planning Production, Inventories, and Work Force*. Englewood Cliffs, N.J.: Prentice-Hall, Inc., 1960.

Lee, W. B. and B. M. Khumawala. "Simulation Testing of Aggregate Production Planning Models in an Implementation Methodology." *Management Science* 20, no. 6 (February 1974): 903–11.

Moskowitz, H. "The Value of Information in Aggregate Production Planning." *AIIE Transactions* 4, no. 4 (December 1972): 290–97.

Starcevich, M. M. "Job Factor Importance for Job Satisfaction and Dissatisfaction Across Different Occupational Levels." *Journal of Applied Psychology* 56, no. 6 (December 1972): 467–71.

Starr, M. K. *Production Management: Systems and Synthesis*. 2nd ed. Englewood Cliffs, N.J.: Prentice-Hall, Inc., 1972.

Taubert, W. H. "Search Decision Rule for the Aggregate Scheduling Problem." *Management Science* 14, no. 6 (February 1968):343–59.

Intermittent (Job Shop) Scheduling

12

Intermittent, or job shop, conversion systems are commonly encountered in many business and governmental organizations. These systems present different types of management problems than do mass production, continuous flow systems. In this chapter we examine the nature of intermittent systems and introduce some concepts, models, and behavioral considerations that enter into planning their use. Figure 12-1 shows how job shop scheduling relates to the overall framework of the book. Because scheduling is a planning subfunction, our primary emphasis in this chapter will be on planning. We'll also have some discussion of control, however, because planning and controlling are interrelated.

WHAT ARE INTERMITTENT SYSTEMS?

Conversion systems can be broadly classified as either continuous or intermittent, depending on the characteristics of the conversion process and the product or service. A continuous system is one in which a large or indefinite number of units of a homogeneous product is being produced. Intermittent systems, on the other hand, produce a variety of products one at a time (in which case they are custom made) or finite numbers of different products in batches to customer order. Many conversion facilities are neither strictly intermittent nor solely continuous but a combination of both.

In Chapter 7 we observed the features of process-oriented layouts for intermittent systems. As you may remember, processing stations (work centers) are grouped together according to the type of function they perform. Each work order may travel through a unique flow path of work centers to meet the customer's requirements. Since the product specifications for each order are different, a separate routing through the system must be

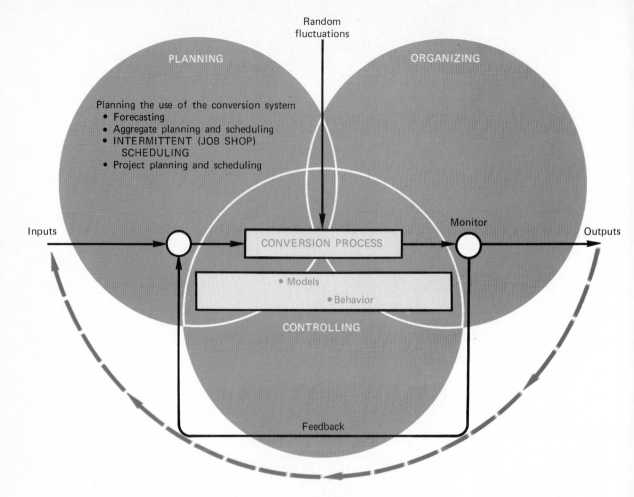

Figure 12-1 **Production/operations management activities**

developed for each one. Separate records must be kept on each job, and the progress of jobs must be closely monitored. In short, each job may differ in completion schedule, routing, input materials, type of transformation, and due date.

In a manufacturing context, intermittent systems are traditionally referred to as job shops. As work orders arrive, the work load on the facility increases. Some work centers may be idle at the same time that others are severely overloaded. A work center may experience a large buildup of "to-be-done" orders awaiting processing. When one order is completed, the equipment may have to be reset or adjusted before the next order can be processed.

The *sequence* in which waiting jobs are processed is important in determining the efficiency and effectiveness of the intermittent system. Sequencing determines the amount of job lateness, costs incurred for setup and changeover, delivery lead times, inventory costs, and the degree of congestion in the facility. Indeed, the scheduling of intermittent systems poses a challenging problem for operations managers.

━━━━━ EXAMPLE ━━━━━

As manager of Matchless Machining Company, you are responsible for processing jobs requiring metal fabrication and forming to customer order. Some jobs, such as thread cutting on metal pipe, are simple. Other jobs are considerably more complex and require intricate metal machining in many stages at different work centers. Your facility consists of 200 work centers specializing in various aspects of machining and supporting services. Ten foremen and 150 skilled employees provide the human resources for your operation. An average of 100 new customer orders arrives daily. On average, a job spends 45 days in the shop. You wish to process the jobs in such a way that customers' orders are finished on time and that Matchless Machining achieves its profit objectives.

Matchless Machining Company must deal with complex problems. Since new orders arrive at irregular rates and consist of different requirements, work loads are seldom evenly distributed across the various work centers; while lengthy delays are occurring at some, others are idle. Of the thousands of jobs in the system, which should you give top priority? For each job, how do you select the sequence in which its various operations are to be performed? Who keeps track of its current status? How do you decide when to switch labor skills from one area to another?

The decisions you make are important because they determine the quality of service to your customers and the costs you will incur for processing their orders. These decisions affect the average number of jobs in the system and hence the amount of in-process inventories on hand. In addition to inventory costs, your decisions affect the efficiency of work force utilization. Further, the sequence in which jobs are processed through the various work stations can result in high setup costs (costs incurred to prepare the work center for the next job to be processed). In some instances, setup costs are negligible, but in other situations they are significant.

In service organizations, intermittent systems are somewhat different in form from job shops in manufacturing. Intermittent service systems frequently offer "provided-to-order" services. In restaurants offering meals served to customer order and in watch repair shops, for example, conversion systems are similar to those in job shops.

Intermittent scheduling is a process involving several activities. Ultimately the purpose of scheduling is to allocate resources to meet demand for goods or services when the goods or services are demanded. The final detailed schedule shows the calendar times at which input and output activities within the process are supposed to occur.

INTERMITTENT SCHEDULING CONCEPTS, TERMINOLOGY, AND SOLUTION PROCEDURES

Overview of the Scheduling Process

Our discussion follows the outline in Figure 12-2. Beginning at the top are the broader levels of planning and scheduling. As the discussion proceeds downward through successively more detailed scheduling levels, we begin to consider system control as it relates to the scheduling process.

Aggregate planning (scheduling)

In this phase, the organization's overall level of output and the resource inputs for achieving it for each of several future time periods are determined. On a monthly basis, for example, the plan may call for producing 1,000 units of output with 20 workers. At this fairly broad level of planning, some more detailed decisions remain unmade. The plan does not make distinctions among each of the 1,000 units; each is treated the same as the next. Further, the plan does not specify when during the month each of the 1,000 units is to be produced, nor in what order, nor which of the 1,000 units is to be made by which of the 20 workers.

Loading

More specific and detailed than aggregate planning, loading differentiates among different work centers within the overall facility. The planned units (specific jobs) to be produced during the month are allocated among the work centers, thus establishing how much of a load each work center must carry during the coming planning period. This assigning of jobs to work centers and the committing of work centers to jobs is known as *loading* (sometimes called *shop loading* or *machine loading*). "The following 15 jobs will be processed on work center *x* during the coming month" is a loading statement. Notice that only the due date of the jobs (one month hence) is specified; the detailed sequence of the jobs is not. Loading determines which jobs processed at which work centers will minimize processing costs; it doesn't specify in what order they should be processed.

Sequencing

This stage establishes the priorities for jobs in the queues (waiting lines) at the work centers. Priority sequencing specifies the order in which the waiting jobs will be processed; it requires the adoption of a priority sequencing rule, a concept we'll discuss later.

Detailed (supplementary) scheduling

Calendar times are specified when job orders, employees, and materials (inputs), as well as job completion (outputs), should occur at each work center. This scheduling supplements preceding scheduling; detailed dates and times are usually not specified until loading and sequencing have been completed. After the priority sequencing rule has been applied, the sequence for processing waiting jobs can be determined. Using estimates of processing durations for all jobs, schedulers can establish their beginning and ending dates and develop the detailed schedule. Then the jobs can

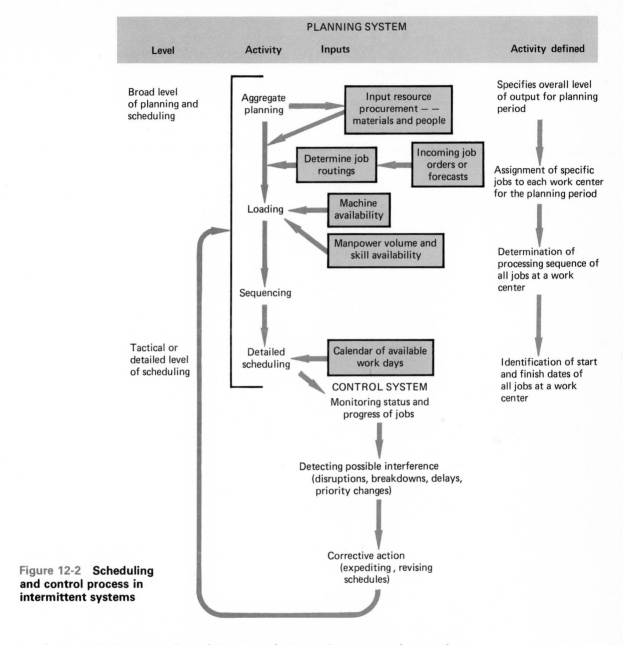

PLANNING SYSTEM

| Level | Activity | Inputs | | Activity defined |

Broad level of planning and scheduling

Aggregate planning → Input resource procurement — — materials and people

Specifies overall level of output for planning period

Determine job routings ← Incoming job orders or forecasts

Assignment of specific jobs to each work center for the planning period

Loading ← Machine availability

Manpower volume and skill availability

Determination of processing sequence of all jobs at a work center

Sequencing

Tactical or detailed level of scheduling

Detailed scheduling ← Calendar of available work days

Identification of start and finish dates of all jobs at a work center

CONTROL SYSTEM
Monitoring status and progress of jobs

Detecting possible interference (disruptions, breakdowns, delays, priority changes)

Corrective action (expediting, revising schedules)

Figure 12-2 Scheduling and control process in intermittent systems

be dispatched, that is, released from production planning and control to the shop floor. Dispatching, transferring the schedule from staff to line personnel, can be accomplished by either physically delivering the schedule or transferring it electronically.

Although the detailed schedule is the end product, the entire *process* of aggregate planning, routing, sequencing, and developing the final detailed schedule is usually meant when we say "scheduling."

408

Part IV

Planning Use
of Conversion
System

Aggregate Planning Level

Chapter 11 considered aggregate scheduling primarily in the context of flow systems. It also applies to intermittent systems, however, and usually in this sequence:

1. In the long-run planning of the conversion process, the overall capacity and processing technology of the facility for meeting long-run market demand are determined.
2. In the shorter run, the capacity and processes are fixed. In intermittent systems, we must consider how capacity and process should be used. This is accomplished in two steps:
   (a) A short-run planning horizon is selected. Maximum processing capacity is compared to forecasted (or known) demand over each period of the planning horizon. Demand is allocated to capacity across periods of the planning horizon. This step determines overall output levels for each period.
   (b) Materials procurement and human resource acquisition are planned to meet the overall output levels.

These steps complete the aggregate planning phase as it applies to intermittent systems. After this broad level of aggregate planning is underway, the more detailed aspects of planning, scheduling, and controlling can be begun.

Loading Concepts and Models

Given the existence of several work centers capable of processing a finite number of new customer orders, which jobs should be assigned to which centers? If we have only one work center capable of meeting the technical processing requirements of a specific job order, we have no choice. In other instances, several work centers may be able to meet the job requirements, and we have to decide which to use. Many techniques are available to help in the decision. The Gantt load chart, a graphical method, is discussed here, and a second method, the assignment algorithm, can be found in the supplement to this chapter.

The Gantt load chart   This graphical procedure is shown in its simplest form in Figure 12-3. The aircraft repair facility has four work centers through which five jobs (aircraft) must be processed. Aircraft *A, B, C, D,* and *E* require sheet metal work; *A, B,* and *D* are the only aircraft needing electronics work. The chart shows the total work load that all waiting jobs require at all work centers. Thus, 55 days of cumulative work lie ahead of the sheet metal center; the paint center faces a 32-day load, and so on. The chart does not specify which job will be completed at which time, nor does it show the sequence in which the jobs should be processed.

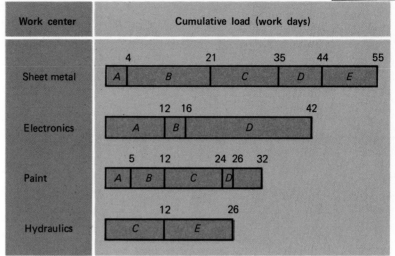

Load Chart for   Aircraft repair
Date prepared   10/27/76
Prepared by   D.J. Rodgers

Figure 12-3 **Gantt load chart for aircraft repair facility**

The Gantt load chart offers the advantages of ease and clarity in communicating important shop information. The existing shop load can be used to develop the more detailed schedules or work activities. It does have some important limitations, however. Since the chart is a deterministic device, it does not convey the variabilities of task duration, equipment (including breakdowns), and human performance times, any of which can cause the estimated load to be inaccurate. Also, the chart is static and must be updated periodically to account for new job arrivals and revised time estimates for existing jobs.

The Gantt chart, whether applied to several departments, machines, or facilities, clearly displays the relative work loads in the system. It signals the need for reassigning resources when the load at one work center becomes too large. Employees from a low load center may be temporarily shifted to high load areas, or, alternatively, excessive load buildup may be alleviated by temporarily increasing the size of work force. Multipurpose equipment can be shifted among work centers. If the waiting jobs can be processed at any of several work centers, some of the jobs at high load centers can be reassigned to low load centers. Later we will show how the Gantt chart can be applied to detailed scheduling as well as to loading. First, however, we will briefly consider how the assignment algorithm can be applied to the loading problem.

Loading with the assignment algorithm   Occasionally a special case of the linear programming algorithm can be useful for assisting in the loading problem. This can be done when the number of jobs equals the number of work centers or machines on which the jobs must be processed.

══════════════ EXAMPLE ══════════════

The metalworking work center of a job shop has been assigned the task of processing four job orders. Four machines in the work center are all capable of processing any of the orders. The foreman must decide which job to allocate to each machine.

This method requires that each machine be assigned one and only one job. Furthermore, some criterion must be chosen to evaluate the "goodness" of the assignments that will eventually be made. The foreman may wish to assign in such a way that profit is maximized, operating cost is minimized, or completion time is minimized.

══════════════ EXAMPLE ══════════════

Suppose the foreman wishes to minimize total processing time in the work center. The estimated days required to process each job on each machine are recorded in the matrix.

Job	Machine			
	1	2	3	4
1	13	16	21	14
2	17	13	19	14
3	12	16	20	16
4	20	12	17	11

For job 3, machine 1 is preferred, because the processing time is only 12 days. However, machine 1 is also preferred for job 1 because this job can be processed fastest on that machine. Since machine 1 can be assigned only one job, a conflict exists.

The assignment algorithm can be used to resolve this problem. It involves four simple steps in which the *opportunity* costs of different assignments are considered. The details of the method are presented in the supplement to this chapter. The optimal assignments are shown here.

Optimal Assignments and Times

Job	Machine	Time (days)
1	4	14
2	2	13
3	1	12
4	3	17
		56

Limitations of the algorithm

The applicability of this procedure has some limitations. First, if the number of jobs is not equal to the number of machines, certain adjustments must be made (these are beyond the scope of this book). Second, this approach does not consider that new jobs, with their loading decisions, may arrive continually; it is a *static* approach. Suppose this algorithm is applied weekly to all new jobs arriving during that week. Over a series of weeks, a heavy work load may accumulate at one machine and a relatively low load at another. A simple updated Gantt chart could detect when the loads are becoming unbalanced. Depending upon the due-dates of the individual jobs, reassignments of jobs to machines may be necessary to even out the loads. Finally, it is commonly found that all jobs cannot be processed on all machines in intermittent systems. Some jobs can be done on only a particular machine or by only one process. When this is the case, no choice exists, and the algorithm cannot be applied. The algorithm may still be applicable, however, to those remaining jobs for which alternatives are available.

Now let's examine the next level of scheduling decisions, priority sequencing.

Priority Sequencing

We can visualize an intermittent system of work centers as a system of waiting lines (queues). As a result of routing, orders waiting to be processed build up in front of each system of work centers. At some point, decisions must be made as to which order to process next at each station. This process of determining the processing sequence of jobs in a queue is known as *sequencing,* or *priority sequencing.*

Why is this decision important? Let us use an example to see the implications of priority sequencing. Consider the five orders awaiting sheet metal operations in the aircraft repair facility we discussed earlier. Customers submitted these job orders during the past week. As sheet metal foreman, you must decide on the processing sequence through your department. There are 5! or 120 different processing sequences for these five jobs.

First-come-first-served (FCFS) sequencing

In a sense of fairness to the customers, you decide to use a first-come-first-served (FCFS) sequencing rule. Say that job orders arrived alphabetically, and customers requested that their sheet metal work be completed at the times listed under "due date" in Table 12-1.

The "job flow time" for this processing sequence measures the length of time each job spends in the system to complete that job. Thus, flow time includes waiting time and processing time for each unit. Job B, for example, waits 4 days while *A* is being processed and then takes 17 days operation time itself. Job *B* is therefore to be completed in 21 days, its flow time.

Our FCFS sequencing rule will result in the following:

1. *Total completion time.* All jobs will have been completed in 55 days.

2. *Average completion time.* The average number of days a job spends in the system is 31.8. This figure is calculated by summing the flow times for all jobs and dividing by the number of jobs:

$$(4 + 21 + 35 + 44 + 55)/5 = 31.8$$

3. *Average number of jobs in the system.* The average number of jobs in the system from the beginning of the sequence through the time when the last job is finished is 2.89. For the first 4 days, 5 jobs are in the system; for the next 17 days, 4 jobs are in the system; for days 22 to 35, 3 jobs are in the system, and so forth. There are 55 total days for the sequence. Hence,

$$[5(4) + 4(17) + 3(14) + 2(9) + 1(11)]/55$$
$$= 2.89 \text{ jobs per day in the system}$$

4. *Average job lateness.* The average lateness of the jobs is 18.6 days. The lateness for each job is obtained by comparing its flow time with its due date. Thus, job *A* is completed at day 4; since its due date is day 6, there's no lateness. Job *B* is completed at day 21, and its due date is day 20; this job is one day late. Similarly, lateness for jobs *C*, *D*, and *E* is 17, 32, and 43 days. Average lateness is:

$$(0 + 1 + 17 + 32 + 43)/5 = 18.6 \text{ days}$$

The FCFS sequencing rule has the advantage of simplicity, and in some respects it provides a sense of "fair play" from the customer's viewpoint. However, some other rules are more desirable from the productive system's viewpoint.

Shortest processing time (SPT)

Consider the "shortest processing time" (SPT) rule: sequence the orders according to processing time, and assign highest priority to the order with the shortest processing time.

The SPT rule yields the data in Table 12-2 and the following performance by using the sequence *A, D, E, C, B:*

1. *Total completion time.* All jobs will have been completed in 55 days.

2. *Average completion time.* The sum of flow times is (4 + 13 + 24 + 38 + 55) = 134. Average completion time is 134/5 = 26.8 days.

3. *Average number of jobs in the system.* Over the entire span of 55 days, 5 jobs are in the system (waiting or being processed) for 4 days

━━━━━━━ TABLE 12-1 ━━━━━━━

SEQUENCING DATA FOR A FIRST-COME-FIRST-SERVE (FCFS) PRIORITY RULE

Job sequence	Job operation time (days)	Job flow time	Job due date
A	4	4	6
B	17	21	20
C	14	35	18
D	9	44	12
E	11	55	12
	55		

━━━━━━━ TABLE 12-2 ━━━━━━━

SEQUENCING DATA FOR A SHORTEST PROCESSING TIME (SPT) PRIORITY RULE

Job sequence	Job operation time (days)	Job flow time	Job due date
A	4	4	6
D	9	13	12
E	11	24	12
C	14	38	18
B	17	55	20

while job *A* is being processed; 4 jobs are in the system while job *B* is being processed for 9 days, and so on. Thus, the average number of jobs in the system each day is:

$$[5(4) + 4(9) + 3(11) + 2(14) + 1(17)]/55$$

$$= 2.44 \text{ jobs}$$

4. *Average job lateness.* The days late for each job in this sequence are 0, 1, 12, 20, and 35 days, respectively. Average lateness is

$$(0 + 1 + 12 + 20 + 35)/5 = 13.6 \text{ days}$$

When we compare the performance of the two rules, we can see that SPT is superior. Although total completion time is 55 days for both sequences, SPT offers a lower average completion time. This means that inventories are tied up to a lesser extent, and quicker service can be provided to customers. With SPT, the average number of jobs in the system is reduced; this reduction can lead to less shop congestion and lower inventory levels. Finally, since average lateness in deliveries to customers is reduced, overall service is improved.

The superior performance of the SPT rule in our example was not an accident. For jobs to be processed in one facility, it is consistently superior to other rules; it is optimal for minimizing average completion time, average number of jobs in the system, and average job lateness.

Setup dependence   In some instances an additional cost factor at the work station, the setup, or changeover, cost must be considered in sequencing. Our previous example assumed these costs to be negligible or independent of the job sequence. But this is not always the case. If a substantial setup cost is incurred, the scheduler should consider this factor, as minimizing overall setup costs for the sequence may be a goal. A family of rolled aluminum parts, for example, might require only a 15-minute setup cost, since the only difference between parts is length, and length can be changed by a minor adjustment of a cut-off press. Changing to a part of another family, however, may require a major setup, since that change requires eight hours to insert and adjust different rolling machine dies.

Table 12-3 shows that overall setup costs for the aircraft repair facility depend on the sequence in which the five jobs are processed. These data show the setup cost when job j is processed after job i. It assumes that job A is already being processed and jobs B, C, D, and E remain to be done. If we choose job B to follow A, a high setup cost (\$29) is incurred. If job D follows A, the setup cost is only \$18. Which sequence of all jobs minimizes total setup costs?

Although optimal solution techniques exist for solving small-scale problems of this type, they are often not feasible for larger size real-world problems. Of more practical value are some heuristic approaches.

The next best rule   One such heuristic, the "next best rule" (NB) states,
(NB)   "given that job i is being processed, select next the unassigned job j for which setup cost is minimum."
For example, if job A is currently being processed, job D would be selected next, since it has the lowest setup cost following job A. After job D, job C or E (\$10 setup cost) would be selected next. The NB rule would yield two sequences:

Sequence	Cost
NB_1: $A - D - C - E - B$	\$18 + 10 + 26 + 18 = \$72
NB_2: $A - D - E - C - B$	\$18 + 10 + 16 + 35 = \$79

TABLE 12-3

415
Chapter 12
Intermittent
Scheduling

MATRIX OF SETUP COSTS

Follower Job *j*

		A	B	C	D	E
Predecessor	A	$0	$29	$20	$18	$24
Job *i*	B	0	0	14	19	15
	C	0	35	0	37	26
	D	0	15	10	0	10
	E	0	18	16	40	0

NB_1 is preferred, since its cost is lower than NB_2. This NB_1 sequence is not optimal. An enumeration of all 24 possible sequences shows that the optimal sequence is $A - D - E - B - C$, with a cost of $60. However, NB_1 may be considered *satisfactory*, especially if we were dealing with larger problems for which complete enumeration of all alternatives was not feasible.

In this example, sequence NB_2 happens to be identical to the SPT (shortest processing time) sequence. In general, however, the NB and SPT sequences are not expected to coincide. If they do not, you must choose between the two rules. Your choice will depend on the relative importance you place on costs of machine setup (NB) as opposed to the value of gaining overall shop effectiveness (SPT).

Sequencing through two work centers
Our previous discussion focused on sequencing several jobs through a single work center. What happens when each job must be processed at two successive centers?

In these cases, we use an optimal procedure that minimizes the completion time for the last job through the process.

Suppose the five jobs, *A* through *E*, in the aircraft repair facility must each pass through the sheetmetal center and then through the paint center. We wish to find the sequence that minimizes completion time of the last job. The processing time (PT) for each job in each center is shown in Table 12-4.

Since there are five jobs, there will be five positions in the processing sequence. These steps tell how to allocate the jobs to the five positions in the sequence:

1. Determine the minimum of all the processing times, PT_{ij}.
2. If the minimum PT_{ij} is associated with work center 1, place the corresponding job in the earliest available position in the sequence; if the minimum PT_{ij} is associated with work center 2, place the corresponding job in the latest remaining position in the sequence.

TABLE 12-4

PROCESSING TIMES (IN DAYS) FOR JOBS IN TWO WORK CENTERS*

Job	Work center 1 (sheet metal)	Work center 2 (paint)
A	4	5
B	17	7
C	14	12
D	9	2
E	11	6

*PT_{ij} = processing time of job i in center j, where i = A, B, C, D, E and j = 1, 2.

3. Cross out both times of the job just assigned to omit that job from further consideration. Cross out the PT_{ij} for the job i just assigned, across all work centers, j.

4. Now return to step 1 and repeat the procedure by identifying the minimum of all remaining PT_{ij}.

Using the data from Table 12-4, the assignments proceed as follows:

1. PT_{D2} is the minimum, 2 days.

2. Since PT_{D2} is associated with center 2, job D is assigned to the last (5th) position in the sequence.

3. Since job D has been assigned, its times are crossed out and only jobs A, B, C, and E require further consideration.

4. (Return to step 1). Of the remaining eight PT_{ij}, PT_{A1} = 4 is the smallest. Since it is associated with center 1, job A is assigned to position 1 in the sequence. Then the times for job A are crossed out, and only jobs B, C, and E have yet to be assigned to remaining positions 2, 3, and 4 in the sequence.

5. (Repeat). Of the remaining six PT_{ij}, PT_{E2} = 6 is minimum. Since it is associated with center 2, job E is assigned to the last available position in the sequence (position 4).

Continuing in this manner, we find that the desired sequence turns out to be $A - C - B - E - D$. The time-phased flow of this job sequence is shown graphically in Figure 12-4. Completion of job D, the last job in the sequence, occurs in 57 days, the minimum.

It is important to remember that this rule applies when all jobs must be processed *in the same order on both work centers*, first on center 1, then on center 2.

Sequencing through two or more work centers

As we expand our discussion to include the types of situations faced by real-world intermittent facilities, the inadequacies of our existing solution techniques become apparent. Most facilities aren't faced with having several jobs to be processed on a single work center; they have many jobs to be done on multiple (often as many as a hundred) centers. Further, all jobs are not going to follow identical routings; some pass through a few work centers, but others pass through many. In addition, jobs arrive at facilities in a variety of patterns, often in a continuous rather than an intermittent manner. They must be routed to work centers as they arrive. Thus the composition of jobs in the waiting line at a work center may change continuously, and priority sequencing becomes a dynamic ongoing process.

For instances like these, optimal analytic solution procedures do not exist. The most common approach by mathematicians and operations researchers has been to apply queueing theory to jobs as they form waiting lines (queues) in advance of being served (processed). The strength of queueing theory is that it provides optimal solutions. Application of queueing theory is severely limited because the mathematical complexity becomes insurmountable once such assumptions as arrival times and service times are relaxed from a few well-known distributions (exponential and Poisson, for example) to more realistic empirical distributions. Queueing theory is not advanced enough to handle the complex job shops encountered in reality. This is not intended to downplay the efforts and accomplishments of mathematicians who have brought queueing theory to its current state, but rather to explain why the technique is not presented and discussed in the context of job shop scheduling. Queueing theory just can't handle the problem complexity encountered in this application.

Some systematic *approximation* procedures, however, have been found. Computer simulation techniques have been used to test the effectiveness of various sequencing rules in these complex situations. Some general guidelines for sequencing have resulted from these efforts. First, most systems are very sensitive to the type of sequencing rule selected, so care must be taken to choose the best one. Second, it will usually benefit the organization to systematically study and develop tailor-made sequencing rules rather than to use untested rule-of-thumb approaches to sequencing in complex intermittent systems.

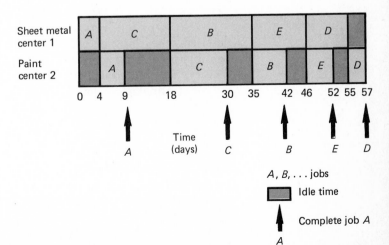

Figure 12-4 **Work flow for sequencing five jobs in two centers in sequence** *A-C-B-E-D*

Dispatching   Frequently, production scheduling literature refers to
                priority sequencing as *priority dispatching.* We have
accepted a more general usage of the term *dispatching,* "to send off."
We accept the traditional process management use of dispatching to mean
the sending off of the final detailed schedule, which was developed in
a staff capacity in production planning and control, to line operating
personnel. Some confusion arises when the priority sequencing is done
by the line operating personnel. In these cases, there is no dispatching
as we've defined it here. Say that a dispatcher in a trucking terminal
priority sequences the drivers to trucks that have been loaded for a given
route. In sending out the drivers, he also is establishing a priority sequence.
The point we want to establish is that in production scheduling studies,
the terms *sequencing* and *dispatching* will occasionally be used interchangeably. We caution you to be careful to see how dispatching is defined.

Detailed Scheduling

Having discussed the aggregate planning, loading, and sequencing
levels of intermittent system scheduling, let's now examine how the
supplementary scheduling is accomplished. This process provides the detailed schedule required by operating personnel so that they know when
to start what job and when it should be finished. One approach is to
make detailed listings of jobs and their required completion dates. From
this list one can "back through" the work centers in the shop and assign
start dates based upon completion requirements. Although we've observed
experienced schedulers do this quite well, it can become very confusing.
We suggest graphical scheduling aids as a plausible and more useful
alternative.

Graphical Scheduling Aids

Gantt charts   We previously showed a Gantt load chart. Another
                version of the Gantt chart can be helpful for visualizing
detailed scheduling of orders. Figure 12-5 is an example; it shows one
possible processing schedule for jobs A through E in the aircraft repair
facility. We must ask you to accept the schedule shown in Figure 12-5
without technological details as to why jobs were scheduled in this manner.
Each pair of brackets denotes on the time scale the estimated beginning
and ending of the activity enclosed within it at each work center. The
solid bars beneath the brackets show the cumulated work loads that
currently exist at each work center. The hydraulics center, for example,
has a scheduled load of 26 days of work, 12 days for job C and 14 days
for job E. The sheet metal center faces the heaviest scheduled load, 55
days. This 55-day load, however, is spread over a time span of 76 days.

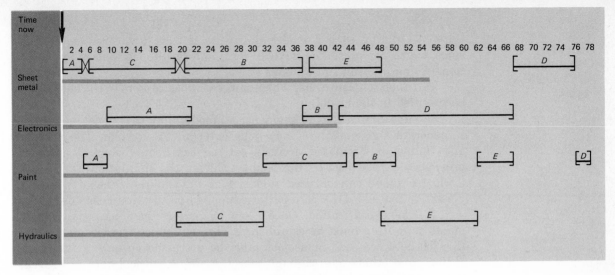

Figure 12-5 **Gantt chart for order scheduling (job sequence: *A-C-B-E-D*)**

Why? First, because job *D* cannot be started in sheet metal until it is finished in electronics on day 67. Thus, days 49 through 67 are currently scheduled to be idle, or open and available for new jobs, in the sheet metal center. Second, two days of setup or changeover time are scheduled in sheet metal. After job *A* is completed, one day of setup is required in preparation for job *B*. Overall, then, 55 days of job processing, two days of setup, and 19 days of idle time constitute the 76-day sheet metal schedule. As work is completed, the "Time now" arrow moves to the right, and a heavier or color-coded line may be used between the schedule brackets to denote work actually accomplished. Scheduled and completed work can thus be compared.

In practice, many refinements of this charting procedure are used. The chart may be updated daily or weekly to show which orders are behind, ahead of, or on schedule, and why. Updating assists in monitoring the progress of orders, points out bottleneck operations, records reasons for progress interruptions (lack of appropriate materials, delays due to tool trouble, delays from improper operator performance, and so on), provides a basis for estimating promise dates to customers with new orders, in some situations indicates the need for shifting work loads from some departments to others when possible, and signals the need for hiring additional employees or working overtime when completion schedules do not meet due-date requirements.

In the supplement to Chapter 4, we discussed the rudiments of computer simulation for a single-channel waiting line system as customers arrived and were processed at a bank teller's window. The same basic concepts are applicable to more complex systems. Even if you have not read the supplement on simulation, you should be able to follow the fundamental

SIMULATION MODELING IN INTERMITTENT (JOB SHOP) SYSTEMS

steps in building such a model and using it to test various sequencing rules, which are presented next. In outline form the simulation approach to modeling intermittent systems is:

1. *Shop configuration.* The number of work centers in the shop must be specified in the model.

2. *Job arrivals.* One segment, or module, of the model is needed to generate the arrivals of new jobs entering the system. The pattern and timing of simulated arrivals can be based on historical patterns previously experienced by the facility. During the simulation, the Monte Carlo technique can be used to select at random the time of the next job arrival based on the data pattern supplied by the simulation designer.

3. *Job classification.* Once a new job arrives, its processing requirements or routing must be established. Through which work centers must this job be processed? Some jobs must be processed on only a few work centers, and others pass through many. Again, historical data can reveal patterns of processing (routing) requirements that may be built into the model. When a new simulated job arrives, its routing is determined in the simulator, often using the Monte Carlo technique.

4. *Processing times.* In the simulator, the time required to process a job at a work center can be determined based on historical service time patterns supplied by the simulation designer. Often, the service (processing) time for a job is randomly selected from a service time distribution that is representative of that work center. The Monte Carlo technique is often used for this purpose.

5. *Specification of shop performance parameters.* The designer must specify the shop performance characteristics of interest. These are the statistics that will be collected to evaluate subsequent alternatives. Such statistics might include percent of idle time at each center, length of job queues throughout the system, average waiting times for jobs, value of inventories in process, measures of job lateness, and measures of job flow times through the system.

6. *Specification of dispatching rule.* The priority sequencing rule to be tested must be selected and built into the model.

7. *Simulation.* The simulation is conducted over time (this is called a simulation run). It is executed by generating new job arrival times, determining their routings, loading them to the appropriate work centers, sequencing them by use of the priority dispatching rule, and creating the representative service times for each job at each center. This simulation is done for a large number of job arrivals, say 10,000 or more. Typically, simulation is accomplished utilizing a digital computer, all of the above having been programmed in a general purpose or special purpose simulation language. When a job is finished at one center, it is placed in the waiting line at the next center in its routing to await processing there. When a work center finishes one job, it is free to begin servicing one of the jobs in its waiting line. The awaiting job with highest priority (based on the priority dispatching rule) is selected for processing next on the open work center.

8. *Recording shop performance parameters.* After all jobs have been processed, the resulting shop performance statistics are recorded and saved for later evaluation and comparison. The simulation run has been completed.

9. *Replication.* At this point, the original dispatching rule can be replaced with an alternative rule in the model. Then, with all other model components unchanged, the simulation can be repeated. The shop performance characteristics from the second run can be compared with those of the first run to determine which of the two dispatching rules performs better. Systematic replications can be made for any number of different rules.

Disadvantages of the Simulation Approach

The primary difficulties of using simulation revolve around tradeoffs of validity and cost. Remember, the model is a *representation* of a real system. One attempts to include the main features of the real system in the model, but many real factors are omitted or are only roughly approximated. The modeler exercises judgment in choosing what to include in and omit from the model. If the final model is judged to be too unrealistic, its results must be given little credibility. On the other hand, realism can be obtained by obtaining more precise data and by expanding the model to include many additional variables that exist in the real-world system. Expanding the model, however, can dramatically increase the costs of model building and computer run time. Many simulation studies have shown that the results obtained from a highly sophisticated model do not differ appreciably from those of a cruder, less costly model.

Advantages of the Simulation Approach

For moderately complex or larger intermittent systems, computer simulation is the least costly systematic procedure for evaluating dispatching rules. Optimal mathematical procedures are not available. Experimentation with a real-world intermittent system is impractical for two reasons. First, a valid testing of a priority rule would require that it be used for an extensive period of time, for months or even years. To test several rules, a prohibitive length of time would be needed for purposes of comparison. Computer models can simulate many years of operation in a matter of minutes. Second, if different priority rules were studied in the real system for long periods of time, it would be difficult to determine the effects of the different rules. Why? Because the performance characteristics of a real system would be caused by many factors and events other than just the priority rule. Variations in people, equipment, communications systems, organizational structure, and numerous other elements cause system performance to change from time to time. If such factors cause performance to improve, the change might be erroneously interpreted to be the result of a newly implemented priority rule. Simulation models avoid such misinterpretations by controlling for these extraneous factors. The only variable that changes from one simulation run to the next is the priority rule being used. Thus, any differences in performance are due solely to the priority rules.

Results of Simulation Research

In this section we briefly discuss some well-known studies on intermittent systems in which various sequencing rules were evaluated. Each of these studies used computer simulation methodologies; all incorporated all nine phases of the simulation model outline presented earlier.

At the outset, a common feature of these research results should be noted: the shortest processing time (SPT) priority rule generally dominates as the single best sequencing rule. In many instances it is clearly superior, and in other situations it is superior to most of the rules and only slightly less effective than the best rule.

Performance
criteria

Various performance criteria can be identified for measuring system effectiveness under different priority scheduling rules. Some of the more common criteria are:

- setup costs
- in-process inventory costs
- station idle time, percent
- percentage of jobs late
- average job lateness
- standard deviation of job lateness
- average number of jobs waiting
- average or mean job completion time
- standard deviation of job completion time

Selection of one or more of these criteria assumes that the overall goal of providing good customer service and/or satisfactory profitability will be met. Three of the criteria (setup costs, in-process inventory costs, and station idle time) are primarily concerned with internal facility efficiency. The more these are minimized without jeopardizing service to customers, the better the use of limited resources and chances for improved profitability. Three of the criteria (percentage of jobs late, average job lateness, and variance of job lateness) are more customer or service oriented than internally oriented. To the extent that these criteria increase, service to customers deteriorates. Finally, three of the criteria (number of jobs waiting, average job completion time, and variance of job completion time) reflect both a customer service and internal efficiency orientation that are hard to separate.

It is difficult, if not impossible, to find a sequencing rule that best satisfies all these criteria simultaneously. If we wish to reduce setup costs, we may have to increase job lateness. This is another example of criterion conflict, which has arisen in many production/operations management functional activities. The relative importance of the criteria must be judged by the operations manager and carefully considered when selecting a sequencing rule.

A study of job completion time   One study tested ten different priority dispatching rules in six different job shop configurations using computer simulation.[1] The results are based on processing over two million simulated jobs through the system. Our main interest in the results has to do with the *job completion* characteristics of the different rules, an important concern to shop managers.

Job completion time is commonly measured in two ways: by measuring the *average* processing or flow time of jobs through the system; and by measuring the *dispersion* of job flow times through the system (measured by a standard deviation or variance). Ideally, one would desire a system with small measures on both dimensions; that is, a small average processing time and a small dispersion as well. This would mean that a given volume of jobs would pass quickly through the system, giving good customer service, reducing in-process inventories, and freeing the facility for processing a larger volume of new customer orders.

The study examined the performances of ten sequencing rules:

Rule 1: FCFS: Jobs are processed at a work center in their order of arrival, first-come-first-served.

Rule 2: SPT: The awaiting job with the shortest processing time is processed next.

Rule 3: SS: The awaiting job with smallest static slack is processed next. Static slack is the difference between the job due date and the time of its arrival at the work center. Thus, a job that arrives far in advance of its due date has a large SS and is processed later.

Rule 4: SS/PT: Static slack is divided by remaining processing time for each job. This rule considers the estimated amount of processing time that remains for a job relative to the amount of slack time. As the SS/PT ratio gets smaller, the job gets a higher priority.

Rule 5: SS/RO: Static slack is divided by the remaining number of operations to be performed on the job. Given equal SS, the job with a higher number of remaining operations receives higher priority.

Rule 6: FISFS: Processing is based on job due date; first in system, first served.

Rule 7: LCFS: Jobs are processed in reverse order of arrival; last job into system is serviced first.

[1]See Y. R. Nanot, "An Experimental Investigation and Comparative Evaluation of Priority Disciplines in Job Shop-Like Queueing Networks" (Ph.D. diss., UCLA, 1963).

Rule 8: DS: Jobs with the smallest amount of dynamic slack are given top priority. Dynamic slack is time remaining to due date less expected processing times for remaining operations.

Rule 9: DS/PT: Dynamic slack is divided by remaining processing time for each job. As this ratio becomes smaller, the job is given higher priority.

Rule 10: DS/RO: Dynamic slack is divided by the remaining number of operations for the job. As this ratio becomes smaller, the job is given higher priority.

The results were obtained for a shop with four work centers. Average (mean) flow time per job ranged from a low of 0.99 for the SPT rule to a high of 2.54 for Rule 9. The standard deviation of flow time ranged from 1.55 to 5.43. Although the standard deviation of flow time was lower for two of the other rules, SPT did well on this dimension also. These results are not surprising when you consider how the SPT rule works. Since the job selected for processing next is the one with the smallest expected completion time, this job doesn't have to wait long in the queue; its flow time (waiting plus processing time) is low. After all the low-time jobs are processed, those with intermediate times are processed. As you can see, jobs with long processing times are continually given low priority and consequently have long waiting times. Eventually, after the quicker jobs are processed, the jobs with long processing times are worked off, but only after considerable waiting time. As a result of these long waits, some of these jobs accumulate a very long flow time. Overall, then, a few jobs have very long flow times, whereas many others have short flow times; this results in a somewhat higher standard deviation of flow times than might be desired. This system behavior is portrayed visually in Figure 12-6. In the figure, two good rules are compared. SPT has the lower mean flow time but a higher variance, as is shown by the standard deviation about the mean (the wider distribution).

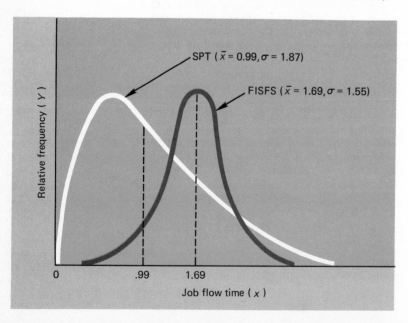

Figure 12-6 Comparative forms of flow time distributions for SPT rule and FOSFS rule

As a final note, two comparative features of these results should be mentioned. First, it is often thought that a first-come-first-served (FCFS) rule offers "fairness" to the customer. The results indicate, overall, that this belief is not true. Since FCFS leads to higher average flow times and a higher dispersion as well, the customer doesn't fare so well as one might think. Second, many practitioners believe that job due-date should be a primary consideration in assigning priorities. In the study, however, although rules 3, 4, 5, 6, 8, 9, and 10 all use some measure of due-date, the SPT rule does better on average flow time, even though it is not a due-date rule.

Job lateness and work-in-process inventories   Using a computer simulation methodology, another researcher examined how well 39 different priority rules performed in terms of job lateness and in-process inventories in the facility.[2] We merely summarize some of the major results here. In terms of percentage of jobs late (that is, jobs not completed by due date), SPT performed far better than most other rules tested. Occasionally, under a few selected conditions, another rule was slightly better than SPT, but overall, SPT was better than the other rules.

There are several ways of measuring work-in-process. The total number of jobs in the shop is sometimes used as a measure. Another is the total work content, the sum of all processing times for all jobs in the shop. Using several measures of work-in-process, this same study found that the SPT rule was not optimal for minimizing work-in-process, although its performance was still relatively good. The optimal rules are called "compound rules." They require somewhat more complex calculations than does the SPT rule. These compound rules are a weighted combination of the SPT and other rules, all combined into one.[3] In short, the SPT, although not optimal, performed well, and it did so without requiring the extensive calculations necessary in the more complex rules.

Truncated SPT   In general, SPT is the best simple sequencing rule discovered to date. Its primary drawback is the dispersion of flow times caused by lengthier jobs being held up in the waiting line. Attempting to overcome this difficulty, some analysts proposed and tested a modified SPT rule.[4] Called the "truncated SPT," the rule works

[2]See R. W. Conway, "Priority Dispatching and Job Lateness in a Job Shop," *Journal of Industrial Engineering* 16, no. 4 (July–August 1965), pp. 228–37, and "Priority Dispatching and Work-in-Process Inventory in a Job Shop," *Journal of Industrial Engineering* 16, no. 2 (March–April 1965), pp. 123–30.

[3]For examples of combination rules see E. LeGrande, "The Development of a Factory Simulation Using Actual Operating Data," in *Readings in Production and Operations Management,* ed. E. S. Buffa (New York: John Wiley and Sons, Inc., 1966); also J. C. Hershauer and R. J. Ebert, "Search and Simulation Selection of a Job-Shop Sequencing Rule," *Management Science* 21, no. 7 (March 1975), pp. 833–43.

[4]This work is reported by R. W. Conway and W. L. Maxwell, "Network Scheduling by the Shortest Operation Discipline," *Operations Research* 10, no. 1 (1962), pp. 51–73.

as follows: "Apply the SPT rule as usual unless a job ends up waiting longer than x time periods to be processed; then give that job top priority." The value for x is set by management. What this does is to interrupt occasionally the normal SPT processing sequence to "work in" jobs that would otherwise continue to wait in line. It helps to avoid the otherwise extremely long flow times possible with the simple SPT. What happens as a result? The standard deviation of flow time gets smaller, as expected. However, average job flow time becomes longer, an undesirable feature in many shops. In summary, in choosing between the simple and truncated SPT, the operations manager must carefully evaluate which is most desired, low average flow time or low dispersion of flow time. A careful, systematic analysis is usually warranted.

Labor limited job shops　The research we have summarized has focused on machine constrained work centers. Often in job shops, there are more machines than employees; employees thus become the limiting factor. In many cases both employees and machines are limitations, and then there is a dual constraint.

Several studies of this problem illustrate that:

1. shop performance is affected by labor assignment policies as well as dispatching rules,
2. the relative importance of due-date assignment, dispatching, and labor assignment decision rules is dependent upon the measure of performance considered,
3. the configuration of labor control at two levels, the shop floor and the higher divisional level, has a major impact on the shop performance, and
4. labor flexibility, the ease with which labor can be shifted among units and organization levels, impacts shop performance.[5]

In summary, the dual constrained job shop is more realistic than the single, machine constrained shop that we've presented here. This added dimension affects job shop performance as it is traditionally measured.

SCHEDULING AND CONTROL　**Rescheduling and Expediting**

Let's say that we have accomplished all the activities we've discussed so far. We have finished aggregate planning, loading, sequencing, and detailed scheduling. In short, we have established a system for *planning the use of* our intermittent system. But we are not done yet. Disruptions

[5]See R. T. Nelson, "Labor and Machine Limited Production Systems," *Management Science* 13, no. 9 (May 1967), pp. 648–71. Also see John S. Fryer, "Operating Policies in Multiechelon Dual-Constrained Job Shops," *Management Science* 19, no. 9 (May 1973), pp. 1001–12; "Labor Flexibility in Multiechelon Dual-Constrained Job Shops," *Management Science* 20, no. 7 (March 1974), pp. 1073–80; and James K. Weeks and John S. Fryer, "A Simulation Study of Operating Policies in a Hypothetical Dual-Constrained Job Shop," *Management Science* 22, no. 12 (August 1976), pp. 1362–71.

may prohibit our plans from being implemented to some extent. Necessary materials or manpower may not be available as planned; equipment may break down; a particularly important customer may desire special treatment. Any of these and other contingencies may cause disruptions and result in rescheduling, a form of corrective action that is part of the *control* process.

Often, the progress and status of each job are monitored as it flows through the system. If the progress of a job is unsatisfactory, the job may be *expedited*. Special attention is devoted to it, and priorities may be shifted at work centers to "hustle the job through" ahead of others. Foremen are notified in advance that the job is coming and is to be given special treatment. Materials needed to do the job may be obtained from suppliers on a special-order basis instead of waiting for receipt of a routine shipment. All this monitoring, special procurement, and advance notification of shop personnel is often done by one person, the expeditor, who is responsible for seeing this particular job through to completion. Certainly expediting is sometimes necessary; but caution should be exercised lest it tend to be overused. Some intermittent shops have been known gradually to increase the use of expediting to the point where most of the jobs are considered "hot jobs" requiring expediting, and attention is given only to "hot hot" lists. Confusion, shop congestion, and inefficiencies are magnified as a result.

Planning for the Scheduling and Control System

The objectives of detailed scheduling, job monitoring, and expediting are to provide services and products to customers in a profitable manner. To accomplish these objectives, an organization needs an overall coordinated effort. The many different job orders must be matched with a large number of machines or work centers; these, in turn, require the prudent use of available human skills and resources. These internal operating subsystems must be integrated with materials procurement and human resource procurement subsystems. To maintain control over the efficiency and effectiveness of the intermittent systems operations, these diverse activities must be coordinated. We'll discuss two fundamentally different approaches to scheduling and control systems: the loading system and the detailed operation scheduling system. These systems differ in the degree of centralized control and information flows they use.

Loading Systems

Loading systems tend to emphasize decentralization of detailed scheduling. Accompanied by schedules expressed in terms of job due dates, new orders are usually loaded into machine or work centers. Decisions about establishing job starting times, assigning jobs to specific people, and assigning jobs to specific machines in the work center are made *locally*, as the load develops at each work center. The individual foremen or supervisors responsible for the successful operation of the center make these decisions based on the current situation and conditions. Usually, however, management at some higher level prescribes the priority dispatching rules to be used on a shopwide basis, except under unusual circumstances.

The Hughes Aircraft Company is one example of an intermittent system that employs a loading system. The Hughes system consists of a shop with anywhere from 2,000 to 3,000 orders in process daily. It has about 1,000 machines situated in roughly 120 work centers. At the heart of this activity is an extensive, integrated computer-based scheduling and control system. One system subcomponent is a computerized simulator that incorporates a priority dispatching rule and develops a detailed schedule for the coming day for each foreman. It is not mandatory that the foremen use this schedule; rather, it is one feasible schedule that may assist them in their local decision making. The results of installing and using this system have been reported to be successful; the number of job orders completed by due-date increased; average order cycle time was reduced; in-process inventories declined; and the amount of expediting efforts was reduced substantially.

Detailed Scheduling System

For decades, managers have tried to implement centralized, detailed scheduling systems. At the extreme, a production control center issues detailed work orders on a shopwide basis directly to all operators who perform the assigned tasks. After completing current jobs, operators return for reassignment to new jobs. This system carries to an extreme Frederick Taylor's concept of separating the planning and doing of work.

Before computers, these systems were difficult to implement and manage. The complexities of monitoring and controlling job orders became enormous for moderate and large intermittent systems. Although Gantt scheduling charts were a major tool used in the production control center to coordinate shop efforts, they were inadequate. They became obsolete as soon as new orders arrived, unexpected machine delays occurred, or other disruptions were experienced. Since these charting procedures were done manually, there were lengthy time delays while people tried to update them. Accurate, up-to-date progress reporting of individual jobs was conspicuously absent.

In recent years, the large data-processing capacities of computers have rekindled the prospects for successful centralized scheduling systems. One was used in a job shop consisting of about 1,000 machines used to produce metal gears.[6] Each gear needed anywhere from a few up to 50 operations on different machines, depending on customers' specifications.

---

[6]See S. Reiter, "A System for Managing Job-Shop Production," *Journal of Business* 39, no. 3 (July 1966), pp. 371–93.

The computer-based system focused on promise dates to customers in developing shopwide detailed schedules. The system incorporated a promise-date priority dispatching rule. Every third day a new six-day shop schedule was prepared, and a complete job-progress report was issued. For each work center, the shop schedule showed the start and finish times for each job. As a result of this system, more jobs met due dates; there was a higher volume of job throughput for the facility; management had greater control of shop operations, and fewer costly overtime operations were needed.

One of the primary problems that we've observed with large-scale computerized operating systems is lack of integrity of the data base. The studies we've cited assume that accurate records concerning such data as completed units, hours worked, machines utilized, workers assigned, start date, and finish date are reported. It is our experience with computerized planning, scheduling, and material control systems, however, that accurate, complete data are not automatically fed into the data collection system on the shop floor. A great deal of production/operations management training time, direction, pressure, and follow-up are necessary to assure data integrity. Without careful checking, the computer may churn out reams of useless information. If employees on the shop floor have supplied incomplete data, no one knows better than they that the schedules built on that data are worthless. Data integrity must be maintained in a computerized intermittent scheduling system.

SELECTED BEHAVIORAL ELEMENTS IN INTERMITTENT SYSTEMS

The operations manager must be keenly aware of some prominent behavioral considerations in intermittent systems. These factors are *part of* the system, and they arise from two sources: the sheer technical complexities of having large numbers of jobs at various stages of completion, and the organization of and role relationships in the system. Although these two sources of behavioral considerations are interrelated, we will consider them separately.

Complexity of Job Status

When you must decide how to process a few jobs through a small number of work centers, your problem is manageable. When the number of jobs increases to hundreds or thousands, each with different routings among hundreds of processing stations, however, your problems are magnified many times. Not only must you process all these jobs, you want to satisfy customers with on-time deliveries, and you want to do so smoothly and efficiently. A single individual is incapable of accomplishing all this. Our limited mental capacities prohibit total awareness of current job status and how that status changes over time. For these reasons, the tools presented earlier have great value to managers of intermittent systems. Gantt load charts and scheduling charts, although simplistic in concept and appearance, serve as memory supplements. They graphically portray the load on the system (and system subcomponents) and the current and projected status of individual job orders.

For decision making, priority dispatching rules play a similar role. The existence of so many jobs and the enormous number of their possible processing sequences pose an unmanageable decision-making problem for people's limited capabilities. We need a simplification process to reduce this decision problem to manageable proportions. By systematically applying priority rules, we get the simplified process we need. Although the rules do not ensure optimal system performance, they do help achieve satisfactory performance, and they are usually better than alternative approaches, including human intuition.

System Organization and Role Relationships

A more pervasive set of problems emerges when one considers the entire intermittent system and the relationships among its subcomponents. The behaviors of individual employees, groups, and work centers or departments must all be integrated in an effective system. Some factors affecting these behaviors can be identified.

Individual characteristics You may remember that intermittent systems, as compared to continuous flow systems, contain a high degree of task variety. Different types of employee skills and work orientations are necessary. Generally, jobs in intermittent systems are already "enlarged"; work content varies, and a higher degree of employee responsibility is emphasized in executing the tasks. Viewed another way, the variety of tasks in intermittent systems is a form of built-in job rotation, one of the methods proposed to enhance employee satisfaction. In hiring, managers should seek employees who have high skill levels and who can work independently without a great deal of supervision. Once employees who are highly skilled and oriented with values of responsibility and occupational achievement have been hired, management must establish a working environment to encourage these individual orientations. Through monetary reward systems, by facilitating group relationships, and through various methods of allocating work among employees, management can create a working environment that enhances the security and fulfills the social needs of the employee. Fulfillment of these needs increases motivation in job performance.

Group characteristics In discussing facility layout (Chapter 7), we pointed out that intermittent systems consist of departments or work centers sharing common processes. A facility might have three departmental groupings consisting of machining, painting, and photography, for example. In these different departments are found different skill or craft groups, and group affiliations are often established. There are three reasons for these group affiliations: command structure, physical proximity, and shared craft interest. As a *formal* basis for group affiliation among machinists, for example, the organizational structures may specify that all machinists report to a machining foreman. Departmental members must communicate and interact with one another to some extent in accomplishing departmental tasks. Second, the physical proximity of machinists in the facility, since they usually work near one another, tends to facilitate interaction and communication, both work-related and personal. Since this is likely to occur on a regular basis, strong group bonds may form. Finally, the existence of an important shared interest, the craft or skill of the department employees, provides a basis for interaction. Unions facilitate this last affiliation; it is likely that in a unionized facility of any size, more than one union will represent differing groups of employees.

The existence of a work group has significant implications for the operations of the system. Although the employees in a group usually adopt a set of shared norms and strive toward satisfying member needs, the group goals may or may not be consistent with organizational goals. Group norms can strongly influence the kinds and amounts of productive activities of its members, especially in highly cohesive groups. A set of research studies found that highly cohesive groups whose goals are consistent with management's goals tend to produce at higher levels.[7] When group and management goals are at odds, however, lower productivity can be expected. The relationship between group goals and productivity is not so strong for groups with low cohesiveness.

Centralized versus decentralized decision making

An interesting question about employee motivation arises when we consider decentralized loading systems and the more centralized detailed scheduling systems. The decentralized loading system provides an important dimension of managerial discretion for the first-line supervisor: *the supervisor decides which employees will work on which job orders.* This type of action prerogative doesn't exist in more centralized systems. In an environment in which wages are hourly and fixed, the decentralized system might be one of the few devices directly available to the supervisor for rewarding and motivating employees. In the more centralized systems, job assignments are often made on a relatively depersonalized basis by the production control center. Any gains from better interdepartmental

---

[7]Stanley E. Seashore, *Group Cohesiveness in the Industrial Work Group* (Ann Arbor, Mich.: University of Michigan, Institute for Social Research, 1954).

coordination could be offset by losses in intradepartmental dissatisfaction and/or productivity.

A potential advantage of decentralized systems is the first-line supervisor's awareness of the local situation and how it might be matched with the work load. The supervisor is aware of employee and equipment capabilities, individual needs, and group norms and values. Employees are easily motivated if their supervisor assigns them to jobs that fulfill their needs. In many companies, bargaining between subordinates and foremen for job assignments is a traditionally accepted interpersonal process. Without it, the prestige attributed to the supervisors' role and the respected craftsmen's esteem may both diminish. Unless other adjustments are made, the diminution of the process could lead to frustration and defensive behavior by supervisors and subordinates alike. Failure to recognize and incorporate behavioral dimensions like these into the design of the intermittent system can seriously damage its chances for efficient and effective operation.

SUMMARY

Intermittent systems have several distinctive characteristics. The types of processes, job orders, work flows, and human skills contrast sharply with those of continuous, or mass-production, systems. Generally, intermittent systems have to deal with diversified customer requests and irregular work flows.

The intermittent scheduling process involves aggregate planning (scheduling), loading, priority sequencing, and detailed scheduling. Loading methods include Gantt load charts and the assignment algorithm. Two sequencing methods are first-come-first-served and the shortest processing time rule. Managers must also consider the problem of priority sequencing in two or more sequential work centers.

The striking feature of the intermittent scheduling and sequencing problem is the elusiveness of its resolution. Although an enormous amount of research effort has been devoted to it for over two decades, from a practical viewpoint the results are disappointing. Generally, companies have found successful systems only through experience and systematic trial and error. Since we have no optimal design procedures, we lack suitable standards for evaluating the true effectiveness of existing intermittent systems. Computer simulation seems to offer the best current approach for systematically evaluating design alternatives, but it holds little promise for optimal solutions.

Intermittent systems entail important behavioral aspects at both the individual and group levels. Management should recognize individual capacity limitations and try to supplement them with graphical aids and systematic decision rules. The needs of individuals and groups as they relate to motivation, productivity, and role relationships are important managerial considerations in intermittent systems. These factors may be substantially affected by management's choices between centralized and decentralized scheduling and control systems.

Determining an appropriate intermittent (job shop) scheduling system design is as tough a problem as will be faced by the production/operations manager. It involves aspects of human behavior, a high diversity of customer requests, and irregularity of work flows. The many challenges of this problem might well persist for decades to come.

Hidesign

After pursuing it as a hobby for many years, in 1957 Bill Withers began to make custom furniture in his garage on a full-time basis. Bill's work had been greatly admired by friends and neighbors, and he was often requested to make special pieces for them. In 1960, Bill leased a facility previously occupied by a supermarket. As his operation expanded, he hired two additional craftsmen, a woodworker and a leather specialist. His high-quality custom-made pieces were well received, and by 1964, Hidesign was incorporated and had 11 employees.

Today, Hidesign serves a custom furniture market covering the entire northwest region of the United States. Bill Withers, the president, has a staff of 37 employees. Custom-made furniture is the sole product, and the company has prided itself on high product quality and timely delivery services. Organizationally, in addition to processing departments, Hidesign has sales, purchasing, shipping, and design departments. Internal processing departments include wood framing, wood preparation, wood finishing, metal finishing, leather, glass, plastics, and cloth fabrics.

This past year anywhere from 350 to 400 jobs were processed in the facility on any given day. Although product quality remains high, on-time deliveries have begun to deteriorate, and although specific data have not yet been compiled, average job lateness seems to be 4 to 7 weeks. Bill Arnold, an employee since 1962, does the shop loading as a special assistant to the shop manager. His job also includes coordinating the overall shop efforts with those of the sales and design departments.

Detailed scheduling of orders has always been the responsibility of the three shop foremen. Larry Cline is foreman of the wood preparation, framing, and finishing departments. Isaac Trumbolt has the leather department and cloth fabrics. Willie Heft is foreman of three departments, metal, glass, and plastics.

Bill Withers is concerned about job lateness. He feels deteriorating customer service might well affect future sales. He has requested George Herring to design a plan for analyzing the current situation and recommending changes. George, whose primary experience has been coordinating a new physical distribution system, is uncertain which factors should be considered and what data will be needed.

1. What is a job shop (intermittent system)?

2. Outline and describe the critical parameters of the job shop scheduling problem.

3. Identify elements of human behavior that are affected by job shop scheduling.

4. Is job shop scheduling a planning activity or a control activity? Explain.

5. Three levels of the scheduling process are loading, sequencing, and detailed scheduling. What are the distinctions among these three activities?

6. What are priority sequencing rules? Why are they needed?

7. Discuss the advantages and limitations of using the Gantt load chart.

8. Interactions among foremen and operative employees can be affected by the type of scheduling and control system that is used in an intermittent system. What differences might be expected between a loading system and a detailed scheduling system?

9. What is the significance of maintaining data integrity in computerized scheduling systems?

10. What is a labor-limited intermittent system? A machine-limited system?

11. Describe the limitations of models for scheduling intermittent systems.

12. Explain why various modeling techniques can be of assistance in scheduling intermittent systems. In what ways are they beneficial?

13. How does a Gantt chart for detailed scheduling differ from a Gantt load chart?

14. Why do most organizations settle for priority rules yielding satisfactory, rather than optimal, system performance?

15. Employee skills and orientation in intermittent systems differ from those in continuous flow systems. Identify some of these differences. Why do the differences exist?

16. Compare the implications of centralized versus decentralized scheduling systems with regard to group behavior and employee job satisfaction.

PROBLEMS

1. Arline Industries is an intermittent manufacturing facility, processing jobs to customer order. Currently, eight new orders are awaiting processing. All jobs must be processed at the same facility.

Waiting orders (in order of arrival)	Estimated processing time (days)	Due date (days from now)
A	23	28
B	16	35
C	5	15
D	31	40
E	11	30
F	20	45
G	2	8
H	27	50

    (a) Develop a Gantt load chart for the facility.
    (b) How many different processing sequences are possible?

2. (a) Apply the first-come-first-served (FCFS) priority sequencing rule to the Arline facility of problem 1. Calculate total completion time, average completion time, average number of jobs per day in the system, and average job lateness.
    (b) Apply the shortest processing time (SPT) rule and perform the same calculations as in part *a*.
    (c) Develop Gantt scheduling charts for the FCFS and SPT rules.

3. Apply the last-come-first-served (LCFS) priority sequencing rule to the Arline facility of problem 1. Compare these results with those of problem 2.

4. At Arline Industries, eight jobs await processing at a single facility. After one job is finished, facility setup costs are incurred before the next job can be processed. Setup costs depend on the processing sequence.

Facility Setup Costs (dollars)

Predecessor job	Follower job							
	A	B	C	D	E	F	G	H
A	—	15	15	20	10	25	15	20
B	15	—	5	10	20	15	5	10
C	5	20	—	30	15	10	10	10
D	25	10	15	—	25	5	5	15
E	20	25	15	30	—	10	30	20
F	30	15	20	25	35	—	10	15
G	15	30	5	10	25	5	—	35
H	10	5	15	20	10	25	10	—

(a) Assuming job A is currently being processed, determine the minimum cost sequence for processing the remaining jobs.

(b) For the sequence obtained in part a, calculate total completion time, average completion time, average number of jobs per day in the system, and average job lateness.

(c) Compare your results for part (b) with your results of part (b) of problem 2.

(d) Calculate setup costs for the processing sequence obtained from the SPT rule in part (b) of problem 2.

5. Eight new projects await processing by Environmental Impact Affiliates. Each job requires an empirical research evaluation before it can be assessed by the legal advisor. All projects must be evaluated empirically and legally. Estimates of processing times (days) for the empirical and legal phases are:

Project	Empirical phase	Legal phase
A	23	7
B	16	21
C	5	36
D	31	9
E	11	12
F	20	17
G	2	8
H	27	22

(a) Develop a Gantt load chart for the work centers (empirical and legal).

(b) Find the processing sequence that minimizes the completion time of the last project processed.

(c) Draw the Gantt chart for order scheduling based on the results for part (b).

(d) What is the completion time of the last project to be processed?

6. Suppose, for the data in problem 5, that each project must pass through both processing phases but does not have to be processed through them in any particular order. A project may go through either the empirical or the legal phase first, and then go through the other phase. Assume the projects were received in alphabetical order. Job due dates are: 60 for A,

75 for B, 32 for C, 85 for D, 70 for E, 95 for F, 25 for G, and 110 for H. Determine the processing sequence for the projects using the following sequencing heuristic:
1. Assign an awaiting project to a work center whenever the work center becomes available.
2. If both work centers become available simultaneously, the next assignment is made to the empirical research phase.
3. At each work center, unstarted projects have priority over projects that have completed one phase of processing.
4. Awaiting projects are assigned to work centers on a first-come-first-served basis.
(a) Determine the sequence in which projects are processed and completed.
(b) Calculate total completion time, flow times, average completion time, and average job lateness for the sequence obtained in part (a).
(c) Determine the sequence in which projects are processed and completed, using the following sequencing heuristic:
    1. Assign a project to a work center whenever the work center becomes available.
    2. If both work centers become available simultaneously, the next assignment is made to the empirical research phase.
    3. Projects are assigned to work centers on the basis of processing time; the awaiting project with the shortest processing time (SPT) is given highest priority, regardless of whether or not it has completed one phase of processing.
(d) For the sequence obtained in part (c), calculate total completion time, flow times, average completion time, and average job lateness.
(e) Compare the results of parts (b) and (d).

GLOSSARY **Assignment algorithm:** A particular version of linear programming used to assign jobs to facilities such that a specific criterion is optimized

Dispatching: transferring the schedule from staff to line personnel

Sequencing rule: a systematic guide for assigning priorities to jobs, thereby determining the sequence in which jobs will be processed

Flow time: total time that a job is in the system; the sum of waiting and processing times

Gantt chart: a graphical procedure showing work loads and/or scheduled activities on a time scale

Load: cumulative amount of work currently assigned to a work center for future processing

Motivation: inner state and desires of an individual that activate behavior and actions

Need hierarchy: types of human needs and their order of importance

Priority sequencing: process of determining processing sequence of jobs in a queue

Queue: a waiting line

Routing: identifying the processing steps or stages needed to create a product

Setup cost: cost of revising and preparing a facility or department for processing a job

Work center: a facility, machine, or work station that provides a service or transformation needed by a job or a customer order

Buffa, E. S. and William H. Taubert. *Production-Inventory Systems: Planning and Control.* Rev. ed. Homewood, Ill.: Richard D. Irwin, Inc., 1972.

Conway, R. W., W. L. Maxwell, and L. W. Miller. *Theory of Scheduling.* Reading, Mass.: Addison-Wesley Pub. Co., Inc., 1967.

Donnelley, James H., Jr., James L. Gibson, and John M. Ivancevich. *Fundamentals of Management: Functions, Behavior, Models.* Rev. ed. Dallas: Business Publications, Inc., 1975.

Fryer, John S. "Labor Flexibility in Multiechelon Dual-Constrained Job Shops." *Management Science* 20, no. 7 (March 1974): 1073–80.

———. "Operating Policies in Multiechelon Dual-Constrained Job Shops." *Management Science* 19, no. 9 (May 1973): 1001–12.

Gavett, J. William. "Three Heuristic Rules for Sequencing Jobs to a Single Production Facility." *Management Science* 11, no. 8 (June 1965): B166–76.

Hershauer, James C. and Ronald J. Ebert. "Search and Simulation Selection of a Job-Shop Sequencing Rule." *Management Science* 21, no. 7 (March 1975): 833–43.

Nanot, Y. R. "An Experimental Investigation and Comparative Evaluation of Priority Disciplines in Job Shop-Like Queueing Networks." Ph.D. diss., UCLA, 1963.

Seashore, Stanley E. *Group Cohesiveness in the Industrial Work Group.* Ann Arbor: University of Michigan, Institute of Research, 1954.

Starr, Martin K. *Systems Management of Operations.* Englewood Cliffs, N.J.: Prentice-Hall, Inc., 1971.

Weeks, J. K. and J. S. Fryer. "A Methodology for Assigning Minimum Cost Due-Dates." *Management Science* 23, no. 8 (April 1977): 872–81.

——— and J. S. Fryer. "A Simulation Study of Operating Policies in a Hypothetical Dual-Constrained Job Shop." *Management Science* 22, no. 12 (August 1976): 1362–71.

LOADING WITH THE ASSIGNMENT ALGORITHM

Occasionally a special case of the linear programming algorithm can be useful for assisting in the loading problem. It can be used when the number of jobs equals the number of work centers or machines on which the jobs must be processed.

=== EXAMPLE ===

The metal working work center of a job shop has been assigned the task of processing four job orders. Four machines in the work center are capable of processing any of the orders. The foreman must decide which job to allocate to each machine.

This method requires that each machine be assigned one and only one job. Furthermore, some criterion must be chosen to evaluate the "goodness" of the assignments that will eventually be made. The foreman may wish to assign in such a way that profit is maximized, operating cost is minimized, or completion time is minimized.

=== EXAMPLE ===

Suppose the foreman wishes to minimize total processing time in the work center. The estimated days required to process each job on each machine are recorded in the matrix.

Job	Machine			
	1	2	3	4
1	13	16	21	14
2	17	13	19	14
3	12	16	20	16
4	20	12	17	11

For job 3, machine 1 is preferred, since the processing time is only 12 days. However, machine 1 is also preferred for job 1, because the job can be processed fastest on that machine. Since machine 1 can be assigned only one job, there is a conflict.

The assignment algorithm is used to resolve this problem. It involves four simple steps that consider the *opportunity* costs of different assignments.

1. *Column reduction.* Subtract the lowest cost in each column from every cost element in that column. Do this for every column. This new matrix of *opportunity* costs is now used in the next step.

2. *Row reduction.* Subtract the lowest cost in each row from every cost element in that row. Do this for every row. This new matrix of opportunity costs is now used in the next step.

3. *Cover the zeros.* Cover all the zero elements in the matrix with horizontal and/or vertical lines. Find the *minimum* number of lines necessary to cover all zeros. If the number of lines required is equal to the number of machines available, an optimal solution has been reached. The optimal assignments are found by examining the zero elements in the matrix. If the number of lines is fewer than the number of machines, go to step 4.

4. *Create new zeros.* Begin with the matrix and the lines from step 3. Find the smallest uncovered cost element (not covered by a line) and *subtract* it from all uncovered cost elements, including itself; add it to all cost elements at the line intersections. All other cost elements remain unchanged. Now erase all horizontal and vertical lines and return to step 3.

Applied to the foreman's problem, the results of step 1 are shown below. It shows that if we assign machine 1 to process job 3, there is no opportunity cost. However, there is still a conflict because machines 2, 3, and 4 would be best utilized by processing job 4, and only one machine can be assigned to process job 4.

Job	Machine			
	1	2	3	4
1	1	4	4	3
2	5	1	2	3
3	0	4	3	5
4	8	0	0	0

Proceeding further, we find that step 2 results in the following matrix, which indicates the job opportunity costs (expressed in time units) with respect to the various machines. For example, the opportunity cost of job 3 with respect to machine 1 is zero and with respect to machine 2 is 4 days.

Job	Machine			
	1	2	3	4
1	0	3	3	2
2	4	0	1	2
3	0	4	3	5
4	8	0	0	0

Now we apply step 3. A minimum of 3 lines is required to cover all zeros. Since the number of lines (3) is fewer than the number of machines (4), a satisfactory solution has not been reached.

Job	Machine			
	1	2	3	4
1	0	3	3	2
2	4	0	1	2
3	0	4	3	5
4	9	0	0	0

In this matrix, the smallest uncovered cost element is the 1 in row 2, column 3. The results of step 4 are:

Job	Machine			
	1	2	3	4
1	0	3	2	1
2	4	0	0	1
3	0	4	2	4
4	9	1	0	0

Step 4 directs us to return to step 3, where we find that only 3 lines are required to cover the zeros. An optimal solution has not yet been found.

Job	Machine			
	1	2	3	4
1	0	3	2	1
2	4	0	0	1
3	0	4	2	4
4	9	1	0	0

Reapplying step 4, we get the next matrix. You can see that a minimum of 4 lines is required to cover all the zeros in this final matrix. A satisfactory solution now exists. The optimal assignments are found by examining the zero elements in the matrix; the optimal assignments lie at these locations. Begin by looking at unique jobs or machines, where only one zero exists for the row or column. For example, looking at jobs (rows), you see that job 3 must be processed on machine 1 if a zero opportunity cost is to be obtained. If so, job 1 must be processed on machine 4, since that is the only remaining machine for job 1.

Job	Machine			
	1	2	3	4
1	0	2	1	0
2	5	0	0	1
3	0	3	1	3
4	10	1	0	0

Continuing with the same logic, we get the following optimal assignments and processing times. Times for each assignment are taken from the original matrix. Since all assignments are made in zero cells, the optimal solution has an overall opportunity cost of zero. The minimum possible processing time for the four jobs is 56 days. This means that 56 machine days are required to process the 4 jobs; it does not necessarily mean that 56 calendar days are necessary to complete all jobs. If the foreman uses this algorithm to resolve his or her machine loading problem, the overall processing time will be minimized.

Optimal Assignments and Times

Job	Machine	Time (days)
1	4	14
2	2	13
3	1	12
4	3	17
		56

The following example illustrates that the assignment algorithm can be used for service sector application. Gantt chart loading is also applicable in the service sector. Just remember to make analogies to the machine (server) and job (item or person processed). These processes could also be used in assigning jobs to typists in a word processing center, assigning inspection tasks to inspectors in a government health service inspection unit, and assigning migrant farm workers to farm work centers that have varying maching/labor skill requirements.

An Additional Illustration

━━━━━━━━━━━━━━━ EXAMPLE ━━━━━━━━━━━━━━━

In the Beef Eater Restaurant, management must decide how to direct different types of customers into different waitress service areas. Management knows that various customer types/waitress combinations will result in different service costs because of varying customer traits and waitress' skills and personality traits. Let's use the assignment technique to illustrate how a satisfactory loading can be arranged when costs for Beef Eater are given in the following matrix.

	Waitresses		
Customer type	Sally	Wanda	Bertha
1	$12.90	$11.90	$12.10
2	15.30	15.50	14.30
3	13.90	13.90	13.00

Our first matrix would be for column reduction, the second for row reduction.

	S	W	B			S	W	B
1	0	0	0		1	0̶	0̶	0̸
2	2.40	3.60	2.20	→	2	0.20	1.40	0̸
3	1.00	2.00	0.90		3	0.10	1.10	0̸

The minimum number of lines required to cover all zeros is 2, a number that does not equal the number of servers. (Servers are analogous to machines and customers to jobs in the algorithm.) We proceed to step 4.

	S	W	B
1	0̶	0̶	0̶.1̶0̶
2	0.10	1.30	0̸
3	0̶	1̶.0̶0̶	0̸

The minimum lines now equal the number of servers and the optimal solution is:

Customer type	Waitress	Cost
1	Wanda	$11.90
2	Bertha	14.30
3	Sally	13.90
		$40.10

1. The costs of processing each of five jobs on five different machines are shown here. Use the assignment algorithm to determine the job-to-machine assignments that will minimize costs.

Job	Machine				
	A	B	C	D	E
1	$100	$ 75	$ 70	$110	$120
2	120	130	115	90	100
3	90	90	110	115	115
4	60	65	40	80	70
5	140	150	170	160	155

2. Architectural Design Associates has six jobs to be assigned to six architects. The expected effectiveness of each architect on each job has been estimated on a rating scale from 1 to 100; a rating of 1 is high effectiveness, and 100 represents low effectiveness. Make the six assignments that will maximize overall effectiveness.

	Effectiveness Ratings					
Job	Louise	William	Ken	Mary	Carl	Patricia
1	33	40	19	24	58	36
2	57	61	8	29	3	24
3	25	56	12	20	10	14
4	44	72	22	37	47	27
5	62	42	31	20	10	33
6	49	33	30	15	22	41

13 Project Planning and Scheduling

As operations managers plan, organize, and control the conversion of inputs into outputs, they must engage in various activities. Figure 13-1 reminds us that although these activities are classified in one category or another, they are all interrelated. Project planning and scheduling, like forecasting, aggregate planning and scheduling, and job shop scheduling, is part of the general process of planning the use of the conversion facilities. Like other planning functions, it affects organizing and controlling, and like them it requires certain behavioral considerations. In this chapter we will emphasize modeling, because project planning and scheduling lends itself to the logic of the modeling approach. But let's begin by finding out what project planning and scheduling is.

PROJECT PLANNING

Project Defined

A project is a one-shot set of activities with a definite beginning and ending point. The activities must be done in a particular order (they have precedence relationships), and they take place in real time. The key concept that differentiates project planning from other types of planning and scheduling is that the project is a one-time occurrence, an occurrence that will not be repeated daily, weekly, or monthly in converting resources into goods and services.

A rush party at a fraternity or sorority, a church or temple picnic, municipal construction of new tennis courts at a park, and initial production of a new product are all projects. Each is a one-shot set of activities; each has a definite beginning and ending point, and each has a series of activities with precedence relationships.

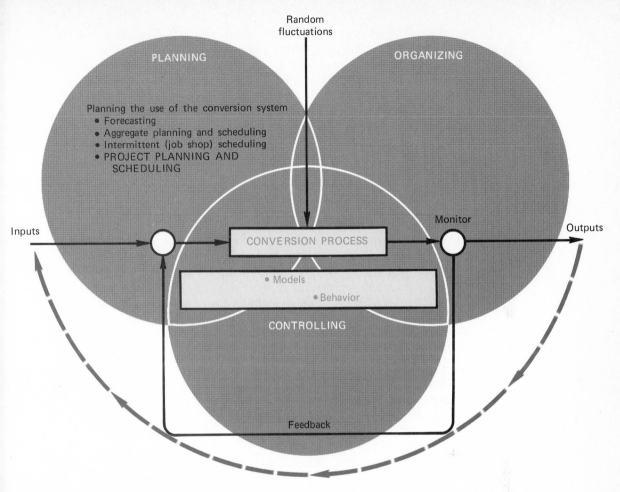

Figure 13-1 **Operations management activities**

━━━━━━━━━ EXAMPLE ━━━━━━━━━

First Christian Church has an annual Sunday School picnic in June. This year the men's club is the host organization. The picnic has been set for Sunday, June 14, and will begin at 4:00 P.M. and end at 9:00 P.M. Activities that must be planned for this project include publicity; providing ice cream, soft drinks, games, and prizes; arranging for a potluck meal; obtaining a facility (location); and coordinating the evening's activities.

Project Planning: A Special Case of General Planning

In general, planning includes all those activities that result in developing a course of action. These activities guide future decision making. Similarly, project planning includes all those activities that result in developing a course of action for a one-shot occurrence with a specific beginning and ending point. These planning activities guide the project manager in future decision making about the project.

Just as general planning is done in phases, so is project planning. *Goals* for the project, including resources to be committed, completion times, and results, must be set and their priorities established. Actual work responsibilities must be identified and assigned. Time estimates and resources required to perform the work activities must be *forecast. Budgets* are as useful in planning projects and in controlling their costs as they are in any other operations management activity. Finally, the project manager must make *policies* to determine which activities are most critical for project completion, how resources should be used, and how additional monies for "crash" completion, should that course of action become necessary, should be spent.

Furthermore, just as the environment forces changes in general planning, it also forces changes in project planning. Project staff (teams) may be formed with the intent of working on a project until completion, only to have team members taken from the project to perform other duties at crucial times within the project. Budget conditions can change dramatically during a project. Poor profitability may cause cash flow problems for the project budget; or unexpected high project costs on some activities may strain the overall project budget. Another key feature of a project may unfold as the project nears completion, and flexibility can be reduced substantially. If environmental forces come at a time when only a few activities remain to be done in a project, the manager has fewer alternatives to choose from, and his or her ability to react is reduced substantially.

Project Planning Versus Routine Planning

Since it focuses on tasks that arise infrequently, project planning deserves special consideration. In operations management, the most prevalent problems are found in the ongoing, repetitive tasks of aggregate planning and scheduling, the planning and scheduling of continuous manufacturing, and the scheduling of intermittent job shop systems. As we have seen, these repeated scheduling situations lend themselves quite nicely to modeling.

We might reason that the project planning situation, since it occurs infrequently and for only one time, is not worth the effort of modeling. This is not the case. When a project misses a completion date and overruns budget, cost consequences can be high indeed.

Typically, the results of project planning efforts become a part of ongoing operations. In construction projects, new product introductions, and large scale maintenance projects—all typical operating management projects—effective project planning and control can and will affect the more routine planning and scheduling problems that follow the project's completion.

Project *planning,* which includes all the managerial activities that result in developing a course of action, is broad in scope. Project *scheduling* is more specific. It establishes times and phases goals and is therefore part of the process of goal setting. Since establishing goals is a planning subfunction, project scheduling may be viewed as a subphase of overall project planning.

In project scheduling, the manager considers the many activities of an overall project, the tasks that must be accomplished, and relates them coherently to one another and to the calendar.

EXAMPLE

Slick Wilson, a first semester freshman at State, is receiving advice from his sophomore roommate on how to study for finals, which start in two weeks. Slick, who has ignored the entire problem until now, is advised to list all his courses and estimate how much time he needs to study for the final in each course, Next, Slick's roommate suggests, he should look in the final exam schedule. When he has determined the order in which he must take his finals, Slick should study for the first one first, the second one next, and so on until he has prepared for all his exams. Slick follows this advice, and he decides that upon completion of the last final, he will throw the schedule away and forget about finals, school, and his introduction to scheduling for a few weeks.

What is the *project* in this example? To study for finals. What were the *beginning and ending points* of Slick's project? The ending point is clear: when Slick steps in to take the last final. The beginning point is not so clear. Since Slick has started planning and scheduling for finals so late, the starting point is now, two weeks before his first final. What are the *activities*? The project activities are studying for various courses. These activities must be *time sequenced against each other,* so that Slick can be prepared for his finals in the order he has to take them, and they also have to be *time sequenced against a calendar.* Had Slick failed to ask his roommate's advice, another week might have slipped by before he started hitting the books for finals. Viewing final exam preparation as a project, how could you improve the scheduling of your study time at the end of this semester (or term)?

There are various methods for scheduling projects. If a mechanic, telling a friend how to repair his car over the weekend, provides an explanation and a sequence of tasks, the mechanic is giving his friend a verbal model. At the other extreme, *mathematical* models can schedule projects using probability and network theory; these might be applied if resource commitments are high and the project consists of hundreds or even thousands of activities. In between these extremes are schematic models, pictorial diagrams. Schematic models are the most common and perhaps the most useful methods of analyzing a project and establishing a schedule to be used as a guide in directing and controlling project progress.

In this section we will look at two simple project scheduling models, Gantt charting and the Program Evaluation and Review Technique (PERT). Both are schematic models, but PERT also has some mathematical model adaptations.

Gantt Charts

Probably you have already developed or seen a schedule that utilizes the basics of a Gantt chart. A Gantt chart, as you may remember from Chapter 12, is essentially a bar chart that schematically shows the relationship of activities over time. Project activities are listed down the page and time across the page.

Figure 13-2 shows a Gantt chart developed for a student preparing for final exams. The project activities are studying for exams in English, history, math, and psychology. Math is broken into two subactivities, studying new concepts since the last exam and studying material on exams one and two for review. By examining the horizontal time axis we see that all activities must be completed in three and a half weeks.

Table 13-1 shows some common Gantt chart symbols. Opening a bracket indicates the scheduled start of the activity, and closing a bracket indicates the scheduled completion. Studying English 1, for example, is scheduled to start at the beginning of week 1 and end after one and a half weeks. The heavy line indicates the currently completed portion of the activity.

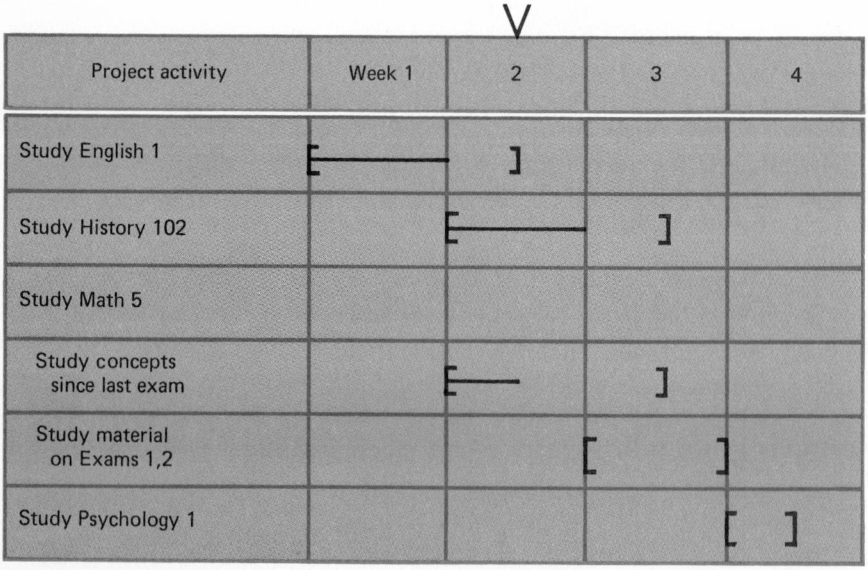

Figure 13-2 **Gantt chart for project scheduling**

Project activity	Week 1	2	3	4
Study English 1	[————	]		
Study History 102		[————	]	
Study Math 5				
Study concepts since last exam		[—	]	
Study material on Exams 1,2			[	]
Study Psychology 1				[ ]

TABLE 13-1

GANTT CHART SYMBOLS

Symbol	Symbol meaning
[	Start of an activity
]	End of an activity
⊢———⊣	Actual progress of the activity
v	Point in time where the project is now

For English 1, one of the one and a half weeks of studying has been completed. Finally, the caret at the top of the chart indicates current time on the time scale. In Figure 13-2, calendar time is at the end of one and a half weeks.

How is this student doing on his studying? What adjustments should he make if he is to meet his schedule? To answer these questions, look down the activities at the point of the arrow. As we've observed, he is behind one-half week in studying English 1. He is also ahead one-half week in studying history and right on schedule in math. He should stop studying history the next half-week and put that time into catching up in English.

EXAMPLE

A new manufacturing facility, which required an expenditure of about $2 million in plant and equipment, was built in Kentucky. The general contractor was a local, nonunion contractor who had had previous project experience; but the largest of his projects had been about half this size. The contractor, a competent builder, had never used formal scheduling techniques. To help him, Gantt charts were drawn up by the company representative with the cooperation of the general contractor. These charts included both an overview chart listing major general and subcontractor activities and more detailed charts for critical activities from the overview chart. The charts forced the general contractor to plan in a way he hadn't done before.

After explaining the charts and providing copies for the general contractor, the company representative saw the contractor using the charts to communicate with his foremen and subcontractors.

The Gantt charts were also valuable for the company representative, a recent civil engineering and business school graduate. The process of constructing the chart provided him with an understanding of project activities, their precedence relationships, and how in real time the project would be completed by the target date. The charts were, for him, a critical model for subsequent project control.

One of the strengths of project scheduling with Gantt charts is the simplicity of the schematic model. In this construction example, contractors, foremen, and company management could readily read and understand the model.

Network Modeling

Many production/operations management problems, including project scheduling, lend themselves to network modeling. Although network models are based on rigorous theory and precise definitions, we will touch on only a few terms and concepts here. Network modeling allows us to address project scheduling a little more formally than we can with the Gantt chart.

Figure 13-3 illustrates the essential features we want to cover in network modeling. *A node is a circle on the graph that designates the beginning and/or ending of an arc;* there are 6 nodes in Figure 13-3. *An arc is the arrow that begins at one node and ends at another;* arcs in Figure 13-3 are 1–2, 1–3, 2–4, 2–5, 4–6, 5–6, and 3–6. On an arc, the arrowhead defines direction; the head is at the ending point. Arc 1–2, for example, begins at node 1 and is completed at node 2. By convention, the diagram is constructed to flow generally from left to right, but arrow *length* is of no significance.

The purpose of the diagram is to depict precedence relationships among the arcs. Some arcs must occur before others. *Precedence is indicated at each node; all arc arrowheads (which lead into the node) must be completed before new arcs may begin (before an arrow from the node can begin).* In Figure 13-3, for example, arc 1–2 precedes arcs 2–4 and 2–5 but does not precede arc 1–3. Arcs 1–2 and 1–3 are parallel arcs with no precedence relationship. All these network concepts will be used when we discuss PERT.

Program Evaluation and Review Technique (PERT)

Development of
PERT

Program Evaluation and Review Technique, commonly referred to as PERT, is a project scheduling technique that is an application of network modeling. PERT was developed for the U.S. Navy in 1958 for planning and control of the Polaris project. The results of using PERT in that application, where some 3,000 contractors were involved, is generally reported to have reduced by two years the project completion time for the Polaris nuclear submarine project. In both government and industry today, PERT is widely used. The Defense Department, the National Aeronautics and Space Administration, and other government agencies require a PERT analysis for companies now doing project work with them.

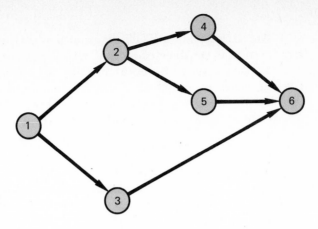

Figure 13-3 **Network of nodes and arcs**

A similar modeling approach called the Critical Path Method (CPM) is also used by business and government. Since CPM and PERT are essentially equivalent, we will concentrate on only one of the two, PERT.

Bar charts and PERT

PERT can be viewed as an extension of a simple bar chart, upon which Gantt charts are conceptually based. Consider the illustration in Figure 13-4. The bar chart (part (a)) shows that all activities in this project can be completed by time 6. Activity B does not start until activity A has been completed, and activity D does not start until activity C has been completed. Activities A and B, however, can take place at the same times that C and D are taking place as long as the B to A and D to C precedence relationships are maintained.

Figure13-4 **Bar chart and PERT diagram comparisons**

(a) Bar chart

(b) PERT diagram

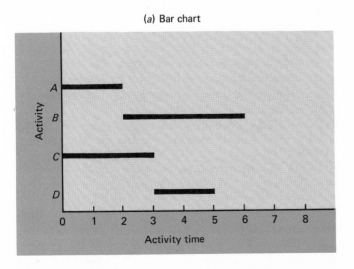

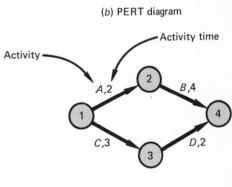

The corresponding PERT diagram is illustrated in part (*b*). Note that the diagram is constructed so that all precedence relationships are maintained. Each activity is represented by a unique arc. The time scale in the bar chart is absent in the PERT diagram; the times are recorded directly on the activity arcs (arrows). Thus, the lengths of the arrows are meaningless; the arrows portray sequential relationships only.

Application of
PERT

First we should clarify when PERT may be used. If your situation lacks the following features, PERT application will have little benefit. First, the scheduling problem must be a project with identifiable activities. Second, the project and activities must all have clear starting and ending points. Third, PERT is most beneficial for projects that are complicated by having many interrelated tasks. Fourth, PERT is good for projects with alternative possible arrangements and sequences of activities and time durations.

The language of
PERT

Basically, the PERT language is an interpretation of simple symbols. Table 13-2 explains the symbols and terms that make up PERT's vocabulary. Key symbols include the *activity* designation, which is an arc or an arrow, and the *event* designation, which is a node. The nodes' only function is to designate the starting and finishing of the activities. Nodes represent a point in time; activities consume time.

The *critical path* is the path taking the longest time through the network from beginning to end. Since it requires the longest time, management should watch it most closely to avoid unnecessary project delays. This path is therefore critical, because it's dangerous or risky.

Logic of PERT

How does PERT work? It works by following these steps:

1. All activities in the project must be clearly identified.
2. The sequencing requirements among activities must be designated.
3. A diagram reflecting the sequence relationships must be constructed.
4. Time estimates for each activity must be obtained.
5. The network is evaluated by calculating the critical path and similar management decision variables. The evaluation is the schedule and plan for subsequent control.
6. As time passes and actual experience is recorded, the schedule is revised and reevaluated.

Step 1 is important because it forces planning on the production/operations manager. Often, the time when the activities are listed is the first time managers become aware of the complexity of the project.

TABLE 13-2

PERT GLOSSARY

Symbol	Term	Meaning
	PERT	Program Evaluation and Review Technique
$\rightarrow$	Activity	A work component needed to be accomplished; a task within the overall project that has a definite beginning and ending point. The activity consumes time. There is no scale for an activity; the length of the arrow has no meaning. A network arc.
$\bigcirc$	Event	A node in the network that designates the beginning and/or ending of activities. A point in time.
$\bigcirc\!\!\rightarrow\!\!\bigcirc$	Network	Combination of nodes and arcs that describes the logic of the project. There is one definite starting and ending point for the entire project.
	Critical path	The path through the network consisting of several activities whose total activity times are the longest of any path through the network. The most pressing, dangerous, risky path through the network. Usually denoted by heavy lines or dashed lines through the activities on that path.
	Critical path time	Total time of all activities on the critical path.
t_e	Expected time of an activity	Expected completion time of an activity. The time estimate with a 50–50 chance of being over- or underachieved. The mean time for the activity.
t_o	Optimistic time	Time estimate for fast activity completion. There is very little chance (say 1 in 100) of completing the activity in less than that time. Will occur only under rare favorable conditions.
t_p	Pessimistic time	Estimated time in which there is very little chance (say 1 in 100) of completing the activity in more than that time. Will occur only under rare unfavorable conditions.
t_m	Most likely time	Estimated time that is the single best guess for activity completion. The "mode" of the distribution of activity times; the most likely time.
T_E	Earliest expected time	Summation of t_e times up to that event. Calculated at an event. Earliest time expected to complete all previous activities.
T_L	Latest allowable time	Latest time an activity can be started that still allows the project to be completed on time. Calculated at an event that designates the start of an activity.
T_s	Slack time	Difference between T_E and T_L; the amount of freedom or latitude available in deciding when to start an activity without jeopardizing the timely completion of the overall project. $T_s = T_L - T_E$.

Steps 2 and 3 also force planning, since precedence relationships must be established and recorded. In step 4, the manager is forced to estimate time for each activity in the project. Table 13-3 explains some typical precedence relationships used in PERT.

Necessary time estimates are obtained from either past data or the experience of those responsible for completing a particular activity. In

TABLE 13-3

PRECEDENCE RELATIONSHIP IN PERT

Network	Meaning
(A) ——→ (B)	Represents an activity AB, where A is the event "Start activity AB", and B is the event "End (complete) activity AB". Activity AB may take 10 hours, but events A and B take *no* hours.
(A) → (B) → (C)	Represents activities AB and BC, where activity AB *must* be completed before activity BC may begin.
(A) (B) → (C) → (D)	Represents activities AC, BC, and CD, where activity CD may not begin until *both* AC and BC have been completed. Activities AC and BC may occur concurrently and are called *parallel activities*.
(A) → (B) (C) → (D)	BD may not begin until AB is completed. CD may not begin until AC is completed. AB–BD and AC–CD are *parallel paths*. However, AC does not have to begin at the same instant that AB begins, although it may. Similarly, BD does not have to be completed at the same instant that CD is completed, although it may. Similarly, it may be completed before AC is completed.
(A) (B) ⋮ (C) (D) OR (A) (B) (C=O) (D)	BC is a "dummy" activity, used when necessary to preserve the logic of the network. It may be represented in two ways, as shown. A dummy activity requires *no* time. The use of a dummy allows all activities to have unique identities.
	Activity CD cannot begin until activities AB and AC are completed. This network has two paths: AB–BC–CD and AC–CD.
ILLEGAL (A) → (B OR C) → (D)	Were the dummy not available, we would have two activities with the same beginning and ending nodes. Since these activities don't have unique identities, confusion would result.

some instances, the times will simply be educated guesses by management. Optimistic (t_o), pessimistic (t_p), and most likely (t_m) times must be estimated so that the expected (average) activity time can be calculated from this equation:

$$t_e = \frac{(t_o + 4t_m + t_p)}{6} \tag{13-1}$$

Calculating t_e in this manner is common practice. As you can see, the most likely estimate is given 4 times more weight than the most optimistic and pessimistic times.[1] This equation allows us to consider a *distribution* of times for any one activity rather than just a single time

[1] Equation 13-1 is an approximation of the Beta distribution, as is the variance calculation discussed next. Although these equations approximate the Beta distribution, we are unaware of empirical evidence suggesting that activity times on projects are Beta distributed. We accept these formulas based on practices and intuitive appeal, rather than evidence concerning the actual distribution of activity times.

estimate. It's not necessary for the optimistic and pessimistic times to be equal distance from the most likely time. The equation reflects the *shape* of the activity time distribution and provides more information than the most likely time, which is a *point estimation.* If we wanted to calculate the variances of the activity times, we could use equation 13-2.

$$\sigma_e^2 = \left(\frac{t_p - t_o}{6} \right)^2 \qquad (13\text{-}2)$$

Managers use step 5, the analysis step, for scheduling, planning, resource allocation, and control. Generally speaking, at least the critical path, critical path time, and event slacks are calculated. Later, we'll touch on some extensions of PERT analysis, time/cost tradeoffs, probabilistic PERT, and PERT with limited resources. But first let's use the five PERT steps in an example.

=== EXAMPLE ===

The Long-Term Care situation. **Long-Term Care, Inc., is a Professional II nursing home aspiring to become a Professional I nursing home. It wants to provide the ultimate in nursing care for patients, but because of recent federal regulations it will need a new, specially designed facility. The administrator at Long-Term Care, Inc., has been so busy with current operations that she has not had time to generate an overall project schedule.**

The first thing the administrator must do is to identify all activities. Let's presume that as consultants we assist the administrator in doing so.

=== EXAMPLE ===

Long-Term Care activities. **The administrator prepares this list of activities:**

A. Perform pilot services for 6 patients in new facility.
B. Build the facility.
C. Install all equipment and furnishings.
D. Recruit workers.
E. Train workers.
F. Pass safety inspection of Municipal Building Authority.

These activities are very general, which is acceptable, but are they in the proper sequence? As consultants, we encourage the administrator to establish precedence relationships. After much thought she identifies the necessary sequence of activities shown here.

Long-Term Care sequencing of activities. **The predecessor activities are:**

	Activity	Predecessor activity
B.	Build facility	None
F.	Safety inspection	B
C.	Install equipment	B
D.	Recruit workers	None
E.	Train workers	D
A.	Perform pilot	C, E, F

Figure 13-5 accomplishes step 3, diagramming the sequence relationships. Note that there must be a node to *begin* (node 10) and to *end* (node 60) the project. Most people find it helpful to use alphabetic characters for coding activities and numbers for nodes, so that activity times may be placed beside activity identification letters without confusion. Figure 13-5, constructed directly from the example sequence of activities, also adds the time estimates.

Note that activity *A*, which also can be called activity 50–60, must be preceded by activities *E, C,* and *F*. The only way we can logically arrange those precedents is to use the dummy activity, 40–50. Look at node 50. Before activity 50–60 can begin from the node, activities 20–50, 30–50, and 40–50 must be completed. All arrowheads coming into a node must be completed before new arrows may leave the node. This assures that the dummy activity is completed. If we move to node 40 and apply the same logic, we assume that activity 20–40 is completed before activity 40–50. If we didn't use the dummy, activities *C* and *F* would both begin at node 20 and end at node 50; they would not have unique identities. This use of a dummy activity assures logical precedence relationships in PERT analysis.

Figure 13-5 **PERT diagram for Long-Term Care, Inc.**

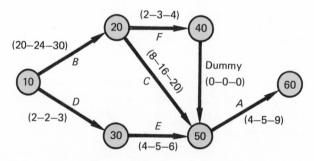

Our next step is to get the administrator to establish time estimates for each activity. Where can she find these times? She can ask building contractors, equipment manufacturers, and her own staff for their estimates of recruitment, training, and pilot program times.

=== EXAMPLE ===

Long-Term Care time estimates. The administrator obtained the time estimates (in weeks):

Activity		t_o	t_m	t_p
B.	Build facility	20	24	30
F.	Safety inspection	2	3	4
C.	Install equipment	8	16	20
D.	Recruit workers	2	2	3
E.	Train workers	4	5	6
A.	Perform pilot	4	5	9

We recorded these time estimates for each activity in Figure 13-5. Since the dummy activity consumes no time, it is assigned times of 0–0–0.

Next we perform step 5, finding the critical path, critical path time, and slack times. First we must calculate, using equation 13-1, the expected time, t_e, for each activity. For activity 10–20 this calculation is:

$$t_e = \frac{(t_o + 4t_m + t_p)}{6}$$

$$= \frac{(20 + 4(24) + 30)}{6} = \frac{(20 + 96 + 30)}{6}$$

$$t_e = 24.3$$

Similar calculations are made for each activity, and the expected times are shown in Figure 13-6.

Figure 13-6 **Expected activity times (in weeks) for Long-Term Care, Inc.**

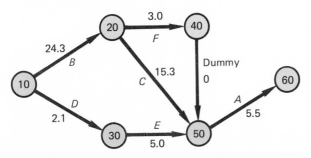

The critical path is the path with the longest time through the network. There are three paths, 10–20–40–50–60, 10–20–50–60, and 10–30–50–60. The total expected time for the first path is (24.3 + 3.0 + 0 + 5.5), or 32.8 weeks. The expected time for the second path is (24.3 + 15.3 + 5.5), or 45.1 weeks. The total expected time for the third path is (2.1 + 5.0 + 5.5), or 12.6 weeks. Therefore, the critical path is 10–20–50–60, and the critical path time is 45.1 weeks. The administrator had better focus her attention on activities on the critical path and allow for a completion time of 45.1 weeks. In Figure 13-7, we have shown the critical path on the PERT diagram.

Figure 13-7 also calculates the earliest expected times (T_E) and latest allowable times (T_L) *at each event,* allowing us to calculate the *event slack,* the extra time available at each event if we arrive as soon as possible and leave as late as possible and still be able to finish the Professional I nursing home facility on time. First we calculate the earliest expected time (T_E) for each node in the network beginning with node 10. To calculate T_E for a node, sum all previous t_e's up to that node on that path. T_E for node 10, set for convenience to time zero, will occur when the project starts. At node 20, T_E is equal to the preceding T_E plus the t_e of activity 10–20 (24.3 weeks). Thus, T_E at node 20 is (0 + 24.3), or 24.3. At node 40, T_E is 27.3 weeks, the sum of t_e's for activities 10–20 and 20–40; alternatively, T_E at node 40 is the sum of T_E at node 20 and the t_e of activity 20–40, or (24.3 + 3.0). Notice that T_E at event 50 is 39.6. The sum of t_e's for the path 10–20–40–50 is 27.3, and the sum of t_e's for path 10–30–50, an alternative way to get to event 50, is 7.1. The sum of t_e's for the other alternate path, 10–20–50, is 39.6. Since T_E represents the earliest expected completion time of *all* activities up to that node, it must be 39.6 weeks until event 50 occurs, rather than 7.1 or 27.3 weeks. Continuing in this manner, T_E for event 60 is 45.1 weeks, the earliest expected completion time for the entire project. As we have shown, T_E calculations begin at the front end (the source) of the network and continue on through until all T_E's for the entire network have been determined.

The reverse procedure is used for the T_L calculations; we begin at the end (the sink) of the network and proceed backwards, node by node, to the beginning. First consider node 60. Its earliest expected completion time is 45.1. If it can be completed in that time, we conveniently designate 45.1 as the *latest* permissible finish time. This is recorded as T_L for node 60 in Figure 13-7. Next we work backwards to node 50. Since activity 50–60 will require 5.5 days, event 50 must occur no later than time 39.6 if event 60 is to occur by time 45.1. Thus, T_L for event 50 equals T_L for event 60 minus t_e for activity 50–60: (45.1 − 5.5), or 39.6. The latest allowable time for node 40 is T_L for node 50 less t_e for activity 40–50: (39.6 − 0), or 39.6 weeks. Similarly, at node 30, T_L equals T_L at node 50 minus t_e of activity 30–50: (39.6 − 5.0), or 34.6 weeks. T_L for node 20 requires special consideration; two activities must be considered, 20–40 and 20–50. First let's consider activity 20–40. T_L for node 20 equals T_L for node 40 minus t_e of activity 20–40: (39.6 − 3.0) or 36.6 weeks. Next,

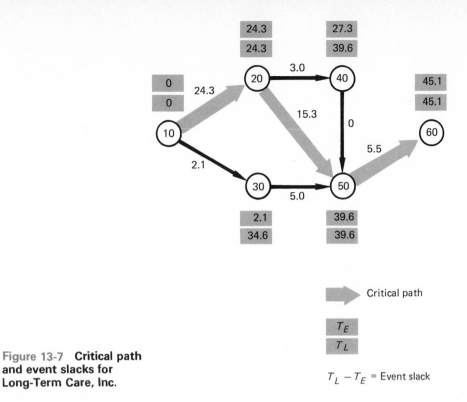

Figure 13-7 Critical path and event slacks for Long-Term Care, Inc.

Critical path

T_E

T_L

$T_L - T_E$ = Event slack

for activity 20–50, T_L for node 20 equals T_L for node 50 minus t_e of activity 20–50: (39.6 − 15.3), or 24.3 weeks. The smaller of these two T_L choices for node 20 is selected. Thus, T_L for node 20 is 24.3 weeks. Had we chosen T_L of 36.6, event 50 could not occur by its latest permissible time of 39.6. Following the same logic, we find T_L for node 10 is zero.

Now we can calculate the event slack, which is $T_L - T_E$ for each event. If we look at Figure 13-7, we see that event slack is zero for most events. Event 30, however, has slack of (34.6 − 2.1), or 32.5 weeks, and event 40 has slack of (39.6 − 27.3), or 12.3 weeks. Why is slack zero at events 10, 20, 50, and 60? *Because slack will always be zero on the critical path.* That is why that path is critical; there is no "fool-around," or slack time.

At event 30 we may recruit workers (10–30) as soon as we start the building (10–20). If we start then, in 2.1 weeks we can expect to be finished recruiting workers. What is the very latest we need to start training the workers (30–50)? We must have the project completed in 45.1 weeks less 5.5 weeks for pilot runs and 5.0 weeks for training. Therefore, we must begin training no later than at (45.1 − 5.5 − 5.0), or 34.6 weeks. *The slack time at event 30 is therefore the difference between latest start and earliest start (34.6 − 2.1), or 32.5 weeks.* Since management attention and resources may be shifted to the critical path from paths that have a good bit of slack, this is an important concept. There is also slack time for activity 20–40. See if you can identify the amount of slack and explain its implications for project management.

PERT scheduling

Once a PERT analysis has been completed, the project manager may schedule the activities that have to be accomplished. He or she schedules, or time sequences, the activities by focusing attention on the critical path. The first activity on the critical path is scheduled first, the second critical path activity scheduled second, and so on until all critical path activities have been sequentially scheduled. The sequencing decision must emphasize the longest path through the network to avoid unnecessary project delays.

Now the project manager starts at the beginning of the network and schedules the remaining activities, considering each activity's latest allowable time—the latest time an activity can be started and still allow the project to be completed on time. The manager works from the start (source) toward the end (sink) of the network so that the precedence relationships among noncritical path activities can be maintained. When scheduling of noncritical path activities has been completed, the manager's schedule is finished.

Notice that we have assumed there are ample resources to schedule critical path and noncritical path activities simultaneously. Generally, resources will not be so plentiful. Later in this chapter, we'll discuss what to do when resources are limited.

Time / cost tradeoffs

In network scheduling models, PERT included, managers often want to reduce critical path times, even if it costs extra money to make the reductions. PERT/COST procedures, formal approaches to reducing critical path times, can be used, but they are very expensive and therefore appropriate only

---

==== EXAMPLE ====

The facilities manager of Home State Insurance Company's two-year-old facility addition (a new office wing) finds that the air conditioning unit is not functioning after the normal May trial. The compressor is out; the fan is out; and because the system was improperly wired, the manufacturer will not cover any losses. After much discussion, the general contractor has agreed to replace the whole system, the cost to be shared between the general contractor and Home State. Of course, the manager wants to know how quickly the job can be done. He has received bids, which are summarized in Table 13-4.

The manager has decided that it would be helpful to schedule this project. He intends to construct a PERT diagram to assist in planning the work by finding the critical path and critical path time. He also intends to spend $400 expediting if it is economical to do so.

The facilities manager is experienced in PERT diagramming and constructs the diagram in Figure 13-8 from data in columns 1 through 4. The critical path is comprised of activities *A, D, G, H,* and *I* with a critical path time of 19 days.

for complex projects with tremendous resources. Although we won't discuss these formal methods here, we will consider basic time/cost tradeoff concepts.

In projects that need time reduction, there are two costs. *Indirect project costs*, costs of overhead, facilities, and resource opportunity costs that can be eliminated if the project is shortened, can also involve lost opportunity costs if market opportunities are missed. These costs result from lack of production output and may be expressed as dollars per time period. Monthly overhead costs of maintaining a house trailer at a construction site, for example, might be $700 per month for heat, light, telephone, clerical help, and other *indirect* construction costs.

A second cost is the *activity direct cost* associated with expediting (speeding up) the project. These expediting costs are direct; they include overtime work, hiring extra labor, retaining an expeditor, long-distance telephone calls, and leasing more equipment.

The essence of the time/cost tradeoff in projects is allocating resources (spending money) to reduce project time only to the point where further expenditures equal indirect project costs. Beyond this point, the cost of expediting exceeds the benefit of reduced indirect project costs gained from reducing project times. The procedure we will use for such an analysis in PERT is straightforward:

1. *Obtain costs.* For each activity, determine indirect project costs and expediting costs. Find these costs per time period ($/day, $/week) corresponding to the PERT time scale.
2. *Determine crash times.* For each activity, find the shortest possible activity time.
3. *Identify activities on the critical path.*

Now the facilities manager wants to expedite. Steps 1 through 3 have been completed in our cost/tradeoff analysis. To reduce the critical path time according to step 4–1, the manager can expedite only activities *A* at $50 per day for 1 possible day and *G* at $120 per day for 4 possible days. *A* is reduced for one day at a cost of $50. The critical path has still not changed, but project completion time has been reduced to 18 days. *G* is reduced by 2 days at a cost of $240. Now two paths become critical: path 1–2–5–6–7–8 and path 1–2–4–6–7–8. Up to this point, project completion time has been reduced to 16 days. The manager has spent a total of ($50 + $120 + $120), or $290 of the $400 allowable for expediting. To reduce one more day, he must spend $120 on *G* and $80 on *F* (the cheaper of *C* and *F*) simultaneously. To take the fourth day from the project, he must spend ($120 + $80), or $200. He cannot do so; he is constrained by step 4–3 of our procedure. The new PERT diagram (spending $290 and keeping $110) is shown in Figure 13-9.

4. *Evaluate the PERT network.* Reduce the critical path (CP) activity times observing these restrictions:

   4-1. Begin expediting the CP activity with the least expediting cost, continuing to the second least costly, and so on to the most costly, or until

   4-2. the target expedited time has been reached, or

   4-3. the resources for expediting ($) have been exhausted, or

   4-4. the indirect activity costs exceed the expediting costs for each activity on the critical path.

In this procedure, you must be careful to keep an eye on the critical path. As the original path is reduced, other paths may also become critical. Should two or more paths have to be expedited simultaneously, the procedure may become too costly. We have gone through an example to illustrate this procedure.

Figure 13-8 Home State Insurance Company PERT diagram

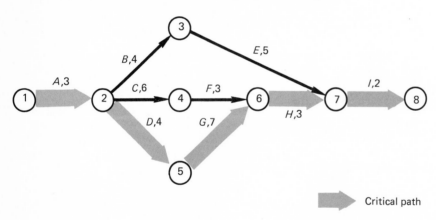

Critical path

Figure 13-9 Home State Insurance Company PERT diagram after expediting

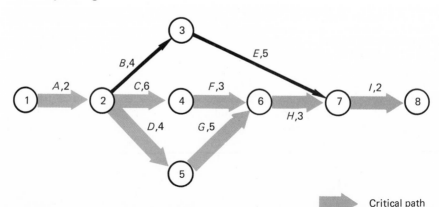

Critical path

TABLE 13-4

HOME STATE INSURANCE COMPANY DATA

Activity	Activity identi-fication	Immediate predeces-sors	Expect-ed dura-tion (t_e) (days)	Standard deviation of dura-tion (σ_e) (days)	Mini-mum duration (crash time) (days)	Cost per day to expedite
Place order	A	—	3	1	2	$ 50
Pull old compressor	B	A	4	0	2	100
Pull and remove old fan	C	A	6	0	4	200
Manufacture new unit	D	A	4	3	4	—
Remove old compressor	E	B	5	5	2	400
Modify duct work	F	C	3	2	2	80
Ship new unit	G	D	7	1	3	120
Install new unit	H	F,G	3	2	3	—
Start up new unit	I	E,H	2	1	2	—

Probabilistic PERT   PERT can readily be modified to consider the variance (σ_e^2) as well as the mean (t_e) of the activity times. To modify PERT, we make the two assumptions that activities are independent and that project completion time is normally distributed. The independence assumption allows us to add the activity variances to obtain a total project variance. The normality assumption lets us use the normal distribution in our analysis.

The mean of the distribution of project completion time is the sum of the individual t_e's on the critical path; it is the expected critical path time. The total variance for the critical path is the sum of the individual critical path activity variances:

$$\sigma_{cp}^2 = \sum_{e=1}^{n} \sigma_e^2 \qquad (13\text{-}3)$$

Consider the Home State Insurance Company example. In the data for Home State Insurance (Table 13-4), the standard deviations for the critical path activities were 1 for A, 3 for D, 1 for G, 2 for H, and 1 for I. From equation 13-3, we see the critical path variance (σ_{cp}^2) is:

$$\sigma_{cp}^2 = \sum_{e=1}^{5} \sigma_e^2$$
$$= [(1)^2 + (3)^2 + (1)^2 + (2)^2 + (1)^2]$$
$$= 16$$

The critical path probability distribution then has a mean (the critical path time) and standard deviation:

$$\mu_{cp} = 19$$
$$\sigma_{cp} = 4$$

Suppose now that the facilities manager wants the project to be completed by July 5th, which is 16 days away. Using X to represent project completion time, he wants to find the probability

$$P(X \leq 16)$$

This is illustrated in Figure 13-10. We can find the standard deviate, Z, by:

$$Z = \frac{X - \mu_{cp}}{\sigma_{cp}}$$

$$Z = \frac{16 - 19}{4} = -0.75$$

In the normal table in the appendices, we find for $Z = -0.75$ the corresponding probability of 0.2734, which is the $P(16 \leq X \leq 19)$. Subtracting from the mean:

$$P(X \leq 16) = 0.5000 - P(16 \leq X \leq 19)$$
$$= 0.5000 - 0.2734$$
$$P(X \leq 16) = 0.2266$$

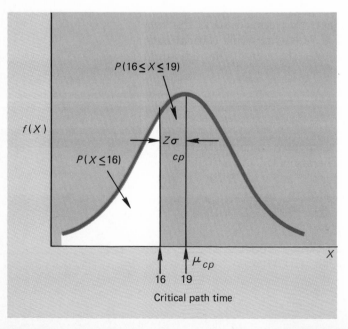

Figure 13-10 Critical path time and variance for Home State Insurance Company

The chance of finishing the project by July 5th is only about 22.7 percent. The manager might now want either to expedite or to generate some contingency plan.

Since probabilistic PERT allows managers to use simple statistics to consider a whole range of possibilities, it's a useful procedure. In our example, the manager was able to take advantage of the *shape* of the distribution of activity times as well as the *mean*, the critical path time.

Limited resources   PERT assumes that there are sufficient resources available to complete simultaneously all activities that are scheduled. This is often not the case. If there are conflicts, limited amounts of labor, for example, some rule is needed to allocate resources among competing activities. Although there are models for approaching this problem, we suspect that heuristics are generally used in practice. Some heuristics for limited resources might be:

- Schedule the shortest activity first.
- Schedule the activity with the lowest variance (most certain) first.
- Schedule the jobs for a particular organization unit (division, department) first.

A project, unlike routine functions that are repeated, has attributes that require a somewhat unique management style. In particular, project management, project organization, and behaviors of managers and subordinates in a project setting need attention.

MANAGING THE
PROJECT:
BEHAVIORS IN
IMPLEMENTATION

Project Management

Focusing on the managerial processes of planning, organizing, controlling, coordinating, and motivating, the essentials of project management parallel those of general management. Project managers must *plan;* they must specify alternative courses of action for possible environmental conditions. They must *organize,* focusing on individual jobs, the grouping of jobs, and the relationships among departments or functions. After project activities have been performed, managers must exercise *control;* they need feedback on results so they can adjust the plan if necessary.

Because the project manager does not normally have position power (by nature of his organization position) over key functional staff, a considerable amount of *coordination* is necessary. To blend several functional areas with various skilled employees, managers need some special traits and techniques. *Motivating* employees, some of whom are peers and some of whom are subordinates but most of whom are not under the project manager's direct control, can become a difficult and critical issue. Persuading employees both on the project team and in auxiliary positions to accept the project manager's goals as their own is critical to project success. It's the crux of motivation.

Measurement   The project manager plans and controls two crucial activities, scheduling and costs. The productivity of the project is often measured as some ratio of these two activities. Managers can measure scheduling performance by comparing scheduled completion against actual completion times. Costs can be measured as a ratio of budgeted to actual costs. A multiplicative relationship between the schedule (time) and costs yields a productivity index (PI) for the project:

$$PI = \left(\frac{\text{Weeks from start as scheduled}}{\text{Weeks from start minus PERT slack}}\right)\left(\frac{\text{Budgeted costs}}{\text{Actual costs}}\right) \qquad (13\text{-}4)$$

If positive slack accumulates as a result of good performance, the denominator of the first term will be smaller, and the PI will be increased. Similarly, if the actual costs (the denominator of the second term) are lowered as a result of good performance, the PI will increase. Therefore, the higher the PI, the better actual project performance compared to planned performance.

The productivity index is helpful because it provides a general guide of time/cost relationships either for varying activities within a project or for an entire project. Remember, however, that it is a gross simplification of project performance. We would hesitate, for example, to make such drastic resource allocation decisions as firing or transferring personnel based solely upon the PI. More detailed investigation would certainly be necessary first.

=== EXAMPLE ===

Two major activities in a project are at the actual 20-week completion stage (20 weeks have transpired since the project started). We know for activities A and B:

Activity	Slack status (weeks)	Budget to date	Actual costs
A	+1	$2,000	$2,000
B	−5	1,000	1,200

As project managers, we are interested in comparative performances for the activities, each of which is directed by a separate supervisor. The productivity index for A can be calculated:

$$PI(A) = \frac{20}{20 - (+1)} \times \frac{2,000}{2,000}$$

$$= \frac{20}{19}$$

$$= 1.052$$

Project Organization

Matrix
organization

The matrix organization is a combination line-staff relationship. In Chapter 8, you may remember, we defined line and staff functions. *A matrix organization is a staff organization that cuts across line functions.* Figure 13-11 shows a matrix organization chart.

The matrix, or project, organization is typically composed of a project manager, who works full-time on the project if it is of any size at all, and a project team. The project team is normally composed of part-time staff, who split time between regular line duties and the project, and full-time staff. It's not unusual, for example, for a research and development project team to consist of a full-time project manager, two full-time technicians, a part-time chemist, a part-time electrical engineer, and a part-time industrial engineer.

Although project teams had been used in the Manhattan Project during World War II, it wasn't until the cold war period in the 1950s and 1960s that project teams were used extensively. For the Minuteman, Polaris, and Apollo space flights and later for various defense projects, both the government and American firms have increasingly used project organization.

Several factors seem to have been responsible for this trend toward project organization and project management. Rapid technological advances in capabilities and reaction times forced organizations to minimize lead

and for *B*:

$$PI(B) = \frac{20}{20 - (-5)} \times \frac{1,000}{1,200}$$

$$= \frac{20}{25} \times \frac{10}{12}$$

$$= 0.667$$

It is clear that activity *A* is on budget and is building a slight positive slack, resulting in a slight positive ratio (1.052). Activity *B* is in trouble. Negative slack is developing, and costs are overrunning, so *PI* is less than 1 (0.667). Management should focus attention on activity *B*.

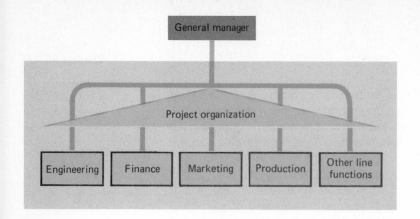

Figure 13-11 **Matrix (project) organization chart**

times and avoid obsolesence. Changing theories and philosophies of national defense and prestige and the need to produce project products at minimum expense encouraged project use. The combination of these environmental trends and the one-time characteristic of projects resulted in the need for a kind of organization that could cut across functional areas. The matrix (project) organization fills that need.

Forming and dissolving the matrix organization

As a prerequisite to project organization, general management must identify and commit resources. Once this commitment has been made, resources can be converted into labor; management of the project team can be assigned; and materials, plant, and equipment can be transferred to project use.

Project managers need both the *technical competence* to understand and meet project goals and the *managerial skills* to complete the project with a diverse group of employees, most of whom are not under their direct control. Although project managers need not have project experience, it is not unusual for them to have technical backgrounds in accounting, finance, engineering, science, or production/operations and experience in industry.

When the goals have been met and the product or service delivered, projects are dissolved and team members transferred to other projects or line functions. If project managers are uncertain about their teams' futures, they may "make work" to keep the project going. Management must be sure to avoid this kind of inefficiency by dissolving the team or redefining its mission as soon as the project has been completed.

Authority, responsibility, and delegation

In Chapter 8 we defined authority as the right to command and responsibility as the duty to command. A critical concept in project management is delegation of authority by the supervisor to the subordinate. The subordinate, in turn, becomes responsible for tasks delegated to him. Since project managers have the authority to complete the projects delegated to them by general management, they are responsible for completion. *They do not, however, have line authority.* Such major work groups as engineering, finance, marketing, and production (see Figure 13-11) are line functions not responsible to the project manager. The project manager, therefore, has the staff function of coordination.

Project managers must have substantial interpersonal behavioral skills. They cannot succeed on technical competence alone. With their functions of planning, organizing, coordinating, motivating, and monitoring performance, project managers are responsible for the projects they're assigned to. But their latitude in directing and controlling projects is limited to monitoring output and advising line managers. Since project managers are responsible for projects but have no direct control over line activities critical to success, their job can be difficult and trying.

Behaviors in a Project Environment

Project managers must have many of the same skills that are exhibited by successful production/operations managers. They must not only be competent technically but must also be skilled in analysis and decision making. Both project managers and production/operations managers (who in some cases are the same person) must act in such a way that the project is completed in an efficient and effective manner. Let's briefly examine a few key behaviors within project teams.

Communication

Project leaders must be able to communicate freely with both team members and line employees who are not regular team members. Within the immediate project team, communication should be frequent. Short daily meetings, written correspondence, and one-on-one problem solving sessions are often necessary for the sorts of tasks required of project teams. We aren't suggesting that everyone on a team should stop working so they can communicate. But the nonroutine, diverse, often ill-structured tasks that project teams engage in require exceptional communication to avoid duplication of effort and costly project delays.

We suggest project managers develop a formal communication system. Such a system can be as loose as carbon copying correspondence and verbally exchanging messages or as formal as team meetings and group work sessions.

Motivation

The several motivators that can be used by a project leader are not substantially different from those available to other managers. Key motivators can be either extrinsic or intrinsic rewards.

Extrinsic rewards are rewards that come from outside the individual. They include, among others, monetary rewards, insurance and other fringe benefits, job titles and project status. Typically, extrinsic rewards can be seen by others. The primary motivator, in our opinion, is a monetary reward. Since money can be used to acquire such a variety of extrinsic rewards, widely different goods and services, we believe it is of paramount importance. Unfortunately, project managers may not have sufficient latitude to give monetary rewards to employees working on the project, particulary employees in line positions. They may be able, however, to see that monetary rewards as incentives for cost control and completion time are given to full-time project team members. Another extrinsic motivator is often competition. When a productivity index is calculated on a departmental basis and posted for everyone to see, less productive departments often complain about the index but try to improve their performance before the next one is posted. Within limits, competition of this sort is healthy for the project.

Intrinsic rewards are rewards coming from within the individual. These include satisfaction from project tasks accomplished, pride in quality workmanship, pleasure from job flexibility, and pride in the team effort. All of these are available in most projects.

Group cohesiveness

When group members are willing to stay together, to develop bonds that hold them together, the group is cohesive. Group size, goal achievement orientation, group status, members' dependence on the group for satisfaction of their needs, and management demands and pressures all affect group cohesiveness and apply to project teams.

As project team and overall group size increase, group cohesiveness decreases. Groups that have achieved stated goals have more of a tendency to remain together than do project groups or subgroups whose goals are not being realized. The higher a group ranks in organization status (measured by project importance, skills required, and job flexibility) the more cohesive the group tends to be. If group members' social, economic, or psychological needs are met by a group, they tend to feel strong ties to the group. The more a project team fills these needs, the more cohesive the team. Finally, management pressures for group members to work in close proximity to one another under stress conditions usually contribute to group cohesiveness.

Overall, the more cohesive the group the better the chances a project can be completed on budget and on time. Because of both the diversity of team members and the one-shot nature of the project, group cohesiveness is difficult to obtain in project teams. But project teams that exhibit cohesiveness have an increased chance of achieving their primary goals.

Project Organization Advantages and
Disadvantages

471
Chapter 13
Project Planning
and Scheduling

Perhaps the one overriding advantage of project organization is that by grouping people and tasks, the organization can take on jobs outside the main stream of its activities. Firms can form interdisciplinary teams to increase their capabilities. Without major reorganization, firms can fix responsibility and centrally control costs.

There are disadvantages too, however. Building and dispersing project teams can be upsetting to the routine of most employees. Furthermore, project managers often feel considerable constraints in having to accept responsibility for completing the project without being given line authority to control it. A final disadvantage is that the matrix (or project) form of organization can lead to more bureaucracy:

> While it may be an extreme case (and there may be other contributing factors), one aerospace company found significant changes when it contrasted its organization structure one year before project organizations were established with the structure two years after this form of organization was used initially. While total company employment had declined about 6 percent, the number of departments, the number of managers, and the number of second-level supervisors had about doubled.[2]

SUMMARY

Project planning includes all those activities resulting in a course of action for a one-shot occurrence with specific beginning and ending points. Project planning, distinctly different from routine operations planning, requires different procedures from those used in job shop and continuous manufacturing environments.

Project scheduling is the time sequencing of the project activities. It can be viewed as a subphase of overall project planning. In project scheduling, the activities of the project are identified and related to one another and to the calendar.

Techniques for project scheduling include Gantt charts and PERT analysis. Gantt charts are visual aids whose strength lies in their simplicity and ease of understanding. Program Evaluation and Review Technique (PERT) analysis is an application of basic network analysis. Activities, represented as network arcs, are related sequentially to one another and represented schematically. Such statistics as critical path time, critical path variance, and event slack are calculated to enhance the value of PERT analysis as a basis for project control.

Critical to project management is measurement of project performance. The PERT analysis focuses upon scheduling, which precedes actual activity

---

[2]Stephen R. Michael and Halsey R. Jones, *Organizational Management: Concepts and Practice* (New York: Intext Publishers Group, 1973), pp. 153–54.

completion. A productivity index, which relates *scheduled* performance time and *budgeted* costs to *actual* performance time and costs, can be helpful to management in adjusting resources for performance improvement.

The project organization focuses on a matrix approach to grouping jobs. Under this approach, staff functions cut across line activities in an attempt at coordination. In a situation somewhat unique to projects, the project manager assumes responsibility for project goals without commensurate authority over line activities. Thus the project manager needs skills in communication, coordination, motivation, and maintaining a cohesive project work group.

CASE

Tranelec Manufacturing, Ltd.

Tranelec Manufacturing, Ltd., is a diversified manufacturer in two primary fields, transportation equipment and electronic applications. In the transportation field, Tranelec products are in the forefront of technological applications, especially in terms of electrical circuitry and component packages. Tranelec management takes great pride in its technological leadership and has decided to retain earnings to support a substantial research and development (R&D) effort.

Currently 74 persons are employed full-time in the R&D division, and at any one time at least twice that many more are involved to some degree in research or development projects. These employees are assigned primarily to line operations in such functional areas as engineering, finance, marketing, and production.

Tranelec organizes its R&D effort by functional area within the division. Engineers, scientists, and technicians are grouped separately. Additionally, within each of these technical specialities, employees are grouped and housed together. Electrical engineers, mechanical engineers, and metallurgical engineers, for example, are each grouped and located together. Projects rotate from group to group, depending upon what work needs to be accomplished. There is a department head for each of the engineering, science, and technical support areas, and three additional project managers have individual project responsibility. There is considerable pressure on project managers for project completion, but they have limited control over staff within the R&D division and even less control over the approximately 150 employees who assist in product development on an occasional basis. The R&D division manager has recently read a brief article about matrix organization. He wonders if matrix organization might be helpful in relieving some of the burden from his project managers and in enhancing division productivity.

One of the three project managers is trying to grasp the basis of PERT. He has assembled the following data for a project soon to be started. He wants to establish a PERT diagram for the project, determine the earliest completion date from project start using expected times, and find the minimum cost plan. This project manager doesn's know whether he has enough data to proceed; even if he does have enough data, he doesn't know how to analyze it and apply the results.

Activity	Immediate predecessor activity	Expected completion time (days)	Minimum expedited time (days)	Expedited cost per day
1	—	10	5	$ 80
2	1	20	15	65
3	2	25	15	40
4	2	20	15	70
5	3,4	15	13	90
6	5	15	10	105
7	1	60	45	30
8	6,7	5	4	85

The project has fixed costs per day of $100; that is, each day that the completion time is shortened from the expected time, the firm saves $100.

1. Differentiate between project and other types of planning.

2. Explain how project planning and project scheduling relate.

3. Provide an example, not given in this chapter, of a project. Describe the project, identifying the beginning and ending points, the activities, and the time sequencing of the activities against each other and the calendar.

4. Discuss how a Gantt chart can be used as a scheduling tool. What type of model is a Gantt chart?

5. PERT has characteristics of both a mathematical model and a schematic model. Explain.

6. Explain how the scheduling and cost performance of a project might be measured. When might such a measure be useful?

7. Relate authority, responsibility, and delegation to project management.

8. Discuss the key behaviors that occur within project teams. In your discussion, explain who the people are who exhibit each behavior and explain the possible conse-

quences of such behavior on project goal accomplishment.

9. Contrast the advantages and disadvantages of project organization.

10. Provide the features that a situation should present before PERT may be used.

11. In PERT, the terms are important. Explain the difference between an activity and an event. What is a critical path?

12. Present the logic of PERT. (How does PERT work?)

13. Explain how a time/cost tradeoff could exist in a project involving the construction, staffing, and opening of a new clubhouse at an existing country club.

14. Managers often complain that statistical analysis is too complicated. Suppose that although your supervisor exhibits such an attitude, he likes PERT. In minimally technical terms explain the advantages of probabilistic PERT to your supervisor and try to convince him to accept it.

1. A veterinarian would like to put drains for collecting animal waste and a septic tank in his animal shelter. He has identified the following activities and estimated their times (in days): planning (2), obtaining contractor (7), excavating (2), laying drainage tile (2), concrete work (3), landscaping (1).

All activities are sequential except for laying the drainage tile and concrete work, which may be done at the same time but must be done after excavation.
(a) Prepare a Gantt chart.
(b) Prepare a PERT chart.
(c) Which chart do you believe would be most useful on this project? Why?

2. Compare the following projects by computing a productivity index for each. You are the general manager responsible for all three projects. What can you conclude?

Activity	Transpired time (weeks)	Slack	Budget	Actual cost
Sales training program	6	−1	$3,650	$2,840
Machine repairs	15	+2	1,500	2,000
Changing filing system	20	−2	8,475	8,475

3. Oscar Thompson, a project manager, is very upset with the productivity index used to measure performance of his group. He is ahead of schedule by three weeks on a project that is 120 weeks in duration and one-third completed. The ratio, 0.94, is still less than one, however. Explain to Oscar where his problem lies.

4. Given the following PERT activities:

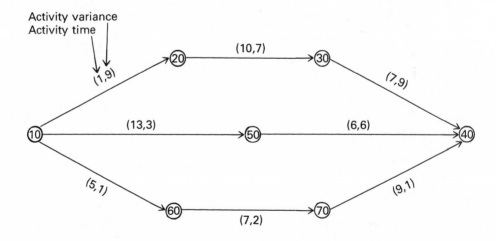

Activity variance
Activity time

(1,9)   (10,7)   (7,9)

(13,3)   (6,6)

(5,1)   (7,2)   (9,1)

(a) What is the critical path?
(b) Construct a Gantt chart for this project.
(c) Examine the activity variances. Which path through the network would you suggest that the project manager watch most closely? Why?

5. Given the following PERT diagram with times in days:

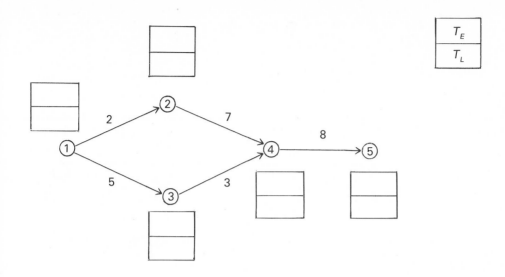

(a) Compute the values for the earliest expected times (T_E) and the latest allowable times (T_L).
(b) Find the event slack at event 2.
(c) The penalty cost per day for each day over 15 days is $10. The costs of expediting, for those activities that allow it, are:

Activity	Expediting cost per day	Maximum days that can be reduced by expediting
2–4	$ 7	2
3–4	6	1
4–5	15	3

Which activities (and by how many days), *if any*, would you expedite?

6. A project manager for Electromagnet, Inc., has constructed the following PERT network.

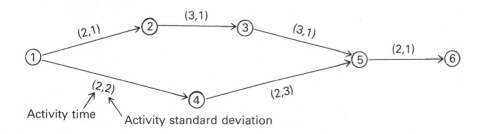

Assist the manager by determining:
(a) the critical path and critical path time
(b) the probability of completing this project in 9 days or fewer and the probability of completing the project in 11 days or more (assuming independent activities and normally distributed completion times)
(c) the expected gain (or loss) from this project if completed, given the following payoff table:

Alternatives	State of Nature		
	Finish 9 days or fewer	Finish between 9 and 11 days	Finish 11 days or more
Complete the project	+$800	+$200	−$100
Don't start the project	$0	$0	$0

7. For a Research and Development project, the following PERT network was constructed. Activity times are in months.

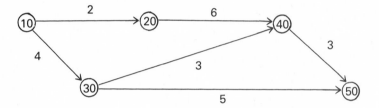

(a) What is the critical path?
(b) What is the event slack at event 30? What does that mean?
(c) Two activities have to be added due to a change in project definition. An activity of two months must precede the entire project, and an activity of two months must precede activity 10–30. What impact, if any, will this have on the critical path and on the event slack at event 30?

8. A public accounting firm has described an audit program at a bank in terms of activities and events and has calculated the expected activity times (t_e) and their variances (σ_e^2) as shown (for example, activity 10–20 has $t_e = 8$ and $\sigma_e^2 = 3$). The activity times are in days in the PERT network.

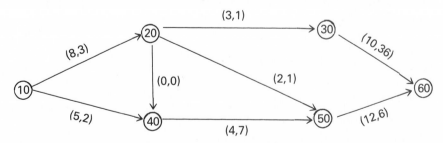

(a) Find the critical path and the mean critical path time for the audit program.

(b) If activity times are assumed to be independent and normally distributed, what is the probability that the audit is completed in 22 days or fewer? Of what value is this information to a partner in the firm?

(c) What can you tell about activity 30–60 as it relates to the critical path?

(d) What is the event slack at event 50? Why?

9. A market research project for Consumer Planning Corporation (CPC) is being planned as shown below. For the market research manager:

(a) Construct a PERT diagram.

(b) Explain the critical path concept and what the critical path is for this project.

(c) Tell how you would spend $200 of expediting money to benefit CPC most.

Activity	Immediate predecessor	Expected time (days)	Cost per day to expedite
A–B	—	2	$100
A–C	—	4	80
A–D	—	5	70
B–E	A–B, A–C	3	100
E–F	B–E	6	150
F–H	E–F	2	50
D–H	A–D,	11	100
H–I	F–H, D–H	1	100

10. Temple Hospital is designing and implementing a wage incentive program. Included are the activities of this project and other project information. Activity times are independent and normally distributed.

(a) Construct a PERT network and mark the critical path. What does the critical path mean?

(b) What is the probability of completion in more than 15 weeks?

(c) You have $1,000 to spend expediting. Where would you spend it? Why?

Activity	Immediate predecessor	Expected time (weeks)	Expected standard deviation	Minimum time	Cost per week to expedite
Project planning 1–2	—	3	1	3	—
Job analysis 2–3	1–2	5	2	2	$ 500
Performance analysis 2–4	1–2	4	2	2	500
Market wage survey 2–5	1–2	7	3	6	300
Structure internal wage program 3–5	2–3,2–4	3	2	2	1,000
Finalize incentive program 5–6	2–5,3–5	4	2	4	—

GLOSSARY

Arc: in networks, the arrow that begins at one node and ends at another

Matrix organization: a project organization that combines staff and line relationships; a staff organization that cuts across line functions

Node: in networks, a circle that designates the beginning and/or ending of an arc

PERT: Program Evaluation and Review Technique; a project scheduling technique that is an application of network modeling

PERT activity: work needed to be accomplished; designated by an arc

PERT critical path: the path through the network consisting of several activities whose total activity times are the longest of any path through the network

PERT event: a point in time on the project; designated by a node; designates the beginning and/or ending of activities

PERT slack time: event slack or time that can be used in nonwork if an event is arrived at as soon as possible and left as late as possible, still allowing the project to finish on time

Probabilistic PERT: a modification of PERT to consider the variance (σ^2) and the mean (t_e) of the activity time

Project: a one-shot set of activities with a definite beginning and ending point

Project planning: All activities that result in developing a course of action for a one-shot occurrence with a specific beginning and ending point

Project scheduling: time sequencing of project activities

SELECTED READINGS

Baumgartner, John S. *Project Management.* Homewood, Ill.: Richard D. Irwin, Inc., 1963.

Buffa, Elwood S. *Modern Production Management.* 4th ed. New York: John Wiley & Sons, Inc., 1973.

Chase, Richard B. and Nicholas J. Aquilano. *Production and Operations Management.* Homewood, Ill.: Richard D. Irwin, Inc., 1973.

Donnelley, James H., James L. Gibson, and John M. Ivancevich. *Fundamentals of Management: Functions, Behavior, Mod-els.* Rev. ed. Dallas: Business Publications, Inc., 1975.

George, Claude S., Jr. *Management for Business and Industry.* Englewood Cliffs, N.J.: Prentice-Hall, Inc., 1970.

Greene, James H. *Production and Inventory Control.* Rev. ed. Homewood, Ill.: Richard D. Irwin, Inc., 1974.

Michael, Stephen R. and Halsey R. Jones. *Organization Management: Concepts and Practices.* New York: Intext Publishers Group, 1973.

CONTROLLING THE CONVERSION SYSTEM

14 Controlling Operations

With this chapter, we change our emphasis from planning to controlling operations in the conversion process (see Figure 14-1). Once the conversion process has begun, production/operations managers must make decisions to keep operations on a steady course toward planned goals. As unexpected events develop, they must revise goals, adjust process inputs, or change conversion activities to keep overall performance in tune with production/operations objectives. Later in this chapter, we'll discuss specific problems managers must deal with in their controlling activities. First, however, let's consider some concepts basic to control.

BASIC CONTROL CONCEPTS

In recent decades, the control process has been developed conceptually, theoretically, and mathematically by engineers and scientists. Not all these developments can be transferred directly to management settings because organizational complexities create conditions different from the pure theoretical systems studied by scientists. Indirectly, however, the basics of control theory provide operations managers a valuable background for analyzing, understanding, and controlling the systems they manage. For this reason, production/operations managers should be acquainted with the elements, types, and characteristics of control systems.

Elements of a Control System

Controlling is a process by which some aspect of a system is modified to achieve desired system performance. A homeowner, for example, may lower the thermostat setting at night to hold monthly heating bills within

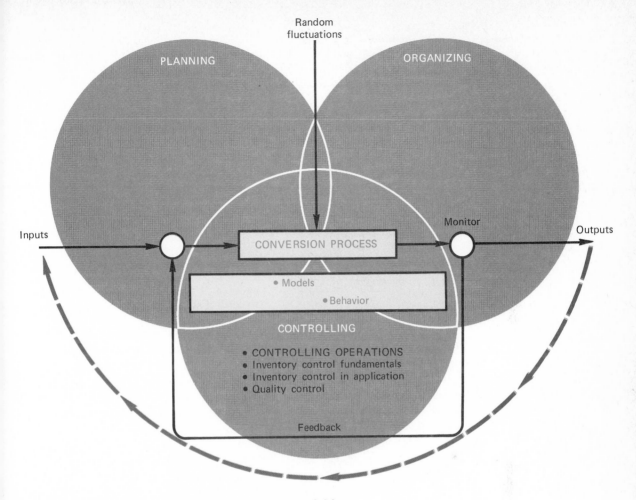

Figure 14-1 **Production/operations management activities**

a budgeted amount. A manufacturer of luggage may decide to purchase leather from a new supplier when it discovers that present suppliers are providing inferior leather. The purpose of the control process is to cause the system to run true to its objectives. Control is not an end itself but rather a means to an end—improving system operation.

Conceptually, many kinds of systems—biological, social, mechanical, political, and economic—have control subsystems that share certain elements. These include system inputs, outputs, a sensor, a comparator, a memory, and an activator. The relationships among these subsystem elements are shown in Figure 14-2.

Let's consider some aspects of control in manufacturing luggage. Overall, inputs (such as leather) provided to the conversion system are processed or converted for the purpose of creating desired outputs (luggage). The outputs (luggage) are monitored and measured by a sensing device (a human inspector and/or test equipment). The resulting measurement (leather thickness or impact resistance) is used in the comparator to detect discrepancies between the measured output and a prespecified standard

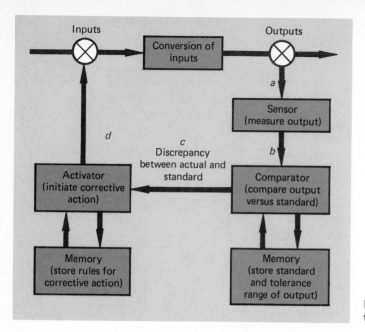

Inputs Outputs

Conversion of inputs

a

Sensor (measure output)

b

d

c
Discrepancy between actual and standard

Activator (initiate corrective action)

Comparator (compare output versus standard)

Memory (store rules for corrective action)

Memory (store standard and tolerance range of output)

Figure 14-2 Elements of the control subsystem

(luggage design specifications) for output. The performance standard, and allowable ranges of deviation from it, are stored in the memory element (in a book, a chart, blueprints, human memory, or some other form). The activator (foreman, manager, or mechanical device) receives information from the comparator and initiates corrective action when the comparator indicates discrepancies outside the tolerance range. The activator has a memory element containing rules for the type of corrective action ("Call the leather supplier to get a new shipment of leather") and the amount of corrective action (the quality and thickness of replacement leather needed). By modifying (correcting) the system inputs, managers change system output and monitor it again. Thus the entire process is repeated.

Information flows are essential to a control system. Without them, a system simply cannot exist—or if it does, it is certainly inoperable. In manufacturing luggage, the inspector (sensor) must gather information about leather thickness. When this information is compared to standard thickness, new information is created. This new information is passed on to the manager, who, in turn, relays it to the leather supplier. Information must flow into and out of each element. The elements cannot perform their intended functions unless they have the information. Unless the manager has received information about the quality of existing leather, he or she is unable to purchase leather that meets the organization's standards.

To be effective, information must flow along an accepted path. Control elements must be arranged to encourage communication of information. In Figure 14-2, the information segments (*a*) through (*d*) comprise an information feedback loop. This feedback is the basis for all control systems. Information from the output side of the conversion process is transformed and fed back into the input side in a steady flow. In this way, management is continually able to compare actual performance with planned results.

Although we may be unaware of them, control systems operate around us all the time. When the pupils in your eyes enlarge or contract as light intensity changes, your body is using a control system. When your automatic thermostat turns on the furnace because the room is cooler than you want it to be, it is operating a control system. Look again at Figure 14-2 and see if you can identify the subcomponents of these or other control systems.

Types of Control Systems

Although all control systems share the features we've described, there are some differences among types of control systems.

Open- versus closed-loop systems
One useful way of classifying control systems has to do with whether they are "open" or "closed." In open-loop systems, some or all of the control elements are not self-contained within the system being controlled; they are not an integral part of the system. As a result, intervention from outside the system is required to maintain control. Consider a simple lighting system intended to maintain an appropriate level of brightness in a room. An electric timing device closes the circuit at 5 P.M. and activates the lights. The same device opens the circuit at 7 A.M., and the lights shut off. Sensing, comparing, and activating are performed according to time, not brightness. Since sensing, comparing, and activating according to brightness are absent from the system, it is an open-loop system. Weather conditions and seasonal differences affecting brightness are not considered. To assure a desired level of brightness, some source of sensing, comparing, and action from outside the existing control system must intervene; the clock governs when the lights go on.

A closed system, on the other hand, might contain a photoelectric cell that continuously monitors room brightness. When brightness falls outside the predetermined tolerance range (which is stored in comparator memory), the lighting circuit is either opened or closed. All the control elements are self-contained within this closed-loop system. Outdoor lights controlled by a closed system are popular with farmers, municipalities, and industries.

Positive versus negative feedback
In this book, we emphasize negative feedback, or goal-seeking systems. Systems with negative feedback loops are oriented toward eliminating or correcting deviations from goals whenever the deviations fall outside tolerable limits. System output is compared to performance standards. When deviations arise, the system responds with an *opposing* action, hence the term "negative." Consider an airplane pilot trying to fly a shortest route from west to east. When a strong wind from the south causes the plane to drift northward, the pilot steers toward the southeast to compensate for the wind. By trial and error the pilot learns how much opposing action

is necessary to keep the plane flying east. When actual flight direction deviates from the desired path, pilots use compensating adjustments to oppose the cause of deviation from system goals. In general, this same type of behavior can be observed in most systems. Outputs falling above prescribed standards initiate actions to bring outputs down. Outputs below the standard initiate upward control action. The system operates to seek or maintain outputs near the prescribed standard.

The positive feedback system, also called the growth system, works differently. As you may know from your own experience, positive feedback is reinforcing. Successful students, for example, begin their college careers with limited knowledge. As they take courses, however, they learn and grow; and as they do, they are able to select higher and higher levels of courses and experiences to increase their knowledge even more. A successful college career is an example of a positive feedback system. Such a system does not seek a constant status, as does a negative feedback system; with positive feedback, the system tends to grow.

Characteristics of control systems

How well does the control system perform? Is the system capable of behaving in the ways we want it to? Can we obtain the desired output? The answers to these questions require us to examine and measure characteristics of system performance. Three attributes of system performance are commonly used: stability, sensitivity, and responsiveness.

Stability

The predictability of the system behavior pattern over time, *stability,* is a hallmark of properly designed negative feedback systems. Figure 14-3 shows examples of stable and unstable system behavior.

In part (*a*), output initially coincides with system goals. Say that (*a*) represents the level of water in a reservoir. A disturbance (such as heavy rainfall) causes output (water level) to rise above the norm, and the control system responds with counteractions (opening the spillway) that cause output to return toward the norm. As time passes, system output (water level) continuously oscillates near the norm as rain falls and the spillway is activated. Since output falls within standard limits, the system is "in control." The pattern of system response is steady and predictable, it exhibits a stable pattern of oscillation. The ability to achieve stability depends on several things: regularity and intensity of disturbances, types of control actions available, and the sensitivity and responsiveness of the system.

Unlike system (*a*), the system in part (*b*) is unstable; it has a highly irregular response pattern, and output may have shifted to a lower level. The system in part (*c*) has two different kinds of stability, transient and steady state. Before the disturbance, output was steady. After disturbance,

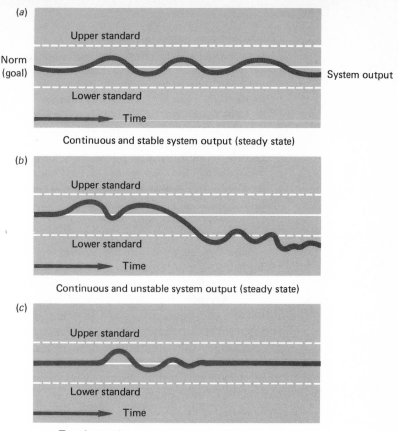

(a)

Upper standard

Norm (goal)

System output

Lower standard

Time

Continuous and stable system output (steady state)

(b)

Upper standard

Lower standard

Time

Continuous and unstable system output (steady state)

(c)

Upper standard

Lower standard

Time

Transient and steady state stability of system output

Figure 14-3 **Examples of system stability**

the control actions resulted in stable system oscillation. After a while, the oscillation decreased as outputs again settled down toward the norm. Finally, the effects of the disturbance disappeared, and the stable steady state behavior returned.

Sometimes corrective actions can themselves result in output deviations greater than the initial problems calling for control action. This is known as "overcompensation," exaggerated responses that can lead to unstable system oscillation. In part (c), both types of responses (transient and steady state) are stable. Transient behavior occurs during the first few time intervals after system disturbance. Steady state behavior is the limiting response for a large number of time periods after system disturbance. Control systems in organizations are established to seek process outputs with both transient and steady state stability.

Sensitivity   System sensitivity is usually measured according to the amount of error necessary before control action is initiated. By how much must output deviate from the goal to evoke a control response?

EXAMPLE

A municipal public safety director is concerned with traffic accidents. The accident rate at Main and Elm Streets is normally about six accidents per year (a satisfactory level), but it is not unusual to experience as many as nine per year. If the accident rate were to become unusually high, the director could invoke some control action to restore the accident rate to a more tolerable lower level. The tolerance range for accidents might be stated as follows: "If the number of accidents exceeds ten per year, initiate control action to reduce the accident rate." Additional traffic signals could be installed, the streets could be widened for a safer flow pattern, or additional traffic surveillance by police could be initiated.

The degree of deviation necessary to initiate a control response is reflected in a predetermined tolerance range stored in the comparator's memory element. This range must be prescribed by the designer and built into the system. Because status is seldom constant over successive time intervals, the tolerance range is a major factor in determining how well the system will behave. Natural variations must be expected; indeed, they are necessary for smooth operation in many systems. Sometimes a control response to these normal variations can disrupt the system and cause unnecessary oscillation. On the other hand, unattended extreme variations can result in even more extreme deviations. Highly sensitive systems result in frequent control actions of small magnitude. Insensitive systems call for occasional but extreme control actions. Managers should give careful thought to the sensitivity of their systems before the tolerance range has been built in. A smooth-running system with the right amount of sensitivity is worth taking a little trouble to get.

Responsiveness   Responsiveness measures how quickly the control response is invoked after an error has been detected. Seldom are control actions taken instantaneously; time delays in the system prohibit immediate action. Sensing, comparing, and taking action all require time, and during this time, system status changes again. The timing of control action must be properly phased with changing system status.

Consider Figure 14-4. In part (a), system output has been in stable and undampened oscillation up to time 1, when the sensor and comparator detect an error. The system is underachieving, and the activator calls for a response to increase output. Because of time delay Δt, the control response is not implemented until time 2, and during this time interval (Δt) the unadjusted system output rises above the goal. Now (at time 2) the delayed control response (to increase output) is superimposed on outputs that are already too high. As a result, output rises beyond the tolerance range at time 3. This calls for more drastic control action, which can lead to more serious detrimental oscillation.

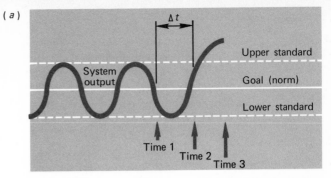

(a)

System output

Upper standard

Goal (norm)

Lower standard

Time 1 Time 2 Time 3

Control implementation delay not synchronized with output pattern

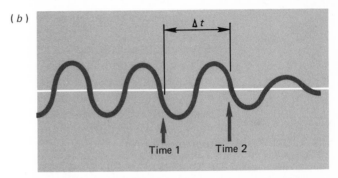

(b)

Time 1 Time 2

Control delay extended to synchronize with output pattern

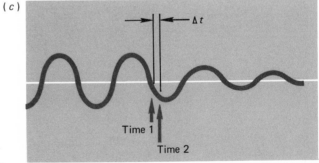

(c)

Time 1 Time 2

Control delay reduced to synchronize with output pattern

Figure 14-4 **Phase relationships between control actions and system responses**

This situation can be corrected in several ways, two of which are illustrated in Figure 14-4. In part (b), the designer is aware of the system's stable oscillation pattern and the implementation time lag; they have been incorporated into the system. Corrective action, when needed, is intentionally delayed (extended) to prevent the system from working against itself. In this way the amplitude of oscillation is reduced, not magnified. Another way to correct the situation in part (a) is to find ways of reducing response delays. Although it is not always possible to do this, in part (c), the designer was able to reduce time delay Δt sufficiently to obtain the desired dampening effect.

The production/operations manager must determine ideal responsiveness for a specific system. Ideal responsiveness depends on both whether delays are avoidable or inherent and the stability of system behavior. Systems that respond rapidly to error may increase the likelihood of overresponse; systems with slow response can remain out of control longer.

Intrinsic control   The basic objective of most control systems is to make error as small as is reasonably possible. No human being is perfect, and neither is any system. We expect errors; the question is how to deal with them. *Reactive* control systems initiate corrective action after errors have taken place. *Intrinsic,* or self-regulation, control processes attempt to anticipate the need for corrective action and adjust the system in advance. If disruptions or changes can be anticipated, say by the use of forecasting techniques, then prior adjustments may allow system outputs to continue at the desired level. Thus we can avoid the transient response of a reactive process. Remember, for example, our discussion of aggregate planning and scheduling as an important control technique for responding to variations in product demand. As demand changes, new levels of output become appropriate. But the effectiveness or productivity of the work force can also change, and this change can dictate the need for revised responses in seeking desired output levels. By anticipating changes in worker productivity, we can determine appropriate control responses.[1]

Intrinsic systems have two major drawbacks. First, they are expensive to design because decision rules for the activator element are usually elaborate and extensive. Second, appropriate devices (forecasting techniques) for anticipating must be selected and developed. If the information from the anticipation devices is unreliable, inappropriate control actions may be initiated.

Changing Goals

Thus far our discussion has focused on controlling systems with a constant goal. The goals of some systems change, however, and control processes are needed to ensure their attainment. In recent years, engineers have attempted to develop control systems that respond to changing conditions by revising system goals automatically. These systems are sometimes called "second order feedback systems." Memory elements of both the comparator and the activator take on a much more significant role in such systems. They require recall capabilities from a repertoire of action alternatives and sets of rules for selecting and applying them. In a sense, such systems may require some "learning" capabilities to permit automatic changing of response patterns.

[1] For methods of incorporating productivity changes into the control system, see R. J. Ebert, "Aggregate Planning With Learning Curve Productivity," *Management Science* 23, no. 2 (October 1976), pp. 171–82.

Organizations are technological and social systems in pursuit of prescribed goals. Accordingly, we find control subsystems—formal and informal, open and closed—throughout. Productive organizations, those of most interest to us, are so complex that automatic closed-loop control processes are seldom feasible. Nevertheless, the basic concepts of control abound throughout the organization; control processes are continuously active.

Controlling People Versus Controlling Technology

A major variable determining the nature of control processes is the presence of people in the organizational system. Insurance companies, health care systems, and automobile repair facilities are examples of productive systems whose goal attainment is highly dependent on the actions of people in the system. Continuous conversion processes found in petroleum refineries, bottling plants, and glass manufacturing, on the other hand, depend more on technology than on people. Their technologies are more capital intense and routinized, and outputs are achieved with less variability.

When people (including customers or clients) dominate the conversion process, several control problems arise. System goals and performance standards are often stated in relatively vague terms, and people's performance varies substantially from time to time. Since many aspects of system performance are nonquantifiable, evaluation and measurement must be subjective. Both inputs and outputs are difficult to measure in any precise way. All these factors tend to prohibit automatic closed-loop control processes.

When conversion processes are mechanized to produce standardized units of output, a different set of problems arises. Although implementing precise control processes is more feasible, these control systems must be very complex. Problems that arise are more often engineering than social in nature. Information flows, inputs and outputs are, however, more amenable to precise measurement than are systems dominated by people.

Organizational Versus Operational Control

Two different types of control activities, organizational and operational, are prevalent in firms today. Organizational control, related to the broad overall design of the system and its structure, is directed toward reviewing, evaluating, and revising relationships among subcomponents to maintain balance and coordination of activities within the system.

Operational control deals with day-to-day evaluation and adjustment of inputs and outputs to attain goals within the established structure. Operations personnel typically devote more time and effort to operational control, although, since they are interrelated, involvement in both types is essential. Differences between operational and organizational control can be clarified by examining the relationships of controlling to planning and organizing.

Relationship of controlling to planning

You may remember that planning includes goal setting, forecasting, and budgeting activities and that operations management is concerned with planning and using the conversion process. Overall goals are refined into hierarchies of supporting subgoals, which become more highly specified at the operational levels. Assigning priorities to the multiple goals provides guidance in selecting which aspects of operations should receive control attention. Those day-to-day operations that tend to facilitate or impede attainment of high priority goals are prime candidates for control efforts. Since resources available for controlling are limited, they should be used wisely. Focusing on those few variables that have the greatest impact on goal attainment can show managers where to concentrate their efforts.

Budgeting is the primary process for making plans operational. Detailed budgeting determines the standards and measurement techniques that provide the basis for control. To budget properly, managers must set goals and subgoals for quantity, quality, and labor effectiveness. Costs must be measurable in some sense. To permit daily monitoring and evaluation of performance and to provide guidance for control actions, managers must specify acceptable cost limits.

At the broadest level, goal setting, general forecasting, and establishing budgeting procedures are forms of organizational control. After these goals have been established, they must be operationalized. Then detailed forecasts and budgets can be used for day-to-day operational control.

Relationship of controlling to organizing

Organizing is the means by which individuals, groups, and facilities are combined in a formal structure of tasks and authority. The necessity for division of labor leads to the formation of groups, departments, and individual jobs, whose efforts must be coordinated to achieve planned goals. Thus, work methods and job design determine job content and the distribution of work within and among organizational units. Establishing productivity and other standards for individual units is not enough to ensure proper performance. Rather, the formal allocation of authority and responsibility for staffing and for directing and motivating employees is the basis of management control. Furthermore, efforts must be made to coordinate the many organizational units so that overall system effectiveness can be achieved. Often, the basic organization structure must be revised to enable system goals to be met. New departments or divisions may be created, and reallocations of authority may be made among organizational units. These control actions, taken by high level management, are forms of organizational control. Similar operational control actions at lower levels include consolidating, redesigning, or even eliminating jobs.

When system performance is inadequate, changes in system structure may be needed. New legislation, changes in societal values, and consumer tastes are all environmental variables that can lead to goal modification that, in turn, can lead to modification of system structure.

Perfect control systems seldom exist in actual productive organizations. We can understand why if we look at some major characteristics that would be integral parts of a perfect system.

CONTROL PROBLEMS IN ORGANIZATIONS

Deciding Which Characteristics To Control

Although there are general guidelines, there is no satisfactory way of knowing for sure that the appropriate system characteristics are being controlled. Sometimes the decision about what to control is based on convenience or expediency; we select characteristics that are readily visible and measurable rather than those more directly related to system objectives. Universities seeking research and teaching goals, for example, may choose convenient output measures like number of faculty publications and classroom contact hours, even though maximizing these measures could be detrimental to goal attainment of quality research and student learning.

Subjective Measurement

When there are people in organizations, there are problems of measurement. Outputs often depend on human creativity, interpersonal group efforts, and employee-machine interactions. In some organizations, human decisions, artistic designs, legal opinions, and other intangible outputs are difficult to evaluate and measure because explicit bases for comparison do not exist. How, then, can managers get the precise information they need for the sensing and comparision elements of a control system? Although personnel evaluation techniques have been attempted to allow subjective evaluation, the scaling and construct assumptions raise questions as to their measurement validity. In short, perfect control systems cannot exist in many organizations because subjective, rather than precise, measurements of output are the only ones that exist.

Information Flows

The nature of information flows in organizations inhibits refined control systems. Feedback is often delayed, distorted (biased), or unclear (contains noise). Were these attributes stable, perhaps the system could compensate accordingly. Often, however, when they will occur and in what degree are unpredictable.

The time lapse between error detection and correction depends on the time required to discover the errors, the time needed to initiate action, and the time needed to implement corrective action once it is initiated. Information is easily distorted, intentionally or not, especially when it is received, interpreted, and/or transmitted through human beings in the communication channel. Finally, indicators of system inputs and outputs contain some randomness and uncertainty. What appears to be an undesirable system deviation may in reality be a measurement error, and undue corrective action may be taken.

Frequency of information flows is also important. Should sensing be intermittent or continuous? If resources are restricted, sensing must often be intermittent, and the result is periodic, delayed feedback.

Standards

The comparator element uses predetermined standards, including limits of permissible variation. These may be hard to establish in technical systems, and they are sometimes impossible in social systems. Standards of human behavior and system performance simply cannot be spelled out and communicated in every detail (see Chapter 9 for discussion of establishing standards in production/operations). Although many standards are established by managers and supervisors, others emerge informally from employees interacting in groups. Changes in the formal system may spawn new codes of behavior and productivity norms as well.

CONTROL LIMITATIONS IN ORGANIZATIONS

Law of Requisite Variety

Because of these many problems, overall control systems are incomplete, although the extent to which formal control is possible varies among systems. Some are more susceptible to control than others.

Ashby's Law of Requisite Variety contends that susceptibility to control depends on the complexity of the system—on the variety of possible events that can occur in the system.[2] According to Ashby's Law, control is feasible when the number of action (control) alternatives is at least as large as the number of possible conditions that can exist in the system being controlled.

As the variety of products and conversion processes increases, so does system complexity. If the system variety is large, the control process must

---

[2] W. Ross Ashby, *An Introduction to Cybernetics* (New York: John Wiley & Sons, Inc., 1956).

also have a large capacity if it is to be effective. Thus, we find that industries with low variety have more sophisticated control systems. In industries in which the variety of processes and products is large, it becomes impossible to measure objectively all possible conditions that might exist; it is hard to determine when a measurement represents true system status versus noise. Error is hard to recognize. Under these conditions, Ashby's Law implies two major types of effort that would be required to develop sophisticated control processes. First, one could try to increase the variety of action alternatives in the control process. This would result in a very complex, expensive control system, if it could be done at all. The second approach would involve decreasing the variety (complexity) of the system being controlled. Since it would require changing products and/or conversion processes, this cost would also be enormous, however.

Management Realism in Control

Managers are responsible for operating ongoing productive facilities. They don't have the luxury of waiting until perfect plans and control systems can be designed and implemented. Under these conditions, plans must necessarily be incomplete. Control processes must be selectively designed and built into the productive process as time and resources allow. Many open-loop control processes allow employees to serve as the source of outside intervention. Such systems give flexibility in operating the productive system and provide a workable way of living with unexpected changes or disturbances. At the same time, these systems meet their ongoing output commitments. Extensive operational control is often established on selected key input and output variables: cost, inventory, and product quality.

Managers must operate the conversion process with restricted resources; and they must establish realistic objectives within these resource constraints. To get maximum output from input resources, managers must carefully scrutinize resource utilization relative to output accomplishments. Let's examine three production/operational areas where control assists in this effort.

CRITICAL PRODUCTION/ OPERATIONS CONTROL ACTIVITIES

Cost Control

After conversion systems have been planned and constructed, they must be operated effectively and efficiently. Forecasts and budgets can help determine desired output levels and resource requirements. To garner the resources and, once obtained, to get maximum benefit from them, cost control processes must be established. Accounting techniques play a vital role in cost control systems for operations.

Facility, process, and product planning lead to projected levels of output. Market research and cost analysis lead to tentative estimates of revenues and operational costs. These can be evaluated and refined through breakeven analysis. Once the desired cost-volume-profit relationships have been established, procedures are needed to ensure their attainment. Although the conversion process is designed and staffed to reach desired output volume, planned selling price (and therefore revenues) are often determined in the marketplace by factors outside the organization's immediate control. Typically, production/operations managers are not dominant participants in the pricing decision. This leaves cost of operation as the variable most directly controllable by the organization for meeting its cost-volume-profit goals. Consequently, operation cost is the basis for many imposed production management pressures.

Operational cost goals are reflected in operating budgets for each division, department, and work unit. Costs at these different levels are periodically monitored and compared against cost standards, and deviations beyond the allowable range initiate search for control actions to bring costs back into line. Unusually low costs may indicate that products are being improperly processed, or they may indicate that some new work methods or standards have been adopted informally. Perhaps the original work or cost standards are obsolete and need revision. If so, information to that effect must be fed back to higher level planning units and profit-volume-cost relationships must be reevaluated. If the desired objective is higher profitability, perhaps lowering the product price would lead to larger output volume. If so, profits and growth would both increase.

Usually, however, costs exceed the allowable range. Excess costs require corrective action because they threaten profit goals. With excessive costs, however, management faces a dilemma. If they don't increase the product selling price, profit will fall. But if they do increase the selling price, sales volume may fall, and the organization's very existence may be threatened. Therefore, when high costs are discovered, management must begin an intensive search for actions leading to cost reduction. Adjustments of work methods, job assignments, materials, or departmental relationships are a few of the many actions that may be needed. The operations manager has primary responsibility for all aspects of operations cost control.

In most private service organizations, this same process holds. Financial institutions, communications firms, and transportation firms must control costs to remain viable. Governmental agencies also experience pressures for cost control as they seek to provide the services needed by the public. Operations managers in these settings have the same needs as their counterparts in the private sector for accounting techniques to assist in controlling costs.

Basic accounting costs

For purposes of decision making and control, operations managers must distinguish between nonvariable (fixed), semivariable, and variable costs. Although some cost elements don't fall cleanly into these categories, many others do.

Nonvariable costs over some relevant range of output are inevitable regardless of output volume. A company may know, for example, that nonvariable costs of $200,000 per year will be incurred whether it produces 1,000 or 20,000 units of its product. An administrative and marketing staff must be maintained; property taxes must be paid; facilities always depreciate. So long as the facility remains operational, the operations manager has relatively little direct control over nonvariable costs.

Variable costs increase in direct proportion to output volume. If each unit of output requires standard amounts of material and labor, when output volume doubles, direct labor and material costs also double.

Semivariable costs increase as volume increases, although not in direct proportion. Maintenance, supplies, materials handling, and other indirect labor are semivariable costs. If output volume doubles, these semivariable costs may increase by 10 or 20 percent.

The relative magnitudes of these basic cost components depend on the particular industry and organization. A small car washing operation may have low fixed costs but high semivariable costs in the form of manual labor. Automobile manufacturers have high fixed costs but also high direct labor and materials costs. Operations managers should learn which costs are directly controllable so that they can institute proper control procedures on the critical cost elements.

Cost centers   One accepted method of cost control is to establish cost centers and to assign responsibility for cost performance. Cost centers, those work units where costs originate, may be at a machine, in a work group, in a department, or on an even broader level. Supervisors with authority over job assignments and scheduling are responsible for efficient labor and materials utilization at the cost center.

Standard costs   A control system for costs must include a standard for comparison so that the manager knows when control action is needed. Standard costs for direct materials, direct labor, and overhead are developed and used for this purpose. Standard overhead costs are established by a variety of methods presented in many accounting textbooks.

Standard costs for direct labor are based on worker productivity standards determined by the work measurement techniques discussed in Chapter 9. The estimated labor content (hours) per unit is multiplied by the standard wage rate to obtain standard direct labor cost per unit. Because variations in materials, workers, the fatigue effects of overtime, and so on are not included in the standards, direct labor costs generally deviate around the standard to some extent.

Standard direct materials costs are based on product analysis studies that determine the standard materials content for an average unit of output.

When materials content is multiplied times the cost per foot, pound, or other appropriate measure, the standard cost is determined. Again, individual output units normally deviate somewhat because of measurement error, waste, worker variations, and so on.

Periodically, say weekly, daily, or monthly, records indicating material and labor inputs and product outflows from each cost center should be updated. Comparisons of cost performance relative to cost standards detect areas of cost improvement. In many cases, since these standards are only approximations, they are not rigidly enforced. They do, however, provide a useful basis for guiding managerial cost control efforts.

Inventory Control

Inventories of materials, supplies, and finished products are important resources in many conversion operations. They are a vital asset requiring large amounts of working capital to maintain. Since working capital is a scarce resource, managers seek to use it wisely by establishing inventory control systems. (Inventory control is covered in detail in Chapters 15 and 16.) All the elements of a general control system—sensors, comparators, action rules, time delays, and feedback—are used in inventory control.

One of the problems in examining any subsystem, including inventory, is the tendency to not recognize its relationship to the total productive system. As you will see, decisions resulting in desirable inventory performance can cause disturbances in other subsystems of the organization. The stability of the overall system is sensitive to actions in various subsystems.

Quality Control

System effectiveness depends on whether or not goals are accomplished. One important goal is to provide products or services that meet predetermined standards. To ensure that output conforms to desired standards, many organizations use quality control systems, as we will discuss in detail in Chapter 17. Of particular interest is the role that statistics can play in helping the manager decide when control action is warranted. This analysis tool, which has been applied more frequently in quality control than in many other operations subsystems, affects sensitivity, responsiveness, and stability of the quality subsystem.

SUMMARY

Control systems in organizations are created to assist management's attainment of goals. In general, all control systems share certain elements. Sensors, comparators, and activators are linked together by information flows.

Control systems can be differentiated according to whether they employ negative or positive feedback. Closed, self-contained systems and open systems requiring outside intervention are two prevalent types. Systems can be generally described in terms of their stability, sensitivity, responsiveness, and goal-changing capacities.

When people are integrally involved in a system, or when organizations are particularly complex, production/operations control systems require special design. Some major problems involve choosing which conversion characteristics to control, measurement difficulties, vagueness of standards, and quality and timing of information flows. Cost, quality, and inventories are often the focus of control efforts in production/operations conversion processes.

Plainview Water Department

CASE

Plainview, a community of about 50,000 residents, has a municipally owned and operated water supply. Bill Shockter, the newly appointed city manager, has determined that the water department should be revamped so that water services pay for themselves and the existing quality of service to residents is improved. Bill has discovered that existing revenue and cost data are sketchy and that the water department's billing practices are less than satisfactory. Customer water usage is approximated monthly with a "standard usage table" and then adjusted by actual meter readings twice a year in January and July. This practice has resulted in numerous citizen complaints regarding both estimated usage and month-to-month fluctuations in water bills. The water department attempts to reduce customer ill will by sending its seven meter readers on site to complaining customers so as to obtain accurate, up-to-date usage readings.

The Plainview Chamber of Commerce expects the population will increase to 70,000 residents within 10 years as a result of new industry's entrance into the community. This projection is of concern to Bill Shockter since the costs of providing necessary governmental services are expected to increase accordingly.

The entire water department problem is of such concern that Bill has hired Kim Mason, a recent college graduate in public administration, to study the situation and make recommendations for improvement. In one week, Kim is to discuss, in outline form, her plan of action with Bill Shockter. Kim's thoughts immediately turned to some basic control concepts that might be useful in formulating the problem.

The following data were given to Kim.

Number of Customer Complaints

	1975	1976	1977
Jan	192	116	247
Feb	1,134	1,326	1,497
Mar	407	514	483
Apr	210	306	183
May	184	92	206
June	311	211	118
July	302	392	207
Aug	1,011	1,222	1,573
Sept	609	414	532
Oct	83	116	208
Nov	72	136	101
Dec	204	118	209

Plainview Water Department Data			
	1975	1976	1977
Average number of customers (households, businesses, etc.)	12,201	12,874	13,247
Plainview population	45,500	47,500	50,000

REVIEW AND DISCUSSION QUESTIONS

1. What is a system?
2. What is control?
3. What is a control system?
4. Identify and describe the elements of control systems.
5. Give an example of a nonorganizational control system. Identify its goal, its control elements, and its information flows.
6. Give an example of an organizational control system. Identify its goals, its control elements, and its information flows.
7. Give examples of open-loop and closed-loop control systems.
8. Discuss the significance of the system stability concept in operations management.
9. Mathematical models are often used to help operations managers anticipate the effects of proposed changes in operations. A frequent criticism is that such models are concentrated on steady state rather than on transient effects. Discuss the importance of this issue and give suggestions for resolving it.
10. Several methods and actions are available to managers for increasing job satisfaction and motivation of employees. How might the control concepts, system sensitivity and responsiveness, be useful to a manager who wishes to increase employee job satisfaction and motivation?
11. What are the major distinctions between organizational and operational control activities?
12. Using an example organization of your choice, identify the most important system characteristics to be controlled. Justify your choices of characteristics and specify how you would measure each characteristic.
13. In an organizational system, where and how does human behavior affect control system stability, sensitivity, and responsiveness?
14. In designing an organizational control system, the designer must choose between a human activator and an electromechanical activator. Outline and discuss the merits and disadvantages of both. What variables will determine which is best?

PROBLEMS

1. The following equation represents the response behavior of a system:

$$X_{t+1} = 1.4X_t + .1y_t$$

X_{t+1} is a numeric measure of the system's condition in time period $t + 1$. This numeric status depends on two things, the system's status, X_t, in the previous time period and the decision, y_t, made in period t. Hence, the previous status and the current decision determine the next status. The decisions, y_t, can be any positive or negative values you choose. Each time you make decisions to change the status of the system, costs are incurred:

$$C_t = (0.1)(y_t^2 + X_{t+1}^2)$$

The costs resulting from a decision made in period t are obtained by squaring the numeric decision and squaring the resulting system status, summing these squares, and then multiplying the sum by 0.1.

(a) Using trial and error, make a sequence of 10 monthly decisions, trying to minimize costs for the entire 10 periods. Assume the initial system status $X_0 = 1$.

(b) Repeat part (a); try to improve your initial decisions.

(c) After doing part (b), reflect on the overall process you went through. Which elements of a control system were present in your mental process? Which ones were not present? Identify each as explicitly as possible.

(d) In making your decisions, was your mental process a positive feedback system or a negative feedback system? Explain.

2. Reconsider the aggregate plan you developed for the Randolf Corporation, problem 7 in Chapter 11. As time passes, you find that actual monthly demands do not coincide with your original estimates of monthly demand used in formulating your plan. Subsequently, to compensate for forecast errors, you modify next month's planned production; and you do this as each month expires. Suppose the actual demands are 9,000; 13,000; 15,000; 19,000; 29,000; 23,000; 27,000; 19,000; 21,000; 10,000; 12,000; and 9,000 for January through December.

(a) Determine a revised production schedule using the following rule:
   1. If actual demand (A) in month i is less than forecasted demand (F), the production originally planned for month $i + 1$ will be reduced by 25 percent of ($Fi - Ai$).
   2. If actual demand in month i is greater than forecasted demand, the production originally planned for month $i + 1$ will be increased by 25 percent of ($Ai - Fi$).
   Calculate the costs of this production schedule.

(b) Determine a revised production schedule using the adjustment rule in part (a) using 75 percent as the amount of error compensation (instead of 25 percent). Compare the costs of this production schedule with those of part (a).

GLOSSARY

Activator: control element that initiates corrective action

Closed-loop system: all control elements are self-contained within the system being controlled

Comparator: control element that compares measured output with standard output

Control: a process by which system components are modified to achieve system goals

Intrinsic system: one in which control actions are initiated prior to and in anticipation of error

Memory: control element that stores performance standards and/or corrective decision rules

Negative feedback: a goal-seeking response characteristic in which system deviations are met with opposing actions

Open-loop system: system in which all control elements are not self-contained within the system being controlled

Overcompensation: corrective actions that cause output deviations of greater severity than the deviations that initiated control action

Positive feedback: a growth response characteristic in which feedback has a reinforcing effect on system status

Reactive system: one in which control actions are initiated in response to error detection

Responsiveness: quickness with which control action is invoked following error detection

Sensitivity: degree of error or deviation needed to initiate control action

Sensor: control element that monitors and measures system output

Stability: predictability of the system behavior pattern over time

Steady state behavior: the limiting response many periods after system disturbance

Transient behavior: system response during time periods immediately after system disturbance

SELECTED
READINGS

Ackoff, R. L. "Towards a System of System Concepts." *Management Science* 17, no. 11 (July 1971): 661–67.

Ashby, W. Ross. *An Introduction to Cybernetics.* New York: John Wiley & Sons, Inc., 1956.

DeGreene, K., ed. *Systems Psychology.* New York: McGraw-Hill Book Company, 1970.

Drake, A. W., R. L. Keeney, and P. M. Morse, eds. *Analysis of Public Systems.* Cambridge, Mass.: MIT Press, 1972.

Ebert, Ronald J. "Aggregate Planning With Learning Curve Productivity." *Management Science* 23, no. 2 (October 1976): 171–82.

Johnson, Richard A., Fremont E. Kast, and James E. Rosenzweig. *The Theory and Management of Systems.* 3rd ed. New York: McGraw-Hill Book Co., 1973.

Kast, F. E. and J. E. Rosenzweig. "General Systems Theory: Applications for Organization and Management." *Academy of Management Journal* 15, no. 4 (December 1972): 447–65.

Klir, G. J., ed. *Trends in General Systems Theory.* New York: John Wiley & Sons, Inc., 1972.

Litterer, J. A., ed. *Organizations: Systems, Control and Adaptation.* 2nd ed. Vol. II. New York: John Wiley & Sons, Inc., 1969.

Miles, R. F. Jr. *Systems Concepts.* New York: John Wiley & Sons, Inc., 1973.

Schoderbek, Peter P., ed. *Management Systems.* 2nd ed. New York: John Wiley & Sons, Inc., 1971.

von Bertalanffy, L. *General System Theory.* New York: George Braziller, Inc., 1968.

Inventory Control Fundamentals

Production/operations managers are responsible for operations cost control. One critical cost of operations is investment in raw materials, supplies, work-in-process, and finished products not yet shipped. If this investment becomes excessive, the results are high capital costs, high operating costs, and decreased production efficiency when too much space is used for inventory. Usually, operations managers develop a plan specifying desired levels for these materials and organize jobs to carry out this plan. Because of environmental influences, however, actual performance generally does not conform to planned performance, and managers must exercise material (or inventory) control. Operations managers must monitor output, compare actual with planned output, and take corrective action through feedback mechanisms. The basics of inventory control are simply an application of control theory. As we have noted in this discussion and illustrated in Figure 15-1, inventory control relates closely to planning and organizing.

In most other functional production/operations areas, there is more of a balance between modeling and behavioral considerations than there is in inventory control. Inventory theory and modeling have been developed so thoroughly by applied mathematicians that one often is left in awe at the level of model sophistication. In this and the next chapter, we will focus on fundamental modeling, the richest approach for learning the basics of inventory control.

Inventory Defined

INVENTORY CONCEPTS

Inventories play a major part in the economy of the United States, as Table 15-1 shows. These data alone suggest that operating managers

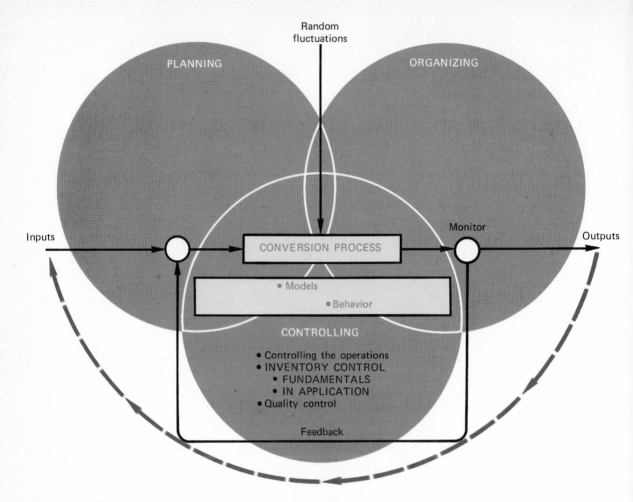

Figure 15-1 Production/operations management activities

should find inventory management a fruitful area for cost control. From the firm's viewpoint, inventories represent an investment; capital is required to hold materials at any stage of completion. Inventories should be evaluated in the same manner as other investments available to the firm and should be retained or increased only if they offer a favorable return on invested capital. Most firms have inventories, but there are widely varying views as to how much inventory to maintain in different firms and among various industries and technologies.

Inventory is stores of goods and stocks. In manufacturing, inventories are called stockkeeping items and are held at a stock (storage) point. One primary inventory function is to decouple, or break apart, successive stages

TABLE 15-1

503

Chapter 15
Inventory Control
Fundamentals

UNITED STATES GROSS NATIONAL PRODUCT (GNP) AND INVENTORIES
(BILLIONS OF DOLLARS)

Year	GNP	Inventories*	Inventories as a % of GNP
1945	128.4	30.6	24%
1955	391.7	82.2	21
1965	684.9	121.1	18
1970	982.4	175.6	18
1975	1516.3	264.8	17

*Book value, end of period, seasonally adjusted.

of operations. (Other important inventory functions are discussed later.) Stockkeeping items usually consist of:

- raw materials,
- work-in-process,
- finished products, and
- supplies

Inventory control is the technique of maintaining stockkeeping items at desired levels.

These examples illustrate some of the many forms inventories take in the conversion process. There are considerably more inventory situations in the diecasting company than there are in the bank. Generally, product-oriented manufacturing organizations experience more tangible inventory situations than do labor intense service-oriented organizations. In manufacturing, since the focus is on a physical product, emphasis is on materials

---

EXAMPLE

First National Bank is a typical commercial bank with full line services. The typical individual account includes various transactions: checking, savings, lock boxes, and loan transactions. Focusing on the teller operation, it is difficult to distinguish raw material, work-in-process and finished goods inventories. The technical operation is to convert labor and material into the service of caring for money. The service is consumed as it is generated. Such materials as deposit slips, withdrawal slips, and loan payment coupons are more like operating supplies than raw materials, work-in-process, and finished goods inventory.

St. Louis Diecasting Company is an aluminum and zinc diecasting company. It is an intermittent manufacturing company, a typical job shop. This company maintains an inventory mix typical of many firms. *Raw materials* **include primary metal alloys of aluminum and zinc in ingot form. This bulk metal is subsequently melted and diecast into parts, and the diecast parts are custom fabricated.** *Work-in-process* **includes diecastings being transported by automatic conveyers, diecastings sitting idle awaiting fabrication (drilling, deburring, etc.), and diecastings awaiting packing. After packing,** *finished goods* **inventories are stored in pallets of boxes awaiting shipment to such customers as Caterpiller and General Motors, who use the diecastings in assembly operations.** *Supplies* **that support manufacturing include gloves, buffer wheels, drill bits, and packing materials.**

and material control; in the service sector, the focus is on a service, and there is very little emphasis on materials or stocks. In many cases, services are consumed as they are generated rather than stocked for later consumption. Thus, in manufacturing more than in services, we can expect considerable attention to be given to inventory control.

In service-oriented organizations that are not so highly labor-intense, inventories assume more importance. Community blood banks must keep inventories of blood types; military organizations and transit systems maintain inventories of equipment and replacement parts. In local department stores, inventories must be substantial to encourage sales. Regardless of the specific institutional setting, the basic concept of production/operations management focuses on conversion of inputs into outputs of goods or services. This conversion process is reexamined with emphasis on material input in Figure 15-2. Note that there may be stock points at the input (raw material), conversion (work-in-process), and output (product) stages. Now, think about the definition of inventory control. Perhaps you can visualize a manufacturing or service facility where you have seen these inventory points and witnessed inventory control.

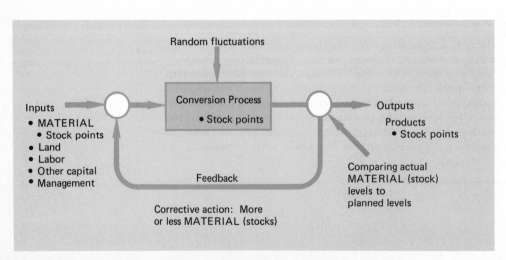

Figure 15-2
The conversion process: materials conversion

Inventory management is that part of operations management concerned with making policies to be met by an inventory control system. To be effective, the operations manager must have a basic understanding of the inventory phenomenon and associated benefits and costs. The rest of this chapter is devoted to helping you gain that understanding.

Why Inventories?

The fundamental reason for carrying inventories is that *it is physically impossible and economically impractical for each stock item to arrive exactly where it is needed exactly when it is needed.* Even were it physically possible for Alcoa to deliver aluminum ingots to St. Louis Diecasting every few hours, for example, it would still be prohibitively expensive. St. Louis Diecasting must therefore keep extra ingots in its supply of raw material inventory for use when they're needed in the conversion process.

Other reasons for carrying inventories are summarized in Table 15-2. Inventory should be viewed as an investment and should compete for funds with other investments contemplated by the firm. If you have studied finance, you have been introduced to the concept of the marginal efficiency of capital (MEC). This concept holds that a firm should invest in those alternatives that provide a greater return than capital costs to borrow. Look at Figure 15-3, which shows a marginal efficiency of capital curve. This figure shows the rates of return on various inventory investment alternatives (shown as a percentage of total investment alternatives). The

---

TABLE 15-2

WHY ORGANIZATIONS CARRY INVENTORY

Level	Reason
Fundamental (primary)	Physical impossibility of getting right amount of stock at exact time of need
	Economical impracticality of getting right amount of stock at exact time of need
Secondary	Favorable return on investment
	Buffer to reduce uncertainty
	Decouple operations
	Level or smooth production
	Reduce material handling costs
	Allow production of family of parts
	Price changes (can be disadvantage)
	Bulk purchases
	Display to customers

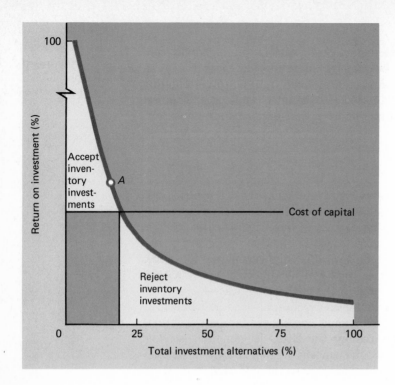

Figure 15-3 **Typical marginal efficiency of capital curve (MEC)**

MEC curve for this firm shows that about 20 percent of the inventory investment alternatives will give a return on investment above the cost of capital. That is, about 20 percent of the firm's inventory alternatives will bring the firm more money than it would have to spend if it borrowed money. These 20 percent of investments should be accepted. The 80 percent of the investment alternatives that would bring in less than the cost of capital should be rejected.

Inventory investments, like other investments the firm may contemplate, must be justified on this basis. By documenting the cost savings for the investment required and computing the return on the investment, managers can determine whether that return is higher than the cost of capital. Inventory investment alternative A in Figure 15-3, for example, is an acceptable investment.

Imagine a firm's MEC curve for *all* investment alternatives. If inventory cannot compete on this same basis with other uses of funds (plant, equipment, land, advertising, bonds, etc.), then inventory should be reduced until it becomes an attractive alternative for the firm. With sound economic analysis, proper levels of inventory can be agreed upon quickly. When demand is unusually high, some protection is needed against the prospects of high stockout costs. Inventory can be used to "buffer" against such uncertainties. Likewise, procurement *lead time*, the time between ordering and receiving goods, is not always constant. Buffer stocks are justifiable if the firm faces uncertain demand or if procurement lead time varies. With buffer stocks, the firm may be able to reduce stockouts.

Inventories are also useful when they *decouple* operations, when they break operations apart so that one operation's supply is independent of another's supply. This decoupling function serves two purposes. First, inventories are needed to reduce the dependencies among successive stages of operations so that breakdowns, material shortages, or other production fluctuations at one stage do not cause later stages of operations to shut down. Figure 15-4 illustrates this concept in a diecasting firm. The diagram shows that although the drilling operation has no diecasts stored as in-process inventories, deburring and packing do have inventory waiting for them. Since deburring and packing could continue to operate from inventories should diecasting and drilling be shut down, they can be decoupled from the production processes that precede them. They could operate independently for a while if need be.

A second purpose of decoupling through inventories is to let one organization unit schedule its operations independently of another. In automobile manufacturing, for example, engine buildup can be scheduled separately from seat assembly, and each can be decoupled from final automobile assembly operations through in-process inventories. Thus, inventories assist in accomplishing the micro objective, operation decoupling, as well as the macro objective, organization unit decoupling.

Inventories can also assist in leveling production. When we examined aggregate planning and scheduling in Chapter 11, we noted that products can be built through slack demand periods and used in peak demand periods. Thus high costs of production rate and work force level changes can be avoided.

In some manufacturing and service operations, material handling costs can be reduced by accumulating parts between operations. This is particularly true of intermittent systems, since they involve less automation of material handling than do continuous systems. Parts can be accumulated and inventoried in tote boxes or baskets and transported by hand-jack dollies or fork-lift trucks much more economically than they can be carried by hand. In continuous manufacturing, automated material handling systems, rather than larger work-in-process inventories, are designed to reduce overall handling costs.

Inventories are also useful in the production of similar parts, called a family of parts. Here, inventories enable operations to be conducted more economically.

Figure 15-4 **Decoupling of operations by using inventory**

Inventory   Inventory

=============== EXAMPLE ===============

In the production of roll-formed aluminum trim pieces for refrigerator shelves, often the only difference among parts is length (various refrigerator models use parts of different lengths). The setup of a rolling machine requires from 8 to 16 hours. Thousands of pieces per hour can be manufactured once a setup has been made. Thirty minutes or less are required to change the cutoff press at the end of the rolling machine for various part lengths. Therefore, for the costs and volumes involved in this low unit cost roll form, it is best to schedule and produce a family of many different parts, perhaps a dozen, for as much as six-months ahead of demand at any one setup.

Obviously, the strategy in this example increases in-process and finished goods inventories. Since overall savings in setup costs more than offset the added investment in inventories, however, the strategy provides a favorable return on investment.

Inventories can also be carried to take advantage of price increases.

=============== EXAMPLE ===============

An executive in charge of crude oil acquisition for a major oil company said that his firm's large supplies of foreign crude oil stored on barges around the world resulted in a substantial one-time gain when the mid-Eastern oil cartel first made a major boost in crude oil prices about 1974. He was, however, susceptible to equally large losses had his inventory hedge been the victim of price decreases rather than increases. The executive took a calculated business risk by carrying excess inventories; this risk put his company in a position to gain from a favorable price change.

With bulk purchases, quantity discounts can be arranged, thus providing another cost advantage of inventories. If firms practice economies of scale in production by producing large volumes, or if a firm's transportation costs are lower for bulk shipments, those firms often offer quantity discounts. If it's feasible to do so, production managers can often save money by buying in bulk.

Merchandising firms often use inventories for customer displays. Since retailers' customers often base their purchases on displayed goods, the retail trade often uses inventory in this way.

Inventory System Concepts

Multistage inventories   When parts are stocked at more than one stage in the sequential production process, there are multistage inventories. Figure 15-4 illustrated several stages of production in a diecasting facility. Since there is interaction between inventory items in the various stages (raw material, diecastings, drilled parts, etc.), it is a difficult problem to establish balanced inventory levels at each stage and for the system overall. Our introductory treatment will focus on inventory at a single stage, with little consideration of interactions of the various stages.

Multiechelon inventories   In inventory systems, multiple institutional levels are involved in converting raw materials into consumer products. The factory level, for example, supplies products to the warehouse level, and the warehouse supplies the retailer who, in turn, supplies the customer. Each level is called an echelon. Multiechelon inventories, illustrated in Figure 15-5, include products stocked at the various levels in the distribution system. Interactions among the echelons determine how much inventory is carried in the system. Our introductory discussion will center on inventory problems at individual echelons.

EXAMPLE

In a large medical center composed of a hospital, a medical school, a school of nursing, and auxiliary research units, the annual expenditure for disposable surgical gloves exceeded $75,000. The stores clerk, who set reorder points and stock levels for the gloves, said that she carried high volumes because demand to central stores was erratic, with occasional large withdrawals. Further examination uncovered two additional echelons of glove inventory in the hospital: stocked gloves on the hospital floor or wing housing a surgery room and stocked gloves in the doctors' and nurses' offices and desks. Thus, demand in central stores was buffered by storerooms near surgery, and storerooms were buffered by emergency supplies in offices.

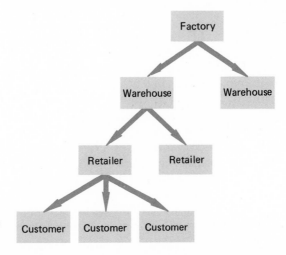

Figure 15-5 **Multiechelon inventory systems**

Reaction to
demand changes
The system should not have to react to rising demand by changing inventories in direct proportion to the increase in demand. As the hospital example illustrated, this is sometimes a complication in a multiechelon inventory structure. One statistical study of inventory-sales ratios in selected firms in Australia and the United States concluded there was strong evidence of economies of scale.[1] After examining several models, this study concluded that *an increase in demand can be serviced by a less than proportional increase in inventories.* The converse is also true; when demand decreases, inventories cannot be decreased in direct proportion. Many firms became aware of this concept first hand in the 1974–1975 recession. As demand weakened during this period, many firms reduced their inventories too much and suffered substantial production cost increases as a result.

The Operating Doctrine

Operations managers must make two basic inventory policy decisions: *when* to reorder stocks and *how much* stock to reorder. These decisions are referred to as the *inventory control operating doctrine.*

The time to reorder is called the reorder point. A system signal, usually a predetermined inventory level, tells clerical or other responsible personnel when it is time to reorder stocks. The amount that should be reordered is called the order quantity. *The inventory level that signals the need to reorder and the reorder quantity selected are economic decisions at the heart of the operations manager's inventory control function.* Although the manager may not actually operate the control system, he or she is responsible for setting the operating doctrine.

Inventory Systems

Q/R inventory
system
One practical way to establish an inventory system is to keep count of every item issued from stores and place an order for more stock when inventories dwindle to a predetermined level, the reorder point. The order is fixed in size (volume), size having been predetermined. Thus, for a quantity-reorder point (Q/R) system, the operating doctrine is established by specifying both when and how much to reorder. Once established, the doctrine is continuously reapplied.

Figure 15-6 illustrates a Q/R inventory system in which the demand for inventories, the usage rate, is known and constant. Replenishment inventories are assumed to be received at the stock point the moment

[1] See J. M. Samuels and D. J. Smyth, "Statistical Evidence on the Relationship Between a Company's Sales and Its Inventories," *International Journal of Production Research* 6, no. 3 (1968), pp. 249–56.

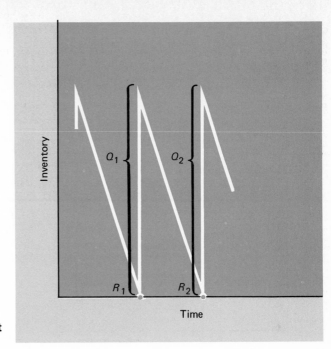

Figure 15-6 **Q/R**
inventory system (constant usage rate)

they have been ordered. Notice that at the beginning of the time axis (far left) an order seems just to have arrived. As time goes by, inventory is steadily depleted until a level of R_1 units is reached. At R_1, the reorder point (also called the trigger level), another order is placed for Q_1 units from the supplier. These units arrive at the instant they are ordered. Procurement lead time is zero. The usage pattern is then repeated, and at level R_2, quantity Q_2 is ordered. In a simple case like this, there would be no need to carry buffer stocks; delivery is instantaneous, and the demand for the inventory item is known for certain. Thus R_1 is set at zero units.

In a Q/R system, both the reorder quantity and the reorder point are fixed. For Figure 15-6, then:

$$R_1 = R_2 \quad \text{and} \quad Q_1 = Q_2$$

A slightly more complex inventory situation is shown in Figure 15-7. Usage (demand) is variable; we do not know in advance how rapidly inventory will be depleted. Here again, a reorder quantity and reorder point have been established as the operating doctrine. Again, $R_1 = R_2$ and $Q_1 = Q_2$; however, as you can see, somewhat different procedures are used to determine their values. It is difficult to establish the most economical operating doctrine when demand varies, as it does in Figure 15-7, and even more difficult when lead time varies too. Since lead time is the time between placing and receiving an order, it is shown as t_{L1} and t_{L2} on the graph. When either demand or lead time varies, the time interval between orders varies—but the order quantity always remains constant.

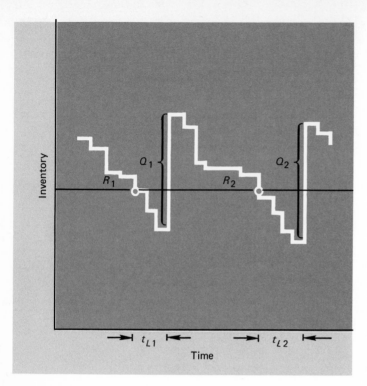

Figure 15-7 **Q/R inventory system (variable usage)**

As the inventory situation and the analysis required to establish the operating doctrine become more realistic, they also become more complex. We'll get to some situations found in practice soon, but first it's necessary to continue with some basic concepts.

Periodic inventory system

Another practical inventory control method is to examine inventories only at set time intervals, periodically, and to then reorder an amount equal to some preestablished base stock level. In periodic systems the time interval between reviews is always constant, but the order quantity varies. As Figure 15-8 illustrates, the level of inventory is examined at times T_1 and T_2, and orders are placed for quantities Q_1 and Q_2. The base stock level and the time between orders, t_1 and t_2, are set by operations management and comprise the inventory system's operating doctrine. In the periodic system $t_1 = t_2$, but Q_1 does not necessarily equal Q_2. Although Figure 15-8 shows constant demand and lead time, these conditions could be relaxed and still allow the periodic inventory system concepts to be retained.

In this book, we will emphasize Q/R systems. Although we will concentrate on determining economic order quantities and reorder points, however, remember that the procedures are similar for the periodic system. Economic order quantity in the Q/R system and base stock levels in the periodic system both determine how much to order; reorder point in the Q/R system and time between orders in the periodic system both determine when to order.

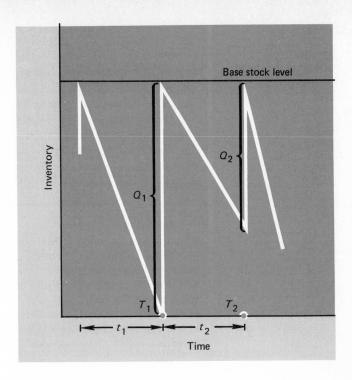

Figure 15-8 **Periodic inventory system**

In operating an inventory system managers should consider *only those costs that vary as the operating doctrine is changed.* Only those costs that vary directly with the operating doctrine are relevant in deciding when and how much to reorder; costs independent of the operating doctrine are irrelevant. Once the relevant costs have been identified, managers can seek an operating doctrine that will result in cost minimization. Basically, there are five types of relevant costs:

1. the cost of the item itself,
2. the costs associated with procuring the stocks,
3. the costs of carrying the stock items in inventory,
4. the costs associated with being out of stock when units are demanded but are unavailable, and
5. operating costs associated with data gathering and control procedures for the inventory system.

Often these five costs are combined in one way or another, but let's discuss them separately before we consider combinations that may be used in different inventory situations.

Cost of Item

The cost, or value, of the item is the sum paid to the supplier for the item received. It is normally equal to the purchase price. In some instances, costs also include other costs that vary directly with each item. Transportation, receiving, and inspection costs, for example, may be included as part of the costs of the item. If the item unit cost is constant for all quantities ordered, the total cost of purchased goods needed during the planning horizon is irrelevant to the operating doctrine. (We shall see how it drops out of the total cost equation when we model this situation.) If the unit cost varies with the quantity ordered, however, this cost is relevant. Often, in practice, price per unit decreases for larger order quantities; a price reduction called a quantity discount.

=== **EXAMPLE** ===

At Busy Bee Laundry, shirts are laundered for 40¢ each with a minimum charge for finishing a shirt order of $1.50. Customers may purchase a coupon book, however, that allows them to pay only $12.60 for three dozen shirts. Without the coupons, one unit (one shirt) costs $1.50, two shirts 75¢ each, three shirts 50¢ each, and four or more shirts 40¢ each. With the coupon book, each of the thirty-six shirts is 35¢, regardless of the number laundered at any one time. Busy Bee's quantity discounts allow customers to purchase a service, rather than a product, at reduced rates in large quantities.

Procurement Costs

Procurement costs are those incurred by placing a purchase order. These costs vary directly with each purchase order placed. Procurement costs include costs of postage, perhaps telephone calls to the vendor, labor costs in purchasing and accounting, receiving costs, computer time for record keeping, and purchase order supplies. While it is not exactly true that all labor, supplies, and overhead vary directly with the number of orders placed in any real world situation, for our considerations in model development, we will assume that they do. Usually the reality is a close approximation of the situation we'll assume for our model.

Inventory Carrying Costs

Carrying, or holding, costs are the real out-of-pocket costs associated with having inventory on hand. Typical out-of-pocket costs include insurance, warehouse rental, heat, light, taxes, and losses due to pilferage, spoilage, or breakage. Another opportunity cost while not an out-of-pocket cost, must be considered—the cost incurred by having capital tied up in inventory. If funds are borrowed to finance the inventory purchase, interest payments are direct costs. The size of all these carrying costs usually increases or decreases in proportion to the amount of inventory that is carried.

Stockout costs, associated with demand when stocks have been depleted, take the form of lost sales costs or backorder costs. When sales are lost because of stockouts, the firm loses both the profit margin on actual unmade sales and customer good will. If customers take their business elsewhere, future profit margins may also be lost.

When customers agree to come back after inventories have been replenished, they make backorders. Backorder costs include loss of good will and money paid to reorder goods and notify customers when goods arrive. Losses associated with backorders are difficult to assess; as the time of the unfilled backorder lengthens, the costs increase, but the increase can be nonlinear. Backorder costs can increase at an escalating rate over time.

EXAMPLE

A customer at First National Bank had two unpleasant banking experiences this year. First, he went to a teller to get six rolls each of dimes and quarters. At this drive-in banking facility, the teller was out of rolls of dimes; she substituted two rolls of nickels but could spare no more. This forced the customer to make another stop at a competitor bank. The second experience was an attempt to obtain an $8,000 commercial rate loan to purchase some land. The customer agreed to provide adequate stocks and bonds as collateral but was refused the loan because loan funds were not available, not because he was a bad risk. The customer received the loan at a competitor bank and thereafter did all his banking at the competitor.

As this example shows, stockouts can and do occur in the service industries as well as in manufacturing. Stockouts can result in lost service opportunities, lost interest or profit, and lost customer good will.

Cost of Operating the Information Processing System

Whether by hand or by computer, someone must update records as stock levels change. In those systems in which inventory levels are not recorded daily, this operating cost is primarily incurred in obtaining accurate physical counts of inventories. Frequently, these operating costs are more *fixed* than variable over a wide quantity (volume) range. Therefore, since fixed costs are not relevant in establishing the operating doctrine, we will not consider them further.

Cost Tradeoffs

Our objective in inventory control is to find the *minimum cost operating doctrine* over some planning horizon. To find the minimum cost, we need to add all relevant costs—the cost of the item, procurement costs, carrying costs, and stockout costs. Using an annual planning horizon, these costs can be expressed in a general cost equation:

$$
\begin{array}{c}
\text{Total} \\
\text{annual} \\
\text{relevant} \\
\text{costs}
\end{array}
=
\begin{array}{c}
\text{Cost of} \\
\text{the item}
\end{array}
+
\begin{array}{c}
\text{Procure-} \\
\text{ment} \\
\text{costs}
\end{array}
+
\begin{array}{c}
\text{Carrying} \\
\text{Costs} \\
\bullet \text{Cycle stocks} \\
\bullet \text{Buffer stocks}
\end{array}
+
\begin{array}{c}
\text{Stockout} \\
\text{costs} \\
\bullet \text{Lost sales} \\
\bullet \text{Backorders}
\end{array}
\quad (15\text{-}1)
$$

Each of the costs in the equation can be expressed in terms of order quantity and reorder point for a given inventory situation. The solution method is then to *minimize* the total cost situation. This can be accomplished graphically; by tabular analysis using trial and error; or by using the calculus, the most accurate method. Using the calculus, operations researchers have developed a wide range of optimal formulas, which vary with changes in the actual inventory situation.

Graphically, the minimization of this equation consists of cost tradeoffs. For a simple model in which costs of purchased goods (items) and stockouts are irrelevant, the tradeoff is between only two cost components, procurement and carrying costs (see Figure 15-9). Notice that annual carrying costs increase with larger values of order quantity, Q. This is logical; large values of Q result in large average inventory levels and, therefore, large carrying costs. Likewise, when Q increases, fewer orders must be placed during the year and annual ordering costs decrease. Therefore, as shown in Figure 15-9, procurement costs decrease as carrying costs increase. There is a *cost tradeoff* between the two. If we add the costs graphically, we obtain a total cost curve. The optimal order quantity is the point at which annual total cost is at a minimum, Q^* in this case.

For more complex cost situations, the cost curves become difficult to graph and analyze tabularly, *but the cost tradeoff concepts remain the same.* In practice, although many inventory situations are never formally analyzed, successful operations managers take into account relevant costs and the tradeoffs between these costs as they attempt to control inventory. Intuitive decision makers in inventory control must consider these costs if they are to operate successfully.

INVENTORY MODELING

The methodology for modeling inventory situations is straightforward. The purpose is to derive an operating doctrine, and four simple steps are involved:

1. examine the inventory situation carefully, listing characteristics and assumptions concerning the situation,
2. develop the total annual relevant cost equation in narrative,

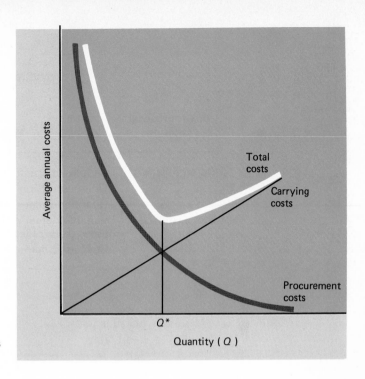

Figure 15-9 **Cost tradeoffs in inventory control**

3. transform the total annual cost equation from narrative into the shorthand logic of mathematics, and

4. optimize the cost equation, finding the optimum for how much to order (order quantity) and when to reorder (reorder point).

We could state the operating doctrine for various models without illustration, but you would be shortchanged should we do so. It is important that you go through these four steps to understand inventory cost tradeoffs and how these tradeoffs are expressed in the operating doctrine.

As we mentioned in our discussion of inventory systems, we will develop models only for the Q/R system, although the general methodology holds for the periodic system as well. Remember, too, that inventory situations can be classified as either *deterministic* (variables are known with certainty) or *stochastic* (variables are probabilistic). In this chapter we'll discuss deterministic models, especially the simple lot size formula, saving our discussion of stochastic models until Chapter 16. Table 15-3 summarizes some inventory model characteristics and illustrates how model complexity changes with environmental conditions.

Variables in inventory models   For model development and discussion, we will use the following notation.

D = Annual demand in units
Q = Quantity ordered
Q^* = Optimal order quantity

TABLE 15-3

INVENTORY MODELS

Environmental conditions	Model	Model complexity
Deterministic	Simple lot size formula	Simple
	Finite correction model	Simple
	Quantity discounts	Moderately complex
Stochastic	Variable demand, constant lead times, service level specified	Moderately complex
	Stochastic demand and lead times	Complex

R = Reorder point
t_L = Lead time
S = Setup or procurement cost per order
I = Carrying charge per unit, expressed as a percentage rate
C = Cost of the individual item; the purchase cost per item
K = Stockout cost per unit out of stock
P = Production rate; units per period of time
d_L = Demand per unit of time during lead time
D_L = Demand during lead time; total demand during lead time

DETERMINISTIC INVENTORY MODELS

The Simple Lot Size Formula

The earliest derivation of what is often called the simple lot size formula was developed by Ford Harris in 1915.[2] Apparently, it was again independently derived by R. H. Wilson, who popularized it. In his honor, it is sometimes referred to as the *Wilson formula*.

This inventory situation assumes that:

1. inventory is being controlled at one point (in a stockroom or in raw materials, for example),
2. demand is deterministic and at a constant known rate per year,
3. no stockouts are allowed,
4. lead time is constant and independent of demand, and
5. the purchase cost per unit is fixed.

[2]Ford Harris, *Operations and Cost* (Chicago: A. W. Shaw Company, 1915), pp. 48–52.

To simplify the case even further, lead time can be assumed to be zero; that is, delivery is instantaneous.

What will the total annual relevant cost equation look like? Let's modify equation 15-1 to fit this situation:

$$\begin{matrix}\text{Total annual} \\ \text{relevant costs}\end{matrix} = \begin{matrix}\text{Procurement} \\ \text{costs}\end{matrix} + \begin{matrix}\text{Carrying} \\ \text{costs}\end{matrix} \qquad (15\text{-}2)$$

Stockouts do not occur, and the annual cost of purchased goods is excluded, since the purchase price per unit is fixed. Only those costs that can be affected by our choice of Q are included.

Examining these terms one at a time, we can see that procurement costs are the cost per order times the number of orders placed in a year. If there are no stockouts, buffer stocks are unnecessary. Carrying costs are the average number of units in inventory each year times the cost of carrying an inventory unit. The total cost equation becomes:

$$\begin{matrix}\text{Total} \\ \text{annual} \\ \text{relevant} \\ \text{costs}\end{matrix} = \begin{pmatrix}\text{Cost of} \\ \text{ordering}\end{pmatrix}\begin{pmatrix}\text{Number of} \\ \text{orders} \\ \text{placed/yr}\end{pmatrix} + \begin{pmatrix}\text{Cost of} \\ \text{carrying} \\ \text{one unit}\end{pmatrix}\begin{pmatrix}\text{Average} \\ \text{number of} \\ \text{units carried}\end{pmatrix} \qquad (15\text{-}3)$$

$$TC = S\begin{pmatrix}\text{Number of} \\ \text{orders placed/yr}\end{pmatrix} + IC\begin{pmatrix}\text{Average number} \\ \text{of units}\end{pmatrix}$$

Remember that we are actually seeking to derive an operating doctrine. How can the number of orders placed per year and average inventory carried be expressed in terms of such variables of interest as demand (D), order quantity (Q), and reorder point (R)?

The number of orders placed per year can be expressed in terms of annual demand and order quantity. Since

$$\text{Annual demand} = \begin{pmatrix}\text{Quantity ordered} \\ \text{in each order}\end{pmatrix}\begin{pmatrix}\text{Number of orders} \\ \text{placed per year}\end{pmatrix} \qquad (15\text{-}4)$$

then

$$\begin{matrix}\text{Number of orders} \\ \text{placed per year}\end{matrix} = \frac{\text{Annual demand}}{\text{Quantity ordered in each order}}$$

$$= \frac{D}{Q}$$

How can we determine the average inventory per year? Look again at Figure 15-6. What is the maximum inventory, the highest that inventory will ever be? It is the order quantity, Q. What is the lowest inventory? Since we reorder when the stock is fully depleted, the lowest is zero. This intermittent pattern, in which inventories vary from maximum to minimum and then back to maximum, is called a cycle. For *any one cycle,* the average inventory would be:

$$\text{Average inventory per cycle} = \frac{\text{Maximum inventory} - \text{Minimum inventory}}{2}$$

$$= \frac{Q - 0}{2}$$

$$= \frac{Q}{2}$$

Think about the several cycles of inventory orders in Figure 15-6. The average for any *one* of these cycles is $Q/2$, but what is the average inventory per year? It is still $Q/2$. *Average inventory is time independent.*

EXAMPLE

Morrison, Inc., orders new trays and issues them to various cafeterias from central stores. If Morrison orders 1,000 trays eight times a year, what is the *annual average inventory* in trays, presuming all the assumptions for the simple lot size formula hold? The average inventory for the first, second, and so on to the eighth cycle would be 1,000/2, or 500. Try to picture the cycling of inventories eight times and the annual effect of this cycling. For the *entire year,* the maximum would be 1,000 and the minimum 0, and the uniform usage would produce an average inventory of 500 new trays.

Substituting our expressions for the number of orders placed per year and average inventory into equation 15-4, our total cost equation becomes

$$TC = S\frac{D}{Q} + IC\frac{Q}{2} \tag{15-5}$$

From this total cost equation evolves the formula for the optimal order quantity:

$$Q^* = \sqrt{\frac{2DS}{IC}} \tag{15-6}$$

What happens was illustrated graphically in Figure 15-9. The total annual costs of this situation involve a tradeoff between annual carrying costs and annual procurement costs. The optimal economic order quantity, Q^*, is located at the low point of the total cost curve, also the point of intersection of the procurement and carrying cost curves.

Since delivery is instantaneous, the reorder point should be set at the lowest point possible, zero, to avoid carrying excess stocks. The operating doctrine, then is:

$$\text{Order} \qquad Q^* = \sqrt{\frac{2DS}{IC}}$$

At the point $\quad R^* = 0$

The calculus is not necessary for understanding the cost tradeoffs illustrated in Figure 15-9 nor for understanding that a low point in the total cost curve is where the optimal order quantity, Q^*, occurs. If you want to see how the calculus is used in this derivation, you may read the supplement at the end of this chapter.

EXAMPLE

Our Redeemer Catholic Church orders candles periodically, and delivery is essentially instantaneous. Annual demand, estimated to be 180 candles, is constant. Candles cost $8 per dozen; the cost of placing the order is estimated to be $9; and the annual carrying charge is estimated to be 15 percent of the candle cost. What quantity should the priest order, and when should he reorder? Calculating the economic order quantity:

$$Q^* = \sqrt{\frac{2DS}{IC}}$$

$$= \sqrt{\frac{2\left(\dfrac{180}{12}\right)(9)}{.15\,(8)}}$$

$$= \sqrt{225}$$

$$Q^* = 15 \text{ dozen}$$

The priest should order 15 dozen. Since delivery is instantaneous, he should order only upon depleting stock, which happens exactly once a year. The operating doctrine is $Q^* = 15$ dozen candles at the point $R^* = 0$.

In our example, the priest is ordering periodically, perhaps intuitively. Possibly he considers that the reasonable cost of candles ($8 per dozen) and the high cost of placing an order ($9) mean that he needn't order very frequently. This raises an important question. How *sensitive* are costs to optimal order quantity? When he's intuitively ordering candles, how far away from optimal order quantity could the priest be and still have relatively low costs? Let's examine the sensitivity of the simple lot size formula.

Model sensitivity   We can compare the sensitivity of total costs (TC) for any operating system with the total costs for an optimal inventory system (TC^*) by using the ratio TC/TC^*. To do this, we compute TC/TC^* as a function of Q/Q^*.

$$\frac{TC}{TC^*} = \frac{S\dfrac{D}{Q} + IC\dfrac{Q}{2}}{S\dfrac{D}{Q^*} + IC\dfrac{Q^*}{2}} \qquad (15\text{-}7)$$

Substituting $Q^* = \sqrt{2DS/IC}$ into equation 15-7 and solving algebraically, we find the general relationship

$$\frac{TC}{TC^*} = \frac{1}{2}\left[\frac{Q^*}{Q} + \frac{Q}{Q^*}\right] \qquad (15\text{-}8)$$

Note that the total cost ratio in this equation is expressed solely in terms of Q and Q^*. If our existing order quantity (Q) is very close to optimal (Q^*), the ratio TC/TC^* is slightly larger than unity. As Q departs farther from Q^*, we expect TC/TC^* also to grow. Graphically, the relation between Q/Q^* and TC/TC^* for the simple lot size case (equation 15-7) is shown in Figure 15-10. Note the flatness of the curve around the minimum point, 1.0 on each axis. If actual Q is off from optimal either direction by a factor of two, costs are increased by only 25 percent. This has important practical implications. For cases that fit the assumptions of the simple lot size model, improving ordering rules won't save much money. Correcting an ordering rule, even one far from optimal, might not result in a very large dollar savings.

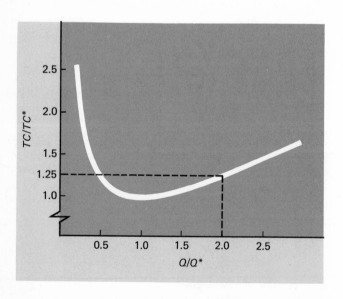

Figure 15-10 Inventory sensitivity—simple lot size case

Source: G. Hadley and T. M. Whitin, *Analysis of Inventory Systems* (Englewood Cliffs, N.J.: Prentice-Hall, Inc., 1963), p. 36.

EXAMPLE

523
Chapter 15
Inventory Control
Fundamentals

Thompson Tooling has a Department of Defense contract for 150,000 bushings a year. Thompson orders the metal for the bushings in lots of 40,000 units from a supplier. It costs $40 to place an order, and estimated carrying costs are 20 percent of the item cost, 15¢. Thompson wants to know what the percent variation their order quantity is from optimal and what this variation is costing them, if anything. Finding optimal order quantity:

$$Q^* = \sqrt{\frac{2DS}{IC}}$$

$$= \sqrt{\frac{2(150,000)(40)}{.2(.15)}}$$

$$= \sqrt{4(10)^8}$$

$$Q^* = 20,000$$

Comparing optimal order quantity to current order quantity, Q:

$$\frac{TC}{TC^*} = \frac{1}{2}\left[\frac{Q^*}{Q} + \frac{Q}{Q^*}\right]$$

$$= \frac{1}{2}\left[\frac{20,000}{40,000} + \frac{40,000}{20,000}\right]$$

$$= \frac{1}{2}[2.5]$$

$$\frac{TC}{TC^*} = 1.25$$

This calculation shows that even though order quantity deviates from optimal by 20,000 units, or 100 percent, the costs are only 25 percent higher than optimal. The excess (marginal) costs of the nonoptimal order quantity can be found as follows:

Marginal costs $= 0.25\,(TC^*)$

$$= 0.25\left(S\frac{D}{Q^*} + IC\frac{Q^*}{2}\right)$$

$$= 0.25\left(\frac{40(150,000)}{20,000} + \frac{.2(.15)(20,000)}{2}\right)$$

$$= 0.25\,(300 + 300)$$

$$= \$150$$

═══════ **EXAMPLE (cont.)** ═══════

Alternatively,

$$TC^* = S\frac{D}{Q^*} + IC\frac{Q^*}{2}$$

$$= \frac{(40)(150,000)}{20,000} + \frac{(.20)(.15)(20,000)}{2}$$

$$= 300 + 300$$

$$= \$600$$

and

$$TC\,\text{actual} = \frac{(40)(150,000)}{40,000} + \frac{(.20)(.15)(40,000)}{2}$$

$$= 150 + 600$$

$$= \$750$$

Marginal cost of the nonoptimal policy is $750 − $600, or $150.

Notice from this example that for annual purchases valued at $22,500, even though order quantity was off *100 percent*, the cost to Thompson Tooling was only an additional $150. You may also note that for the *TC** calculation, ordering costs are equal to carrying costs, each being $300. This is just what we illustrated graphically earlier.

Finite Correction Model

Sometimes, part of the delivery is instantaneous upon ordering, but the rest of the units are sent little by little over time. When the order is placed, the supplier begins producing units, which are supplied continuously to the purchaser. While these units are being added into inventory (causing it to grow), customers are drawing units out of inventory (causing it to diminish). Consider the case in which replenishment rate exceeds withdrawal rates. After some time, the order quantity has been produced, and net inventories have increased. The inventory level, however, never reaches the same high level as the simple lot size model, the order quantity. This situation is illustrated in Figure 15-11. During the time t_p, the slope of inventory accumulation is not vertical, as it was in the simple lot size model. This is the case because the entire order is not received at one time. Here, the production rate (ability to supply) must always be greater than the demand rate $(P > D)$. This means that during the time t_p, inventory is consumed as well as built up, and this situation continues until the initial order quantity, Q, has been produced and delivered. At that point,

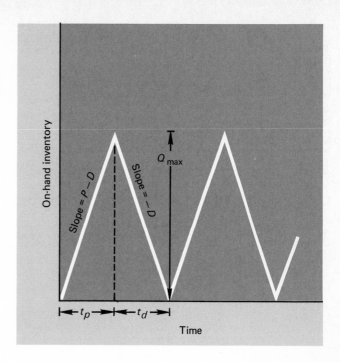

Figure 15-11 **Finite production rate inventory situation**

inventory is at its maximum. Thereafter, during time t_d, demand occurs while the process used for production is idle or shifts to other jobs. At the end of time t_d, another order for Q is placed, production startup is instantaneous, and the cycle repeats.

As with the simple lot size case, we assume demand is known with certainty, and production (delivery) begins instantaneously upon placing an order. However, the order for the entire lot is filled continuously over time, not immediately as was the case with the simple lot size model.

Still applying the other assumptions of the lot size model, the total annual cost equation for this model is:

$$\begin{matrix} \text{Total annual} \\ \text{relevant costs} \end{matrix} = \text{Procurement costs} + \text{Carrying costs} \qquad (15\text{-}9)$$

$$\begin{matrix} \text{Total annual} \\ \text{relevant costs} \end{matrix} = \left(\begin{matrix} \text{Cost of} \\ \text{ordering} \end{matrix} \right) \left(\begin{matrix} \text{Number of} \\ \text{orders} \\ \text{placed} \\ \text{per year} \end{matrix} \right)$$

$$+ \left(\begin{matrix} \text{Cost of} \\ \text{carrying one unit} \end{matrix} \right) \left(\begin{matrix} \text{Average number} \\ \text{of units} \end{matrix} \right)$$

It can be written:

$$TC = S\frac{D}{Q} + IC \left(\begin{matrix} \text{Average number} \\ \text{of units} \end{matrix} \right)$$

As we have noted, maximum inventory never reaches Q but is something less. Therefore, average inventory carried will not be $Q/2$. Realizing that the positive slope of the graph is $P - D$ and the negative slope is $-D$, we can find the maximum inventory, $Q_{\max}$, from

$$\text{Slope} = \frac{\text{Rise}}{\text{Run}}$$

$$P - D = \frac{Q_{max}}{t_p}$$

But the length of time required to produce a lot is

$$t_p = \frac{Q}{P}$$

Substituting

$$P - D = \frac{Q_{max}}{\dfrac{Q}{P}}$$

$$Q_{max} = (P - D)\frac{Q}{P} = Q\left(\frac{P - D}{P}\right)$$

Average inventory is then:

$$\frac{\text{Average}}{\text{inventory}} = \frac{\text{Maximum inventory} + \text{Minimum inventory}}{2}$$

$$= \frac{\dfrac{Q(P - D)}{P} + 0}{2}$$

$$\frac{\text{Average}}{\text{inventory}} = \frac{Q}{2}\left(\frac{P - D}{P}\right)$$

The total cost equation to be minimized for the finite correction case is:

$$TC = S\frac{D}{Q} + IC\left(\frac{Q}{2}\left(\frac{P - D}{P}\right)\right) \tag{15-10}$$

which yields

$$Q^* = \sqrt{\frac{2DS}{IC}\left(\frac{P}{P - D}\right)} \tag{15-11}$$

Since production and resupply begin instantaneously, the optimal reorder point would again be at $R^* = 0$. Note that for this operating doctrine, the formula for Q^* is identical to Q^* for the simple lot size model (equation 15-6) except for the *finite correction factor*, $(P/(P - D))^{1/2}$. Will this finite correction result in Q^* being greater here than in the simple lot size formula? Examine the factor and remember that $P > D$.

=== EXAMPLE ===

A large hotel serves banquets and several restaurants from a central kitchen in which labor is shifted among various stations and jobs. Salad consumption (demand) is virtually constant and known to be 30,000 salads per year. Salads can be produced at a rate of 45,000 per year. Salads cost 40¢ each, and it costs $4 to set up the salad line. Carrying costs of salads, high because of spoilage, are estimated to be 90 percent of the cost of a salad. No stockouts are allowed. The hotel would like to establish an operating doctrine for salad preparation.

First, we can set the reorder point at $R^* = 0$ because labor can be shifted to the salad operation instantaneously, and the production rate is greater than the demand rate. Finding Q^*:

$$Q^* = \sqrt{\frac{2DS}{IC}\left(\frac{P}{P-D}\right)}$$

$$= \sqrt{\frac{2(30{,}000)(4)}{.9(.4)}\left(\frac{45{,}000}{45{,}000-30{,}000}\right)}$$

$$= \sqrt{2(10)^6}$$

$$Q^* = 1{,}414$$

In this example, an order should be placed for 1,414 salads when there are no salads on hand. If salads are served 365 days a year, the daily usage is a little less than 83 salads; production capability is slightly over 123 salads per day. When 1,414 salads are ordered, it takes about 11.5 days to produce them and about 17 days to consume them. A salad may be kept fresh, however, for a maximum of 5.5 days. The manager should therefore question whether it is feasible to meet the restriction. This situation illustrates for us how inaccurate costs or an inappropriate inventory model can distort reality. If a salad *cannot* be kept long enough, something must be changed. Carrying costs may have to be increased; this would force smaller order quantities. Production rates may have to be reduced to be more in line with demand. Or perhaps a more appropriate inventory model should be used to reflect more accurately the cost of perishable goods. We suspect the carrying costs are unrealistically low. This model is valid and the calculations correct for the information given in the illustration. As the example shows, however, you should always make validity checks in applying inventory or other models to production/operations situations.

Quantity Discounts

When demand is known for certain, delivery is instantaneous (no stockouts), and item cost varies with volume ordered, the result is a modified simple lot size situation called the *quantity discount* case. Although the concept of quantity discounts is also applicable to other inventory situations, for our introductory treatment we will modify only the simple lot size situation.

Figure 15-12 illustrates the quantity discount concept, the basis of which is examination of price breaks. As volume ordered (Q) increases, the supplier can often produce and ship more economically. To encourage volume purchases, the supplier shares the economies of scale with the customer.

=== EXAMPLE ===

Safeway, a grocery store chain, recently advertised grapefruits at the price of 12 for $1.00. Customers could buy grapefruits for 10¢ each in quantities fewer than 12, 12 for $1.00 as advertised up to 49, or in large bags of 50 for $3.50. Thus, unit prices decreased as volume increased (10¢ each for fewer than 12, 8.33¢ each for 12 to 49, and 7¢ each for 50 or more).

In Figure 15-12, the solid lines represent average annual costs for various feasible order quantities. Note, however, that the solid lines are *discontinuous* at the price breaks; for different ranges of Q values, different cost curves apply.

In the operating doctrine for quantity discounts, reorder point is still at zero inventory, since delivery is assumed to be instantaneous. The general procedure for determining the reorder quantity starts by checking the lowest cost curve for an optimal Q. If that is unsuccessful, each higher

Figure 15-12
Quantity discounts

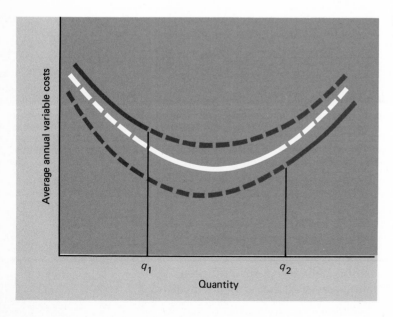

cost curve is systematically checked until optimal is found. Follow these steps:

1. Calculate the economic order quantity (EOQ) using the simple lot size formula for the lowest unit price.
2. Determine if the EOQ in step 1 is feasible by determining whether it is in the quantity range for that price. *If it is feasible,* stop here. Compute the total cost for this quantity, compute the lowest total cost at each price break, and choose the quantity with the lowest total cost.
3. If the EOQ in step 1 is not feasible, compute the total cost for the lowest *feasible* quantity for the lowest unit price.
4. Perform the first and second steps for the next highest unit price. If there is a feasible solution, stop and follow the procedure in step 2. If not, perform the third step. The "best" price/quantity to date will be for the *lowest total cost* of all costs evaluated in step 3.
5. Repeat step 4 until a feasible solution is found or all prices are evaluated. If no feasible optimal quantity is found with the EOQ, choose the price break with the lowest total cost.

Essentially, this procedure finds the lowest cost point on the lowest cost curve, checks feasibility, and if nothing is feasible, computes a cost at the price break that allows a feasible solution. Then we move to the next highest cost curve (see Figure 15-12) and repeat the procedures. In this way, all *minimum cost* EOQ's will be calculated, and all price breaks will eventually be checked, provided an optimal feasible solution is not discovered earlier. As in all inventory operating doctrines, the optimal order quantity is the *quantity that offers the lowest total cost.* An example should help clarify this procedure.

═══════ **EXAMPLE** ═══════

Consider an inventory situation in a medical center where disposable sanitary packs are ordered in boxes of 5 dozen per box. Annual demand is 400 boxes; the cost of placing an order is $12; and the inventory carrying charge is 20 percent. There are two price breaks; price per box is $29 for 1–49 boxes, $28.50 for 50–99 boxes, and $28 for an order of 100 or more boxes.

To determine the optimal quantity, we begin on the lowest cost curve and compute Q for a price of $28 per unit.

$$Q = \sqrt{\frac{2DS}{IC}} = \sqrt{\frac{2(400)(12)}{.2(28)}} = 41.40$$

$$Q = 42 \text{ boxes}$$

Since 100 or more boxes must be ordered to realize a price of $28 per box, our $Q = 41$ is not feasible. Computing the total cost at the lowest feasible quantity, 100, we get:

$$TC = CD + S\frac{D}{Q} + IC\frac{Q}{2}$$

$$= 28(400) + 12\left(\frac{400}{100}\right) + .2(28)\left(\frac{100}{2}\right)$$

$$= \$11,528$$

Moving to the next highest curve,

$$Q = \sqrt{\frac{2DS}{IC}} = \sqrt{\frac{2(400)(12)}{.2(28.5)}} = 41.04$$

$$Q = 41 \text{ boxes}$$

The price of $28.50 is for a volume of 50–99 boxes, so $Q = 41$ is not feasible. Computing the total cost at the first feasible quantity (50) in this range:

$$TC = CD + S\frac{D}{Q} + IC\frac{Q}{2}$$

$$= 28.50(400) + 12\left(\frac{400}{50}\right) + .2(28.50)\left(\frac{50}{2}\right)$$

$$= \$11,638.50$$

Moving to the next highest and last cost curve:

$$Q = \sqrt{\frac{2DS}{IC}} = \sqrt{\frac{2(400)(12)}{.2(29)}} = 40.68$$

$$Q = 41 \text{ boxes}$$

This is a feasible quantity, since $29 is the price for a volume of 1–49 units. Now we must compute the total cost for $Q = 41$:

$$TC^* = CD + S\frac{D}{Q^*} + IC\frac{Q^*}{2}$$

$$= 29(400) + 12\left(\frac{400}{41}\right) + .2(29)\left(\frac{41}{2}\right)$$

$$= \$11,835.97$$

Comparing all total costs, we see that the lowest total cost is $11,528 for an order quantity of 100. Therefore the operating doctrine for disposable sanitary packs is:

$$Q^* = 100$$
$$R^* = 0$$
$$TC^* = \$11{,}528$$

The quantity discount overcame higher ordering and carrying costs. The total of ordering and carrying costs were \$328 for $Q = 100$, \$238.50 for $Q = 50$, and \$235.97 for $Q = 41$. However, the quantity discount of \$1 per box for 400 boxes (comparing $Q = 100$ to $Q = 41$) overcame the additional \$92.03 in ordering and carrying costs, making $Q = 100$ the more attractive choice.

Lead Time in Deterministic Models

Deterministic models can easily be adjusted for lead times known with certainty. The reorder point is calculated:

R^* = Buffer stock + Demand during lead time

   = 0 + (Lead time) (Demand per unit time)

$R^* = t_L d_L$ **(15-12)**

Reorder point is now set and shown in Figure 15-13. Note that total demand during lead time, d_L, is lead time times demand per unit time. At R^*, an order will be placed for Q^* units. The actual order for quantity Q^* will arrive t_L later. During the time between ordering and arrival, d_L units will be demanded, and inventory will be reduced accordingly.

Figure 15-13 Reorder points with lead times

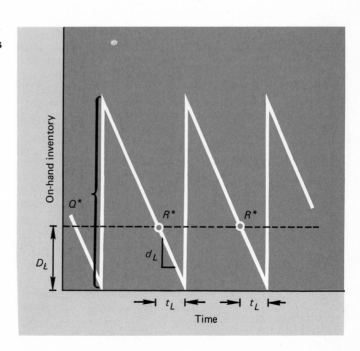

━━━━━ EXAMPLE ━━━━━

A hamburger chain has a local retail outlet that uses 730 cases of six-ounce paper cups annually. Ordering costs are $15; carrying costs are 30 percent of average inventory investment; and a case costs $12. Delivery lead time is known with certainty to be 5 days. Establishing the optimal operating doctrine:

$$Q^* = \sqrt{\frac{2DS}{IC}} = \sqrt{\frac{2(730)(15)}{.3(12)}}$$

$$= 77.99$$

$$Q^* = 78$$

$$R^* = t_L d_L$$

$$= 5d_L$$

$$= 5\left(\frac{730}{365}\right)$$

$$R^* = 10$$

The operating doctrine would be to order 78 cases when stocks on hand reach 10 boxes.

SUMMARY

In most industrial societies, inventories are necessities. Inventory control is a technique that focuses on maintaining stocks at desired levels within a firm. The responsibility for establishing inventory policy and subsequent control in operations typically rests with the production/operations manager.

Inventories are necessary for a number of reasons, the fundamental reason being that it is physically impossible and economically impractical for every stock item to be delivered exactly when it is needed. In controlling inventories it is necessary to establish an operating doctrine, policy decisions concerning *when* to replenish stocks and *how much* stock to replenish.

These decisions are usually made within the framework of either a quantity/reorder inventory system or a periodic inventory system. In the Q/R system, when stock is depleted to an established reorder point, a predetermined quantity is ordered. In the periodic system, after an established time interval has passed, stock is replenished up to a predetermined base stock level.

Inventory costs that are relevant in selecting the operating doctrine are the cost of the item, costs associated with procurement, costs of carrying the item in inventory, and costs associated with being out of stock when units are demanded. Formally or informally, inventory control decisions must consider these cost components and their tradeoffs.

The methodology for establishing the operating doctrine is to develop the total relevant cost equation for a particular inventory situation and then to optimize that cost equation by finding the minimum cost operating doctrine. In quantity/reorder point systems, the minimum cost economic order quantity (Q^*) and reorder point (R^*) must be determined.

For inventories with deterministic demands and lead times, some helpful models are the simple lot size formula (Wilson EOQ), the finite correction model, and the quantity discount case. When demand and lead times are known, there is no need to carry buffer stock, since stockouts would never occur. This simplifies the models considerably.

1. Differentiate between multistage and multiechelon inventories. Must you have only one or the other? Explain.

2. What is meant by the inventory operating doctrine? In the operating doctrine, why are *two* decisions necessary?

3. Contrast the periodic and quantity/reorder inventory system operating doctrines.

4. Explain the steps in the modeling methodology for inventory situations. Why is the understanding of this methodology important to the practicing manager?

5. In Figure 15-12, why are the lines dotted? Will the optimal cost always be at the lowest point on a cost curve? Why or why not?

6. Define inventory control in the context of an automobile repair facility employing four mechanics. For any technical terms used in your definition, provide examples.

7. Refer to Figure 15-2 (the materials conversion process). For a general purpose farming operation, provide one example of a material item for each stock point.

8. Why are inventories necessary? Discuss.

9. What kinds of items should be selected when managers are attempting to improve inventory systems? Why?

10. Explain the cost tradeoffs of equation 15-5 in essay form, utilizing a graph if it is helpful.

11. Explain how the finite production rate inventory situation differs from the simple lot size situation. What impact does the cost of the item have on each situation? Explain.

12. In deterministic inventory models, total costs are relatively insensitive to deviations from the optimal operating doctrine. Explain.

1. Delicious Donut Shop orders 100 fifty-pound bags of flour every three months.
   (a) What is the average inventory for three months (in bags)?
   (b) What is the average inventory for a year (in bags)?
   (c) What is the average monthly inventory (in pounds)?

2. Delicious Donut Shop requires 50 bags of flour every three months. The costs of ordering are $12 per order placed and a carrying charge of 22 percent of the flour cost. A bag of flour costs $27. Flour can be delivered virtually instantaneously from a local warehouse. Determine the operating doctrine for a quantity-reorder point inventory system.

3. A manufacturing firm requires 35,000 two-centimeter-long pieces of wire every month for an assembly. Ordering costs are estimated at $36, and the cost of carrying is 30 percent of the unit price, which is 6¢. Assuming delivery is instantaneous, find the reorder point and economic order quantity.

4. The owner of Delicious Donut Shop (see problem 2) has been ordering 100 bags of flour at one time.
   (a) What percentage is the owner away from optimal order quantity? How much is this deviation costing per year?
   (b) Considering the total cost of flour per year, what can you conclude about deviations from optimal order quantity? Should the owner continue to investigate similar situations? Why or why not?

5. A bookstore orders blue books (exam booklets) in boxes of one gross. Annual demand is even throughout the year and known with certainty to be 600 boxes. Lead time is known to be exactly one month. The cost of placing an order is $16, and annual carrying charges are 36 percent. The wholesaler gives the bookstore a quantity discount as follows:

Quantity (boxes)	Price per box
1–49	$7.50
50–99	7.35
100 or more	7.00

Establish the economic operating doctrine.

6. A textile manufacturer is interested in optimally determined inventories for cutting operations for a children's product line. The production manager would like to establish the optimal reorder point and order quantity for each item in the line. Garment 78A201, a typical product, is demanded uniformly throughout the year, total demand being 14,000 items. The production rate is 2,000 items per month. Sewing, the operation following cutting, is staffed to meet annual demand exactly. Setup costs for cutting are $240, and the cost of carrying one item for a year is 50¢. Since cutting and sewing are done in the same plant, delivery of cut items to sewing is essentially instantaneous. Determine the cutting operation operating doctrine for garment 78A201.

7. A printing company annually uses 640 bundles of cardboard for packing. Ordering costs are $12; carrying costs are 10 percent of average inventory investment; and a bundle costs $3.10. Delivery time is known with certainty to be 14 days. Establish the optimal operating doctrine.

8. Trinidad Co. is interested in the economical order quantity for a production subassembly that is currently purchased from another company. The final assembly made by Trinidad Co. is for a parent company, under an annual contract, with the year's demand set at 50,000 units. Two purchased subassemblies are required for one final assembly. The cost of a subassembly is $10, and the cost of placing an order with the supplier is $3.60. The annual inventory holding charge is 20¢. Trinidad currently orders 750 units at one time. Can you save them any money by recommending a new order quantity? If so, how much can they save and what quantity should they order?

9. An electrical motor housing has an annual usage rate of 75,000 units per year, an ordering cost of $20, and annual unit carrying charge of 15.4 percent of the unit price. For lot sizes of fewer than 10,000 the unit price is 50¢; for 10,000 or more the unit price is 45¢. Delivery lead time is known with certainty to be two weeks. Determine the optimal operating doctrine.

10. A bakery that supplies a large number of retail outlets uses an ingredient at the rate of 2,000 pounds a day, 250 days a year. Delivery is virtually constant and requires five days. A three-day usage of safety stock is set by management and cannot be changed. Ordering costs are $49 per order, and the cost of carrying inventory charge is $0.001 per pound per day. Determine

   (a) the economic order quantity,
   (b) the reorder point,
   (c) the maximum inventory level, and
   (d) the total annual carrying costs.

11. Teletex, Inc., purchases all metal needed in bar stock form. With an annual demand of 3,000 units, a purchase ordering cost of $60, and storage costs of 20 percent of the unit cost, what is the optimal order quantity given these price breaks:
   (a) 0–299, $50 per unit
   (b) 300–499, $40 per unit
   (c) 500 or more, $30 per unit.

Buffer stocks: inventories to protect against the uncertainties of unusual product demands and uncertain lead times

Carrying costs: real out-of-pocket costs associated with having inventory on hand; include opportunity costs, heat, light, breakage, and taxes

Decoupling: use of inventories to break apart operations so that one operation's supply is independent of another's supply

Inventory: stores of goods and stocks

Inventory control: technique of maintaining stockkeeping items at desired levels

Lead time: time between ordering and receiving goods

Multiechelon inventories: products stocked at various levels (factory, warehouse, customer) in a distribution system

Multistage inventories: parts stocked at more than one stage in the sequential production process

Operating doctrine: basic inventory policy decisions made by operations managers concerning when to reorder stocks and how much stock to reorder

Periodic inventory system: operating doctrine of replenishing stocks up to a base stock level after an established time period has elapsed

Procurement costs: costs of placing an order, including postage, telephone calls to vendor, labor, and computer costs associated with purchasing

Q/R inventory system: operating doctrine of replenishing stocks by ordering an economic order quantity (Q) when the reorder point (R) is reached

Quantity discounts: policy of allowing item cost to vary with the volume ordered; usually the item cost decreases as volume increases due to economies of scale in production and distribution

Stockout costs: costs associated with demand when stocks have been depleted; generally lost sales or backorder costs

SELECTED READINGS

Buffa, E. S. and W. H. Taubert. *Production-Inventory Systems: Planning and Control.* Rev. ed. Homewood, Ill.: Richard D. Irwin, Inc., 1972.

Hadley, G. and T. M. Whitin. *Analysis of Inventory Systems.* Englewood Cliffs, N.J.: Prentice-Hall, Inc., 1963.

Harris, F. W. *Operations and Costs.* Chicago: A. W. Shaw Company, 1915.

Magee, J. F. and D. M. Boodman. *Production Planning and Inventory Control.* 2nd ed. New York: McGraw-Hill Book Co., 1967.

Starr, M. K. and D. W. Miller. *Inventory Control: Theory and Practice.* Englewood Cliffs, N.J.: Prentice-Hall, Inc., 1962.

OPTIMIZATION AND INVENTORY CONTROL

In this supplement we briefly present several optimization concepts from the calculus and relate them to inventory control. The calculus concepts will not be thoroughly understood by the reader who has never been exposed to the calculus; they are stated to provide a brief review for those understanding the basics of classical optimization.

The only inventory case derived here is the simple lot size formula, the first inventory model presented in the chapter. The derivation is started where the chapter stopped; development of the model terms will not be repeated.

Classical Optimization

The derivative

The concept of a derivative is to differentiate with respect to a variable. Differentials that are required for this supplement are

$$d(a) = 0$$
$$d(ax) = a\,dx$$
$$d(x + y - z) = dx + dy - dz$$
$$d(x^n) = nx^{n-1}\,dx$$

where a represents a constant and x, y, and z are variables.

Let's find the first derivative of the expression $y = 3x^2 + x - 3$ with respect to the variable x:

$$\frac{d(y)}{dx} = \frac{d}{dx}(3x^2) + \frac{d}{dx}(x) - \frac{d}{dx}(3)$$

$$\frac{d(y)}{dx} = 6x + 1$$

In this example, each of the differentials was used to find the first derivative, $d(y)/dx$. The second derivative would be found by taking the derivative of the first derivative:

$$\frac{d^2(y)}{dx^2} = \frac{d}{dx}(6x) + \frac{d}{dx}(1)$$

$$\frac{d^2(y)}{dx^2} = 6$$

Optimization

In the calculus, the derivative is taken to find the optimal point for the decision variable. The general procedure is to take the first derivative of a function with respect to a decision variable and set the result equal to zero. The equation is then solved for the decision variable in terms of the other parameters in the equation. To determine whether the optimal point is a maximum or a minimum, the second derivative is taken. If the second derivative is positive, the optimal point is a minimum. If the second derivative is negative, the optimal point is a maximum. If the second derivative is zero, the point is an inflection point.

In the previous example,

$$\frac{d(y)}{dx} = 6x + 1$$

The optimal value of x is found by setting this equation equal to zero and solving for x:

$$0 = 6x + 1$$

$$x = -\frac{1}{6}$$

When the second derivative was found, it was $+6$. Therefore, $x = -1/6$ is a minimum point.

Partial derivatives   The object of a partial derivative is to hold all variables as constants except the one that is being differentiated. We partially differentiate, viewing all other variables as constants rather than variables.

For example, if $y = zx^3 - x^2 + 2x$, let's find the first partial derivative of y with respect to x. To do this, we treat z as though it were a constant and differentiate:

$$\frac{\delta y}{\delta x} = \frac{\delta}{\delta x}(zx^3) - \frac{\delta}{\delta x}(x^2) + \frac{\delta}{\delta x}(2x)$$

$$= z\frac{\delta}{\delta x}(x^3) - \frac{\delta}{\delta x}(x^2) + 2\frac{\delta}{\delta x}(x)$$

$$= 3zx^2 - 2x + 2$$

Optimizing the simple lot size formula   The total cost equation for the simple lot size formula was developed to be:

$$TC = CD + S\frac{D}{Q} + IC\frac{Q}{2}$$

$$= CD + SDQ^{-1} + \frac{IC}{2}Q$$

Taking the partial derivative of total cost with respect to order quantity, Q,

$$\frac{\delta(TC)}{\delta Q} = 0 + (-SDQ^{-2}) + \frac{IC}{2}$$

Setting the first derivative equal to zero, and solving for Q:

$$0 = \frac{-DS}{Q^2} + \frac{IC}{2}$$

$$\frac{SD}{Q^2} = \frac{IC}{2}$$

$$Q^* = \sqrt{\frac{2DS}{IC}}$$

Checking the second derivative to assure a minimum of the cost function:

$$\frac{\delta^2(TC)}{\delta Q} = \frac{\delta}{\delta Q}\left(-\frac{SD}{Q^2}\right) + \frac{\delta}{\delta Q}\left(\frac{IC}{2}\right) = -(-2)\frac{SD}{Q^3} + 0$$

$$= \frac{2DS}{Q^3}$$

a positive value results, thus assuring a minimum. Notice that the term *CD*, the item cost, dropped out of the first equation in the first derivative. This illustrates that this cost component is constant with regard to changes in order quantity.

Again, we can see the power of the logic in calculus, but you need not be overwhelmed if you cannot follow all the mathematics. Clearly, the logic of mathematics is useful when applied to the many rational problems in productions/operations.

PROBLEMS

1. **For the following total cost (*TC*), find the optimal order quantity, *Q**. *A* is a constant. Is this a minimum or a maximum cost point? Why?**

$$TC = (27 + A)Q + \frac{100}{Q} + 274$$

2. **Given a (*Q, R*) item control system in which:**
    (a) **Delivery is instantaneous.**
    (b) **The vendor quotes a price (*c*) as twice the variable charge (*V*) plus the ratio of the fixed charge (*F*) divided by the order quantity (*Q*).**
    (c) **The inventory storage rate (*i*) is applied to the value of the *maximum* inventory.**
    (d) **No stockouts are permitted.**
    (e) **The demand per year (*d*) and the cost of ordering per order (*S*) are both known.**
    Define any additional notation used.
    (a) **Explain the basic approach one should take in proceeding to analyze this type of system. Determination of the *optimal* operating doctrine is the goal.**
    (b) **Write a verbal total cost equation for the entire system.**
    (c) **Solve the system for the optimal operating doctrine (*Q** and *R**).**

Inventory Control in Application

In Chapter 15, in which we discussed the fundamentals of inventory control, we explained several deterministic models. In reality we rarely encounter the simplified conditions of these models, and they therefore are of limited value. In this chapter, we'll relax the deterministic conditions and examine some models of a more practical nature, stochastic inventory models. We'll also consider some inventory applications and material requirements planning.

Variable Demand, Variable Lead Time, and Variable Demand During Lead Time

STOCHASTIC INVENTORY MODELS

Variable demand For simple inventory models, we assumed that future demand is known with certainty. Generally, however, this is not the case; demand must be estimated. The most common way to estimate demand is to collect data about past experiences and forecast future demand based on that data. Here is a summary of the most recent seven days' demand for a part used in manufacturing:

Actual daily demand (units)	Number of occurrences (days)	Relative frequency of occurrence
1–200	3	42.8%
201–400	2	28.6
401–600	1	14.3
601–800	1	14.3
	7	100.0%

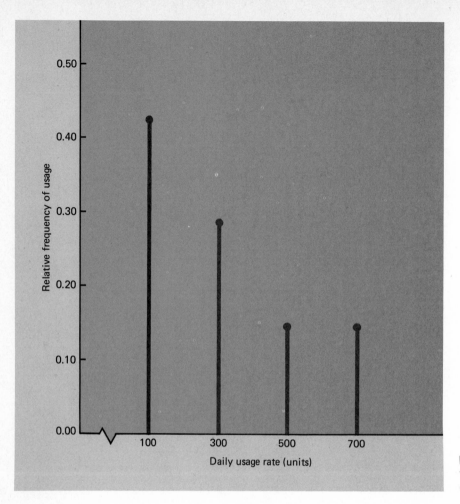

Figure 16-1 **Relative frequency distribution of daily usage**

For three of the seven days (42.8 percent of the days), usage ranged between 1 and 200 units; it exceeded 600 units per day on only one of the seven days. Records like this one can be useful for estimating future usage rates; they reveal historical usage patterns that might otherwise go unnoticed. Should the usage rates be highly variable, we can take this variability into consideration when we decide how much inventory to carry.

In the conventional method for measuring variability of usage, we:

1. calculate the average usage rate from historical data, and
2. calculate the standard deviation of usage about the average.

In the data for the manufacturing part, the usage rate intervals are very wide; each interval covers a 200-unit range. To obtain some very approximate indicators of the demand pattern, we will calculate the mean and standard deviation of these data using only the midpoints of the intervals. Average, or expected, demand is calculated as follows:

$$\text{Expected demand} = \frac{100(3) + 300(2) + 500(1) + 700(1)}{7}$$

$$= 300 \text{ units per day}$$

We find the variability in demand by computing the standard deviation of demand about the mean:

$$\text{Standard deviation of demand} = \sqrt{\sum_{i=1}^{n} \frac{(\text{Demand}_i - \text{Expected demand})^2}{n}}$$

$$= \sqrt{\frac{3(100-300)^2 + 2(300-300)^2 + (500-300)^2 + (700-300)^2}{7}}$$

$$= 214 \text{ units}$$

Finally, we can get a visual portrayal of usage and its variability by constructing a relative frequency distribution of daily demand shown, as we have done in Figure 16–1. As you can see, lower levels of usage have a greater chance of occurring than do higher levels.

Lead time   Like demand, lead time is often uncertain rather than constant. If it is uncertain, the length of lead time takes on some distribution. Extending our manufacturing part example, we find that the lead time distribution is:

Actual lead time (days)	Number of occurrences	Relative frequency of occurrence
2	2	28.6%
3	3	42.8
4	2	28.6
	7	100.0%

Of the seven recent lead times observed, two were of two days' duration; three were of three days' duration; and two were of four days' duration. The expected lead time is found like this:

$$\text{Expected lead time} = \frac{2(2) + 3(3) + 4(2)}{7}$$

$$= 3 \text{ days}$$

The standard deviation can be found like this:

$$\text{Standard deviation of lead time} = \sqrt{\sum_{i=1}^{n} \frac{(\text{Lead time}_i - \text{Expected lead time})^2}{n}}$$

$$= \sqrt{\frac{2(2-3)^2 + 3(3-3)^2 + 2(4-3)^2}{7}}$$

$$= 0.75 \text{ days}$$

We can describe the lead time distribution in terms of its mean, three days, and standard deviation, 0.75 days. A relative frequency distribution of lead time duration is shown in Figure 16–2.

Demand during lead time There are two sources of demand variation during lead time, the length of lead time itself and the demand per time period of lead time. Continuing with our example, we find that what is really important is the interaction between

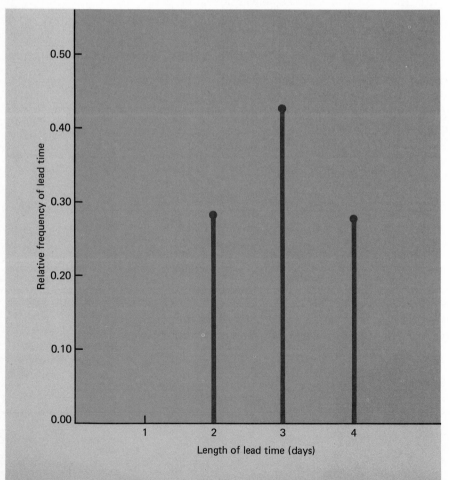

Figure 16-2 **Relative frequency distribution of lead times**

demand (mean of 300 units and standard deviation of 214 units) and *lead time* (mean of three days and standard deviation of 0.75 days). If we had expected demand per day during each day of the expected lead time, we would experience "expected demand during lead time." For the manufacturing part:

$$\text{Expected demand during lead time} = (300)(3) = 900 \text{ units}$$

If we had the lowest demand for each day of the shortest lead time, we would have a low demand of:

$$\text{Lowest demand during lead time} = (100 \text{ units per day})(2 \text{ days per lead time})$$
$$= 200 \text{ units}$$

Likewise, if the most demanding condition prevailed, highest demand per day and longest lead time, then:

$$\text{Highest demand during lead time} = 700(4)$$
$$= 2,800 \text{ units}$$

As you can see, between these extreme points, there can be various levels of demand. We can calculate all possible combinations of lead time duration and daily demand, and see what values are possible for demand during lead time. We can also calculate the probabilities of these demands and use them to construct a probability distribution of demand during lead time. For larger problems involving many classification intervals of demand and lead time, hand calculations become tedious. An alternative method for generating the distribution of demand during lead time is to simulate the operation of the inventory system over time on the computer. By drawing a demand, drawing a lead time, computing a demand during lead time, and repeating the process dozens of times, we could classify the data into a distribution of lead time demands and compute a mean and standard deviation to describe that distribution.

Figure 16–3 illustrates how inventory levels are affected by variations in lead time demand. After the first reorder point, R_1, expected demand and expected lead time occur. After R_2, the second lead time, t_{L_2}, occurs. Although t_{L_2} is shorter than expected, daily demand during the lead time is considerably greater than expected; thus, overall lead time demand is greater than expected. At R_3, both lead time, t_{L_3}, and daily demand are different from what was expected; demand is much lower than expected, and lead time is much greater than expected. As the figure shows, the two random variables, demand and lead time, interact. This interaction is common in actual inventory situations.

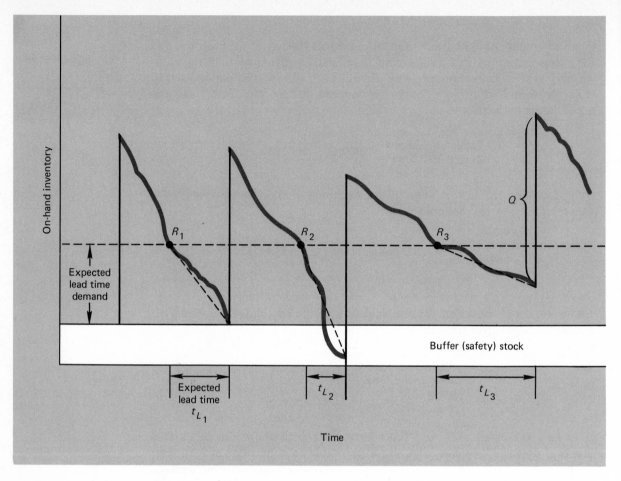

Figure 16-3   Q/R model with varying demand and lead times

A Model for Variable Demand and Constant Lead Time, with Specified Service Level

Now let's examine a moderately complex quantity-reorder point model in which lead time does not vary, but demand is variable. In this model, we want to find an operating doctrine that takes into account the possibility of a stockout. We want to establish buffer stocks that are adequate for providing a specified level of protection for service to customers when demand is uncertain.

We'll define a few additional variables to those defined in the previous chapter:

μ = random variable representing demand during lead time

σ_μ = standard deviation of demand during lead time

$\bar{\mu}$ = expected lead time demand

$\bar{d}$ = average daily demand

σ_d = standard deviation of daily demand

D = expected annual demand

B = buffer stock

z = number of standard deviations needed for a specified confidence level

Look closely at the first cycle in Figure 16–3. Several relationships exist. First, we can see that the expected lead time demand ($\bar{\mu}$) plus the buffer stock (B) equals the reorder point (R_1). This general relationship holds:

$$R = \bar{\mu} + B \qquad (16\text{-}1)$$

Second, we know that if lead time (t_L) is constant, which it is for the model being developed, expected lead time demand is expected demand times lead time:

$$\bar{\mu} = \bar{d}t_L$$

We also know that the buffer stock is the *protection* for the service level specified, $z\sigma_\mu$ units. Buffer stock is z standard deviates of protection for a given *variability* of demand during lead time. Substituting, the reorder point for our operating doctrine is now:

$$R = \bar{\mu} + B$$
$$R^* = \bar{d}t_L + z\sigma_\mu \qquad (16\text{-}2)$$

The order quantity is simply the simple lot size formula with expected annual demand substituted for annual demand:

$$Q^* = \sqrt{\frac{2\bar{D}S}{IC}} \qquad (16\text{-}3)$$

The use of average demand in equation 16-3 is appropriate for this model regardless of the shape of the demand distribution. Because of its variable nature, demand may take on many shapes. It may be a very unconventional empirical distribution, or it may be normally distributed, Poisson distributed, or negatively exponentially distributed. You may not be familiar with all of these distributions; we mention them only because they have been found to be reasonable representations of demand at various levels of production-wholesale-distribution systems. There is some evidence, for example, that the normal distribution describes many inventory situations at the production level; the negative exponential describes many at the wholesale and retail levels; and the Poisson describes many retail situations.[1]

[1] J. Buchan and E. Koenigsberg, *Scientific Inventory Control* (Englewood Cliffs, N.J.: Prentice Hall, Inc., 1963).

=== EXAMPLE ===

Daily demand for product EPD101 is normally distributed with a mean of 50 units and a standard deviation of 5. Supply is virtually certain with a lead time of six days. The cost of placing an order is $8, and annual holding costs are 20 percent of the unit price of $1.20. A 95-percent service level is desired for the customers who place orders during the reorder period. Backorders are allowed; once stocks are depleted, orders are filled as soon as the stocks arrive. There are no stockout costs. We can assume sales are made over the entire year.

Determining the operating doctrine, we calculate order quantity to be:

$$Q^* = \sqrt{\frac{2\bar{D}S}{IC}} = \sqrt{\frac{2(50)\,(365)\,(8)}{.2(1.20)}}$$

$$= 1{,}103$$

From the normal distribution, a 0.95 confidence interval gives $z = 1.645$ (see Appendix A). Thus:

$$R^* = \bar{d}t_L + z\sigma_\mu$$
$$R^* = 50(6) + 1.645\sigma_\mu$$

From statistics, we know that for an independent variable the total variance is the sum of the individual variances. The variance of demand during lead time is:

$$\sigma_\mu^2 = \sum_{i=1}^{6} \sigma_i^2 = 6(5)^2$$
$$\sigma_\mu = \sqrt{6(5)^2} = 12.2$$

Therefore:

$$R^* = 50(6) + 1.645(12.2)$$
$$= 300 + 20$$
$$= 320 \text{ units}$$

Our operating doctrine is to order 1,103 units when we reach an order point of 320.

How was the reorder point established in this example? Look at the distribution of demand during lead time shown in Figure 16–4. How was this normal distribution obtained? It comes from the distribution of *daily* demands. Since demand per day is normally distributed, and since lead time is six days, the lead time demand distribution is the sum of six normal daily demand distributions. We can draw Figure 16–4 because we know from statistics that the sum of independent normal distributions is itself a normal distribution.

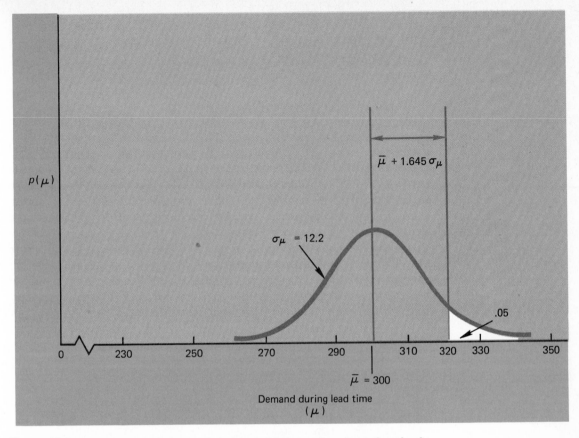

$p(\mu)$

$\bar{\mu} + 1.645\,\sigma_\mu$

$\sigma_\mu = 12.2$

.05

| 0 | 230 | 250 | 270 | 290 | 310 | 320 | 330 | 350 |

$\bar{\mu} = 300$

Demand during lead time
(μ)

Figure 16-4 Distribution of demand during lead time when lead time is six days and daily demand is normally distributed with mean of 50 units and standard deviation of 5 units

Next we determine the number of units that will provide the desired 95 percent protection level. We seek that level of demand μ such that the probability of μ or more units being demanded is .05 during lead time. From a normal probability table, we find that $z = 1.645$ is the desired number of standard normal deviates above the mean. As you can see in Figure 16–4, only 5 percent of the area under the curves lies beyond this point.

In our example for product EDP101 the operating doctrine accomplishes two things. First, it results in economical levels of cycle stocks because our choice of Q^* provides a proper balance between ordering costs and inventory carrying costs throughout the year. Second, it provides the desired level of customer service during lead times while we are waiting to receive a replenishment order from our suppliers. The 320 units we have on hand when we place an order provide a 95 percent assurance of being able to meet customer demand until the new shipment is received. We expect only 300 units to be demanded, but we carry an extra 20 units of buffer stock to provide the desired service level. How much do we pay to obtain this extra level of protection? Our average inventory levels for the year are 20 units higher than they otherwise would have been. Therefore, the annual cost of carrying buffer stock is:

$$(B)(I)(C) = (20 \text{ units})(.20)(\$1.20 \text{ per unit})$$
$$= \$4.80$$

Variable demands and lead times   The basic procedure for finding operating doctrines when *both* daily demands and lead times vary is a convergence procedure; we use directed trial and error. For the quantity-reorder point model, we compute an order quantity assuming constant demand. Then we calculate a reorder point using the order quantity we have just computed. We then use this reorder point to revise the previous estimate of order quantity and recalculate the reorder point. Eventually, the order quantity and reorder point converge upon their optimal values. This process is necessary because two random variables, lead time and demand, are interacting. Although a detailed treatment of these models is beyond our introductory treatment, we believe you should be aware of their existence.

INVENTORY CONTROL IN APPLICATION

Concepts for the Practitioner

Dynamic inventory levels   The simple lot size formula

$$Q^* = \sqrt{\frac{2DS}{IC}}$$

illustrates that the relationship between demand (D) and order quantity (Q^*) varies with the square root of demand. Table 16–1 illustrates this relationship for several demand levels. Note that as demand increases 100 percent, inventory order quantity, and subsequently maximum inventory levels, increase only 41 percent. In Table 16–1, demand increases from 1,000 to 2,000 (100%), and order quantity increases from 31.62 times a constant factor to 44.72 times the same constant factor (41%). You may remember that in Chapter 15, we also found that an increase in demand can be served by less than proportional increases in inventory levels. *Demand changes should not cause rapid, wide fluctuations in inventory.* If operations managers find in application that work-in-process and finished goods inventories are building rapidly, the problem may very well be caused by scheduling and loading difficulties, not by increases in demand.

TABLE 16-1

549
Chapter 16
Inventory Control
in Application

RELATIONSHIP BETWEEN DEMAND AND ORDER QUANTITY IN THE SIMPLE LOT SIZE SITUATION: EXAMPLE DEMANDS

Demand	Change in demand	Order quantity	Change in order quantity
1,000	—	$31.62\sqrt{2S/IC}$	—
1,500	50%	$38.72\sqrt{2S/IC}$	20%
2,000	100	$44.72\sqrt{2S/IC}$	41
3,000	200	$54.77\sqrt{2S/IC}$	73
4,000	300	$63.24\sqrt{2S/IC}$	100

Service level   Service levels, treatment policies for customers when there may be stockouts, can be established and measured in several different ways. Two of the most common are:

1. the ratio of the number of *customers* receiving the product to the number of customers demanding the product and
2. the ratio of the number of *units* supplied to the number of units demanded.

Suppose four customers each demanded 100 units and demand was met. When a fifth demanded 200 units, however, demand was not met. Service level as a customer ratio in this case is 4/5, or 80 percent serviced; service level as a unit ratio is 400/600, or 67 percent serviced. Whether a firm uses a customer or a unit ratio depends on what use general management wants to make of buffer stocks. If management wants buffer stocks to protect against units demanded, a unit ratio is used. If buffer stocks are meant to protect against customers demanding units, a customer ratio is used. As an operations manager, you must make sure that marketing and general management understand the way service level is being measured so that internal disagreements can be minimized. Our example in Figure 16–4 used the number of units as the service level criterion.

Inventory as a   Because demand is not always certain but must be
system input   projected in some way, forecasting is a requirement for inventory systems. Similarly, inventory levels established with the operating doctrine are necessary inputs for production/operations management decisions in many other functional areas. Table 16–2 illustrates some of the production/operations management activities that depend heavily upon inventory levels in operations. As you can see, inventory control and other major planning and control activities interact in operations. Poor inventory control, whether it allows rapidly changing inventory levels or fails to account accurately for inventories, results in wide variations in other operations subfunctions. In a later section

TABLE 16-2

INVENTORY AS A SYSTEM INPUT

Production/operations management activity	Role of inventory
Aggregate output planning	Input to establish work force levels and production rates
Material requirements planning	Input to establish on-hand inventories preceding ordering
Physical distribution	Input as actual finished goods stocks; the basis for shipping schedules
Scheduling and loading operations	Input to determine *net* production requirements

of this chapter, we will see how the inventory status file is a direct input into the material requirements planning system, for example. Poor inventory control increases the variability of decisions in many functions and increases costs and operations inefficiency throughout the organization. In many instances, poor performance is a direct result of poor inventory control.

Saving Money in Inventory Systems

Suppose your first assignment on your first job is to evaluate the current inventory system and procedures at a major distribution center for a national company. Where would you begin? What would you do? In this section, we hope to provide you with a general guide toward saving money in inventory systems. As you read it, remember that this is a general guide, not a solution procedure for all inventory problems. With that in mind, we suggest you consider these possible cost saving areas.

ABC classification   When an organization's inventory is listed by dollar volume, generally a small number of items account for a large dollar volume, and a large number of items account for a small dollar volume.

The ABC inventory concept divides inventories into three groupings, an *A* grouping for those few items with large dollar volume; a *B* grouping for items with moderate unit and dollar volume; and a *C* grouping for the large number of items accounting for a small dollar volume. The *A* group might contain, for example, about 15 percent of the items, the *B* group 35 percent, and the *C* group 50 percent.

Table 16–3 lists a number of stock items according to decreasing dollar usage, and Table 16–4 groups these items into an ABC classification. The *A* items comprise 79.5 percent of the total dollar volume, the *B* items 17.6 percent, and the *C* items only 2.9 percent. Notice, however, that the *A* items are only 22.2 percent of the total items, the *B* items 22.2 percent, and the *C* items 55.6 percent. Figure 16–5 graphically illustrates the dollar value classification for this example.

TABLE 16-3

EXAMPLE ANNUAL USAGE OF INVENTORY BY VALUE

Item stock number	Annual dollar usage	Percent of total value
2704	$125,000	46.2
1511	90,000	33.3
0012	32,000	11.8
2100	15,500	5.8
0301	6,200	2.3
0721	650	0.2
8764	525	0.2
7402	325	0.1
3520	300	0.1
	$270,500	100.0

TABLE 16-4

EXAMPLE ABC GROUPING OF INVENTORY BY VALUE

Classification	Item stock number	Annual dollar usage	Percent of total dollar usage	Number of items	Percent of total number of items
A	2704, 1511	215,000	79.5	2	22.2
B	0012, 2100	47,500	17.6	2	22.2
C	0301, 0721, 8764, 7402, 3520	8,000	2.9	5	55.6
Totals		270,500	100.0	9	100.0

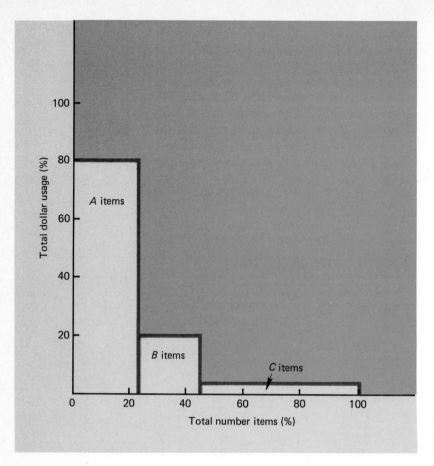

Figure 16-5 **Example ABC inventory classification: percent inventory value vs. percent of items**

If you are trying to reduce costs in an inventory system, which class would you concentrate on? The high dollar volume group, the A class, should receive your attention first; one of the major costs of inventory is annual carrying costs, and your money is invested largely in class A. Tight control, sound operating doctrine, and attention to security on these items would allow you to control a large dollar volume with a reasonable amount of time and effort. Items in this class are usually either high unit cost items or high volume items with at least moderate costs.

A good start in examining an inventory system is to make an ABC classification and focus initially on the A items—unit cost/volume combinations that account for high dollar volumes.

Blanket rules   When blanket rules, general rules, are being used in inventory systems, they are often good places to investigate for cost savings. Such rules as "always carry a month's supply on all items," "reorder when you take out the last case of any item," and "don't order any inventory that won't fit in this stock room" almost always provide an opportunity for cost savings. Try to think of individual items and families of parts that by violating the rule would reduce costs.

Sometimes comptrollers send such directives as "Reduce all inventories 33 percent" to operations managers. If you can prove that current inventories costs are reasonable by justifying inventory as a return on investment (see Chapter 15), you may be able to challenge such a directive successfully.

Stochastic demand and lead time   It is very unlikely that you will observe many situations in which the deterministic simple lot size formula applies. Even if it does apply, you probably will not save much money; stock clerks can be off on order quantities a good bit without incurring excessive costs. Nevertheless, you can use your understanding of the modeling approach and cost tradeoffs to attack situations with these characteristics:

1. High variability in demand. It is likely that with wide variations in demand, systematic evaluation and buffer stock calculations can reduce the erratic reactions to demand that result in repeated overstock and understock situations.
2. High variability in lead times. Essentially, the same is true for lead times; we want to have good estimates of the mean and variability of demand during lead time in our inventory system to reduce overstock and understock situations.

High stockout costs   When stockout costs are high, buffer stocks should be increased accordingly. It is costlier for stockouts in some items than it is in others. Focus on items that have high cost consequences to the organization when they are out of stock. For these high stockout cost items, examine the operating doctrine to see how buffer stocks are set and see that inventories are adequate.

Safety stocks   Evaluate safety stock levels to be sure that they relate to the variability of demand and lead time and to the costs of stockouts. If demand variability, lead time variability, and stockout costs are not high, buffer stocks are unnecessary. Remember, buffer stocks should be demand and cost dependent; they should not be set intuitively.

Decoupling operations   One common use of inventories is to decouple operations. This use of inventories can become excessive, however, if work-in-process continues to rise at the expense of inadequate finished goods inventories and shipments. There are several ways to reduce excessive buildups and reduce costs. A special housecleaning effort (moving items off the shop floor and forcing foremen to process them on through the shop) is one way to reduce in-process inventories. Another is to remove a small number of tote boxes (boxes used for in-process inventory) from operations weekly for several months. If tote boxes are removed from the plant and placed in unaccessible storage, foremen have no place to store their work-in-process. Usually they simply finish the work and send it to the next department or operation. Gradually but significantly, work-in-process is reduced.

Raw material and finished goods inventory   Excessive inventories at the beginning or the end of the production process can lead not only to high carrying costs but also to increased risk of obsolescence.

Furthermore, when physical inventory records are collected for tax and auditing purposes, as they are periodically, it is unpleasant and embarrassing to have accountants and marketing staff find that you are carrying obsolete raw material or finished goods. Such a situation shows that control is poor and often results in a write-off against production/operations' profitability.

Table 16–5 summarizes some of the ways managers can save money in inventory control.

Inventory Control Procedures

Inventory control procedures for operating systems vary in complexity and accuracy from the absence of any noticeable control to computerized systems for distribution and production. In between these extremes are simple visual controls, the two-bin system, and cardex systems. We'll briefly examine two of the systems, a cardex file and IBM's computerized COPICS system. The two-bin system, which needs no extended explanation, consists simply of filling two bins with units of the same item. One bin is used first; when it is empty, the quantity necessary to replenish the empty bin is reordered, and stock from the second bin is used.

Cardex file system   The cardex file system has variations, but the essential features are:

1. There is a card for every stock item; the cards are filed on a rotating drum in a central location.
2. On the top of each card is the computed operating doctrine. For a Q/R system, the economic order quantity and reorder point are listed. For a periodic system, the time between orders and the base stock level are listed. The supply source (vendor) may be listed here also.
3. A ledger comprises the balance of the card. It states beginning inventory, orders placed, orders received, issues from stores, and current inventory levels. Each time a transaction is made, an entry with the corresponding date is recorded. When physical inventories are taken, cards are adjusted to reflect current actual inventories.

Table 16–6 shows a cardex file card for one stock item.

TABLE 16-5

A GENERAL GUIDE FOR SAVING MONEY IN INVENTORY CONTROL

Inventory situation	Operating guides
No priority for inventory items	Classify by ABC; examine high dollar volumes first, low dollar volumes last.
Blanket rules applied	Challenge on cost basis by examining items and families of parts; justify by return on investment.
Stochastic (variable) demand and lead times	Obtain estimates of mean and variance of demand, lead time, and especially demand during lead time; adjust buffer stocks, reorder point, and order quantity to avoid continued overstock or understock situations.
High stockout costs	Identify high stockout cost items by questioning staff; adjust buffer stocks on cost tradeoff basis.
Safety stocks	Evaluate reasons for safety stocks; levels should be based on demand, lead times, and cost tradeoff among ordering, carrying, and stockout costs; do not set intuitively.
Decoupling operations	Justify in-process inventory levels as basis for cost reductions and efficiency in operations; reduce levels if too much inventory results in inefficiencies due to space limitations.
Raw material and finished goods inventory	Examine physical inventories carefully; accept obsolescence write-offs but reduce future obsolescence through more careful scheduling and control; coordinate closely with purchasing on raw materials and marketing on finished goods inventories.

The primary advantage of this procedure is simplicity. Because records are on hand, any part may be checked quickly. This procedure is especially good for inventory situations that do not have more than 500 or 1,000 items. A primary problem with the cardex file system is the validity of the data; it's difficult to ensure that *all transactions* are recorded and current levels computed accurately. If withdrawals are made when the stock clerk is either absent or busy, the transaction may not be recorded, and the records are invalid. Furthermore, it can become expensive both to maintain credibility in the data and, for large inventory situations with many items, to maintain the system itself.

Recently, remote terminal access computer facilities with central processing capabilities have made this cardex procedure obsolete for multi-location distribution and manufacturing firms. Computers are less costly than cardex systems. Cardex files are still useful, however, for small and medium-sized organizations with no computer access.

TABLE 16-6

CARDEX FILE CARD FOR ONE INVENTORY ITEM

ARTOTURF, INC.

PART #:3799
ITEM DESCRIPTION: Vinyl back artificial turf

UNITS: Square yard
COST: $4.25/sq yd

Date	Invoice #	Purchases	Sales	Adjustments Dr.	Cr.	Balance (sq yd)
11/15/76	Beg inventory					256172
11/15	3033, 3035		3767			
11/16	3039		3424			
11/17	3041, 3042, 3049		14040			
11/18	3047, 3048		11618			
11/19	3050		8547			
11/22	3051, 3052		10354			
11/23	3053, 3054, 3056, 3062		13854			190568
11/24	3064		4933			
11/29	3066, 3068, 3069		10459			
11/30	3077		11467			163709

IBM's COPICS The Communications Oriented Production Information and Control System (COPICS) is a series of concepts outlining an approach to an integrated manufacturing system.[2] COPICS deals with problems common to manufacturing companies—forecasting, master production scheduling, inventory management, and plant monitoring and control. The computer is not the system but rather a tool management can use in operating the system. COPICS focuses on data communication technology in manufacturing subsystems; its key element is the manufacturing *data base*, a common data base with which all production subsystems interact.

The essential features of COPICS are shown in Figure 16–6. Note the relationship between the subfunctions from order entry through shipment of goods. We'll illustrate this system by discussing the inventory management module.

The inventory management module is designed to serve as a comprehensive tool through which management can plan and control inventories at the level of finished goods, work-in-process, and raw materials. The inventory management control objectives are to improve customer service by reducing the number of shortages and late customer deliveries through

[2]This section is based on IBM's COPICS manuals G320-1974 (Vol. 1: *Management Overview*) and G320-1977 (Vol 4: *Inventory Management*), White Plains, N.Y., 1972.

improved timing of component part deliveries and to reduce investment in all types of inventory, including maintenance parts and tools. This is accomplished through a system that is flow-charted in Figure 16–7. Notice that embedded in the system are functions for calculating the operating doctrine.

Volume IV of COPICS includes a complete discussion of the inventory system and a presentation of order point versus material requirements planning (MRP). MRP, discussed in the next section, appears most appropriate for complex assembled parts in which inventory requirements can be exploded from a complex product structure.

Several other computer systems are available, none of which we will discuss here. Production/operations managers will find computer firms' representatives eager to help them find a system that will fit their needs.

Quantity-Reorder Versus Periodic Inventory Systems

To practice inventory control, production/operations managers must select either a quantity/reorder (Q/R) system or periodic inventory system. The following points might assist you in making that decision.

1. *The periodic system requires less manpower to operate than the Q/R system.* In the Q/R system, each item must be counted as it is issued or demanded. This requires a person to record the transaction. In the periodic system, no person is required in the inventory area except at the end of the period, when a physical inventory must be taken. The periodic is especially good for raw material and supply inventory systems for which tight security is not necessary.

2. *The periodic system requires less calculating time than the Q/R system.* In the Q/R system, each issue or demand from stock must be subtracted to obtain net inventory. If this is not done, a reorder point might be skipped. Use of the computer for receiving data on issued items and for making the calculation of on-hand inventory can greatly reduce this clerical time in the Q/R system and largely cancel out the advantage of the periodic. *Systemic costs,* the costs of running the system, are generally fewer with the periodic system.

3. *The periodic system may require more buffer stock to protect against uncertainties of demand and lead time.* If the quantity-reorder point and corresponding base stock level-reorder time are set mathematically, in a minimum cost framework, there is no advantage to one system over the other. However, often in the periodic system, the reorder time is set to correspond with a weekly or monthly physical inventory. For example, if an optimal 2.7 days between orders were rounded to a week (7 days), either considerable stockouts or excessive buffer stock to protect against stockouts would result. In either case, costs tend to be excessive in that periodic system.

4. *The periodic system can result in more stockouts when unusually high demand occurs.* When an unusually large demand occurs, because

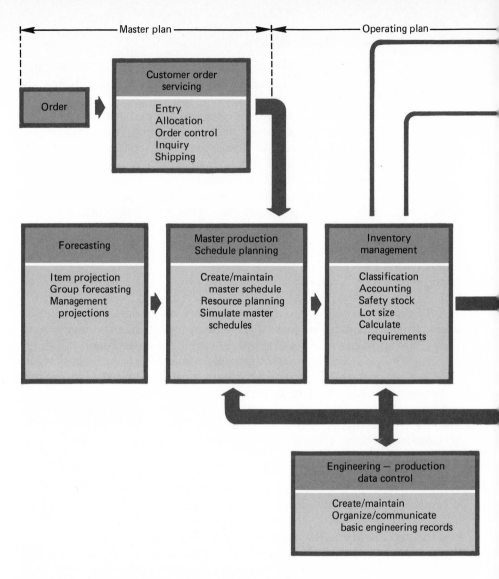

Figure 16-6 COPICS manufacturing—functional flow

Source: IBM, *Communications Oriented Production
Information and Control Systems (COPICS),* Vol 1:
Management Overview and Vol 4: *Inventory Management.*
(IBM order numbers 6320-1974 and 6320-1977).

the Q/R system keeps track of a net inventory with each unit demanded,
it can react more quickly. If two or three random high demands occur
in succession, there is a better chance of avoiding a stockout with immediate
ordering, or reducing the time during which there is a stockout with the
Q/R system. With the periodic, stock is simply gone until an order is
placed at physical inventory time.

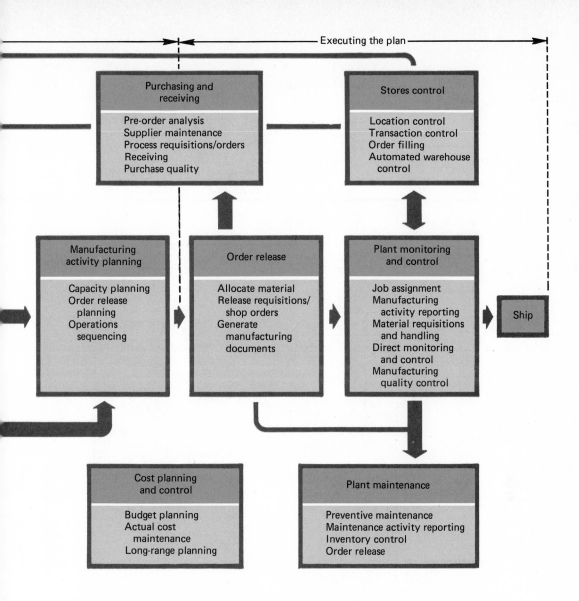

The tradeoffs among these advantages and disadvantages are unique to any one application. Within any one medium or large organization (a hospital, a steel fabricator, an automotive dealer, or a nursery, for example), more than likely both periodic and Q/R systems are useful for different inventory situations.

Material requirements planning (MRP), which we'll discuss next, is an information system for planning and control. MRP is not unique to inventory control and not an inventory control system. We present it here simply because the information in the system relates to inventory; MRP could just as well have been presented alone or with production control and scheduling.

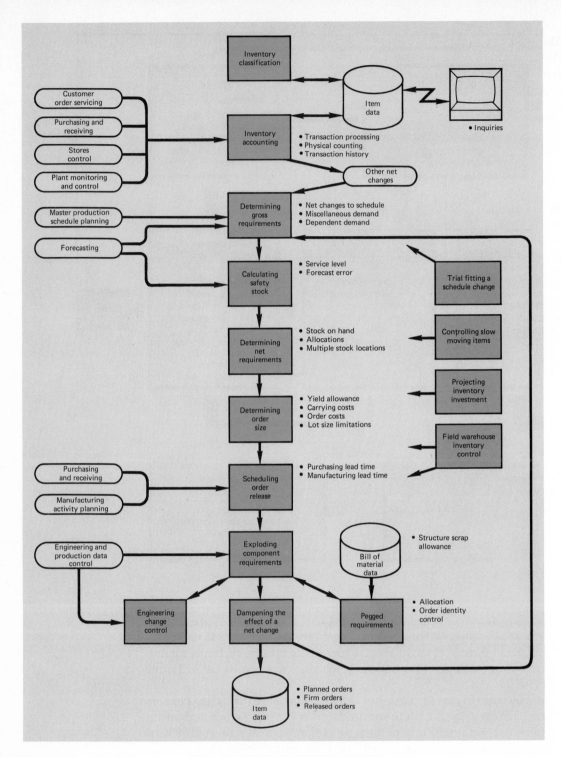

Figure 16-7 **Basic functions of inventory management in COPICS**

Material requirements planning (MRP) is a computerized data information system that can support scheduling and inventory manufacturing functions. The MRP system is a logical means of taking an assembled end item (product) and exploding the item into its component parts. The component parts (materials) are then aggregated according to their due dates (planning). This is the essence of MRP: material (component parts) requirements planning (aggregating all component parts and item sequencing or time phasing them).

**The MRP
environment**

The MRP environment is almost exclusively an assembly manufacturing situation. The assembly can be either continuous manufacturing, as in appliances and automobile manufacturing, or intermittent manufacturing, as in a printing job shop. Figure 16–8 shows how MRP relates to the subsystems required for its operation. These subsystems include a master schedule, an inventory status file, and a bill of material file for product structure. The outputs from the MRP system are order release requirements, order rescheduling, and planned orders (these indicate future capacity utilization).

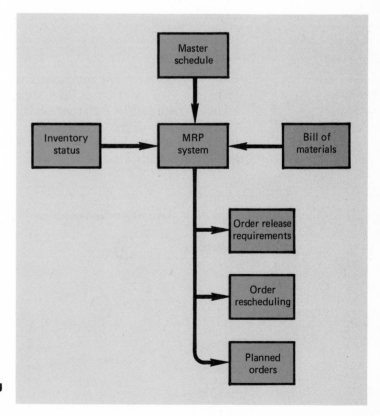

Figure 16-8 **Material
requirements planning
system**

Assumptions underlying MRP

There are several assumptions underlying MRP systems, some of which are not initially obvious. Key assumptions are:

1. A *computer* is readily available to perform the logic calculations in MRP and handle data files.
2. The *product structure* is one having an end item with component parts.
3. An up-to-date, accurate *bill of materials* exists for each part, and it *is computerized.*
4. The *master schedule* is accurate and viewed as deterministic; what is planned will happen.

When these conditions apply to the scheduling/inventory environment in the firm, MRP has demonstrated that it can enhance the efficiency of operations.

Assumptions 1 and 3 are especially critical. Companies that have used computers *before* going to an MRP system are often better prepared for it than companies that have never used computers. It is helpful to have had experience with data files, data integrity, and shop floor control before initiating an MRP system. Computerizing the bill of materials (a listing of all the materials in a given part) file is no small task; it alone can set MRP implementation back a full year if it has been improperly planned.

Product structure

The computerized bill of materials allows the aggregation of like subcomponent parts, even though they might be required in different end items. Look at Figure 16–9. For one A and one D end product, a total of two B subcomponents and three C subcomponents would be required. For complex product structures with tens of thousands of subcomponent parts, the collection (aggregation) of

Figure 16-9 **Two assembled products**

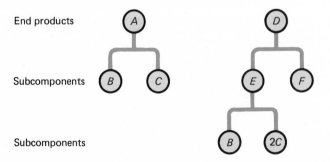

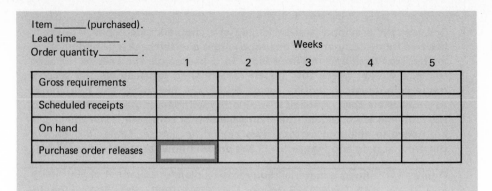

Figure 16-10   **MRP computer printout**

parts by quantity is no small task. It is precisely this kind of task that MRP packages handle very well.

The logic of MRP   The MRP package, which is offered by computer software companies, performs the logic, explodes requirements into the future, offsets lead times, and nets out (computes) on-hand and order balances.[3]

The logic of MRP has been around a long time in production planning; it is simply the perpetual inventory approach:

$$\begin{matrix} \text{Quantity available} \\ \text{for the future} \end{matrix} = \begin{matrix} \text{Quantity} \\ \text{on hand} \end{matrix} + \begin{matrix} \text{Quantity} \\ \text{on order} \end{matrix} - \begin{matrix} \text{Period} \\ \text{requirements} \end{matrix} \qquad (16\text{--}4)$$

An inventory status report provides the clues for material requirements planners. It gives them current on-hand quantities, open orders, and lead times.

Requirements are exploded into the future by combining the master schedule requirements with due dates on the bill of material. Since lead times are known from the inventory file, lead times for the required material can be calculated. Finally, with the MRP system, the on-hand and on-order balances are used to calculate the quantity available for the future. A computer printout for a purchased part may take the general form shown in Figure 16–10. The cell for purchase order releases for the current period, week 1 in Figure 16–10, is called the *action bucket,* since it is this cell that triggers some ordering activity.

---

[3]See Jeffrey G. Miller and Linda G. Sprague, "Behind the Growth in Materials Requirements Planning," *Harvard Business Review* 52, no. 5 (September–October 1975), p. 84.

EXAMPLE

Consider the assembly and packaging of a simple kitchen chair. The chair has two frame components, one for the seat and the back legs and another for the seat back and the front legs. To subassemble the seat to the seat frame, a worker needs four fasteners. Similarly, to assemble the second frame component, a worker needs four more fasteners. The two frame assemblies are then attached to each other with four more fasteners. When the four legs are attached, the chair assembly is complete. Then the chairs are boxed in shipping cartons, two chairs per carton. Table 16–7 shows the product data and Figure 16–11 the product flow for the chair assembly.

Figure 16–12 shows a material requirements plan for shipment of 500 chairs in 8 weeks, and Table 16–8 defines the terms. Items A–G have different on-hand balances, safety stocks, allocations, and lead times. One thing is common—they must all be present in sufficient quantity to support assembly seven weeks from now so that the one-week assembly may be accomplished to meet delivery.

Examining Figure 16–12, we see that item A, the seat frame and back legs, has 50 on hand; 500 are required in seven weeks. However, a safety stock of 20 is required for unexpected demand, and 30 frames have been previously allocated to offer production runs. Thus, the net available for the 500 requirement is zero. Since the lead time for item A is four weeks, the order for 500 must be placed four weeks before required, or in three weeks. Note that the figure reflects a planned order release in week 3 for 500 units.

This figure reflects *a point in time,* in this case eight weeks before required shipment. As time progresses, week by week, for example, the components of the figure can change considerably. If between now and next week 600 additional chairs are ordered to be delivered in week 7, and 20 item A units are allocated to a repair order, two significant changes will be required for item A, and one of these affects the entire figure.

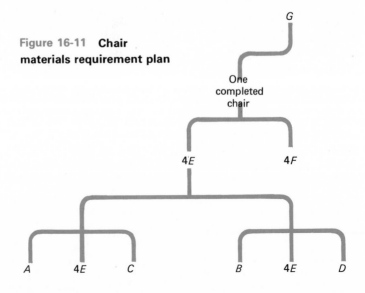

Figure 16-11 Chair materials requirement plan

TABLE 16-7

PRODUCT DATA

Product: Kitchen chair
Ordered quantity: 500

Shipment date: Week 8
Production time: One week

Component items	Description	Average lead time (weeks)	Number of components to produce one chair
A	Frame—seat frame and back legs	4	1
B	Frame—seat back and front legs	4	1
C	Seat base—completed	2	1
D	Seat back—completed	2	1
E	Fasteners	1	12
F	Leg caps	1	4
G	Shipping carton	3	$1/2$

TABLE 16-8

MRP TERMINOLOGY

Term	Definition
On hand	Quantity currently on hand
Safety stock	Required safety stock
Allocated	Previously allocated to other production
Gross requirements	Total need
Scheduled receipt	An open order (either a shop order or a purchase order) from available components; does not represent an order to fabricate or procure the components
Available	Quantity available during a specific time period
Planned order receipts	An order oriented by its due date
Planned order release	An order oriented by its start date

Disadvantages and advantages of MRP

The disadvantages of MRP lie primarily in the assumptions that must be met before MRP can be utilized. A computer is necessary; the product structure must be assembly oriented; bill of materials and inventory

On hand	Safety stock	Allocation	Item number		Week 1	Week 2	Week 3	Week 4	Week 5	Week 6	Week 7	Week 8
50	20	30	A	Gross requirements							500	
				Scheduled receipts								
				Available	-0-	-0-	-0-	-0-	-0-	-0-	-0-	-0-
				Net requirements							500	
				Planned order receipts							500	
				Planned order releases			500					
150	20	30	B	Gross requirements							500	
				Scheduled receipts								
				Available	100	100	100	100	100	100	-0-	-0-
				Net requirements							400	
				Planned order receipts							400	
				Planned order releases			400					
60	20	30	C	Gross requirements							500	
				Scheduled receipts								
				Available	10	10	10	10	10	10	-0-	-0-
				Net requirements							490	
				Planned order receipts							490	
				Planned order releases					490			
52	20	30	D	Gross requirements							500	
				Scheduled receipts								
				Available	2	2	2	2	2	2	-0-	-0-
				Net requirements							498	
				Planned order receipts							498	
				Planned order releases					498			
500	300	150	E	Gross requirements							6000	
				Scheduled receipts								
				Available	50	50	50	50	50	50	-0-	-0-
				Net requirements							5950	
				Planned order receipts							5950	
				Planned order releases						5950		
2000	400	200	F	Gross requirements							2000	
				Scheduled receipts								
				Available	1400	1400	1400	1400	1400	1400	-0-	-0-
				Net requirements							600	
				Planned order receipts							600	
				Planned order releases						600		
200	50	50	G	Gross requirements							250	
				Scheduled receipts								
				Available	100	100	100	100	100	100	-0-	-0-
				Net requirements							150	
				Planned order receipts							150	
				Planned order releases				150				

Figure 16-12 **Product component flow**

status must be assembled and computerized; and a valid master schedule must exist. This last assumption, a required master schedule, *drives the entire MRP system.* The requirement for master scheduling is neither new nor unique to MRP systems. Converting customer orders and/or forecasts into a master schedule is a key part of any manual or computerized production/inventory control system. *The master schedule is critically dependent upon good forecasts or firm orders concerning future demand.* Another disadvantage has to do with data integrity. Unreliable inventory data from the shop floor can wreck a well-planned MRP system. Training personnel to keep accurate records is not an easy task, but it is critical to successful MRP implementation.

MRP has several advantages. The computational power of the digital computer can be utilized on a large scale manufacturing problem. The end product need is exploded *exactly* into the component part needs. The materials information system is *time phased;* the necessary parts information is computed for several periods into the future, not just one period ahead. Finally, the MRP system is dynamic.

The dynamic nature of the MRP system is vital. The MRP system reacts well to changing conditions; it thrives on change. Changing conditions from the master schedule for several periods into the future can affect not only the final required part but also dozens, even hundreds, of component parts. Because the production/inventory data system is computerized, a new MRP computer run can be made, and plans can be revised based on this new information. Since runs might take several hours of computer time for reasonably complex manufacturing environments, however, and since computer costs are high, the MRP system might well be changed as infrequently as once a week. With a dedicated computer or high priority processing, the MRP system could conceivably react almost instantly to changes in customer demands as reflected in the master schedule.

What MRP is not   It is important to understand that MRP is a production/inventory information system. *MRP is not a scheduling approach for aggregate scheduling or for shop day-to-day scheduling.* No standards or actual shop production experience required for scheduling are in the MRP system. *MRP is not an inventory control system.* How much to order and when to order are not a part of the MRP system. The inventory operating doctrine must still be established based on economic criteria, costs that play no part in an MRP system. The MRP information system, however, can allow inventory planning to be extended several periods into the future.[4]

MRP does not do capacity planning. For capacity planning the route sheet must be computerized. (The route sheet shows how many pieces per hour can be produced by machines and/or work centers and gives the technological ordering of tasks needed to complete a part.) The route sheet file is not a prerequisite for an MRP system.

In short, if the assumptions required for implementing any MRP system are met, MRP is an effective production/inventory information system. It can be used to find the time-phased material requirements that

---

[4]See William A. Ruch, "Economic Lot Sizing in MRP: The Marriage of EOQ and MRP." (Paper presented at the 19th Annual Conference, American Production and Inventory Control Society, Atlanta, Georgia, October 1976).

are important input information for production planning, scheduling, and inventory control decisions.[5]

BEHAVIORAL PITFALLS IN INVENTORY CONTROL

Rational decision making

Establishing the inventory operating doctrine involves a decision process that is rational, logical, and unemotional. This decision, based on cost tradeoffs, is typical of the decisions Frederick Taylor thought managers should make. But Taylor believed that people are rational and unemotional, and we know that such is not always the case. As operations managers, you should be aware that people making inventory decisions interject their own biases and individual traits into the decision-making process from time to time. The people you work with are complex, with wants and desires of their own, and they should not be expected to behave like machines. The inventory management *process* is rational, but the people involved in the process are not always rational.

Chain-of-command

It is not unusual to establish rules and methods for inventory control only to find, because of the random nature of demand and lead times, that exceptions occur in demand and lead times. When these exceptions occur, they can usually be resolved at the shop floor, at low levels in the organization. Unfortunately, those in such other organization subsystems as marketing and finance tend to stress particular shortage or overstock situations. Frequently, significant and unnecessary jumps in the chain-of-command are encouraged within the operations subsystem, and operations managers at a policy level start making decisions best made by those near the inventory situation, who are closely acquainted with the variables involved. Often top management makes schedule changes that upset the careful plans of diligent, hard working, intelligent clerical and lower-level supervisors. As a result, severe oscillations in the overall schedule can occur.

Feedback

Operations managers must monitor inventory levels and make adjustments within the production planning and control process when they discover that actual output deviates from planned output. These adjustments might well involve decisions to build inventory, reduce inventory, or change inventory procedures and operating doctrines. There can be no *control* in inventory without three activities:

---

[5] For more details on MRP, see W. L. Berry and D. Clay Whybark, "Research Perspecting for Material Requirements Planning System," *Production and Inventory Management* (June 1975), pp. 19–25, James H. Green, *Production and Inventory Control, Systems and Decisions* (Homewood, Ill.: Richard D. Irwin, Inc., 1974), pp. 243–67; and Joseph A. Orlicky, *Materials Requirements Planning* (New York: McGraw Hill Book Co., 1975).

1. monitoring of performance and inventory levels,
2. feedback to decision makers comparing actual performance and material usage with planned performance and usage, and
3. adjustment of inputs to the conversion process, especially the capital inputs of inventory.

Feedback should include formal status reports, prepared manually or by the computer, as well as visual feedback obtained by touring the facility. There is no good substitute for walking through the conversion process yourself—whether your organization is a bank, a restaurant, a school, or a manufacturing facility. When you see the conversion process yourself, you can compare your first-hand observations with planned conditions and quickly make adjustments for discrepancies you may find.

Inventory policy   Often, top management adjusts aggregate inventory levels. These manufacturing and operations policy decisions should be well grounded in cost analysis. The policy decisions about aggregate levels of inventory changes should then be converted to specific items by middle management, first-line management, and clerical personnel. Again, we need to emphasize the dynamic nature of inventory. Overreacting to a problem by changing inventory levels can result in higher costs in aggregate planning, material requirements planning, physical distribution, and scheduling. All these activities and subsystems depend upon production/operations management inventory decisions that are not themselves dynamic.

Individual risk-taking propensity   As you probably know from your own experience, people vary considerably in their tendencies to take chances. Some people thrive on taking risks; others are risk-averse. Any banker can tell you that among checking account customers are a certain percentage who keep far too many cash reserves in noninterest-bearing accounts because they are afraid of future uncertainty. Operating managers can also be risk-averse. In their overreactions to the possibility of a stockout, they may carry excessive buffer stocks.

On the other hand, some people are high rollers, risk takers. As operations managers or supervisors, people who take excessive risks are just as damaging to inventory control as are people who are too risk-averse. They may allow inventory levels to vary drastically and cause stockouts, high costs, and adverse effects in other operations subsystems. Individual propensity to take risks within the organization's inventory control procedures should be assessed carefully. Extreme behaviors are costly to operations.

SUMMARY   Stochastic (variable) inventory models are required when demand is variable, lead time is variable, or both demand and lead time vary. A distribution of demand, lead time, or demand during lead time can be described by its mean and standard deviation.

The operations manager is most interested in the distribution of demand during lead time; this is a critical factor in establishing buffer stocks and the reorder point. When *both* demand and lead time vary, we must use trial-and-error in establishing the operating doctrine.

Money can be saved in inventory systems by evaluating the ABC classification, blanket rules, stochastic demand and lead times, high stockout cost items, safety stocks, decoupled operations, and raw material and finished goods inventory.

There are numerous inventory control procedures for practical application, among them the cardex file system and IBM's COPICS. The cardex file system is a manually operated system in which an inventory card represents each stock item and transactions are kept on the card. The COPICS system is a manufacturing information system with a common data base. Inventory management is one module that utilizes this data base.

Material requirements planning is a computerized data information system that can support scheduling and inventory manufacturing functions. Specific assumptions or conditions must be met before MRP is applicable. MRP is not an inventory control system; it is a data information system.

Primarily, inventory control is a rational process that lends itself to logical procedures. Behavioral pitfalls in inventory control involve the irrationality of decision makers, a tendency to jump the chain-of-command in reaction to stockout conditions, lack of control, irrationally established inventory policies, and the variability in people's propensity to take risks.

Good Shepherd Home

CASE   The Good Shepherd Home is a long-term care facility with an 80 bed capacity located in San Mateo, California. Mr. Scott, the administrator, is concerned about rising food costs. He questions whether administration is as efficient as it might be and realizes that food, a "raw material" for his food services, has increased in price significantly. Mr. Scott decides to investigate food services more closely.

Analyzing last month's purchased items, Mr. Scott summarizes a random selection of items. Mr. Scott wonders what interpretation he should make about these typical items. He has looked at 100 stock items and is considering tighter controls on the 40 stock items that resulted in 400 quantities (dozen, cases, pounds, etc.) being ordered.

GOOD SHEPHERD TYPICAL INVENTORY ITEMS

Number of stock items	Quantity ordered	Total cost	Average inventory
3	50	$3,500	$1,200
12	150	2,500	900
20	200	1,500	600
40	400	2,000	200
25	200	500	100

Of particular interest is a problem with a perishable good, bread. Since the home has residents from independent living units eating at the home irregularly, bread demand is uneven. Bread is delivered daily and is only used that day for table meal service; the day-old bread is salvaged for dressings and similar items. Scott estimates the cost of bread to be 30¢/loaf and the cost of day-old bread to be 10¢/loaf. Scott says, "We should not be out of fresh bread at the table. Although man cannot live by bread alone, it is very important to our residents. I put a high cost on being out of bread—considerably more than the cost of a loaf. In fact, I think every time we run out of bread, it costs a dollar per loaf short in good will lost from our residents." Knowing he feels this way, the food services supervisor has a standing order for 30 loaves per day and twice that amount on Sunday. The demand for bread the last two weeks is shown below.

GOOD SHEPHERD BREAD DEMAND

	Week 1		Week 2	
Day	Bread demand	Day		Bread demand
Mon	20	Mon		19
Tue	15	Tue		27
Wed	21	Wed		20
Thu	30	Thu		32
Fri	31	Fri		27
Sat	19	Sat		16
Sun	42	Sun		39

In conversation with Mr. Scott, the supervisor says, "I recently heard about cost tradeoffs in food service inventory. I don't really see what item cost, carrying cost, ordering costs, and stockout costs have to do with proper nutrition. I try to buy good quality foods and spend less than $3.00 per day per resident on food. That's my objective." Mr. Scott has heard about cost tradeoffs too, but he wonders what they mean and how they could assist in a nursing home environment. To try to understand this better he talked to his bookkeeper. The supervisor says that she knows with certainty that demand for hamburger over a menu cycle is 200 pounds. Further, the bookkeeper estimates it costs $10 to place an order and 20 percent of the hamburger cost to carry hamburger in inventory. Hamburger costs 70¢ per pound. The dietitian says a menu cycle lasts 2 weeks, and we currently order hamburger every week. Mr. Scott is puzzled by all this.

1. Explain two common ways to measure and establish service levels, giving an example of each.

2. Discuss the primary assumptions underlying a material requirements planning (MRP) system.

3. What is meant by the ABC classification? How might an organization's inventory be analyzed using the ABC classification?

4. Discuss at least three advantages and disadvantages of a material requirements planning (MRP) system.

5. Inventory control is a rational process in which decisions are often made irrationally. Explain.

6. Given a probability distribution of demand and a distribution of lead time, what alternatives exist for finding the probability distribution of demand during lead time? Select one alternative and explain how it works. Why is the distribution of demand during lead time important?

7. For Figure 16–3, explain how lead time and demand vary. What impact does such variation have on buffer stocks, if any?

8. Suppose a directive comes to a manufacturing facility from the controller strongly suggesting a 35-percent across the board reduction in inventory levels. The plant manager asks you to assist him in explaining the need for inventories in manufacturing. What points would you make in favor of having inventories to as-sist the plant manager in answering the controller?

9. Select two general areas in which money might be saved in inventory control and explain how you would plan a cost study for each.

10. Discuss the advantages and disadvantages of the periodic inventory system compared to the quantity-reorder inventory system.

11. Explain the essential features of a material requirements planning (MRP) system. A flow chart or diagram might be useful to organize your discussion.

12. Relate the perpetual inventory logic of MRP to the example in the chapter on planning kitchen chair assemblies. Illustrate how the logic was utilized in Figure 16–12.

13. Relate individual propensity for risk taking to decision making in inventory control.

PROBLEMS

1. The daily demand for a component assembly item is normally distributed with a mean of 60 and standard deviation of 7. Further, the source of supply is reliable and maintains a constant lead time of three days. If the cost of placing the order is $20 and annual holding costs are 50¢ per unit, find the order quantity and reorder point to satisfy 75 percent of the customers who place orders during the reorder period. There are no stockout costs, and unfilled orders are filled as soon as an order arrives. Assume sales occur over the entire year.

2. Daily demand for pickles for a local chain of fast food restaurants is normally distributed with a mean of 30 jars and a standard deviation of 7. Supply is virtually certain with a lead time of two days; the cost of placing an order is $2.50, and annual holding costs are 80 percent of the unit price of 60¢ per jar. A 98-percent service level is desired. The restaurant chain serves 365 days a year.
    (a) Determine the operating doctrine for ordering pickles.
    (b) Construct graphs similar to Figures 16–3 and 16–4 to portray this situation.
    (c) What is the annual cost for pickle buffer stocks? Does this cost seem reasonable for a 98-percent service level?

3. For the fast food restaurant chain in problem 2, suppose that exactly the same situation exists for coffee as did for pickles, except that coffee costs ten times as much per can as do pickles per jar.
    (a) What is the operating doctrine for coffee?
    (b) What is the annual cost for coffee buffer stocks?

(c) What conclusions can you reach concerning the effect price has on operating doctrine and buffer stocks (by comparing your answer to problem 2)?

4. For the fast food restaurant chain in problem 2 suppose that exactly the same situation exists for chocolate syrup as did for pickles, except that chocolate syrup demand is 30 cans per day with a standard deviation of 28 cans.
   (a) What is the operating doctrine for chocolate syrup?
   (b) What is the annual cost for chocolate syrup buffer stocks?
   (c) What impact does the variability of demand (the standard deviation) seem to have on buffer stocks (by comparing your answer to problem 2)?

5. Consider the assembly and packaging of a kitchen chair in the MRP example provided in the chapter (including Tables 16–7 and 16–8 and Figures 16–11 and 16–12). Trace the impact of each of the following on the material requirements plan. (Consider each to be an independent change to the example; these are not a sequence of changes.)
   (a) The lead time on fasteners has increased to three weeks, and the lead time on frame-seat frame and back legs decreased to two weeks.
   (b) You are currently in week 2, seven weeks before planned shipment of 500 chairs. You have the opportunity to double the order to 1,000 chairs. Marketing needs a decision quickly on accepting or rejecting the order. Can material plans be changed to support acceptance of the order?
   (c) Safety stock on items E and F must be increased to 1,000 and 900 units as soon as possible. You are still in week 1. What should be done?
   (d) Engineering has issued a change notice to include an extra leg cap with each chair for customer replacement. You are at the beginning of week 7. What impact will this change have on delivery if it is honored?

6. The demand per period for an inventory item seems to have the following probability distribution:

Demand (D)	Probability of demand occurring
5	0.2
6	0.4
7	0.3
8	0.1

All stock to meet the demand for a period must be acquired at the start of the period. The product costs $4 per unit and sells for $7 per unit. Any leftover at the end of a period must be disposed of as "seconds" at a selling price of $3 per unit. On the other hand, if the stock becomes depleted, there is no cost associated with the shortage.
   (a) Under the above conditions, will it be more profitable to stock six or seven units at the start of each period?
   (b) If there were a cost associated with a shortage and a probability of a shortage for each demand level, how would you modify part (a)?

7. You find yourself, as operations manager of a group of stock market analysts for a small brokerage firm, faced with the following problem. The company's market research group suggests you "follow" (analyze) some "risky" stocks, as some customers desire this kind of investment. They estimate maximum demand from any one "high risk taker" to be in any one month:

Number of risky stocks demanded	Probability of this number being demanded
2	0.30
4	0.20
5	0.10
6	0.30
8	0.10

They also assess a cost associated with not having the number of risky stocks demanded to be $100 (loss of customer possibilities). Further, you know that your unit costs per month (C) to "follow" stocks are:

$$C = \left\{ \begin{array}{l} \$25D \text{ for } D \leq 4 \\ \$15D \text{ elsewhere} \end{array} \right\}$$

where D is the number of risky stocks demanded. How many risky stocks should you "follow" each month?

GLOSSARY

ABC classification: inventory division with three groupings, an A grouping for a few items with a large dollar volume, a B grouping for items with moderate volume and moderate dollar volume, and a C grouping for items with a large volume and small dollar volume

Bill of materials: a listing of all materials required to produce a part

Cardex file: manually operated system when an inventory card represents each stock item with transactions kept on the card

COPICS: Communications Oriented Production Information and Control System; IBM's computerized common data base manufacturing information system

Individual risk taking propensity: degree to which individuals tend to take or avoid chances

Lead time demand: units of stock demanded during lead time; can be described by a probability distribution in stochastic situations

Master schedule: the conversion of customer orders and/or forecasts into time phased quantities due

MRP: Material Requirements Planning; a computerized data information system that can support scheduling and inventory manufacturing functions

Service level: treatment policy for customers when there are stockouts; commonly established either as a ratio of *customers* served to demanded or a ratio of *units* supplied to demanded

SELECTED
READINGS

Berry, W.L. and D. Clay Whybark. "Research Perspectives for Material Requirements Planning Systems." *Production and Inventory Management* (June 1975): 19–25.

Buchan, J. and E. Koenigsberg. *Scientific Inventory Control.* Englewood Cliffs, N.J.: Prentice-Hall, Inc., 1963.

Buffa, E.S. and W.H. Taubert. *Production-Inventory Systems: Planning and Control.* Homewood, Ill.: Richard D. Irwin, Inc., 1972.

Green, James H. *Production and Inventory Control Systems and Decisions.* Rev. Ed.

Homewood, Ill.: Richard D. Irwin, Inc., 1974.

Hadley, G. and T.M. Whitin. *Analysis of Inventory Systems.* Englewood Cliffs, N.J.: Prentice-Hall, Inc., 1963.

IBM. *Communications Oriented Production Information and Control Systems (COPICS).* Vol. 1. *Management Overview* and Vol. 4. *Inventory Management.* (Order numbers G320-1974 and G320-1977). White Plains, N.Y., 1972.

Magee, J.F. and D.M. Boodman. *Production Planning and Inventory Control.* 2nd ed. New York: McGraw-Hill Book Co., 1967.

Miller, Jeffrey G. and Linda G. Sprague. "Behind the Growth in Material Requirements Planning." *Harvard Business Review* 53, no. 5 (September–October 1975): 83–91.

Orlicky, Joseph A. *Material Requirements Planning.* New York: McGraw-Hill Book Co., 1975.

Plossl, George W. and Oliver W. Wight. *Material Requirements Planning by Computer.* Washington, D.C.: American Production and Inventory Control Society, 1971.

Ruch, William A. "Economic Lot Sizing in MRP: The Marriage of EOQ and MRP." Paper presented at the 19th Annual Conference, American Production and Inventory Control Society. Atlanta, Georgia, 1976.

Starr, Martin K. and D.W. Miller. *Inventory Control: Theory and Practice.* Englewood Cliffs, N.J.: Prentice-Hall, Inc., 1962.

17 Quality Control

In examining the fundamentals of production/operations management we have discussed planning, organizing, and, in the last three chapters, control. We have stressed efficiency and effectiveness in the conversion of resources into goods or services. Efficiency requires as little waste as possible in the proper use of employees, materials, equipment, and other resources. It is often measured as an *actual* quantity relative to a *desired* quantity. Effectiveness has to do with goal accomplishment. The goals of operations managers are often related to quantity of output, cost, and quality. In this chapter we'll examine one of these goals, establishing and maintaining an acceptable quality level. Quality control, like all the other aspects of production/operations management, is intertwined with the planning, organizing, and other controlling activities of P/OM managers (see Figure 17–1).

The behavioral and modeling aspects of planning, organizing, and controlling quality have special meaning. Traditionally in operations management, quality control has been approached as a problem lending itself to solution with statistical techniques. Certainly statistical techniques are very useful in modeling quality control; both sampling theory and statistical inference have made major contributions. But quality control requires the application of some specific behavioral considerations too. In this chapter we'll stress both modeling and behavior. Using the two together can help managers meet their quality goals.

PRODUCT QUALITY

Product (output) quality

The conversion process is operated to produce a product—not just any product but one possessing specific characteristics. The product's important characteristics

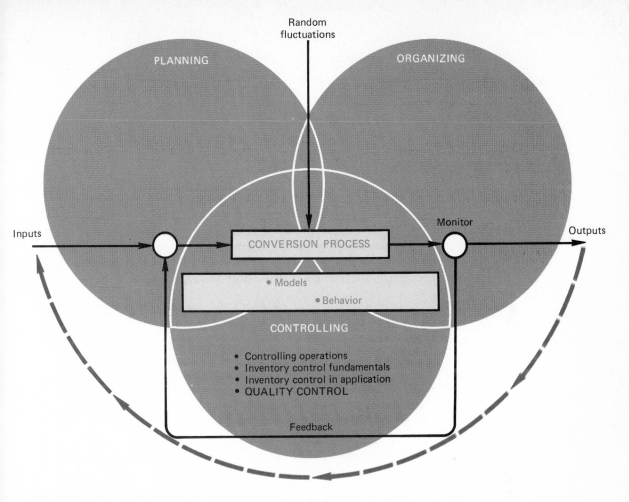

Figure 17-1 **Production/operations management activities**

are specified when it is designed prior to its manufacture. These characteristics are called the *design specifications*. After the product has been produced, we can observe the extent to which it conforms to or deviates from the design specifications. *Product (output) quality is the degree to which the product conforms to the design specifications.*

When there is close conformance between design and output characteristics, there is a high degree of product (output) quality. When there are important discrepancies, there is a low level of quality. Product quality can be seen to fall on a continuum ranging from very low to very high, as Figure 17–2 shows.

Product characteristics   All aspects of the product are not equally important to our customers. Usually, only some of them need be considered when assessing the level of quality. But which aspects are most important? Weight? Size? Shape? Color? Functional performance? *The important product characteristics are determined by the*

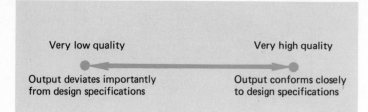

Figure 17-2 **Degrees of output quality**

specific market goals of the organization and by the technical requirements of the important stages of the transformation process. Often we must compromise between these two sources of quality requirements.

A well-founded decision to create a product is based on an identification of the market for which the product will be produced; product characteristics are shaped by the specific market goals of the organization.

EXAMPLE

Not all financial institutions, magazines, or automobiles are similar in product quality or market goals. Credit unions, for example, provide financial services to a different market from that serviced by banks and savings and loan institutions. *Playboy* magazine was designed to appeal to readers with a different set of interests from those who read *Mechanics Illustrated*. Likewise, Mercedes automobiles appeal to a market segment distinctly different from that Volkswagon aims at.

In each of these cases we can identify some major characteristics distinguishing one product from another. These distinguishing features identify the product characteristics that are aimed at a particular market. A magazine's important characteristics might include a prescribed balance among pictorial content, fiction writing, and current events. The magazine's goals may also specify the level of sophistication of its articles and the clarity and tone of its photographs. These are identifiable critical product characteristics. Market success depends upon the organization's ability to obtain a suitable level of adherence to these attributes; that is, its ability to attain an acceptable quality level.

The second source for identifying crucial product characteristics is the conversion process that creates the product. Conversion processes often consist of a sequence of successive stages, in which quality requirements for one technical stage are imposed on other stages. Consider the hospital transformation process in Figure 17-3. This diagram shows several substages of the technical processes required to obtain the desired output, a well patient. Follow the sequence of subprocesses in reverse order, beginning with the final stage, dismissal. Prior to dismissal the patient must have treatment which may take the form of physical therapy, radiology, surgery, and so on. The proper choice among these treatments must be based on the physician's skills and experience. In making diagnoses, physicians frequently rely on information received from analyses performed in earlier stages (X-ray and lab tests). In many instances this information must be of a certain form and content. If it does not conform, the physician's ability to accomplish the product quality goals may be hindered. Satisfactory processing in the diagnosis stage, then, often depends on the previous stages. We can therefore expect specific procedural and/or performance requirements to be imposed on the X-ray and laboratory stages. Requirements might include, for example, size, clarity, and number of photographs, and specific items of information and their forms. The point is clear. Many of the product specifications imposed on early stages are dictated by the needs of succeeding stages. Furthermore, to accomplish a specific output goal the *technical processes* at some stages are more important than those at other stages. Certainly, proper diagnosis and treatment are of greater importance than the kinds of forms used in admitting. Why? Because the potential consequences of a diagnostic or treatment error may be grave indeed. The technical requirements of the important stages in the transformation process clearly shape product quality characteristics.

Process capability   A maximum quality level, or upper capability limit, can be established for every technical process. If the operations manager can select the best material and the best operator in the plant and arrange for all the equipment to be properly set-up and operated, output can be produced under carefully controlled, ideal conditions. Say that under these conditions, output averages 1 percent defective (1 percent of the units produced are unacceptable). In this case, 1 percent defective is the upper bound on quality level; it is the *process capability*. Two things are important to remember about process capability. First, in general there are errors in conversion operations because of the random variability of materials, people, and equipment. Process capability is *not* necessarily zero errors. Second, the process capability is not necessarily the most efficient level of production. In fact, most processes should be priced and operated for a higher quantity and lower quality level than the process capability. The costs of producing at the upper limit of capability can be exorbitant.

Now let us return for a moment to the operations manager's basic functions: planning, organizing, and controlling. If quality goals are to be met, all three activities must be performed.

Figure 17-3   **Hospital transformation process**

Planning

Output quality cannot be left to chance; goals for quality must be established. As quality goals are established, management becomes involved in quality design considerations, product reliability, and quality assurance, systematic efforts to assess overall final output quality.

Design

Of two firms producing the same product, one may have to pay high costs to maintain an acceptable quality level while its competitor can maintain the same quality at a much lower cost. The difference is often a result of the emphasis placed on quality considerations in the design phases of product development, prior to full-scale production. The old adage, "quality is *designed into* the product," holds true. Seemingly minor modifications in product design can dramatically increase ability to reach desired output quality once production has begun. The number of stages in the conversion process, the types of input resources needed, and the types of technical processes required to produce the output are all largely determined in the product design phase. All these, in turn, play a large role in determining the costs of controlling output quality throughout the life of the product. It is not surprising, then, that organizations often have a quality specialist as part of the product-and-process-design team. Quality is not inspected into a Rolls-Royce; it is designed and built in. Only when rigorous specifications are set and met does a product of high quality emerge. The same design-for-production strategy can hold for other cars with less rigorous specifications, as we know from General Motors Corporation's successful market strategy of designing and producing cars for various market segments.

Of course product-and-process design does not end when production begins. Design often continues throughout the product life in the form of various redesign activities. Redesign may be initiated in response /to unplanned or unexpected circumstances that arise after the original product design phase. These redesign needs are signaled by reliability studies, quality assurance programs, and customer complaints.

Reliability

The product's useful life span, or the expected duration of its performance, makes up its reliability. Products like bandages, nails, and food are expected to have short lives or to be used only once. Other products, refrigerators, for instance, consist of many subcomponents expected to function in concert over extended time periods. Life expectancies for these products are not left to chance; the products and their subcomponents are designed to meet minimum reliability standards. Our product must be sufficiently reliable to enable us to compete effectively in the marketplace. Once we have determined the desired reliability for our product, two basic design questions arise: What reliability is required of each of its subcomponents if we wish to achieve the reliability goal for the final product? Which subcomponents should be used?

Often a final product does not perform properly unless *all* of its subcomponents function correctly. As soon as one or more subcomponents fail, the total product is disabled; the useful life of the product is ended. In cases such as these the reliabilities of individual subcomponents must be greater than the reliability desired for the final product. This situation exists whenever the chances of failure of each subcomponent are independent of each other.

Product reliability is usually expressed in terms of a probability. The probability of the system functioning successfully equals the product of the probabilities of all its subcomponents.

In the design strategy, then, we first specify the desired reliability of the final product. Then we determine what subcomponent reliability is required to accomplish this overall reliability. Once reliability has been met, we can base subcomponent selection on economic considerations.

========== EXAMPLE ==========

Suppose we wish to produce a product consisting of two subcomponents. We want the product to have a useful life expectancy of one year with .90 probability. The product functions successfully only as long as *both* subcomponents function. Upon failure of one (or both) subcomponents the product ceases to function. How reliable must each subcomponent be? Usually the more reliable the subcomponent the greater its cost. Furthermore, the increase in cost is often greater than the increase in reliability. This is reflected in the table, which shows the prices we must pay vendors to supply the two subcomponents for various levels of reliability.

Subcomponent	Reliability of subcomponent		
	.90	.95	.98
A	$50	$90	$140
B	$70	$90	$110

Although subcomponent failure rates are independent, the success of our product depends on both operating successfully. Since we want a product reliability of .90, we select subcomponents each having .90 reliability. The resulting product will meet our reliability standard if subcomponent *A* operates successfully for one year and subcomponent *B* operates successfully for one year. These two events each have .90 probability of occurring. The probability of *both* events occurring is $.90 \times .90 = .81$, which is the reliability of the final product. We see, then, that subcomponent reliability must be greater than the desired reliability of the final product.

What would be the result of using subcomponents *A* and *B* when each has .98 reliability? Multiplying subcomponent probabilities we find the overall probability to be:

$$P = (.98)(.98)$$
$$= .9604$$

For *A* and *B* having .95 reliabilities:

$$P = (.95) (.95)$$
$$= .9025$$

Both of these options would meet or exceed the desired product reliability. It is important to note that as the number of subcomponents in the system increases, the reliability of each must be increased if final product reliability is to be met. As we said before, these greater requirements are usually obtained only at greater subcomponent cost. As product reliability standards are increased, the costs of supplying such a product can increase dramatically.

Which versions of subcomponents *A* and *B* should be used in our product? We answer the question by first identifying all combinations of *A* and *B* that satisfy our overall reliability goal. Then we pick the combination of *A* and *B* that is least costly. Four alternative combinations of *A* and *B* meet or exceed the product reliability goal; five combinations are unsatisfactory.

Overall Reliabilities

Alternative	Subcomponents		Overall reliability
	A	*B*	
1	.95	.95	.9025
2	.98	.98	.9604
3	.95	.98	.9310
4	.98	.95	.9310
5	.90	.90	.8100 (unsatisfactory)
6	.90	.95	.8550 (unsatisfactory)
7	.90	.98	.8820 (unsatisfactory)
8	.95	.90	.8550 (unsatisfactory)
9	.98	.90	.8820 (unsatisfactory)

We now use cost criteria to evaluate the satisfactory alternatives, 1 through 4:

Costs for Different Subcomponent Reliabilities

Alternative	Cost
1	$ 90 + 90 = $180
2	140 + 110 = 250
3	90 + 110 = 200
4	140 + 70 = 210

We would select alternative 1 on the basis of economic criteria.

As you can see, reliability analysis requires probabilities of successful operation of subcomponents. This information, called failure-rate data, is obtained from test results. An evaluation of how subcomponent failures can affect overall system reliability helps in evaluating alternative changes in product design.

Quality assurance   Like product design and reliability, quality assurance is part of the quality planning function. Quality assurance programs commonly involve systematic efforts to assess the overall level of output (final product) quality. They determine current quality levels and trends in these levels, and they make comparisons with the quality levels of competitors. This information is used in product and process redesign, market strategy, and product pricing decisions. Organized information sources for assurance may include:

- product life tests, or accelerated life tests that can include destructive testing,
- analysis laboratories for determining the causes of product failures,
- sampling of finished products to detect deficiencies, and
- establishment of field representatives to examine "in-use" product performance.

After product standards have been set by management, they must be checked. Since these product standards involve so many aspects of quality control, the costs of quality assurance are high. Prevention, appraisal, and internal and external failure costs, outlined in Table 17-1, are all quality assurance costs.

Another way to visualize costs of quality assurance is in terms of cost tradeoffs. These are similar to total cost and cost components tradeoffs in inventory control. There is a basic tradeoff between *control costs* (those in Table 17-1) and the *cost of undetected defects*. Figure 17-4 illustrates these tradeoffs in general form. Although operations managers may not have precise cost data, they will have at least a rough idea of how these costs behave. They may have to be quite astute to find where an optimal or even a good cost tradeoff position is located. A real curve certainly will not be so smooth as the simple curve of total costs in Figure 17-4. As this curve vividly illustrates, perfect output is usually not a wise goal; costs of achieving it would be prohibitive. Reasonably accurate cost data will show that some degree of output imperfection should be tolerated.

Organizing

Often, quality control in manufacturing firms is organized in a way distinctly different from the way it is organized in service organizations. Usually, quality control in manufacturing is a staff function established

TABLE 17-1

COSTS OF QUALITY ASSURANCE

Prevention (costs associated with design and planning of a quality control (QC) program)	Appraisal (costs involved in the direct appraisal of quality both in the plant and in the field)	Internal failure (costs directly related to the occurrence of defective production within the plant)	External failure (costs associated with the failure of a product or service in the field)

QC administration and systems planning
Quality training
Quality planning (QC engineering work)
  Incoming, in-process, final inspection, and test planning
  Special processes planning
  Quality data analysis and feedback
  Procurement planning
  Vendor surveys, audit and surveillance planning
  Reliability studies
Design and development of quality measurement and control equipment
Qualification of material
	Testing
	Inspection
	Quality audits
	Incoming test and inspection and laboratory acceptance
	Checking labor
	Laboratory or other measurement service
	Setup for test and inspection
	Test and inspection material
	Outside endorsements
	Maintenance and calibration
	Product engineering review and shipping release
	Field testing
		Scrap, at full shop cost
		Rework, at full shop cost
		Scrap and rework, fault of vendor
		Material procurement
		Factory contact engineering
		QC investigations (of failures)
		Material review activity
		Repair and troubleshooting
			Complaints and loss of customer good will
			Warranty costs
			Field maintenance and product service
			Returned material processing and repair
			Replacement inventories
			Strained distributor relations

Adapted from J. W. Gavett, *Production and Operations Management* (New York: Harcourt Brace Jovanovich, Inc., 1968), pp. 401–402.

to monitor, police, and assist in corrective action. Figure 17-5 illustrates a quality control organization that is common in medium to large companies. Within the quality control group are a manager, quality assurance engineers, quality technicians, and an inspection function. Occasionally, process engineers are also grouped here. Note that the quality control function reports directly to the plant manager and indirectly also to the works manager. Quality control responsibilities are usually separated from line production responsibilities so as to obtain unbiased assessments of product quality. Consequently, conflict sometimes arises between quality control and production personnel. When this happens it's the plant manager's responsibility to manage and mediate the conflict situation. Whether the

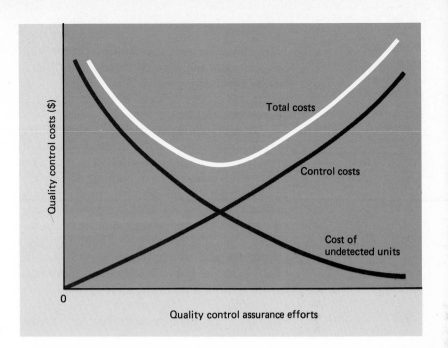

Figure 17-4 **Quality assurance cost tradeoffs**

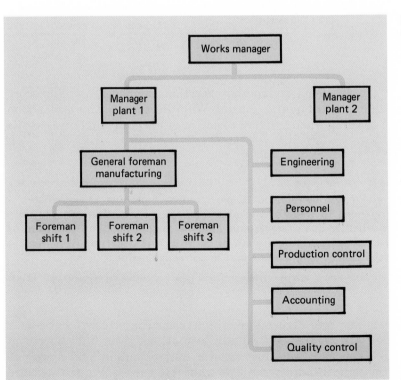

Figure 17-5 **Organizing quality control in manufacturing**

plant manager can maintain a proper balance between product quality and production quantity in these conflict situations depends to a large extent upon the person. Some plant managers handle it very well and others not so well. This example organization structure is only one of several possibilities.

In service organizations, quality control is frequently maintained by operating personnel without additional staff. The organization structure may therefore be somewhat different from manufacturing firms. The burdens of measurement, comparison feedback, and correction fall upon line managers or administrators. Since quality is determined in the line in the first place, it seems reasonable for line personnel to be directly responsible for overseeing quality. Often, however, line personnel feel pressure to meet production schedules; they feel that time is not available to monitor and control the process adequately. When this is true, output quality may suffer. Nonetheless, many service organizations rely on the integrity and conscientiousness of line employees to attain quality of output. In a university or a college, for example, there is little if any formal quality control, aside from the teachers' own efforts, of the teaching function. Perhaps some of your professors could use some occasional monitoring of their teaching by staff or even by direct supervisors.

All the things we've discussed so far—different ways of defining lines of authority and responsibility, grouping quality control and inspection people together—influence product or service quality. But quality is still inadequate, even if it has been planned and organized, unless it is also controlled.

Controlling

Of all the problems facing the operations manager, none is more demanding than product quality control. Why? Because control is an action process, and deciding when and how to activate this process requires astute judgment.

=== **EXAMPLE** ===

Suppose you have identified a single important product characteristic, length. You need to monitor the output of your conversion process to determine whether this characteristic adheres to specifications. If it does, the process is operating in a state of control. If it does not, you must entertain the idea of taking some sort of corrective action.

This process is shown in Figure 17-6. Think of the characteristics of length as you review the figure. Several things must exist for the process to be complete. Obviously, we must have a unit of output and a way of measuring the critical characteristic we want it to possess. We can measure

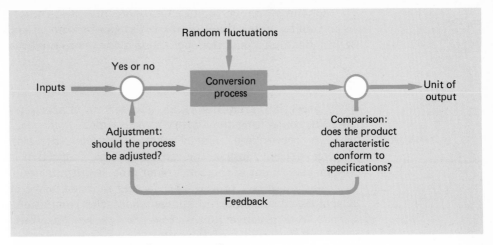

Figure 17-6   **Feedback of output quality**

length in feet, inches, or centimeters. This measurement provides sufficient information for concluding what actually exists. Next we enter a comparison phase, in which we compare what actually exists with what is desired. If the length measurement conforms satisfactorily to product standards (length specifications), we transmit the conformance information to those operating the conversion process and no action follows. On the other hand, deviations between what actually exists and what is desired signal the need for further activity.

All these preliminary phases lead up to and support the action phase. You may remember from Chapter 14 that control involves action in response to the comparison phase of the process. The distinguishing feature of control is its *action* content. When the conversion process is operating, product quality always exists. It may be very high, low, or intermediate, but it is always there. Quality *control*, however, does not always exist. It exists only when *deliberate action* is undertaken to cause output characteristics to conform to desired levels.

Measurement plays an important role in quality control. In our example, we noted that length was a critical characteristic. We could check the length of the product in two ways: we could measure and record actual length, or we could test to see if actual length falls within upper and lower limits. If we measure by actual length, we measure by *variable*; this requires some specified scaled physical dimension—weight, volume, length, or sound. If we test to see whether length falls within upper and lower limits, we measure by *attribute*. When we measure by attribute, the product is either good or bad; either it falls within the limits, or it doesn't. With attribute measurements, we have only two choices, accept or reject; with variable measurement, we have a wide continuum of choices. Deciding whether to measure by variable or by attribute depends on matters we will discuss later, when we consider control charts. The kind of measurement we use determines the kind of control chart we select.

Of the planning, organizing, and controlling functions none is more important to quality than control. Let's examine some models and behavioral techniques that assist the operations manager in quality control.

MODELS IN QUALITY CONTROL

Inspection, sampling plans, and control charts are all used daily to assist in controlling the quality of operations. *Inspection* of raw material, work-in-process, and finished products provides the basic data needed for the comparison phase of the control process. Inspection is the observation and measurement of the conversion process outputs and inputs.

Sampling is a process of selecting representative observations from a population to make inferences about the population. We sample the output from a conversion process for two reasons. First, sampling tells us about the quality of the output itself. Examining only a few ears of corn can give us an idea about the quality of the entire wagon load of corn from which the ears were taken. The usual model for this is called a *sampling plan.* Secondly, we can sample the output to tell us about the process that produced it. We might examine the quality of a sample of corn to tell us some things about the agricultural system from which it came; is this farm producing at the same quality level it was in previous years? The usual devices for this sort of control are called *control charts.*

Inspection

Inspection can be done either visually or mechanically; its purpose is to see whether the physical characteristics of the good or service conform with specifications. Inspection usually involves checking actual output units against product specifications and recording whether the product was good or bad as well as the degree of deviation from the specifications. Inspection is commonly divided into three areas: receiving inspection, work-in-process inspection, and finished goods inspection.

Receiving inspection

The quality of outputs from a conversion process can be no better than the inputs from which they are generated, unless excessive costs are first incurred to modify the inputs. Inputs are often built up, over a succession of stages, into the final product. At the end of this progression, we sometimes find that defective inputs used in initial stages result in an unacceptable final product. This requires subsequent costly repair, which could have been avoided. Therefore, management often establishes programs to monitor the inputs prior to their use. At *receiving inspection,* incoming shipments of raw materials subcomponents from vendors or other inputs are observed and evaluated against predetermined quality standards. These materials are often physically separated from work-in-process materials and are only released to operations after passing the initial inspection.

Often management inserts special inspection points between successive stages of the conversion sequence; this is called *work-in-process inspection.* The outputs of one or more stages are screened before they are used in subsequent operations. The operations manager must develop inspection plans for each of these monitoring stations. The plan may call for inspection of every unit produced (100 percent inspection), or it may incorporate a sampling plan in which only some of the outputs are examined. The intensity of inspection depends on the volume of output, the cost of inspecting, and the cost consequences (in subsequent stages) of not inspecting.

An important decision for the operations manager is how many inspection stations to have and where to locate them. A very simple heuristic can be used to help make this decision. Two key factors must be considered, the *percent of defective* output expected at each stage of the conversion process and the *cost* of inspection. Ideally, you would want to inspect at locations where inspection costs are low and percent defective is high. This would give a low cost of inspection per percent defectives detected. Table 17-2 illustrates the possibilities. We can use a simple three-step procedure for selecting the locations of inspection stations:

1. Identify all stages of the conversion process that are potential locations for inspection stations. Estimate the inspection costs and gather historical percent defective information for these stations.
2. Compute the critical ratio for each potential inspection station:

$$\text{Critical ratio} = \frac{\text{Cost of inspection}}{\% \text{ defective}} \qquad (17\text{-}1)$$

3. Rank the inspection stations by critical ratio. The lowest critical ratio is the most desirable location, the second lowest critical ratio second most desirable, etc. With limited resources, locate inspection stations until funds are depleted.

TABLE 17-2

LOCATION OF INSPECTION STATIONS

Percent defective in conversion process	Cost of inspection	
	Low	High
Low	Acceptable location; analyze carefully	Poorest location
High	Best location	Acceptable location; analyze carefully

━━━━━━━━━━ EXAMPLE ━━━━━━━━━━

A process has three possible location sites for inspection, *A*, *B*, and *C*.
Process percent defectives are 10 percent for site *A*, 5 percent for site
B, and 6 percent for site *C*. The cost of inspection at *A* is $150, at *B*
is $200, and at *C* is $100. Critical ratios are

$$A = \frac{\$150}{.10} = \$1,500$$

$$B = \frac{\$200}{.05} = \$4,000$$

$$C = \frac{\$100}{.06} = \$1,667$$

Inspection stations should be located first at station *A*, second at station
C, and finally at station *B*. If funds are limited, locate in that order until
funds for inspection are depleted.

Although this procedure seems simple, it has some hidden complexities
that warrant caution. Estimates of inspection costs and defective rates
needed in step 1 are difficult to obtain. Also, our example assumed that
the cost of a defective unit passing through the process is constant for
all stages of the conversion process. Is it? Usually in most organizations
it is not. How would you revise the procedure to take this factor into
account? We're not going to answer this question here; instead, we ask
you to answer it in the questions at the end of the chapter. If you understand
the concepts we've discussed so far, you should be able to modify the
procedure to take unequal costs into account.

In labor-intense organizations, substages of the conversion process
consist of people. Inspection of these processes is also useful for detecting
shifts or changes. Bank tellers, for instance, may be viewed as a subcomponent of bank operations. Procedures may be used to monitor a teller's
transactions for the preceding day, an after-the-fact inspection, or for
periodically monitoring while transactions are occurring.

Obviously, the current "process setting" of the bank teller is not
measurable in any precise sense. This difficulty is commonly encountered
when people are the dominant component of the conversion process.
Nonetheless, such a monitoring program serves an important quality control
function. It notifies the teller that certain selected conversion characteristics
are important for attaining high quality outputs. It is a means by which
output quality standards are meaningfully conveyed to the teller. And
if consistently applied, it can signal desirable or undesirable trends in
performance so that action can be taken by operations managers.

================= EXAMPLE =================

One bank used a simple rating system, shown here, to daily assess three characteristics. This rating can be thought of as an inspection of work-in-process by the head teller.

Date: 2-7-78   Teller: Jim Ross

Process characteristic	Grade
Speed	B
Accuracy	A
Personality	B
Overall	B

Finished goods inspection

For conversion processes that produce identifiable final products (such as physical goods), finished goods inspection is often used. This is a special kind of monitoring. Work-in-process inspection was concerned with subcomponents of the final product. Now, however, all of the subcomponents have been combined into a completed total product. It is this total product, not the subcomponents, that the organization and its customers are most concerned with. Various testing procedures can be used to determine whether the product conforms to functional and appearance standards. If it does not, sources of discrepancy must be identified, and corrective measures must be initiated. Without an inspection of the finished goods, customers may be very dissatisfied, and their dissatisfaction can cost your organization good will and profits.

Sampling Plans

Sampling plans are an important statistical application in quality control. These modeling procedures are often used to monitor the quality of incoming materials and parts and for final acceptance sampling of finished goods. They help us make judgments about output quality in an economical manner.

We'll focus on sampling plans as they might apply to receiving inspection. When a large shipment of a purchased item arrives, someone must decide whether to accept or reject the shipment. Rather than inspecting all units in the shipment, we can systematically sample a few units. A systematic sampling can provide the information needed for the accept/reject decision for the entire shipment. Thus the time, effort, and cost of more extensive inspection are avoided. Of course, there are some risks involved because of possible sampling errors.

Two kinds of errors can result from sampling. A shipment of good quality can be mistakenly rejected if a disproportionately large number of defective units from the shipment is selected at random. It is also possible to select at random mostly good units from a shipment of poor quality overall. The first type of risk is α, the "producer's risk"; the second is β, the "consumer's risk." We want a sampling procedure that assures that each of these risks is no greater than a specified chosen level.

For large shipments consisting of many units, say 5,000, we must determine a sample size (n) and an acceptance number (c) such that we obtain satisfactory assurance that our accept/reject decision, based on the sample, is correct. The n and c determine the characteristics of our sampling plan. First, randomly select n units from the shipment and determine the quality of each unit. If the quality of more than c of the units is incorrect, reject the entire shipment. If the quality of c or fewer of the units is incorrect, accept the shipment.

Standard procedures are available for determining the sampling plan parameters, n and c, that will meet the performance requirements specified by the user. The details of these procedures are presented in the supplement to this chapter.

=== EXAMPLE ===

A large medical clinic purchases quantity shipments of pregnancy test kits (PTKs). A shipment contains 10,000 PTKs. Each kit contains a specified chemical mixture. The kit is used by the physician to determine whether a patient is pregnant. If the chemical composition of the PTK is incorrect, the results of the test can lead to erroneous conclusions. Therefore, it is important that the PTK shipment be evaluated with respect to its chemical composition.

Physicians have found in the past that a shipment is of good quality if no more than 2 percent of the PTKs in it are of incorrect chemical composition; i.e., if the percentage of defective units is not in excess of 2 percent (.02). They consider shipments with 5 percent or more defectives to be an extremely bad quality shipment. We want a plan that has a .95 probability of accepting good shipments but only a .10 probability of accepting extremely bad shipments. These performance specifications for the sampling plan are summarized on the left side of Table 17-3. A sampling plan was derived to meet these performance requirements. The plan calls for 308 PTKs to be sampled from each shipment (right side of Table 17-3). If more than 10 of these are defective, the entire shipment is rejected. If 10 or fewer defectives are found, the shipment is accepted. In this way shipments consisting of 2 percent defectives have only 5 chances out of 100 of being rejected, while shipments with 5 percent defectives have only 10 chances out of 100 of being accepted. This sampling plan includes procedures for determining the probability of accepting the shipment if percents defective are between 2 and 5. These probabilities are shown in Figure 17-7.

TABLE 17-3

SAMPLING PLAN AND SPECIFICATIONS FOR PTKs

Performance specifications	Parameters of sampling plan
Good quality = 2% or fewer defectives	
Desired probability of accepting a good quality shipment = .95	$n = 308$
Risk: probability of α errors = .05	$c = 10$
Bad quality = 5% or more defective	
Desired probability of accepting a bad quality shipment = .10	
Risk: probability of β errors = .10	

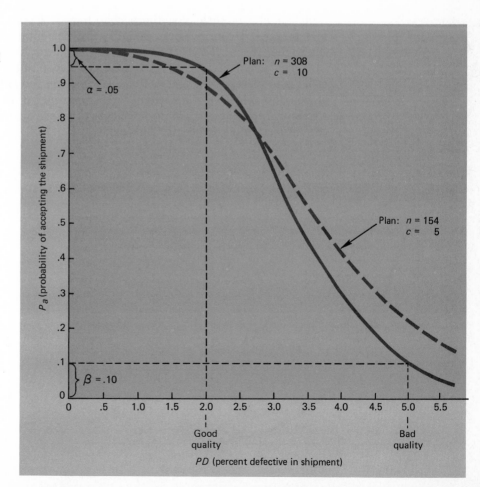

Figure 17-7
Probability of accepting a PTK shipment (OC curve)

The solid curve in Figure 17-7, called the "OC curve" (operating characteristics curve), reveals how a sampling plan will discriminate when used on incoming shipments. If a shipment is of high quality (low percent defectives), a good sampling plan gives us a high probability of accepting the shipment. Shipments of poorer quality (high percent defectives) have a lower probability of being accepted by the plan.

You can see from the solid OC curve in Figure 17-7 that the desired probabilities of accepting good and bad PTK shipments have been obtained. The second sampling plan, $n = 154$ and $c = 5$, will not meet desired performance specifications. The supplement to this chapter presents the details of how the desired plan was found.

General effects of
n and c

Each sampling plan consisting of n and c has a unique OC curve. Sampling plans with large sample sizes are more discriminating than plans with smaller sample sizes. Figure 17-7 shows OC curves for two sampling plans with different sample sizes and acceptance numbers. For both plans the acceptance number, c, is in constant proportion to n. For plans with larger n's the probability of accepting good quality lots is higher than for plans with smaller n's. Also, for bad quality lots, the probability of acceptance decreases when n is larger. Of course, these benefits are not obtained without incurring the higher inspection costs associated with larger sample sizes.

The effect of increasing the acceptance number (for a given value of n) is to increase the probability of accepting the shipment for all levels of percent defective other than zero (Figure 17-8). By using a larger c, we allow shipments with more defectives to pass inspection. As c is decreased, the inspection plan becomes tighter.

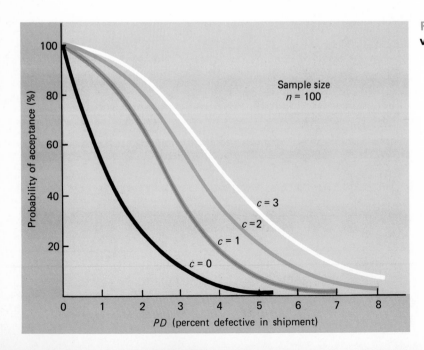

Figure 17-8 **Effect of variations in c**

In general, a sampling plan is specified by n and c. The selection of n and c determines the behavior of the plan. The resulting probabilities of acceptance are determined from sampling theory. Higher values of c result in "looser" performance, increasing the probability of accepting a shipment with a given level of defectives. Increasing n results in greater confidence that we have correctly discriminated between good and bad shipments. However, inspection costs are also increased with larger values of n. The task of quality management is to find the proper balance between the costs and benefits of alternative sampling plans.

From a practical standpoint, as an operations manager you will not have to develop sampling plans. Your quality control technician, or you in his absence, can refer to *Military Standard 104 (MSTD 104D)*, a widely accepted manual of sampling plans. For most applications this manual specifies both sample size and rejection and acceptance levels. You need only be an informed user—not a statistician—to use statistical quality control techniques. With them, we are convinced, you can operate the operations process more effectively and efficiently.

Deciding on good and bad quality

Choosing what percents defective constitute good and bad quality is a vital management decision. The sampling plan is designed around this decision. If managers are too stringent in defining good quality, the costs of obtaining (purchasing) such high quality shipments can become exorbitant. At the other extreme, a high percent defective can result in conversion disruptions, high scrap and rework costs, and higher costs of customer ill will. If it's possible to negotiate good and bad quality levels when you're purchasing shipments from suppliers, you can arrange for the vendor's finished goods inspection to have the same sampling plan that the customer's receiving inspection uses. Such a procedure can simplify matters considerably, and we recommend it.

Quality Control Charts

Detecting shifts when they occur is a major difficulty in the surveillance of process and product characteristics. When a conversion process begins to shift out of control, we would like to know as soon as possible so we can initiate corrective action. Although one would think it would be a simple matter to detect a shift by observation, it usually isn't. Occasionally, random variability in the process may make it seem that process output is bad when actually there has been no basic change. At other times, real shifts are mistakenly attributed to random variability. If a basic change occurs we want to detect and correct it so we can avoid costs of producing faulty products. On the other hand, we do not want to waste resources trying to correct a process that is already operating properly. To help avoid interpretive errors and detect when real shifts have occurred, quality control charts are very useful.

Control charts are used in some form in many manufacturing facilities. We have seen them in automobile manufacturing, appliance production, diecasting operations, pet food production, metal stamping, and petroleum refining. More recently, service industries have adopted this useful technique in various settings; accident rates provide measures of goodness of traffic control processes, numbers of robberies as a measure of public safety systems, sickness rates as measures of health care systems, and accident rates as measures of safety in ski slope recreation systems. Banks, hospitals, and other service organizations could make use of them too.

Control charts are based on the statistical concept of the *central limit theorem*. This theorem allows us the convenience of using the standard normal distribution in making judgments about changes in the process we are monitoring. With it, we can conveniently determine the chances that some important characteristic of our process has changed, and we can express these chances explicitly. To use this theorem, we take a randomly selected sample of several units of output from some stage of the conversion process. For each unit sampled we measure the critical characteristic, say its length, and compute the arithmetic average of the observed lengths. We then use this *average* to make our judgments regarding *system performance*. The central limit theorem specifies that if we compute many such averages, they will be approximately normally distributed regardless of the shape of the distribution of individual lengths, and this approximation to normality improves as the size of our sample is increased.

A control chart is unique to the operation that it is describing. Figure 17-9 shows a control chart for the temperature of a chemical plating operation. This chart has three important parameters, which were determined from historical data: mean (average) temperature, upper control limit (UCL), and lower control limit (LCL). In the past, the mean, or average, temperature for the process has been 86°C. The upper and lower control limits have been set at 89° and 83°. After the chart had been constructed, three more days of operation transpired. Sample temperature readings for these days were measured and then recorded on the chart. Temperature averages for the first two days were near the mean; the third sample average was near the upper control limit. An operations manager could glance at this chart and say, "The process is in control based upon the last three days' performance." With this overview of what control charts are, let's outline the steps for constructing and interpreting them. A more detailed presentation is given in the supplement to this chapter.

Here are the steps in developing quality control charts:

1. Determine whether *measurement* in the process is by variable or attribute. The type of measurement dictates which calculating formulas to use.
2. Partition the *historical data*. A control chart is constructed from historical data; current or future performance is compared with this past performance. You must have two distinctly different data sets, one for control chart *construction* and a second to reflect most recent performance.
3. Using the data for control chart construction, *calculate* a process mean and upper and lower control limits.

4. *Graph* the control chart. The chart will be some measurement (on the y-axis) versus time (on the *x*-axis).

5. *Plot* current or most recent performance on the graph.

6. *Interpret* the chart to see if (a) the process is in control and no action is required, (b) the process is out of control and an assignable cause should be sought, or (c) the process is in control but trends are occurring that should alert the manager to possible out-of-control conditions.

7. *Update* the control chart. After a reasonable period of time, often a month, the control chart is reconstructed by returning to step 2 above. You can repartition the data by discarding the oldest historical data and replacing it with historical data collected since the last updating.

Look at step 3. After a mean has been calculated, management must decide how certain we want to be that when the process appears out of control, it really is out of control. Managers may desire different degrees of certainty based upon their knowledge of the importance of an error in the process. Table 17-4 lists three of the many choices available in setting the control limits. These choices are expressed in terms of standard deviations (σ) of the bell-shaped unit normal curve shown in Figure 17-10. With narrow control limits ($\bar{x} \pm 1\sigma$), there is a reasonable chance that when the process appears to be out of control it may not actually be out of control (probability .317). This probability is equal to the shaded area in part (*a*). With wide control limits ($\bar{x} \pm 3\sigma$), there is little chance of a sampling error (0.3 percent). This is the shaded area in part (*b*); when a sample mean falls outside these limits, the process is very likely out of control. The selection of control limits involves tradeoffs between two types of risks. With the first type, α, the *producer's risk,* there is a possibility of concluding that the process is out of control when it is actually in a state of statistical control. (This is the same terminology used in sampling plans.) The producer's risk is reduced by using wide control limits; it is increased by using narrower control limits.

The second type of risk, β, the *consumer's risk,* describes the situation in which an out of control process is mistakenly adjudged to be in control. This risk increases as the control limits are widened and decreases as they are narrowed. Ultimately, the choice of control limit width must

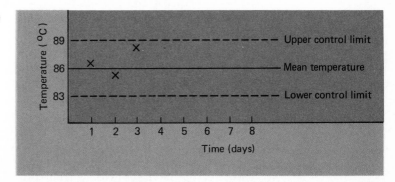

Figure 17-9 Example control chart

TABLE 17-4

NORMAL DISTRIBUTION PATTERNS FOR SETTING CONTROL LIMITS

Normal curve standard deviate	Area under curve: confidence level	Control limits	Action of manager when process is in control
± 1	68.3%	± 1 σ	Frequent adjustment
± 2	95.5	± 2 σ	Moderate adjustment
± 3	99.7	± 3 σ	Infrequent adjustment

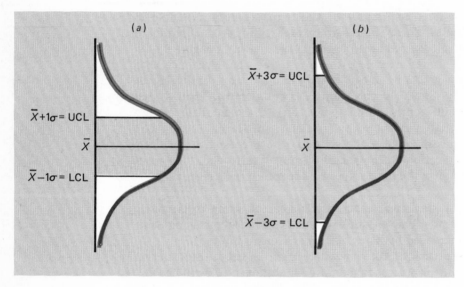

Figure 17-10
Probabilities of α error for control limits set at 1 standard deviation (a) and 3 standard deviations (b)

be based on these risks and the costs associated with them. If the costs of undetected shifts are extremely high relative to the costs of correcting the process, narrow limits (lower consumer risk) are appropriate. If the costs of restoring the process to the desired state are very high compared to the costs of producing defective output, wider limits (lower producer's risk) are appropriate.

Control charts for attributes   When sample units are classified into one of two categories (good or bad, success or failure, etc.), measurement is by attribute. Suppose we observe a sample of units from some process and classify each as either defective or acceptable. We can calculate the fraction of defective units in the sample and compare it to the historical fraction defective in the process. If the sample fraction defective (p) deviates widely from the historic process fraction defective

($\bar{p}$), we may conclude that some change in the process has occurred, that the current fraction defective is either higher or lower than usual. Attributes control charts are used for this purpose. If the process is under control, the sample fraction defective (p) is an estimate of the underlying process fraction defective. Several such sample estimates tend to be normally distributed, and the control chart has the form shown in Figure 17-11.

To construct an attribute control chart, we begin by inspecting a sample of n units to determine what fraction of those units is defective. We do this with equation 17-2, where x is the number of defective units:

$$p = \frac{x}{n} \qquad (17\text{-}2)$$

If this process is repeated, say m times, we get several estimates of fraction defective. Then, using these m estimates of p, we calculate the historical *average* fraction defective for the process using equation 17-3.

$$\bar{p} = \frac{\sum_{i=1}^{m} p_i}{m} \qquad (17\text{-}3)$$

Several such sample estimates of p will tend to be normally distributed with a standard deviation given by equation 17-4. In this equation, $\bar{p}$ is the average fraction defective, and n is the sample size used in each sample that was taken.

$$\sigma_{\bar{p}} = \sqrt{\frac{\bar{p}(1-\bar{p})}{n}} \qquad (17\text{-}4)$$

If we want a small α error, the control limits might be set at three standard deviations:

$$\begin{array}{c} \text{Control limits} \\ \text{(UCL and LCL)} \end{array} = \bar{p} \pm 3\sigma_{\bar{p}}$$

for a process in which we desire reasonably tight control.

Figure 17-11 **Attribute control chart**

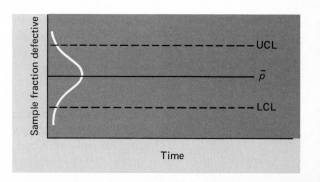

━━━━━━━━━━━━━ **EXAMPLE** ━━━━━━━━━━━━━

A visual inspection for scratches (each unit is judged good or bad) on a decorative paint trim operation produced the following data for last week.

Day	Number of units sampled	Number defective
Mon	30	3
Tue	30	10
Wed	30	6
Thurs	30	2
Fri	30	3

This week we have worked two days, Monday and Tuesday, and 30 pieces were sampled each day. Six pieces were found defective Monday and nine Tuesday. As operations manager, you are wondering if the process is in control this week. Is the number of defectives found Monday and Tuesday unusually high or low compared to last week's typical process performance?

To find a solution, construct a fraction defectives control chart based on last week's typical process performance. Last week's data are used to calculate average fraction defective ($\bar{p}$), the standard deviation of average fraction defective ($\sigma_{\bar{p}}$), and the control limits (UCL and LCL). Then you can plot the percent defective for this week's Monday (p_m) and Tuesday (p_t) against last week's control chart. The required calculations are shown here.

Control charts for variables In some situations we're interested in obtaining the actual measurement of an important characteristic, such as length, weight, or volume. After we have identified the variable of interest, we can use control charts to monitor its mean value and its variability. Since most frequently the process *average* is of greatest concern, we will restrict our discussion to controlling this process mean. To obtain an estimate of the current process mean, average the sampled values of a variable. We could measure temperature, for example, three times on the hour and average these three readings to estimate the mean temperature per hour of the heating process. The average hourly temperature over an entire day could be calculated by averaging 24 different hourly averages, the result being a mean of means. The distribution of these hourly means is approximately normal. These temperature data can also be used to calculate the standard deviation of this normal distribution and establish control limits. (The computations are illustrated in the supplement to this chapter.) After calculating control limits, we can implement steps 4 through 7 of the control chart procedure.

$$\bar{p} \text{ (for last week)} = \frac{\Sigma x}{\Sigma n} = \frac{24}{150} = .16$$

$$\sigma_{\bar{p}} = \sqrt{\frac{\bar{p}(1 - \bar{p})}{n}} = \sqrt{\frac{.16(1 - .16)}{30}} = .067$$

$$\text{UCL} = \bar{p} + 3\sigma_{\bar{p}} = .16 + 3(.067) = +.361$$

$$\text{LCL} = \bar{p} - 3\sigma_{\bar{p}} = .16 - 3(.067) = -.041$$

Since fraction defective cannot be less than zero, the LCL will be set at zero.

$$\text{Sample defectives: Monday } p_m = \frac{6}{30} = 0.20; \text{ Tuesday } p_t = \frac{9}{30} = .30$$

Now you can construct the resulting control chart:

Sample fraction defective

0.361		x			
0.160	x				
0.0					

Mon Tue Wed Thurs Fri

Time (days)

Monday's fraction defective is close to the historical process average. Tuesday's sample indicates that the process is still in a state of control. If a future sample falls outside the control limits, the operating manager can be quite confident (99.7 percent) that he should look for an assignable cause.

Temperature can be monitored periodically, and undesired temperature changes can be detected economically. Then action can be undertaken to restore temperature to desired levels.

Other control chart considerations As Figure 17-12 shows, control charts can be used in many ongoing situations. Notice that "normal behavior" features sample observations that are randomly scattered around the central value of the chart. When successive sample points form an identifiable pattern or fall outside the control limits, very likely something other than random effects are in operation. Subsequently management should launch an investigation to determine the cause of this nonrandom behavior.

Step 7 in the construction of control charts, you may remember, is updating the charts. When the charts are periodically updated, they become dynamic rather than static. The control limits and/or the central tendency of the chart change as the process changes over time. Look at Figure

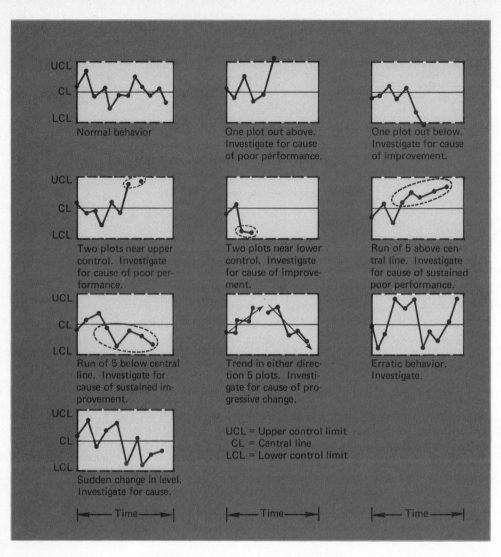

UCL
CL
LCL
Normal behavior

One plot out above.
Investigate for cause
of poor performance.

One plot out below.
Investigate for cause
of improvement.

UCL
CL
LCL
Two plots near upper
control. Investigate
for cause of poor per-
formance.

Two plots near lower
control. Investigate
for cause of improve-
ment.

Run of 5 above cen-
tral line. Investigate
for cause of sustained
poor performance.

UCL
CL
LCL
Run of 5 below central
line. Investigate for
cause of sustained im-
provement.

Trend in either direc-
tion 5 plots. Investi-
gate for cause of pro-
gressive change.

Erratic behavior.
Investigate.

UCL
CL
LCL
Sudden change in level.
Investigate for cause.

UCL = Upper control limit
 CL = Central line
LCL = Lower control limit

|←— Time —→| |←— Time —→| |←— Time —→|

Figure 17-12
**Control chart
evidence for
investigation**

Source: B. L.
Hansen, *Quality
Control* (Englewood
Cliffs, N.J.:
Prentice-Hall, Inc.,
1973).

17-13. During June and July, the UCL and the LCL were updated daily. August and September's control limits were not updated daily, but September's control limits and central tendency were determined from the behavior that was experienced in August. The point is that over four months, the process changes, in this case stabilizes. Since the control charts simply reflect process performance, they change too; in this case they get narrower.

One may establish and use a control chart in a variety of ways. After we have identified the product (or process) characteristic to be controlled, we must resolve a number of other design questions. What sample size should be used? How often should a sample be taken? What control limits should be selected? We know that the answers to these and other design questions are important because they determine both the effectiveness and the cost of the control process. Specific answers to these design questions depend to a great extent on the specific organization, on the peculiarities and nature of its processes and products. In general, choices among alternative design parameters involve tradeoffs among opposing costs and risks, and these economic design considerations must be evaluated.

Large sample sizes provide greater precision than small sample sizes. Since the resulting sampling distribution more closely meets the assumption of a normal distribution, the estimate of the current process average is more reliable, and we can place greater confidence in the sample results; the risk of error is reduced. There are, however, offsetting disadvantages

Figure 17-13 **Control chart for percent defective—four months' production of an electrical device**

Source: Eugene L Grant, *Statistical Quality Control*, 3rd ed. (New York: McGraw-Hill Book Co., 1964).

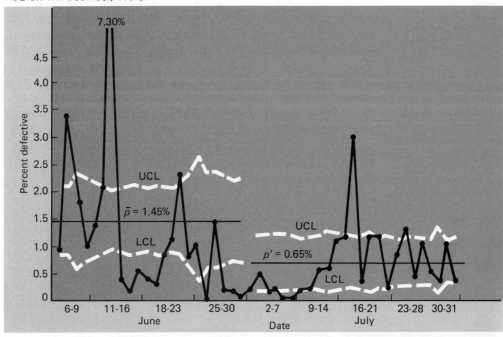

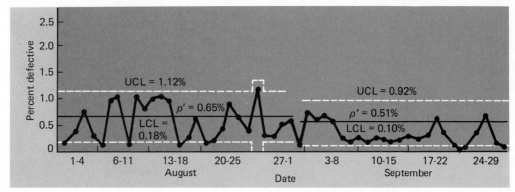

to large sample sizes. First, the direct costs of sampling are related to sample size. Large samples may result in higher sampling costs because of lengthier disruptions of the conversion process while samples are taken. Measurement of the characteristic of interest may require destructive testing of the items in the sample. If these items are expensive, large samples result in high costs of inspection. Finally, the results obtained from very large samples may be deceptive because the process may have shifted during the sampling process. Figure 17-14 shows what can happen with prolonged sampling. The dotted line reveals that the process mean is shifting over time. Under these conditions, it is possible for the long-run sample mean to be very close to the overall process average $\bar{x}$; the process shifts may therefore go undetected. Smaller sample sizes stand a better chance of detecting such shifts.

How frequently should samples be taken? It depends partly on the cost consequences of allowing process shifts to go undetected and partly on the performance history of the process. Processes with long historical periods of stability and infrequent out of control conditions might require only occasional sampling. For processes with more erratic and unpredictable histories, more frequent sampling may be necessary. At the same time, consideration must be given to the costs of undetected shifts. If the process runs continuously for long intervals without sampling, a large number of defective outputs may result. Should these defectives be easily detected and inexpensive to correct, infrequent sampling may be economically justifiable. If, however, it is expensive to detect and correct defectives, or if the consequences of supplying defectives to customers are significant, the added costs of more frequent sampling are justified.

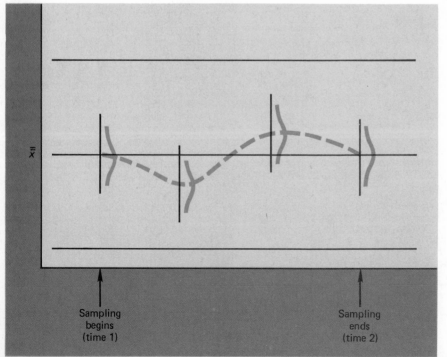

Figure 17-14 Prolonged sampling from a shifting process

Process capability   So far, our discussion of control charts has been restricted to processes performing under normal conditions. Control charts can also show process capability. Since process capability uses the best employees, equipment, and material, some of the random nature of the process is removed. Although control chart procedures for establishing limits are the same under both normal and tightly controlled conditions, the limits will necessarily differ. If both actual and process capability limits are shown on the same chart, there's likely to be some confusion. We recommend that you use separate charts. Process capability control charts can be very helpful to the marketing staff when they are bidding or selling jobs based on process quality capabilities.

Specification versus control limits   One final point needs to be made in our discussion of control charts. Control limits on a control chart reflect actual quality performance. *Specification* limits, on the other hand, are statements of what the product characteristics should be. Thus, product specification limits might be less than, equal to, or greater than the quality control limits. We want to caution you to distinguish between the concepts of quality *control* chart limits and quality *specification* limits.

BEHAVIORAL DIMENSIONS IN QUALITY CONTROL

When quality levels fail to meet specifications, the quality control technician knows to look for some "assignable cause." Defective materials, improper setup of equipment, technology-related problems, operator error, or many other factors could all be assignable causes. By the time an error has been detected by internal inspection efforts, from customer complaints, or from product failure, it is possible that a large number of similarly defective units has also been produced. Clearly, a fundamental limitation of statistical quality control is its historical orientation. Inspection involves examining products or services *after* they have been produced. Contrary to arguments often received by quality control personnel from production personnel, quality is *not* inspected into the product. The quality level is put there by operating line personnel. Thus, the attainment of suitable quality depends upon appropriate human performance or behavior when the product is being made.

If the product is made correctly in the first place, the needs for inspection and corrective changes are substantially reduced. In recent years much effort has been devoted to instilling a "quality orientation" into the work behavior of the people who work in the conversion process. Behavioral change procedures directed at changing performance quality *before* rather than after the fact, however, have met with limited success. We will discuss some of these attempts and the inherent behavioral problems that relate to quality in the following few paragraphs.

Quality/Quantity Tradeoffs

Very few studies have specifically investigated the relationships between quantity and quality of output. A review of the literature suggests there is no simple inherent relationship between these two factors. Especially for such routine, repetitive tasks as typing, bank proofing, or collating, operators tend to emphasize one over the other. If quality improves, quantity decreases; if quantity goes up, quality suffers. For tasks involving more complex and diverse physical and mental processes, the relationships between quantity and quality are not nearly so clear; therefore, our conclusions cannot be firm. In these more complex tasks, when does the operator emphasize quality at the expense of quantity? When does the reverse occur? Although task design, individual mental and physical abilities, degree of task automation, instructions to the worker, and the behavior that is rewarded or punished by the organization all have some effect, the complexities of these many factors tell us there is no simple answer to our questions. The quantity/quality tradeoff is usually determined by how the conversion processes are designed, staffed, and managed.

Zero Defects

Zero Defects programs, which attempt to improve quality by changing workers' attitudes, are popular in contemporary organizations. Their theme, "Do it right the first time," stresses error-free performance. Unfortunately, however, production/operation processes inevitably result in some undesirable output. Defects in materials, tooling, and equipment and operator errors are inherent in the process. Error-free performance is, for most processes, economically and practically infeasible. Although many people assume that errors are made because employees are not conscientious enough about their work, attempts to change employee attitudes have met with very limited success. Banners, slogans, Zero Defect days, and the like generally improve performance only temporarily; in about six months, employees' performance returns to its previous level.[1] Nevertheless, this sort of approach has some value. "Quality motivation" focuses the organization's attention on the human variable in product quality; it attempts to influence, rather than simply report, behavior that affects quality.

Quality Motivation

The American Society for Quality Control's *Quality Motivation Workbook* stresses some basic concepts for motivating employees. The idea is to apply techniques of motivation and management to obtain improved product quality.

---

[1]See Everett E. Adam, Jr., "An Analysis of Changes in Performance Quality with Operant Conditioning Procedures," *Journal of Applied Psychology* 56, no. 6 (1972), pp. 480–86, for a review of studies about Zero Defects by quality control specialists.

To supplement this booklet, managers should try to be familiar with some recent basic behavioral contributions that provide a systematic way of thinking about the many factors that determine employees' performance on the job. Consider the basic expectancy model in Figure 17-15. This model suggests that effort leads to performance, which, in turn, leads to satisfaction. Satisfaction then leads to future efforts. Basic to the individuals' efforts are their perceptions of how much they will be rewarded—and the chances of their being rewarded—for their efforts. Effort, together with abilities and role perceptions, leads to performance, or accomplishment. Individuals are rewarded according to their performance. The rewards, and how equitable they seem to the employees, determine their satisfaction; the degree of satisfaction then affects how much effort individuals will expend in the future. How could all this apply to the quality of an individual's work performance? Let's look at an example.

EXAMPLE

A student working as a stock clerk for a grocery chain can exercise some control over the quality of his work by checking prices before stocking, cleaning shelves, facing groceries properly (labels out) when stocking, and being friendly and courteous with customers. The degree to which this PERFORMANCE QUALITY is attained is a function of his abilities, role perception, and the effort he extends. The effort he extends may be a function of how much he needs money (reward) to continue his education and the relationship he perceives between his effort and rewards. If the stock clerk notices, for example, that the manager gives more hours of work to clerks who extend the greatest effort, he may extend more effort himself. Performance leads to money (extrinsic reward) and to the satisfaction of looking at full, clean shelves and pleased customers (intrinsic rewards). If the rewards seem equitable to the stock clerks, if wages are fair and just, job satisfaction is likely. The result of these behavioral processes is a positively motivated stock clerk.

Figure 17-15 **Expectancy model of motivation**
Adapted from L. W. Porter and E. E. Lawler III,
Managerial Attitudes and Performance (Homewood, Ill.:
Richard D. Irwin, Inc., 1968), p. 17

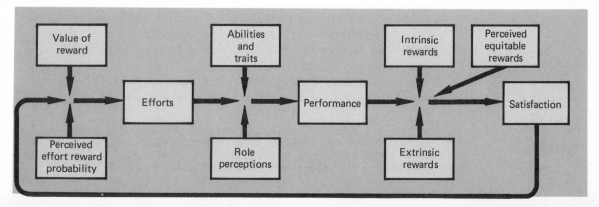

608
Part V
Controlling
the Conversion
System

Behavioral Modification in Quality Control

Recently, there have been several attempts to influence performance quality on routine repetitive tasks by employing operant conditioning procedures.[2] Operant conditioning assumes that people's behavior can be modified by a series of rewards. People act as a result of habits, built-up associations between a particular situation or set of circumstances and the response it generates, When faced with a situation, people react predictably because of the response they have received in the past. If the response is changed, behavior can be changed. Studies in the behavioral laboratory and in organizations provide some generalizations about influencing performance quality with behavior modification procedures. First, it appears that performance *quality* is more difficult to change than performance *quantity*. Second, it is clear that financial rewards more often result in improved quality than nonfinancial rewards. Once reasonable quality performance levels have been reached, however, continued financial rewards do not obtain significant additional quality improvement. Third, actual behavior is influenced more greatly by direct rewards than by attitude change procedures. We should be aware, finally, that these procedures provide, at best, mixed results.

EXAMPLE

In an attempt to influence quality in a diecasting department of some 36 men, one company succeeded in obtaining a significant quantity increase but no significant change in quality. Figure 17-16 shows weekly changes in the department as the result of a formal program involving weekly individual meetings between the supervisor and each employee. Quantity is measured as percent of standard, and quality is measured by percent defective. Overall, the company, with a $73,000 first-year cost reduction in this department, judged the program successful and implemented it in other departments. The fact remains, however, that quality did not improve, even though emphasis was given to performance quality at least weekly.

This entire discussion of quality motivation should illustrate that an extremely difficult productivity question remains unresolved—how to motivate employees to improve substantially their performance quality. We have many techniques and procedures to influence performance quantity (efficiency) but a considerable way to go with regard to performance quality (effectiveness).

Several other important quality-related behavioral problems remain unsolved. Human error in inspection is a common occurrence. A 100 percent

---

[2]See Everett E. Adam, Jr., "Behavior Modification in Quality Control," *Academy of Management Journal* 18, no. 4 (December 1975), pp. 662–79. This work provides references to the related works of George A. Johnson, William A. Ruch, William E. Scott, Jr., and James B. Shein, all of whom have contributed to recent quality motivation research.

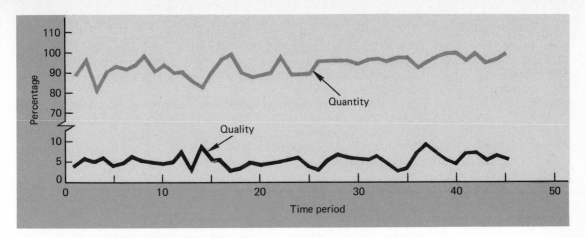

Figure 17-16 **Weekly diecasting quality (percent scrap) and quantity (percent performance) performance**

inspection certainly does not mean that *all* defective parts are observed and discarded by the inspector. This is particularly true for the routine, repetitive vigilance tasks that typify many inspection situations. Another difficulty arises from ambiguous quality standards (specifications) in some monitoring tasks. Our previous examples assumed that standards were clear and unambiguous, and that a unit of output could be adjudged either definitely suitable or definitely unsuitable (defective). In many real situations, however, precisely defined standards do not exist. The acceptability or unacceptability of output requires judgmental evaluation on a case-by-case basis. Product characteristics must sometimes be evaluated against *general* , rather than specific, criteria, particularly in the service sector.

Another quality problem is often found in group situations. If several inspectors are all monitoring the same items, there may be a "group effect." In such settings, group norms often emerge, and group members apply sanctions to obtain compliance with these norms. From the organization's viewpoint it is desirable for the group norm to coincide with the desired or intended quality standard. If the desired standard is ambiguous, however, the group's adopted standard may deviate from it. The problem for the manager is to detect the group standard and direct it toward the desired standard. Even when the desired and adopted standards coincide, they may diverge with the passage of time. The consequences of such deviations can be significant and disruptive. By instituting surveillance programs, employee training, group discussion, and methods of clarifying and communicating desired standards, the operations manager may be able to reduce the deviations from them.

SUMMARY

In this quality control chapter we have discussed concepts of product quality, including assurance and reliability; models useful in quality control, including inspection, sampling, and control charts; and behavioral dimensions in quality control. Quality control can be facilitated by management's planning and organizing efforts. Operations managers should locate inspection stations, set up sampling plans, and construct control charts. But they must be aware that all these control procedures are used by people. Quality motivation and behavioral modification techniques are some ways that operations managers can encourage employees to improve quality.

It is our belief that the most important aspects of an introduction to quality control are understanding concepts in quality control, being able to apply basic control models, and understanding that quality control is not totally a statistical problem. If you have mastered these, you have a grasp of the fundamentals of quality control.

CASE

Aqualock, Inc.

In 1970 George Thrall founded Aqualock, Inc., a manufacturing company producing small rubber gaskets used in hydraulics systems. His gaskets were simple in design and relatively easy to produce in large quantities. In 1977, gross sales from servicing customers throughout North America with large quantity shipments reached $8 million.

Demand for Aqualock products has increased so rapidly thAt the manufacturing facility is constantly under pressure to increase output around the clock. Customers and sales personnel in the field often call the home facility to determine estimated lead times for prospective orders and estimated delivery times for existing orders. In response, production foremen have increasingly emphasized to employees the need for increasing output to meet demand.

In late 1977, George Thrall began experiencing a new problem, an increase in customer complaints about the quality of shipments being received. George decided to add a quality control analyst to the Aqualock staff in hopes of finding and correcting the sources of customer dissatisfaction.

In his first two weeks the quality analyst uncovered some data that a production foreman had recorded two years previously.

Data for gasket YB4 (1976)

Sample number	Sample size	Number of defective gaskets in sample
1	40	6
2	40	1
3	40	0
4	40	2
5	40	1
6	40	4
7	40	3
8	40	2
9	40	6
10	40	0
11	40	3
12	40	2

The analyst began gathering data on current production of the same gasket. Samples were taken once each day for five consecutive work days with these results.

Data for gasket YB4 (1978)

Sample number	Sample size	Number of defective gaskets in sample
1	40	4
2	40	8
3	40	6
4	40	2
5	40	8

If you were the new analyst, what ideas would you entertain for getting to the bottom of George Thrall's quality problem? Of what value are the data at hand? What avenues of exploration would you recommend?

REVIEW AND
DISCUSSION
QUESTIONS

1. Define product quality.

2. Define product reliability.

3. If you were to design a portable radio, what product characteristics would you specify as critical for enhancing sales? What characteristics are less important?

4. What product characteristics and quality control procedures are important in a dormitory cafeteria? Which of these is most important? Which is least important?

5. Define process capability.

6. Discuss the roles of reliability and quality assurance in quality planning.

7. In some organizations, quality control responsibilities are separated from line production responsibilities; in other organizations they are not separated. Why?

8. Identify different types of inspection and discuss their roles in the quality control process.

9. What are the distinctions between inspection and sampling?

10. How does inspection by variables differ from inspection by attributes?

11. What is an acceptance sampling plan? How does it work, what factors must be considered in designing it, and what costs are incurred in using it?

12. What is an OC curve?

13. How do control charts differ from acceptance sampling plans? Under what circumstances is each appropriate?

14. Give examples of control chart patterns that would lead you to conclude that control action may be warranted.

15. "If our employees are requested to increase output quality, the quantity of output is going to suffer." Discuss this statement.

16. What are the merits and disadvantages of Zero Defects programs?

17. Discuss the relative importance of intrinsic and extrinsic rewards in the expectancy model of motivation (Figure 17-15) as they relate to the quality goals of the organization.

18. Reconsider the statement in question 15 in the context of the expectancy model of motivation.

19. Is operant conditioning an effective management technique for quality motivation in nonroutine, nonrepetitive tasks?

PROBLEMS

1. Tripod Instruments, Inc., has been examining a lens during production for scratches. If there are, in the inspector's opinion, too many scratches, the lens is "bad" and rejected. Otherwise the lens is good. Construct a control chart for last month's inspected lenses.

Last month	Pieces inspected	Pieces rejected
Week 1	50	5
2	50	15
3	50	12
4	50	8

2. A product has two subcomponents, *A* and *B*. Failure of either *A* or *B* results in failure of the product. The probabilities of *A* and *B* performing successfully for 1,000 times are .92 and .93, respectively, and are independent.
   (a) What is the probability that the product will operate properly 1,000 or more times?
   (b) What is your answer to (a) if the probabilities for *A* and *B* are .85 and .75, respectively?

3. A relatively new test, a Gravindex Test, has been used by our lab for the past ten weeks. This test indicates pregnancy by determining whether hormones are present in the urine. If hormones are present, the test is positive; in the absence of hormones, the test result is negative. We know the test is about 90 percent reliable, and we believe we now have the test well under control. We want to establish some means of checking *future* test results to see if the test appears to be staying in control. Our results to date using a sample size of 10 tests each week, are:

Negative	Positive	Total tests
30	70	100

   (a) Construct a control chart for this test.
   (b) Suppose we collect the following data over the *next* four weeks for our Gravindex Test.

Week	Negative results	Positive results
1	3	7
2	2	8
3	2	8
4	6	4

Is the process (test) in control during these four weeks? If not, what do you do?

613
Chapter 17
Quality Control

4. In conjunction with a class assignment, two industrious operations management students decided to study book returns to the campus library by library users. The students collected their data by sitting on the library steps on Wednesday and Thursday and watching books being returned. They observed the following:

   Wednesday: 40 people entered the library, 5 of whom were returning books
   Thursday: 60 people entered the library, 15 of whom were returning books

   These students need your help in constructing a control chart of this "process." After hearing about this, you go over on two successive Mondays and observe:

   Monday: 10 people enter the library, 5 of whom are returning books
   Monday: 10 people enter the library, 4 of whom are returning books

   What inferences can you make concerning your observations based on the data of your fellow students?

5. Peanuts, Inc., has asked you to check the automatic temperature control of its main baking oven; manufacturing personnel claim the control is broken. Having a business school background (and not an electrical engineering background), you have decided to approach the problem from a statistical quality control standpoint. You have gathered the following data.

Date	Sample mean of three temperature readings	Date	Sample mean of three temperature readings
6/1	120° F	7/26	125° F
6/2	122° F	7/27	127° F
6/3	116° F	7/28	128° F
6/4	118° F	7/29	131° F
6/5	124° F	7/30	131° F

   Specifications:

   Manufacturer's guarantee on equipment is for any setting between 100° F–150° F with a variance of $\pm 7°$ F from the setting.

   Product (peanut) specifications are 120° F $\pm$ 5° F.

   Specifically, you have been asked to determine as of 12/31 if Peanuts, Inc., has a baking oven problem. If so, what do you recommend?

6. Relectro Corporation produces a miniature electric motor consisting of four basic subcomponents: coil, prime circuit, switch, and simo-wire. Relectro promises its customers a two-year motor life with a probability of .95. Failure of any of the basic components renders the motor useless. Consideration is being given to redesigning the product for purposes of cost reduction. Engineers have gathered the following reliability and cost data for components that could be purchased from new vendors.

Data for Existing Components

Component	Unit cost	Two-year failure probability
Coil	$17.00	0.01
Prime circuit	8.50	0.03
Switch	1.50	0.05
Simo-wire	4.00	0.01

Data for New Vendors

Component	Vendor X Unit cost	Vendor X Two-year failure probabilty	Vendor Y Unit cost	Vendor Y Two-year failure probability
Coil	$16.25	0.010	$21.00	0.005
Prime circuit	12.00	0.020	15.00	0.001
Switch	2.50	0.030	4.00	0.025
Simo-wire	4.00	0.010	4.50	0.010

Perform a reliability and cost analysis to support your recommendations for redesign of the motor.

7. A manufacturing facility consists of three work stations for which there are currently no inspection stations. You have estimated the cost of adding inspection stations and gathered some additional information summarized below.

Work station	Output per day (units)	Average percent defective	Estimated inspection cost per day	Estimated cost of each undetected defective
A	1,000	5%	$20	$6
B	1,000	10	30	4
C	1,000	3	25	2

(a) As quality manager your limited budget will allow you to add only one inspection station in your conversion process. Which location would you select from the three possibile locations?
(b) What would be your choice if the output rates at A, B, and C were 1,000, 1,500, and 2,000 units per day, respectively?
(c) Develop a heuristic for inspection station selection that considers all of the variables in the problem.

8. An appliance manufacturer has just hired you to evaluate and set up a quality control program in their manufacturing facility that supplies their anodized aluminum decorative trim parts. You report in a staff capacity to the plant manager. In-process inspection and finished goods inspection are currently being performed by some 30 inspectors in a facility employing 500; but little is being done with this data other than recording pieces sampled, number defective, and reasons for defects by employee and job.

(a) What type of information might you want to gather to assess current quality levels?

(b) What variables do you want to measure and start systematically providing to supervisors throughout manufacturing? (Example: Provide OC curves or plant percent defective.)

(c) How would you implement your program?

9. The control charts on p. 616 were attached to an extrusion machine at the facility of a major dog chow manufacturer's production facility. This extruding machine combined inputs of various grains, heat, and water, put the mixture under pressure and extruded ("squeezed out") dog chow that was put into chunks upon extrusion. This is the key machine in the production process and, as shown, five variables are constantly watched and recorded hourly. Realizing the actual charts are incomplete in labeling and detail, answer the following questions as best you can.

(a) The day shift started at 7 A.M. and ended at 2 P.M. Then operators changed. Did the second shift operators make any significant changes in inputs?

(b) Which, if any, attributes being measured are out of control on the first shift (7 A.M.–2 P.M.)?

(c) What can the shift foreman do when he observes the control chart during period 1 (1 P.M.)?

GLOSSARY

Acceptance number: one parameter of a single sampling plan; the largest number of defectives allowed in the sample that still permits acceptance of the shipment

Attributes measurement: type of measurement in which a product characteristic is classified into one of two categories: success or failure, accept or reject, etc.

Consumer's risk: probability of concluding that a poor quality shipment of inputs is of good quality

Control chart: a graphical device, based on sampling results, used to make inferences about the control status of a process

Control limits: upper and lower bounds of a control chart; used to indicate the control status of the productive process

Design specifications: detailed requirements of a product specifying its important desired characteristics

Inspection: observation and measurement of conversion inputs and outputs

OC curve: operating characteristics curve; the relationship of acceptance probability to level of incoming quality for a specified sampling plan

Process capability: maximum level of output quality performance of a productive process that can occur under ideal operating conditions

Producer's risk: probability of concluding that a good quality shipment of inputs is of poor quality

Product quality: degree to which the product conforms to design specifications

Quality motivation: application of management motivation techniques to workers to improve quality

Receiving inspection: inspection subfunction that focuses on assessing the quality of conversion inputs

Reliability: a product's useful life span; usually expressed as a probability of its ability to perform its intended function for a specified length of time

Sampling: process of selecting representative observations from a population

Sampling plan: specific procedure that incorporates sampling to permit inferences to be made about some population characteristic

Product	Location		Date
Dog Chow	13-10 North		2/7/78

Inspector	Inspector	Inspector
Hirsch	Coder	Votino

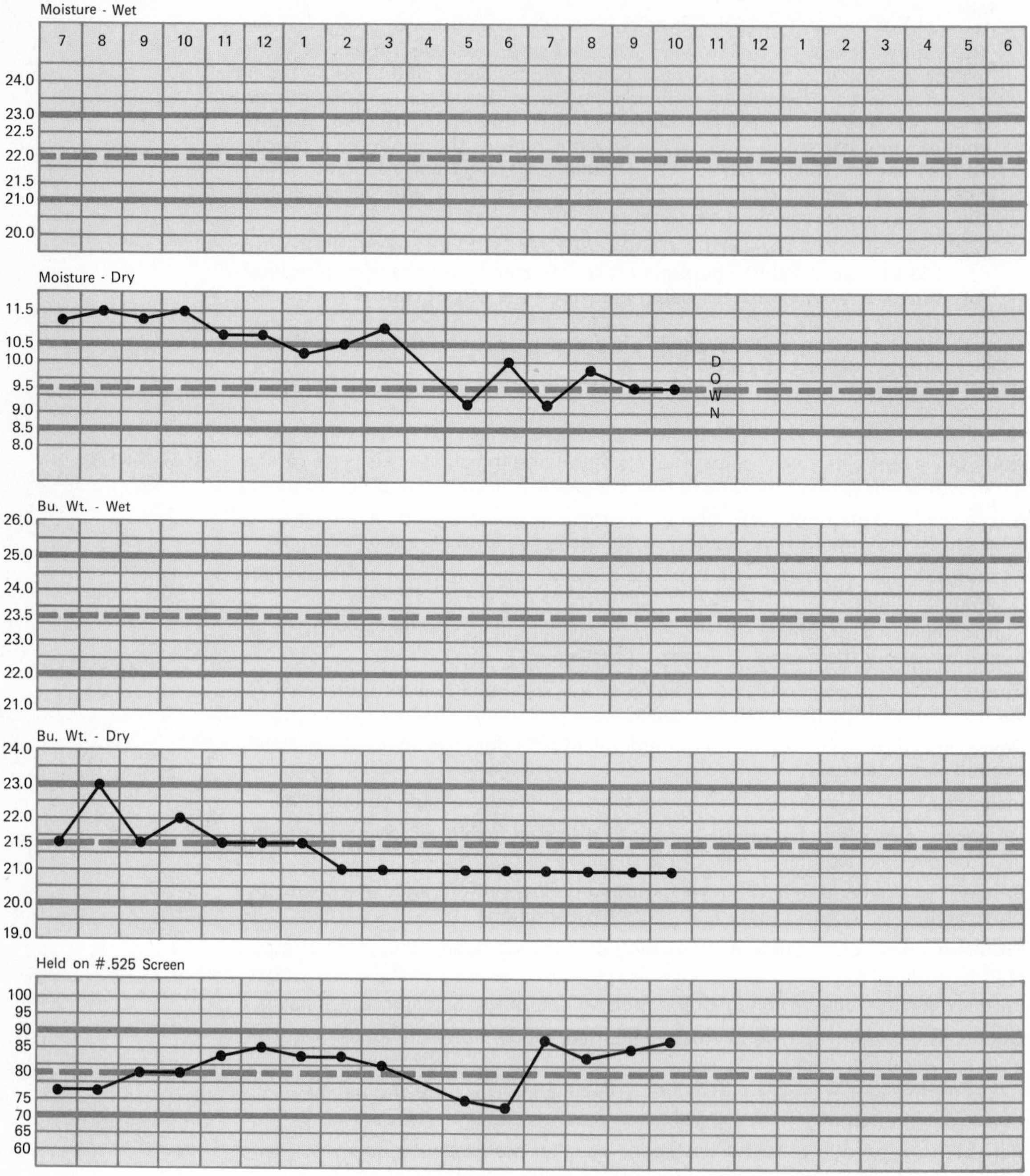

Moisture - Wet

Moisture - Dry

Bu. Wt. - Wet

Bu. Wt. - Dry

Held on #.525 Screen

Specification limits: boundaries that define the limits of variation for a product characteristic; any output outside these boundaries is unacceptable

Variables measurement: type of measurement in which a product characteristic is classified according to its degree of conformance on some measurement scale

Zero Defects: formal programs adopted by organizations to change worker attitudes toward quality improvement

Adam, E. E. "An Analysis of the Change in Performance Quality Employing Operant Conditioning Procedures." *Journal of Applied Psychology* 56, no.6 (December 1972): 480–86.

Adam, E. E. "Behavior Modification in Quality Control." *The Academy of Management Journal* 18, no. 4 (December 1975): 662–79.

Adam, E. E. and W. E. Scott. "The Application of Behavioral Conditioning Procedures to the Problems of Quality Control." *The Academy of Management Journal* 14, no. 2 (June 1971): 175–93.

American Management Association. *Zero Defects: Doing It Right The First Time.* New York: A.M.A. Manufacturing Division, 1965.

American Society for Quality Control. *Quality Motivation Workbook.* Milwaukee, Wisconsin: ASQC, 1967.

Dodge, H. F. and H. G. Romig. *Sampling Inspection Tables.* New York: John Wiley & Sons, Inc., 1959.

Duncan, A. J. *Quality Control and Industrial Statistics.* 3rd ed. Homewood, Illinois: Richard D. Irwin, Inc., 1965.

Fetter, Robert B. *The Quality Control System.* Homewood, Illinois: Richard D. Irwin, Inc., 1967.

Gavett, J. W. *Production and Operations Management.* New York: Harcourt Brace Jovanovich, Inc., 1968.

Grant, E. L. *Statistical Quality Control.* 3rd ed. New York: McGraw-Hill Book Company, 1964.

U.S. Department of Defense. *A Guide to Zero Defects.* Quality and Reliability Assurance Handbook 4115.12, 1965.

SELECTED READINGS

CONSTRUCTING SAMPLING PLANS AND CONTROL CHARTS

The purpose of this supplement is to present briefly the more detailed aspects of sampling plans and control charts and to identify some underlying concepts and techniques.

Sampling Plans

The sampling plans discussed in this book are based on the Poisson probability distribution. We assume a random sample of size n is taken from a Poisson population that has a fraction defective p'. Then we use tables or graphs to calculate the probability of obtaining c or fewer defectives in the sample or of obtaining more than c defectives in the sample. This general approach is adopted here to derive a sampling plan.

First, let's summarize again the process of acceptance sampling. We wish to make an accept/reject decision about the overall quality of a large shipment of items. To avoid the high costs of 100 percent inspection, we devise a systematic sampling procedure in which only a randomly selected subset of the total shipment is inspected. The sampling plan consists of a sample size (n) and an acceptance number (c), and it is designed to provide us the level of risk protection that we desire. As we shall see, our choices of n and c are very important.

To determine suitable values for n and c, we need four additional items of information: α, β, AQL, and $LTPD$. Two of these, α (alpha) and β (beta), are measures of the degree of risk that is desired in the sampling plan. AQL and $LTPD$ are parameters that define what constitutes "good" quality and "bad" quality for a shipment. AQL is conventional notation meaning "acceptable quality level," or "good" quality. $LTPD$ is "lot tolerance percent defective," or "poor" quality level. Assigning numeric values to these four parameters is largely a matter of managerial judgment. As soon as their numeric values have been decided, values for n and c can be determined.

After we have specified what constitutes good and poor quality, we must specify acceptable degrees of risk for each type of error in our sampling plan. If the shipment is actually of "good" quality, for instance, we wish our sampling plan to offer a high probability of accepting the shipment and a low probability of rejecting it. α is used to represent the probability we will tolerate for rejecting good (AQL) shipments. An $\alpha = .05$, for example, might be selected. Similarly, we specify a probability for the risk that our sampling plan will accept shipments of poor $(LTPD)$ quality. This probability is represented by β; assume for this example that $\beta = .10$. The values of α and β are often negotiated but are commonly assumed to be .05 and .10.

Repeating the previous example for the pregnancy test kits (PTKs), let's derive the sampling plan that eventually called for $n = 308$, $c = 10$. First, the design parameters are identified (see Table S17-1).

Approximate values for n and c are found by calculating the desired ratio, $LTPD/AQL$, which in our example is $.05/.02 = 2.5$. From Table S17-2 (column 4) we find that $c = 10$ gives the desired ratio. Having found $c = 10$, we now find the desired sample size n. This is done by making two calculations using columns 2 and 3 of Table S17-2. First, the value of $p'n_{0.95}$ for $c = 10$ must be divided by AQL: $6.169/.02 = 308$, the suggested sample size n. What are we

DESIGN SPECIFICATIONS FOR PTK PLAN

AQL	α	LTPD	β
.02; a shipment in which no more than 2% of the PTKs are defective is a good quality shipment.	.05, the desired producer's risk for the sampling plan. If a shipment is of good (AQL) quality, we want no more than a .05 probability of concluding that it is bad.	.05; a shipment in which 5% of the PTKs are defective is a bad quality shipment.	.10, the desired consumer's risk for the sampling plan. If a shipment is of bad (LTPD) quality, we want no more than a .10 probability of concluding that it is good.

doing when we are making this calculation? We are finding a sample size n that gives a 0.95 probability of accepting a shipment that contains an *AQL* percent defective when $c = 10$. In Table S17-2, the values of $p'n_{0.95}$ have been precalculated from a Poisson probability chart, which will be shown below. The calculation made above is really $p'n_{0.95}/p' = n_{0.95}$ when p' is chosen to be at the *AQL* level.

TABLE S17-2

FACTORS FOR SELECTING A SAMPLING PLAN (n AND c) THAT APPROXIMATES THE DESIRED AQL AND LTPD WHEN $\alpha = 0.05$ AND $\beta = 0.10$*

C	$p'n_{0.95}$	$p'n_{0.10}$	$p'n_{0.10}/p'n_{0.95}$ = LTPD/AQL
0	0.051	2.30	45.10
1	0.355	3.89	10.96
2	0.818	5.32	6.50
3	1.366	6.68	4.89
4	1.970	7.99	4.06
5	2.613	9.28	3.55
6	3.285	10.53	3.21
7	3.981	11.77	2.96
8	4.695	12.99	2.77
9	5.425	14.21	2.62
10	6.169	15.41	2.50
11	6.924	16.60	2.40
12	7.690	17.78	2.31
13	8.464	18.96	2.24
14	9.246	20.13	2.18
15	10.04	21.29	2.12

*Source: Frank E. Grubbs, "On Designing Single Sampling Inspection Plans," *The Annals of Mathematical Statistics* (1949), p. 256.

The second required calculation is similar to the previous one, except that column 3, $p'n_{0.10'}$, is used with *LTPD*. The value of $p'n_{0.10}$ for $c = 10$ is divided by *LTPD*: $15.41/.05 = 308$, the suggested sample size. This shows that a sample size of 308 gives a 0.10 probability of accepting a shipment that contains an *LTPD* (10 percent) percent defective when $c = 10$.

In our example, we were fortunate that both calculations led to a sample size of 308 units for $c = 10$. Often it is impossible to find one set of n and c that simultaneously satisfies all the desired design parameters α, *AQL*, β, and *LTPD*. In such cases we must be willing to sacrifice (modify) α or β, and the calculations become somewhat more tedious. If α or β is modified, we can no longer rely on the tabulated values in Table S17-2, since these apply only for $\alpha = 0.05$, $\beta = 0.10$. Instead we must use the Poisson prabability chart, Figure S17-1. Let's use another example to illustrate.

Suppose we want a plan that satisfies the following: $AQL = 0.02$, $\alpha = 0.05$, $LTPD = 0.06$, $\beta = 0.10$. The desired ratio, $LTPD/AQL$, is $.06/.02 = 3.0$. From Table S17-2 (column 4) we find that the desired ratio falls between $c = 6$ and $c = 7$. Now we must evaluate four sampling plans that will come close to our desires. These are summarized in Table S17-3.

In plan 1, for $c = 6$, β is held at the desired value of 0.10, but the desired α is not obtained. In plan 2, α is held at the desired value of .05, but β deviates from the desired level. Corresponding conditions exist in plans 3 and 4, except

Figure S17-1   Probability curves for Poisson distribution

Source: H. F. Dodge and H. G. Romig, *Sampling Inspection Tables* (New York: John Wiley & Sons, Inc., 1959).

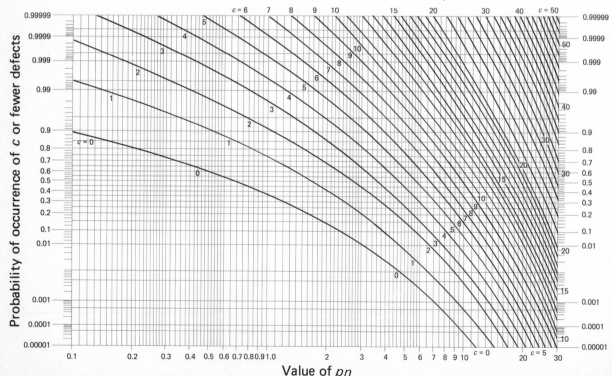

FOUR ALTERNATIVE SAMPLING PLANS THAT APPROXIMATE DESIRED SPECIFICATIONS

If $c = 6$		If $c = 7$	
Plan 1	**Plan 2**	**Plan 3**	**Plan 4**
$\beta = 0.10$ α modified	$\alpha = 0.05$ β modified	$\beta = 0.10$ α modified	$\alpha = 0.05$ β modified
$n = \dfrac{p'n_{0.10}}{LTPD}$	$n = \dfrac{p'n_{0.95}}{AQL}$	$n = \dfrac{p'n_{0.95}}{LTPD}$	$n = \dfrac{p'n_{0.95}}{AQL}$
$= \dfrac{10.53}{.06}$	$= \dfrac{3.285}{.02}$	$= \dfrac{11.77}{.06}$	$= \dfrac{3.981}{.02}$
$\doteq 175$	$\doteq 164$	$\doteq 196$	$\doteq 199$

that $c = 7$. For each plan an approximate sample size was obtained from the appropriate value in column 2 or 3 of Table S17-2.

Since either α or β has been modified in each plan, we must determine how much they have been changed. For example, plan 1 calls for $c = 6$ and $n = 175$. What value of α results? The answer can be found by calculating $p'n$ and entering this value in Figure S17-1. In this case $p'n = (AQL)(175) = (.02)(175) = 3.50$. After entering 3.50 at the bottom of the chart, we proceed upward until intersecting the curved line for $c = 6$. To the far left of this intersection we can read the probability of acceptance, 0.94. Hence, the α risk is $1.00 - 0.94 = .06$ for this plan. In a similar manner the unknown α or β for each plan has been calculated and summarized in Table S17-4.

Although all four plans come close to meeting desired specifications, none meets them exactly. As manager, you must choose the plan you feel is most suitable.

Control Charts for Variables

In some situations we're interested in obtaining actual measurements of lengths, weights, or volumes. In these cases we use control charts for variables. Our discussion focuses on charts for controlling the process *average*.

Let x_i be the measured value for the ith unit in a sample of size n, and $\bar{x}$ be the average value of these n measurements. Now instead of sampling only once, suppose we sample m times and obtain m sample averages always picking samples of size n. Each sample average is then denoted as $\bar{x}_j$. We can then calculate the average and the standard deviation of these sample averages. Equations S17-1 through S17-4 are the fundamental equations used for constructing a variables control chart.

$$\bar{x} = \frac{\sum\limits_{i=1}^{n} x_i}{n} \tag{S17-1}$$

$$\bar{\bar{x}} = \frac{\sum\limits_{j=1}^{m} \bar{x}_j}{m} \tag{S17-2}$$

$$s_{\bar{x}} = \sqrt{\frac{\sum\limits_{j=1}^{m} (\bar{x}_j - \bar{\bar{x}})^2}{m-1}} \tag{S17-3}$$

$$\text{Control limits} \atop \text{(UCL and LCL)} = \bar{\bar{x}} \pm 3s_{\bar{x}} \tag{S17-4}$$

The control chart takes the form shown in Figure S17-2.

EXAMPLE

Micron Distribution Center, Inc., packages imported cameras in cartons for shipment to retailers throughout the United States. They wish to use adequate packing materials in each carton to minimize shipping and handling damage, but they do not want to overpack the cartons. Management has decided that current packing procedures are desirable and want to document the current packing process for future comparisons. A control chart will be constructed given the following data. These data were obtained by sampling the current packing process.

Packing date	Ounces of packing material per carton (x_i)
May 1	8, 7, 5, 9, 11
3	8, 8, 7, 7, 5
4	8, 4, 7, 13, 8
5	10, 12, 8, 9, 11
7	9, 9, 10, 9, 8

Note that measurement is by variables (interval scaled data). We first find the sample averages when $\bar{x}_j = \Sigma x_i/n$:

Date	Sample average ($\bar{x}_j$)
May 1	40/5 = 8.0
3	35/5 = 7.0
4	40/5 = 8.0
5	50/5 = 10.0
7	45/5 = 9.0

CALCULATION OF UNKNOWN α OR β FOR EACH OF FOUR SAMPLING PLANS

Plan 1	Plan 2	Plan 3	Plan 4
$\beta = 0.10$: determine α for $c=6$, $n=175$	$\alpha = 0.05$; determine β for $c=6$, $n=164$	$\beta = 0.10$: determine α for $c=7$, $n=196$	$\alpha = 0.05$: determine β for $c=7$, $n=199$
$p'n = (AQL)\,(n)$ $= (.02)\,(175)$ $= 3.50$	$p'n = (LTPD)\,(n)$ $= (.06)\,(164)$ $= 9.84$	$p'n = (AQL)\,(n)$ $= (.02)\,(196)$ $= 3.92$	$p'n = (LTPD)\,(n)$ $= (.06)\,(199)$ $= 11.94$
Probability* of acceptance = .94	Probability* of acceptance = .14	Probability* of acceptance = .955	Probability* of acceptance = .095
$\alpha = 0.06$	$\beta = 0.14$	$\alpha = 0.045$	$\beta = 0.095$

*Probability obtained from Figure S17-1.

Then we find:

$$\bar{\bar{x}} = \frac{\Sigma \bar{x}_j}{m} = \frac{8.0 + 7.0 + 8.0 + 10.0 + 9.0}{5} = 8.4$$

$$s_{\bar{x}} = \sqrt{\frac{\Sigma(\bar{x}_j - \bar{\bar{x}})^2}{m-1}} = \sqrt{\frac{(8.0 - 8.4)^2 + \ldots}{4}} = 1.2$$

Then:

$$UCL = \bar{\bar{x}} + 3S_{\bar{x}} = 8.4 + 3(1.2) = 12.0$$
$$LCL = \bar{\bar{x}} - 3S_{\bar{x}} = 8.4 - 3(1.2) = 4.8$$

Our packing material control chart, which can be used to plot future daily performance, is:

Sample average		
12.0	----------------	UCL
8.4	————————————	$\bar{\bar{x}}$
4.8	----------------	LCL

Time (days)

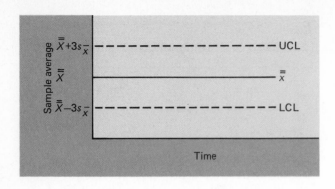

Figure S17-2 **Variable control chart**

REVIEW AND DISCUSSION QUESTIONS

1. What parameters must be specified to develop an acceptance sampling plan?

2. How does one's choice of AQL, LTPD, α, and β affect the cost of acceptance sampling?

3. How is the OC curve affected by changes in n and c?

4. Discuss the cost tradeoffs involved in selecting the control limits of a variables control chart.

5. What sample size should be used for a variables control chart?

PROBLEMS

1. Thompson Metal Works manufactures metal screws. The following shows the diameters for part #2735, a standard metal screw, the last time the part was produced two months ago.

Date	Screw diameters (cm)
8/5	0.5, 0.6, 0.4, 0.3
8/6	0.5, 0.5, 0.4, 0.6
8/7	0.7, 0.5, 0.5, 0.6
8/8	0.5, 0.5, 0.5, 0.5

(a) Construct a control chart for the last production run.
(b) A sample was taken today, the first day of production in two months on this part. Metal screws diameters were 0.5, 0.9, 0.5, 0.9. Based on the control chart developed above, what can you tell the general foreman about his process?

2. Your reputation as an analyst has gained widespread acclaim in the Allstate University athletic department. The basketball coach asks you to help him with the following problem. Coach Stewart believes that the lack of success of the team in conference play has been because of the way nonconference foes defensed Smith (games 4–8) and the way conference foes defensed him (games 9–13). He gives you the following data concerning the average of Smith's first 11 shots of each game:

Game	Sample mean of distance from basket	Game	Sample mean of distance from basket
4	6.0	9	6.0
5	8.0	10	8.0
6	5.0	11	5.0
7	4.0	12	9.0
8	7.0	13	10.0

You are asked to apply what you have learned in quality control, viewing Smith's performance as a process. Provide Coach Stewart with an answer as to whether Smith's conference performance is in control based upon his performance during nonconference games.

3. The results of four samples concerning a shaft diameter were taken three weeks ago when our process was running smoothly ($n = 3$). It is shown here. Since then we have experienced a labor strike, and some business school students are running our production line. Results of two samples taken today are: sample 1—2.30, 2.15, and 1.91; sample 2—1.85, 1.87, 1.78. What can we tell our plant manager about the process today compared to our previous base? What does this mean he should now do? Support your decision with analysis.

Sample	Diameter (inches)		
1	2.10	2.08	1.96
2	1.97	1.98	2.05
3	1.95	1.91	1.98
4	2.07	2.08	2.03

4. Construct OC curves for the following sampling plans:
   (a) $n = 100$, $C = 1$
   (b) $n = 200$, $C = 2$
   (c) $n = 300$, $C = 3$

5. Construct OC curves for the following sampling plans:
   (a) $n = 100$, $C = 1$
   (b) $n = 100$, $C = 2$
   (c) $n = 100$, $C = 3$

6. Find an acceptance sampling plan that meets the following specifications:

$$\alpha = .05 \qquad AQL = .01$$
$$\beta = .10 \qquad LTPD = .08$$

7. Find an acceptance sampling plan that meets the following specifications:

$$\alpha = .03 \qquad AQL = .01$$
$$\beta = .05 \qquad LTPD = .08$$

DYNAMICS OF OPERATIONS MANAGEMENT

18 The Conversion Process in Change

Organizations and their conversion subsystems are dynamic. Both because there always seems to be room for further improvement and because new demands are placed on the organization from various sources, managerial processes and actions are continually in motion. To make improvements and meet new demands, managers must make changes. Whether large or small, changes are the rule rather than the exception. A continual process, change becomes a way of life in the organization. Because it is so pervasive and has important effects on system operation and output, change deserves special consideration by the manager.

Open Versus Closed Systems

Let's digress for a moment and discuss "closed" versus "open" systems to see how each has been used in our coverage of P/OM. Conceptually, a closed system is a self-contained entity within a definable boundary. Within the boundary are the interrelated subcomponents of the system. Since it is self-contained, the system does not depend on exchanges of inputs and outputs with its environment. It is sealed off from environmental encroachments.

The open system, on the other hand, exchanges energy and/or matter with its environment. Although it retains its unique wholeness, it is an integral part of the larger environment; its continued viability requires that the system adjust to the varied energy inputs from the environment. All organizations can realistically be viewed as open systems—systems that are integral parts of larger social systems. Their continued existence depends upon successful exchanges of material and energy with the environment.

In introducing the operations subsystem, we have often treated it as if it were a *closed* system consisting of many separate subcomponents. In this way we have been able to concentrate on basic concepts of selected problems faced by the operations manager and to learn about these problems in an uncomplicated manner. Only after we had studied the basics of such topics as facility location, layout, job design, and scheduling as if they were independent problems, each in a closed system, did we begin discussing their interrelationships. Neither has our discussion emphasized environmental influences on the operations subsystem. In Figure 18-1, our general framework, inputs, outputs, and random fluctuations are the only representations of environment/subsystem exchanges. Except for mentioning these, we have viewed the operations subsystem as sheltered off from, or closed to, the external environment.

Figure 18-1   General model for production/operations management

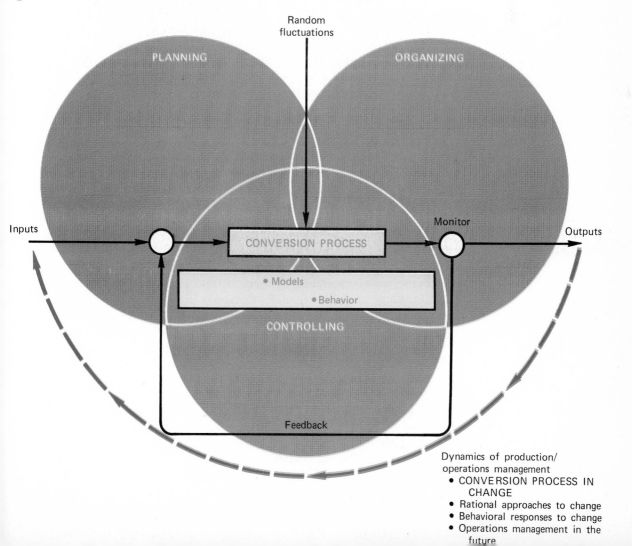

In this chapter the emphasis shifts from analysis to synthesis. We wish to emphasize the dynamics of operations that arise from system interrelationships and to stress the openness of the operations subsystem to the environment. We hope to enable you to recognize how the need for change occurs and why adjustments in the subsystem are necessary for survival.

Think about the dynamics of production/operations management as it fits into our general framework in Figure 18-1. Beginning at the far right of the figure, outputs are inspected by the organization and received by consumers; both the organization and customers serve as initiators of change. Based on their observations, management makes modifications of inputs, the conversion process, and/or outputs. The need for these changes activates management's planning, organizing, and controlling activities in a formal sense and often involves the use of models. Further, changes influence human behavior, both formally and informally. In fact, the process of change has such widespread effects on the organization that ultimate outcomes of change are difficult to predict precisely. This presents a management dilemma. On the one hand, we want a closed system orientation; on the other hand, reality forces an open system. Management desires a predictable or stable conversion process that allows the goal of economic efficiency to be met; nevertheless, as an open system we must recognize the need for changes in order to remain a viable organization. As a production/operations manager, you must strike a proper balance between stability and adaptability in your organization. If you understand the dynamics of organizational change, you may be able to balance stability and adaptability in a more enlightened way.

DYNAMICS OF
PRODUCTION/
OPERATIONS
MANAGEMENT

Changes in the conversion process do not occur one at a time. Usually, multiple changes of various magnitudes are occurring simultaneously. Further, these changes are not independent of one another; they have the interdependencies expected of any system. Since a system is a web of interwoven subcomponents, changes in one part result in changes in other parts. Some of these "ripple" effects are predictable; others are not. In short, organizational change can rapidly become a "can of worms" if not approached cautiously. In Chapter 1 we stated that managing the total system is a job of identifying subsystem relationships, predicting the effects of changes in the system, and properly implementing the system change. For these reasons we suggest a somewhat systematic approach to studying the dynamics of the conversion process. The framework we suggest is shown in Figure 18-2. The broad dimensions of change flow from left to right in Figure 18-2. Recognition of the need for change, targets for change, the change process, and the desired results of change are distinct phases usually identifiable in any change situation.

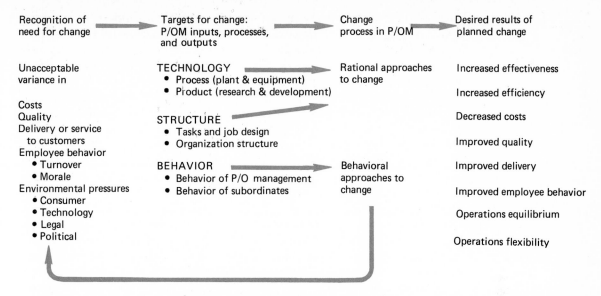

| Recognition of need for change | → | Targets for change: P/OM inputs, processes, and outputs | → | Change process in P/OM | → | Desired results of planned change |

Recognition of need for change → Targets for change: P/OM inputs, processes, and outputs → Change process in P/OM → Desired results of planned change

Unacceptable variance in

TECHNOLOGY
• Process (plant & equipment)
• Product (research & development)

Rational approaches to change

Increased effectiveness

Increased efficiency

Costs
Quality
Delivery or service
 to customers

STRUCTURE
• Tasks and job design
• Organization structure

Decreased costs

Improved quality

Employee behavior
• Turnover
• Morale

BEHAVIOR
• Behavior of P/O management
• Behavior of subordinates

Behavioral approaches to change

Improved delivery

Improved employee behavior

Environmental pressures
• Consumer
• Technology
• Legal
• Political

Operations equilibrium

Operations flexibility

Figure 18-2 **Dynamics of production/operations management: the conversion process in change**

Recognition of Need for Change

Before we can plan and initiate change, we have to recognize that a change is needed, and we have to know why it is needed. In a broad sense, this recognition activity is part of the overall management information and control system. Indicators that change is needed can come from internal sources or from sources that are external to the organization. Random fluctuations, unplanned and/or uncontrollable environmental influences that tend to cause actual output to differ from planned output in the conversion process, are necessary in our model because they happen so often in reality. We may have to make changes to meet existing organizational goals; or it may be necessary to change the goals themselves.

Internal indicators The conversion process operates to meet predetermined goals and sets performance standards that are consistent with goal attainment. Most commonly, management establishes goals for profitability, product quality, customer service, and commitments to employees. It is not surprising, then, that measures that are closely related to these goals are the primary internal indicators of the need for change. Some of the most commonly used indicators are:

- costs
- product quality
- delivery or service to customers
- employee behaviors

When actual system performance varies from the standard or planned tolerance range on any of these dimensions, the manager should be prepared for imminent change of some sort.

Some of these indicators are readily quantifiable; others are not. Reports of direct and indirect labor expenses (costs), scrap rates (quality), and employee absences and quitting rates (employee behaviors), for example, are usually reported periodically in standard report forms. These can easily be compared against performance standards, and deviations can be noted and investigated. Some indicators are much more subtle, however. Not all costs are recognized; some aspects of product quality or customer service are not conveniently measurable; and employee dissatisfaction may surface in nonquantifiable form. When the indicators are subtle, formal change may not occur until the underlying problem magnifies itself to such an extent that it becomes more easily recognized. By this time, remedial changes may be very costly to implement, much more so than if the indicators had been recognized earlier. Sometimes even though the need for change is not formally recognized, the change is made anyway.

=== EXAMPLE ===

During the 1960s a regional library system had developed job descriptions for all its job positions. Hiring and training practices for the next ten years were based on these job descriptions. In 1973, because of excessive operating costs and budgetary cutbacks, the library completely reevaluated the jobs. Job analysis revealed that the old job descriptions were not at all consistent with the actual job responsibilities. Employees had recognized the obsolete nature of the job descriptions and had taken it upon themselves to redefine their own job responsibilities. As a result, job content was changed informally. Further analysis revealed considerable duplication of activities among employees.

This example shows how informal changes can occur gradually. By the time needs are formally addressed, the costs of making necessary changes can be large in terms of dollars and employee discontent. To be aware of the subtle as well as the more obvious indicators of the need for change, managers must do more than merely read reports. They must be aware of and appreciate the feelings of their employees and their customers, and they must be able to communicate with them effectively.

At this point a distinction should be made between the indicators of change and the type of change that is needed. Unacceptable variations in costs, product quality, customer service, and employee behaviors must be interpreted cautiously. Although they are *indicators* of problems, they do not necessarily *identify* what the problem is. They are merely symptoms; the problem remains to be identified. High operating costs (the indicator), for example, may be due to excessively high product quality from overly diligent workers. Or they may be traced to high scrap and rework and indicate low employee morale. In each case the indicator merely signals that a problem exists. Further search is needed to identify the problem so that appropriate changes can be made.

External indicators In general, the conversion process is designed to enable efficient operation shielded from external pressures or impingements. The system can never be totally closed, however; as the external environment changes, it imposes changes on internal operations. An obvious example is the change in consumer tastes and desires in a competitive market. If CB radios are the rage, organizations with the technological and financial capability will begin producing CB radios if they wish to establish or improve their market position. The development of transistor circuitry made vacuum tubes obsolete; electronics manufacturers either changed with the new technology or went out of business because of deficient product demand.

In some instances, external indicators arise in a more direct way. This is particularly true in service industries making products to suit the needs of particular customers rather than mass markets. Here a close degree of customer-supplier cooperation results in new product designs. Changes in products or processes are often made on a regular basis.

Besides consumer tastes and technological innovations, there are also significant environmental sources of change. Broad societal changes in values are often reflected in new laws and governmental regulations that require compliance. Today's concern over environmental pollution has a direct impact on the internal operations of most organizations. Scarce energy resources force changes that have been of little concern to operations managers in the past. Legal and political pressures for change are also evident to the perceptive production/operations manager.

Targets for Change

Once the need for change has been recognized, the manager can identify one or more aspects of the conversion process that must be modified. In general either the technology, the organization structure, or employee behavior in the conversion process is the target for change.

Technology The technology of the operations subsystem consists of the physical or mental processes by which conversion from inputs to outputs is accomplished. The technology for manufacturing refrigerators is dominated by cutting, forming, and assembling of sheet metal, manufacturing electronic and mechanical components, assembly (including the compressors and refrigeration components), painting, and packing. The technology of an automatic car wash includes soap and water sprays, roller brushes, chain drives, and blower-dryers.

In dental clinics, the human components of the technology are more directly visible. Knowledge and skills of dentists and technicians are directly witnessed by the customer (patient). The physical aspects of the dentist's technology range from materials used in treating the patient (drilling equipment, teeth-cleaning preparations, and so on) to elaborate laboratory equipment never seen by the patient.

When change is needed, the modifications may be directed primarily toward the technology by which inputs are converted into outputs. These kinds of modifications often involve redesign of plant and equipment to process existing products as new processes or materials are developed. The development of plastics, for example, resulted in displacement of many refrigerator components formerly made of metals. This necessitated the replacement of metal rolling and forming with plastics extrusion processes. A similar, but accentuated, switch from metal to plastic is currently taking place in the automobile industry as firms attempt to reduce weight for increased gasoline mileage so that government standards and consumer demands can be met. The decision to switch from one processing technology to another because of changes in inputs or because of processing innovations can be analyzed from an engineering/economic viewpoint. Some methods for doing this will be presented in the next chapter.

Often, the basic product itself must be modified to meet changing consumer needs or to comply with external requirements. The annual model changes and new product introductions practiced by many industries represent frequent pressures for change in individual operating systems. In fact, one way to compete in some industries is to be effective in quick development, manufacture, and delivery of new products (operations flexibility). The product line, consequently, is very volatile. In the manufacturing equipment industry, it is not unusual for customer-supplier cooperation to produce new designs, features of which will be incorporated in future editions of the supplier's "regular" products. In these cases operating system effectiveness is measured in terms of flexibility, the ability to work with product and customer engineers to develop and manufacture unique products that, in some cases, are later produced in volume. Often, then, new products and processes are necessary from a strategic viewpoint. Developing new products and processes can be undertaken systematically rather than on a hit-or-miss basis. A rational approach for these changes is discussed more fully in Chapter 19.

Structure

Sometimes the organization structure, tasks and jobs within the organization, become the targets for change. When costs, quality, or employee satisfaction indicates that changes are warranted, individual jobs may be redesigned. Job analysis and work methods studies may reveal that some job elements should be eliminated, others simplified, and still others expanded.

Task redesign may also be appropriate when new products and processes are developed. Unless the new product is very similar to the old one, old tasks cannot simply be reapplied to new products. Consider the changes in job design faced by an aircraft manufacturer who is gearing up to mass-produce a new, larger model. Although the fundamental conversion technology from the old model remains unchanged, the sequence and content of individual jobs must be modified. The basic skills of some employees, such as riveters, can be readily transferred to the new model from the old, but the details of the jobs must be modified. Under these conditions the manager can estimate the overall effects of such changes on output performance by using "learning curve analysis," which we will discuss in Chapter 19.

At a broader level, the entire organizational structure may need changing. If goals are not met, new departments and divisions may be formed and old ones dissolved. Perhaps the quality control function may be reassigned from the manager of manufacturing to the vice-president of operations to obtain higher level control of quality. Job shop scheduling and dispatching may be centralized to improve overall shop throughput; or a new customer relations department may be created to improve service to customers.

New products and technological changes may also necessitate structural adjustments. Many manufacturing organizations have created environmental engineering groups to redesign conversion processes and facilities so that environmental contamination is reduced. The computer expertise developed by many organizations has led to computer services departments that serve not only the operations function but the other functional areas of the organization as well.

Many organizations are changing the structure of the marketing/production interface, the distribution system. Traditionally, production maintains control of products until they have been shipped from the plant, when they enter the marketing distribution channels. The marketing staff then determines stock points and quantities at various warehouse locations. Many firms have a *physical distribution* function that cuts across traditional production and marketing functions. The physical distribution manager may be responsible for in-plant purchasing, receiving, inventory control, and finished goods inventory. He or she normally determines modes of transportation for finished goods, warehousing points, and shipment sizes and oversees the distribution system. This function represents tremendous potential dollar savings to the firm. To change from traditional to the physical distribution concept requires a major structural change in the organization, however.

As companies grow and product markets expand, structures are changed accordingly. Organizations may diversify along product lines to gain greater efficiencies; others may decentralize as a means of developing future managerial skills and experience. In Chapter 19 we will show how "system dynamics" models can be used to evaluate the effects of structural changes like these.

Behavior From the operations manager's viewpoint, behavior is a third target for change. Very often, goal attainment is possible by modifying employee behavior rather than by changing the technology or the structure of the conversion process. Product quality and efficiency goals may be enhanced through on-the-job training of operative employees. These training efforts are designed to modify behavior in favorable directions. Similarly, managerial effectiveness can be improved by development and training programs in such areas as decision making, leadership, and employee/supervisor relationships.

When behavior is the primary target for change the manager may use several change strategies. How successful the change is depends upon human learning capabilities and the reinforcement/reward procedure that is used. These procedures and the methods by which change is introduced affect how readily change is accepted or resisted in the organization. These topics are presented in detail in Chapter 20.

The Change Process in Production/Operations

Obviously, the three targets for change are not independent of one another. In most cases, change in one area is accompanied by changes in the others. Of the three, behavioral change is the most pervasive. It is difficult to conceive of technological and structural changes that do not also result in the need for behavioral change. You have witnessed many such situations, perhaps unknowingly. Consider the computerized checkout systems in many large hardware stores and supermarkets. The technological change from the old system to the new one brought about the need for modified skills and behaviors of employees, particularly as they relate to inventory procedures. Previously, inventory counts of shelf items were periodically updated by hand. In the computer-based system, each transaction is recorded by stock number at the cash register, where inventory levels are updated and reordering may be automatic. Store managers and other employees now focus their skills and efforts on other tasks than counting stock items. Certainly some retraining and reorientation of work behavior is required when such a change is made.

At the present time, the change process in organizations is more an art than a science. Although managers attempt to be systematic and rational in planning for change, complete rationality and predictability of the effects of change are not possible. At best, we can be aware of some general concepts and procedures to help smooth out the transitions that occur in organizations. In advance of the change, we can make rough estimates of its potential effects by asking some "what if" questions about system behavior and economic consequences. These approaches are elaborated in the two chapters that follow. In general, the unpredictable nature of change arises from the complexities of the organization. These complexities, examined below, illustrate the varied secondary effects that can result from change.

Change's ultimate effects on the organization revolve around the interrelationships inherent in such systems. Three types of interrelationships are readily apparent: the subfunctions of the management process, the functional areas of the organization, and the basic operations problems.

Subfunctions of the Management Process

Throughout this book we have emphasized the planning, organizing, and controlling subfunctions of the managerial process and their interrelationships. By now it should be clear that since they are complementary activities, changes in any one can cause corresponding adjustments in the others. New control procedures necessitate replanning and possibly reorganizing. Changes in plans necessitate reallocating resources, which involves reconsideration of authority/responsibility relationships and the design of control processes. A change in one subfunction introduces the prospect of changes in the others.

Functional Areas of the Organization

Although our focus is on the production/operations subsystem, we cannot overemphasize our interdependence with the other subsystems, Including marketing and finance. Consider the implications of a major marketing decision, the introduction of a new product or service. This change introduces accompanying changes in operations; changes in the conversion process, including job design and the organization structure, must be made. These conversion changes then necessitate further changes in the finance subsystem, because sources of capital and credit must be arranged and working capital and cash flow requirements must be estimated.

When new processing innovations occur, they cannot be adopted unilaterally within the operations subsystem. The decision to change must be made jointly after management has ascertained that the necessary investment meets the organization's return requirements and that the financial resource requirement is obtainable.

For manufacturing firms that produce several products, there are efficiency advantages to producing large quantities of one before changing over to produce another. When the operations manager decides to deviate from past changeover practices, the effects are felt in the marketing and finance areas. The marketing and distribution function may find shortages of some products and excess quantities of others relative to market demand. Finance may witness substantial changes in the cost of carrying inventories and changes in working capital requirements and cash flows. Conversely, changes in a company's financial picture may require that production schedules be altered dramatically so that profitability goals can be attained. Similarly, a new promotional campaign by marketing may necessitate that traditional production schedules be revised so that output is coordinated with anticipated market response. In these and many other ways, changes in one functional area can have an impact on others.

Basic Operations Problems

Because the basic operations problem areas are interrelated within an operations subsystem, changes in one facet stimulate changes in others. Many of these relationships have been presented in our discussions throughout this book. New inventory control doctrines result in output scheduling changes. New location decisions affect procurement and delivery lead time requirements and may result in new transactions patterns among units in the production/distribution system. Changes in product quality standards may mean that employees must be retrained, jobs redesigned, equipment and processes renovated, and inventory control doctrines changed. Let us consider an inventory/scheduling example to illustrate how a change in one area can affect changes in others.

EXAMPLE

An assembly department uses component part number $X131$, which is manufactured in the fabrication department. Historically, the assembly department supervisor orders an optimal quantity ($Q*$) of 10,000 units and uses them at a constant rate of 200 units per day (d). The fabrication department requires a 5 day lead time (after receiving the request) before it can begin producing and supplying the units at a continuous rate of 500 units per day (p). Thus, the assembly department uses a reorder point of 1,000 units, just enough to meet its assembly needs for 5 days until the new shipment begins to arrive from fabrication. This same pattern of ordering and replenishment, shown in Figure 18-3, has existed for several years. Because of changes in inventory-related costs, the assembly supervisor has decided to begin using a new optimal order quantity of 15,000 units.

Historically, the fabrication supervisor has been accustomed to the inventory replenishment pattern in Figure 18-3. During each inventory cycle, 20 days of productive time are devoted to manufacturing component $X131$. During the remaining 30 days of the cycle, the fabrication department is scheduled to work on jobs for other customers. How is the fabrication schedule affected by the assembly supervisor's revision of order quantity?

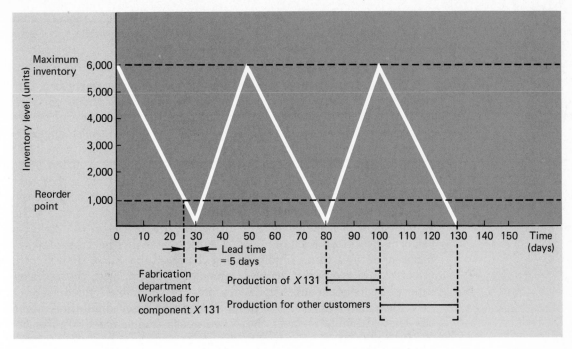

Figure 18-3 **Existing inventory pattern for component X131 in assembly department**

The new order quantity (15,000 units) will require 30 instead of 20 days of productive time in fabrication. Since annual demand for $X131$ is unchanged, the number of orders placed per year will be smaller than they were, but the run lengths will be longer. Because established scheduling patterns have been disrupted, the fabrication supervisor must determine how to schedule other jobs through the department so that a smooth, efficient overall flow of jobs will result. We are focusing on operating problems; but think of the impact of this change on the functional areas of finance and marketing as well.

Perhaps you recognize this inventory example as the finite production model developed in an earlier chapter. Like this example, most of the models used in production/operations management are limited; since they are abstractions, they treat only selected aspects of real system problems. As you use them, you must remember their limitations and estimate how the actions suggested by the models will affect other aspects of the operating subsystem.

In light of the many considerations we've discussed, it is no surprise to find that organizations are often hesitant to change; sometimes they avoid dramatic change until it becomes a real necessity. It is more comfortable to live with established relationships than to face the uncertainties that accompany change. Most managers give careful consideration to the types of interrelationships we've discussed before they initiate change. Their abilities to assess and prepare for the impacts of change are based on intuition and experience. Recently, computer simulations of organizations have begun being used to explore the implications of proposed changes in a more explicit manner. Let's look at this approach next.

<table>
<tr><td>SYSTEM
DYNAMICS</td><td>

The examination of overall system behavior is important for two reasons. First, many individuals make decisions in various parts of the organization. The *combined* effects of these decisions determine overall system performance. Although any individual decision may appear to be a good one when considered by itself, it may have detrimental effects overall when it is combined with others. Second, any decision or policy should be judged on how it affects the system over time rather than on its effects at one point in time. While static modeling emphasizes one point in time, dynamic modeling focuses on changes over time. Although as managers of systems we are ultimately interested in the steady-state performance after a change, we are interested in the transient system behavior as well. Since implementing changes takes time, their significant effects usually are not realized immediately. Similarly, the reactions of interrelated system subcomponents may not be visible immediately.

System dynamics is a term for a computer-based simulation methodology that attempts to meet these two needs. Pioneered by Professor Jay W. Forrester at M.I.T., system dynamics is a quantitative methodology for developing and analyzing models of systems and their behavior.[1] We won't concern ourselves with the technical details of system dynamics but discuss instead its general potential for management.

</td></tr>
</table>

An Example System Dynamics Study

In our discussion, we'll outline a research report that illustrates both the general form of simulation results from system dynamics models and the artificiality of system boundaries chosen for purposes of analysis and decision making.[2] It will help you see the advantages of viewing an organization as an open system rather than as a closed system. In using this systems approach, managers can improve internal operations by considering the organization's interactions with organizations and people in its external environment. In this example, internal organizational changes acting through external organizations result in smoother overall operations. As we discuss the example, we will relate it to our model for change, Figure 18-2.

The system under consideration is an industrial components manufacturer with no formal production-inventory-employment control system. Internal operating policies and decision rules are made on the basis of managerial intuition and experience. Adjustments of production rates, inventory levels, and employment levels are primarily reactive. When

---

[1] Jay W. Forrester, *Industrial Dynamics* (Cambridge, Mass.: The M.I.T. Press, 1961).

[2] See Edward B. Roberts, "Industrial Dynamics and the Design of Management Control Systems," *Management Technology* 3, no. 2 (December 1963), pp. 100-118.

customers periodically complain about slow deliveries, for example, management reacts by hiring more production employees, increasing production rate, and thereby increasing inventory levels and improving deliveries to customers. Customer complaints are an external indicator of the need for change; behavior and/or structure are the targets for change; improved deliveries are the desired result of change. On other occasions, when bad financial reports show excessive inventories, management reacts by reducing employment levels, reducing production, and thereby reducing inventories to more favorable levels. When this occurs, the financial reports are the internal indicators of need for change, and internal behavioral changes are directed toward the end result of decreasing operating costs. This mode of operation is not unusual.

A system dynamics model of this situation was constructed; it included representations of incoming customer orders, manufacturing rates, employment changes, inventory levels, and product deliveries of the components manufacturer. A computer program was developed reflecting the logic of what actually happened in the firm. A simulation run of this computer program model over hypothetical future time periods was conducted, and system performance was recorded on the following dimensions: on-hand inventory level, manpower (employment) levels, volume of incoming customer orders, and backlog of customer orders. The resulting system performance is shown in Figure 18-4 (a).

Let us examine and interpret these results. First, system performance is recorded over 300 simulated weeks. Incoming customer orders declined during the initial 20 weeks, increased during the next 20 weeks, and continued to show considerable variability for the remainder of the simulation run. The variations in employment, inventory, and backlogs were even more dramatic. Notice that as inventories decline, employment increases, but with a lag; as inventories increase, employment decreases. Further, as time passes, the amplitudes (heights of peaks and depths of valleys) of employment, inventory, and backlogs increase substantially. These wide variations can be very costly, and there is obviously room for considerable improvement. Goals of operations equilibrium, reasonable costs, and customer deliveries are not being met. The system performance is a further indicator of the need for change.

A new, more formal management control system was proposed for the components manufacturer, with the goal of reducing existing wide variations. Its primary features were designed to:

- gather better information on sales,
- smooth the sales estimates, thereby reducing the chances of direct factory responses to random sales variations,
- periodically review inventories and implement reordering policies that would bring actual inventories into line with target inventory levels,
- monitor order backlogs so they don't drift afar from normal levels, and
- adjust work force to meet the desired production rate in consideration of current sales volume and manufacturing backlog conditions.

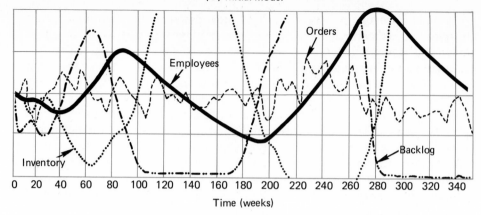

(a) Initial model

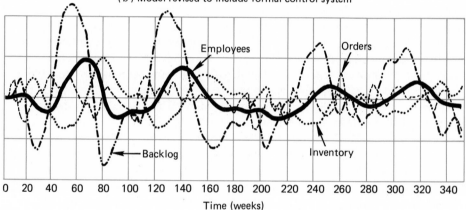

(b) Model revised to include formal control system

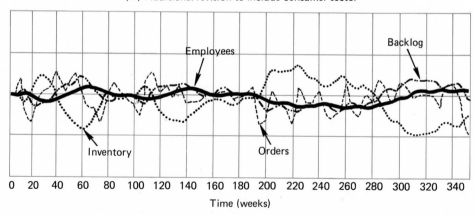

(c) Additional revision to include consumer sector

Figure 18-4 **Results of three system simulation runs**

Source: Edward B. Roberts, "Industrial Dynamics and the Design of Management Control Systems," *Management Technology 3,* no. 2 (December 1963), pp. 109 and 113. Printed by permission from *Management Science.*

This proposal involves changes in managerial technology and structure (targets) to achieve operations equilibrium, lower costs, and improved deliveries (desired results). From the manufacturer's viewpoint, all these changes can be accomplished internally within the manufacturing system. Would this new management control system improve the manufacturer's performance? To find out, the analyst revised the previous model, incorporated the features under consideration, and computer-programmed the logic of the revision. The revised model was then run over 300 simulated weeks with the results shown in part (b) of Figure 18-4. As you can see, system performance has generally improved, variations in employment, inventory, and backlogs are substantially reduced. Still, the basic dynamic pattern remains—the sales fluctuations are followed by even larger fluctuations in inventories, employment, and backlogs. These results are an indicator of need for further change.

At this point, management considered an additional modification, adding to the model a representation of the consumer sector of the industry (the addition of an external factor). The customers of this components manufacturer are themselves manufacturers of military and other consumer electronics products. It seemed appropriate to consider the consumer sector because fluctuations in incoming consumer orders seemed to be the driving force behind the other fluctuations in the manufacturer's system. This suggested that a better understanding of consumer ordering practices might be worthwhile. The results of an investigation revealed that consumer ordering practices were related to the manufacturer's delivery lead time. On this basis the consumer sector, including representations of the consumer's components inventory, production rate, engineering evaluation process, and order release policies, was added to the simulation model. While developing these new additions to the model, management discovered that the customer's rate of releasing new orders (to the manufacturer) is affected by the manufacturer's delivery delay (to the customer), and the manufacturer's delivery delay is influenced by the rate of new orders received from customers. The revised model was computer programmed to recognize this interrelationship and was tested over 300 simulated weeks. Performance of the manufacturing system under these conditions was improved, as shown in Figure 18-4 (c). Overall, the dynamic behavior of the system under these conditions is much more stable than it was under the previous two conditions.

The results indicate that the greatest improvement in the manufacturer's system performance could be obtained by adjusting the factory lead time for deliveries. This is an *internally* controllable parameter of the manufacturer. Even more noteworthy, however, is the thought process necessary to recognize the significance of this parameter. *This awareness occurred only after someone was willing to look at environmental elements, in this case the structure of consumer policies, outside the system of immediate concern.* Thus, a useful internal change was identified when management took an "open" systems approach to the problem.

SUMMARY
Since organizations and their conversion subsystems are dynamic open systems in constant interaction with their environments, changes of varying magnitude are constantly occurring. Managers must be aware of the process of change and its role in the organization.

Several aspects of change must be understood if change is to be successfully managed. First, one must recognize the need for change as signalled by either internal or external indicators. Next, the targets for change—technology, structure, and behavior—must be identified. Any or all of these are directly involved in the organizational change process.

The unpredictable nature of the overall effects of change arise from the complexities of organizations. There are three sources of complexity. First are those arising from interrelationships among the subfunctions of the management process (planning, organizing, and controlling). Second are those stemming from the interactions among functional areas (operations, finance, and marketing, for example). Third, complexities arise from the inherent interrelationships among operations subproblems (scheduling, layout, location, and inventory).

Since many decisions and changes occur simultaneously, and since they are ultimately interrelated, it is difficult in advance to predict their overall effects on system effectiveness. Consequently, some systemic methods are desirable for assessing the overall impacts of proposed changes. System dynamics is one methodology for accomplishing this. Still, the state of the art remains relatively underdeveloped, and managerial intuition and experience remain the main means used for predicting the overall effects of change.

CASE

Hidesign

After pursuing it as a hobby for many years, in 1957, Bill Withers began to make custom furniture in his garage on a full-time basis. Bill's work had been greatly admired by friends and neighbors, and he was often requested to make special pieces for them. In 1960, Bill leased a facility previously occupied by a supermarket. As his operation expanded, he hired two additional craftsmen, a woodworker and a leather specialist. His high-quality, custom-made pieces were well received, and by 1964, Hidesign was incorporated and had 11 employees.

Today, Hidesign serves a custom furniture market covering the entire northwest region of the United States. Bill Withers, the president, has a staff of 37 employees. Custom-made furniture is the sole product, and the company has prided itself on high product quality and timely delivery services. Organizationally, in addition to processing departments, Hidesign has sales, purchasing, shipping, and design departments. Internal processing departments include wood framing, wood preparation, wood finishing, metal finishing, leather, glass, plastics, and cloth fabrics.

This past year, anywhere from 350 to 400 jobs were processed in the facility on any given day. Although product quality remains high, on-time deliveries have begun to deteriorate, and although specific data have not yet been compiled, average job lateness seems to be about 4 to 7 weeks. Bill Arnold, an employee since 1962, does the shop loading as a special assistant to the shop manager. His job also includes coordinating the overall shop efforts with those of the sales and design departments.

Detailed scheduling of orders has always been the responsibility of the three shop foremen. Larry Cline is foreman of the wood preparation, framing, and finishing departments. Isaac Trumbolt has the leather department and cloth fabrics. Willie Heft is foreman of three departments, metal, glass, and plastics.

Bill Withers is concerned about job lateness. He feels deteriorating customer service might well affect future sales. He has requested George Herring to design a plan for analyzing the current situation and recommending changes. George, whose primary experience has been coordinating a new physical distribution system, is uncertain which factors should be considered and what data will be needed.

Reanalyze Hidesign's situation by applying the concepts of change presented in this chapter and by using your previous analysis of Hidesign from Chapter 12.

1. In some situations it is useful to view operations as a closed subsystem, while in other situations an open system view is more useful. Give examples of both.

2. What factors contribute to the dynamic nature of operations in an organization?

3. Using Figure 18-2 as a guide, analyze the dynamics of the conversion process of a college of business and administration.

4. Using Figure 18-2 as a guide, contrast the dynamics of the conversion processes of a manufacturing firm and an urban transit system.

5. How does a manager decide which indicators of the need for change are most important?

6. Reliable National Bank is considering the installation of automatic teller units at several locations throughout the city. What indicators of the need for change and what desired results Led to considering this change?

7. Suppose you are requested to predict the results of Reliable National Bank's contemplated change (see question 6). Outline your approach for making such a prediction, including a list of the main factors that must be considered.

8. Identify two organizations for which external indicators of the need for change are of minimal importance. List two others for which external indicators are dominant.

9. Some managers contend that the three targets for change are substitutable; when the need for change arises, a manager usually has a choice of making changes In any or all of the target areas. Discuss this statement.

10. Identify and discuss the behavioral implications of decisions to change job shop priority rules, facility layout, and facility location.

11. Identify and discuss the behavioral implications of changes in technology and organizational structure.

12. Give examples showing how changes in the finance and marketing subsystems necessitate changes in the operations subsystem of the organization.

13. Facility location is a major planning decision in operations management. Show how it is interrelated with organizing and controlling of operations.

GLOSSARY

Analysis: process of decomposing a "whole" into separate subparts to permit a better understanding of the individual subcomponents

Closed system: a self-contained entity within definable boundaries; a system that has no exchanges (inputs or outputs) of energy with its environment

Open system: a system that is an integral part of a larger system; its viability depends upon successful adjustments to varied inputs from and outputs to its environment

Synthesis: process of constructing or reconstructing the "whole" by combining various subparts; attempts to understand how the "whole" will behave once it has been created from interrelated subcomponents

System dynamics: a computer-based simulation methodology for developing and analyzing models of systems and their behavior

SELECTED READINGS

Abernathy, W.J. "Production Process Structure and Technological Change." *Decision Sciences* 7, no. 4 (October 1976): 607-19.

Aldrich, H. and D. Herker. "Boundary Spanning Roles and Organization Structure." *Academy of Management Review* 2, no. 2 (April 1977): 217-30.

Anderson, C.R. and F.T. Paine. "Managerial Perceptions and Strategic Behavior." *Academy of Management Journal* 18, no. 4 (December 1975): 811-23.

Buehler, V.M. and Y.K. Shetty. "Managerial Response to Social Responsibility Challenge." *Academy of Management Journal* 19, no. 1 (March 1976): 66-78

Forrester, Jay W. *Industrial Dynamics.* Cambridge, Mass.: The M.I.T. Press, 1961.

Guetzkow, H., P. Kotler, and R.L. Schultz, eds. *Simulation in Social and Administrative Systems.* Englewood Cliffs, N.J.: Prentice-Hall, Inc., 1972.

Lee, J.A. "Leader Power for Managing Change." *Academy of Management Review* 2, no. 1 (January 1977): 73-80.

Roberts, Edward B. "Industrial Dynamics and the Design of Management Control Systems." *Management Technology* 3, no. 2 (December 1963): 100-118.

Schrieber, A.N., ed. *Corporate Simulation Models.* Seattle: Graduate School of Business Administration, University of Washington, 1970.

Scott, W.G. "Organization Theory: A Reassessment." *Academy of Management Journal* 17, no. 2 (June 1974): 242-54.

Rational Approaches to Change

Managers of organizations must expect change. The question is not whether change will be necessary but how to deal with it. In Chapter 18, we considered three target areas for change, technology, structure, and behavior, as we put the process of change into an overall, integrative framework. Now we can begin to think about these targets from a managerial point of view. In this chapter, we'll discuss rational approaches to change in technology and structure; in Chapter 20, we'll consider rational approaches to change in behavioral situations. As Figures 19-1 and 19-2 show, change is a necessary part of all conversion processes. If we can learn to deal with change in a rational way, not only will our organizations be better; our lives will be easier.

THE ROLE OF RATIONALITY

Managerial intuition, judgment, and experience play major roles in change decisions. Whether these decisions are based on hunch or thoughtful analysis, the full effects of significant change are usually unpredictable to some extent. But managers need not be discouraged by the absence of complete predictability; once we have recognized the need for change, we can take some careful, systematic steps to increase predictability somewhat and help ourselves cope with change.

One procedure that lends rationality to the change process is the scientific approach to decision problems. Six steps in this approach are:

1. problem recognition and definition,
2. statement of objectives,
3. formulation of alternative solutions,

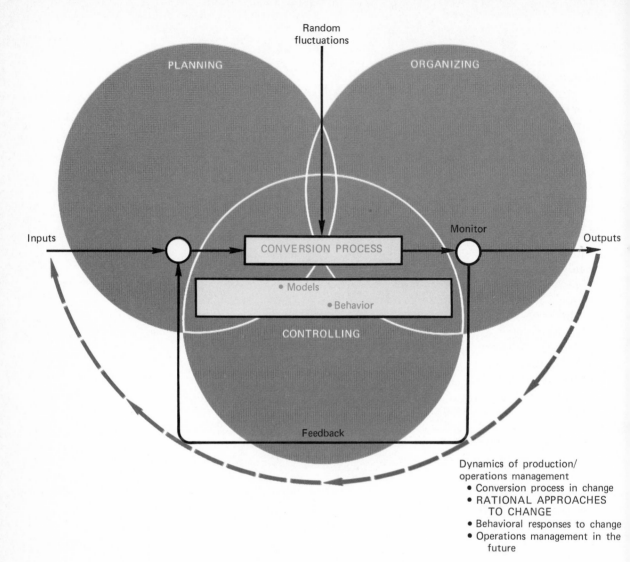

Random
fluctuations

PLANNING   ORGANIZING

Inputs   Monitor   Outputs

CONVERSION PROCESS

• Models
    • Behavior

CONTROLLING

Feedback

Dynamics of production/
operations management
• Conversion process in change
• RATIONAL APPROACHES
    TO CHANGE
• Behavioral responses to change
• Operations management in the
    future

Figure 19-1 **General model for production/operations management**

4. data collection,
5. evaluation of alternatives, and
6. decision or choice.

We can recognize and define a problem only after the indicators of the
need for change have appeared. Then we state our objectives in terms
of the desired results of planned change (Figure 19-2). It is the final four
steps of the scientific approach to change that we want to emphasize in
this chapter. As managers learn to formulate alternative solutions, collect

data, and evaluate alternatives, they become better able to make rational decisions.

By a "rational" approach, we mean the process of carefully identifying change alternatives, analyzing their effects from a financial, economic, or other logical point of view, comparing the alternatives on this basis, and identifying the best of the alternatives. Typically, this kind of approach involves quantitative analysis. Thereafter, additional nonquantifiable factors can be introduced and considered before the final choice is made. This procedure allows managers to put those logical, typically quantifiable aspects of the total change problem in proper perspective.

Of the three targets for change—technology, structure, and behavior—behavior is least susceptible to quantitative analysis, technology is most susceptible, and the effects of structural modification are somewhere in between. When technology is the target, changes in products, processes, equipment and/or facilities are considered. Ordinarily, formal or rational analysis in these instances is of a financial or engineering nature. When organizational structure or policy is the target, some attempts are made to measure change in financial terms, but to a lesser extent; the impact of these changes can't always be captured in financial terms. Nevertheless, the rational approach is still applicable. We are generally forced to employ nonfinancial measures of system performance, however; changes in crime rate, service to customers, reduction in procurement lead times, and similar patterns often reflect system performance. Let's begin our discussion of changes in conversion technology with a look at financial and economic analysis.

Figure 19-2 Dynamics of production/operations management: the conversion process in change

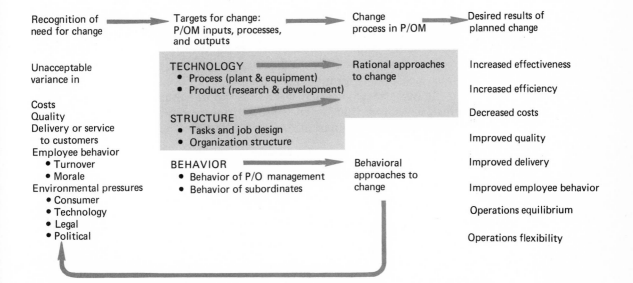

To almost every organization in both the public and private sectors, financial analysis is vital. Public agencies operating on limited budgets want to provide as much service as possible to the public. Private firms strive to provide suitable returns on capital invested by their owners. Whenever proposals are made to change products, processes, equipment, or facilities, some financial implications must be considered. Operations managers are concerned with proposals for revising facility layouts, changing the system capacity, deciding facility location, revising inventory systems, and so on. Proposals for change are almost always made in the hope that some benefits will result; but the benefits can't be realized unless the necessary resources are committed first. Are the anticipated benefits of change worth the anticipated costs? This is the central question of financial and economic analysis.

The financial change problem in production/operations management differs from the initial investment problem, although we use similiar solution procedures for both. In the initial investment situation, the manager has a certain amount of resources to be spent either on the investment or on other alternative investments. For the financial change problem, the manager again has a certain amount of resources and again must compare the proposed alternative with the competing alternatives. But the manager also has another option. He or she can choose to make no change at all. The "no change" alternative is sometimes called the *defender* and the alternative the *challenger.*

We can compare one alternative with competing alternatives with a marginal efficiency of capital curve. Look at Figure 19-3. Say that the overall cost of capital to the firm is 10 percent. Assuming investment alternatives are numbered *1, 2, 3,* and so on by decreasing return on investment, the first 12 investments faced by the firm in this time period would return a rate above the cost of capital. The firm would marginally invest in the first, then the second, and so forth until available funds were depleted. Even if funds were still available after the first 12 investments, the firm would not invest further. Actually, as this example is constructed, the return on investment for the twelfth alternative just equals the cost of capital, and the firm would be neutral about investing in it. It's also possible to graph total investment dollars (cumulative) rather than the investment alternatives as we did in Figure 19-3. Whatever the method, remember that for each project there is an associated investment dollar, and the dollar amounts vary considerably from project to project.

Terminology and Concepts

Although it's not always possible to do so, decision makers try to evaluate alternatives logically and comparably. Toward this end, economic analysis borrows some standard terminology from finance and accounting.

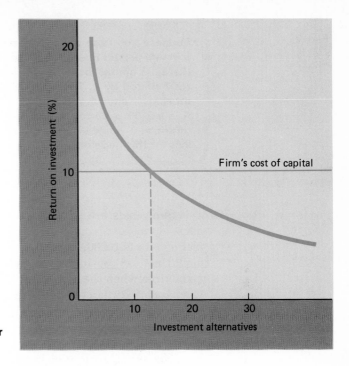

Figure 19-3 **Return on investment for investment alternatives**

When considering existing or prospective equipment and facilities, the manager is interested in the costs associated with their ownership and operation. This information is needed, for example, to decide whether old equipment should be retained or replaced by newer models. What is the old equipment worth? Although sometimes the relevant information can be obtained from accounting data, often it cannot be. Frequently, accounting cost data are not relevant for use in investment decisions because they are historic rather than current. By reflecting what has occurred in the past in a standard, orderly fashion, they give some measure of current operating status. They do not reflect changes in market values of existing equipment or the costs of replacing old equipment and facilities with new. For financial analyses of investment proposals, accounting costs play a secondary role. *The costs that are used in economic analysis are current costs, actual costs.* Let's examine a few costs that become important to us in analysis.

Opportunity costs are the returns that are lost or foregone as a result of selecting one alternative instead of another. The amount of the opportunity cost is determined by comparing the benefits or advantages of a choice with those of the best alternative. Selection of one alternative usually involves foregoing the opportunity of gaining benefits offered by other alternatives.

================= EXAMPLE =================

Suppose you wish to sell your car and person A offers you $900. Then a friend, person B, offers $800. If you select alternative A, you must forego the $800 offered by B. If you select alternative B, you must forego the $900 offered by A. Thus alternative A offers a $100 net advantage. Stated otherwise, should you choose B, the loss from passing over alternative A is a $100 opportunity cost to you. If you wish to maximize your dollar return, you would select alternative A, thereby minimizing the opportunity loss for this decision.

Sunk costs are past expenditures that are irrelevant to current decisions. Suppose a company purchased a special piece of equipment one year ago for $10,000. Since the purchase is a past event, the cost of $10,000 should not be considered in future choices. Prior to the investment, up to the time when the decision was made to buy the equipment, the $10,000 purchase price was a relevant consideration. Thereafter, it became irrelevant for any future decisions. Should you now be interested in replacing the piece of equipment, its salvage value is important, but the initial sunk cost of $10,000 is not.

The salvage value of facilities and equipment is a relevant revenue (a negative cost), since existing assets that are abandoned or replaced may be saleable. The income received from an asset sale is the *salvage value.* Thus, when a decision alternative involves income from the sale of existing assets, salvage value is a relevant consideration. Salvage value is a market value, similiar to the concept of current, actual costs.

Salvage value provides a good example of how accounting records can be inappropriate for financial decision making. The book value of an asset, in an accounting sense, is usually not an accurate indicator of the asset salvage value. Although the company's book value may be thousands of dollars, the market value may be higher, lower, or even zero. The market or salvage value, not the book value, is relevant for decision analysis.

To assist in decision analysis, current and future salvage values are estimated for the asset under consideration. A schedule of salvage values, an example of which is shown in Table 19-1, shows the estimated salvage value for an existing piece of equipment that is being considered for replacement. Current salvage value is $10,000; year-end salvage values are shown for each of three succeeding years. Suppose the company is examining the financial impact of selling the equipment now versus selling it at the end of each of the three ensuing years. Notice that salvage value is expected to decrease annually and that opportunity costs can be calculated for each of the decision alternatives. From the viewpoint of salvage income, the best alternative is to sell now; current salvage value is highest, and the proceeds can be invested during year 1 at 8 percent for an additional $800 in income. By selling at the end of year 1, the company foregoes

TABLE 19-1

A SCHEDULE OF ESTIMATED SALVAGE VALUE OF AN EXISTING PIECE OF EQUIPMENT

| Sell at end of year | Expected salvage value at year end | Annual opportunity costs | | Total lost income |
		Income lost due to decrease in salvage value from previous year	Income lost from not investing salvage funds at 8% during succeeding year	
0 (now)	$10,000	$ 0	$ 0	$ 0
1	8,000	2,000	800	2,800
2	5,000	3,000	640	3,640
3	1,000	4,000	400	4,400

$2,000 of salvage income and the $800 interest income. Compared to selling now, the total first year opportunity cost is $2,800. Of course, other relevant costs besides those associated with salvage value must also be considered, and so should the revenues that can be generated each year with the equipment.

Depreciation is an accounting concept for recovering outlays (expenditures) for assets over their lives. Depreciation, a bookkeeping concept, does not reflect market values. Since we are interested only in market values, of what value is depreciation to the economics of change (replacement)? Depreciation is important only in that the depreciation schedule affects income tax rates, and income taxes affect actual cash flows. The higher the depreciation in any one period, the lower the taxes paid and the greater the cash flows (revenues less expenses). Although we will cover depreciation and taxes in some detail in the supplement to this chapter, for our purposes here we will simplify matters by ignoring them both.

Incremental cash flows

Later, when we evaluate and compare investment opportunities, we'll have to consider the alternatives' incremental cash flows. When we do a cost comparison of two alternatives, we are interested only in the cost differences, or increments, between them; obviously, cost elements that are shared in common are irrelevant.

Cash flows are of central interest in evaluating any investment proposal. What are all the cash flows associated with an alternative? Some involve only outlays of funds with no anticipated additional revenues. If we assume, for example, that new and old equipment generates the same revenues, investing in replacement equipment involves only outlays of funds. Other proposals offer both new revenues and outflows. If we decided to open a wine and cheese shop at a new shopping center, we could expect both new cash outflows and inflows. All inflows and outflows that result from adopting an alternative should enter into the analysis, including not only initial outlays but also ongoing outlays expected throughout the asset life. Anticipated costs of owning, operating, and maintaining the asset should therefore be considered. To determine incremental cash flows, we must also consider expected revenue from sales and possible salvage decisions. Also important are the *magnitude* (size) of cash flows, the *direction* (revenue or expense) of cash flows, and the *patterns* (exactly when) cash flows take place over the life of the asset.

Life of the Asset

There are several ways of viewing the life of an asset. Consider the life of a piece of equipment. First, we can determine its *accounting life,* the life used to develop a depreciation schedule. Second, we can consider its *machine life,* the length of time the machine could actually function. At the end of the machine life, there might or might not be some salvage value. Machine life typically is of secondary interest to us in economic analysis. We are primarily interested in *economic life,* the period of time the asset performs its useful economic service to the organization. These three measurements may be widely divergent.

═══════════ EXAMPLE ═══════════

A national diamond wholesaler, who considers it absolutely necessary for his firm to convey a prosperous image, requires his salespeople to drive either Lincoln Continentals or Cadillacs. He has established a policy of purchasing only new automobiles and retaining them for two years. At the end of that time, the economic usefulness of the luxury car ends. The accounting department, on the other hand, sets up a depreciation schedule based on a three-year life; and the automobile manufacturers' data suggest that properly maintained Continentals and Cadillacs should last ten years. For these cars, then, machine life is ten years, accounting life three years, and economic life two years. When management undertakes an economic analysis of fleet replacement, economic life is critical.

Time Value of Money

When analysts speak of the time value of money, they mean the revenues that may be received for money over time. A sum of money held as cash may either depreciate or appreciate in value over time, but it will not earn any revenues while it is being held. If the same sum of money is invested over time for a specified amount with a guarantee of repayment of the principal, the original sum of money has value over time. The original sum itself may have depreciated or appreciated in value, just as though it were held as cash. This idea of money having value over time is frequently overlooked by individuals, businesses, and, of special interest to us, by production/operations managers.

===== EXAMPLE =====

Suppose you are given $100 as a birthday gift. You decide to invest now for two years in a bank paying 8 percent annual interest. At the time of initial investment, time zero for purposes of analysis, the bank owes you $100. After one year, the bank owes you not only the initial amount but 8 percent of that amount as well. At the end of year one, the amount due you is $108, or $100 + (.08)($100). Thus, at the beginning of year two you have an investment of $108, which will remain in the bank during year two. At the end of year two, the bank owes you not only the $108 you had at the beginning of that year, but also an additional 8 percent of that amount, interest on your investment during the second year. At the end of year two, the amount owed you is $116.64, or $108 + (.08)($108). Your savings have been *compounded*.

Income and Expense Patterns and Associated Compound Interest Factors

Income and expense patterns In equipment and operations replacement situations, there are six basic patterns of income and expense flows. Figure 19-4 shows three of these flow patterns, and since each pattern has a reverse flow as well, there are six possible cash flows. The three not shown (given P to find S, given P to find R, and given S to find R) would have the same graphical patterns as their counterparts, except that the cash flows would be reversed.

Compound interest factors Which income flow pattern applies to our birthday gift example? Given a present sum of money (P) to find a future sum of money (S) after n periods. If we consider the time value of money at interest rate i over the n years, we have the concept of a compound interest factor. Let's call this particular factor a single payment compound amount factor. It could be defined as $CAF(s)_i^n$ and illustrated:

$$
\begin{array}{lll}
P & & S \\
\downarrow & & \downarrow \quad CAF(s)_i^n \\
\hline
0 & & n \\
& \text{Time at } i &
\end{array}
$$

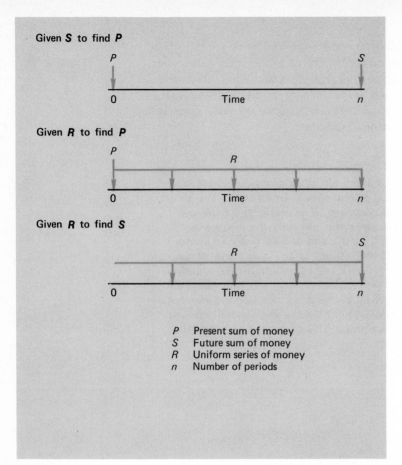

Given **S** to find **P**

P ↓ 0 — Time — S ↓ n

Given **R** to find **P**

P ↓ 0 — R — Time — n

Given **R** to find **S**

0 — R — Time — S ↓ n

P	Present sum of money
S	Future sum of money
R	Uniform series of money
n	Number of periods

Figure 19-4 **Income and expense flow patterns**

In terms of our example, the future sum of money, *S*, is found by looking up the factor in Appendix B (appendices are at the end of the text) and solving for *S* as follows:

$$S = P\,(CAF(s)_i^n) \qquad (19\text{-}1)$$
$$= \$100\,(CAF(s)_{.08}^2)$$
$$= 100\,(1.166)$$
$$= \$116.60$$

Note that the answer we get by using equation 19-1 ($116.60) is not precisely the same as the answer we got by computing each year's interest ($116.64). This is because the factor is rounded in the appendix. The single payment compound amount factor was found by going to Appendix B for an interest rate, *i*, of 8%. Then we look in the *n* column for the appropriate number of periods, in this case 2. Next we find the column that applies to our cash flow situation, in this case given *P* to find *S*. By matching the time periods (2) with the proper column, we find that 1.166 is the factor we are looking for, and we use it in our calculation.

You do not have to remember the name of the factor (the single payment compound amount factor) nor the interest formula from which the factor was derived ($(1 + i)^n$) to use the table. *You need only understand the logic of the investment situation, the cash flow patterns given and sought.* The different compound interest factors associated with varying cash flows are:

Cash flow	Factor name	Factor symbol
given S to find P	present worth factor	$PWF(s)_i^n$
given P to find S	compound amount factor	$CAF(s)_i^n$
given R to find P	present worth factor	$PWF(u)_i^n$
given P to find R	capital recovery factor	CRF_i^n
given R to find S	compound amount factor	$CAF(u)_i^n$
given S to find R	sinking fund factor	SFF_i^n

Note that (s) refers to a single payment and (u) to a uniform annual series for the various factors. Can you find each factor in Appendix B? The factors corresponding to Figure 19-4 are shown in Figure 19-5 along with a more precise definition of terms. The interest formulas for several factors are presented in the supplement to this chapter.

Now let's illustrate another factor.

===== **EXAMPLE** =====

Your brother promises to give you $116.64 two years from now. If money earns 8 percent interest, what is the *present* value to you? This is a cash flow situation in which S is given, P must be found.

$$P \qquad\qquad S = \$116.64$$

```
P                    S  = $116.64
↓                    ↓
0                    2
        n = 2
        i =  .08
```

Solving for P,

$$P = S \text{ (given } S \text{ to find } P \text{ factor)}$$
$$= S(PWF(s)_i^n)$$
$$= \$116.64\,(PWF(s)_{.08}^2)$$
$$= 116.64\,(.8573)$$
$$= 99.995$$
$$P \cong 100.00$$

This is the reverse of our previous example, in which $100 invested for two years equaled $116.64. The present value of $116.64 in two years at 8% is $100.00.

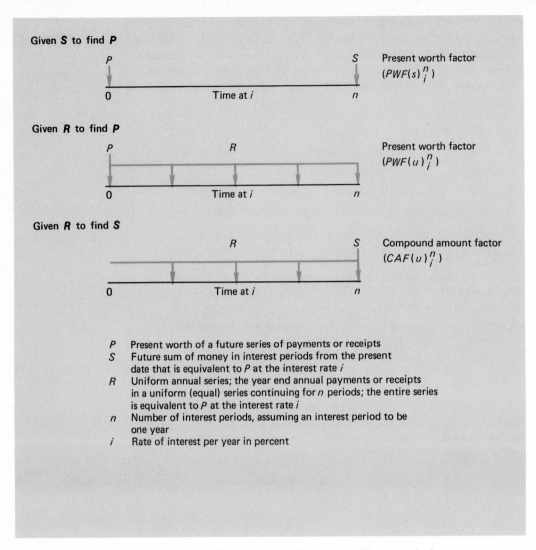

Given **S** to find **P**

P

S Present worth factor

$(PWF(s)\,_i^n)$

0   Time at i n

Given **R** to find **P**

P R

Present worth factor

$(PWF(u)\,_i^n)$

0   Time at i n

Given **R** to find **S**

R S

Compound amount factor

$(CAF(u)\,_i^n)$

0   Time at i n

P Present worth of a future series of payments or receipts
S Future sum of money in interest periods from the present
     date that is equivalent to P at the interest rate i
R Uniform annual series; the year end annual payments or receipts
     in a uniform (equal) series continuing for n periods; the entire series
     is equivalent to P at the interest rate i
n Number of interest periods, assuming an interest period to be
     one year
i Rate of interest per year in percent

Figure 19-5   **Income and expense flow patterns and compound interest factors**

When we use the table, we must expect some rounding errors. Had we multiplied $116.60 by .8573, for example, we would have found a present value of $99.96.

Choosing a
discount rate

The importance of the time value of money is reflected in the choice of i in the compounding and discounting process. How should the value of i be chosen? What should it represent? These questions are not always simple to answer for investment decisions. For some organizations, i represents the interest rate charged by lending institutions that loan the money needed to make the investment in plant or equipment. Many companies interpret i as the "cost of capital," the cost to them of procuring the funds necessary to finance an investment. Some companies, in choosing i, think in terms of opportunity costs—"If I invest in project x it had better offer at least a rate of return of i because an alternative investment offers rate i." Finally, some firms have a blanket investment policy—"No investment will be made unless it offers at least a return of i percent per year." Many of these interpretations will be used as we discuss methods of investment evaluation.

Methods of Evaluation

There are several formal financial methods of evaluating proposed operations changes, and they vary in the degree of simplicity and the type of information they provide. We will focus on the equipment replacement problem, one of several rational operating change problems faced by management. We will choose one model that is simple to calculate, the payback method, and one model that is not as simple to calculate but is often more informative, *net present value.*

Payback   One of the most commonly used methods of evaluating investment proposals is to calculate the payback period of the investment as follows:

$$\left(\begin{array}{c}\text{Payback}\\\text{period}\end{array}\right) = \frac{\text{(Net investment)}}{\left(\begin{array}{c}\text{Net annual income}\\\text{from investment}\end{array}\right)}$$

Net investment, in dollars, includes the purchase price and installation less salvage value of any equipment or other asset that has depleted its economic life. Net annual income is the annual cash flow in dollars per year. The resulting payback period is expressed in terms of time, in this case years.

Payback measures the length of time required to recover one's investment. Organizations may be interested in recovering their investment quickly so that they may use the funds for reinvestment in other alternatives. In these cases, payback periods can be calculated for each alternative, and the one offering the quickest turnover of funds (shortest payback period) can be selected.

For several reasons, managers should use the payback criterion with caution. First, it does not consider the time value of funds. Second, uneven expense and revenue flow patterns cannot be considered. Finally, it ignores all inflows that occur after the payback period. On the other hand, it has the advantages of simplicity and ease of communication. We recommend

━━━━ **EXAMPLE** ━━━━

Two different orange pickers are being considered by Arizona Orchards, Inc., to assist in harvesting the orange crop at the Chandler, Arizona, farm. Alternative A requires a net investment of $10,000 and is expected to return $2,500 in net annual income per year. Investment B is slightly more expensive, $12,000, but is expected to return $2,750 per year in income. Calculating the payback period,

$$\text{Payback } A = \frac{\$10,000}{\$\ 2,500/\text{yr}} = 4 \text{ yr}$$

$$\text{Payback } B = \frac{\$12,000}{\$\ 2,750/\text{yr}} = 4.36 \text{ yr}$$

Arizona Orchards should choose A over B.

it not be used as the sole basis of decision but in conjunction with, or as a supplement to, the other methods of analysis.

Net present value   Net present value considers all cash flows associated with an investment, discounts each unique flow (revenue or expense) back through time by using the appropriate compound interest factor, and then sums the net value of all discounted flows at the present time. The result is a net present value:

$$\text{Net present value} = \Sigma \left[(\text{Revenue})\left(\begin{array}{c}\text{Compound}\\\text{interest}\\\text{factor}\end{array}\right) - (\text{Expense})\left(\begin{array}{c}\text{Compound}\\\text{interest}\\\text{factor}\end{array}\right)\right] \quad (19\text{-}2)$$

$$NPV = \sum_{1}^{T} (v_t - c_t)(PWF(s)_i^t) - P \quad (19\text{-}3)$$

where

$i =$ rate of interest per year in percent
$P =$ initial investment made at present time
$T =$ life of investment
$v_t =$ income or receipts occurring in period t, where $t = 1, 2, ..., T$
$c_t =$ expenses or disbursements made in period t, where $t = 1, 2, ..., T$

The procedure for using net present value is:

1. Separate all data by alternatives. Repeat each of the following steps for each alternative.
2. Grasp the cash flows. (A diagram of cash flow might be helpful.) On the diagram identify the interest rate and time periods.
3. Write a total net present value equation in words to reflect the situation, the cash flow patterns.

4. Substitute the appropriate dollars and compound amount factors for each flow in the equation.
5. Find the compound amount factors in the Appendices and solve, finding the net present value for each alternative.
6. Choose the alternative with the *greatest* net present value.

Once you have solved a few problems, you'll probably be able to shortcut this procedure considerably. In *NPV* analysis we assume that cash flows that occur throughout the year always occur at year end. Let's take one example through the complete procedure. This example involves existing equipment that is deteriorating and must be replaced to sustain operations. The manager can compare decision alternatives on a present value basis using the organization's cost of capital as the discounting rate.

EXAMPLE

Fireway Company must purchase a piece of replacement equipment and is considering models offered by two competing equipment manufacturers. Both models have a useful life expectancy of six years (no expected salvage value), and Fireway has a cost of capital of 10 percent for its investments. Each model provides an income of $4,000 annually. Alternative A requires an initial outlay of $10,000 and requires maintenance expenditures of $1,000 annually. Alternative B, a deluxe model, requires an initial outlay of $12,000 and annual maintenance costs of $500. Which alternative is less costly?

The first step has been completed, as the data are already organized according to investment alternative. The cash flows are:

Model A

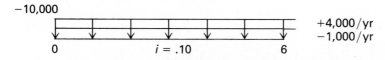

−10,000   +4,000/yr
                                                           −1,000/yr
0            $i = .10$ 6

Model B

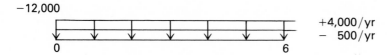

−12,000   +4,000/yr
                                                           − 500/yr
0   6

The net present value equation for *A* would be:

$NPV(A)$ = Sum for each of six years (revenue − expense)(factor) − *P*

= (4,000 − 1,000)(given *R* to find *P*) − *P*

= (4,000 − 1,000) $PWF(u)^6_{.10}$ − 10,000

= 3,000 (4.355) − 10,000

= 13,065 − 10,000

$NPV(A)$ = + $3,065

─────── **EXAMPLE (cont.)** ───────

Similarly, the net present value for *B* would be:

$$NPV(B) = (4,000 - 500) \text{ (given } R \text{ to find } P) - 12,000$$
$$= 3,500 \ PWF \ (u)^6_{.10} - 12,000$$
$$= 3,500 \ (4.355) - 12,000$$
$$= 15,242 - 12,000$$
$$= + \$3,242$$

Choose *B* over *A* because \$3,242 > \$3,065.

As you might have figured out, another method of solution could also be used. With this method, use separate present worth factors for each of the six periods and sum the six amounts and the initial investment at the current time, time zero. The answers should be equivalent or nearly so using the rounded table factors with those we calculated above for alternatives *A* and *B*. Let's look at a more complex example.

─────── **EXAMPLE** ───────

Hopi Trucking has just paid \$16,000 cash for a new truck. Hopi management estimates that the useful life of the truck is four years. At the end of four years, the estimated salvage value will be \$2,500. Maintenance and other operating costs are expected to be \$10,000 per year for three years and \$12,000 in the fourth year. Assuming we can replace the truck in four years for the same price, how much money must be generated each year from this investment to have at least enough to purchase another truck in four years? Money is worth 8 percent to Hopi, and revenues flow in uniformly to the firm.

First, we must recognize that we are being asked for a dollar amount four years hence, not at the present time. Second, we should realize that the \$16,000 truck we now have is a sunk cost. Since we are not considering depreciation and taxes, they will not influence our decision. Let *X* be the dollars of revenue required each year to cover expenses and provide \$16,000 at the end of four years. Our problem then is as follows.

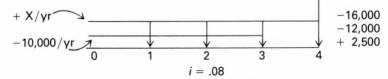

We have −\$10,000 per year occurring for three years and, at the end of the fourth year, −\$12,000 for expenses. We also have −\$16,000 for a new

---

EXAMPLE (cont.)

truck and +$2,500 for salvaging our old truck. The cash inflow we are looking for is X per year for four years. This can be expressed *at year four*:

$$NPV = -10{,}000 \ (R \text{ to find } P) \ (P \text{ to find } S)$$

$$n = 3 \qquad n = 4$$
$$i = .08 \qquad i = .08$$

$$+ \ X \ (R \text{ to find } S) - 16{,}000 - 12{,}000$$

$$n = 4$$
$$i = .08$$

$$+ \ 2{,}500$$

$$= -10{,}000 \ (PWF(u)^3_{.08})(CAF(s)^4_{.08})$$

$$+ \ X(CAF(u)^4_{.08}) - 25{,}500$$

$$= -10{,}000 \ (2.577)(1.360) + 4.506 \ X - 25{,}500$$

$$= 4.506 \ X - (35{,}047 + 25{,}500)$$

$$NPV = 4.506 \ X - 60{,}547$$

Setting $NPV = 0$ (the breakeven for sales and expenses at four years) and solving for X gives:

$$0 = 4.506 \ X - 60{,}547$$
$$X = 60{,}547 / 4.506$$
$$X = \$13{,}437$$

Annual sales revenue will have to be $13,437 to cover expenses and provide $16,000 cash at the end of four years.

With this example, we have solved a problem with a more complex cash flow and an unknown value other than the net present value. Notice that the three-year annual operating expense was brought back to time zero as an annuity and then carried forward four years as a single payment. Although this process was computationally more efficient than taking the $10,000 forward to the fourth year each of three times, the result would be the same in either case.

What should we do if the investment alternatives have *unequal lives*? Clearly, we can't compare them directly. Let's assume that like-for-like replacement can occur at the end of the life of each asset and use the least common multiple of lives over which to compare the investment.

If one alternative has a three year life and one a two year life, we would make the comparison over six years. We are assuming, then, that the first alternative would have two exactly similar (like-for-like) investments and the second alternative three exactly similar investments.

<hr>

EXAMPLE

Yardcare, a lawn care company, can purchase an inexpensive lawn mower for $80 that lasts one year or a more expensive mower for $120 that lasts two years. Neither mower requires maintenance the first year, but in the second year the more expensive mower will require $40 worth of maintenance. Both are essentially worthless at the end of one and two years respectively. Money is worth 10 percent to Yardcare. Currently, Yardcare purchases about 30 mowers every two years with no guiding investment replacement principle. What should they do in the future?

Let the inexpensive model be I, the more expensive E. We need to compare over equal lives, the least multiple being two years. Comparing for one mower, we assume that I is replaced at the end of year one with another I. The patterns and solutions for each are:

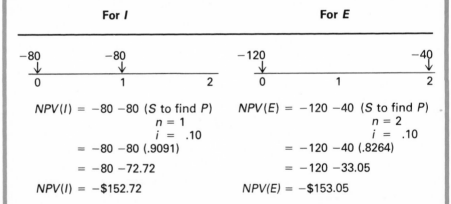

For I

$NPV(I) = -80 - 80$ (S to find P)
$n = 1$
$i = .10$
$= -80 - 80 (.9091)$
$= -80 - 72.72$
$NPV(I) = -\$152.72$

For E

$NPV(E) = -120 - 40$ (S to find P)
$n = 2$
$i = .10$
$= -120 - 40 (.8264)$
$= -120 - 33.05$
$NPV(E) = -\$153.05$

Based on present value, the inexpensive model is favored; the cost is $0.33 less per mower ($153.05 − $152.72). For all practical purposes, Yardcare would be indifferent about the choice. The money saved every two years, 30 times $0.33, or $9.90, is negligible, and it is doubtful cost data used in the analysis are completely accurate. Errors in data concerning maintenance and purchase prices are always likely.

At times, organizations want investments to meet a minimum rate of return. If the *net* present value at that rate of return is positive, the investment provides greater returns than would the rate used in determining the present value. The investment is made. On the other hand, if the present value is negative, the return is less than that provided by the interest rate used, and the investment is unattractive.

━━━━━━ EXAMPLE ━━━━━━

XYZ company is considering adding one truck to its fleet of delivery trucks. The truck can be obtained at a cost of $1,800 if it is purchased for cash now. It is estimated that this used truck will have a useful service life of three years but will require year-end maintenance expenditures of $300 each year. As a result of expanded delivery service, management estimates that annual net revenues will be increased by $1,000 per year for each of the three years. XYZ requires a minimum rate of return of 10 percent and does not wish to make investments that do not offer at least a 10 percent return. The cash flows are:

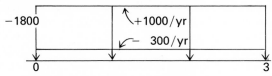

The net present value is calculated:

$$NPV = -1,800 - 300 \text{ (given } R \text{ to find } P) + 1,000 \text{ (given } R \text{ to find } P)$$
$$n = 3 \qquad\qquad n = 3$$
$$i = .10 \qquad\qquad i = .10$$

$$= -1,800 - 300(PWF(u)^3_{.10}) + 1,000\ (PWF(u)^3_{.10})$$

$$= -1,800 + 700\ (PWF(u)^3_{.10})$$

$$= -1,800 + 700\ (2.487)$$

$$NPV = -\$60$$

The net present value is −$60. The negative sign indicates that the proposed investment will not meet XYZ's requirement of a 10 percent return on investment. The investment should not be made.

We could expand this analysis to include the effects of depreciation and taxation. Furthermore, if salvage is expected after the project's useful life, the salvage value should be treated as a future inflow.

Internal rate of return

Suppose you have identified the inflows and outflows of an alternative and wish to determine the rate of return it offers. In this case, *i* is not prescribed but is a variable whose value you are seeking for this alternative. *The internal rate of return is the discount rate i at which net cash flows for the alternative equal zero.* In other words, the process for finding the internal rate of return involves finding the value of *i* for which the present value of outflows equals the present value of inflows. The resultant value of *i* is called the internal rate of return; it is determined by process of trial and error.

We have analyzed XYZ Company's truck purchase proposal and found it had a negative net present value for *i* = .10. What is the internal rate of return offered by this proposal? We know it is less than 10 percent, so we first try something less, say 8 percent. In Appendix B, the annual series present value factor for three years and 8 percent is 2.577. The proposal's present value for $i = .08$ is then:

$$PV \text{ inflows} = (\$1,000)(2.577)$$
$$= \$2,577$$

and

$$PV \text{ outflows} = \$1,800 + (\$300)(2.577)$$
$$= 1,800 + 733$$
$$= \$2,573$$

Since inflows exceed outflows on a present value basis, we know the rate is between 0.08 and 0.10 but very close to 0.08. Although we could interpolate to find the exact rate, the net present value of $4 is so close to zero for 8 percent that we will call the internal rate of return 8 percent for this investment alternative. As manager, you may wish to compute this rate of return for all alternatives and choose the one offering the highest return if it exceeds your cost of capital.

Model selection   We recommend again that you use payback in conjunction with net present value in financial change analysis. In the supplement to this chapter, we'll show you why we recommend using payback with either the risk analysis model, a modification of NPV, or the present value model.

Frailties of Estimation

As manager, you will want to take into account some of the assumptions used in financial analysis of investment proposals. You should recognize, however, that several estimates enter into the analysis, and they may turn out to be erroneous. Actual salvage values, useful lives, and applicable interest rates (costs of capital) may be different from the values assumed at the time of analysis. This is especially true for long-term alternatives. How can we know the salvage value twenty years from now? What difference does it make to the current decision?

One approach to these questions is to perform a multiple analysis of each alternative. Instead of performing one present value analysis for alternative A using a salvage value of $2,000, two or more analyses may be done. The first might be based on a very pessimistic estimate of salvage value, a second on a very optimistic estimate, and the third might incorporate a most likely estimate. Analysis results can then be compared with one another and with those of other alternatives as well. It may turn out that alternative *A*, even under the most pessimistic conditions, is still better than other alternatives. This is a useful piece of information for decision purposes. The risk analysis procedure discussed in the supplement illustrates another approach to solving the estimation problem.

So far we have discussed techniques for systematically and logically evaluating the economic and financial consequences of change. We have noted that these methods are appropriate to use whenever the need for change arises. In Chapter 18 we observed that recognition of the need for change can be either voluntary or imposed by a variety of forces acting on the organization. One target for change is the organizational technology, including the conversion process and the product.

Historically, many organizations have found it beneficial to deal with technological change proactively rather than reactively. If we defer action until the legal, social, or competitive environments demand a change in products and conversion processes, we may lose opportunities. A proactive posture recognizes not only that change is going to occur in the future but that organizational efforts and resources can be used to guide the direction and timing of change to some extent. In other words, we can plan for change so that the results are compatible with system goals. With ample awareness of impending change, we can make transitions with fewer disruptions and at lower cost than we can if we wait passively for change to overtake us.

Product and Process Life Cycles

The demand for a product, its market acceptance, generally tends to follow a predictable pattern.[1] Shown in Figure 19-6, the product life cycle has some important ramifications for managers as they attempt to deal with change in their organizations.

The pattern suggests that most products do not have indefinite lives; they arise from meager beginnings, and they reach ultimate peaks at which the level of demand is substantially higher than it was at the initial stage. The time span over which the stages occur is not specified; it varies considerably across industries. For many novelty products, the time from birth to death may be very short, perhaps a matter of weeks or months. For other products, the life cycle may span many years or even decades. In any case the very nature of this pattern raises significant questions for management. When will the various stages occur? What can we do to influence their occurrence? What facilities, materials, and labor are

---

[1] For a discussion of the product life cycle concept, see C. E. Block and K. J. Roering, *Essentials of Consumer Behavior* (Hinsdale, Ill.: The Dryden Press, 1976), Chapter 15.

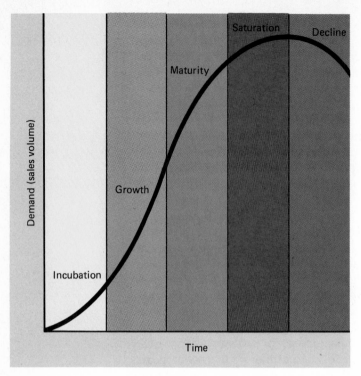

Figure 19-6   **Stages of a product life cycle**

optimal for meeting the anticipated demand? What should be done with existing facilities and conversion processes as demand declines and the product's life ends? Some of these questions are not solely the concern of the operations subsystem; they are an integral part of the marketing and finance subsystems as well. They require coordinated actions by the entire organization.

Phasing multiple products   A general strategy of phasing new products in and old products out is often used to sustain existing processing technology. This concept, previously discussed in Chapter 5, is shown for a hypothetical firm in Figure 19-7. As existing products are demanded less during the later stages of their life cycles, new products are developed and produced. In this way, output capacity can remain stable. Between times t_0 and t_1, product A goes through saturation and begins the decline stages; at the same time, product B completes the incubation stage. Similarly, products C and D are initiated later as earlier products decay.

Of course, actual transitions are not nearly so smooth as in our simple ideal example. Rarely does capacity remain constant; the technologies needed to produce different products are not identical, and at least some changes are almost always necessary. Organizations do not always have a new product waiting for introduction at the precise moment that an existing product begins to decline. Furthermore, the rates of growth and decline may not be highly predictable. With marketing promotional efforts, however, rates of growth and decline can sometimes be influenced. IBM, an expert at planned change, has introduced new computer lines since the late 1950s. Phasing new computers into and old ones out of its basic product line, IBM plans for the changes in its market.

Research and Development

Many organizations, especially larger ones, do not leave the development of new products and processes to chance. They direct formal concerted efforts toward creating new products, finding new uses for existing products, and developing new processes that will reduce capital or manufacturing costs. These are the objectives of research and development (R&D).

Figure 19-7 Ideal use of capacity by time-phasing products

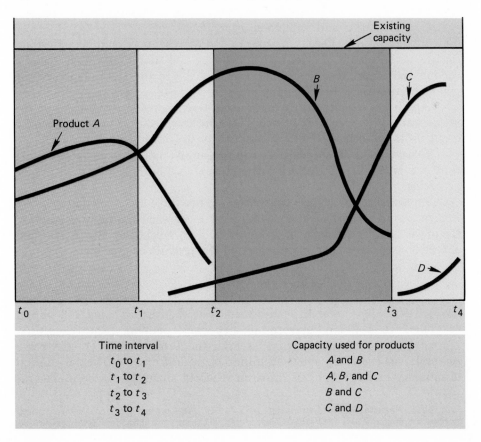

Time interval	Capacity used for products
t_0 to t_1	A and B
t_1 to t_2	A, B, and C
t_2 to t_3	B and C
t_3 to t_4	C and D

Realizing a new successful product or process does not happen overnight. Most often it occurs over a succession of steps and involves the talents and expertise of many people, especially in the initial phase. Consider, for example, a relatively new process for tagging salmon used in wildlife management. Historically the process involved catching the fish, physically handling it, tagging, and physically releasing the fish. The new process consists essentially of "tagging" by remote laser beam, thus eliminating the need for physically catching, tagging, and releasing. Now think of the research and development efforts that were required to bring about this new process. Many years ago the theories of physics underlying the laser were conceptualized. Later, developmental research in physics and electronics resulted in a working laser beam. Since then many scientists and engineers have developed applications of laser beams in space explorations, health, science, industry, and other settings. Only recently, with the help of fish biologists, has this new tagging process been brought into use. Overall we can identify fundamentally different stages of innovation.

Stages of innovation

There are four generic stages of technological innovation: basic research, applied research, development, and implementation.

Basic research: Research projects that represent original investigation for the advancement of scientific knowledge and that do not have specific commercial objectives. They may, however, be in the field of present or potential interest of the company.

Applied research: Research projects that represent investigation directed toward the discovery of new scientific knowledge. They have specific commercial objectives for either products or processes.

Development: Technical activities concerned with nonroutine problems that are encountered in translating research findings into products or processes.

Implementation: Once the other stages have been completed, the innovation process involves building pilot models, designing and building the necessary equipment and facilities, and initiating the marketing channels necessary for dissemination of the product or process.

Who pays for research and development?

In the years 1965 to 1975, the federal government was expending funds at the rate of some $16 billion and private industry was expending about $20 billion annually on research and development.[2] Of this, basic research was receiving about $2 billion of federal and less than $1 billion of industry monies. Applied research received about $3 billion of federal

---

[2]U.S., National Science Foundation (NSF 74-313), *An Analysis of Federal R&D Funding by Function: Fiscal Years 1969–1975* (Washington, D.C.: Surveys of Science Resources Series, 1974).

and $3 billion of industry funds. The overwhelming amounts, $11 billion federal and $16 billion industry, were allocated to development.

Private funds have been paid mainly by larger firms in high technology industries with relatively rapid product turnover. Chemical, electronics, aerospace, and transportation industries, unlike such relatively dormant industries as canning and mining, expend great efforts in research and development. In the more dynamic industries innovation is accepted as an inherent characteristic of organizational life, and R&D is a vital part of it. Annual budgetary allocations are made on a regular basis, often as a percent of sales.

The costs of R&D are typically very high. It often requires investment in such facilities as laboratories with highly specialized, expensive equipment for experimentation and testing. Scientific, engineering, and technical expertise must be procured. Technical libraries and computing facilities are often a necessity. In addition, a supporting staff, including research administrators, is required. Often it is difficult to see the tangible contributions of R&D to corporate goals. Especially for basic research, R&D contributions are infrequent or irregular. In light of the high costs and infrequency of tangible results, it is no wonder that many firms are hesitant to engage in extensive R&D efforts. Consequently, many "research" departments are actually almost completely concerned with development. In fact, a good number of these hardly even concern themselves with development, concentrating instead on *innovation*, which involves simply putting a new twist on an old product.

Organization of
R&D

In most companies R&D is a staff function located at either the corporate or divisional level. Three examples of R&D organizational structure are shown in Figure 19-8. In part (*a*), R&D is centrally located. From this location, R&D can economically serve the needs of all divisions and avoid duplication of effort. A disadvantage is that the R&D unit may be geographically and organizationally remote from the immediate needs of the various divisions. This difficulty is overcome by decentralized R&D (*b*). This structure, however, can tend to raise the overall corporate costs of the R&D effort insofar as duplication across divisions may result. Decentralization is well suited to companies in which applied research and development dominate the overall R&D effort, particularly when the products and processes have a high degree of technological differentiation along divisional lines. Here the development efforts are specialized, tailored to the nature of each specific division.

The combination structure, (*c*), attempts to reap the best of the benefits offered by both centralization and decentralization. R&D units at divisional levels can be specialized toward the special needs at that level, especially in the developmental and applied areas. Some of the applied research and perhaps all of the basic research may be centralized at the corporate level. Development and innovation frequently occur at the divisional level.

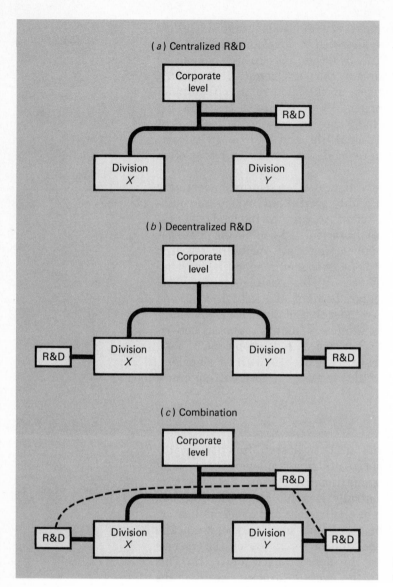

Figure 19-8 **R&D location in organization structure**

The dotted lines among the three R&D units reflect subsidiary relationships among them; relevant results of basic or applied research at one level are transferred to the others. On occasion, the progress of development efforts at a divisional level may be impeded because further applied research is needed. If the corporate R&D unit, for example, is the only one prepared to work in the necessary applied area, the problem must then be referred to it until a solution is reached.

From the R&D process emerge new concepts, ideas, potential projects, and technologies. Then management must decide which potential R&D projects should be adopted within the limited budget in each of the R&D units. As existing products and processes reach new stages in their life cycles, R&D efforts are directed toward bringing new products and processes onstream so that desired overall levels of organizational output can be sustained with minimal disruption.

Thus far we have discussed two common rational approaches to change, investment analysis and research and development of products and processes. Now we must consider changes that occur in organization structure, tasks, and policies. Are rational approaches available for these types of changes? Yes, with two qualifications. First, the effects of policy and structural changes are less predictable because of their potentially widespread influence throughout the organization and because they can affect organization performance in so many diverse ways. Second, the research methodologies for studying policy and structural changes are relatively new and are not yet highly developed or widely used. We will present two methodologies for studying the effects of change, learning curve analysis and system dynamics. These two methodologies differ substantially in focus and orientation. Learning curve analysis is one way of evaluating the effects of changes in tasks; it is based on traditional industrial engineering techniques. In contrast, system dynamics is applicable to a broader range of potential changes in organizational structure and policy. Both methodologies are helpful for identifying and evaluating change alternatives, and they can play an important role in the scientific approach to problem solving.

CHANGES IN ORGANIZATION STRUCTURE, TASKS, AND POLICIES

Learning Curve Analysis

When a new model of an existing product is introduced, especially if the work content is similar, learning curve analysis can be helpful in its manufacture. As an organization gains experience in manufacturing a product, the resource inputs required per unit of output diminish over the life of the product. The hours of labor that go into manufacturing the first unit of a new commercial aircraft are typically much higher than those needed for the one-hundredth unit, for example. As the cumulative output of the model grows, the labor inputs continue to decline. As you know, if you repeat a new task continually, your performance improves. The performance time drops off rather dramatically at first, and it continues to fall at some slower rate until a performance plateau, a leveling off, is reached. This learning phenomenon occurs for groups and organizations

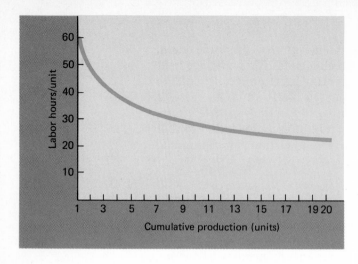

Figure 19-9 **An 80 percent learning curve plotted on arithmetic coordinates: first unit requires 60 labor hours**

as well as for individuals. Furthermore, performance data from many companies show that this learning pattern is often regular and predictable. The general form of this pattern, called the learning curve, is shown on arithmetic coordinates in Figure 19-9. In it, the initial unit output requires 60 labor hours to manufacture. As output and experience continue, labor

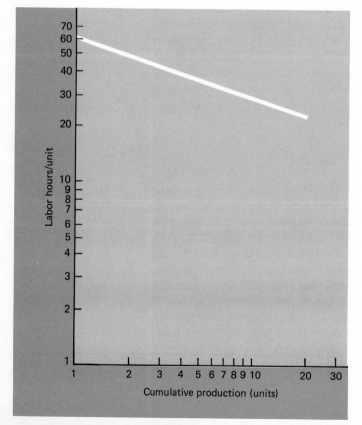

Figure 19-10 **An 80 percent learning curve plotted on logarithmic coordinates: first unit requires 60 labor hours**

hours per unit diminish to about 23 for the twentieth unit. The general equation for this curve is:

$$Y_i = ki^b \qquad\qquad (19\text{-}4)$$

where

Y_i = labor hours required to produce the ith cumulative unit of output

k = labor hours required to produce the first unit of output (initial productivity)

b = index of learning

This exponential curve becomes a straight line when plotted on logarithmic coordinates (Figure 19-10).

Rate of learning   The rate of learning is not the same in all manufacturing applications. Learning occurs at a higher rate in some applications than others and is reflected by a more rapid descent of the curve. By convention the learning rate is specified as a percentage. A 90 percent curve, for example, means that each time cumulative output

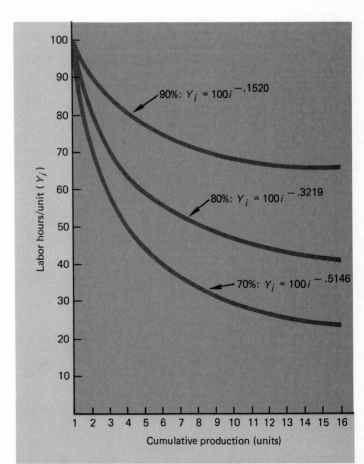

Figure 19-11 Arithmetic coordinates for 70, 80, and 90 percent learning curves: first unit requires 100 labor hours

90%: $Y_i = 100i^{-.1520}$

80%: $Y_i = 100i^{-.3219}$

70%: $Y_i = 100i^{-.5146}$

Labor hours/unit (Y_i)

Cumulative production (units)

doubles, the newest unit of output requires 90 percent of the labor input of the reference unit; if unit 1 requires 100 labor hours, unit 2 will require 90 percent of 100, or 90 hours, unit 4 will require 90 percent of 90 hours, or 81 hours, and so on. Labor hours required for 70, 80, and 90 percent curves are shown here for various levels of cumulative output, assuming 100 labor hours are required for the first unit.

Cumulative output i (units)	Labor hours required for ith cumulative unit		
	70% curve	80% curve	90% curve
1	100.0	100.0	100.0
2	70.0	80.0	90.0
4	49.0	64.0	81.0
8	34.3	51.2	72.9
16	24.0	41.0	65.6

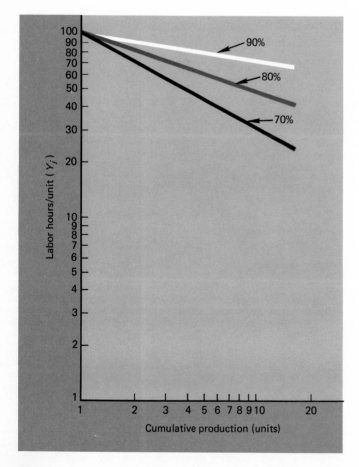

Figure 19-12 Logarithmic coordinates for 70, 80, and 90 percent learning curves: first unit requires 100 labor hours

We have plotted these three curves on arithmetic coordinates (Figure 19-11) and logarithmic coordinates (Figure 19-12) for 16 cumulative units of output. Arithmetically, the rate of learning is reflected by b, the index of learning. The index b is shown in Figure 19-11 for each curve. The index of learning for the 90 percent learning curve is $-.1520$. Table 19-2 shows computed values of i^b for 80 and 90 percent curves. By using equation 19-4, you can extend these calculations to cover any desired level of cumulative output beyond those given in the table.

Equation 19-4 applied to the Surefloat situation in the example on page 678 becomes:

$$y_i = (500)i^{-0.3219} \qquad \text{(19-5)}$$

TABLE 19-2

COMPUTED VALUES OF i^b FOR 80% AND 90% CURVES: 50 UNITS

i (unit number)	80% curve ($b = -.3219$)	90% curve ($b = -.1520$)	i (unit number)	80% curve ($b = -.3219$)	90% curve ($b = -.1520$)
1	1.0000	1.0000	26	.3504	.6094
2	.7999	.9000	27	.3461	.6059
3	.7021	.8462	28	.3421	.6026
4	.6400	.8100	29	.3379	.5994
5	.5957	.7830	30	.3346	.5963
6	.5617	.7616	31	.3311	.5934
7	.5345	.7440	32	.3277	.5905
8	.5120	.7290	33	.3245	.5878
9	.4930	.7161	34	.3214	.5851
10	.4766	.7047	35	.3184	.5825
11	.4621	.6946	36	.3155	.5800
12	.4494	.6854	37	.3128	.5776
13	.4380	.6771	38	.3101	.5753
14	.4276	.6696	39	.3075	.5730
15	.4182	.6626	40	.3050	.5708
16	.4096	.6561	41	.3026	.5687
17	.4017	.6501	42	.3002	.5666
18	.3944	.6445	43	.2980	.5646
19	.3876	.6392	44	.2958	.5626
20	.3819	.6342	45	.2937	.5607
21	.3753	.6295	46	.2916	.5588
22	.3697	.6251	47	.2896	.5570
23	.3645	.6209	48	.2876	.5552
24	.3595	.6169	49	.2857	.5535
25	.3548	.6131	50	.2839	.5518

━━━━━━━━━ EXAMPLE ━━━━━━━━━

Surefloat Boat Builders has been receiving customer orders for a new model yacht. Based on previous experience at introducing new models, Surefloat engineers estimate that an 80 percent improvement curve is applicable and that the first unit of the new model will require 500 hours of labor. Surefloat has received customer orders for delivery in the next 5 months as follows:

Month	Number of yachts ordered
1	2
2	6
3	10
4	10
5	15
	43

The manufacturing manager is concerned about the manpower requirements for meeting these commitments to customers. The manufacturing engineer was asked to provide some information that could be used for manpower planning.

Using equation 19-5 (or tabled values) for the 80 percent curve, the engineer generated the data in Table 19-3. Surefloat management can use these data to decide how many yachts to produce each month so that the manpower requirements are smoothed across months. The data also enable determination of work force size. Notice the effects of learning in the data. Commitments to customers in month 2 are 200 percent greater than in month 1; yet the manpower to accomplish this increases by only 98 percent over the previous month. As the second column shows, labor hours are reduced rather dramatically initially and then taper off to relatively small increments as the effects of learning diminish with experience.

━━━━━━━━━ EXAMPLE ━━━━━━━━━

Surefloat management has decided on a selling price of $12,000 per yacht. It expects to receive payment the month following delivery. Each yacht will be produced and delivered during the month in which it was promised previously. Work force size will equal the monthly manpower equivalents shown in Table 19-4. Standard wages are $1,000 per month per employee. Costs of direct materials, variable materials overhead, and fixed administrative and marketing overhead are also shown in Table 19-4. All these costs will be incurred during the month of production.

TABLE 19-3

ENGINEERING DATA FOR USE IN MANPOWER PLANNING

Yacht (cumulative)	Labor hours* per yacht (rounded)	Month	Number of yachts promised	Labor hours needed for monthly commitments	Change in labor hours from previous month	Change in output from previous month	Monthly** manpower equivalents (number of people)
1	500	1	2	900			5.62
2	400						
3	351	2	6	1,773	+98.1%	+200.0%	11.08
4	320						
5	298						
6	281						
7	267						
8	256						
9	246	3	10	2,185	+23.2	+ 67.7	13.65
10	238						
11	231						
12	225						
13	219						
14	214						
15	209						
16	205						
17	201						
18	197						
19	194	4	10	1,816	−16.8	0	11.35
20	191						
21	188						
22	185						
23	182						
24	180						
25	177						
26	175						
27	173						
28	171						
29	169	5	15	2,373	+31.0	+ 50.0	14.83
30	167						
31	165						
32	164						
33	162						
34	161						
35	159						
36	158						
37	156						
38	155						
39	154						
40	153						
41	151						
42	150						
43	149						

Total labor hours = 9,047   Total yachts = 43

*Obtained from Figure 19-4 and equation 19-4; labor hours for yacht one = $Y_1 = (500)(1.000) = 500$.
**A person is assumed to work 20 days per month, 8 hours per day. Thus, a "manpower equivalent" is $20 \times 8 = 160$ labor hours per month. For each month the manpower equivalent is found by dividing the monthly labor hours by 160. Hence, for month one, $900 \div 160 = 5.62$.

Uses of learning
curves

Just as learning curve analysis can be used for manpower planning, it can also be helpful in cash-flow planning. Cash-flow planning involves identifying the timing of cash outlays and inflows associated with a new product. The analysis indicates when we will need to borrow funds to finance our operations until revenues begin to make the project self-supporting.

Notice that monthly inflows are less than outlays for each of the first 3 months. Cumulative cash flows are negative through month 5, and Surefloat will have to borrow funds or divert them from other projects to finance operations on the new model yacht during these months. By using learning curve analysis, we can estimate manpower needs and the costs (outflows) necessary to complete a cash flow analysis.

TABLE 19-4

CASH FLOW FOR SIX MONTHS: SUREFLOAT BOAT BUILDERS

	Month					
	1	2	3	4	5	6
Units produced and delivered	2	6	10	10	15	15
Cash inflow from sales	—0—	$24,000	$72,000	$120,000	$120,000	$180,000
Outflows						
Wages	$5,620	11,080	13,650	11,350	14,830	13,500
Direct materials ($6,000 per yacht)	12,000	36,000	60,000	60,000	90,000	90,000
Variable materials overhead (10% of direct materials)	1,200	3,600	6,000	6,000	9,000	9,000
Fixed administrative and marketing overhead	10,000	10,000	10,000	10,000	10,000	10,000
Monthly outflow	$28,820	60,680	89,650	87,350	123,830	122,500
Net monthly cash flow (inflow-outflow)	(28,820)*	(36,680)	(17,650)	32,650	(3,830)	57,500
Cumulative cash flow position (month-end)	(28,820)	(65,500)	(83,150)	(50,500)	(54,330)	3,170

*Parentheses denote negative cash flow.

Parameter
estimation

Two parameters, k and b, must be estimated for learning curve analysis. If these parameters are seriously in error, results can be very misleading. Estimates of labor hours for the initial unit are based primarily on staff experience and familiarity with the history of the conversion process. Estimation accuracy will be closely related to the degree of conversion similarity between the new and previous products. Estimation of the appropriate learning rate is typically accomplished by regression analysis on data from experiences with similar past products.

Sources of
improvement

While the learning curve depicts productivity improvement over time, improvement does not take place solely because workers are learning. The sources of productivity changes are numerous, but they include changes in work methods, product engineering modifications, facilities layout improvements, equipment redesign, employee training, and others. We intend the term "learning curve" to subsume the effects of all these sources of productivity progress in summary measure. Learning curve analysis is generally of greatest benefit in labor-intense conversion processes.

System Dynamics

In Chapter 18, when we described system dynamics, we mentioned that system dynamics models can provide information of many kinds to managers. One way these models are often used is for examining the effects of policy and structure changes in the organization. The analysis procedure involves three basic steps: creating a valid model of the system of interest as it currently exists, modifying the model to incorporate new policies or changes in structure, and recording and comparing simulated system performance before and after the changes. With this procedure, we can use such variability measures as service to customers, inventory levels, manpower levels, and output levels to evaluate the overall effects of change in the system.

A system dynamics simulation model is a mathematical representation of some system of interest. Without presenting the mathematics, we will discuss its general structure and form and show how it might be manipulated to provide useful managerial information. To use this model, the major components of the system must first be identified. Next, relationships among the components must be determined; in particular, flows of people, information, and materials within the system must be specified in detail. Usually these flows involve time delays, which must be represented in the model. Finally, the decision rules used for day-to-day operations within the components must be built into the model.

These model characteristics are shown in Figure 19-13 for a hypothetical production-distribution system. In the system is a factory, which sends the finished product to a nearby factory warehouse for storage. From inventory in the warehouse, finished goods are shipped to a few regional distributors, who order (purchase) from the factory warehouse when their existing inventory levels begin to deplete. Similarly, shipments enter local distributors' inventories when they are received from their regional distributors. Local distributors then supply retailers, who sell to the retail customers. Overall there are five sectors in this production-distribution system. In the factory is a production component, which creates the final product; a production decision component; and a purchase decision component. As the diagram shows, the production decision depends on information

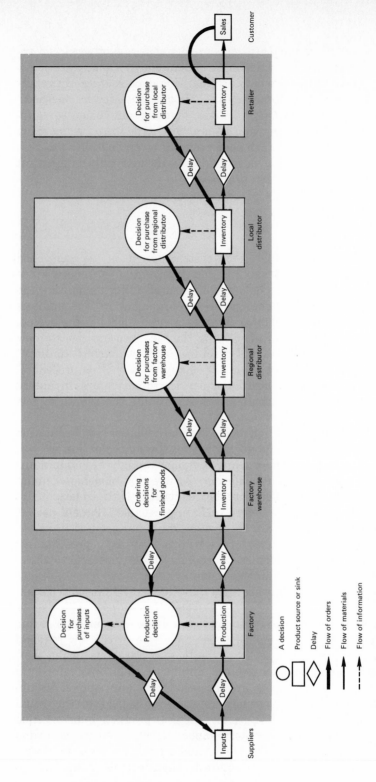

Figure 19-13 Production-distribution system

Legend:
- ○ A decision
- ▭ Product source or sink
- ◇ Delay
- ━► Flow of orders
- ─► Flow of materials
- ┄► Flow of information

Suppliers — Inputs — Delay — Decision for purchases of inputs — Production decision — Production — Delay — Factory

Factory warehouse — Ordering decisions for finished goods — Inventory — Delay — Regional distributor

Regional distributor — Decision for purchases from factory warehouse — Inventory — Delay — Local distributor

Local distributor — Decision for purchase from regional distributor — Inventory — Delay — Retailer

Retailer — Decision for purchase from local distributor — Inventory — Sales — Customer

682

about current production rate and the quantity of new orders received from the factory warehouse. Only after the production decision has been made can managers decide to purchase factory inputs. Each of the other four sectors contains a pool of inventory, which is depleted when orders from downstream are filled and replenished when purchase orders from upstream are filled. In each sector the purchase decision is based on information about the current inventory level in that sector.

Two general characteristics of relationships among sectors should be noted. First, materials and finished goods flow downstream, and orders for goods flow upstream. Second, there are delays in receiving orders and in receiving replenishment supplies. The restricted information flows, the delays, and the use of inventory-based rules for purchasing decisions result in wide fluctuations throughout the system, particularly in those sectors farthest removed from the retail customers. Say that a sudden increase in retail sales causes retail inventories to go below desired levels. The retailer may respond by purchasing both larger amounts from the local distributor to restore inventory and some additional amount in anticipation of higher retail sales demand. After some delay, the local distributor receives the larger orders from retailers, fills them from existing inventory, and then places larger orders to the regional distributor. In each sector inventory levels decline and backorders begin to accumulate; and these variations are amplified as they progress upstream. By the time the factory begins gearing up in response to the large increase in orders from the factory warehouse, retail customer sales may have dropped off. Retailers subsequently reduce orders to local distributors who, in turn, order less from regional distributors, and so on. Meanwhile, back at the factory, production rates and employment levels are beginning to fluctuate wildly as a result of all these changes in demand.

What can management do to improve the performance of this production-distribution system? Can production, inventories, and backorders be stabilized to provide better customer service and lower production costs? By building a simulation model of the existing system, managers can experimentally evaluate proposed changes. Perhaps some proposed changes require only minor modification of the model, while others involve major remodeling efforts. If purchase order decision rules, for example, were tested for each sector within the existing model, the experimental simulation results would reveal the extent to which system performance is affected by these decision rules. The manager may find that they have relatively limited impact and that more extensive model modification is warranted. Say that the manager proposes establishing a new information flow in which current retail consumer demand becomes a direct input to production decisions at the factory. In this way demand information would bypass the three intermediate sectors. The existing model would be modified to incorporate this new information link, and subsequent simulation runs would indicate its potential effect on system behavior. A more extensive managerial proposal might consider restructuring the production-distribution system by consolidating two or more sectors into one. Perhaps by consolidating local and regional distributorships we could eliminate some existing delays in ordering and receiving. This type of system change could be evaluated by restructuring the model and then simulating system performance.

The system dynamics approach is useful because it helps the manager understand the structure and behavior of systems. However, it remains an experimental procedure, and the user has no assurance that the experimental results will materialize when changes suggested by the analysis are implemented. Furthermore, because of the modeling efforts and computer time required the analyses can be expensive. Still, system dynamics is one of the most formalistic approaches to anticipating the effects of policy and structural changes in organizations.

SUMMARY

The operations manager is part of a dynamic organization that requires changes in technology, structure, and behavior. Since the effects of change are so pervasive, the manager seeks to guide change in a rational manner toward the accomplishment of system goals. To help the manager guide change in the organization, financial analysis, research and development, learning curve analysis, and system dynamics are all useful techniques.

With financial analysis the manager can evaluate the economic aspects of proposed changes. He or she can compare alternatives against one another or against a specified criterion before making a choice. The form of the analysis rests on basic concepts used in accounting, economics, and finance. After all the economic consequences of a proposal have been considered, the manager is in a better position to weigh them against noneconomic or nonquantifiable factors and make a more enlightened decision.

The research and development function is a major means by which organizations can plan for change. Proactive rather than reactive, R&D accepts the fact that change is an inherent part of organizational life. At the heart of R&D is the concept of product and process life cycles, a useful idea in phasing new products and processes into adoption so that transitions can be smooth and economical. This process is not cost-free, however; establishing R&D efforts is expensive in terms of the people, equipment, and facilities required. Furthermore, the very nature of the R&D process is risky; we can never be sure that a new product or process will materialize when it is needed.

Learning curves can be useful for manpower planning, cash flow analysis, and product pricing. Manpower planning and cash flow analysis help smooth the transition when new products or new models are introduced in the product line. The product pricing decision is vital to the organization's profitability.

System dynamics is a framework for evaluating changes in policy and structure on an experimental basis. It is applicable when one wishes to evaluate how changes in one or more parts of the system will affect both other parts and system performance overall. Modeling, of great potential value in system dynamics, helps the manager understand system interrelationships and behavior.

CASE

Cleanair Corporation

Cleanair Corporation designs and manufactures small contaminant filtration units. These units are used in various industrial facilities to reduce emissions contributing to air pollution. Cleanair's research and development department has developed and tested a new model, the Minigasp III, which it believes is now suitable for full-scale marketing. Minigasp I has been successfully marketed for eight years and Minigasp II for four, and Cleanair management believes that Minigasp III faces even brighter marketing prospects. Although similar in many ways to its predecessors, Minigasp III contains an innovative chemical processing system that should give Cleanair a competitive edge in the industry. Management must now decide whether or not to add Minigasp III to its product line.

The marketing manager says that a $3,000 per unit selling price would be very competitive and anticipates sales of one unit in each of months one and two, two units in month three, three units in month four, and four units per month thereafter. Payment by the customer is expected during the month of purchase. The operations manager believes he can meet these market demands if the changeover of facilities is started immediately. An initial outlay of $30,000 will be necessary to renovate part of the plant and equipment. Costs of manufacture have been estimated as follows:

Direct materials = $700 per unit

Indirect materials = 10 percent of direct materials cost

Direct labor = $ 7 per man hour

Indirect labor = 20 percent of direct labor cost

Additional administrative and
marketing costs = $3,000 per month

In addition, maintenance expenses will be $1,000 in month one, $750 in month two, and $500 per month thereafter. Production engineers estimate the initial unit of Minigasp III will require 200 hours of labor to manufacture. Thereafter, they believe an 80 percent learning curve is applicable.

The finance manager questions the advisability of adopting the new product because of the risks involved. If new governmental regulations were to be created, always a major factor in this industry, the marketability of Minigasp III could be prematurely damaged. Consequently, he suggests the project not be undertaken unless the funds from sales can fully recover the initial $30,000 outlay during the first year of production. As operations manager you are expected to respond to the finance manager.

REVIEW AND DISCUSSION QUESTIONS

1. What is meant by "rational approaches to change"?
2. Identify three examples of organizational changes for which the rational approach is helpful to the operations manager.
3. Discuss examples for which the rational approaches to change are of limited value.
4. Define "defender" and "challenger" as used in financial and economic analysis.

685

5. Discuss difficulties of applying financial and economic analysis to behavioral changes in organizations.

6. What is the role of return on investment in financial and economic analysis of change alternatives?

7. Define the following:
   (a) opportunity costs
   (b) sunk costs
   (c) salvage value
   (d) depreciation

8. Define accounting life, machine life, and economic life of an asset.

9. How does an organization determine the appropriate discount rate for use in financial analysis?

10. Compare the major features of payback, net present value, and internal rate of return methods of evaluation.

11. The concept of product and process life cycles has implications for both rational approaches to change and organizational structure. Discuss these implications.

12. Under what circumstances is learning curve analysis most applicable?

13. What are the sources of productivity improvement that cause the learning phenomenon?

14. For what kinds of operating decisions can learning curve analysis provide data?

15. Discuss the role of system dynamics in analyzing organizational changes.

PROBLEMS

1. What is the present value of $1,000 to be invested for 5 years at 8 percent interest? At 10 percent interest?

2. What is the present value of $6,500 to be received 8 years from now if the prevailing interest rate is 8 percent? 10 percent?

3. What is the present value of a 10-year series of $500 investments if the interest rate is 8 percent? 10 percent?

4. You are to receive $500 per year for 10 successive years. If the interest rate is 8 percent, to what amount will this series accumulate? At 10 percent?

5. A company is considering two alternative relayout designs. Alternative 1 requires an initial investment of $100,000, will result in $20,000 annual cost savings for the next 10 years, and is expected to have equipment salvage value of $20,000 at the end of 10 years. Alternative 2 requires an $80,000 initial investment, will result in $16,000 annual cost savings, and will have no salvage value after 10 years. The interest rate is 8 percent.
   (a) Which alternative is best using the payback criterion?
   (b) Which alternative is best using the net present value criterion?

6. Hilite Entertainment, Inc., is considering two alternative locations for a new movie theater. Hilite is using a 10-year planning horizon with a 10 percent cost of capital. Location 1 involves a land purchase and construction costs totaling $200,000; this property's estimated resale value after 10 years is $400,000. Annual revenues will be $82,000; annual expenses will be $47,000. Location 2 requires a 10-year lease agreement; in addition to an initial outlay of $20,000, the annual lease payment is $30,000 per year. Annual revenues at location 2 are expected to be $95,000; annual operating expenses will be $37,000. Which location is best?

7. Using an interest rate of 8 percent, calculate the net present value of the following investment proposal.

initial outlay = $200,000

renovation outlay after 5 years of operation = $50,000

annual maintenance costs (years 1 through 5) = $25,000

annual maintenance costs (years 6 through 10) = $35,000

annual revenues (years 1 through 3) = $65,000

annual revenues (years 4 through 6) = $90,000

annual revenues (years 7 through 10) = $70,000

salvage value after year 10 = $50,000

8. **Fastback Trucking Company is considering two alternative types of trucks. Truck *A*, a less expensive used model, has a useful economic life of 2 years, an initial cost of $3,000, estimated salvage value of $300 after 2 years, annual maintenance costs of $800. Truck *B*, a newer and faster model, will have a useful economic life of 4 years, an initial cost of $8,000, estimated salvage value of $2,000 after 4 years, annual maintenance costs of $200, and will increase revenues from deliveries by $500 each year. Which alternative is most attractive?**

9. **In response to a customer inquiry, a manufacturing company is estimating the costs of 25 units of a new product, which is similar to an existing one. Estimates indicate that 400 labor hours will be required to produce the first unit. Draw graphs of labor requirements for units 1 through 25 for 80% and 90% learning curves.**

10. **Reconsider problem 9 using the 80% improvement curve. Direct labor and variable overhead are estimated at $9.00 per labor hour. Direct materials will cost $600 for each unit produced. Initial tooling for the product costs $15,000. Monthly overhead will cost $6,000 per month during the life of the project. The available work force consists of 10 operators, each available for 160 hours per month. If a profit of 10 percent on selling price is desired, what should be the selling price?**

Accounting life: length of an asset's life determined for the purpose of developing a depreciation schedule

GLOSSARY

Applied research: investigation directed to discovery of new scientific knowledge with specific commercial objectives toward products or processes

Basic research: original investigation for the advancement of scientific knowledge

Depreciation: accounting concept used to recover outlays for assets over their lives

Development: technical activities encountered in translating research findings into products or processes

Economic life: useful life of an asset

Internal rate of return: interest rate at which the present value of inflows equals the present value of outflows

Learning curve: pattern of input resources consumed in creating successive units of a product; generally initial units require higher amounts of inputs, and later units require progressively fewer inputs

Life cycle: pattern of demand throughout the product's life; similar patterns and stages can be identified for the useful life of a process.

Machine life: length of time an asset (machine) is capable of functioning

Net present value: technique of discounting all cash flows of an investment back to their present values and netting out the inflows against the outflows

Opportunity costs: returns that are lost or foregone as a result of selecting one alternative over another

Payback period: period of time required for investment net income to equal net outlays

Present value of a future sum: future sum divided by the growth rate of funds over the relevant time period

Research and development: organizational efforts directed toward product and process innovation; includes stages of basic research, applied research, development, and implementation

Salvage value: income received from sale of an asset

Sunk costs: past expenditures that are irrelevant to current decisions

Time value of money: concept that recognizes that a sum of money has the potential for generating returns (revenues) over time

SELECTED READINGS

Abernathy, W. J. "Production Process Structure and Technological Change." *Decision Sciences* 7, no. 4 (October 1976): 607–19.

———— and P. L. Townsend. "Technology, Productivity and Process Change." *Technological Forecasting and Social Change* 7, no. 4 (1975): 379–96.

———— and K. P. King. "The Limits of the Learning Curve." *Harvard Business Review* 52, no. 5 (September–October 1974): 109–19.

Adam, Everett E. Jr. and Michael F. Pohlen. "A Scoring Methodology for Equipment Replacement Model Evaluation." *AIIE Transactions* 6, no. 4 (December 1974): 338–44.

Baloff, N. "Estimating the Parameters of the Startup Model—An Empirical Approach." *Journal of Industrial Engineering* 18 (1967): 248–53.

Conway, R. W. and A. Schultz. "The Manufacturing Progress Function." *The Journal of Industrial Engineering* 10 (1959): 39–54.

Gavett, J. W. *Production and Operations Management.* New York: Harcourt Brace Jovanovich, Inc., 1968.

Hertz, David B. "Risk Analysis in Capital Investment." *Harvard Business Review* 42 (January–February 1964): 95–106.

Hirschman, W. B. "Profit from the Learning Curve." *Harvard Business Review* 42 (January–February 1964): 125–39.

Starr, M. K. *Systems Management of Operations.* Englewood Cliffs, N.J.: Prentice-Hall, Inc., 1971.

Terborgh, George. *Business Investment Management.* Washington, D.C.: Machinery and Allied Products Institute, 1967.

U.S. National Science Foundation (NSF 74-313). *An Analysis of Federal R&D Funding by Function: Fiscal Years 1969–1975.* Washington, D.C.: Surveys of Science Resources Series, 1974.

In this supplement we discuss concepts and models important to financial analysis relating to changes in technology and structure. Capital budgeting and engineering economic concepts in this supplement include depreciation and taxes in replacement, compound interest factors, additional replacement models, and model selection.

RATIONAL APPROACHES TO CHANGE

Depreciation and Taxes

Depreciation Depreciation is an accounting procedure for recovering outlays (expenditures) for assets over their lives. Companies invest in equipment and facilities with the expectation that future income benefits will be realized. The resulting income cannot be called profit until the expenses necessary to generate the income have been deducted. To accomplish this, the initial investment is subdivided across several years and charged off against income in each of those years. When considering investments in new facilities or equipment, management should determine depreciation. Different methods of depreciation can be selected; the choice affects the attractiveness of decision alternatives because of its effect on taxation.

Basically, depreciation methods fall into two categories, straight line and accelerated. Straight line depreciation is used to recover asset expenditures evenly over the asset's expected life. The annual amount of depreciation is determined by using equation S19-1.

$$\frac{\text{Annual amount}}{\text{of depreciation}} = \frac{\text{Asset cost} - \text{salvage value}}{\text{Estimated asset life}} \qquad \text{(S19-1)}$$

Suppose a machine is purchased for $20,000 and has a life expectancy of six years and an expected salvage value of $2,000 after year 6. Using equation S19-1,

$$\frac{\text{Annual amount}}{\text{of depreciation}} = \frac{\$20,000 - 2,000}{6}$$

$$= \$3,000 \text{ per year}$$

As we see in Table S19-1, the company reduces its taxable income each year by $3,000, the annual depreciation amount.

In contrast to the straight line approach are several accelerated methods of depreciation. These methods allow the firm to reduce taxable income by larger amounts in the earlier years of asset life but small amounts in the later years. Although several accelerated methods exist, we will present only one, the sum-of-years-digits. It should be noted that one does not have complete freedom in selecting an accelerated method. Choice is constrained by Internal Revenue Service regulations and depends upon the circumstances involved.

TABLE S19-1

**STRAIGHT LINE DEPRECIATION SCHEDULE FOR MACHINE COSTING
$20,000 INITIALLY WITH SIX YEAR LIFE AND
$2,000 SALVAGE VALUE**

Year	Book value Beginning value of asset	Depreciation	Book value Ending value of asset
1	$20,000	$ 3,000	$17,000
2	17,000	3,000	14,000
3	14,000	3,000	11,000
4	11,000	3,000	8,000
5	8,000	3,000	5,000
6	5,000	3,000	2,000 (salvage value)
		$18,000	

To use sum-of-years-digits, one first determines the total amount to be depreciated: amount to be depreciated (y) = asset cost − salvage value. Next, the number of years over which depreciation is to occur is determined, and the sum of these years is calculated: for n years the sum is $1 + 2 + ... + n = x$. Then the amount of depreciation for each of the n years is determined as follows:

$$\text{First year depreciation} = \left(\frac{n}{x}\right)y$$

$$\text{Second year depreciation} = \left(\frac{n-1}{x}\right)y$$

Continue until the last (nth year), when

$$\text{Final year depreciation} = \left(\frac{1}{x}\right)y$$

Let us use the previous example to illustrate. The amount to be depreciated overall is:

$$y = \text{Asset cost} - \text{salvage value, or}$$
$$y = \$20,000 - \$2,000$$
$$= \$18,000$$

The expected life is six years, the sum of which is $x = 1 + 2 + 3 + 4 + 5 + 6$, or 21. Therefore the amount of depreciation for year 1 is:

$$\left(\frac{n}{x}\right)y = \left(\frac{6}{21}\right)(\$18,000)$$
$$= \$5,143$$

SUM-OF-YEARS-DIGITS DEPRECIATION SCHEDULE

	Book Value			Book Value
Year	Beginning value of asset	Depreciation rate	Depreciation	Ending value of asset
1	$20,000	(6/21) (18,000)	$5,143	$14,857
2	14,857	(5/21) (18,000)	4,286	10,571
3	10,571	(4/21) (18,000)	3,429	7,142
4	7,142	(3/21) (18,000)	2,571	4,571
5	4,571	(2/21) (18,000)	1,714	2,857
6	2,857	(1/21) (18,000)	857	2,000 (salvage value)
		21/21 (18,000) 100%	$18,000	

For the remaining years the depreciation schedule is shown in Table S19-2.

Observe the patterns of annual depreciation for the two methods over the six-year life of the equipment. Overall, the entire $18,000 is depreciated in both cases. Under straight line, it occurs evenly, $3,000 per year; under the accelerated method, the initial year is $5,143, and depreciation diminishes annually thereafter. This means that under accelerated methods there is less taxable income initially. The tax implications of these methods are discussed next.

Taxes   Taxes have a direct effect on the financial benefits associated with investment decisions. In our discussion we consider only federal taxes on income and profit. However, a complete analysis should also consider state, local, and other relevant taxes.

Companies are taxed annually by the federal government in relation to their end of year profit picture. Medium and large companies are taxed at a rate of approximately 50 percent of profit. Recall that annual profit equals annual income minus annual costs of operation. Therefore, for a specified amount of annual income, the appropriate tax payment depends on the level of annual cost of operation. If costs are high, tax payments will be lower than if costs are low. With this in mind, you can see how different depreciation methods affect the benefits of investment proposals. To illustrate this let's calculate the tax implications of the two depreciation methods discussed earlier. Table S19-3 summarizes the calculations assuming a tax rate of 50 percent.

As columns 3 and 5 show, both methods result in an overall tax reduction of $9,000, because the cost of the equipment was charged off against income in determining profit in each year of the asset's life. The two methods differ in the way the $9,000 reduction is dispersed over the six years.

Taxes also enter into the analysis if an asset's selling price differs from its depreciated or book value. For example, if the book value of equipment is $2,000 at the time the equipment is sold for $1,000, a $1,000 loss can be declared, and taxes can be reduced accordingly.

━━━━━━━━━ TABLE S19-3 ━━━━━━━━━

TAX IMPLICATIONS OF TWO DEPRECIATION METHODS

	Straight line		Sum-of-years-digits	
1	**2**	**3**	**4**	**5**
Year	Reduction in taxable income (amount of depreciation)	Reduction in taxes (50%)	Reduction in taxable income (amount of depreciation)	Reduction in taxes (50%)
1	$3,000	$1,500	$5,143	$2,572
2	3,000	1,500	4,286	2,143
3	3,000	1,500	3,429	1,714
4	3,000	1,500	2,571	1,286
5	3,000	1,500	1,714	857
6	3,000	1,500	857	428
		$9,000		$9,000

━━━━━━━━━ TABLE S19–4 ━━━━━━━━━

NET PRESENT VALUE OF TWO ALTERNATIVES FOR COD DEPRECIATION AND TAX EFFECTS ADDED (50 PERCENT TAX RATE)

Machine A

Time (year)	Initial outlay	Annual maintenance	Annual depreciation
0	−$10,000		
1		−$1,000	$1,667
2		−1,000	1,667
3		−1,000	1,667
4		−1,000	1,667
5		−1,000	1,667
6		−1,000	1,667

Machine B

Time (year)	Initial outlay	Annual maintenance	Annual depreciation
0	−$12,000		
1		−$500	$2,000
2		−500	2,000
3		−500	2,000
4		−500	2,000
5		−500	2,000
6		−500	2,000

EXAMPLE

693
Chapter 19
Approaches
to Change

Consider two investment alternatives for Consolidated Dryers, Inc. (COD). Alternatives *A* and *B* are two cut-off machines for manufacturing dryers. Machine *A* costs $10,000 and will require maintenance of $1,000 per year. Machine *B* costs $12,000 but requires maintenance of only $500 per year. COD uses straight line depreciation. The economic life of the asset is six years with no expected salvage value. Which machine should be purchased?

Using net present value, but short-cutting special analysis steps, we can solve the problem as shown in Table S19-4. Note that because of the higher cash flow from more depreciation and lower maintenance costs, machine *B* is the more favorable investment even though *B* had higher initial costs.

Derivation of Compound Interest Factors

Single payment compound amount factor

Often we are interested in determining for a proposed investment the *compound amount* to which it will grow during its life. If I invest P dollars now for n years at an annual interest rate of i, what compound dollar amount

Tax savings		Net outflows		Present value
		$-\$10,000$		$-\$10,000$
$\$833$	$(-\$1,000 + 833) =$	-167		
833		-167		
833		-167	$-\$167 \times 4.355$	
833		-167	$\longrightarrow$	-727
833		-167		
833		-167		

Total = $-\$10,727$

Tax savings		Net outflows		Present value
		$-\$12,000$		$-\$12,000$
$\$1,000$	$(-\$500 + 1,000) =$	500		
1,000		500		
1,000		500	$\$500 \times 4.355$	
1,000		500	$\longrightarrow$	$+2,178$
1,000		500		
1,000		500		

Total = $-\$9,822$

S will result? The general procedure for determining the compound amount is:

Beginning time (beginning of year)	Beginning amount	Ending time (end of year)	Ending amount
0	P	1	$S_1 = P + P_i = P(1 + i)$
1	$P(1 + i)$	2	$S_2 = P(1 + i) + P(1 + i)i$
			$= P(1 + i)(1 + i)$
			$= P(1 + i)^2$
2	$P(1 + i)^2$	3	$S_3 = P(1 + i)^2 (1 + i)$
			$= P(1 + i)^3$
3	$P(1 + i)^3$		
$n - 1$	$P(1 + i)^{n-1}$	n	$S_n = P(1 + i)^n$

We find, then, the general expression for calculating the compound amount, S_n, to which an initial single investment, P, will grow over n years when the interest rate is i percent per year:

$$S_n = S = P(1 + i)^n \qquad \text{(S19-2)}$$

The factor $(1 + i)^n$ is the compound amount factor for a single payment found in Appendices B and C,

$$CAF(s)^n = (1 + i)^n$$

Single payment present worth factor

When you think carefully about the time value of money, you will find that there are two ways of looking at it. Money invested now will compound into a larger amount in the future. But a sum of money to be received by you in the future is worth some smaller amount to you now. In other words, the *present* value of a future receipt is lower than the amount to be received. Why? If you possessed the future amount *now* (at present), rather than later, you could invest it and receive interest payments on it throughout the time of possession. The investment would compound during the waiting period, and you would end up with a larger amount. The process of calculating a present value is called *discounting;* a future sum is discounted (reduced) to some smaller amount, its present value.

Let's now reexamine equation S19-2 in more detail.

$$S = P(1 + i)^n$$

$$\begin{pmatrix} \text{A future amount to} \\ \text{be received after} \\ n \text{ periods} \end{pmatrix} = \begin{pmatrix} \text{Present} \\ \text{value} \\ \text{of an} \\ \text{investment} \end{pmatrix} \begin{pmatrix} \text{Available} \\ \text{investment} \\ \text{growth rate} \end{pmatrix}$$

In words, S19-2 says that a future amount (compound value) is determined by multiplying the investment's present value by its growth rate over the appropriate time span. If P, n, and i are known, we can solve for S, the compound or future amount.

If we divide both sides of equation S19-2 by $(1 + i)^n$, we obtain equation S19-3.

$$P = \frac{S}{(1 + i)^n} \qquad \text{(S19-3)}$$

$$\begin{pmatrix} \text{Present} \\ \text{value} \\ \text{of an} \\ \text{investment} \end{pmatrix} = \begin{pmatrix} \dfrac{\text{A future amount}}{\text{to be received}} \\ \dfrac{\text{after } n \text{ periods}}{\text{Available}} \\ \text{investment} \\ \text{growth rate} \end{pmatrix}$$

In words, equation S19-3 says that the present value of a proposed investment is determined by dividing the future amount to be received at the end of n years by the available investment growth rate dictated by the investment market. Stated another way, the *present* value of a sum of money to be received in the future equals that future sum divided by the growth rate of interest for investments. If S, i, and n are known, we can solve for P, the present value. Appendices B and C illustrate this interest factor. The factor $(1/(1 + i)^n)$ is the single payment present worth factor, $PWF(s)^n$ found in column 2 of the tables.

The preceding discussion related to *single* (one-time) investments and receipts. Sometimes *multiple* outlays or receipts occur annually over several years in equal annual amounts. The same basic rationale applies.

Uniform annual series present worth factor

Suppose you are told you will be given $100 one year from now and another $100 two years hence. This is an equal payment annual series with a total dollar amount of $200.

However, to you the *present* value of the gifts is less than $200 for the same reasons presented in our previous discussion of present value. This is the case of finding the present value for a uniform annual series.

The factor for the present value of a uniform series can be found in Appendices B and C. The factor, $PWF(u)^n$ is the bracketed interest factor of equation S19-4 below.

The general equation that was used to generate the tabled values can be developed as shown.

Year	Amount received at end of year	Present value factor	Present value of amount received
1	R	$\dfrac{1}{(1 + i)}$	$R\left[\dfrac{1}{(1 + i)}\right]$
2	R	$\dfrac{1}{(1 + i)^2}$	$R\left[\dfrac{1}{(1 + i)^2}\right]$
⋮	⋮	⋮	⋮
n	R	$\dfrac{1}{(1 + i)^n}$	$R\left[\dfrac{1}{(1 + i)^n}\right]$

Thus, the present value of an annual series of R dollars per year over n years is the sum of the present values for each payment:

$$P = R\left[\frac{1}{(1 + i)}\right] + R\left[\frac{1}{(1 + i)^2}\right] + \ldots + R\left[\frac{1}{(1 + i)^n}\right]$$

Collecting terms we obtain

$$P = R\left[\frac{1}{(1 + n)^1} + \frac{1}{(1 + n)^2} + \ldots + \frac{1}{(1 + i)^n}\right]$$

This is a geometric series the sum of which is

$$P = R\left[\frac{(1 + i)^n - 1}{i(1 + i)^n}\right] \tag{S19-4}$$

P is the present value of a series of equal annual payments (receipts), R, which occur over n years.

Other compound interest factors

Three uniform annual series factors have not been derived, but they can be derived in a manner similar to what we have just done. Stated without proof, they are:

1. the capital recovery factor, $(CRF)_i^n$, the bracketed factor of equation S19-5,
2. the sinking fund factor, $(SFF)_i^n$, the bracketed factor of equation S19-6, and
3. the compound amount factor, $(CAF(u)_i^n)$, the bracketed factor of equation S19-7.

$$R = P\left[\frac{i(i + 1)^n}{(1 + i)^n - 1}\right] \tag{S19-5}$$

$$R = S\left[\frac{i}{(1 + i)^n - 1}\right] \tag{S19-6}$$

$$R = R\left[\frac{(1 + i)^n - 1}{i}\right] \tag{S19-7}$$

Additional Replacement Models

Risk analysis

Description of the model. Many decisions are based on discounted cash flow calculations. Management might be told, for example, that replacement alternative X has an expected internal rate of return of 9.2 percent and for replacement Y a 10.3 percent return can be expected. With risk analysis, the manager obtains the above information *plus* a distribution of other possible rates of return on each investment. You might tell the managers, for example, that X has 1 chance in 20 of being a total loss, 1 in 10 of earning from 4–5 percent, 2 in 10 of paying 10–12 percent, and 1 chance in 50 of attaining a 30 percent rate of return. From another schedule he learns what the most likely rate of return is from Y. These alternatives are graphically portrayed in Figure S19-1. Notice that the *shape* of the distribution gives the manager additional information about the variability of each proposal.

Figures S19-1 Alternative investment distribution of returns

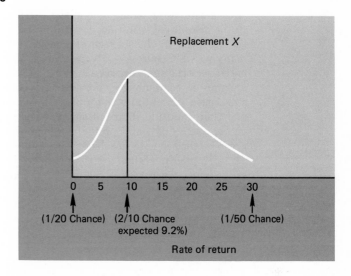

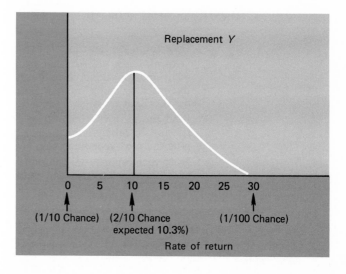

The model. The basic model is present value, present worth, discounted cash flow, or internal rate of return. However, instead of computing only the most likely rate of return, we compute several for each alternative. Data concerning the variables in the model are collected by obtaining estimates through such questions as:

1. Given that the expected annual cost of maintenance is $510, what is the probability that the cost will exceed $550?
2. Is there any chance that the cost will exceed $650?
3. How likely is it that the cost will drop below $475?

Answers to these kinds of questions give a distribution for each variable used in the discounted cash flow determination of return on investment.

As you might suspect, estimation errors can enter into the analysis from many possible sources—salvage values, expenses, and revenues. If we attempted to reiterate the analysis for each source, we could easily end up with an overwhelming amount of computation. Fortunately, risk analysis is adaptable to computer simulation. Essentially the process involves programming the investment model and then inputing distributions of annual cash inflows, cash outflows, salvage value, useful life, and annual interest rate. In one simulation run, the Monte Carlo method is used to select at random a value from each of these distributions. The net present value for that run is calculated and recorded. Each of many such simulation runs, say 500 of them, would be performed, and the result would be 500 net present values. We then classify these observations into a frequency distribution that conveys a picture of just how much variation in net present value is to be expected. This information may be more useful to the operations manager than a single estimate.

The Machinery and Allied Products Institute (MAPI) Model[1]

The MAPI formula may be characterized as an "adjusted" after-tax rate of return criterion. The entire focus of the calculation is to determine a rate of return for the next year on net investment, relative to the conditions that would prevail if the company went on without the proposed project. The steps involved in the MAPI analysis are:

1. Determine the net capital investment in the piece of equipment.
2. Determine the after income tax net operating advantage of the proposed addition. This is actually a calculation to see how much earnings have increased by using the new piece of equipment. This is usually reflected by increased revenue, decreased cost, or a combination of both.
3. Find the next year capital consumption avoided by the project. This is the fall in salvage value from holding an existing asset one more year, plus the next-year allocation of possible capital additions or renewals.
4. Next-year capital consumption incurred is determined. This is the allowance for obsolescence and deterioration of the proposal taken from a

---

[1] See George Terborgh, *Business Investment Management* (Washington, D.C.: Machinery and Allied Products Institute, 1967) and *A Practical Method of Investment Analysis: The MAPI System* (Washington, D.C.: Machinery and Allied Products Institute and Council for Technological Advancement, 1971).

MAPI chart. It is a function of the estimated terminal salvage value as a percent of cost and estimated service life.

5. Next year income tax adjustment is found as the *net* increase in income tax resulting from the project.

6. Now you can calculate the after-tax return, called the "urgency rating." The actual mechanics of calculation vary slightly from this form:

$$\text{After-tax return} = \frac{\text{Net monetary advantage from project}}{\text{Net investment required by project}} \times 100$$

$$= \frac{(2) + (3) - (4) - (5)}{(1)} \times 100$$

To use the MAPI procedure, you need a MAPI summary form and charts (graphs). The details of the procedure are beyond our introductory treatment; if you're interested, the Machinery and Allied Products Institute can provide you with clear procedures to follow.

Model Selection

Further insight into the recommendation of combining payback with net present value is provided by a study on replacement model selection that used this procedure:

A scoring model was developed and used to rate several analytical techniques used in making equipment replacement decisions. The model incorporates both subjective evaluations by users as well as objective performance measures on several actual replacement problems. Among the several models ranked, the payback criterion ranked highest, primarily because of the ease with which it is understood and implemented. Models incorporating present values, including profit maximization and risk analysis, ranked next, while the MAPI technique received the lowest ranking.[2]

This study developed a ranking methodology including the opinion and evaluations of users and actual computational and data requirements regarding each of several models on actual replacement problems.

Criteria that users were asked to evaluate models against were:

1. Recognition of the time value of money. This refers to the allowance for variations in value that money will have in time periods other than the present. It involves the rate used to discount future amounts of money.

2. Recognition of the time pattern of money. The time pattern of money is the order (pattern) in which money is received or expended throughout the replacement life cycle, i.e. the flow of revenue and expenses to and from the equipment in each time period.

3. Treatment of risk and uncertainty. Risk refers to the ability to incorporate probabilities associated with possible outcomes. Uncertainty refers to a lack of any information concerning the probabilities of possible outcomes.

[2] Everett E. Adam, Jr. and Michael F. Pohlen, "A Scoring Methodology for Equipment Replacement Model Evaluation," *AIIE Transactions* 6, no. 4 (December 1974), pp. 338–44.

4. Utilization of market values. This refers primarily to the value assigned to the equipment at the time of purchase or salvage. It involves the question of using market values for the receipts from the equipment to be replaced, as well as expenditures for the new equipment at the time of its purchase as well as its salvage at a later date.

5. Accuracy. Accuracy is to the precision or exactness of the model as it relates to the actual equipment replacement problem. This does not refer to the computational accuracy of the model. It is the state of being free from error as an evaluation device.

6. Simplicity. Simplicity is the degree to which the model is easy to understand and apply. It is the equality or state of not being complex. Simplicity reflects clarity.

These evaluations were combined with actual replacement data, allowing the inclusion of two additional factors: computational difficulty and number of data points. All eight factors were combined in a scoring rule that provided the results shown in Table S19-5. The profit maximization model is the continuous function representation of present value. In Table S19-5, the higher the total score, the better the model *relative to the other models.* No model was "best" in an optimal sense. We can see that payback ranked highest (148), followed by risk analysis (111) and present value (101).

Even though payback was ranked low on three criteria—time pattern of money (−1), treatment of risk (−5), and market values (−8)—the overwhelming high score on simplicity (123) offset those factors. Because of the low scores on three of the factors, the authors felt that the simplicity of payback alone was not enough to recommend the model by itself. On the other hand, we cannot overlook the importance of simplicity to the user and the high ranking that payback received on that criterion. We concur with the authors in their final recommendation: use payback in conjunction with either risk analysis or present value analysis.

TABLE S19-5

WEIGHTING FUNCTION RESULTS*

			Models		
Criteria	**Payback**	**Present value**	**MAPI**	**Risk analysis**	**Profit maximization**
Time value	−18	20	−1	10	4
Time pattern	−1	17	2	3	10
Treatment of risk	−5	0	−9	38	−4
Market values	−8	4	9	1	10
Accuracy	57	80	55	56	74
Simplicity	123	−20	11	3	2
Total score	148	101	67	111	96

*Source: Adam and Pohlen, "A Scoring Methodology for Equipment Replacement Model Evaluation," *AIIE Transactions* 6, no. 4 (December 1974), p. 342. Copyright American Institute of Industrial Engineers, Inc., 25 Technology Park/Atlanta, Norcross, Georgia 30092.

1. Illustrate how depreciation affects the relative financial attractiveness of investment alternatives.

2. Contrast the effects of straight line and accelerated methods of asset depreciation.

3. Define the following:
    (a) single payment compound amount factor
    (b) single payment present worth factor
    (c) uniform annual series present worth factor

4. Of what value is risk analysis in evaluating alternative investment proposals?

5. Describe the main features of the MAPI model.

6. Discuss the major considerations in selecting replacement models.

1. An asset has an initial cost of $150,000, an estimated life of 8 years, and salvage value of $22,000. Develop schedules of depreciation for straight line and sum-of-years-digits methods of depreciation (similar to Tables S19-1 and S19-2).

2. For problem 1, develop a table of tax implications (similar to Table S19-3).

3. Using a 10 percent interest rate, calculate the net present value implications of the two depreciation methods for the data in problem 1.

4. Agribin, Inc., wants to build a new equipment facility but cannot invest in projects returning less than a 10 percent return. Alternative A requires a $300,000 investment, will have an economic useful life of 8 years, and will create net inflows (revenues minus expenses) from operations of $80,000 annually. Alternative B requires a $200,000 initial outlay, is expected to have zero salvage value after 8 years of useful economic life, and will create net inflows of $65,000 per year. None of these estimates includes depreciation and tax considerations.

    (a) Which alternative is best if straight line depreciation is used?
    (b) Which is best if sum-of-years-digits is used?
    (c) Compare after tax net present values for both alternatives.
    (d) Which, if either, of the alternatives should be selected?

20 Behavioral Responses to Change

As production and operations managers plan, organize, and control the conversion process, they are managing a dynamic process, not a static one (see Figure 20-1). After inputs have been converted into outputs, they are transported to the market through some physical distribution system. At this point consumers come into the picture. Whether they accept or reject the goods and services, their reactions and suggested changes are transmitted back to the production/operations environment. This market feedback is important not only to marketing but to production and operations as well, for consumer reactions often force changes upon the production/operations function. And consumers aren't the only ones who suggest changes; government regulations, societal norms, new technology, and economic growth also exert external pressure on the conversion system.

These and other pressures force production/operations managers to operate in dynamic environments even though their internal production function is somewhat static in the short run. Internally, materials, demand, equipment, and employees also vary considerably within a single P/OM process. *The production process must be dynamic to react to the internal variations just as it must be dynamic to react to external pressures.*

In Chapter 18, you may remember, we specified a general framework of the conversion process in change (see Figure 20-2). In Chapter 19, we considered rational approaches to change in two target areas, technology and structure. Now we will concentrate on the third area in which changes can be made, behavior.

The Behavioral Change Process

Consistent with the model of the conversion process in change (Figure 20-2), the behavioral change process includes:

1. Recognition of the need for change.
2. Identification of the behavioral targets for change by production/operations managers and/or their subordinates.
3. Decision to change in a certain way.
4. Strategy for change; the behavioral approach toward change.
5. Implementation of the behavioral change; the actual changing of behaviors of participants in the production process.

Figure 20-1 **General model for production/operations management**

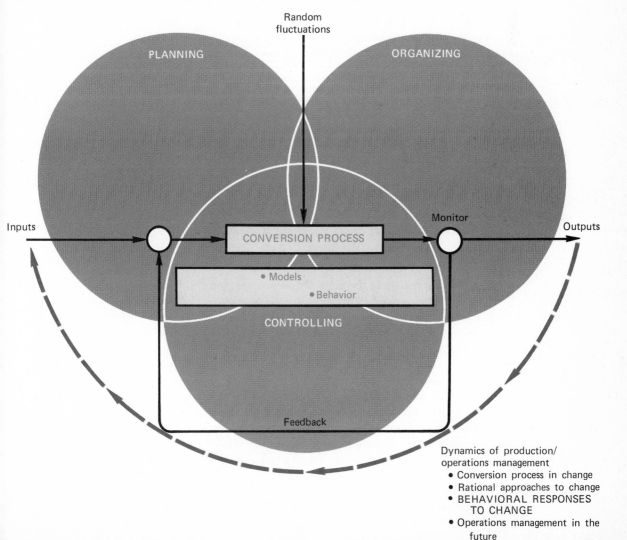

Dynamics of production/operations management
- Conversion process in change
- Rational approaches to change
- BEHAVIORAL RESPONSES TO CHANGE
- Operations management in the future

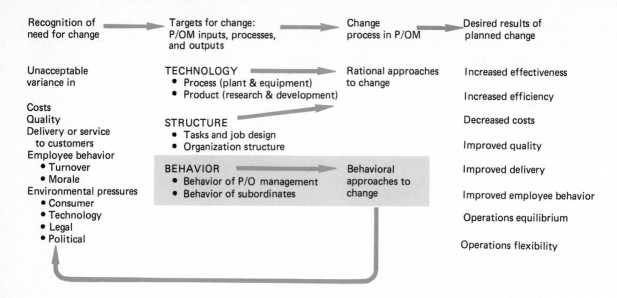

| Recognition of need for change | Targets for change: P/OM inputs, processes, and outputs | Change process in P/OM | Desired results of planned change |

Figure 20-2　**Dynamics of production/operations management: the conversion process in change**

We have already pointed out how to recognize the need for change. If your organization's costs, product quality, delivery dates, customer service, employee turnover, and/or employee morale are unacceptable, you should consider making some changes. In the rest of this chapter, we'll discuss steps 2 through 5 of the behavioral change process, concentrating not only on the process itself but on dealing with resistance to it and management's role in changing behavior for the good of the organization.

Behavioral Targets for Change

The inputs to the conversion process, land, labor, capital, and management, are blended to produce a good or service. Actual output is not always consistent with plans, and the plans themselves also change from time to time. In both instances some reblending of the inputs is required. Consistently, experienced P/O managers find that *it is the reblending of behaviors—the behaviors of labor (the operative worker) and management (operations managers at all levels)—that is the most difficult and challenging of all change problems.* Typical engineering problems faced by production managers can be approached on the basis of economic rationality. Behavioral change problems, however, are an altogether different story. Behavioral change involves people, and people have emotions.

There are, you see, two targets for behavioral change, the production/operations manager and the operative workers or other subordinates. Numerous studies have shown that in order for managers to change their subordinates, they must change themselves first. They must be exposed to new techniques and methods either before their subordinates are expected to learn them or along with their subordinates. If subordinates see that their supervisors are willing to change their behaviors, they are much more willing to change too. Therefore, as production and operations managers, you must think of behavioral change not only in terms of your subordinates but of yourselves as well.

Strategies for Behavioral Change

Three distinct strategies have been suggested for changing behavior.[1] As we discuss them, remember that they may assist managers change the behaviors of both supervisors and operative workers.

Empirical-rational strategies assume that people are rational, that they will act in their own self-interest.

If production and operations managers wish to advance change, they should show employees that the change is not only desirable for the organization but for the employees' self-interest too. When employees understand that change will benefit them, they will change their behavior.

Assume, for example, that a line foreman is personally rewarded when the production costs of his unit are acceptable. If the line foreman is shown rework and scrap cost reports indicating that his department exceeds plant average, he will logically decrease his costs by improving quality because it is in his own self-interest to do so. How will he do this? By explaining to subordinates that it is in their self-interest to improve quality; that is, by using the same empirical-rational approach with them that was used with him.

Normative-reeducative strategies build upon the empirical-rational strategies. Besides assuming that workers are rational, these strategies also presume that people act as a result of attitudes and values they have acquired over time. Since these attitudes and values are normative (beliefs about what "ought" to be), they can be changed only when individuals commit themselves to new behavior patterns. Thus changing behavior involves not only presenting people with facts in their own self-interest but changing their attitudes, skills, and relationships as well.

Suppose that a foreman, for example, has long believed that quantitative analysis is useless for managing product quality. Under this strategy, the foreman might be sent to a series of application sessions teaching

---

[1]Robert Chin and Kenneth D. Benne, "General Strategies for Effecting Changes in Human Systems," in *The Planning of Change*, 3rd ed., Warren G. Bennis, Kenneth D. Benne, Robert Chin, and Kenneth E. Corey, eds. (New York: Holt, Rinehart, and Winston, Inc., 1976), pp. 22–45.

the essentials of sampling and statistical inference. If in these sessions the foreman's own data were used to make up control charts and demonstrate sampling, he might begin to change his attitude toward quantitative analysis.

We feel that we should insert a word of caution here. The authors of this book have used normative-reeducative strategies themselves in a quantitative quality control training program. Our experience was that while some foremen did in fact change their attitudes and behaviors as a result of this strategy, others were completely indifferent and continued to hold the same attitudes they held in the first place.

Power-coercive strategy
This strategy is based on the concept of the application of political, economic, or some other form of power.

Power can be legitimate (the proper use of delegated authority), or it can be informal (without formal organization sanction). Often, power is simply the effective use of leadership and position in the organization. In other cases, power may be brought to bear on individuals from peer groups, informal leaders, economic realities, or fear (fear of job loss, for example). Whatever its form, the result is the same; power can be a very effective way to bring about changes in individual and group behavior.

One good example of power to bring about change in production/operations management is in the collective bargaining process. The production/operations manager has the economic power to persuade change in seniority and management rights, among other things. The union, through the threat of collective withdrawal of labor, has the power to bargain for higher wages and improved fringe benefits, should they elect to do so, at the expense of seniority and management rights.

The Learning Process

Clearly, the key to both the empirical-rational and the normative-reeducative strategies is learning. Let's look into the learning process itself to see what happens when people modify their behavior by learning new skills, attitudes, or facts.

Learning
Learning is really a series of small steps toward a goal. Say that a student wishes to learn to read Chinese. Step by step, she learns each character. After each step she gets a response, feedback, from her teacher. Building on the responses she gets, she continues to learn more characters, to put them together, and finally to read whole sentences. When she has successfully taken all the necessary steps, she has learned.

The basic learning process applies in production/operations as well. Given a new task, employees will learn. The question is whether they will learn behaviors that are beneficial to the organization or behaviors that are disruptive.

Reinforcement   In the learning process, the critical determinants of a broad spectrum of human behaviors are the *environmental consequences of that behavior.* These consequences are called reinforcers.

Positive reinforcers are pleasant, rewarding, and satisfying; they serve to increase the probability that the behavior (response sequence) will occur again. Negative reinforcers are usually unpleasant, undesirable, and even painful. Generally, behaviors with positive consequences tend to be repeated when the situation reoccurs; behaviors with negative consequences tend to be abandoned.

Behavioral effects   Not only the reinforcement itself but also its timing
of reinforcement   is important. One study notes:
schedules

> The effectiveness of a given reinforcer will depend upon its magnitude, its quality, the degree to which it has been associated with other reinforcers, and the manner in which it is scheduled. As a matter of fact, the effectiveness will depend as much upon its *scheduling* as upon any of its other features.

> A schedule of reinforcement is a more-or-less formal specification of the occurrence of a reinforcer in relation to the behavioral sequence to be conditioned. It is fairly easy, even for individuals with a minimum of training, to follow specified schedules of reinforcement in order to generate predictable behavioral patterns.[2]

Schedules of reinforcement may be either continuous or intermittent. Continuous reinforcement occurs after every response sequence that has been chosen for conditioning. Consider a new employee on a mass production line who completes hundreds of units daily. Although many units are assembled correctly, others are not. Under continuous reinforcement, a foreman would observe every unit and provide either a positive or a negative reinforcer. This rarely, if ever, occurs in production/operations because of time and resource limitations. More often, reinforcement is intermittent, occurring occasionally after the response sequence (the behavior). Under continuous reinforcement conditions, although learning takes place more quickly, so does extinction (forgetting the response and reinforcement relationship) once the reinforcement is suddenly withdrawn.

[2]Everett E. Adam, Jr., and W. E. Scott, "The Application of Behavioral Conditioning Procedures to the Problems of Quality Control," *The Academy of Management Journal* 14, no. 2 (June 1971), pp. 175–93.

Intermittent reinforcement schedules are grouped into fixed interval, variable interval, fixed ratio, or variable ratio classifications. Interval schedules are tied to a time dimension; ratio schedules are tied to the number of responses. In *fixed interval* schedules, reinforcement occurs regularly after a fixed period of time has elapsed. An assembler might receive verbal reinforcement once each week, every week, for example. In *variable interval* schedules, the time interval between reinforcements varies. *Fixed ratio* schedules provide reinforcement after a fixed, preplanned number of responses, after each one hundred units of output, for example. *Variable ratio* reinforcements are staggered to occur after various numbers of responses have been made. A foreman might reinforce an assembler's behavior after thirty-seven, then fifty, and then fifteen units of output. With variable schedules, the employee does not know in advance when the next reinforcement will occur.

Typically, production/operations managers reinforce and are themselves reinforced on variable rather than on fixed schedules. Because of the time pressures that exist in operations, managers can't be committed to fixed reinforcement schedules. In fact, this is all to the good, because when reinforcement schedules are variable, behavior patterns, once they have been learned, tend to persist.

Since our interest is changing behavior, we can draw several conclusions from what we've discussed so far. First, new behavior patterns are learned fastest with continuous, or nearly continuous, reinforcement schedules. Second, behavior patterns that have been learned under variable intermittent reinforcement schedules are the most difficult to change. This is true because people continue old behaviors, even when reinforcement has stopped, expecting to be reinforced again; since reinforcement times have varied in the past, they may not be aware that no more reinforcement is coming. Third, negative reinforcement, when properly administered, can be effective. When punishment (the infliction of pain or discomfort) is administered, however, the consequences can be disastrous. Let's look a little closer at punishment and its consequences in operations.

Punishment

There is research to suggest that punishment, under differing circumstances, may increase occurrences of undesirable behavior, cause it to last longer, be a short-lived deterrent, cause people to vary their behavior but be unable to control the direction of the new behavior, and arouse negative feelings. On the other hand, mild punishment may help improve behavior by at least providing negative feedback on performance.[3]

Think of the times you've been punished. Haven't you sometimes revolted and acted even worse? The same holds true in production/opera-

---

[3]See Timothy W. Costello and Sheldon S. Zalkind, *Psychology in Administration* (Englewood Cliffs, N.J.: Prentice-Hall, Inc., 1963), pp. 215–16.

tions situations. Since the effects of punishment are unpredictable and often adverse, we think it might be better to use positive reinforcement instead.

=== EXAMPLE ===

Two foremen in the same production facility employed different reward systems, each beyond normal organizational rewards. The first foreman seemed always upset and irritated at his subordinates, verbally admonishing them for any small reason, often hours or days after the behavior. His employees tended to ignore his behavior, and react neither negatively nor positively over time. The second foreman administered praise and/or candy to his workers intermittently. He was very careful and always praised or offered a piece of candy after outstanding behavior. He was one of the most highly thought of and successful foremen in the facility, and his department was very productive.

Now, of course we aren't recommending that every foreman lay in a supply of candy. The success of the second foreman's reward system resulted not from the magnitude of the reward but from its *systematic administration.* He almost always reinforced acceptable behavior, and often in the presence of others. The real reward was recognition. This is not to say that punishment never brings about beneficial change; but dysfunctional consequences are also a distinct possibility.

Extinction
Much of the research in operant conditioning suggests that desirable behaviors should be rewarded and undesirable behaviors ignored. When positive reinforcement is withdrawn, behaviors supposedly extinguish—but often only after an initial increase in the response that is seeking the old reinforcement. Here is where we get into trouble in production/operations management. If the employee is unaware that the old response-reinforcement contingency has ended, he may continue, even intensify, the old response. Managers inadvertently continue to reinforce the very behaviors that they want to stop. Why? *Because in reality, response-reinforcement contingencies are varied and complex.* A supervisor's verbal reinforcements, for example, are not the only reinforcers at work on the job. Other rewards to the employee come from the task itself. These intrinsic rewards are part of the task being performed. One of these, the "batch traction," is the worker's feeling that he should finish a group of units or a specific part of a task before he takes a voluntary rest period. Seeing a task through to completion results in a pleasant, positive reinforcement. At times, these kinds of intrinsic reinforcements can conflict with extrinsic reinforcements.

━━━━━━━━━ **EXAMPLE** ━━━━━━━━━

Although a manager stresses quality on a daily basis to employees, the employee also enjoys the batch traction effect of seeing quantities of finished products pile up in front of him. As the "to-be-done" pile diminishes and the "finished" pile builds up, the employee tends to let quality slip at the expense of quantity for the final units in the lot. This quality/quantity tradeoff exists for many routine, repetitive tasks.

We suggest that you change behavior by altering positive reinforcers and placing behavior under positive control. Try to communicate *current* response-reinforcement contingencies clearly; remove obsolete reinforcers so that old, undesirable behavior will subside. The manager in our example could arrange for a conveyor to remove each piece of work when it is finished. That way workers wouldn't be reinforced by a pile of completed work.

Resistance to Change

Each of us resists change, some more than others. There are all sorts of reasons why people are reluctant to change. Positive reinforcers for current behavior patterns encourage us to continue acting as we are. Perhaps we're afraid of failing at something new. Often we're anxious about anything unknown and prefer to keep our old ways even if they're unsatisfactory. People like the stability afforded by established patterns of relationships in their personal and professional lives. The security we feel from orderly and familiar ways of doing things can be threatened by change, and so can our status, authority, autonomy, and discretion. Change sometimes makes old skills obsolete and requires us to develop new skills. In general, there are four basic reasons for resisting change:

1. Economic factors—a threat to economic security, such as losing a job.
2. Inconvenience—a threat of making life more difficult, such as having to learn new ways of doing things that were formerly done routinely.
3. Uncertainty—a threat of not knowing the implications of forthcoming change.
4. Interpersonal relationships—a threat of disrupting or destroying customary social relationships, group standards, or socially valued skills.

If training for change disrupts the current work flow, resistance to change is intensified. Work will be initially disrupted, and higher operating costs can be expected temporarily. The initiator of change must be prepared to accept these added costs. Part of the initial decrease in work flow is due to the learning process. Besides that, however, employee resistance to change is high at these initial stages; often the employee does not clearly perceive the need for change in the first place. All he knows is that he is now further behind in his work.

These fears and frustrations may lead to attitude and behavior patterns that can magnify even the most seemingly insignificant changes. Resistance behaviors may take a variety of forms, including aggression, withdrawal, or regression. These manifest themselves in higher absenteeism, requests for transfer, sabotage, or a series of emotional outbursts.

There are several ways to overcome, at least partially, resistance to change. Before examining these techniques, let's look at an abstract of a classic research study concerning resistance to change. Although conducted in the 1940s, the study is still valid for today's organizations, a fact that illustrates for us that good, sound research is timeless.

Harwood
Manufacturing
Company
At the main plant of the Harwood Manufacturing Company, which produced pajamas, researchers studied line operative workers.[4] Like most sewing plants, Harwood employed mostly women, in this plant some 500 women and 100 men. The purpose of the research was to investigate two questions. Why do people resist change so strongly? and What can be done to overcome this resistance?

The plant had an outstanding personnel program with minimal labor unrest and no movement toward unionization. The company worked hard to maintain good employee relations at all levels. Payment was on an incentive system, with an allowance for changing to a new job to offset decreased efficiency during the learning period. Despite this allowance, however, attitudes toward job change in the factory were negative. Turnover was high for employees who were changed to another job; they quit rather than learn a new set of tasks. Among employees who were transferred and remained, these feelings were standard:

> In addition to resentment against the management for transferring them, the employees typically show feelings of frustration, loss of hope of ever regaining their former level of production and status in the factory, feelings of failure, and a very low level of aspiration. In this respect, these transferred operators are similiar to . . . chronically slow workers . . .

On the basis of their preliminary theory that resistance to change is a combination of individual reaction to frustration and strong group-induced forces, the researchers felt that the most appropriate methods for overcoming resistance to change would be group methods. Therefore, they designed several experiments. The first experiment involved three degrees of participation among groups to be transferred to new jobs:

1.   No participation in planning changes; this group was simply told that its members would be transferred to new jobs.

[4]Lester Coch and John R. P. French, Jr., "Overcoming Resistance to Change," *Human Relations* 1 (1948), pp. 512–32.

2. Participation through representation; this group selected one member to help design the new jobs.
3. Total participation by all group members in designing their new jobs.

Two groups were given treatment 3, total participation. Great care was taken to standardize group treatments on dimensions other than degree of participation.

Results of this experiment are shown in Figure 20-3. Output was substantially lower for the no participation group (1) after the transfer than for the three participation groups. There was also a substantial difference in attitude among the three groups. After 40 days, 17 percent of the employees in group 1 quit. Many of the members of this group felt hostility, and several filed grievances about the new rate. Group 2, which enjoyed limited participation, had a substantially better learning curve than did group 1. But the two total participation groups showed even better results. Furthermore, none of the three participation groups (groups 2 and 3) had anyone quit; they received no more training after the second day; and they showed no signs of aggression or hostility at all.

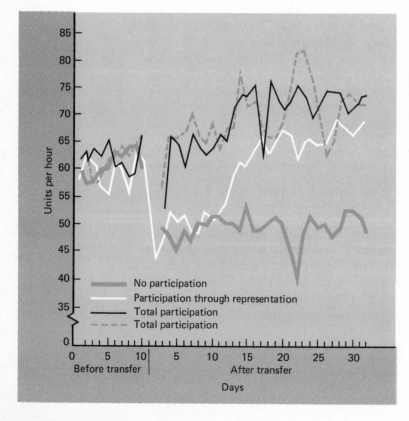

Figure 20-3 **Effects of participation through representation and of total participation on recovery after an easy transfer**

Source: Lester Coch and John R. P. French, Jr., "Overcoming Resistance to Change," *Human Relations* 1 (1948), pp. 512–32, fig. 2.

Then the researchers devised a second experiment, which involved only the members of the no participation group. After the initial 32-day study period, the remaining members of this group were dispersed to new jobs throughout the factory for 75 more days. Then they were brought back together and transferred to a new job, but this time they were allowed to participate in the job design. The results were in sharp contrast to their previous behavior. Output was 35 percent higher than it was before; no one showed any signs of aggression or hostility; and not a single person had quit after 19 days on the new job.

Clearly, participation in designing new jobs overcomes many of the frustrations and aggressions that are typical in resisting change. Further, and most important from a cost standpoint, units of output increased and turnover decreased under conditions of participation. This piece of research has been a basic building block in the foundation of participation as a strategy to overcome resistance to change. We recommend this strategy for production/operations managers today.

Naturally, there have to be limits on the degree of participation. All employees cannot and should not participate in all decisions. What we do suggest is that the effective P/O manager should use the participative approach to gain inputs and ideas for key decisions, especially those affecting the day-to-day duties of subordinates. Although ultimate decisions and responsibilities for performance still rest with production/operations managers, their chances for successful group performance increase substantially if they use a participative approach.

As a final note, we should remind you that resistance to change may appear throughout the organization, from the highest to the lowest levels. Because people occupying high levels within the organization have benefited from the existing system, they may resist changes even more intensely than people at lower levels.

Overcoming resistance to change
As you look over the following suggestions for overcoming resistance to change, remember that each is only a partial solution to the problem. Unfortunately, there is simply no single way to break down all the resistance barriers.[5]

1. *Peer group influences.* In Harwood Manufacturing, the peer group probably encouraged group members to meet the job standards that they had participated in establishing. Peer groups have influences where there is a strong sense of belonging to the group and a perception that the group is superior to others. Groups do significantly influence behavior, and the effective P/O manager attempts to influence the peer group directly or indirectly through the informal group leaders.

[5]James H. Donnelly, James L. Gibson, and John M. Ivancevich, *Fundamentals of Management*, rev. ed. (Dallas, Texas: Business Publications, Inc., 1975), p. 287, and John B. Miner, *The Management Process: Theory, Research, and Practice* (New York: Macmillan Pub. Co., Inc., 1973).

2. *Group discussion.* Participation is most effective if the needs for change are clearly communicated to the group at a level the group members understand, employees want to get involved in the change, and a group meeting is held to encourage discussion and consideration of ideas and suggestions.

3. *Suggestions from employees.* Some employee suggestions should be implemented and the implementation brought to the attention of participants. A superficial "sense of participation" that merely covers an autocratic P/O manager's actions will soon be understood by employees to be no participation; behaviors will adjust accordingly.

4. *Managers' job security.* P/O managers can provide a sense of job security for subordinate supervisors. If supervisors feel that their jobs are secure, they will not perceive employee participation as a threat to their own positions.

5. *Sensitivity (T-Group) training.* Sensitivity training is a group therapy session designed to increase individual awareness of others and to stress authentic relations with others. We question the application of this technique at lower levels in the organization, especially by nonprofessional leaders. Leaders should have strong therapeutic backgrounds in clinical psychology, a background we suggest is missing from most practicing production/operations managers. Transactional analysis, a somewhat similar technique, emphasizes self-awareness. We mention these techniques more to caution against quick adoption than to recommend their value. Research results suggest that such groups may destroy employees' value structures and provide nothing to replace them, the result being dysfunctional job behaviors.

6. *Terminology.* We suggest that certain words, "change," for example, often carry negative connotations and arouse aggressive behaviors unnecessarily from subordinates whose behavior you desire to modify. Walking up to Tom's work area and saying, "Tom, I want you to change your daily scrap reporting system" could arouse more resistance than a softer approach. "Tom, could we talk about the way our daily scrap reporting system works, at your convenience?" is better. Any reference that infers manipulation of an individual is likely to arouse anxieties and create resistance to change. Often, job evaluations cause defensive behavior even by people whose jobs are not affected. Once the employee becomes defensive (usually because the evaluator uses a poor approach or chooses his or her words carelessly), communication is nearly impossible.

7. *Individual characteristics.* Certain types of people resist change no matter what approach is used. These individuals rely heavily on their own personal experience in making decisions, assume the future will be like the past, believe that there is one best way of doing things, and have a low risk-taking propensity. They tend to be more anxious about their work and have poorer educational backgrounds than people who are more willing to change.

Planning for change can be helpful in two ways: it forces careful consideration of the implications of change, and it can facilitate the transition during change. After recognizing the need for change and identifying the goals to be accomplished, managers can choose among several types of change alternatives. Once you are ready to implement a change, you can anticipate potential resistance and develop ways to overcome resistance for each change alternative. To do this, you must have a clear understanding of what the change is to accomplish, whom the change will affect and how, how the change might be resisted, and the resource restrictions with which you are faced.

Although precise models for undertaking planned change do not exist, one can approach these issues in a thoughtful, structured manner. One useful approach for systematically clarifying potential pitfalls is to construct a simple "people-change" matrix like the one in Table 20-1. The left side of the matrix lists all people who will be affected by the change alternative under consideration. Across the top are listed all job-related characteristics that may be modified if the change is adopted. These characteristics are the potential sources of resistance.

Within each cell is the manager's assessment of the importance, to the person affected, of changing each of the job characteristics. Your ability to fill in this matrix depends on your awareness of the needs, desires, capabilities, and aspirations of the people on the left side of the matrix. It also depends on your insights about the potential impact of the change alternative on the various job characteristics. Once you have filled in the matrix, you can begin identifying likely sources of resistance, the reasons for this resistance, and ways for overcoming it. Methods such as these can be very helpful in planning for change.

TABLE 20-1

AN EXAMPLE "PEOPLE-CHANGE" MATRIX FOR ONE CHANGE ALTERNATIVE

People affected	**Job characteristic affected by change**					
	Job skills	Work content	Superior/ subordinate relationship	Work group relationships	Informal relationships	Potential for career mobility
Brown	high	low	high	low	low	medium
Smith	low	low	medium	medium	medium	low
Green	low	low	high	low	high	high
Watts	medium	low	high	medium	low	high
Hone	low	medium	medium	high	low	high

The Change Agent

In behavioral change procedures, it is generally agreed, there are *facilitators* and *learners* of change. In our discussions of the learning process and overcoming resistance to change, we have stressed the production/operations manager's role in initiating change. Essentially, P/O managers are the *facilitators* of change; they are the *change agents.* Production/operations managers continually face the situation of getting changes accomplished through others; operative workers continually face the situation of learning these changes.

Reinforcers

In their efforts to bring about change, production/operations managers are managers of reinforcement. They have to focus on the behavior responses of the participants in the production process, rewarding (reinforcing) those behaviors that they want continued and withdrawing rewards from those behavioral responses that they want diminished.

The rewards, remember, are both extrinsic and intrinsic. Although some, particularly monetary, rewards are generally determined by someone other than first-line supervisors, many powerful reinforcers are under the supervisor's control. Verbal reinforcers can be particularly useful. The key to eliciting change effectively with verbal reinforcers is systematically tying the positive verbal response to work well done. Although it is easy to praise a wide range of behaviors and persons indiscriminately, the effect of the verbal reinforcement is quickly lost if that is done. When properly administered, verbal reinforcement can bring about changes in quality and quantity levels—key output variables in manufacturing and service operations.

Values

Everyone has values and personal beliefs. Sometimes we're hesitant to interject them into conversation unless we are comfortable with the people we're talking to. You would probably be much more outspoken about brutality in football in your parents' living room, for example, than you would in a locker room after a big game. The same is true on our jobs; the more comfortable and secure our surroundings, the more likely we are to interject our values into behavioral change processes.

In their roles as change agents, managers' values may be interjected into the organization whether they want them to be or not. If intervention is on a micro level, managers' value orientations may affect only a few employees. This is the case when managers are retraining people for a few jobs and for procedural changes in production/operations. If intervention is on a macro level, on the other hand, many employees may be affected. Strong beliefs on such broad issues as capitalism, job discrimination, and pollution control can even have an impact on an entire community. Generally, within production/operations management, value systems are interjected into the organization at the micro-intervention level. Top manufacturing and service organization executives have greater position power and more opportunity to influence macro-level issues in accordance with their own values. There are exceptions, of course. A plant manager of a facility employing 1,500 workers in a community of 7,000 can interject his or her values on the community through personal and company support of schools, streets, or social programs.

As changes take place there will necessarily be conflicts in values. In the process of change, the change agent should beware of inadvertently creating threats to personal values concerning basic individual freedoms. On such issues as religion and politics, for example, most organizations do not want to uphold any position that might alienate employees. Caution must be taken so as to avoid substantial value conflict and subsequent employee unrest. We are neither supporting nor condoning the interjection of personal values into organizations; we simply want to make the point that as a production/operations manager, you will have the chance to insert your values into the organization in your role as change agent. Think carefully about your responsibility if and when you do so.

Role of top management If top management does not support change programs at lower levels, change simply will not occur. Management's support must be strong and consistent. We have observed "partial support of change" in management training seminars. Let's look at a case in which top management initially believed that the management training program developed especially for the company did not apply to themselves.

=== EXAMPLE ===

A medium sized corporation instituted a training program that consisted of twenty two-and-a-half day sessions spanning about six months. Top management initially insisted on participating only in a synopsis of the program, which lasted half a day. All 400 managers at other levels took the full training program, and many began implementing changes as a result. About midway through the program—about three months after its inception—top management decided they were missing something and needed the entire program, so they were scheduled as a group for a full two-and-a-half day session at the end. Several times during this session, top level executives commented on changes their subordinates were implementing. They could now see where the impetus for the changes had originated and commented that they would be even more supportive in the future. There was a general feeling from subordinate managers that by having implemented the training program at all, top management showed themselves to be interested in improvement and change. After top management went through the entire program, their support was even clearer.

Several studies indicate that unless top management supports new managerial techniques and approaches, even people exposed to training will continue their old behavior. This is the case because top management continues to reinforce old behavior. In fact, under these conditions, training programs can even make matters worse. At one organization, managers were trained to use a human relations approach to dealing with people. At the end of the program, the managers accepted the idea and decided to use it. After a few months, however, those same managers were found to have become even more autocratic than they had been in the first place. Why? Because top management, uninvolved in the program, continued to reinforce autocratic behavior, and subordinate managers, who had learned through the program to emulate top management's style, had actually learned to be more autocratic than they had been before the program. Had top management supported the use of human relations techniques—even, perhaps, tried it themselves—this unhappy situation would not have taken place.

Awareness

The change agent should assess existing response-reinforcement contingencies (behavior-reward patterns) in the organization. Before instigating change, new production/operations managers should try to get a good idea about current behaviors and rewards. Many experienced managers, when transferred to new facilities, take months to review operations and get to know personnel before they initiate changes. Because existing personnel often view a change of management with anxiety, taking your time before making wholesale changes can reduce tension. If immediate action is required, it must be taken, however, even though you may wish later that it hadn't been necessary.

It is wise to recognize that not all changes are good. Avoid change for the sake of change, and try to be ready to revert to old methods and procedures if you recognize that a poor decision to change has been initiated. Your role as production/operations manager and change agent will be enhanced with your employees by this reversal, and subsequent changes will be more strongly supported.

Communication

Most of the literature concerning the participative approach to change stresses group meetings and careful communication of the need for change. If the change involves only one person, it might be best to have a one-on-one session explaining the need for change as you perceive it, asking for suggestions, and working out the change procedure together. Group meetings may follow the same general procedure. It is important that you, as the change agent, follow up on your initial meeting to get additional inputs and determine if there are barriers to the change that have not been brought out in the open. Openness and honest, straightforward relationships should be fostered; there should be no "hidden reasons" for changes. We've found operative workers to be both shrewd and, if treated fairly, supportive of changes when the reason for change is sound and generally beneficial for the firm.

Production/Operations Changes

Many changes have been successfully carried out in organizations and documented through company records, reports at professional meetings, and professional publications. Many of you have had work experience in complex organizations. In light of our discussion in this chapter, can you think of a successful or an unsuccessful change that you've observed? What was the need for the change? Who was the change agent? Who were the learners? Was there resistance to the change? What strategy led to the success or failure of the change?

As we end this chapter with two reported cases of change in operations, see if you can answer these same questions.

=== EXAMPLE ===

Organization Change: The Effect of Successful Leadership.[6] The Technology Project of the Yale Institute of Human Relations was studying the impact of modern technological methods on work satisfaction and interpersonal relations among hourly rated employees and firstline supervisors in two large automobile plants. Their method of study utilized naturalistic field observation and depended heavily on direct observation of on-the-job performance over a long period of time, on interviews, and on objective performance data.

One of the two plants became the focus of special study because its performance was far below that of the five other plants in the company. The study we report here considers the need for change in this plant and how the change was ultimately accomplished.

On every measure of organizational performance, the plant was last, or next to last, of all the company's plants. It utilized 16 percent more direct labor personnel than standards called for. It exceeded the maximum standards for defects and rejections. Indirect labor costs were higher than for any other plant, as were its rates of absenteeism, accidents, and labor turnover. This was typical of its performance for several preceding years. There was obviously a need for change.

During this period, upper management tried a variety of pressures to improve plant performance. Telephone calls, letters, and memoranda flooded the plant manager. Plant visitations by upper management were frequent. Staff

---

[6]From Costello and Zalkind, *Psychology in Administration*, pp. 197–99. The case was excerpted by the authors from R. H. Guest's *Organizational Change: The Effect of Successful Leadership* (Homewood, Ill.: The Dorsey Press, Inc., and Richard D. Irwin, Inc., 1962), pp. 114–17.

members from headquarters visited and worked with their counterparts in the plant, apparently to no avail. The plant manager and his subordinates knew that things were wrong and needed changing, but the actions they took only seemed to make things worse.

Finally, toward the end of the year, after first considering closing the plant, management retired the plant manager and brought in as a replacement the production manager of one of the other plants. Because this took place only after a costly plant walkout, it illustrates the point that too often, change is initiated only when things get even worse than they have been.

Upper management made no changes other than replacing the old manager. Company management, formal structure in the plant, supervisory personnel, and product line remained the same. The striking improvement that resulted during the next three years seemed largely, if not exclusively, to have resulted from the actions taken by the new manager. We now examine briefly the steps taken by the new manager to accomplish the change. Before doing so, we must point out that once top management had made its own change decision (to replace the previous plant manager), its own behavior toward the plant changed. All the pressure was taken off. The influence of reducing the pressure is difficult to assess, but it certainly must have been helpful. The question is, would such a change (in upper management's behavior) have enabled the previous manager to have done what the new man did? The researchers thought not. The differences between the two men, their different histories, and the behavior of upper management accounted for the changes.

The new manager introduced no dramatic changes; as a matter of fact, he took his time about introducing any changes. He seemed at first to be primarily concerned about getting the men to know him in an informal way and, in turn, getting to know them; for example, very early in his regime he sent a letter to all foremen asking to be invited to visit the foremen's sections. He arranged to meet with the union shop committee. His orientation period soon acquainted him with the emergency and crisis basis of operations in the plant and the need for planning. His response was the initiation, bit by bit, of an extensive set of group meetings involving broader representation and dealing with more significant activity than had ever been the case before. There were monthly meetings of all plant supervision, weekly meetings of the manager with his staff, cost meetings, specialized meetings focusing on quality control, materials control, and so on. The supervisor below the manager soon followed his example, without needing any orders, and meetings became a frequent and scheduled way of getting the plant's work planned and coordinated. Although the new manager clearly avoided the invitation offered him by top management to "clean house," he soon did begin a rather extensive but carefully planned program of transferring supervisory level personnel throughout the plant. This approach apparently avoided either insecurity or resentment. Also

━━━━━━━━━━ EXAMPLE (cont.) ━━━━━━━━━━

there were changes introduced in the physical facilities. First, came improvements in the accommodations (washrooms, lockers, cafeteria) for the employees. Then, systematically, improvements in equipment and changes in systems were introduced. These were introduced gradually and in cooperation with the concerned personnel. Emphasis seemed to be placed on changes that would make it possible for employees to work together more smoothly and more efficiently.

In three years, before the new plant manager was promoted out of the plant, interpersonal intergroup relations had improved, and on most performance criteria the plant was leading the other plants in the company. In this plant, a point had been reached at which it was not capable of changing itself internally. Some agent outside the organization—in this case the new manager—was required.

Although our next example is concerned with a production scheduling problem, the author focused on the implementation process that led to the use of a model rather than on the model itself. Note how the need for a change agent emerged and how the manager subsequently accomplished the model implementation.[7]

━━━━━━━━━━ EXAMPLE ━━━━━━━━━━

A Production Scheduling Change at Baumritter. The Baumritter Corporation is a furniture manufacturer selling primarily under the Ethan Allen brand name. 1970 sales were approximately $65 million with manufacturing in 18 factories. The author and several colleagues at the University of Rhode Island have had a five year research affiliation with Baumritter; the primary orientation is on the process of major system design and implementation. Baumritter has been deeply involved in a system to control materials throughout the organization.

Aggregate   One facet of the research led to the conclusion
Capacity   that a critical need for aggregate capacity plan-
Planning   ning existed and that Baumritter personnel did not
                 fully comprehend the problem. It was felt that this
situation represented a fertile opportunity for the design of an implementation-oriented model. The intent was to plant a seed in the Baumritter system that could be nurtured on a cooperative basis, the research team's relative role decreasing over time. The model was built and demonstrated

[7]Excerpted from Thomas E. Vollman, "A User Oriented Approach to Production Scheduling." (Paper presented at the 3rd Annual American Institute for Decision Sciences Conference, St. Louis, Missouri, 1971).

722

Part VI
Dynamics of
Operations
Management

EXAMPLE (cont.)

to the vice president of manufacturing, assistant vice president of manufacturing, plant managers, assistant plant managers, other manufacturing executives, and systems analysts working on the materials flow system.

The reaction of these people was highly positive; an improved recognition of the seriousness of this problem was felt, and the research team expected that cooperative implementation would take place shortly. However, no amount of prodding on their part caused this to happen.

There is a moral to be learned from this story: the top down approach of selecting the most critical problem first is conceptually elegant, but the bottom up approach of finding a problem of present concern will usually produce implementable results. The place to be studied was a large factory in Orleans, Vermont.

Production Scheduling	The process of scheduling assembly lines at Orleans was somewhat chaotic. All the parts for a complete item were simultaneously started at the cutoff

saws, with the exception that the item would be ready for assembly 8 weeks later. As time elapsed, however, the standard 8-week lead time from cutoff saw to the start of final assembly was often missed. Although the stated goal was to assemble an entire manufacturing lot size upon completion, this goal was rarely met. "Hot list" requirements, poorly constituted finished goods inventories, marketing demands, and pool car shipments all led to sizable variation in the quantities being assembled.

Three of the key manufacturing executives at Orleans attempted to design an assembly schedule on the basis of smaller lot sizes than the cutting lot sizes. They attempted to determine what items to make week-by-week for the next 7 or 8 weeks on each major assembly line. The effort involved 1 or 2 days, or about 5 labor days per week. The procedure was to arrange pieces of paper on a long table; each piece of paper represented a particular assembly lot of an item. Demand forecasts, standard assembly times, part availabilities, pool car requirements, and dollar output objectives were used.

The actual output from the assembly lines was at considerable variance with what the schedule had predicted. As one week's output was off, corrective actions were taken in subsequent weeks; this made the validity of estimates for future time periods ever more dubious.

At this time the author and his colleagues proposed that the production scheduling process be attacked with a time-shared computer model. The reaction to this suggestion was overwhelmingly negative. Comments included: "the computer is no substitute for manufacturing judgment"; "go back o your Ivory Tower"; "you are wasting your time, and I will not permit anyone in my organization to waste his time by cooperating with you." No Orleans employee was forbidden to work with us on the project, but no one was encouraged to do so either.

Implementation   The strategy for designing a model that would be implemented in this environment forced consideration of the relative strengths of insiders, or users who understood the goals, criteria, constraints, and data inputs; and outside experts or designers who have model building skills.

The approach to the problem was to send a research assistant to the factory to stay until someone could be convinced. The entree had to be an individual who could become convinced that the programs could help *him* in the solution of problems with which *he* was personally involved. Finding this kind of individual and getting him on your side is essential.

The individual at Orleans was one of the three men involved in the major assembly scheduling process. His job in the organization was industrial engineer—time study man—assistant to the assistant plant manager. He had had two years of college and no exposure to computers. He didn't see how he could participate in the development of a computer model, nor did he understand why it was necessary for him to be involved. Convincing him of the necessity for his involvement was a key step in the implementation process.

When the inside man or user became convinced that the effort was worth trying, he received a substantial amount of personal harassment from his fellow workers. Some were friendly: "I always knew you was a college professor at heart"; but others were more substantive; he was essentially told that no company time was to be devoted to this project. He did it largely on his own time.

As the model was being developed, considerable interest was being generated around the plant. Most of the interest was negative, and when the first run produced results that were clearly wrong, many individuals had a good time saying I told you so. The user, however, expected the first run to be invalid. He also expected the reason for the lack of validity to be apparent; this proved to be correct. His fellow workers only saw the invalid model, not the glaring inconsistencies that could be remedied. The model's requirement for explicitness quickly pointed out major inconsistencies in data inputs, criteria, and the process of scheduling itself. Within a month these inconsistencies were largely removed, and the model was generating valid assembly schedules 18 weeks into the future.

Once the model became operational at Orleans and actual results began to match the schedule, people who had been openly hostile became believers virtually over night. There was no arguing with success, and the amount of managerial talent freed up to work on other activities was significant. News of the success quickly spread through other Baumritter factories, and the author and his colleagues were besieged with requests for the scheduling model.

EXAMPLE (cont.)

The approach to these requests was to promote the original user to the status of expert major assembly scheduling model builder with the job of transplanting the model to other locations. The researchers helped him in the first two or three transplantations, with their role gradually diminishing. He was thereafter able to implement the system in several factories by himself. Interestingly enough, the problems experienced by Orleans were largely universal, and the model did fit in most other applications. In some of these other applications, new problems were uncovered; at least one of these problems was found also to exist at Orleans. The model went through several stages of generalization, but most of this work was accomplished by Baumritter employees.

Benefits   The benefits from the production scheduling model are somewhat difficult to tie down explicitly. Companies that implement a good system of production planning and inventory control often achieve a 10 to 20 percent increase in productivity due to better utilization of equipment, reduced expediting, etc., and productivity has indeed increased in Baumritter plants since the scheduling system was put in. In addition, major assembly scheduling became so predictable in all factories that order acknowledgment was changed and is now based upon the production schedule. An anticipated problem with filling railway cars did not matter, since improved scheduling allowed for much better planning of railway car needs. Purchasing activities were similarly made easier with a clearer understanding of needs. However, the most fundamental benefit coming from major assembly scheduling model was the clearly perceived need for rationalizing the rest of the production planning and inventory control—materials flow system.

Perhaps most interestingly of all, about a year after major assembly scheduling was working, the vice president of manufacturing became convinced that his most significant problem was aggregate capacity planning; the systems approach had now evolved the problem definition to where the author and his colleagues had seen it two years earlier.

SUMMARY

Pressures for change result from both *external* forces (new government regulations, changing societal norms, new technology, and growth) and *internal* forces (new materials, equipment, products, and personnel). These pressures force the conversion process to be dynamic and the managers and workers involved in this process to change their behaviors.

The behavioral change process involves recognition of the need for change, identification of the behavioral targets for change, decisions to change a certain way, accepting a strategy for change, and implementing the behavioral change.

Strategies for change may be one or a combination of an empirical-rational strategy, a normative-reeducative strategy, or a power-coercive strategy. Regardless of the strategy, the production/operations manager cannot expect a l00 percent behavioral change in subordinate managers and workers.

Subordinates will learn; it is up to the production/operations manager to facilitate learning of behaviors that are supportive of operations goals. To do this, the production/operations manager should focus on the response (worker)-reinforcement (manager) contingency. Positive rewards should be used intermittently to support (reinforce) worker behaviors that the manager wants continued. For behaviors the manager wants eliminated, we suggest extinction as a guide rather than punishment. The manager must correctly evaluate what reinforcement the worker is currently receiving for these undesirable behaviors so that the reinforcements can be withdrawn. This is difficult to do, because in reality the response-reinforcement contingencies are varied and quite complex.

Managers and their subordinates will resist change, some more than others. Worker participation can help reduce the barriers to change. Several other partial solutions exist that can help reduce resistance to change.

Implementation of behavior change rests primarily with production/operations managers in their roles as change agents. They can use extrinsic and intrinsic rewards to bring about change. Operations managers are cautioned not to insert their value systems upon others even though they might have the position power to do so. Top management must be supportive of change. The wise operations manager will solicit and gain support from significant superiors before implementing a major change program. This will clearly enhance the probability of successful change.

CASE

Education Copy Services

Prior to August, 1976, two photocopy machines were available for use by the faculty and secretarial staff of the School of Business. This resource provided easy, quick, and convenient service to faculty in reproducing materials related to personal, teaching, research, and service activities. In an effort to reduce high copying cost, a new policy was implemented. All copying for small jobs was to be done by the secretarial staff, and automatic devices were installed to monitor and count all copies made. The machine would not operate without one of these devices, preset with a department charge account, which a secretary possessed. Some faculty found that access to copying was considerably less convenient than it had been in the past. Last-minute service was not as easily obtained, and a longer planning horizon for copied material was needed. Secretaries found that numerous special trips to the machines were necessary, resulting in interruptions of typing and other office responsibilities.

Then it was announced that as of November 26, 1976, the number of machines would be reduced from two to one. Small jobs (fewer than 11 copies) would continue to be run by secretaries on the one machine. Jobs of eleven or more would be transported across campus to Quick Copy Service for reproduction. This change was to be on a trial basis and offered a handsome cost savings to the college. All indications were that copy service to faculty would be at least as good as had been experienced since August.

The management department chairman and secretarial staff thought about the potential implications of the new system. It was decided that a memo should be sent to faculty identifying some things that could be done to enhance the service obtained from the new system. The essential points presented to the faculty were:

1. Jobs requiring more than 10 copies will be sent to Quick Copy.
2. Generally, the secretarial staff will mail or deliver jobs to Quick Copy twice daily, once in the morning, once in the afternoon.
3. Quick Copy will deliver the finished jobs back to the departmental office.
4. The secretarial staff will continue to process small jobs on the machine here in the building. This will be done once in the morning and once in the afternoon. This will enable the secretaries to perform their other obligations to faculty more effectively.
5. As a result of these 4 steps, the faculty is reminded that some lead time will be necessary for getting the jobs done. The necessary lead time is not expected to be any greater, in general, than it was under the old system. If we allow Quick Copy two to three days lead time, they will be able to get us special emergency service on those exceptional occasions when it is needed.

After thinking about the new system and the memo, the chairman wondered about faculty reaction. The new system seemed to have implications for changes in traditional patterns of behavior. What reactions would you expect if you were chairman? What actions should be taken to ensure smooth adaptation to these changes?

REVIEW AND DISCUSSION QUESTIONS

1. If all employees will learn, why should an operations manager be concerned about learning?

2. Colleges and universities are often bureaucratic in dealing with students. Faculty and staff may be abrupt, inconsiderate, and outright wrong in their behaviors. Think of one experience you've encountered when that was so. Placing yourself in the role of a university operations administrator, use the steps in the behavior change process to show how such an experience could be avoided in the future.

3. State the strategies for behavioral change and briefly explain each. In answering question 2, which strategy for behavior change were you suggesting?

4. Contrast positive reinforcement, negative reinforcement, and punishment. Which holds the most promise for behavioral change in production/operations management? Why?

5. An owner/production manager offers criticism when he observes a mistake, offers praise only at the end of a day, pays for performance weekly on an incentive plan, and provides medical benefits whenever a valid claim occurs. For each of these actions, explain the reinforcement schedule. Utilize continuous-intermittent, fixed-variable, and interval-ratio dichotomies in your answer.

6. It has been stated that as much as 90 percent of what is learned in college is remembered only for a short time. Think about this book on production/operations management and what you have learned in reading it. Why would you expect 90 percent of the material to be soon forgotten? What

could be done in the business school curriculum or in industry to partially offset this extinction process?

7. A claims processing clerk is fearful of losing her job when the new computer system is installed. She has been most reluctant to help the system designers understand her current duties. In fact, she has hidden some of the complex tasks from them. Which of the four basic reasons for resisting change is most prevalent here? Why?

8. Explain the experimental design of the Harwood Manufacturing study that dealt with resistance to change. What were the results in comparing the "no participation" group to the "total participation" groups? Why are the results of this study from the 1940s still of value to operations managers today?

9. Explain in some detail two suggestions for overcoming resistance to change.

10. What is a change agent? Who would this person be in a chemical plant, in a hospital, and on a professional baseball team?

11. Explain the role of top management in bringing about change in the organization.

12. Consider the production scheduling change at Baumritter presented in the chapter. Answer these questions, which were posed at the beginning of that section for the Baumritter situation:
    Can you identify succesful or unsuccessful changes?
    What was the need for change?
    Who was the change agent?
    Who were the learners?
    Was there resistance to the change?
    What strategy led to the success or failure of the change?

13. Explain the occasional failure of using verbal reinforcement. How can this be counteracted in operations applications?

GLOSSARY

Change agent: the facilitator of change; the role the production/operations manager takes in bringing about behavioral change in subordinates

Empirical-rational change strategy: strategy assuming that presented with facts, knowledge, and information, people will act in their own self-interest and rationally change behaviors to that end

Extinction: ignoring, by withdrawing positive reinforcements, unacceptable behaviors in hopes they will diminish and eventually disappear

Extrinsic rewards: social or economic incentives that are external to the task being performed

Intrinsic rewards: internal incentives that are psychologically part of the task being performed; satisfaction inherent in the task

Learning: having a goal, responding to obtain the goal, obtaining feedback from the response, making additional responses, adjusting the responses or goal until the goal is met

Normative-reeducative change strategy: a strategy assuming that people have attitude and value systems; when presented with facts, knowledge, and information directed at attitudes and values, people will change behaviors as they change their attitudes and values

Participation: approach to overcoming resistance to change through employee involvement in planning and implementing the change

Power-coercive change strategy: use of political, economic, or some other form of influence to force change in the behavior of others

Punishment: the infliction of pain or discomfort

Reinforcement: environmental consequences of behavior

Reinforcement schedules: more or less formal specification of the occurrence of a reinforcer in relation to the behavioral sequence to be conditioned; can be continuous or intermittent; intermittent can be interval or ratio and fixed or variable

SELECTED READINGS

Adam, E. E. "An Analysis of the Change in Performance Quality Employing Operant Conditioning Procedures." *Journal of Applied Psychology* 56, no. 6 (December 1972): 480–86.

Adam, E. E. and W. E. Scott. "The Application of Behavioral Conditioning Procedures to the Problems of Quality Control." *The Academy of Management Journal* 14, no. 2 (June 1971): 175–93.

Bandura, A. *Principles of Behavior Modification.* New York: Holt, Rinehart and Winston, Inc., 1969.

Bennis, Warren G., Kenneth D. Benne, Robert Chin, and Kenneth E. Corey. *The Planning of Change.* 3rd ed. New York: Holt, Rinehart and Winston, Inc., 1976.

Chin, Robert and Kenneth D. Benne. "General Strategies for Effecting Changes in Human Systems." in *The Planning of Change,* Warren G. Bennis, Kenneth D. Benne, Robert Chin, and Kenneth E. Corey, eds. 3rd ed. New York: Holt, Rinehart and Winston, Inc., 1976.

Coch, Lester and John R. P. French, Jr. "Overcoming Resistance to Change." *Human Relations* 1 (1948): 512–32.

Costello, Timothy W. and Sheldon S. Zalkind. *Psychology in Administration.* Englewood Cliffs, N.J.: Prentice-Hall, Inc., 1963.

Donnelly, James H., Jr., James L. Gibson, and John M. Ivancevich. *Fundamentals of Management.* Rev. ed. Dallas, Texas: Business Publications, Inc., 1975.

Fitts, P. M. "Cognitive Aspects of Information Processing: III. Set for Speed vs. Accuracy." *Journal of Experimental Psychology* 71 (1969).

Honig, W. K., ed. *Operant Behavior: Areas of Research and Application.* Englewood Cliffs, N.J.: Prentice-Hall, Inc., 1966.

Miner, John B. *The Management Process: Theory, Research, and Practice.* New York: Macmillan Pub. Co., Inc., 1973.

Reese, E. P. *The Analysis of Human Operant Behavior.* Dubuque, Iowa: Wm. C. Brown Co., 1966.

Skinner, E. F. "Operant Behavior." in W. K. Honig, ed. *Operant Behavior: Areas of Research and Application.* Englewood Cliffs, N.J.: Prentice-Hall, Inc., 1966.

Smith, F. C. and C. Lem. "Positive Aspects of Motivation in Repetitive Work: Effects of Lot Size Upon Spacing of Voluntary Work Stoppages." *Journal of Applied Psychology* 39 (1955): 330–33.

Vollman, Thomas E. "A User Oriented Approach to Production Scheduling." (Paper presented at 3rd Annual American Institute for Decision Sciences Conference. St. Louis, Missouri: 1971).

Operations Management in the Future

21

In this, our final chapter, we look to the past, the present, and the future of production and operations management. Whether we agree with Edmund Burke that "You can never plan the future by the past" or with Patrick Henry that "I know of no way of judging the future but by the past," we must at least admit that the past, after all, is all we have. As a basis for prediction, it may be limited, but it is a beginning. Together we'll review the history of production and operations management in the hope it will help us see the future of the field. We'll review current practice (and, incidentally, the content of this book) and speculate on emerging trends and future events that might shape your future role as a production/operations manager.

The Transition from Manufacturing to Operations Management

THE PAST AS A BASIS FOR THE FUTURE

Manufacturing management Manufacturing management was built upon the subdivision and specialization of labor, the recognition of differential skills in labor, and the scientific approach to studying work. With this approach, which spanned the late 1700s to about 1930, the focus was upon technology and logic at the manufacturing core.

Production
management

Production management, the general term used to describe this discipline from the 1930s through the 1950s, emphasized the production of goods and services in industrialized societies. Production management, continuing the application of Frederic Taylor's scientific, logical techniques, developed such areas as time and motion study and scheduling. Statistical applications in quality control, fundamentals of mathematical programming (primarily linear programming), and further development of inventory theory highlight this period. The use of the short-hand logic of mathematics to formulate production problems emerged as a prominent methodology. Finding new ways to produce larger volumes of output efficiently to supply insatiable consumer needs became a necessity.

The Hawthorn studies typify the emergence of a human relations approach to management in the 1940s. During the decades of the 1940s and 1950s, our concept of employees changed from Taylor's mechanistic view to an understanding that people are complex individuals with psychological as well as material needs. In the late 1950s, the digital computer emerged, a significant event for the future of the field. Also during this time, the economy continued to shift employment from agriculture to services. As farm mechanization increased and our society grew in wealth, people began demanding more services.

Operations
management

The digital computer accomplished several things for production managers. First, it relieved a tremendous clerical burden in production planning, costing, and control. Second, it gave production managers more information than ever before about a process that has always been data rich. Finally, in the late 1960s and 1970s, the computer began to be used as an analytical tool to assist in large-scale modeling and understanding of production processes.

Because many felt the word "production" had overly restrictive connotations, operations management became a term used to encompass both the manufacturing segment of the economy and the service sector. To the extent that the conversion process requires management, whether in manufacturing or a service industry, an operations manager is necessary.

The distinguishing feature of operations management is its continuation of the logical analysis developed in production management and the application of these useful techniques to the service sector where, generally, management has not benefited from existing production management procedures. Such applications have helped increase efficiency and quality, while reducing costs and delivery time in service systems. Operations management is not new in itself; it is a broadening of production management to include delivery of services.

Economic Trends and Techniques

Data suggest that the U.S. economy has shifted from a balance among the agriculture, manufacturing, and service sectors toward a manufacturing and service sector orientation. In 1920 in the United States, agriculture employed 30 percent, manufacturing 39 percent, and services 31 percent of the work force. By 1971, the figures had shifted dramatically; agriculture employed only 5 percent, manufacturing 36 percent, and services 59 percent of the work force. Because the service sector is so labor intense, it must pay attention to the management of conversion processes.

Several studies suggest that operating managers believe their discipline should focus foremost on problems in cost control, production control, labor/industrial relations, quality control, and production planning. Further, the techniques managers use most frequently appear to be network analysis (PERT, CPM especially), linear programming, time series analysis (exponential smoothing especially), regression and correlation, and computer simulation.

Notice, again, that most of these operations managers' problems are planning and control oriented. To understand the problems, one must understand the concepts, and to solve the problems, techniques rely heavily on models. Further, it seems clear that the employee's behavior requires our attention in operations management, especially with the shift to the labor intense service sector, where the worker is more critical to the conversion process than are machines and materials. This book has attempted to respond to these expressed current needs of practicing managers and to provide concepts and orientation for those who are preparing for future careers in this area.

Production/Operations Management Activities

As you have seen throughout, Figure 21-1 is the general model of this book. Think about what practicing managers have indicated their major problems to be and the techniques they found most useful as you review this general model. The managerial process, the conversion process, activities of production/operations managers, and models and behavior should now fit together. It is our belief that this general model provides a framework for application that you may rely upon in your career to assist you as a production/operations manager or as a general manager responsible for this function.

Production/Operations Management: The Systems View

During the 1960s, the systems approach emerged as a new framework for studying organizations. Whereas the approaches used during the

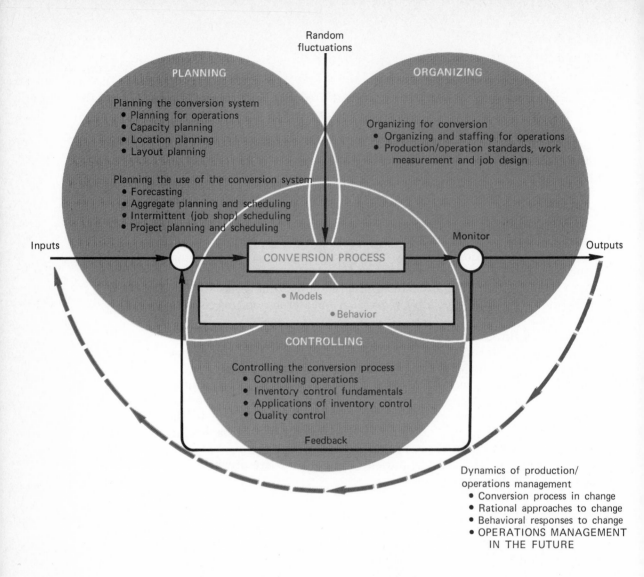

Figure 21-1 General model for production/operations management

preceding half-century emphasized understanding operations by detailed *analysis* of organizational components, the systems approach focuses on *synthesis.* The systems approach encourages managers to view the organization in its entirety rather than becoming preoccupied with a single subcomponent. If managers understand why organizations function as they do overall, they can keep the total organization's goals and objectives in view. The operations subsystem, remember, is but one component in a larger network of interrelated components. Together, all the subsystems, interrelating with one another, make up the larger system, the organization itself.

Still, the systems approach remains largely at a conceptual/descriptive stage of development. We believe that the analysis approach allows us to focus more directly, and in appropriate detail, on the day-to-day problems faced by operations managers. When the daily problems have been solved, operations managers can use the systems approach to interrelate the more major problem areas.

Production/Operations Management: The Life Cycle View

At several places in this book we have talked about life cycles.[1] We've mentioned the product life cycle, an important concept to product design and research and development efforts. The physical facility and equipment also have life cycles. They must be designed, brought on stream in operations, used in the conversion process, and eventually discarded. As an operations manager, you will benefit from an exposure to the field from a life cycle perspective. Although the life cycle orientation differs from ours, the planning, organizing, and controlling subfunctions play vital roles in it too.

Current Practice Overview

When one is studying a discipline like production/operations management, it's sometimes difficult to know which approach to take. Is the managerial process approach best? What about the systems view? The life-cycle approach? Don't get too worried about questions like these. In our own managerial process approach, we have made use of the systems orientation (in discussions of the dynamics of P/O management; interfaces of planning, organizing, and controlling; and interactions of operations, other functions, and the environment) and the life-cycle approach too. Had we emphasized either of these other approaches, we would have found ourselves discussing the managerial, modeling, and behavioral dimensions we have tended to concentrate on in our own approach. *The fact is that within any contemporary framework, regardless of its primary orientation, the focus is on managing the conversion process, which converts economic inputs into outputs of goods and services.*

Service Sector Applications

In recent decades, both the numbers of people employed and the level of economic activity have increased substantially in the service sector. The field of operations management has expanded along with the service

DISCERNIBLE
TRENDS IN
PRODUCTION/
OPERATIONS
MANAGEMENT

[1]The life cycle approach is explained in detail in Richard B. Chase and Nicholas J. Aquilano, *Production and Operations Management* (Homewood, Ill.: Richard D. Irwin, Inc., 1973).

sector. In a discipline that traditionally focused only on manufacturing, managing service sector conversion processes must now be included.

The real challenge to operations managers is transferring existing tools and techniques from the manufacturing sector to the service sector. Unfortunately, existing technology may not be adequate for meeting the challenge. New developments are badly needed, particularly in the area of measurement. Nevertheless, some service sector improvements are possible with what already exists. Insurance companies, banks, savings and loan institutions; schools and universities; local, state, and federal government; long-term care facilities, clinics, hospitals; food services, recreation, motels, and hotels; transportation; communication—these are all large, institutionalized segments of our economy that could fruitfully apply existing operations management techniques.

The challenges are to identify the components of the conversion process; to plan, organize, and control the conversion process; and to deliver services as outputs from the conversion process efficiently and effectively. These are substantial challenges. Convincing general management and administration that the rationality of the production core, and the tools and techniques so useful in analysis there, are often useful in delivery of services is a challenge in itself.

Computerization

Computer trends   Before 1960, a relatively small percentage of organizations in the United States, Canada, and the world were utilizing the digital computer in manufacturing and operations. The digital computer was developed in 1955, and by the mid-1960s most major firms in the United States and Canada were using it in accounting activities and introducing it into manufacturing for data collection and dissemination purposes. The percentage of total firms using the computer for manufacturing and operations activities, however, remained rather low. In the 1970s this situation changed. Significant events increasing computer applications during this period included:

1. *Pricing umbrellas.* In the United States, computer companies were forced to separate the pricing of computer hardware (equipment) and software (programs for application). This appears to have encouraged competition for software applications in general and in production/operations in particular. To date, the major hardware manufacturers continue to lead in software development.
2. *Mini computers.* The push for computers with larger and larger core capacities during the 1960s has been moderated by development of smaller computers, minicomputers, in a price range that smaller companies can now afford.
3. *Time sharing.* Accounting firms, banks, consulting firms, and computer specialty firms are offering computer time to other users. Under time

sharing the user firm buys central processing unit time rather than the entire computer.

4. *Consumer acceptance.* Every year development of computerized systems in government, retailing, and finance continues, the more each of us as consumers accepts computers as a way of life. This same phenomenon is occurring within organizations in which production/operations managers are the consumers. As the computer is accepted more readily, barriers to change are more easily overcome for each new application in production/operations.

Planning and controlling applications
We think the trend for utilizing the computer in manufacturing will continue. Computer utilization will also increase in service organizations, particularly in such areas as scheduling and control of transportation systems and various governmental operations. Critical to production/operations management are capability for large scale integrated data bases, timeliness of information, and computational power, all of which the computer provides with ease.

Systems Modeling and Analysis

Systems view and suboptimization
Accounting, engineering, finance, production/operations, and marketing interact within the organization and within a complex environment. The cruxes of the system concept are feedback and interaction. Today's production/operations managers *cannot* operate solely within the walls of the office or factory; they do not have the luxury of treating conversion as a rational closed process. Forced into a systems viewpoint, operations managers must accept suboptimization in the conversion subsystem as the price of getting closer to optimization for the entire system.

Simulation
Trends in operations analysis include computer simulations of the business firm, the conversion function, such business functions as distribution and finance, and individual processes within the conversion function. These simulations allow analysts and managers to test alternative proposed actions in a hypothetical environment that simulates the real operating process. Decision alternatives can be tested economically, without upsetting existing operations. To the extent that the simulation is logically consistent with and represents the real world situation, the simulation methodology can be a very useful tool for examining production/operations subsystems as they relate to larger systems.

Simulations have been conducted in production/operations on such functional problems as:

- facilities location,
- plant layout,
- aggregate scheduling,
- job shop scheduling,
- project scheduling,
- forecasting,
- inventory control, and
- physical distribution.

Typically, various decision rules are developed and tested to determine if operating costs may be reduced and/or to see if system effectiveness can be improved. Simulation offers a powerful guide for operations decision making.

The use of simulation and other analytical techniques has brought about the existence of the operations analyst, a specialist who is highly skilled in the technical problems in modeling and analysis of operations. These specialists are experts at visualizing the technical structure of operating problems; to improve system design, they can build models that include relationships among the operating subcomponents. Operations analysts, however, are not operations managers. They are resources with whom the manager must communicate and interact in order to plan, organize, and control the operations function.

Government Regulation

In recent years, the government has been taking an ever-increasing role in regulating aspects of production/operations. Price controls, for example, were instituted in the early 1970s, although they were generally lifted, except for the oil industry, by 1976. Utilities, transportation and communications organizations, among other service groups, are continually regulated by the government. Despite periodic grumbling in Congress, we expect this trend to continue.

EEOC and OSHA   By establishing the Equal Employment Opportunity Commission (EEOC) and enacting the Occupational Safety and Health Act (OSHA), the federal government has instituted strong guidelines for production/operations managers in the area of equal employment opportunity and health and safety. Federal legislation has been also enacted regarding pollution control and health care. We see this trend of social and environmental legislation continuing.

Energy

With the increasing dependence on foreign oil by the United States, Canada, Europe, and Japan, most of the industrialized world is experiencing an energy shortage. At a minimum, businesses and consumers must pay considerably higher costs to maintain current consumption patterns.

Pressure is being felt by production/operations managers for fuel economy in plants and equipment used in the conversion process. Although most organizations have fuel conservation programs underway, with strikingly successful results in many cases, the point is that conversion processes and products have had to be changed. Production/operations managers are reacting to this external force by changing equipment and tooling and by retraining workers. We will discuss energy again, since we think the existing energy shortage will continue to challenge production/operations management in the future.

Inflation

Creeping inflation appears to be a fact of life in economies throughout the world. If it is not controlled, inflation can assume runaway proportions, as has happened in Latin America, South America, and Great Britain. Inflation hurts production/operations managers through increased costs and disenchanted employees. In inflationary times, it's hard to determine how much of increased costs are attributable to the inflationary costs of labor, equipment, and materials and what costs are attributable to poor managerial and worker performance. Since operations managers are continually pressured to control costs, inflationary conditions can sometimes encourage managers to shelter poor performance under an inflation umbrella, an action that is not conducive to overall organization effectiveness.

Productivity

Productivity defined   Productivity is the *ratio of outputs* of goods or services from the conversion process *to inputs* consumed in the generation of these outputs. For any system, productivity is simply the ratio of outputs to inputs. For us, the relevant system is a conversion process.

Productivity is a general measure of efficiency receiving a renewed interest by business and government. Examples of this trend are:

1. *Unions.* Unions are interested in sharing productivity improvements with management and owners. Within the steelworkers union, for example, productivity committees have been established to assist in improvement efforts.
2. *Business.* Individual firms have undertaken extensive productivity improvement programs. Collectively, through trade associations, efforts are being made to assess industry productivity and changes within any one industry over time. An unresolved problem is a clear identification of which productivity gains are attributable to capital, which to technology, and which to labor. Productivity institutes to investigate issues of interest to business are being formed on many college campuses and by business

consortiums. One example of the latter is the American Productivity Center, which was formed in 1977 and is located in Houston, Texas. This productivity center is funded by scores of businesses with a general mission of productivity improvement in the private sector.

3. *Government.* There are numerous examples of interest in productivity within government. The Civil Service Commission of the federal government has a productivity group. The U.S. Price Commission has evolved into a national Productivity Commission. The Board of Governors of the Federal Reserve Banking System has underway a productivity measurement and improvement program. Later, we will discuss a productivity program sponsored by the National Science Foundation. These highlights illustrate productivity programs at the national level. There are similar state and municipal programs underway also.

Measurement
One problem in productivity improvement has been the measurement of outputs and inputs. How do you measure outputs of a barber? By the amount of time spent in productive effort? Persons served? Dollars of revenue generated? Further, what are the inputs consumed and how are they measured? Are inputs labor hours? Labor dollars? Is the barber chair to be measured as original cost or depreciated cost? For meaningful comparison, inputs and outputs must be on equivalent scales, and the subcomponents of each must allow aggregation. This is often attempted by using dollars, or some other monetary measure.

Using dollars is a good approach for outputs that can be evaluated in the market, but what about government services? Because of the absence of a clearly identifiable market for the services provided, government services are particularly difficult to measure. Furthermore, the need for measurement is crucial in government because government has no direct responsibility to the owners of capital as is the case in the private sector.

Since a before-and-after comparison is required for evaluation of any improvement procedure, measurement is crucial to productivity improvement. Realizing this, in 1975 and 1976 the Research Applied to National Needs (RANN) sector of the National Science Foundation (NSF) devoted 1.8 million dollars toward productivity measurement. The research is to be completed by 1978. The focus of the program is upon productivity measurement in such administrative services as personnel, purchasing, computer services, and quality control and Inspection. In June 1976, the National Science Foundation presented a seminar in Washington, D.C., to explain the program:

RANN supports research in three major areas of productivity measurement—national economic measures, measures for the delivery of urban services, and productivity measurement systems for administrative services.

The program on productivity measurement systems for administrative services was developed to deal with the changing nature of the U.S. production system. The increasing use of technology in the direct production of goods and services and on the changing nature of organizational structures has resulted in an increased use of resources in nonproduction activities. This trend is reflected in employment statistics. For example, between 1950 and 1970, professional and technical workers increased from 8.7 percent of the workforce to 14.7 percent; managers and officials from 8.9 percent of the workforce to 10.5 percent; and clerical and kindred from 12.3 percent of the workforce to 17.4 percent. Many companies report similar changes. Indeed, in most industries about two-thirds of the employees work in nonproduction areas.

The purpose of the RANN program in productivity measurement systems in administrative services is to develop and to test measurement systems in this area. To date, seven awards have been made and the research is in progress.

Table 21-1 lists the research projects that were started under the program. Results from these projects can be obtained directly from the NSF or the principal investigator.

As we discussed important trends in the preceding section, perhaps you noticed several factors external to the organization: government regulation, energy, and inflation. In our speculations, we'll consider these and other external forces that will mold the character of operations management in the future. Perhaps the greatest single lesson the operations manager can learn from all this is the necessity of being able and ready to adapt to future environmental intrusions. Systems must be designed not only for short-run economies of operation but for flexibility as well.

Energy

Almost any energy forecast suggests that an energy shortage with dependence on foreign oil is likely to continue in the free world for the next ten years. Many oil companies have been attempting to change their identities from oil companies to energy companies, with the implicit idea of diversifying their operations. With the reduction of U.S. and free world reserves in oil, increasing attention is being given to coal, nuclear, and solar energy sources.

Although coal reserves are substantial in the United States, emission standards set by the federal government restrict low quality, high sulfur content coal. The implications of just this kind of environmental dilemma trouble consumers and policy makers alike. What kinds of tradeoffs are we willing to make between *environmental control* and the *benefits from energy?* The benefits from energy are visible everywhere; in transportation, heating, air conditioning, and consumer products, each of us consumes energy daily. How much are we willing to pay in personal effort (walking) or nonconsumption (staying home) for a cleaner environment? Although most of us are willing to sacrifice considerably for a clean environment,

TABLE 21-1

NSF PRODUCTIVITY MEASUREMENT RESEARCH PROJECTS*

Title of project	Grant number	Institution conducting research project	Principal investigator	Project description
"Research on Productivity Measurement Systems for Administrative Service: Budget and Management Analysis"	APR75-20564	ABT Associates, Inc., 55 Wheeler, Cambridge, Mass.	Peter Merrill	Investigated methods of measuring the productivity of the budget and management analysis function in a hospital, a university, and in state government generally. Modelled the central budgeting function of a multicampus university, focusing on measurement of productivity.
"Research on Productivity Measurement Systems for Administrative Services: Purchasing Management"	APR75-20542	City of Detroit in conjunction with Wayne State University	John Cox	Case studies with four states, four cities, and two countries to define the purchasing system to be measured, to determine what is expected from the system, and to determine current methods of measuring the performance of the purchasing system.
"Research on Productivity Measurement Systems for Administrative Services: Personnel Administration and Training"	APR76-08199	Georgetown University	Selma J. Mushkin	Evaluation of eight city personnel systems, focusing on the quality and quantity of performance. Manpower and personnel methods are evaluated, and a research design for future productivity measurement is to be developed.
"Research on Productivity Measurement Systems for Administrative Services: Purchasing Management"	APR75-20557	Michigan State University	Robert M. Monczka	Field research with eighteen organizations in the private and public sectors to survey purchasing performance (including productivity) measures and their use.

*Source: William A. Ruch, ed., *Proceedings of the Grantees Conference on Research on Productivity Measurement Systems for Administrative Services.* Sponsored by the National Science Foundation, Tempe, Arizona (November 1976).

Title of project	Grant number	Institution conducting research project	Principal investigator	Project description
				Approximately 250 measures were identified, and interviews were conducted with approximately 275 purchasing and related personnel.
"Research on Productivity Measurement Systems for Administrative Services: Inspection and Quality Control"	APR76-07140	University of Missouri-Columbia, in conjunction with Arizona State University	Everett E. Adam, Jr.	Develops and field tests an approach toward measuring the quality dimension of productivity that may be generalized in the service sector and service functions in manufacturing. Field testing was conducted in check processing and personnel within the Federal Reserve Banking System.
"Research on Productivity Measurement Systems for Administrative Computing and Information Services"	APR75-20561	The Ohio State University	William T. Morris	Utilizes nominal group techniques and the delphi procedure to elicit productivity measures for computing and information services functions within several organizations.
"Research on Productivity Measurement Systems for Administrative Services: Computing and Information Services"	APR75-20546	Westinghouse Electric Corp., R&D Center, Beulah Road, Pittsburgh, in conjunction with MIT and the University of Pittsburgh	Herman D. Greenberg	Developing models and measuring system for calculating partial (efficiency) and total (effectiveness) productivity indexes for use in computer and information services.

we would like our energy too. We're not so sure we can have both much longer.

What does all this have to do with the production/operations manager? An energy shortage will affect our ability to operate conversion processes, just as much as it affects consumers. Social issues that affect workers, products, and regulation affect variables critical to effective operations too.

Whether the trend in the next ten years is toward foreign oil, shale oil, or such other energy sources as nuclear, solar, or coal, plant and equipment design decisions, product decisions, and conversion process costs will all be affected in a dramatic way. As potential production/operations managers, you must keep aware of current energy developments and trends. Correct interpretation will be essential to decisions you must make in operations.

International Business

The world is shrinking. Improvements in transportation, international banking, and communication have made commerce and trade take place in a smaller world. Increasingly, products are produced in locations where the combination of labor, material, and transportation can be most economically supplied to the consumer. A typical American multinational company, for example, might export its technology in the form of equipment and technical expertise to an underdeveloped country, produce one product component in that country, and then ship the component to the United States for final assembly and ultimate consumption. Perhaps Japan, more than any other country, illustrates how international production can be accomplished in a reasonably short period of time. Since World War II, Japan has recovered enough to influence production in electronics, steel, transportation, and shipbuilding, to name only a few industries, throughout the world.

Production/operations managers can learn from other countries. By comparing their production methods and costs with our own, managers can improve methods and reduce costs. Because of worldwide costs and prices, production executives must be aware of opportunities to make or purchase parts in other countries. International production is significant in operations today, and we believe this phenomenon will increase in the next decade.

Population

Although population is leveling in the United States and Canada, in many countries population explosions make it increasingly difficult to provide the essential food and shelter requirements for subsistence. Should this continue, production must be devoted toward agriculture and basic housing and clothing needs. Population trends have an impact on the allocation of factors of production, and these trends shape the production process, a matter of clear importance to production and operations managers.

Real Worth

Although the Gross National Product, the measure of output for the United States economy, increases annually, real growth was slowed in the 1970s. This situation presents a dilemma for managers. When output increases, new plants and equipment are necessary to keep up with demand. But when real growth slows down, companies tend to hold back on new facilities. What should managers do?

Should the economy in general or a particular industry spurt forward, there could be serious capacity problems unless new plants and equipment are ready. In 1975, for the first time in 25 years, utilization of capacity dipped below 70 percent in the United States. Should we continue to operate below capacity, the equipment that is unused will become obsolete before it is worn out. Furthermore, operating below capacity makes it more difficult to earn enough profits to replace obsolete plants and equipment. And since there is no capacity pressure, there's little incentive to invest in new facilities.

The point is clear. When real growth is slowed capacity remains unused and expenditures for plant and equipment are reduced. Under these conditions, the production/operations manager finds it increasingly difficult to introduce new technology into the conversion process.

Service Sector Technology

In the labor-intense service sector, we believe that job specialization and mechanization will increase. Quasi-manufacturing processes, small assembly lines, and special-purpose equipment will probably be used as much as possible in an effort to reduce high labor costs. Consider the fast-food chains we see everywhere. Compared with traditional restaurants, these chains make use of much more food that has been prepared at a factory located away from where it is consumed, and they employ much more specialized labor. French fries, for example, are precut and frozen at a factory. Then they are transported to the store, where one or two people do nothing but deep fry them. We imagine that parallel examples of specialized labor and location will become increasingly prevalent in financial, health care, educational, and governmental services.

SUMMARY

Although the future of P/OM is not predictable in any precise sense, its general orientation is strongly influenced by its beginnings and its recent history. The basic notions of striving for system efficiency and effectiveness will continue, and the many techniques that have been developed will continue to have useful application.

The most discernible thrust of current and near-term efforts in operations management is in the service sector. Perhaps the greatest increase in application will be in governmental operations at the local and national levels. As economic and environmental issues continue to dominate the world, decisions that were traditionally politically based will be approached more systematically.

As for the future nature of conversion processes themselves, one can only point to the many unpredictable environmental elements that must be recognized and dealt with. We must expect and respond to changes in population, technology, and economic conditions. These requirements point to the need for designing conversion systems that are not only adaptive to changing needs but operated efficiently and effectively. These two sometimes-conflicting requirements will present a challenge of great proportions to the future production/operations manager.

REVIEW AND DISCUSSION QUESTIONS

1. It is helpful in determining the future of production/operations management to remember the past. Trace the transition from manufacturing to operations management.

2. Study Figure 21-1, production/operations management activities. Lay the figure aside and try to reproduce it. Which parts of the figure do you perceive to be essential as a framework for practicing as an operations manager? Why?

3. Several discernible trends in production/operations management were presented in this chapter. Select one that you believe should be expanded and expand it. Likely, one or more trends were overlooked. Select a trend in production/operations that you believe should have been summarized and summarize it.

4. One speculation concerning production/operations management was that energy shortages will impact conversion processes in dramatic ways in the future. Provide some factual evidence not provided in this book that supports or refutes this speculation.

5. Large amounts of effort and resources have been devoted to studying productivity in the service sector in recent years. Why has this occurred?

6. One problem in productivity improvement has been the measurement of system inputs and outputs. Explain why this is a problem, and give examples of it.

7. Is it possible to have an efficient conversion system that is at the same time a flexible system? Discuss this question.

SELECTED READINGS

Britney, Robert R. "Continuing Education in Production/Operations Management." (Paper presented at the 34th Annual Meeting, Academy of Management, Seattle, Washington, 1974).

Chase, Richard B. and Nicholas J. Aquilano. *Production and Operations Management: A Life Cycle Approach.* Homewood, Ill: Richard D. Irwin, Inc., 1973.

Fuchs, Victor. *The Service Economy.* New York: Columbia University Press, 1968.

Gaither, N. "The Adoption of Operations Research Techniques by Manufacturing Organizations." *Decision Sciences* 6, no. 3 (October 1975): 797–813.

Green, Thad B., Walter B. Newsom, and S. Roland Jones. "A Survey of the Application of Quantitative Techniques to Production/Operations Management in Large Corporations." *Proceedings of the 1976 Academy of Management 36th Annual Meeting.* Kansas City, Missouri, August 1976.

AREAS OF A STANDARD NORMAL DISTRIBUTION*

An entry in the table is the proportion under the entire curve which is between $z = 0$ and a positive value of z. Areas for negative values of z are obtained by symmetry.

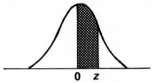

z	.00	.01	.02	.03	.04	.05	.06	.07	.08	.09
0.0	.0000	.0040	.0080	.0120	.0160	.0199	.0239	.0279	.0319	.0359
0.1	.0398	.0438	.0478	.0517	.0557	.0596	.0636	.0675	.0714	.0753
0.2	.0793	.0832	.0871	.0910	.0948	.0987	.1026	.1064	.1103	.1141
0.3	.1179	.1217	.1255	.1293	.1331	.1368	.1406	.1443	.1480	.1517
0.4	.1554	.1591	.1628	.1664	.1700	.1736	.1772	.1808	.1844	.1879
0.5	.1915	.1950	.1985	.2019	.2054	.2088	.2123	.2157	.2190	.2224
0.6	.2257	.2291	.2324	.2357	.2389	.2422	.2454	.2486	.2517	.2549
0.7	.2580	.2611	.2642	.2673	.2703	.2734	.2764	.2794	.2823	.2852
0.8	.2881	.2910	.2939	.2967	.2995	.3023	.3051	.3078	.3106	.3133
0.9	.3159	.3186	.3212	.3238	.3264	.3289	.3315	.3340	.3365	.3389
1.0	.3413	.3438	.3461	.3485	.3508	.3531	.3554	.3577	.3599	.3621
1.1	.3643	.3665	.3686	.3708	.3729	.3749	.3770	.3790	.3810	.3830
1.2	.3849	.3869	.3888	.3907	.3925	.3944	.3962	.3980	.3997	.4015
1.3	.4032	.4049	.4066	.4082	.4099	.4115	.4131	.4147	.4162	.4177
1.4	.4192	.4207	.4222	.4236	.4251	.4265	.4279	.4292	.4306	.4319
1.5	.4332	.4345	.4357	.4370	.4382	.4394	.4406	.4418	.4429	.4441
1.6	.4452	.4463	.4474	.4484	.4495	.4505	.4515	.4525	.4535	.4545
1.7	.4554	.4564	.4573	.4582	.4591	.4599	.4608	.4616	.4625	.4633
1.8	.4641	.4649	.4656	.4664	.4671	.4678	.4686	.4693	.4699	.4706
1.9	.4713	.4719	.4726	.4732	.4738	.4744	.4750	.4756	.4761	.4767
2.0	.4772	.4778	.4783	.4788	.4793	.4798	.4803	.4808	.4812	.4817
2.1	.4821	.4826	.4830	.4834	.4838	.4842	.4846	.4850	.4854	.4857
2.2	.4861	.4864	.4868	.4871	.4875	.4878	.4881	.4884	.4887	.4890
2.3	.4893	.4896	.4898	.4901	.4904	.4906	.4909	.4911	.4913	.4916
2.4	.4918	.4920	.4922	.4925	.4927	.4929	.4931	.4932	.4934	.4936
2.5	.4938	.4940	.4941	.4943	.4945	.4946	.4948	.4949	.4951	.4952
2.6	.4953	.4955	.4956	.4957	.4959	.4960	.4961	.4962	.4963	.4964
2.7	.4965	.4966	.4967	.4968	.4969	.4970	.4971	.4972	.4973	.4974
2.8	.4974	.4975	.4976	.4977	.4977	.4978	.4979	.4979	.4980	.4981
2.9	.4981	.4982	.4982	.4983	.4984	.4984	.4985	.4985	.4986	.4986
3.0	.4987	.4987	.4987	.4988	.4988	.4989	.4989	.4989	.4990	.4990

*Source: Paul G. Hoel, *Elementary Statistics*, 2nd edition (New York: John Wiley & Sons, Inc., 1966), p. 329.

8% COMPOUND INTEREST FACTORS*

	Single payment		Uniform series				
n	Compound amount factor Given P to find S $(1 + i)^n$	Present worth factor Given S to find P $\dfrac{1}{(1 + i)^n}$	Sinking fund factor Given S to find R $\dfrac{i}{(1 + i)^n - 1}$	Capital recovery factor Given P to find R $\dfrac{i(1 + i)^n}{(1 + i)^n - 1}$	Compound amount factor Given R to find S $\dfrac{(1 + i)^n - 1}{i}$	Present worth factor Given R to find P $\dfrac{(1 + i)^n - 1}{i(1 + i)^n}$	n
1	1.0800	0.9259	1.000 00	1.080 00	1.000	0.926	1
2	1.1664	0.8573	0.480 77	0.560 77	2.080	1.783	2
3	1.2597	0.7938	0.308 03	0.388 03	3.246	2.577	3
4	1.3605	0.7350	0.221 92	0.301 92	4.506	3.312	4
5	1.4693	0.6806	0.170 46	0.250 46	5.867	3.993	5
6	1.5869	0.6302	0.136 32	0.216 32	7.336	4.623	6
7	1.7138	0.5835	0.112 07	0.192 07	8.923	5.206	7
8	1.8509	0.5403	0.094 01	0.174 01	10.637	5.747	8
9	1.9990	0.5002	0.080 08	0.160 08	12.488	6.247	9
10	2.1589	0.4632	0.069 03	0.149 03	14.487	6.710	10
11	2.3316	0.4289	0.060 08	0.140 08	16.645	7.139	11
12	2.5182	0.3971	0.052 70	0.132 70	18.977	7.536	12
13	2.7196	0.3677	0.046 52	0.126 52	21.495	7.904	13
14	2.9372	0.3405	0.041 30	0.121 30	24.215	8.244	14
15	3.1722	0.3152	0.036 83	0.116 83	27.152	8.559	15
16	3.4259	0.2919	0.032 98	0.112 98	30.324	8.851	16
17	3.7000	0.2703	0.029 63	0.109 63	33.750	9.122	17
18	3.9960	0.2502	0.026 70	0.106 70	37.450	9.372	18
19	4.3157	0.2317	0.024 13	0.104 13	41.446	9.604	19
20	4.6610	0.2145	0.021 85	0.101 85	45.762	9.818	20
21	5.0338	0.1987	0.019 83	0.099 83	50.423	10.017	21
22	5.4365	0.1839	0.018 03	0.098 03	55.457	10.201	22
23	5.8715	0.1703	0.016 42	0.096 42	60.893	10.371	23
24	6.3412	0.1577	0.014 98	0.094 98	66.765	10.529	24
25	6.8485	0.1460	0.013 68	0.093 68	73.106	10.675	25

*Source: Adapted from Eugene L. Grant, W. Grant Ireson, and Richard S. Leavenworth, *Principles of Engineering Economy*, 6th ed. Copyright © 1976, The Ronald Press Company, New York.

	Single payment		Uniform series				
	Compound amount factor Given P to find S $(1+i)^n$	Present worth factor Given S to find P $\dfrac{1}{(1+i)^n}$	Sinking fund factor Given S to find R $\dfrac{i}{(1+i)^n - 1}$	Capital recovery factor Given P to find R $\dfrac{i(1+i)^n}{(1+i)^n - 1}$	Compound amount factor Given R to find S $\dfrac{(1+i)^n - 1}{i}$	Present worth factor Given R to find P $\dfrac{(1+i)^n - 1}{i(1+i)^n}$	
n							n
26	7.3964	0.1352	0.012 51	0.092 51	79.954	10.810	26
27	7.9881	0.1252	0.011 45	0.091 45	87.351	10.935	27
28	8.6271	0.1159	0.010 49	0.090 49	95.339	11.051	28
29	9.3173	0.1073	0.009 62	0.089 62	103.966	11.158	29
30	10.0627	0.0994	0.008 83	0.088 83	113.283	11.258	30
31	10.8677	0.0920	0.008 11	0.088 11	123.346	11.350	31
32	11.7371	0.0852	0.007 45	0.087 45	134.214	11.435	32
33	12.6760	0.0789	0.006 85	0.086 85	145.951	11.514	33
34	13.6901	0.0730	0.006 30	0.086 30	158.627	11.587	34
35	14.7853	0.0676	0.005 80	0.085 80	172.317	11.655	35
40	21.7245	0.0460	0.003 86	0.083 86	259.057	11.925	40
45	31.9204	0.0313	0.002 59	0.082 59	386.506	12.108	45
50	46.9016	0.0213	0.001 74	0.081 74	573.770	12.233	50
55	68.9139	0.0145	0.001 18	0.081 18	848.923	12.319	55
60	101.2571	0.0099	0.000 80	0.080 80	1 253.213	12.377	60
65	148.7798	0.0067	0.000 54	0.080 54	1 847.248	12.416	65
70	218.6064	0.0046	0.000 37	0.080 37	2 720.080	12.443	70
75	321.2045	0.0031	0.000 25	0.080 25	4 002.557	12.461	75
80	471.9548	0.0021	0.000 17	0.080 17	5 886.935	12.474	80
85	693.4565	0.0014	0.000 12	0.080 12	8 655.706	12.482	85
90	1 018.9151	0.0010	0.000 08	0.080 08	12 723.939	12.488	90
95	1 497.1205	0.0007	0.000 05	0.080 05	18 701.507	12.492	95
100	2 199.7613	0.0005	0.000 04	0.080 04	27 484.516	12.494	100

10% COMPOUND INTEREST FACTORS*

	Single payment		Uniform series			
	Compound amount factor Given P to find S	Present worth factor Given S to find P	Sinking fund factor Given S to find R	Capital recovery factor Given P to find R	Compound amount factor Given R to find S	Present worth factor Given R to find P	
n	$(1 + i)^n$	$\dfrac{1}{(1 + i)^n}$	$\dfrac{i}{(1 + i)^n - 1}$	$\dfrac{i(1 + i)^n}{(1 + i)^n - 1}$	$\dfrac{(1 + i)^n - 1}{i}$	$\dfrac{(1 + i)^n - 1}{i(1 + i)^n}$	n
1	1.1000	0.9091	1.000 00	1.100 00	1.000	0.909	1
2	1.2100	0.8264	0.476 19	0.576 19	2.100	1.736	2
3	1.3310	0.7513	0.302 11	0.402 11	3.310	2.487	3
4	1.4641	0.6830	0.215 47	0.315 47	4.641	3.170	4
5	1.6105	0.6209	0.163 80	0.263 80	6.105	3.791	5
6	1.7716	0.5645	0.129 61	0.229 61	7.716	4.355	6
7	1.9487	0.5132	0.105 41	0.205 41	9.487	4.868	7
8	2.1436	0.4665	0.087 44	0.187 44	11.436	5.335	8
9	2.3579	0.4241	0.073 64	0.173 64	13.579	5.759	9
10	2.5937	0.3855	0.062 75	0.162 75	15.937	6.144	10
11	2.8531	0.3505	0.053 96	0.153 96	18.531	6.495	11
12	3.1384	0.3186	0.046 76	0.146 76	21.384	6.814	12
13	3.4523	0.2897	0.040 78	0.140 78	24.523	7.103	13
14	3.7975	0.2633	0.035 75	0.135 75	27.975	7.367	14
15	4.1772	0.2394	0.031 47	0.131 47	31.772	7.606	15
16	4.5950	0.2176	0.027 82	0.127 82	35.950	7.824	16
17	5.0545	0.1978	0.024 66	0.124 66	40.545	8.022	17
18	5.5599	0.1799	0.021 93	0.121 93	45.599	8.201	18
19	6.1159	0.1635	0.019 55	0.119 55	51.159	8.365	19
20	6.7275	0.1486	0.017 46	0.117 46	57.275	8.514	20
21	7.4002	0.1351	0.015 62	0.115 62	64.002	8.649	21
22	8.1403	0.1228	0.014 01	0.114 01	71.403	8.772	22
23	8.9543	0.1117	0.012 57	0.112 57	79.543	8.883	23
24	9.8497	0.1015	0.011 30	0.111 30	88.497	8.985	24
25	10.8347	0.0923	0.010 17	0.110 17	98.347	9.077	25

*Source: Adapted from Eugene L. Grant, W. Grant Ireson, and Richard S. Leavenworth, *Principles of Engineering Economy*, 6th ed. Copyright © 1976, The Ronald Press Company, New York.

	Single payment		Uniform series				
	Compound amount factor Given P to find S	Present worth factor Given S to find P	Sinking fund factor Given S to find R	Capital recovery factor Given P to find R	Compound amount factor Given R to find S	Present worth factor Given R to find P	
n	$(1 + i)^n$	$\dfrac{1}{(1 + i)^n}$	$\dfrac{i}{(1 + i)^n - 1}$	$\dfrac{i(1 + i)^n}{(1 + i)^n - 1}$	$\dfrac{(1 + i)^n - 1}{i}$	$\dfrac{(1 + i)^n - 1}{i(1 + i)^n}$	n
26	11.9182	0.0839	0.009 16	0.109 16	109.182	9.161	26
27	13.1100	0.0763	0.008 26	0.108 26	121.100	9.237	27
28	14.4210	0.0693	0.007 45	0.107 45	134.210	9.307	28
29	15.8631	0.0630	0.006 73	0.106 73	148.631	9.370	29
30	17.4494	0.0573	0.006 08	0.106 08	164.494	9.427	30
31	19.1943	0.0521	0.005 50	0.105 50	181.943	9.479	31
32	21.1138	0.0474	0.004 97	0.104 97	201.138	9.526	32
33	23.2252	0.0431	0.004 50	0.104 50	222.252	9.569	33
34	25.5477	0.0391	0.004 07	0.104 07	245.477	9.609	34
35	28.1024	0.0356	0.003 69	0.103 69	271.024	9.644	35
40	45.2593	0.0221	0.002 26	0.102 26	442.593	9.779	40
45	72.8905	0.0137	0.001 39	0.101 39	718.905	9.863	45
50	117.3909	0.0085	0.000 86	0.100 86	1 163.909	9.915	50
55	189.0591	0.0053	0.000 53	0.100 53	1 880.591	9.947	55
60	304.4816	0.0033	0.000 33	0.100 33	3 034.816	9.967	60
65	490.3707	0.0020	0.000 20	0.100 20	4 893.707	9.980	65
70	789.7470	0.0013	0.000 13	0.100 13	7 887.470	9.987	70
75	1 271.8952	0.0008	0.000 08	0.100 08	12 708.954	9.992	75
80	2 048.4002	0.0005	0.000 05	0.100 05	20 474.002	9.995	80
85	3 298.9690	0.0003	0.000 03	0.100 03	32 979.690	9.997	85
90	5 313.0226	0.0002	0.000 02	0.100 02	53 120.226	9.998	90
95	8 556.6760	0.0001	0.000 01	0.100 01	85 556.760	9.999	95
100	13 780.6123	0.0001	0.000 01	0.100 01	137 796.123	9.999	100

Index